REPORT FROM BARCELONA, SPAIN

Brave New Worlds — March 15, 2007

FUTURE CONDITIONAL

MAX ANDREWS &
MARIANA CÁNEPA LUNA

Barcelona-based correspondents examine different toilet designs in Europe, particularly the Spanish style, and the Catalan caganer figure. This leads to musings on ways that these may illuminate the country's rapid changes in the midst of a massive demographic transformation and in the wake of terrorist bombings and the election of a radical leftist administration.

page 43

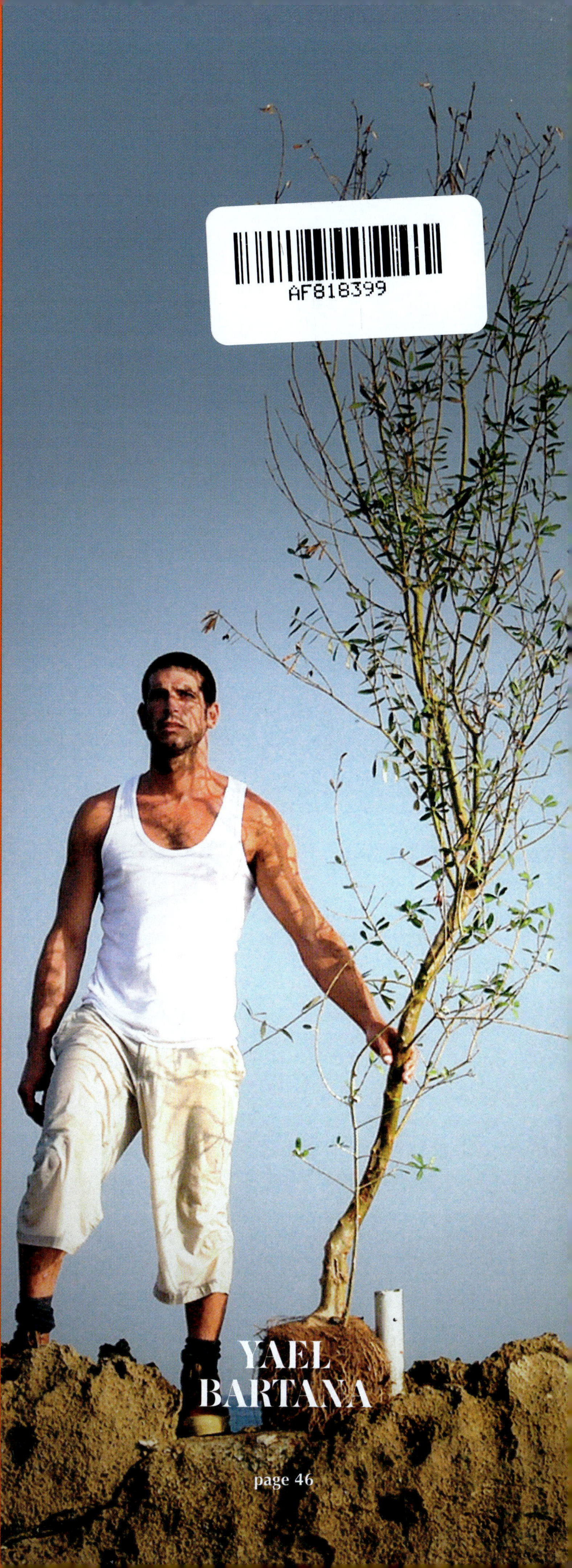

YAEL
BARTANA

page 46

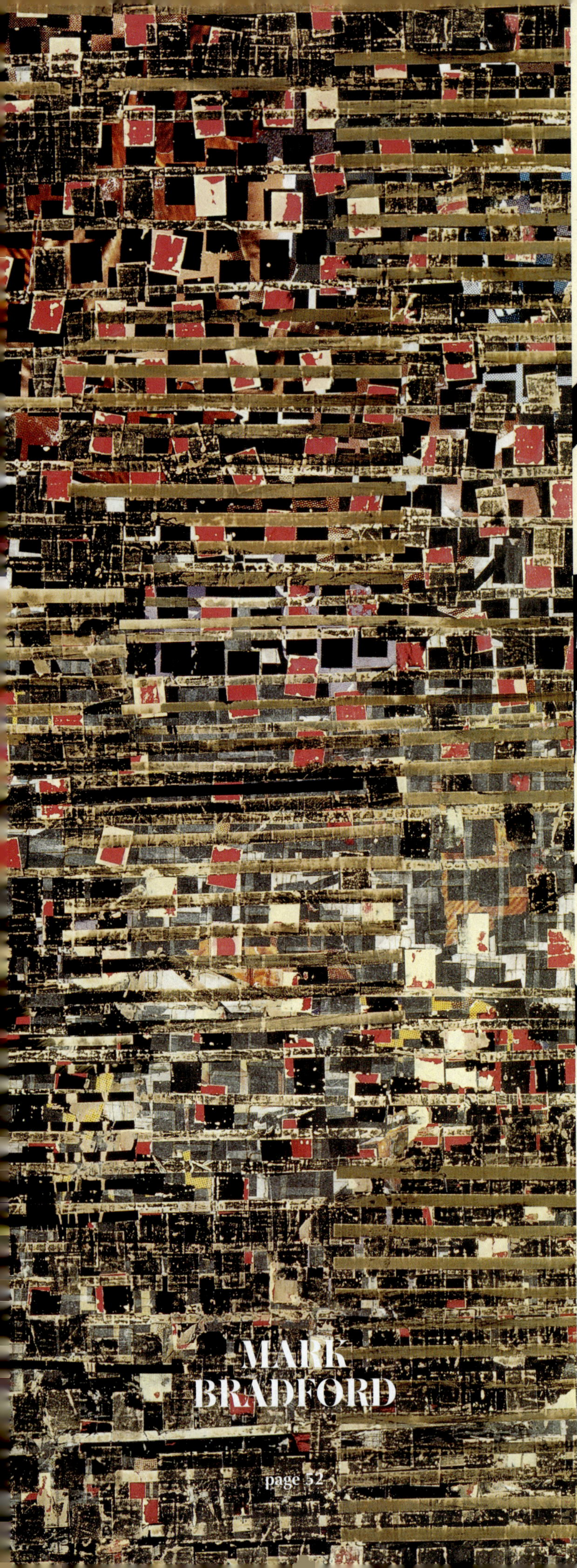

MARK
BRADFORD

page 52

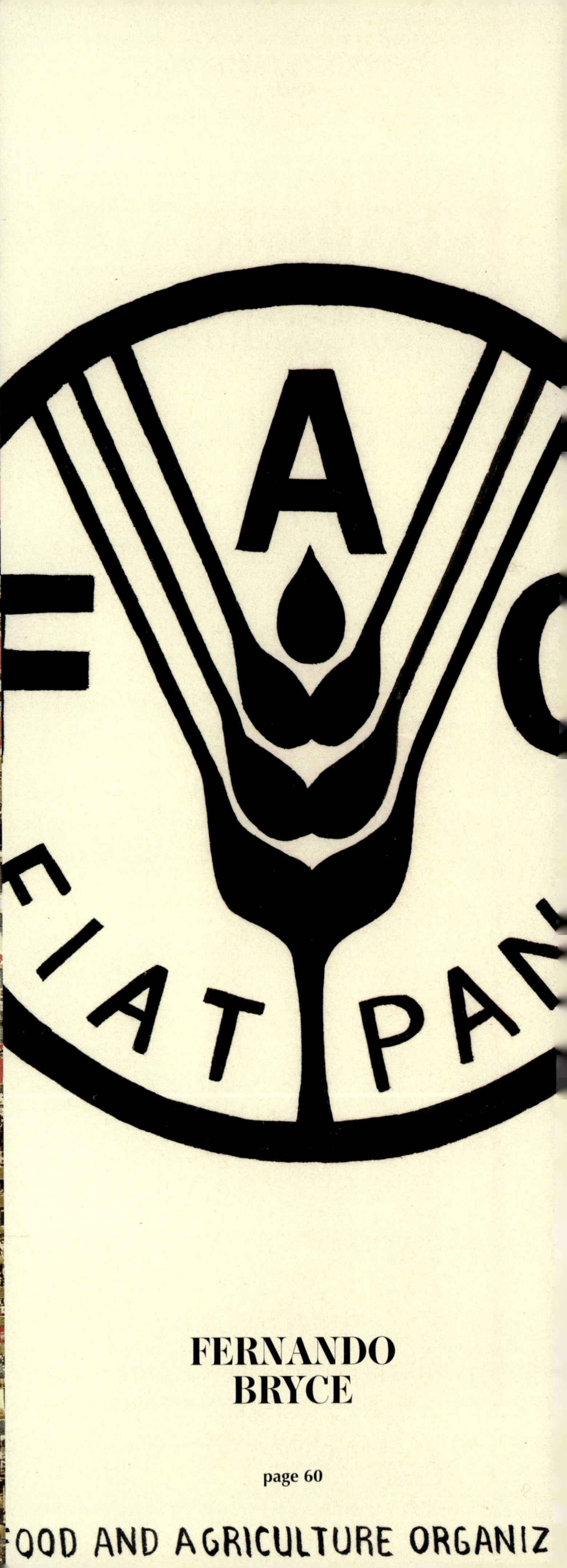

FERNANDO
BRYCE

page 60

REPORT FROM BOGOTÁ, COLOMBIA

Brave New Worlds April 19, 2007

MOCKUS' BOGOTÁ: ART AS PUBLIC POLICY

JOSÉ ROCA

José Roca narrates some of the shocking antics and surreal public mobilizations dreamed up and realized by the former mayor of the capital of Colombia. Can performance art and civic action be one and the same? The answer just might be "yes" in this compelling story.

page 70

REPORT FROM BUCHAREST, ROMANIA

Brave New Worlds April 16, 2017

MONUMENTAL BACKLASH

MIHNEA MIRCAN

What will the capital of Romania look like a decade after the country's entry into the European Union? Will it have rid itself of megalomaniac monuments of the past Communist regime, or will it end up suffering from an even worse overdose? This missive from a delirious reporter from 2017 predicts a requisite monument to Constantin Brancusi and an imagined but not wholly unlikely Guggenheim Museum in Bucharest.

page 75

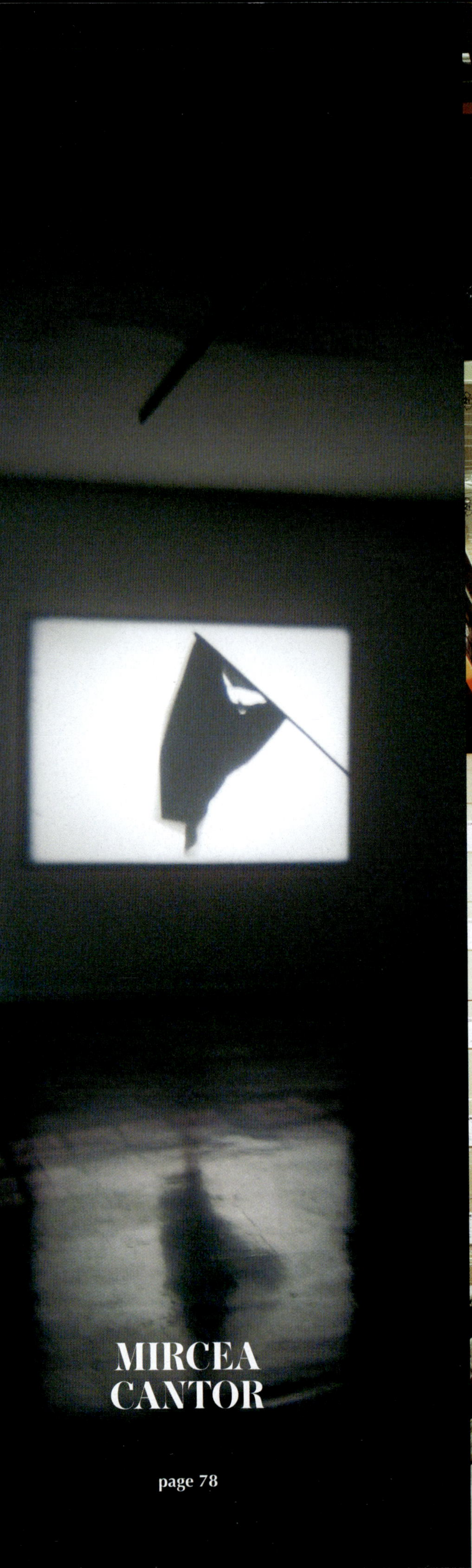

MIRCEA
CANTOR

page 78

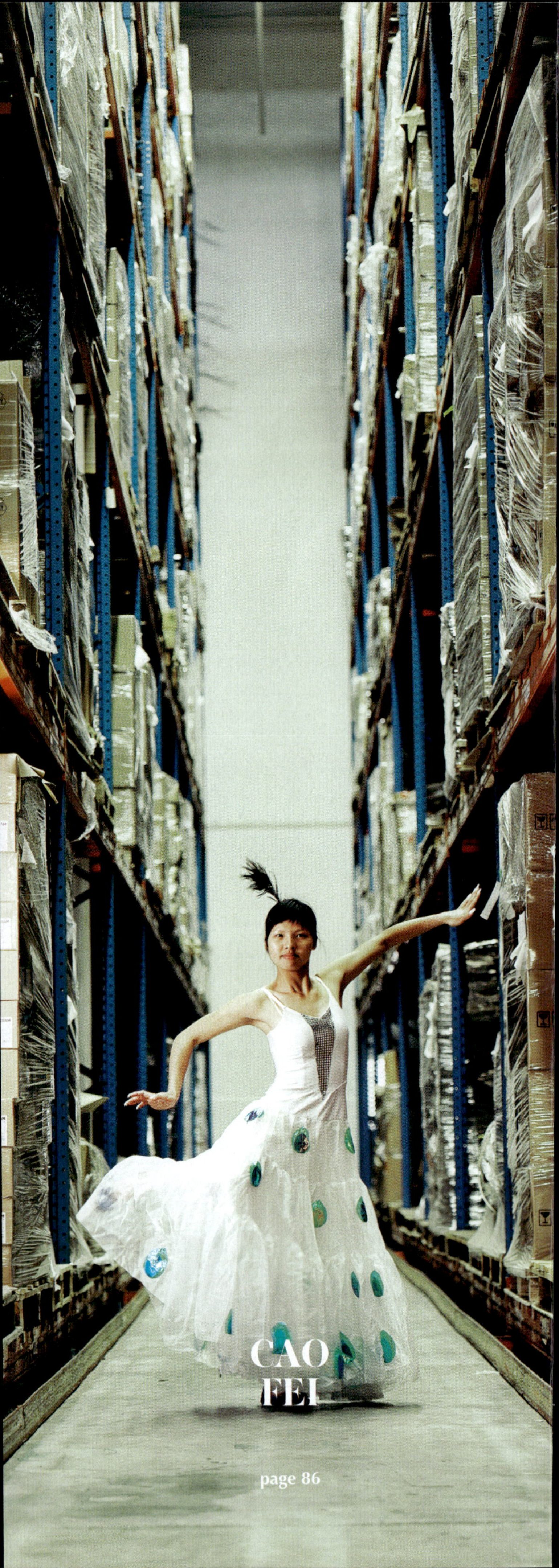

CAO
FEI

page 86

GOODLY CREATURES, BEAUTEOUS MANKIND, O BRAVE NEW WORLDS

§

DORYUN CHONG

George Orwell and Nam June Paik's 1984. Numerology of disasters. Narratives of discovery and loss, violence and redemption by two writers separated by three centuries. Today's artists wrestling with the often amorphous, sometimes overdetermined contour of contemporaneity. These are the author's access points to the world in which we live.

page 94

REPORT FROM OSLO, NORWAY

Brave New Worlds April 26, 2007

MAPPING A NEW TERRAIN

TONE HANSEN

In this sharp analysis, the Oslo-based artist and writer investigates one of the wealthiest countries in the world, which has "outsourced" much of the structure of its vaunted social democracy. The philosophical and practical conflicts between Norway's ideal of public welfare, neo-imperialism, and immigration also have deep ramifications for culture and diversity.

page 103

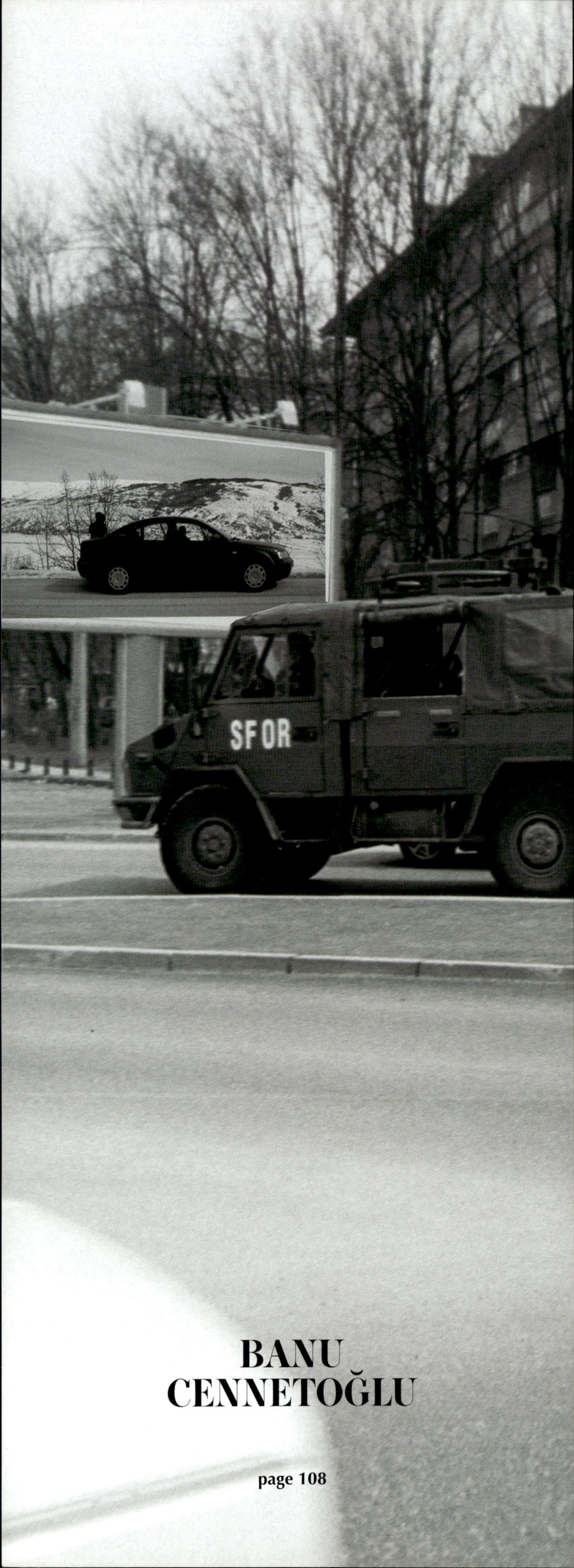

BANU
CENNETOĞLU

page 108

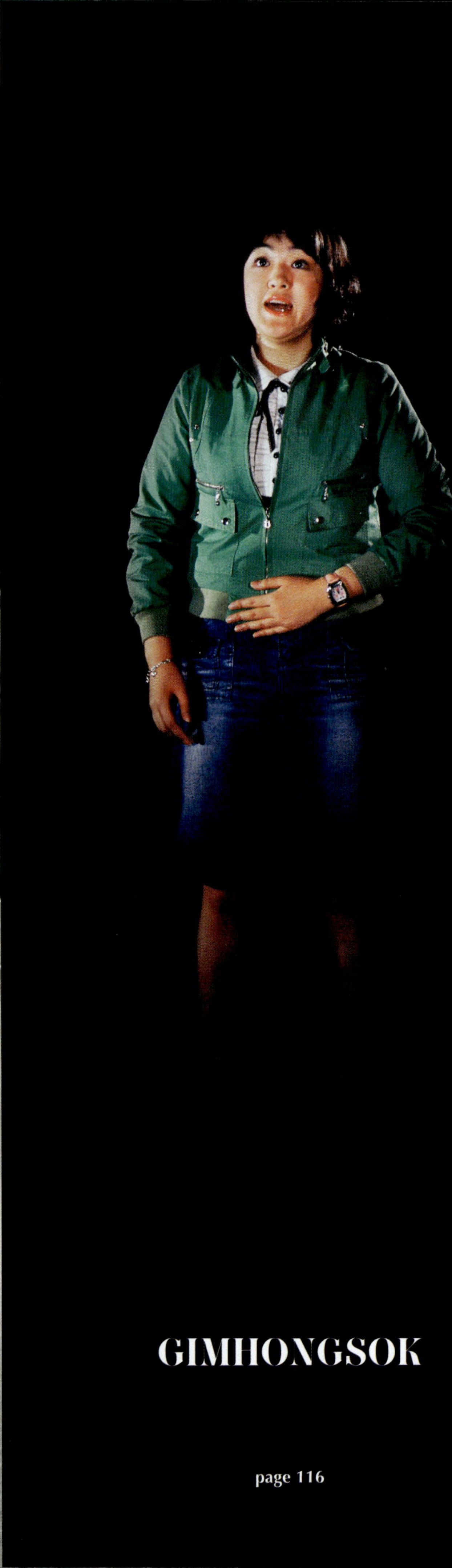

GIMHONGSOK

page 116

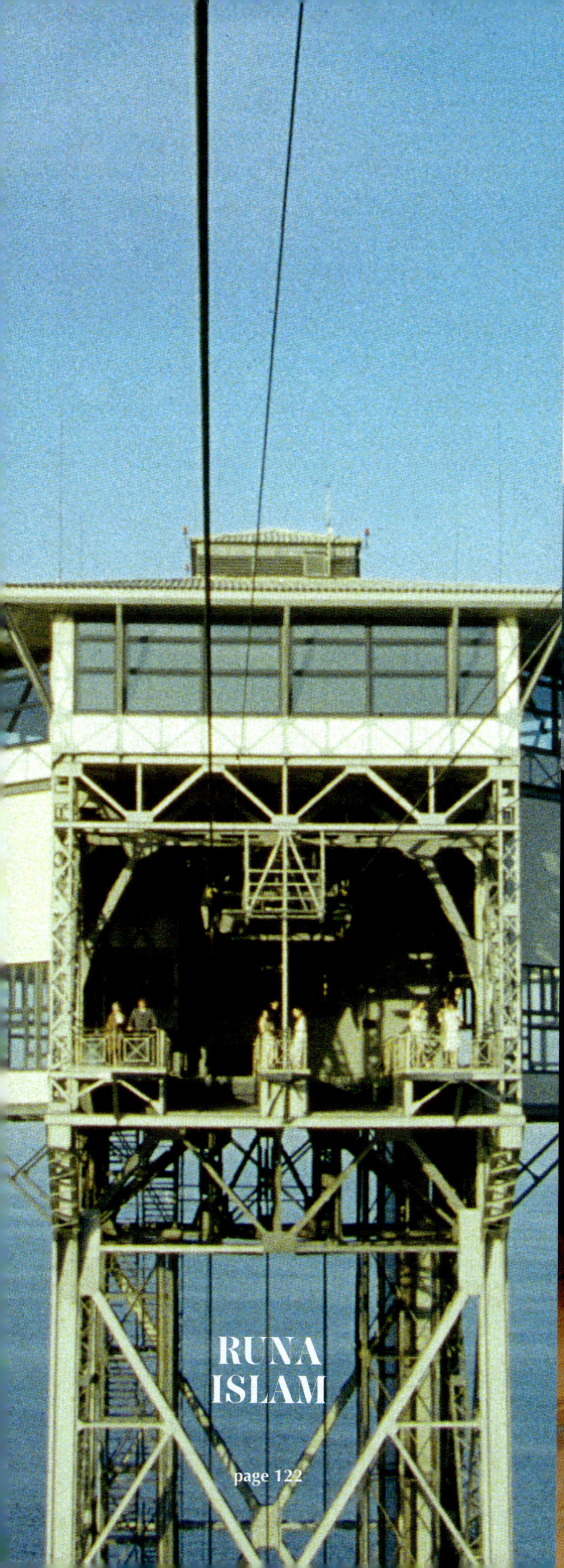

RUNA
ISLAM

page 122

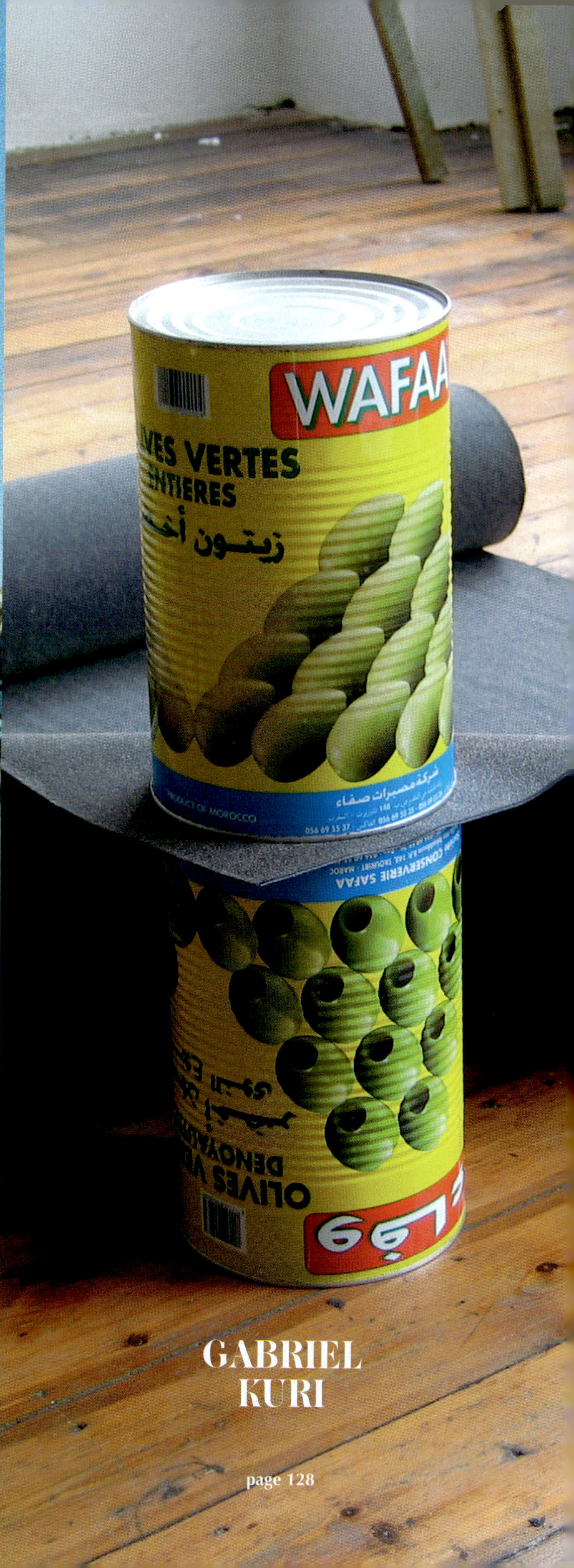

GABRIEL
KURI

page 128

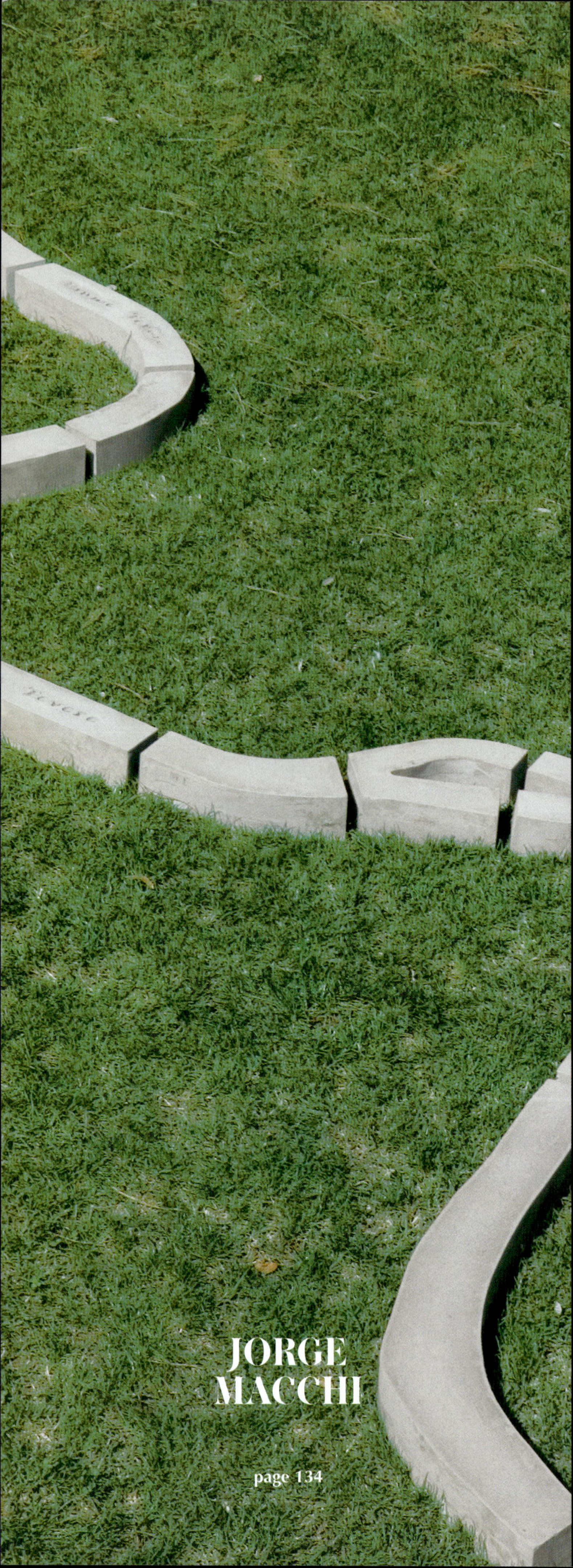

JORGE MACCHI

page 134

The Nation.

THE NEW AMERICAN CENTURY

ARUNDHATI ROY

page 140

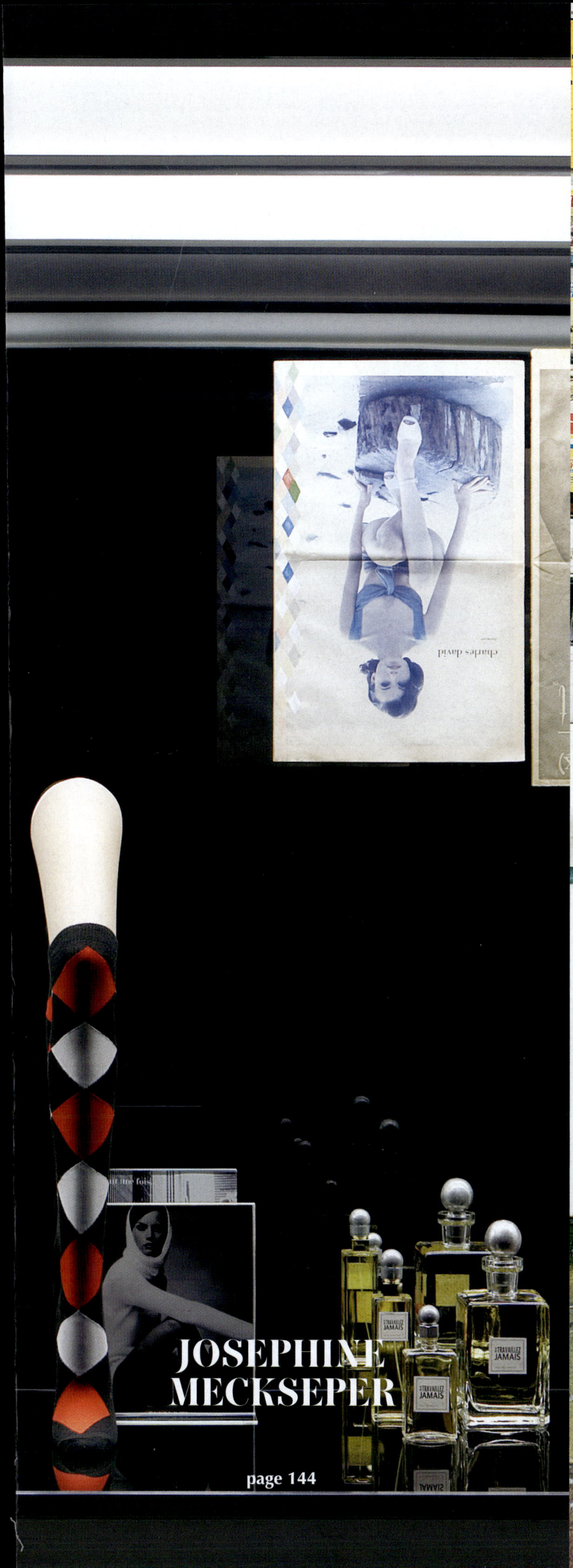

JOSEPHINE MECKSEPER

page 144

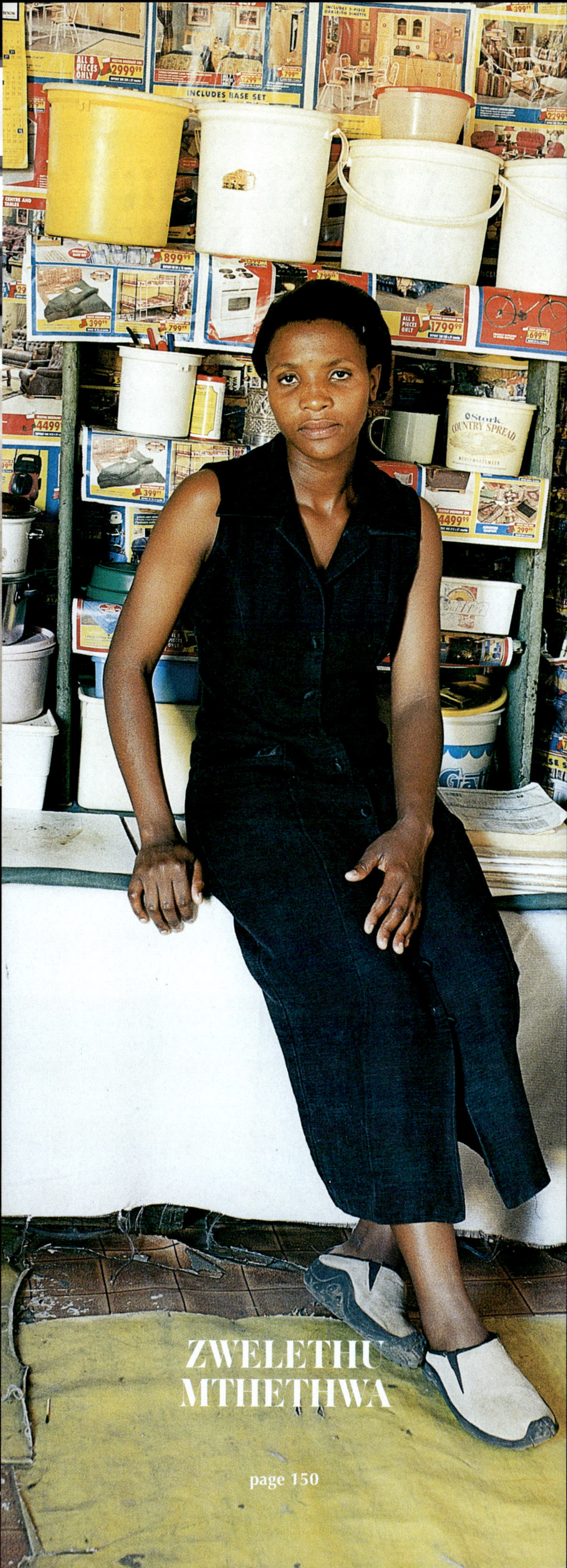

ZWELETHU MTHETHWA

page 150

A ROSE FOR BRAVE NEW WORLDS

§

YASMIL RAYMOND

What is the promise of art? What does art have to do with courage? Is the creative process an antidote to violence? The author ponders these questions through the work of the artists in the exhibition and concludes that peace is inherently a model of action and creation.

page 156

REPORT FROM SANTIAGO, CHILE

Brave New Worlds April 23, 2007

NOTES FROM CHILE: UTOPIA AND MELANCHOLIA

CECILIA BRUNSON

In 1965 a group of Latin American utopianists set out on a journey, under the banner Amereida—their modern answer to Virgil's The Aeneid—traversing the continent from the southernmost point to the edge of the Bolivian Amazon jungle. The expedition was cut short because another revolution was afoot, that of Che Guevara, but this convergence of architects, poets, and artists would have a lasting impact as an important historical avant-garde act.

page 163

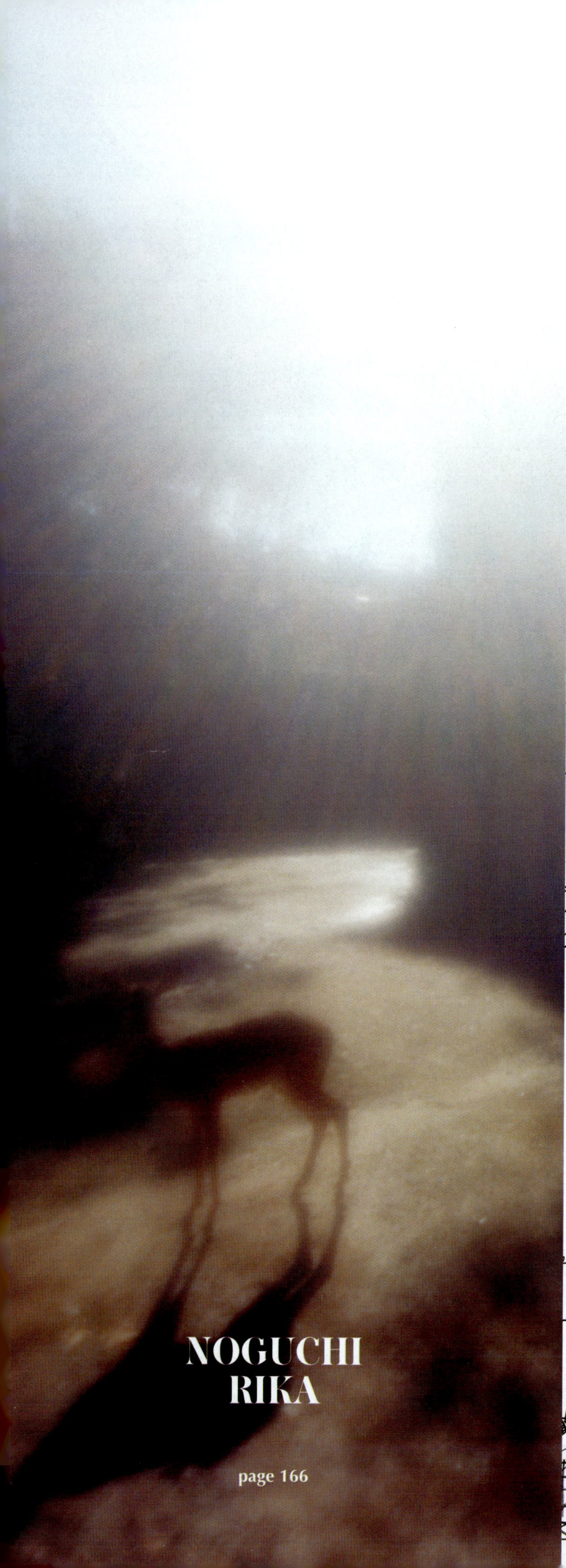

NOGUCHI
RIKA

page 166

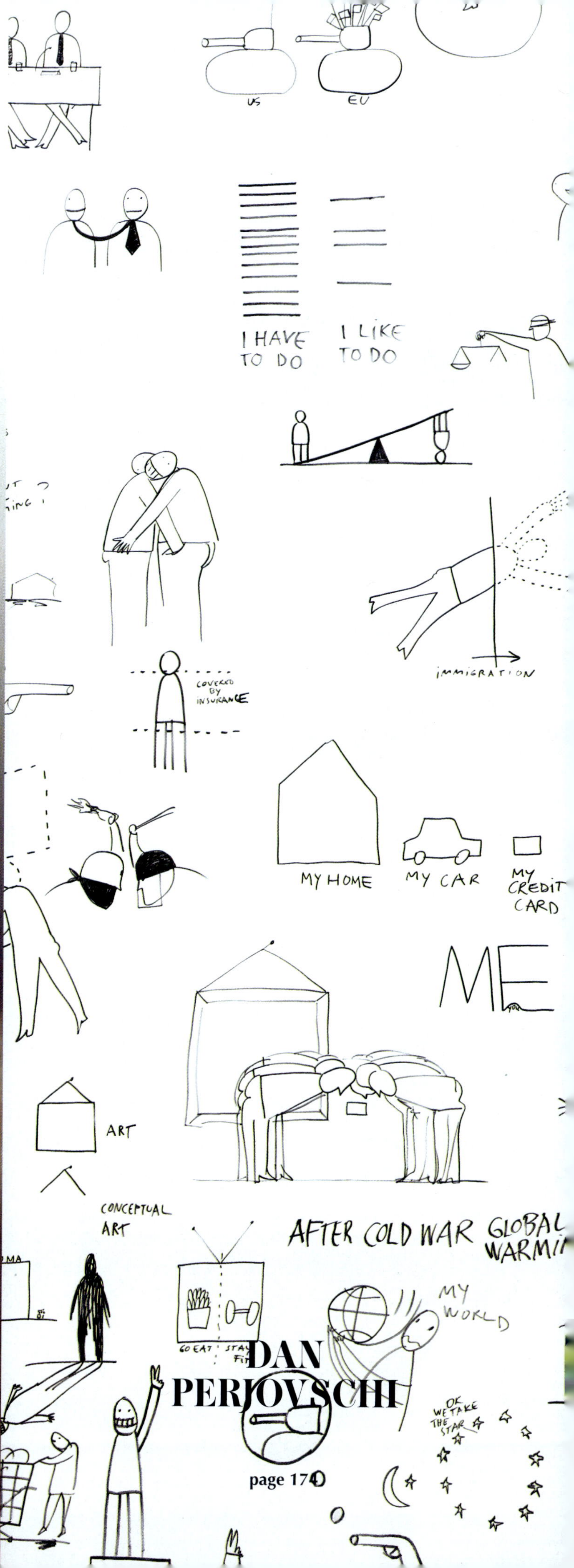

DAN
PERJOVSCHI

page 174

The New York Times Magazine

THE CASE FOR ONTAMINATION

KWAME ANTHONY APPIAH

page 178

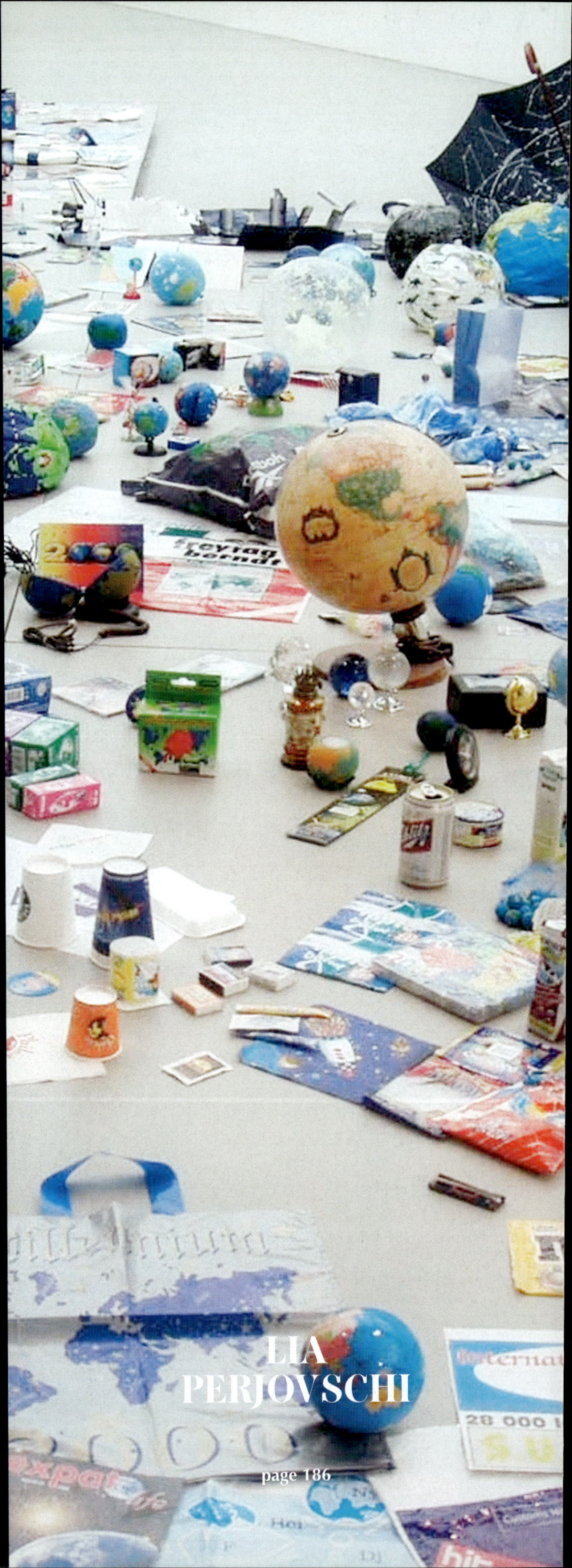

LIA PERJOVSCHI

page 186

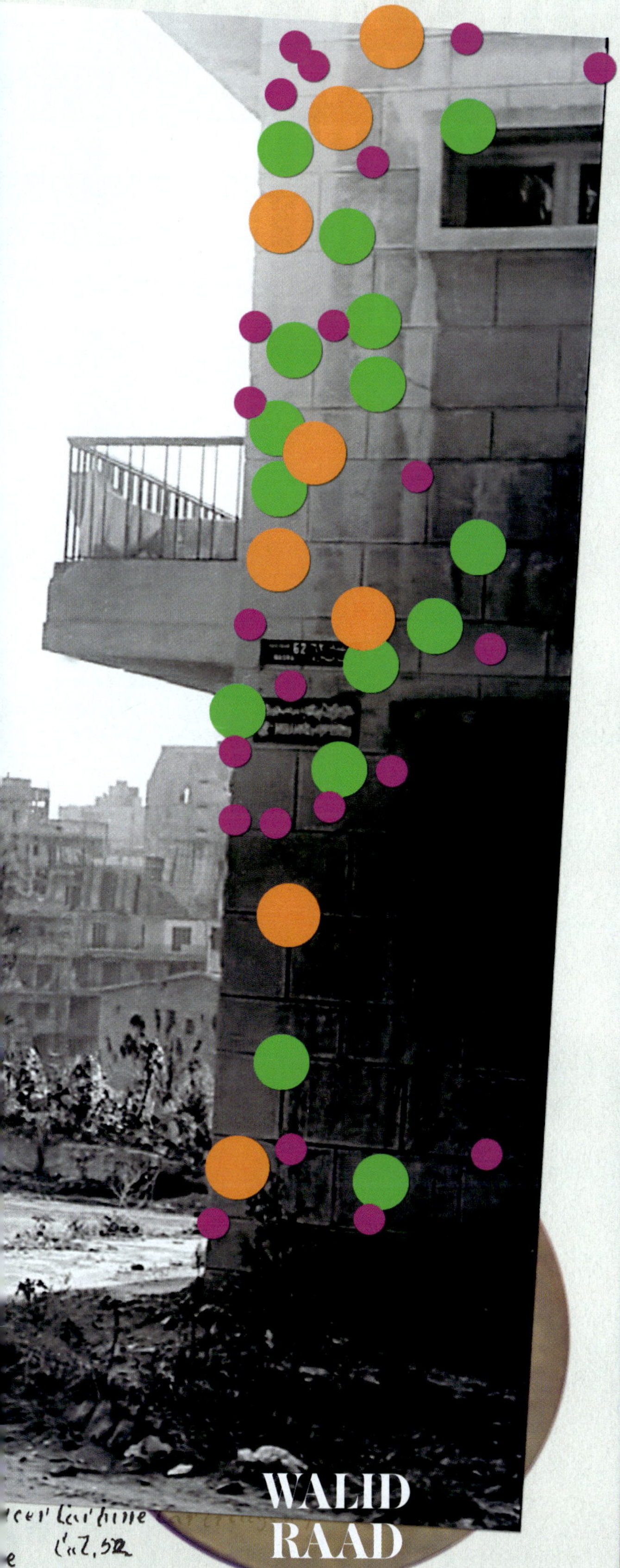

WALID RAAD

page 190

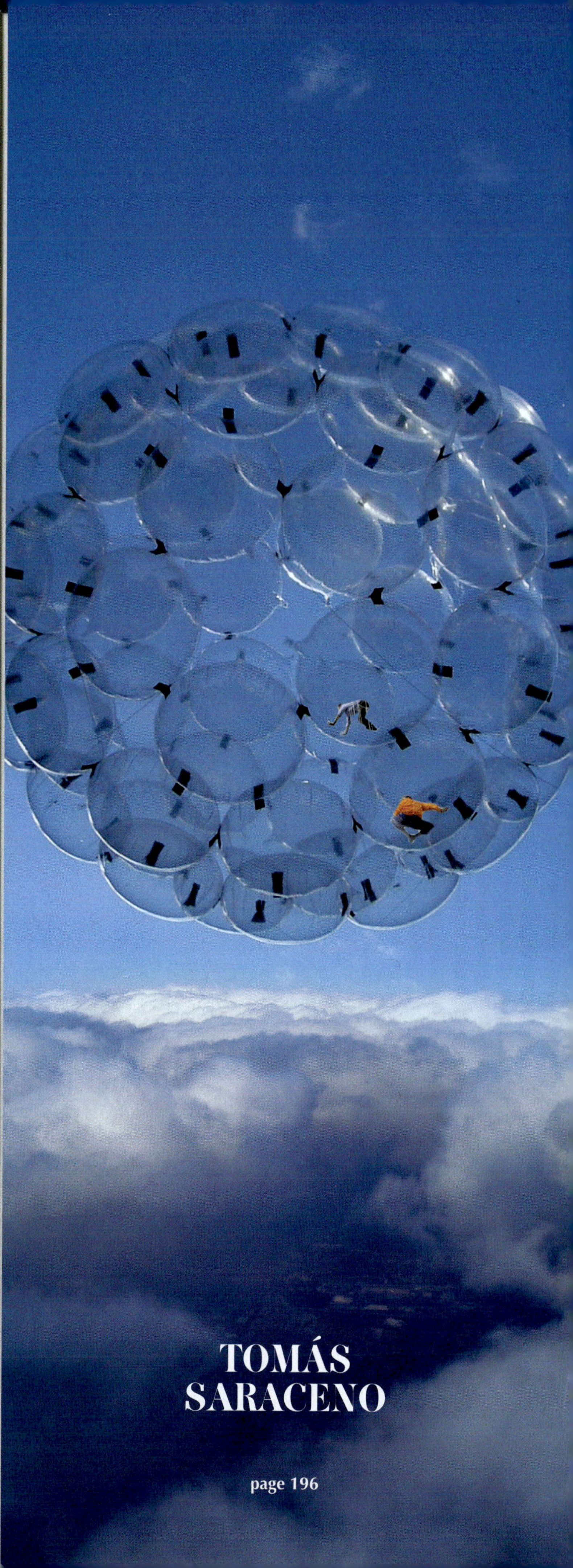

TOMÁS SARACENO

page 196

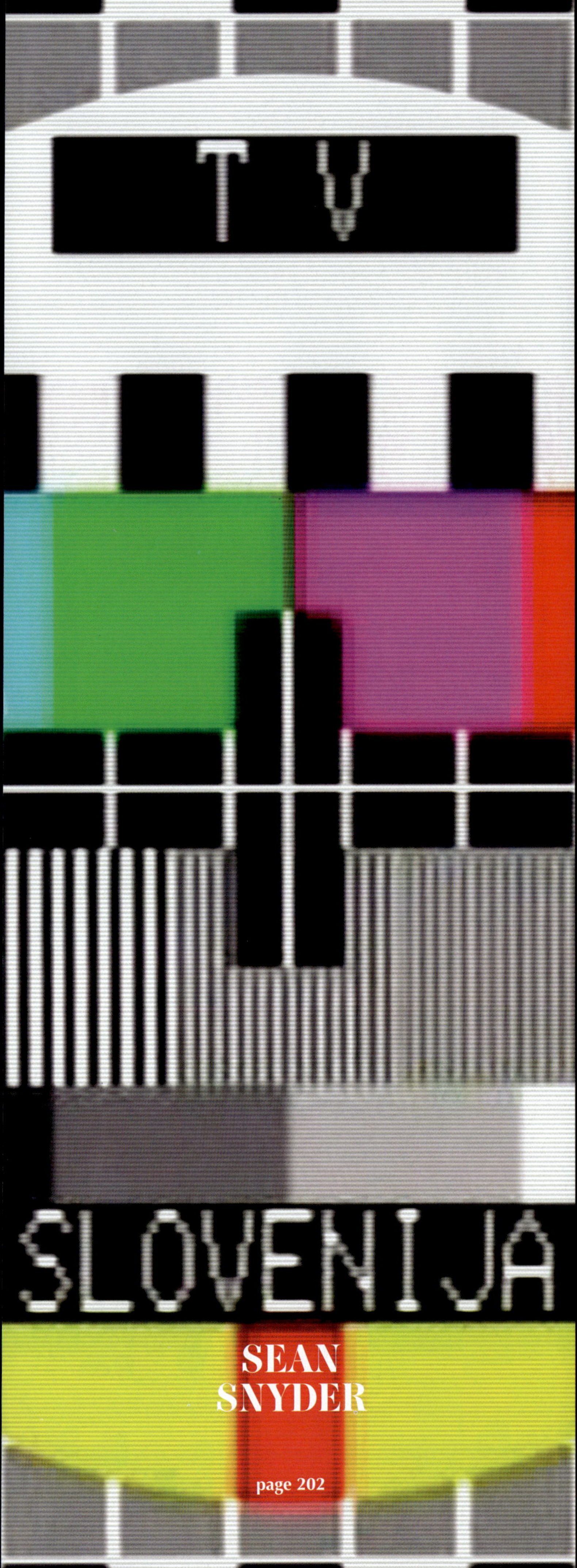

SEAN SNYDER

page 202

WHEN BEARING WITNESS OVERRIDES A REPORTER'S FEAR

JANINE DI GIOVANNI

page 210

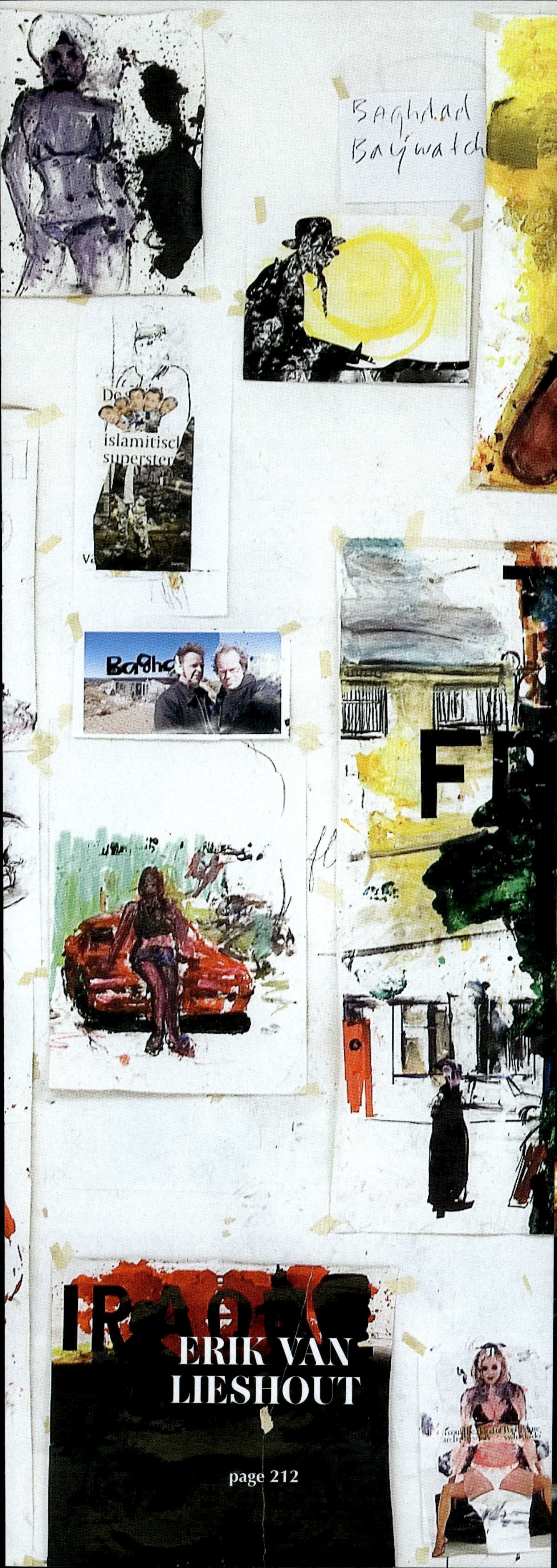

ERIK VAN LIESHOUT

page 212

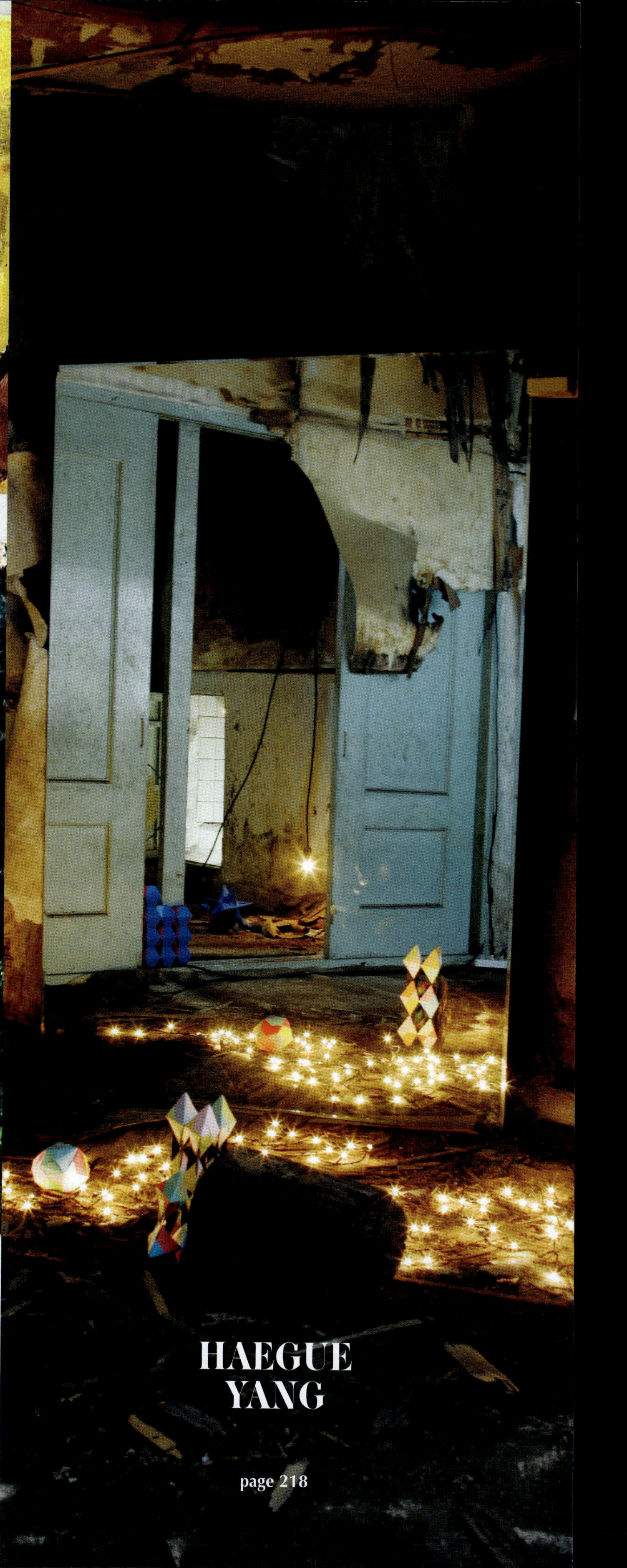

HAEGUE YANG

page 218

REPORT FROM GUANGZHOU, CHINA

Brave New Worlds February 15, 2007

REGARDING THE PAIN AND THE HAPPINESS OF OTHERS

HU FANG

Our Guangzhou-based correspondent often chats with his ailing, elderly mother via the Internet. The July 2004 London bombing, Motorcycle Diaries, Karl Marx's 1835 essay, the online game Second Life, and Susan Sontag's last book are some of the things that inflect this reflection on our heavily mediated existence in reality.

page 224

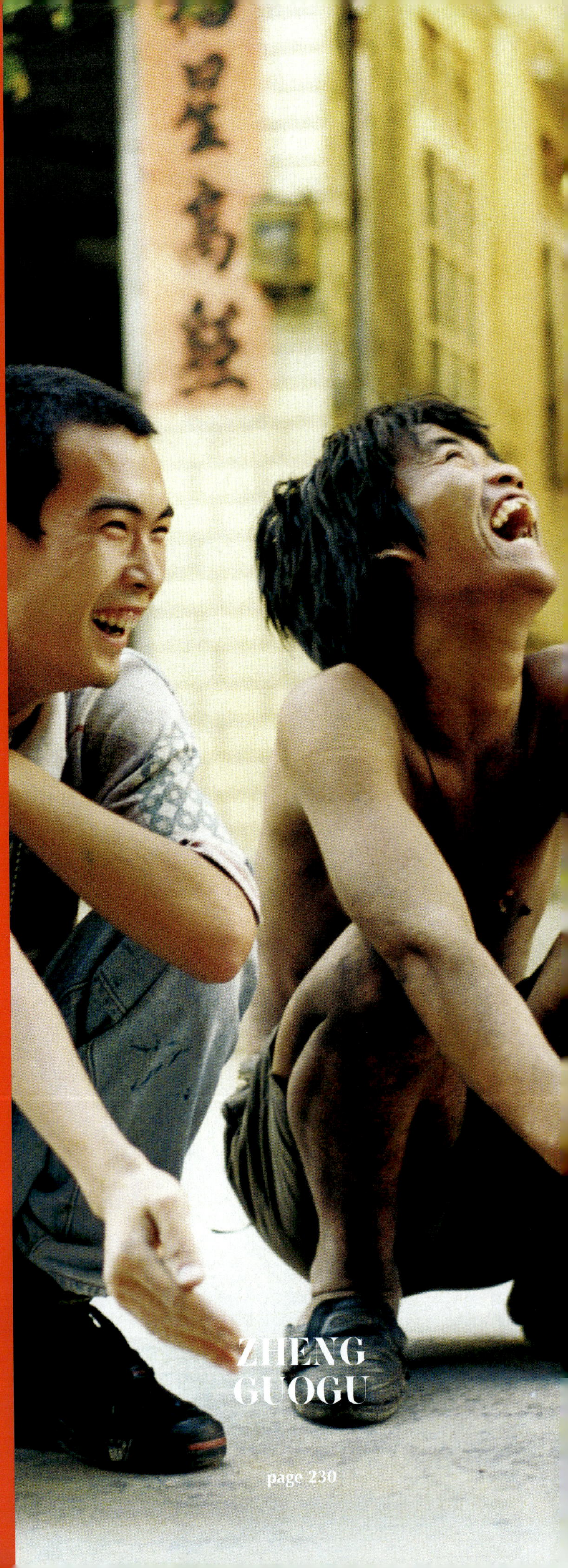

ZHENG GUOGU

page 230

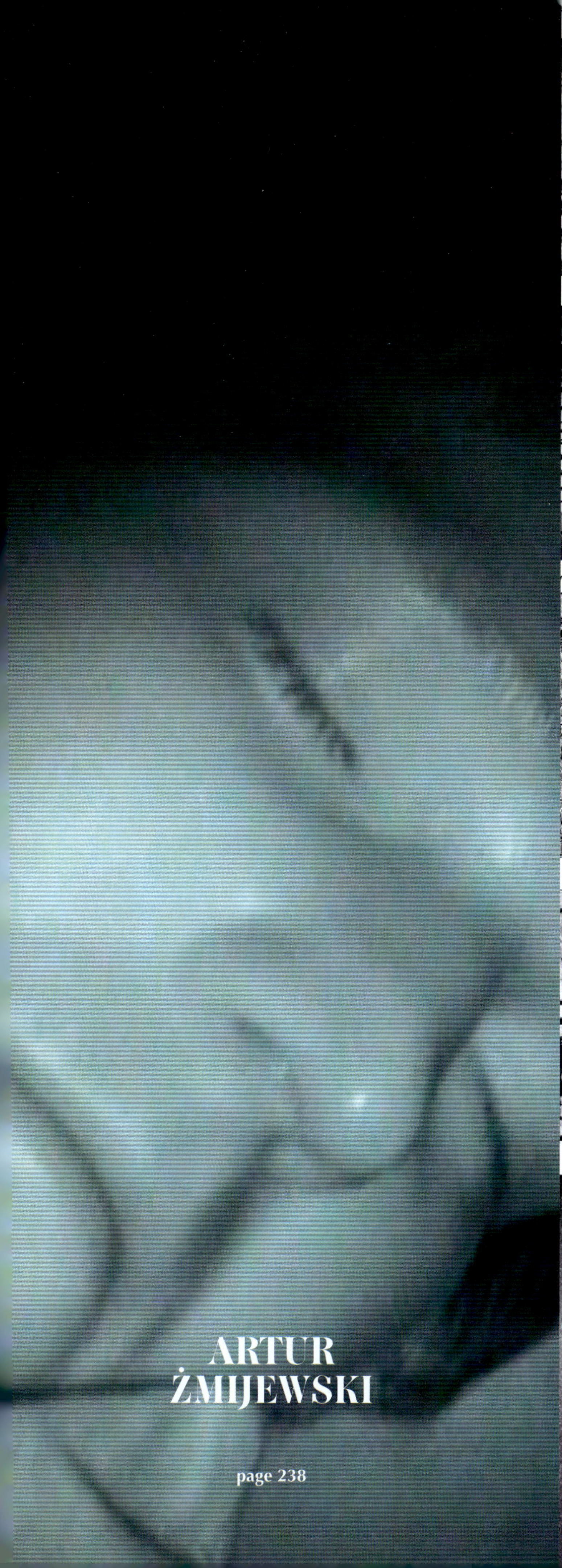

ARTUR ŻMIJEWSKI

page 238

hose who

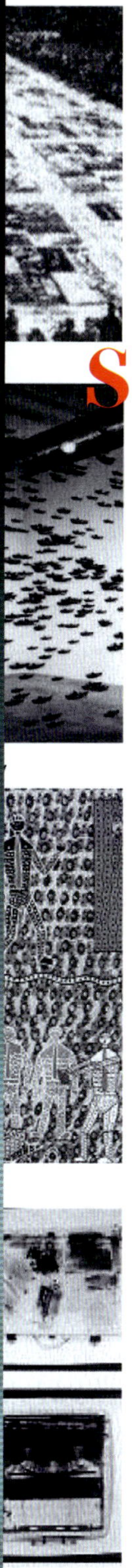

as a form of ultimate struggle against denial and death. “Macro-history” and “micro-history”. Being together. Idea of celebration, the need for desires the innocence of pleasure, the beauty of sharing. “The inclusion of the other in oneself” Charles Arthur Boyer.
Portrait of Marcel Brien 90 kg wrapped candies

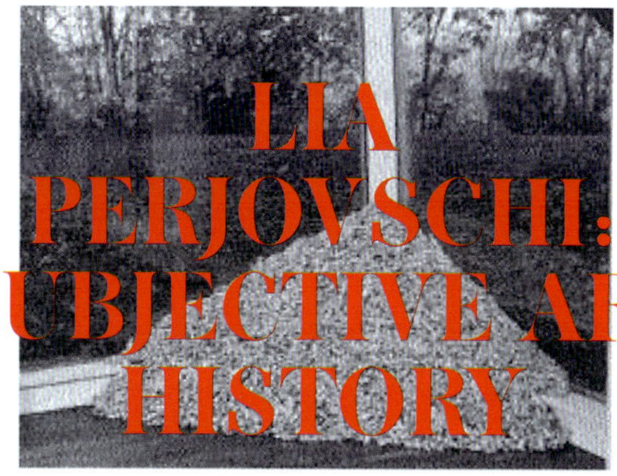

LIA PERJOVSCHI: SUBJECTIVE ART HISTORY

1987**Felix Gonzalez-Torres** Perfect Lovers

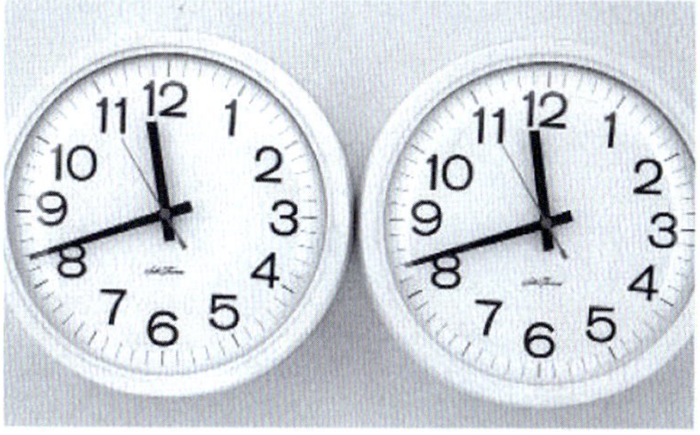

Sonsbeek - **site specific projects** in the city of Arnhem
1988 **Krysztof Wodicszko Unit** for homeless

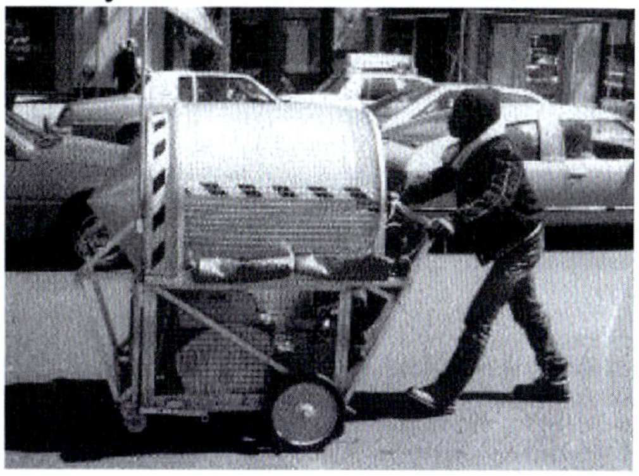

1988 **Katharina Fritsch** Company at Table

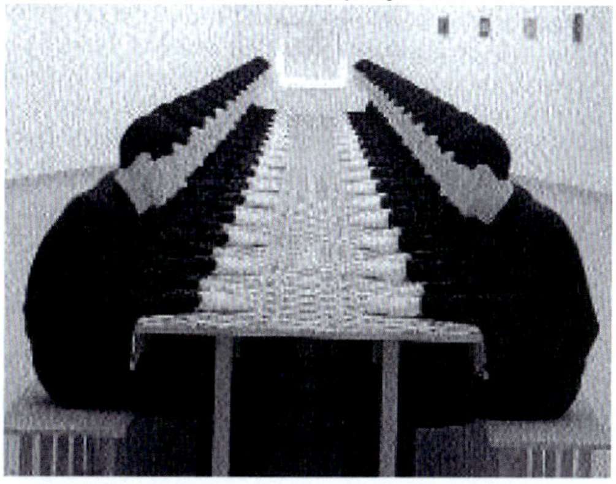

1988 **Joseph Kosuth** A grammatical remark

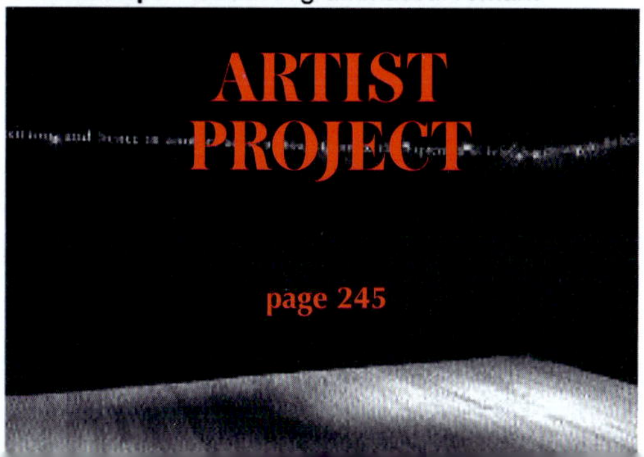

ARTIST PROJECT

page 245

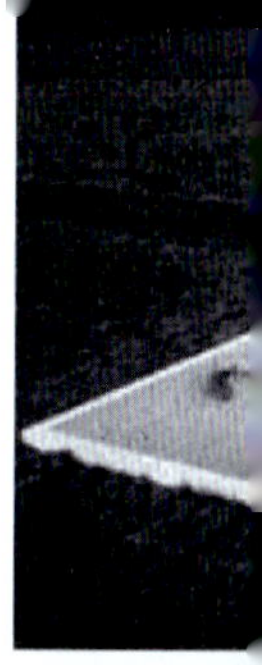

1989 **Ilya Ka**

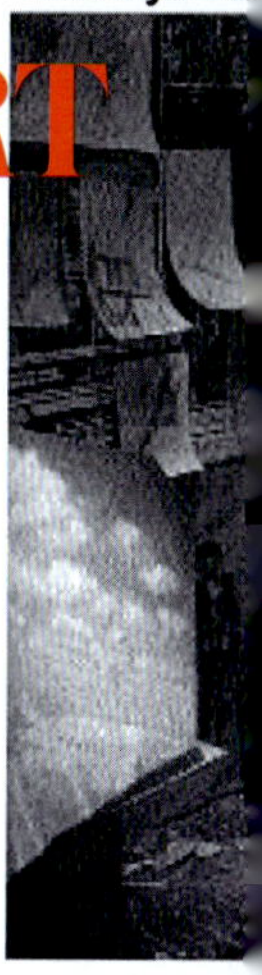

1989 **Fall of**
in East Eur
Jeffrey Sho
work

1989 **Damie**

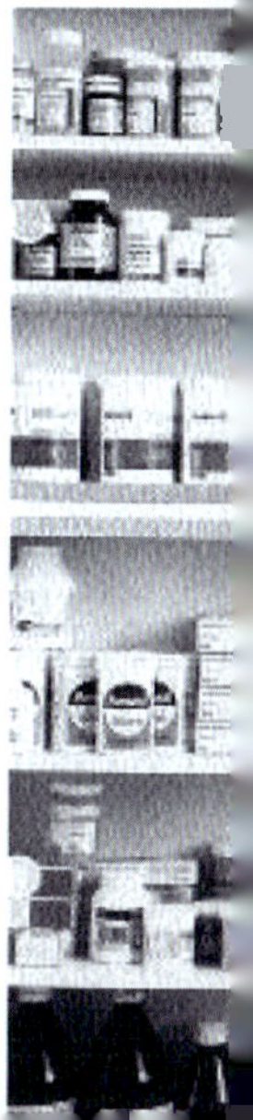

BRAV
WOR

E NEW
LDS

BRAV
WOR

E NEW
LDS

DORYUN CHONG / YASMIL RAYMOND

Walker Art Center, Minneapolis

Published on the occasion of the exhibition *Brave New Worlds*, organized by Doryun Chong and Yasmil Raymond for the Walker Art Center.

Walker Art Center
Minneapolis, Minnesota
October 4, 2007–February 17, 2008

Brave New Worlds is made possible by generous support from Ann M. Hatch and Peter and Annie Remes. Support for artist travel is provided in part by the Consulate General of the Netherlands in New York.

The exhibition catalogue is made possible by a grant from the Andrew W. Mellon Foundation in support of Walker Art Center publications.

Available through D.A.P./Distributed Art Publishers, 155 Sixth Avenue, New York, NY 10013. www.artbook.com

Printed and bound in Minneapolis by Bolger, Inc. and Midwest Editions, Inc.

Library of Congress Cataloging-in-Publication Data

Raymond, Yasmil.
Brave new worlds / Yasmil Raymond, Doryun Chong.—1st ed.
p. cm.
"Walker Art Center, Minneapolis, Minnesota, October 4, 2007-February 17, 2008."
ISBN-13: 978-0-935640-89-2 (pbk. : alk. paper)
ISBN-10: 0-935640-89-4 (pbk. : alk. paper)
1. Art and globalization—History—20th century—Exhibitions. 2. Art and globalization—History—21st century—Exhibitions. I. Chong, Doryun. II. Walker Art Center. III. Title.
N72.G55R39 2007
709.05'074776579—dc22
2007032184

Design Director: Andrew Blauvelt
Designer: Emmet Byrne
Design Fellow: Layla Tweedie-Cullen
Curatorial Fellow: Rachel Hooper
Editors: Pamela Johnson and Kathleen McLean
Publications Manager: Lisa Middag
Image Production: Greg Beckel

Cover: Cao Fei *Mirage* Production still from *COSPlayers* 2004 digital chromogenic print

Editors' Note

Brave New Worlds is an effort to reflect on the current station and meaning of "global art." We began by wondering how this important topic—and state of mind—that has influenced and shaped the topography of contemporary art and its discourse in the past two decades or so may have changed, perhaps radically, during the past few years. And this question is inextricably linked to the ways in which being "American" has also changed. As curators based in an American institution (in one of the so-called "flyover" Midwestern states, to be more precise), we operate with the assumption that our understanding of "global" may very well differ from that of other colleagues and audiences of contemporary art; we'd like to think that the relative geographic isolation of our location also affords us great openness and curiosity. Our experiences during the course of research for the exhibition affirmed, again and again, the utterly mundane and naïve but frequently forgotten fact that we live in a world composed of numerous places and realities that intimately resemble what we know, yet lie beyond our assumptions and comprehensions. As we got acquainted with distinctive portraits of places through our travels, the artists with whom we felt the strongest connections were those whose practice is, by definition and by necessity, political.

So how do artists make art politically? No doubt there are many ways of doing it, and our understanding is utterly and intentionally simple. We wake up every morning and drink coffee or tea while we read the newspaper (increasingly in digital format) to learn about the world. This is often the beginning as well as the foundation of a responsible relationship to reality, community, history, and the environment, and we have come to believe that this is also how some of today's most cogent and relevant art-making starts. That is, to make art is, in the first order, to try to know the world around you. Some artists focus on the diversity of possible gestures to gain such an understanding, while others explore the many avenues of materially experiencing that same world. Then, there are those who doggedly dream of alternative worlds. Ultimately, however, even when their voices seem most quixotic, they are undeniably anchored by their desire to know and experience the world.

As we were getting to know the twenty-four artists in this exhibition and their work, we were also fortunate to come in contact with a number of fellow curators, critics, and writers from across the globe who not only generously shared their knowledge about the artistic landscape of each specific site, but also treated us to cram courses on the broader historical, social, cultural, and even economic contexts that shape artistic tendencies and exigencies in their locales. In the following pages, selected "correspondents" put on the hat of journalist and tell us about the places in which they live. While the itinerary covered in this volume makes stops in physical sites around the world—from the Strait of Gibraltar and the highlands of Northern Israel to a Balkan city and Southern China to Los Angeles and Valparaíso, Chile—you will also encounter in myriad forms multiple references to certain critical subjects: wars, past and present, and their reckonings; labor and migration; national and supranational citizenship; monuments and the media, to name just a few. These are ingredients of our hopes and nightmares—or our everyday reality.

In Aldous Huxley's *Brave New World*, a 1932 novel about a future dystopia, humankind is ruled as a unified body politic called "World State." Our perspective of multitudinous "brave new worlds" may be thought of as an antidote to that terrifying vision of singularity, maintained through all-encompassing social engineering. But also critically, ours is a view of this particular moment. This chorus of voices is but one crystallization of our position vis-à-vis the world, a reality that continues to resolutely exist and indefatigably evolve.

Doryun Chong & Yasmil Raymond
October 2007

Departments

Note to the Reader

The artist entries in this catalogue were written by exhibition co-curators Doryun Chong **(DC)** and Yasmil Raymond **(YR)** and curatorial fellow Rachel Hooper **(RH)** of the Walker Art Center.

Correspondents

Max Andrews and Mariana Cánepa Luna are the directors of Latitudes, an independent curatorial office founded in April 2005. With an operational base in Barcelona (41°23′ N, 2°10′ E), Latitudes explores local, pan-European, and international networks and collaborates with artists, institutions, and organizations to facilitate and produce temporary and sustained projects, including exhibitions, commissions, editorial initiatives, research, and conferences. Most recently, they edited *LAND, ART: A Cultural Ecology Handbook* (Royal Society of Arts/Arts Council England, December 2006) and organized a symposium in partnership with the Royal Society of Arts for Still Life: Art, Ecology and the Politics of Change, Sharjah Biennial 8, United Arab Emirates.

Cecilia Brunson is a curator based in Santiago, Chile, where she directs the curatorial residency program INCUBO. Prior to her independent curatorial work, she was associate curator at the Blanton Museum of Art, Austin, Texas, and exhibition coordinator at the Americas Society, New York. Some of her recent exhibitions include: *Claudio Girola: Invención y Travesías* 1923–1994 (Museum of Fine Arts, Buenos Aires, and Museo Rufino Tamayo, Mexico City, 2007–2008); *Luis Camnitzer: 1968 Masacre de Puerto Montt* (Galería Metropolitana, Santiago); *Cristián Silva: Black Sun–Green Flamingo* (Blanton Museum of Art, Austin); and the 29th Biennial of Pontevedra, Spain, for which she was the curatorial advisor.

Tone Hansen, an artist and writer, lives and works in Oslo, Norway. Currently a research fellow at the Academy of Fine Art in Oslo, she is the editor of the anthology *What Does "Public" Mean? Art as a Participant in the Public Arena* and *The New Administration of Aesthetics: The Reader* (Torpedo Press, Oslo, 2006). Her recent project, *Megamonstermuseum: How to Imagine a Museum of Today?*, was shown at the Photo Gallery in Oslo in 2007. Hansen has written texts for a number of art magazines, including *IASPIS* (Sweden) and *Derivé* (Austria), as well as for newspapers and catalogues.

Hu Fang, based in Guangzhou and Beijing, China, is the cofounder and artistic director of Vitamin Creative Space in Guangzhou as well as a novelist and essayist. His most recent book, *New Arcades*, is a collection of fictional essays, including "Survival Club," "Sensation Fair," and "Cool Shanshui" (Map Office Publishers, Hong Kong, 2006). Hu was also a coordinating editor of *documenta 12* magazines, and is one of the invited "players" at the Lyon Biennial 2007 as well as a member of the curatorial team of the Yokohama Triennale 2008.

Mihnea Mircan is a curator based in Bucharest, Romania. He coordinates *Under Destruction*, a series of site-specific projects at the Museum of Contemporary Art, Bucharest. The third episode, with artist Nedko Solakov, is scheduled for October 2007. Mircan has recently organized the exhibition *Sublime Objects: Works from the Collections of FRAC Grand Est* and curated the Romanian Pavilion at the 2007 Venice Biennale.

José Roca is a curator based in Bogotá, Colombia, where he directs the art program of the Banco de la República. His recent curatorial projects include *Phantasmagoria: Specters of Absence* (Biblioteca Luis Ángel Arango, Bogotá, with traveling exhibition coproduced with Independent Curators International, New York, 2007–2009), and *Botánica política* (Sala Montcada, Fundación La Caixa, Barcelona, 2004). He also co-curated the Trienal Poli/gráfica de San Juan, Puerto Rico (2004) and the 27th São Paulo Biennial (2006). Roca is currently the artistic director of *Philagrafika*, a quadrennial exhibition of contemporary printmaking to be held in Philadelphia in 2010.

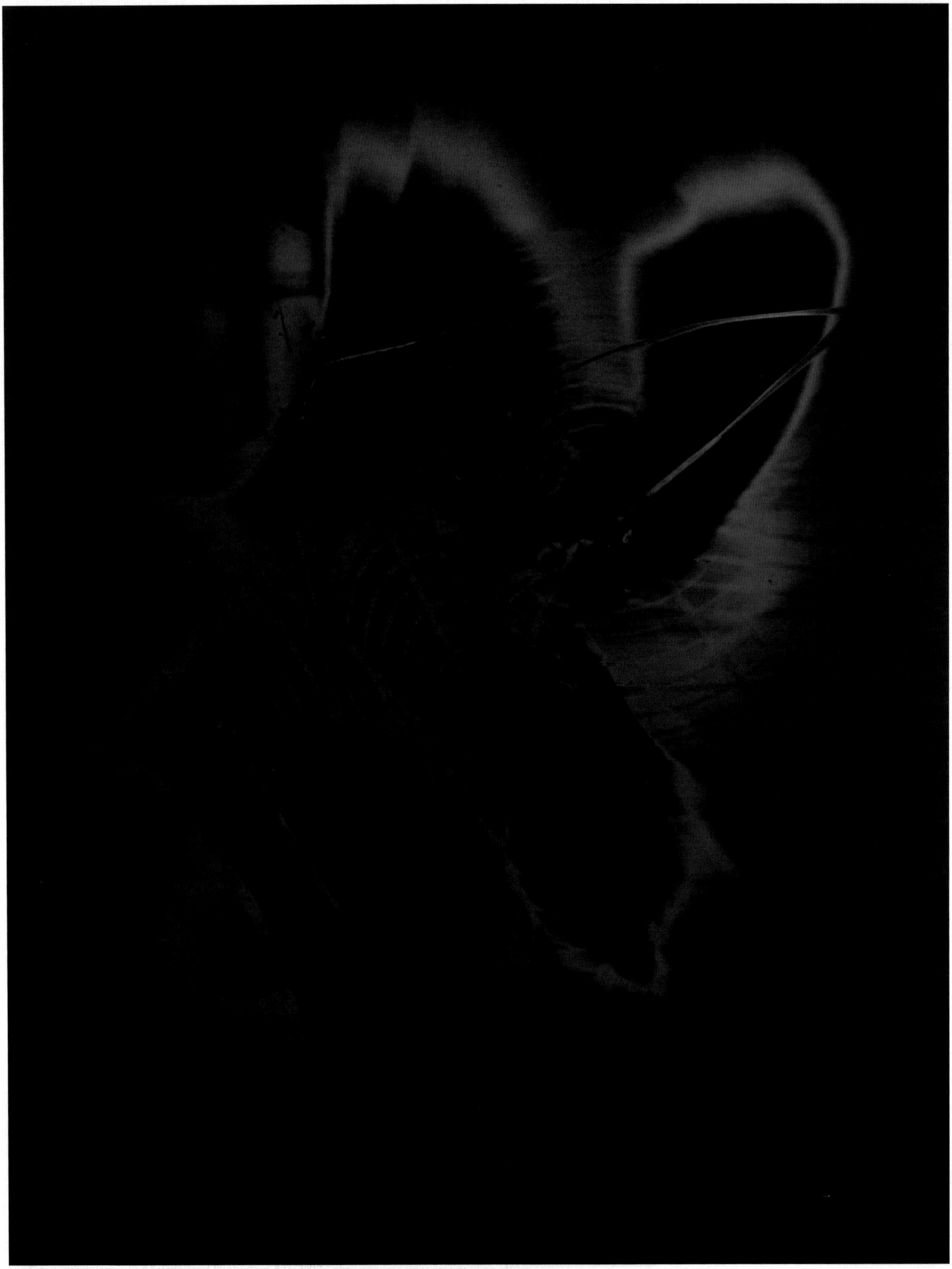

Fotograma solarizado #3 (*Solarized Photogram #3*) 2007 chromogenic print mounted on aluminum

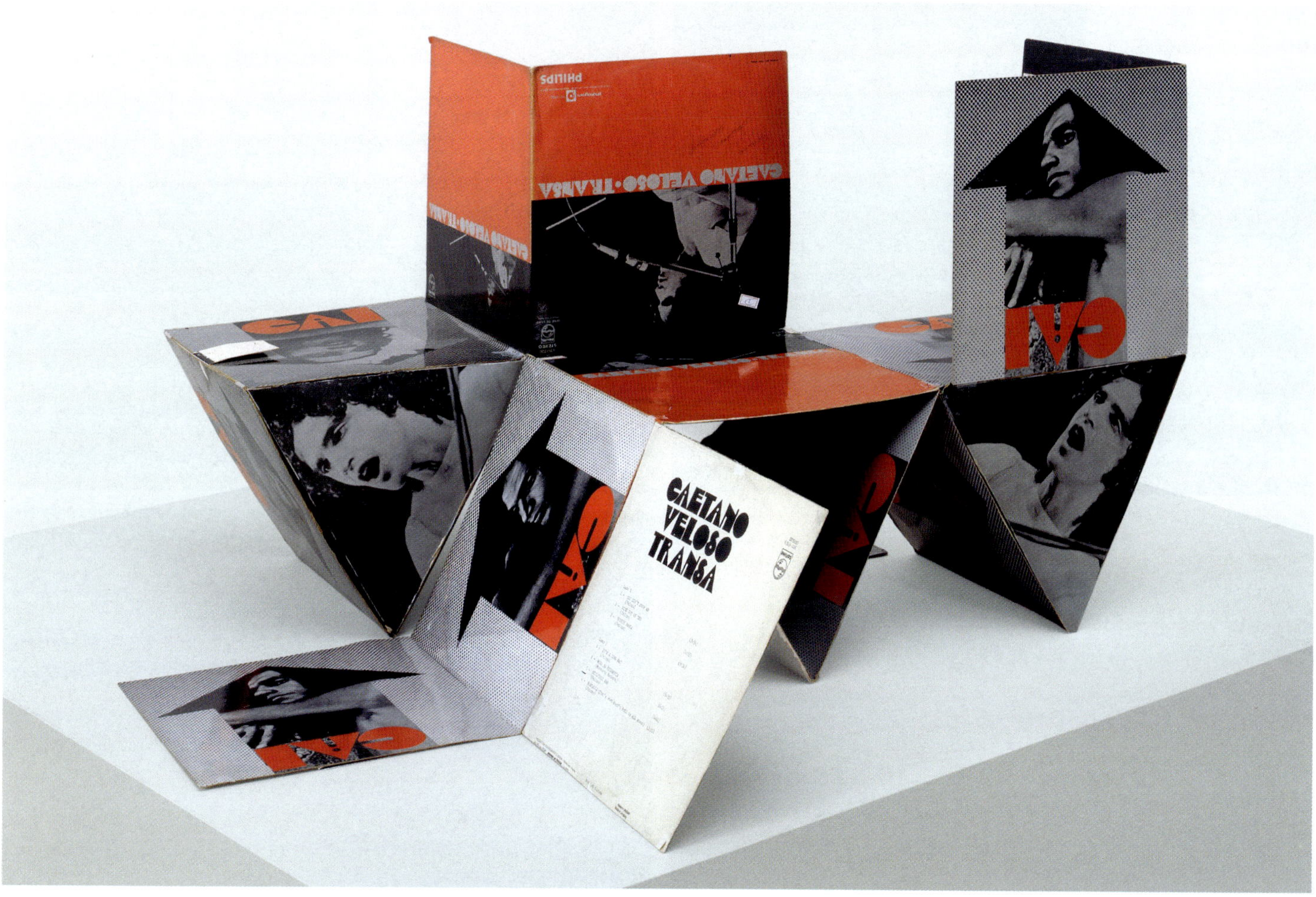

Transa 2005 paper, vinyl

GEOMETRIES OF LIGHT: ARMANDO ANDRADE TUDELA

Born in Peru, 1975. Lives and works in St. Étienne, France.

Armando Andrade Tudela's body of work includes sculpture, photography, video, and works on paper and reflects on cultural information and its various levels of meaning. Playfully asserting the technique of collage in his practice, he juxtaposes geometric and organic forms along with spatial patterns to create crossing layers, common grounds, and intersecting relationships. For the most part, the work starts with an investigation into a structure, which the artist has described as "modules of information that flow through different aspects of culture: history, architecture, [and] vernacular paraphernalia."[1] In *Transa* (2005), for example, he arranged covers of Caetano Veloso's 1972 album of the same title (recorded during his political exile in London) into a balanced structure of zigzag rows of positive and negative black, red, and silver triangles combined with head shots of the singer. Andrade connects the leading voice of the Tropicália movement in Brazil with the avant-garde ideals championed by Veloso's contemporaries such as artists Lygia Clark and Hélio Oiticica, who were preoccupied with breaking down social hierarchies through the sensorial experience of art. Andrade's cardboard construction transposes packaging material into a malleable kinetic sculpture reminiscent of Clark's *Bichos* (1960), a series of pliable structures made of aluminum plates that she described as "living beings," but Andrade's abstract geometry traverses the realm of popular music rendered as hybrid organism.

The artist's exploration of the crossroads of forms, structures, and ideologies responds to his interest in the contextual connections and overlooked histories of his native Peru. His slide projection *Camión* (2003) is a photographic essay on Peruvian abstraction, not in the realm of painting and sculpture but in vernacular street culture. The sixty-photograph endeavor seeks to rectify, not without a touch of humor, the presumption that modernity had a "late arrival" in Latin America. The fifteen-minute slide presentation focuses on bold geometric designs—lines, arrows, circles, triangles—painted on the exteriors of commercial trucks and trailers. The pedagogical overtone implied by the slide show's formality is rapidly deflated by the deliberate pacing of the images—blurry fleeting shots taken on the move as the artist chased down his subjects—transforming the speechless presentation into a rhythmic display of saturated colors and shapes. In *Fotograma solarizado* (*Solarized Photogram*) (2007), a series of black-and-white photograms, Andrade takes his exploration into the contested ground of representation and abstraction in photography. Combining the antiquated Rayogram with traditional photographic techniques, he renders a group of uncanny silhouettes countered by nebulous gray halos that dissolve the objects' origins, liberating them from their concreteness into abstraction of the yet unnamed.

YR

1. Armando Andrade Tudela, interview with Adriano Pedrosa, in Lisette Lagnado and Adriano Pedrosa, eds., *27a. Bienal de São Paulo Guia*, exh. pub. (São Paulo: Fundação Bienal de São Paulo, 2006), 36.

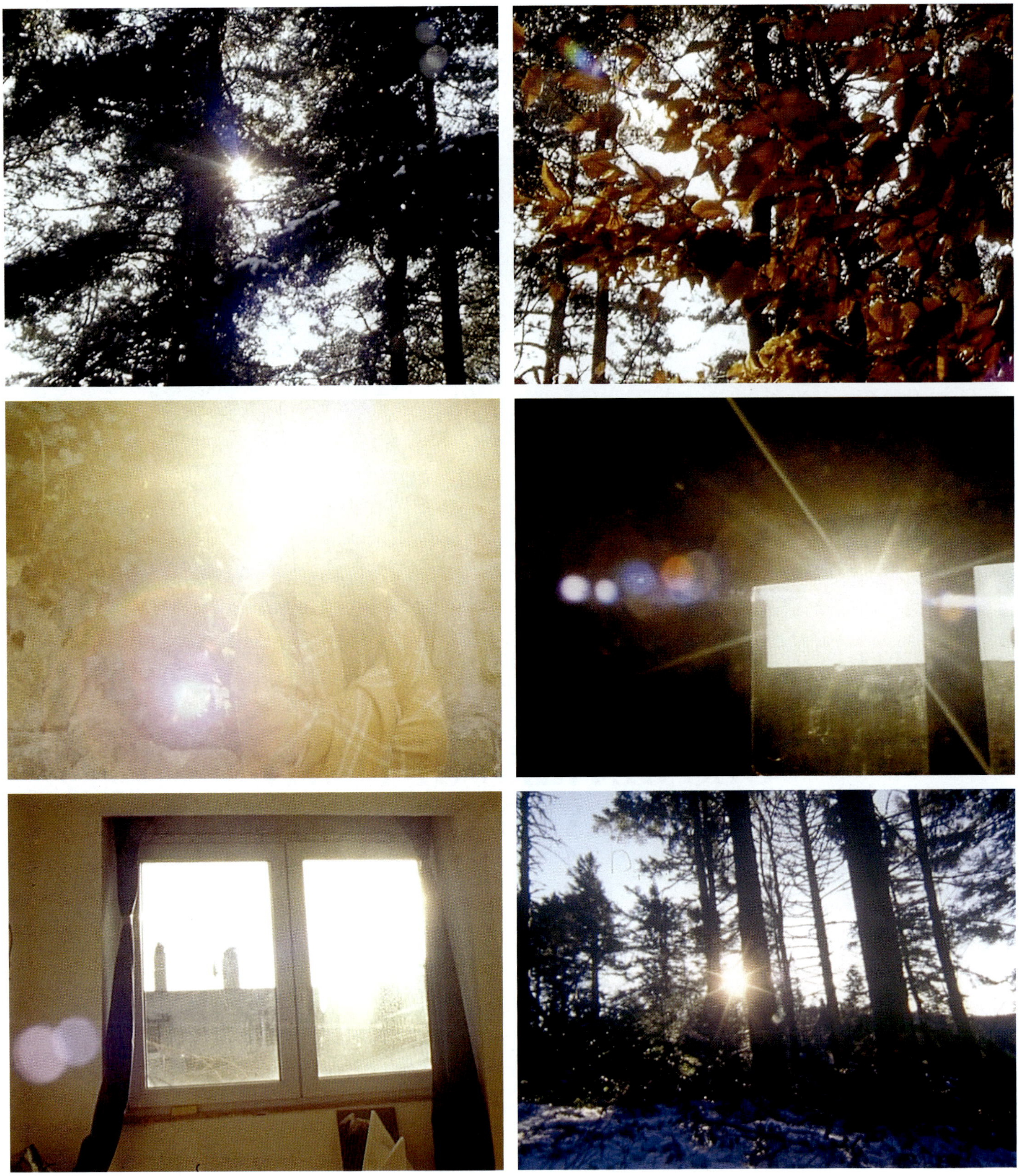

Stills from *Untitled Film #1* 2007 16mm film transferred to DVD (color, silent); 8:08 minutes

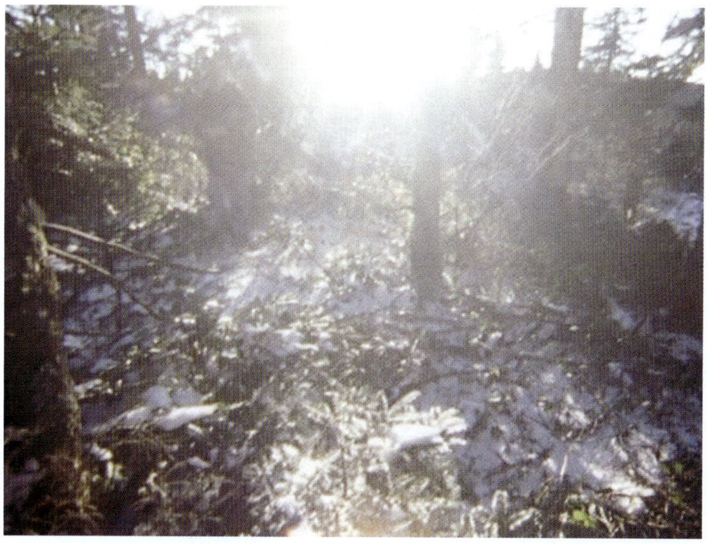
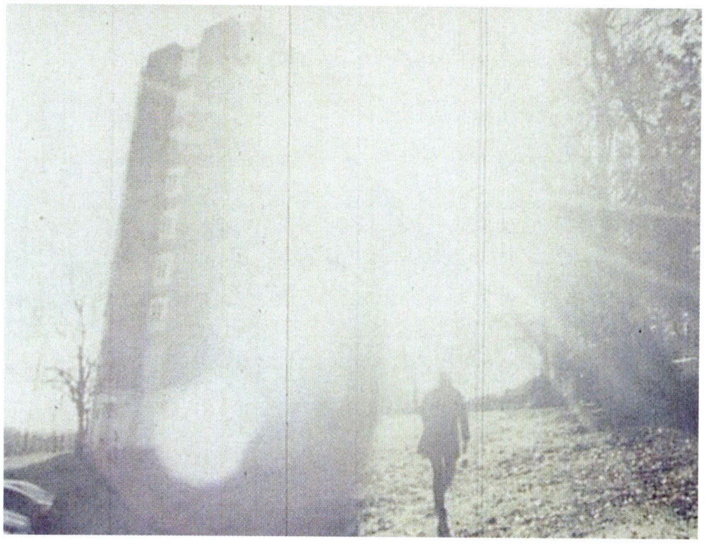
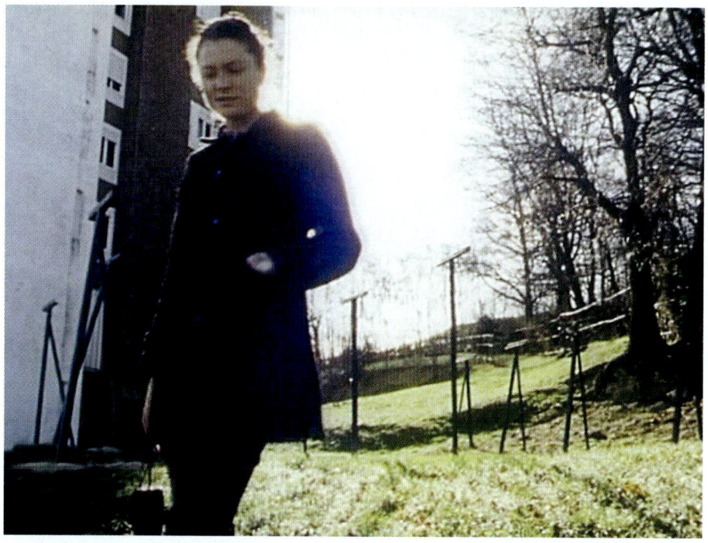
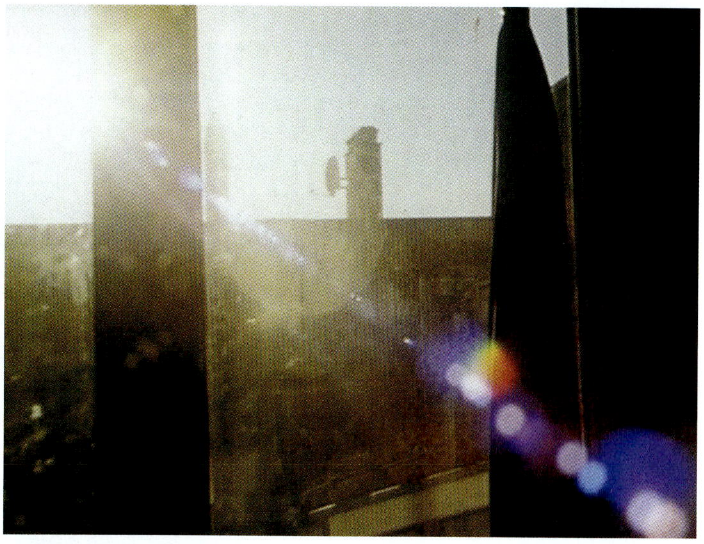
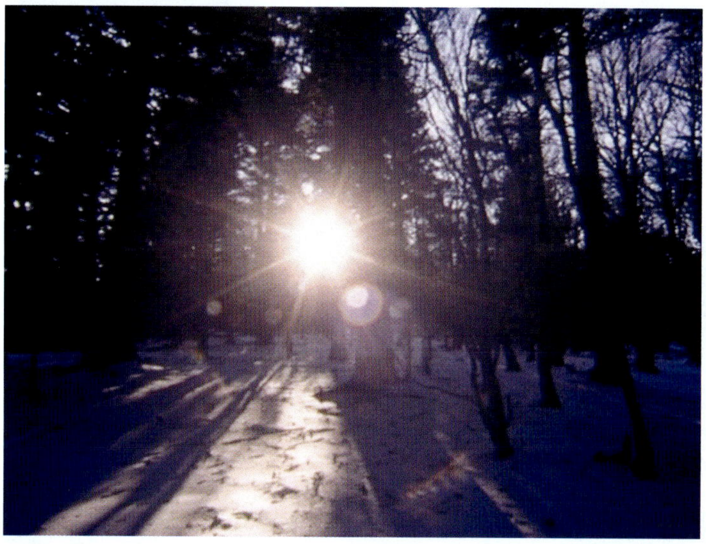
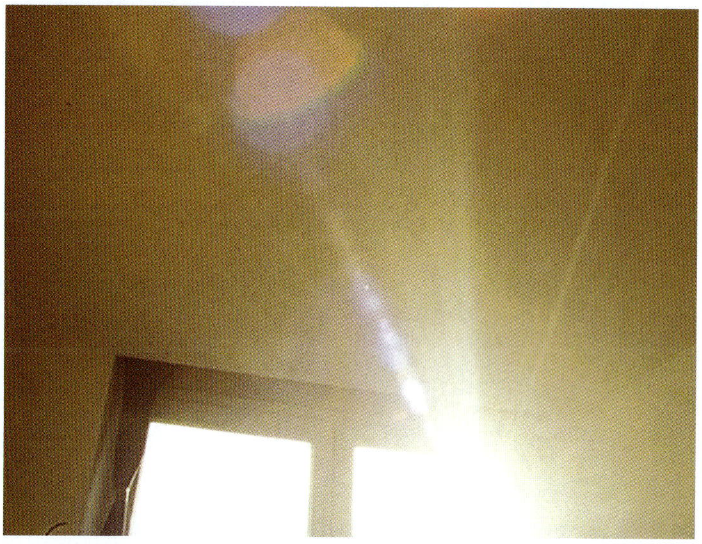

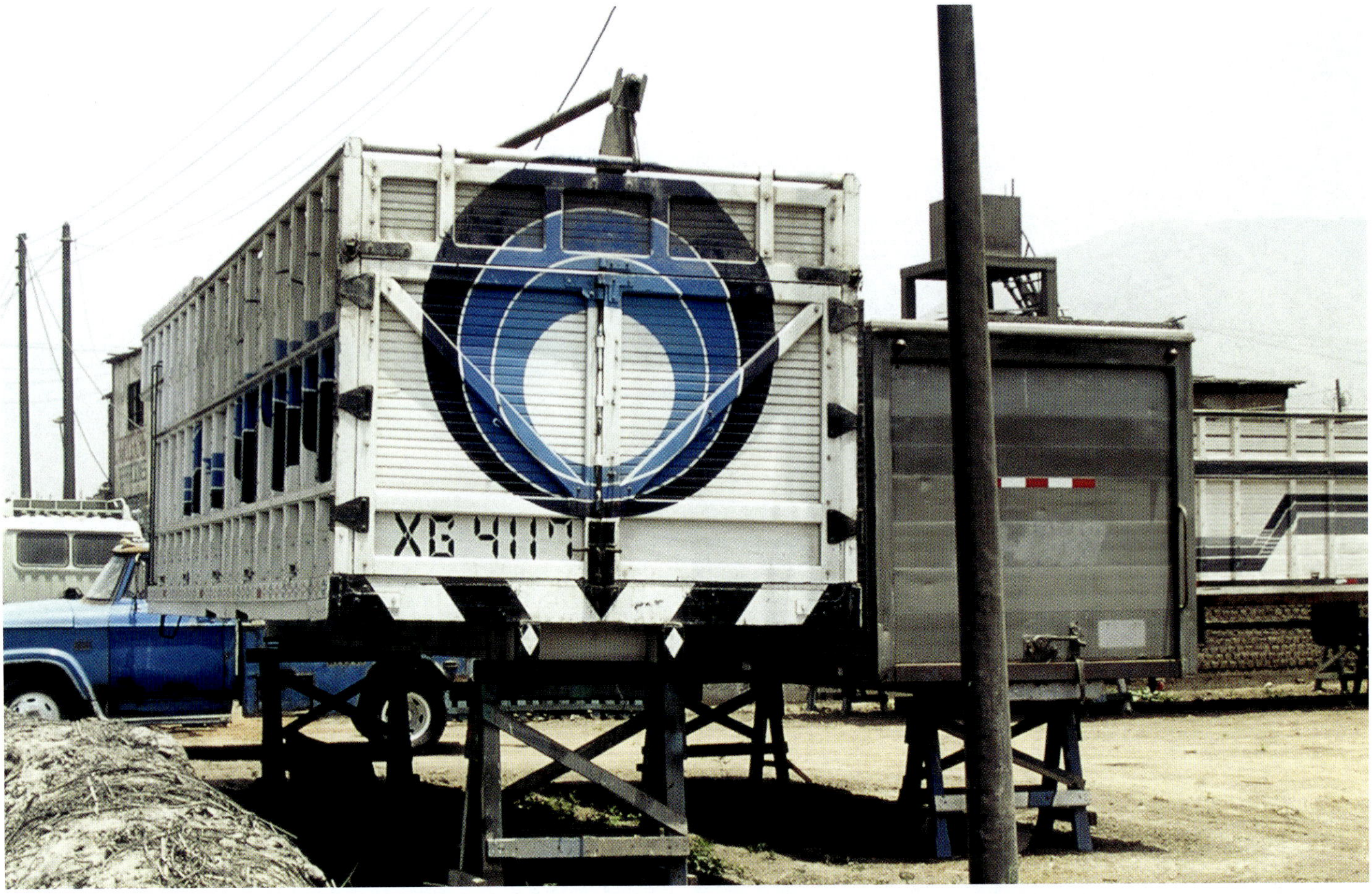

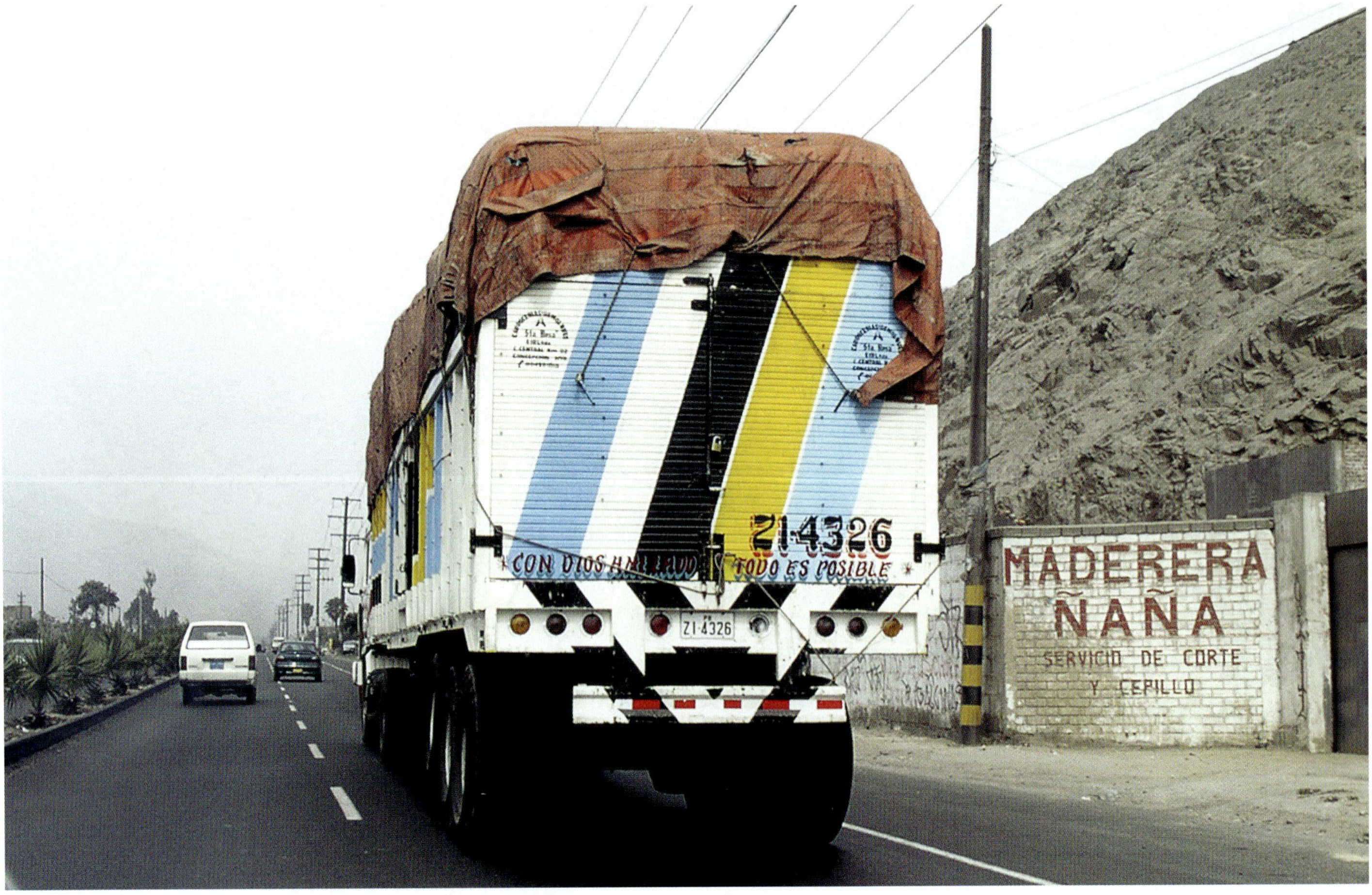

Stills from *Camión* 2003 35mm color slides, plexiglass stand; 15 minutes

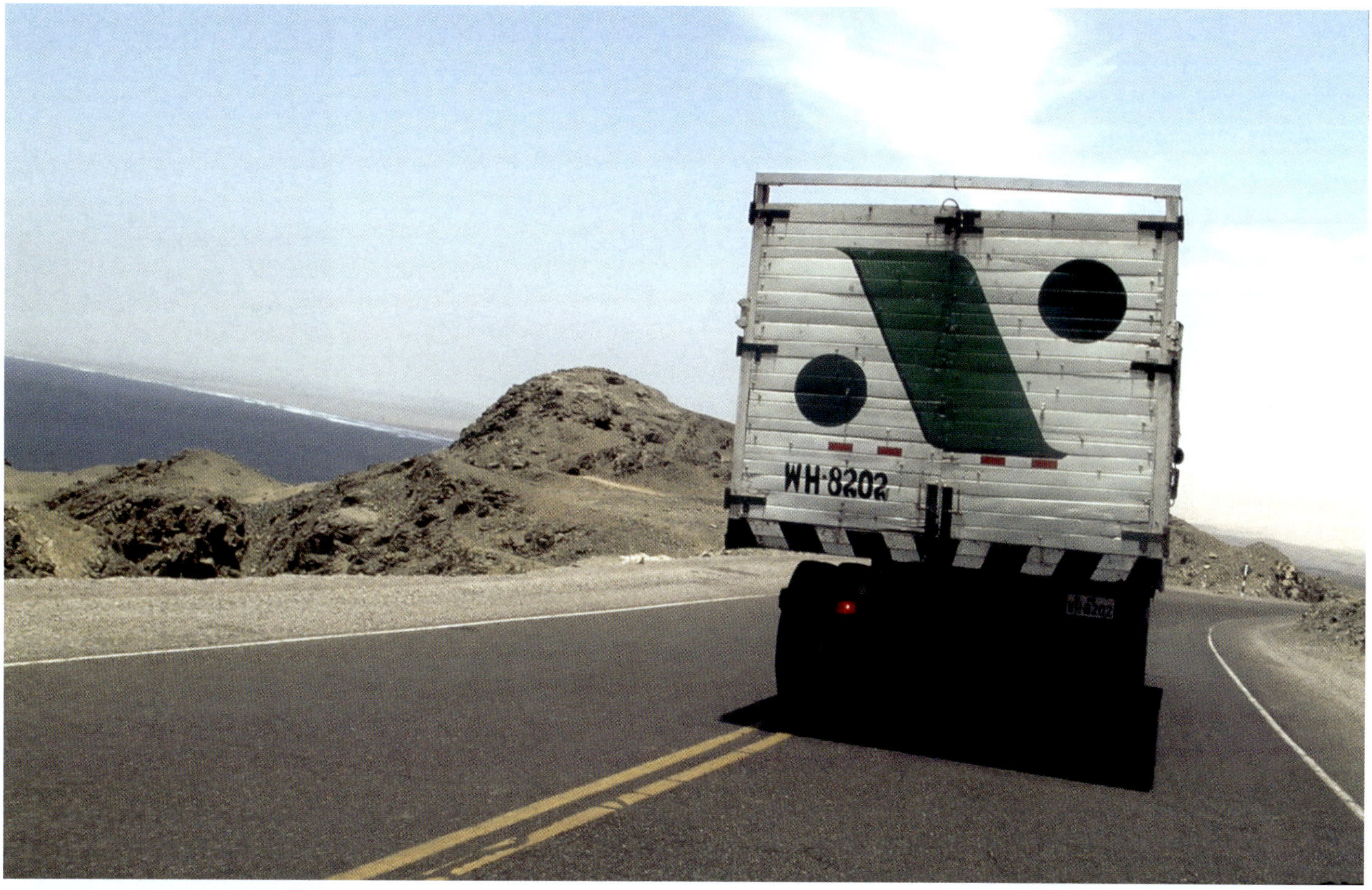
WH-8202

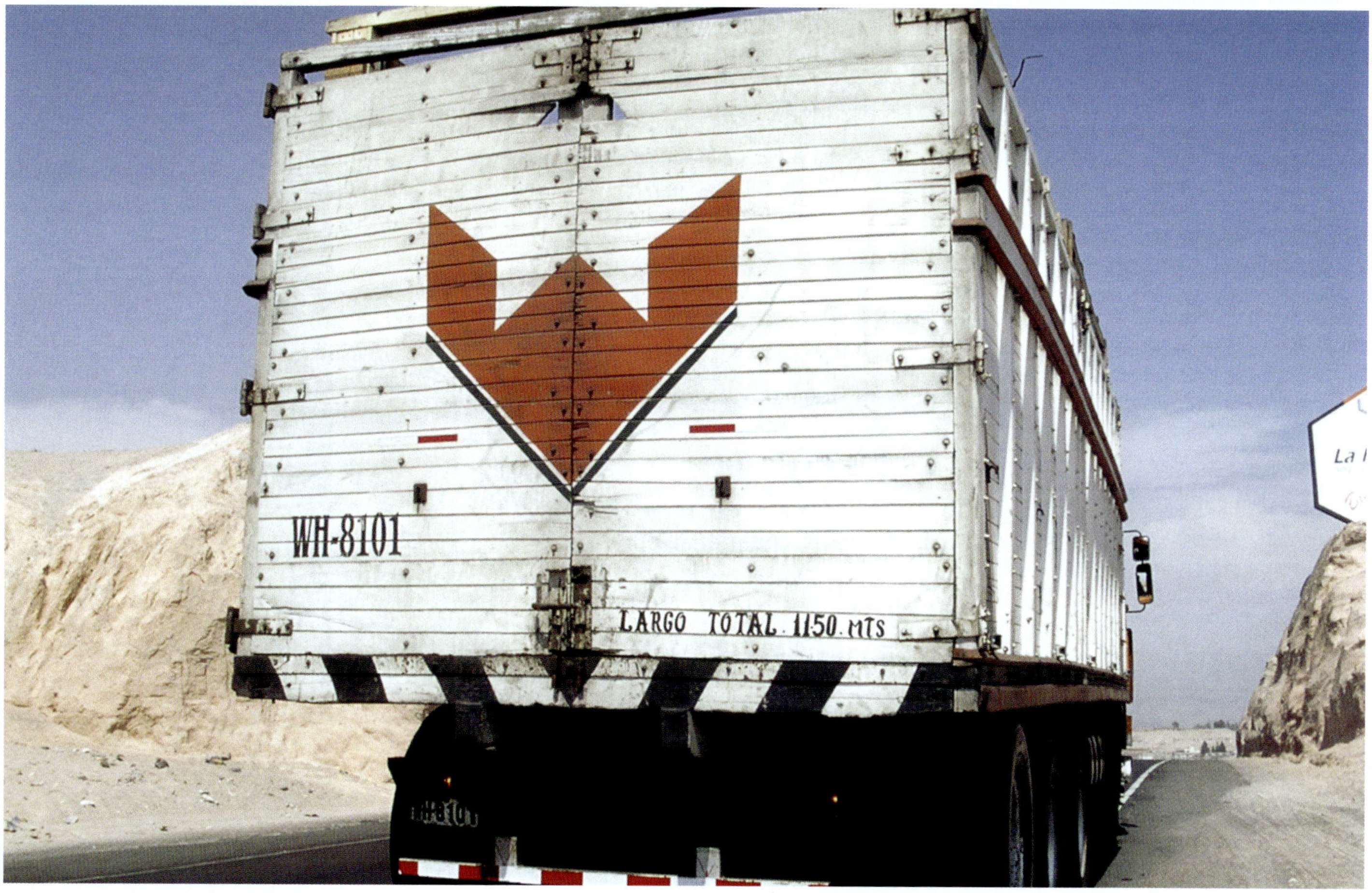
WH-8101
LARGO TOTAL 11.50 MTS

COMPLICATED DESIRES: YTO BARRADA

Born in France, 1971. Lives and works in Paris and Tangier.

On a clear day, you can see the coast of Spain across the Strait of Gibraltar from the beach in Tangier, Morocco. Africa and Europe almost touch, and the political and emotional tension is palpable, especially for the Moroccans who are forbidden from entering Europe without a visa after the European Union's 1985 Schengen Agreement and subsequent Schengen Convention in 1995, which abolished border posts within Europe while tightening its external border control. Even so, those who live in Tangier increasingly long to traverse the Mediterranean Sea, so much so that their will often becomes entirely directed toward this illegal, disruptive, and often fatal goal. In Arabic, when one speaks of an acquaintance who has crossed from North Africa to Europe, one does not say "they immigrated" but rather "they burned," meaning they burned their passport and left their past behind.[1] This was not the case for Yto Barrada, however, who returned to Tangier from her studies abroad and began an ongoing photographic portrait of the Moroccan city in *A Life Full of Holes: The Strait Project* (1998–present). The title comes from a 1964 recording of storyteller Driss Ben Hamed Charhadi made by American author Paul Bowles, who was living in Tangier at the time documenting and translating Moroccan oral traditions. In his tale, Charhadi comments on the Moghrebi adage: "Even a life full of holes, a life of nothing but waiting, is better than no life at all."[2] Like the storyteller's quote, Barrada's photographs evoke the troublesome situation of immigrants and would-be immigrants who abandon one land for another and one set of struggles for another, leaving themselves "empty," in a permanent state of longing.

Born in Paris to Moroccan parents, Barrada has firsthand experience with the liminal existence of immigrants. The photographer/filmmaker's dual citizenship has allowed her to move between Tangier and Paris for most of her life. After spending her youth in Morocco, she left to study political science at the Sorbonne. While researching ways that Palestinians and Israelis negotiate roadblocks in the West Bank, she found herself taking more photographs than notes and determined that her images more fully captured the spirit of the people and their political struggles. Eventually she shifted fields and went to the International Center of Photography in New York to pursue a career as a photographer. Shot in reportage style, Barrada's works are nonetheless more loosely suggestive than strict photojournalism. In *A Life Full of Holes: The Strait Project*, which includes pictures of people floating through the present and yearning for the future, figures are often shown from above, from behind, sleeping in public places, or staring off in the distance, disconnected from their surroundings and in stasis. Their ennui ultimately defies Orientalist stereotypes and depicts Moroccans as full subjects with complicated motivations and desires.

Barrada's long-term examination of Tangier is remarkably open-ended and diverse with a wide variety of subjects that include cityscapes, landscapes, industrial sites, and Aaron Siskind-like abstractions of paint flaking off of shipping containers. Taken as a whole, the series works allegorically and metonymically to present a multifaceted view of Tangier over time, a photomontage that conveys the state of the city as well as African/European migration in general. As the Moroccan and Spanish governments move ever closer to an undersea rail-tunnel connection between the two nations, the artist's meditation on the unfulfilled promise of prosperity through emmigration from Africa and the one-way flow of tourists from Europe is undeniably germane. Of her images, Barrada has said, "They expose a secret code that is a way of confronting disillusionment that, in spite of the obstacles, makes possible—like poetry or playing—the passage from one space to another, from waste ground to playground."[3]

RH

1. Yto Barrada, "A Life Full of Holes: The Strait Project" (artist's statement), in Yto Barrada, *A Life Full of Holes/The Strait Project* (London: Autograph ABP, 2005), 1.

2. See Driss Ben Hamed Charhadi (Larbi Layachi), *A Life Full of Holes*, a novel tape-recorded in Moghrebi and translated into English by Paul Bowles (New York: Grove Press, Inc., 1982), 6.

3. Yto Barrada, interviews with Nadia Tazi, in *Yto Barrada/A Life Full of Holes/The Strait Project*, 60.

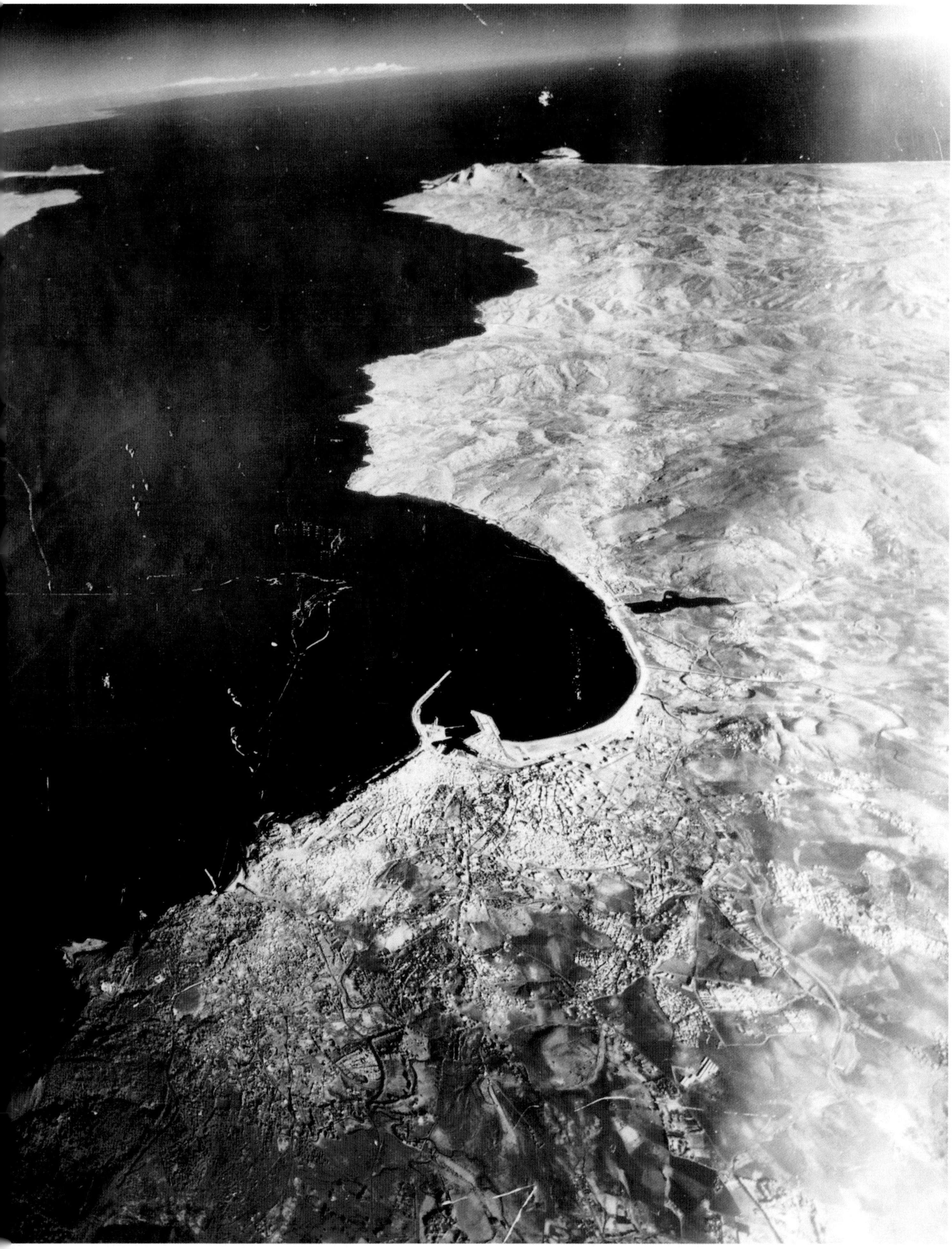

The Strait of Gibraltar from *A Life Full of Holes: The Strait Project* 2003 chromogenic print

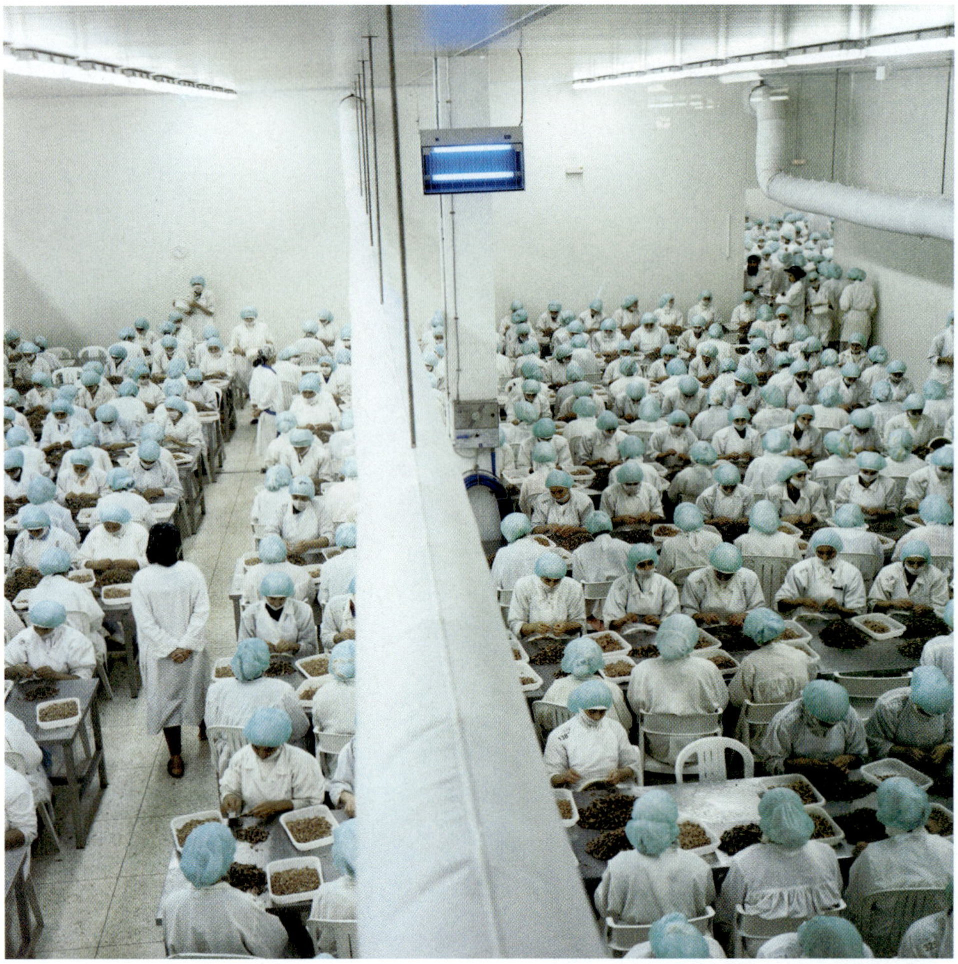

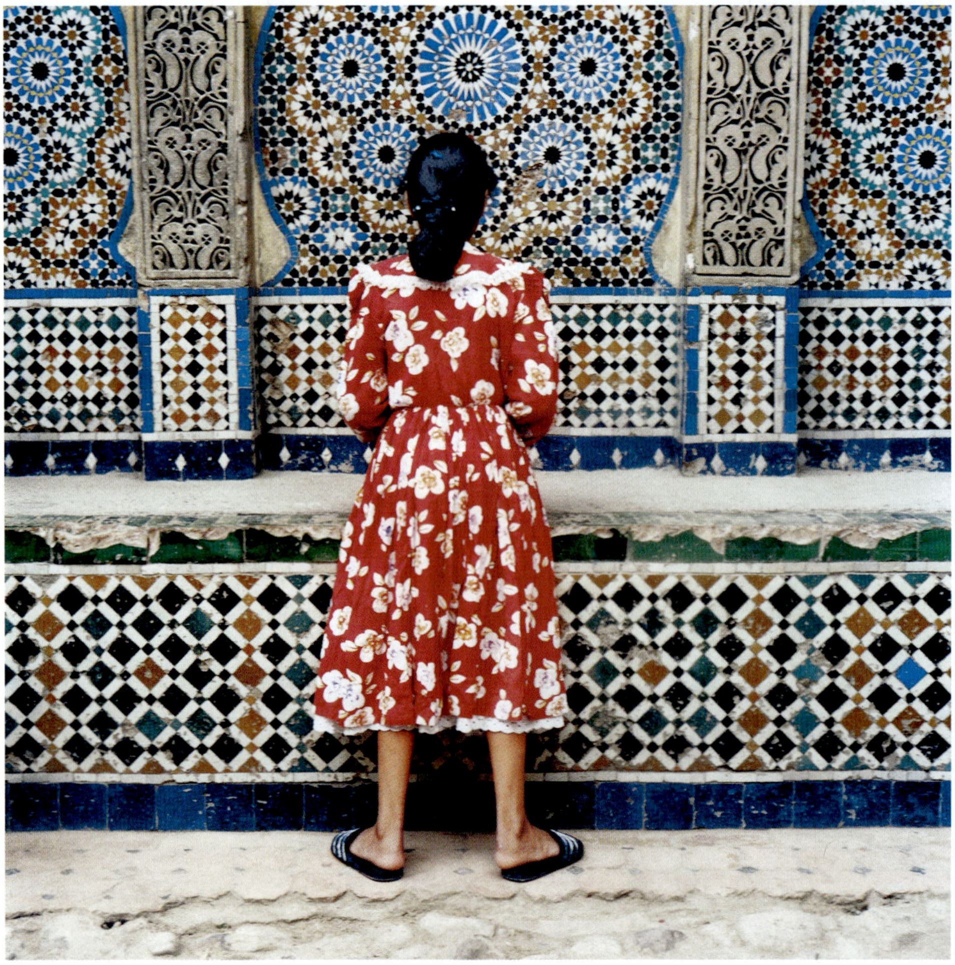

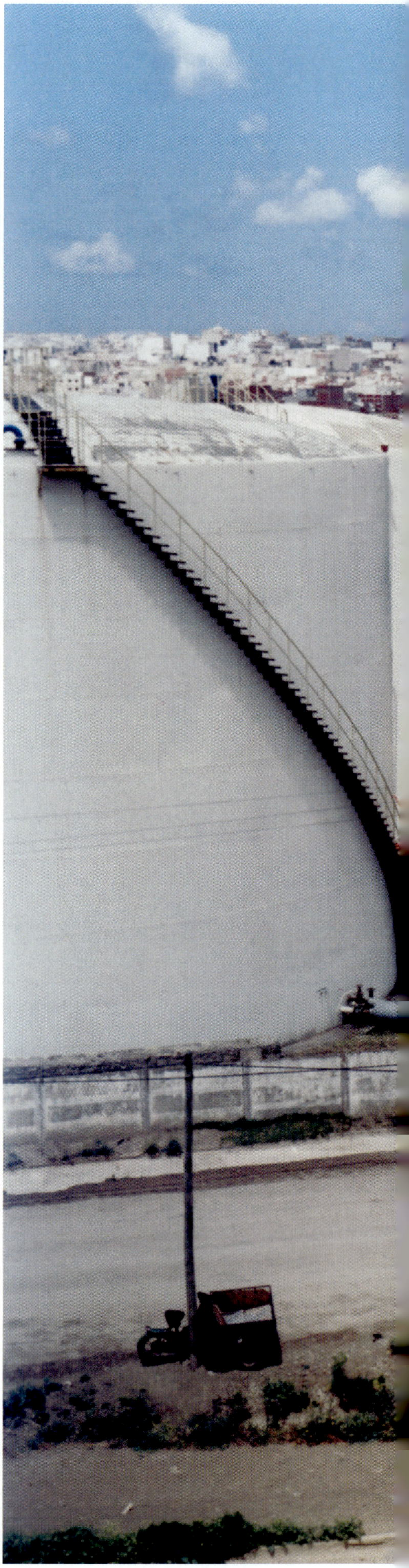

left, top: *Factory 2—Prawn processing plant in the free trade zone* from *A Life Full of Holes: The Strait Project* 1998 chromogenic print bottom: *Girl in Red—Playing Jacks* from *A Life Full of Holes: The Strait Project* 1999 chromogenic print right: *Quartier des épines* from *A Life Full of Holes: The Strait Project* 1998 chromogenic print

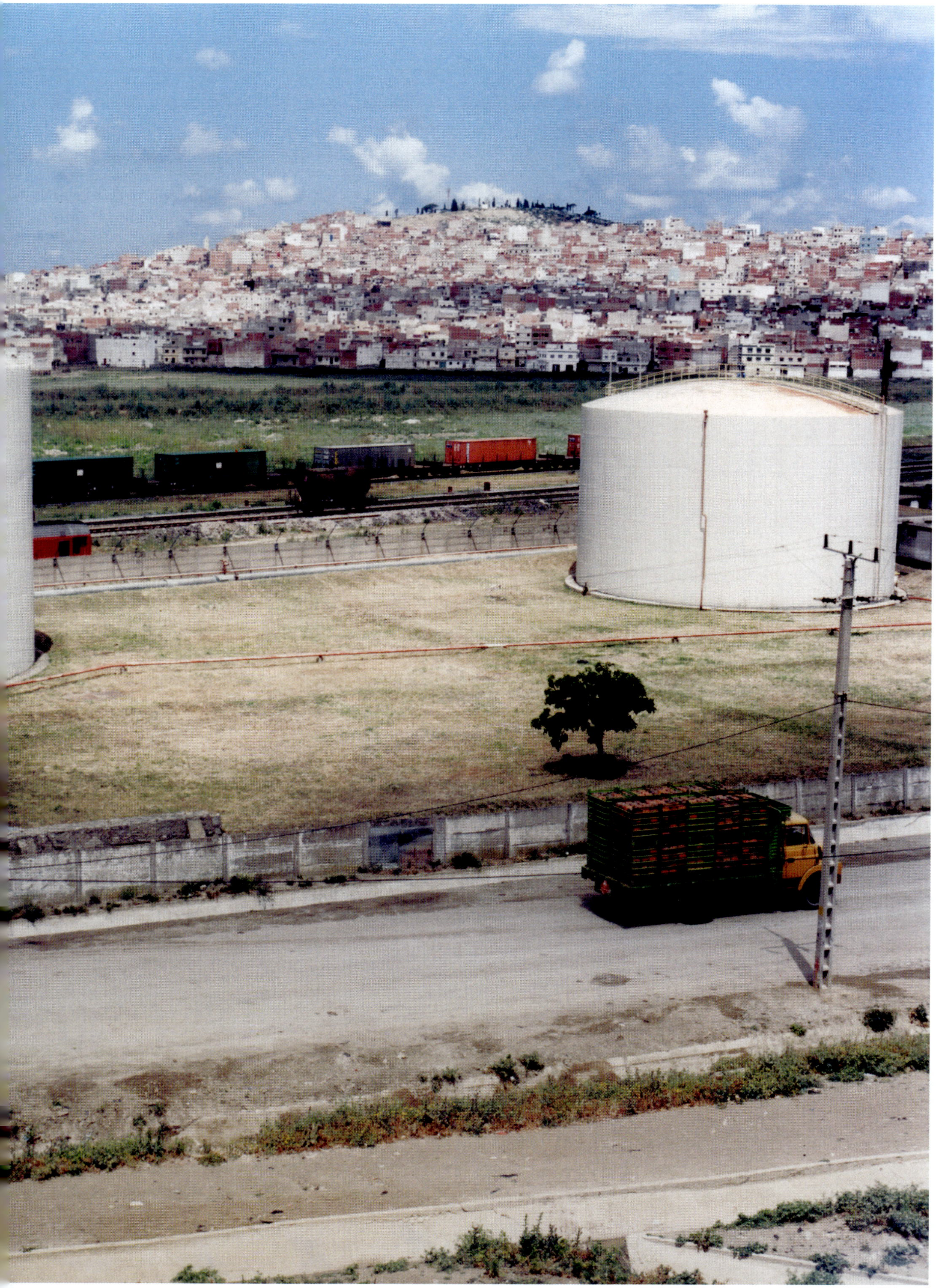

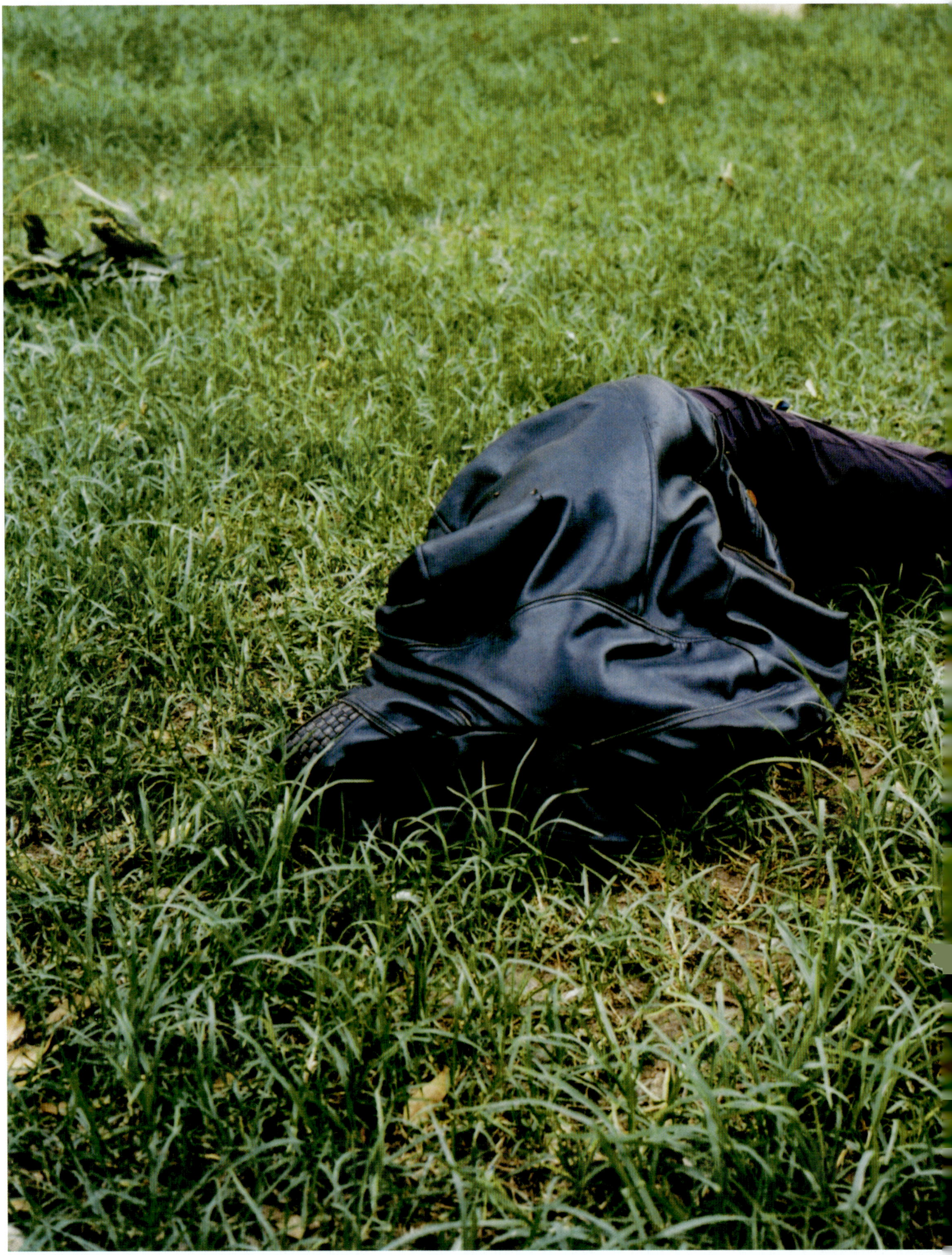

Selections from *The Sleepers, Tangier 2006* from *A Life Full of Holes: The Strait Project* 2006 chromogenic prints

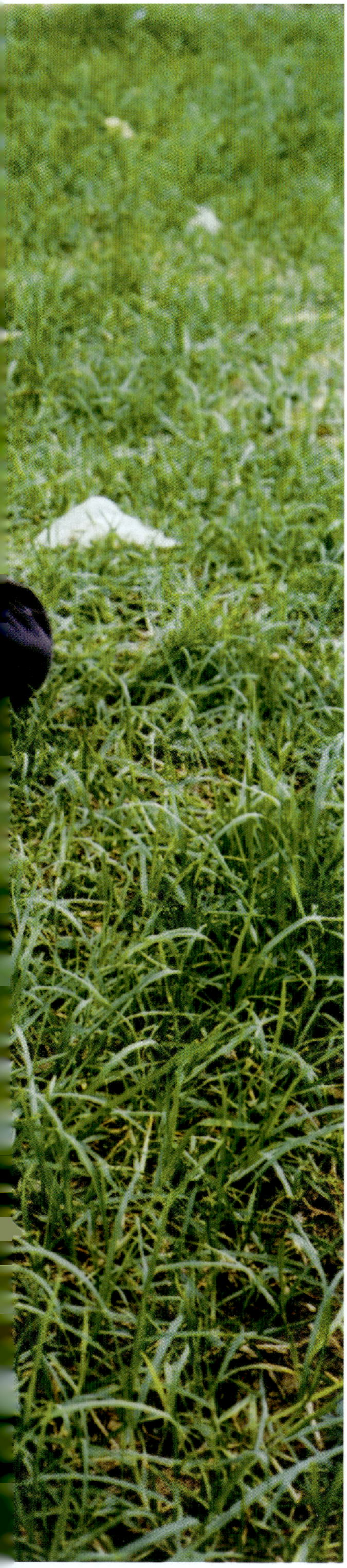

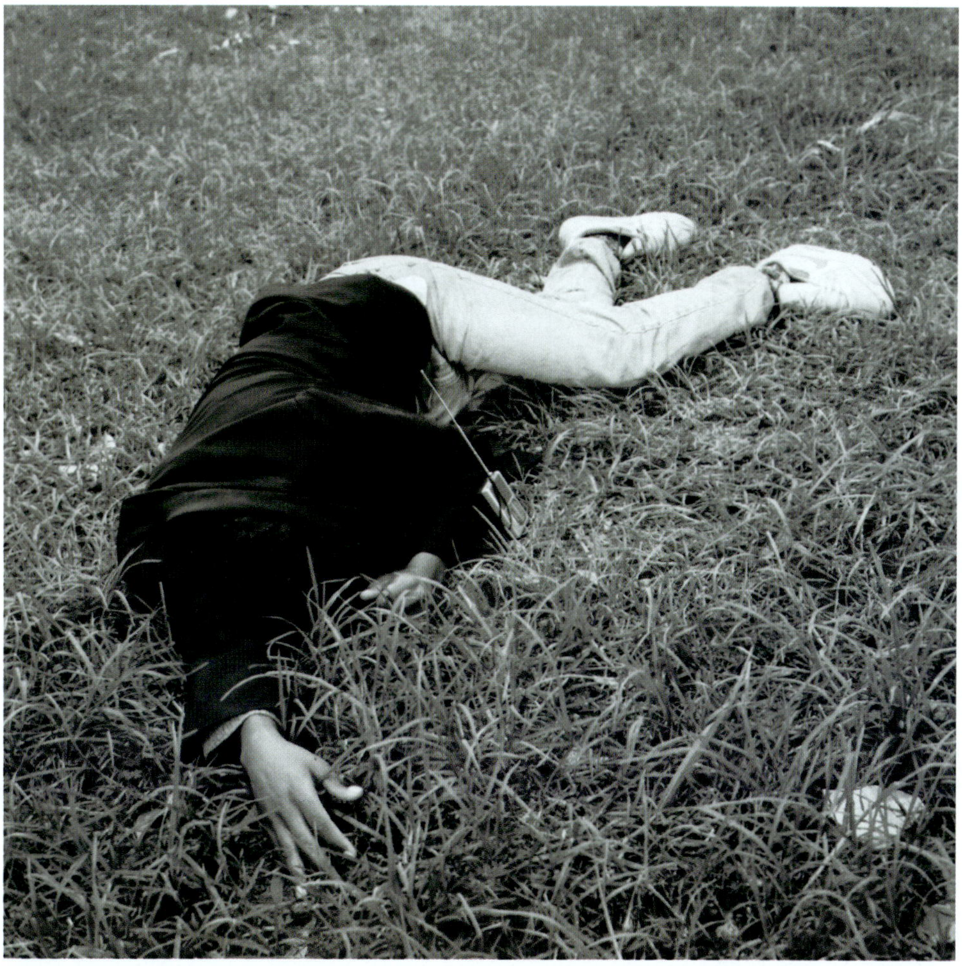

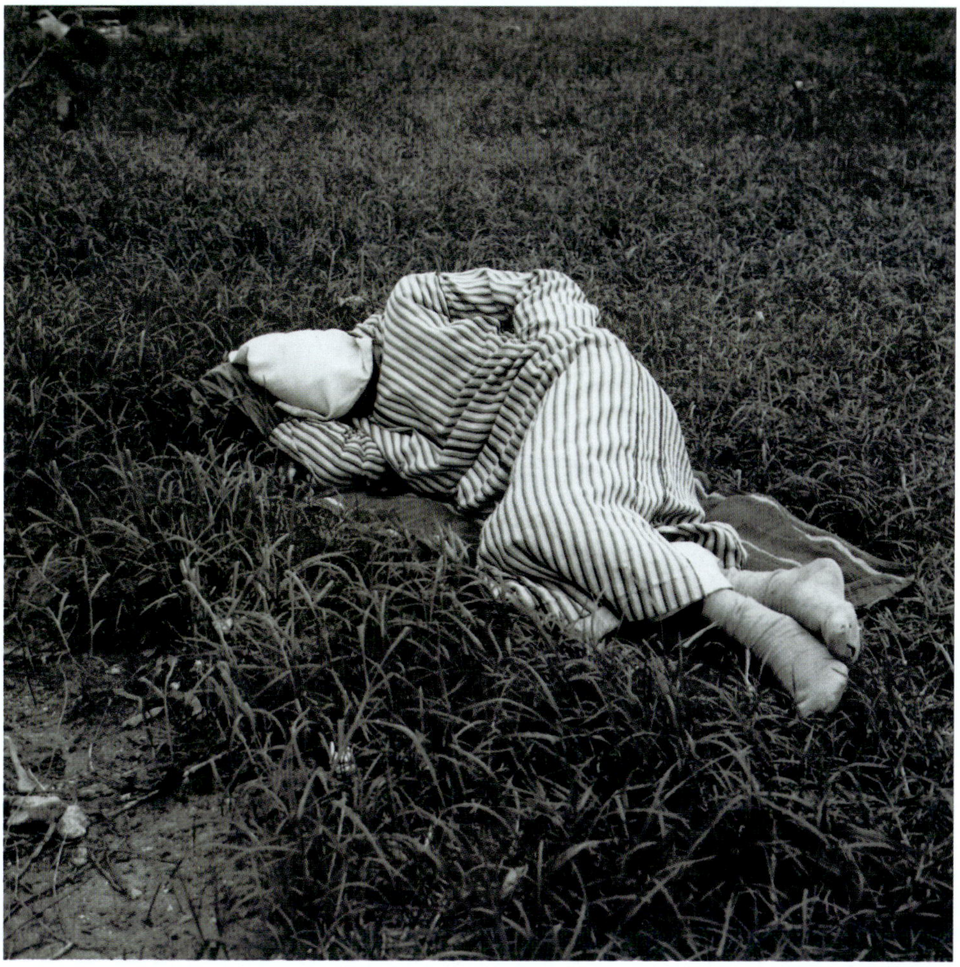

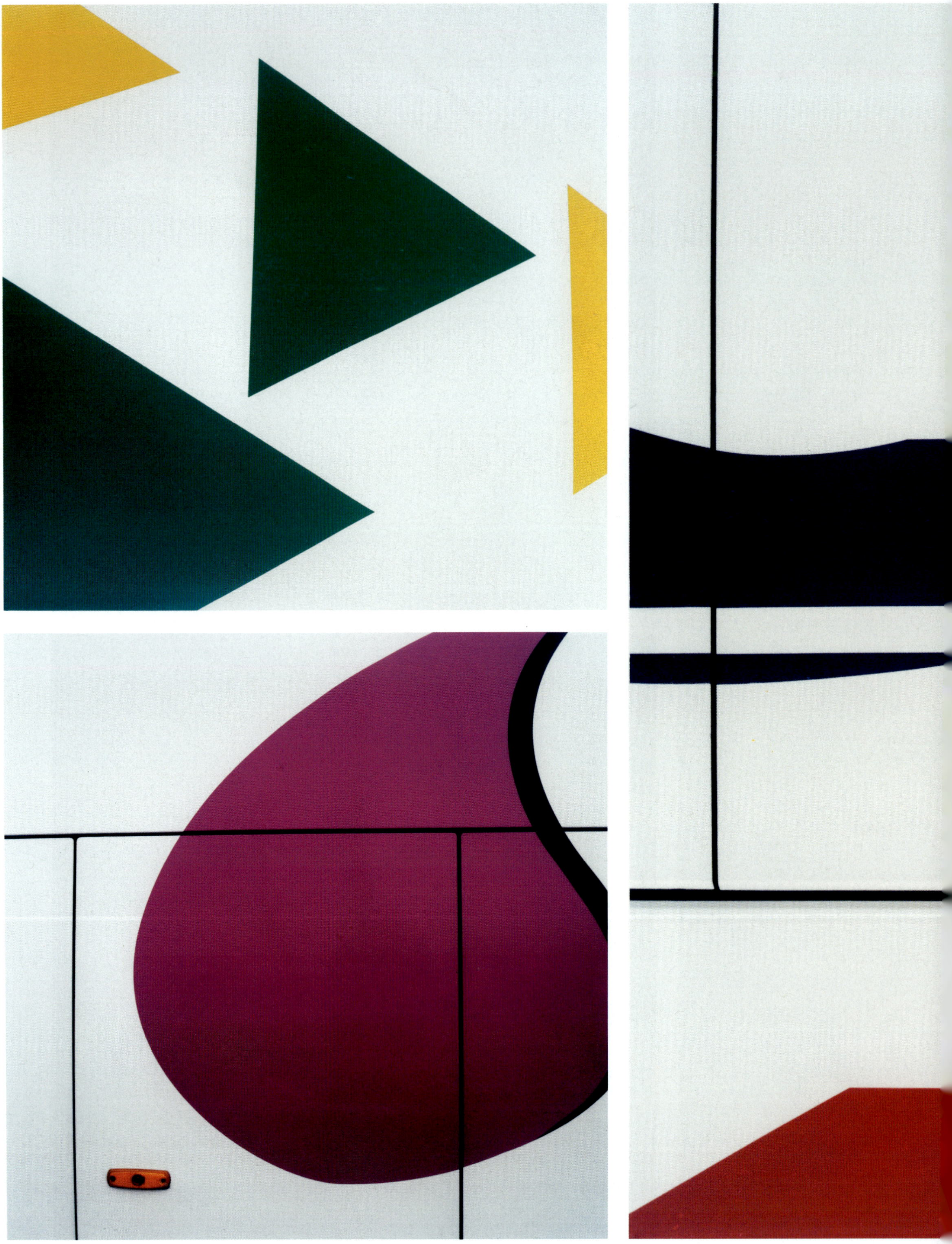

above and following pages: Selections from *AUTOCAR Tangier, 2004* from *A Life Full of Holes: The Strait Project* 2004 chromogenic prints

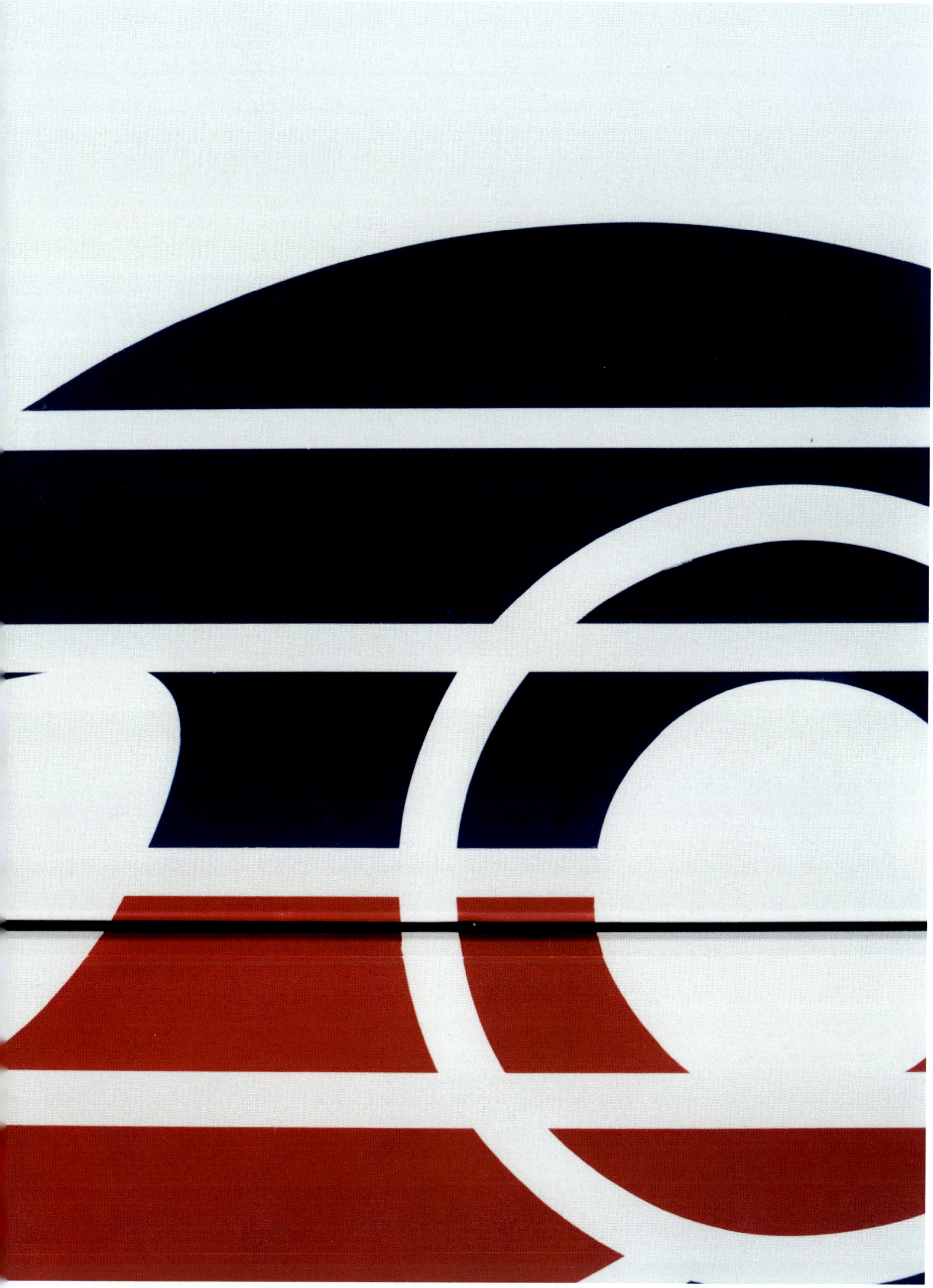

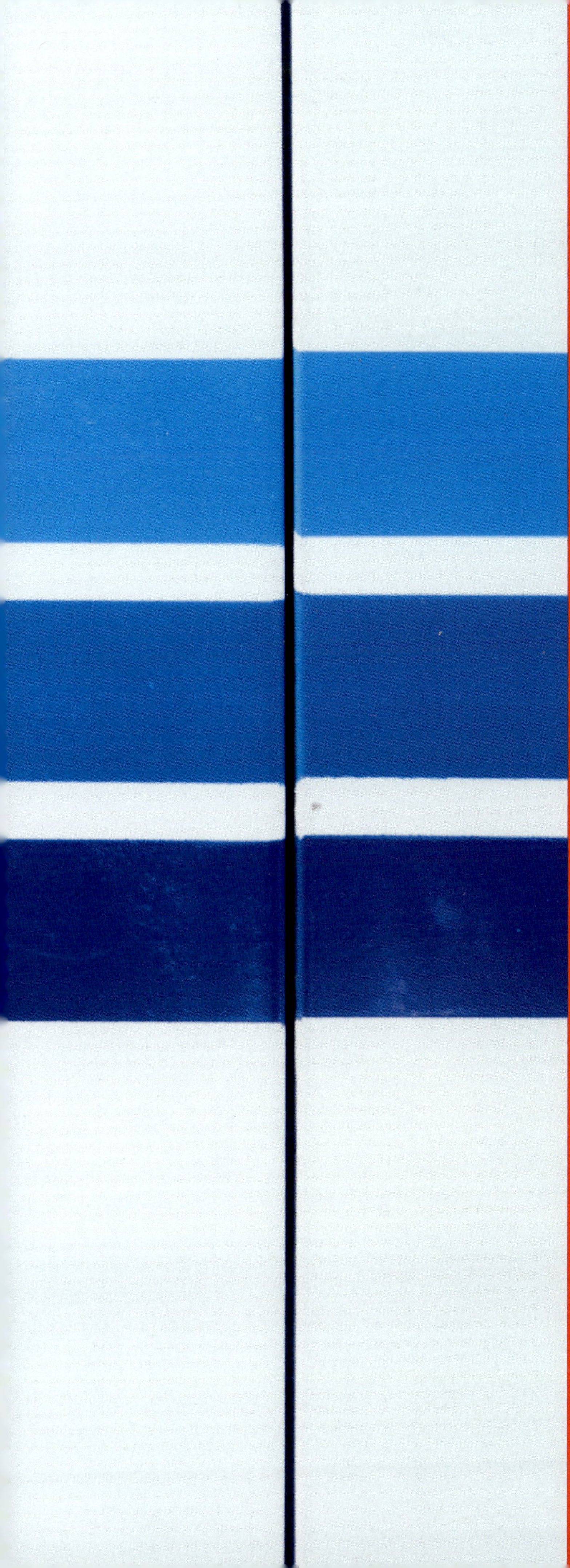

REPORT FROM BARCELONA, SPAIN

Brave New Worlds March 15, 2007

FUTURE CONDITIONAL

MAX ANDREWS &
MARIANA CÁNEPA LUNA

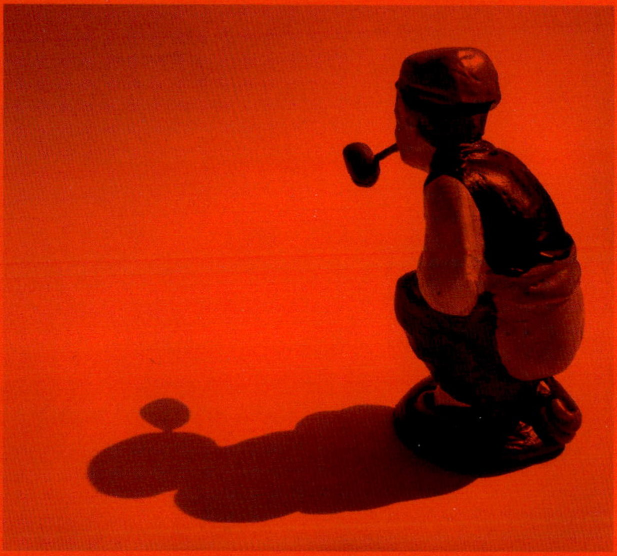

As Slovenian philosopher Slavoj Žižek has remarked, how can ideology be declared dead in a Europe with such a diverse design of toilets? Where the French latrine prompts an immediate, rapid expulsion of one's excrement as if in homage to its flushes of Revolution, a typical German model necessitates a confrontation with what one has left behind, seemingly through obligation to revisit and examine the past, however unpleasant that may be. Žižek didn't mention Spanish toilets. Yet much like Anglo-Saxon ones, their usual pan design allows a condition somewhere between these two ideologies that somewhat indecisively floats between speedy exigency and studied legacy. Spain is barely middle-aged as a modern democracy. The frequently heard jibes that it is some twenty years behind the rest of Western Europe is by and large precipitated by the reality that the country was locked down under the oppressive military dictatorship of General Franco from 1936 to 1975. Thus, in the present we can perceive both the speed of a headlong rush toward popular consumer culture on the one hand, yet on the other a slowness in the task of processing recent history—recovering, archiving, and reconciling what was suffocated and often literally buried.

These two contrasting conditions in contemporary Spanish culture might find their symptoms in two cultural institutions at almost opposite ends of the nation that are certainly at ideological poles with regard to the values they seem to embody. From the outside, the Museo de Arte Contemporáneo de Castilla y León (or MUSAC) in the northern city of León and the Museu d'Art Contemporani de Barcelona (better known as MACBA), a kilometer or so to the west as we write this in the Catalan capital, already make bold statements through their architecture. Unlike the most celebrated (or notorious) marriage of museum ideology, architecture, and city image—Frank Gehry's Guggenheim Bilbao—both MUSAC and MACBA are institutions with a municipal role that are home to publicly financed collections. The mission of the candy-striped MUSAC, designed by Mansilla & Tuñón and opened in April 2005, is to collect art made since 2000. It is an unashamedly youth-oriented approach geared at the post-dictatorial generations raised on foreign pop music, movies, and so on, with an expectation toward entertainment and the representation of street subcultures, and an eye toward usability and interactivity.

If MUSAC's analogous medium is multichannel cable TV, then MACBA's is the typewriter and the sheet of white paper. Richard Meier's blindingly white MACBA edifice, opened in 1995, is directed by the implications of proselytizing the developments in avant-garde art and political change in the late 1960s and early 1970s. Here, art as entertainment is anathema—and skateboarders very definitely belong outside, though they have taken up the adjoining Plaça dels Àngels as a favored haunt. The museum functions as a place of doctrine where postwar Spanish—and more specifically, Catalan—art practice can be sutured into the historical record.

Yet both of these crudely characterized phenomena are dwarfed by the single-biggest architect of the image of Spanish culture: tourism. Barcelona is the preeminent tourist city, a destination that since its much-vaunted hosting of the 1992 Olympic Games has been molded through civic initiatives into a seamlessly legible visitor experience. Trumping the Franco-era touristic images of flamenco and bullfighting (which are actually traditions of the south of Spain) with sun, sea, shopping, and sangria—while scripting and flaunting its historical pedigree, from its so-called "Gothic quarter" to the turn-of-the-century modernism credentials of Antoni Gaudí, Salvador Dalí, Joan Miró, Pablo Picasso, and so on—Barcelona now boasts tourist hordes that far outnumber its residents. Where the city's population hovers around 1.5 million, it hosts more than 5 million visitors every year. While MACBA wears its political and discursive credentials on its sleeve, it also offers a space in opposition to the obedient, prepackaged, predigested logic of this theme-park vision of the city. The lure of the tourist euro clearly played a role in the raison d'être of an initiative such as MUSAC—no doubt (Guggenheim) Bilbao-envy played its part, too—yet in León, it's the wholesale importation of the techniques of youth marketing and brand identity into the realms of the museum that make it a particularly telling touchstone for the speedy impulse in culture.

If there is a "third way" in between these contrasting cultural speeds and historiographies—and between Spain's uneasy relationship with the idea of itself with respect to its dictatorial history and the identity of its regions, as well as the rest of the world's image of it from the outside—then the traumatic events of the morning of March 11, 2004, may well have forced it to look more closely at the realities of the present. The train bombings in Madrid, now known (like 9/11's date-stamped moniker) as 11M, shocked the country and the world, leaving one hundred ninety-one dead and around two thousand injured. In political terms, the landscape changed unrecognizably in a very short period. The center-right Partido Popular (People's Party), led by its then-president José Maria Aznar, maintained the hypothesis that the bombings were an action by Euskadi Ta Askatasuna (Basque Fatherland and Liberty, better known as ETA), the Basque nationalist organization that since its founding in 1959 has been claiming sovereignty and self-determination for the Basque region. The main party of the opposition, the Partido Socialista Obrero Español (Spanish Socialist Workers' Party), the social democrats led by José Luis Rodríguez Zapatero, interpreted the attacks as a punishment for the Spanish support of the war in Iraq. It was later discovered that the perpetrators were local Islamic extremists collaborating with Spanish informants.

The international media reported the assumed Al Qaeda links shortly after, despite most of the national news channels showing old footage of ETA terrorists' actions. The polar opinions of the two main political parties confused and divided the nation and only three days later, on March 14, the general elections gave power to Zapatero. Spanish troops were withdrawn from Iraq soon after, on April 28, 2004. Since then, Zapatero's government has strived to promote the Alliance of Civilizations (a United Nations Secretary General's initiative encouraging alliances between Western and Islamic countries); legalized gay marriage; opened up a peace process with ETA (since stalled due to the December 30, 2006, bombing of the Madrid Barajas Airport's new Terminal 4 that killed two Ecuadorians); and initiated processes of reform with regard to autonomy in the regions, most significantly the expanded independence afforded to Catalonia with the 2006 redefinition of the Estatut—changing the Spanish constitution to define the region as a "nation" and increasingly recognizing economic autonomy and the Catalan language.

The immediate present, too, increasingly concerns immigration. Since the mid-1990s Spain has stabilized and grown its economy and demographics (the country has one of the lowest birth rates in Europe), largely due to a massive influx of immigrants from Morocco, Ecuador, and Romania—the immigrant population is now 8.7 percent of the total population of more than 44 million. The countries of origin have also benefited from this phenomenon: from Madrid alone some 1,500 million euros were transferred, mostly to Latin American countries, in 2006. In 2005 the Zapatero government opened a legal process of official recognition for seven hundred thousand immigrants, the highest annual number to date, and by 2010 it is anticipated that some 20 percent of the active population will have come from overseas. As it is elsewhere in Europe, Spain's lack of recognition of foreigners' qualifications often makes it difficult for this population to find legal jobs and work permits. Cleaning, babysitting, or caring for the elderly are typical employment niches for those "without papers," while those who were dentists, lawyers, executives, or engineers at home can often only find work in restaurants, cleaning toilets, or in the building trade. Though there is a will to transform such situations, there have also been a huge number of repatriations, as the geographic reality of Spain being just fifteen kilometers from the African continent at its nearest point continues to put enormous pressure on the nation as the imagined gateway to the "European dream."

At this point in time, Spain is witnessing an unprecedented mass immigration of people arriving from the Maghreb, Mauritania, Ethiopia, and even further afield, from Pakistan. The Canary Islands, the westernmost outpost of Spain, are now regular witness to a phenomenon analogous to that of the Cuban balseros as thousands of people arrive on the islands' shores after having entrusted their future to hundreds of miles of open ocean and overloaded, rickety boats known as cayucos or pateras. By the summer of 2006—and as the northern region of Galicia was burning with widespread forest fires—eleven thousand Africans had landed in the Canary Islands, a figure already double that of the previous year. July and August saw two graphic, sudden arrivals on La Tejerita beach in southern Tenerife as two cayucos, each loaded with almost one hundred people, made landfall. Newspaper front pages were filled with the surreal image of beach tourists and locals offering their drinks and clothes to the exhausted arrivals, and assisting Red Cross officials in carrying the bodies of their less fortunate compatriots to hospitals. That same summer in the Mediterranean, the crew of the Spanish fishing boat Francisco y Catalina rescued forty-eight sub-Saharans from their stricken vessel near the coast of Malta. Having arrived at the island's port, they were stuck on board for eight days awaiting a European-level political decision about their status. Finally, eighteen went to Spain, ten to Italy, eight remained in Malta, and five now find themselves in the mountains of Andorra, while the fishermen received civic awards for their intervention.

Anticipating neither a rush for an imagined future, or an examination of a historical past—and to return to the ideology of toilets—this inundation by the geopolitical realities of the "here and now" seems to demand another kind of excremental analogy. Fortunately, Catalan tradition has long enshrined its own unique case (overlooked by both Žižek and Dominique Laporte's seminal 1978 History of Shit): not one toilet design or the other, but no toilet at all. The small statue figure of the caganer (defecator) is commonly found squatting in a quiet corner of Bethlehem nativity dioramas, in the act of expelling solid waste en plein air. The ideological implications of this pillar of Catalan culture might call for a pragmatic, sustainable fertilization of the present, and an honest shame-free confrontation with what it means to be human. By laying bare the fundamentals of civilization, the caganer—however unlikely it might seem—provides a brave model for our new world. ■

IMAGE

page 41 A caganer statuette from Spain's Catalonia region depicts a squatting, red-capped peasant, a tradition dating back to the seventeenth-century in an agricultural society where defecation was associated with fertility and health.

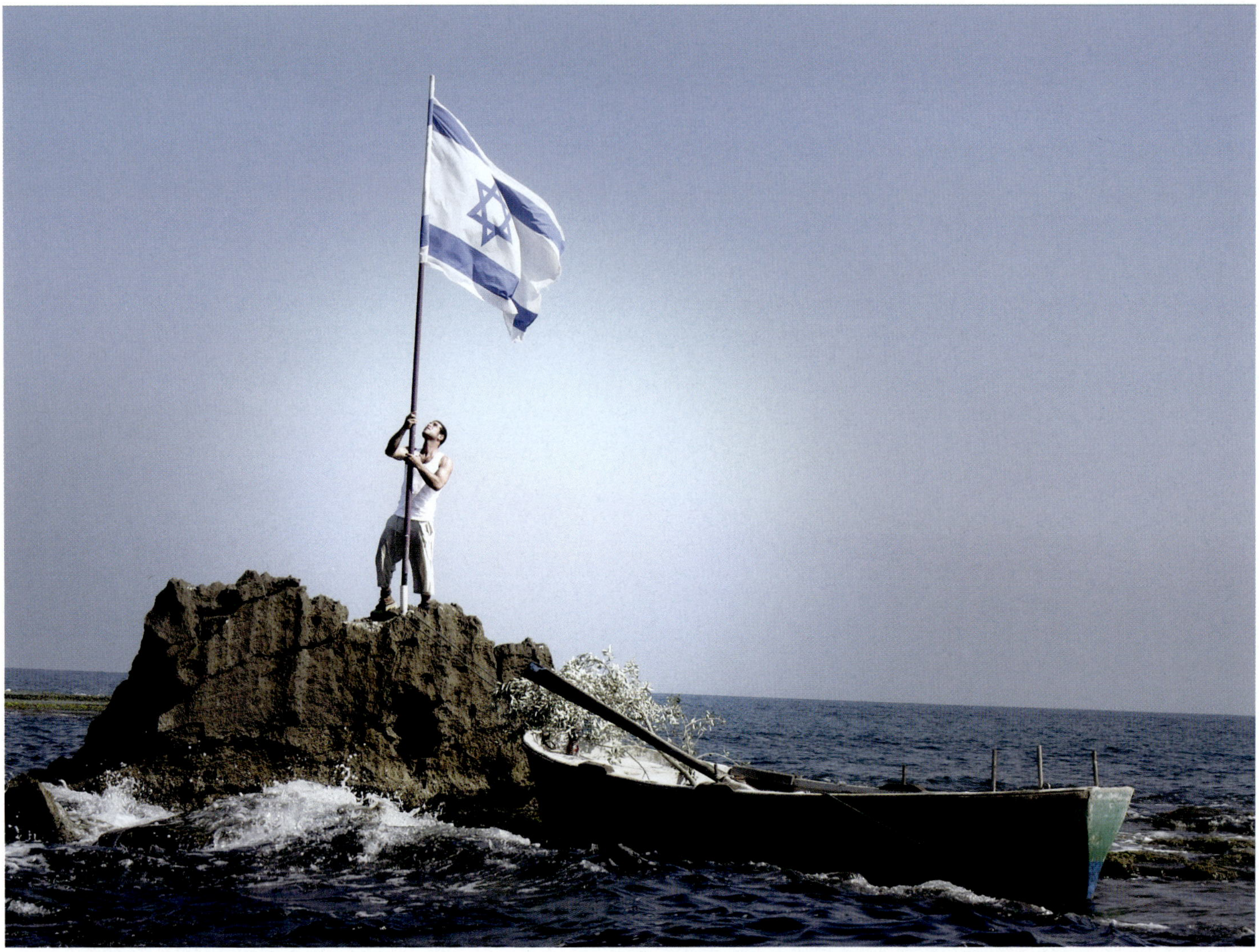

IMPRINTS OF CONFLICT: YAEL BARTANA

Born in Israel, 1970. Lives and works in Amsterdam and Tel-Aviv.

After college, Yael Bartana left Israel for the United States and Europe, and returned years later, almost as an outsider, to the place of her birth. The distance she had gained made her see her country's cultures and rituals in a new and strange light. Her images reveal her perception of the thorough integration of nationalism and violence into the modern state of Israel, and she is keenly sensitive to the ways in which the trauma of the current conflict has imprinted itself on the customs, social identities, and even physical interactions of young Israelis, much as the Holocaust did on preceding generations. In 2000, Bartana began a video/photograph series that captures the holidays, recreational activities, and rituals of Israel's Jewish majority in simply framed shots of landscapes and close-ups—often of teenagers' expressive faces and hands. Working from documentary-style footage, she assembles rhythmical edits, at times slowing the speed to create a lingering, transcendent effect. Many of her videos also draw audiences into the drama with droning or ethereal sounds. By focusing on moments in which individuals teeter on the edge of assimilation into a collective culture, the artist has developed a thoroughly humanistic point of view that searches for an existential meaning often lost in media reports on Israeli politics: "To me this is the concern of the eye society, a society of the eye that fails to see. I think it generates blindness and a lack of awareness to what is important and what is not; just stop for a minute and look at what's here."[1]

After graduating from the Bezalel Academy of Art and Design in Jerusalem, Bartana studied at the School of Visual Arts in New York, where she received her MFA. After a few years, she applied to the Rijksakademie van beeldende kunsten in Amsterdam to study film. Her first project was the three-minute video installation *Profile* (2000). The protagonists are Israeli women soldiers who are standing in a line at target practice. Viewers can hear the gunfire when they put on headphones that mimic the earmuffs worn by the soldiers. Her more recent work continues to reflect poetically on nationalism as in *A Declaration* (2006), in which a young Israeli brings an olive tree in a row boat to replace an Israeli flag on an offshore island.

Installation is an important component of Bartana's projects, such as *Wild Seeds* (2005), a

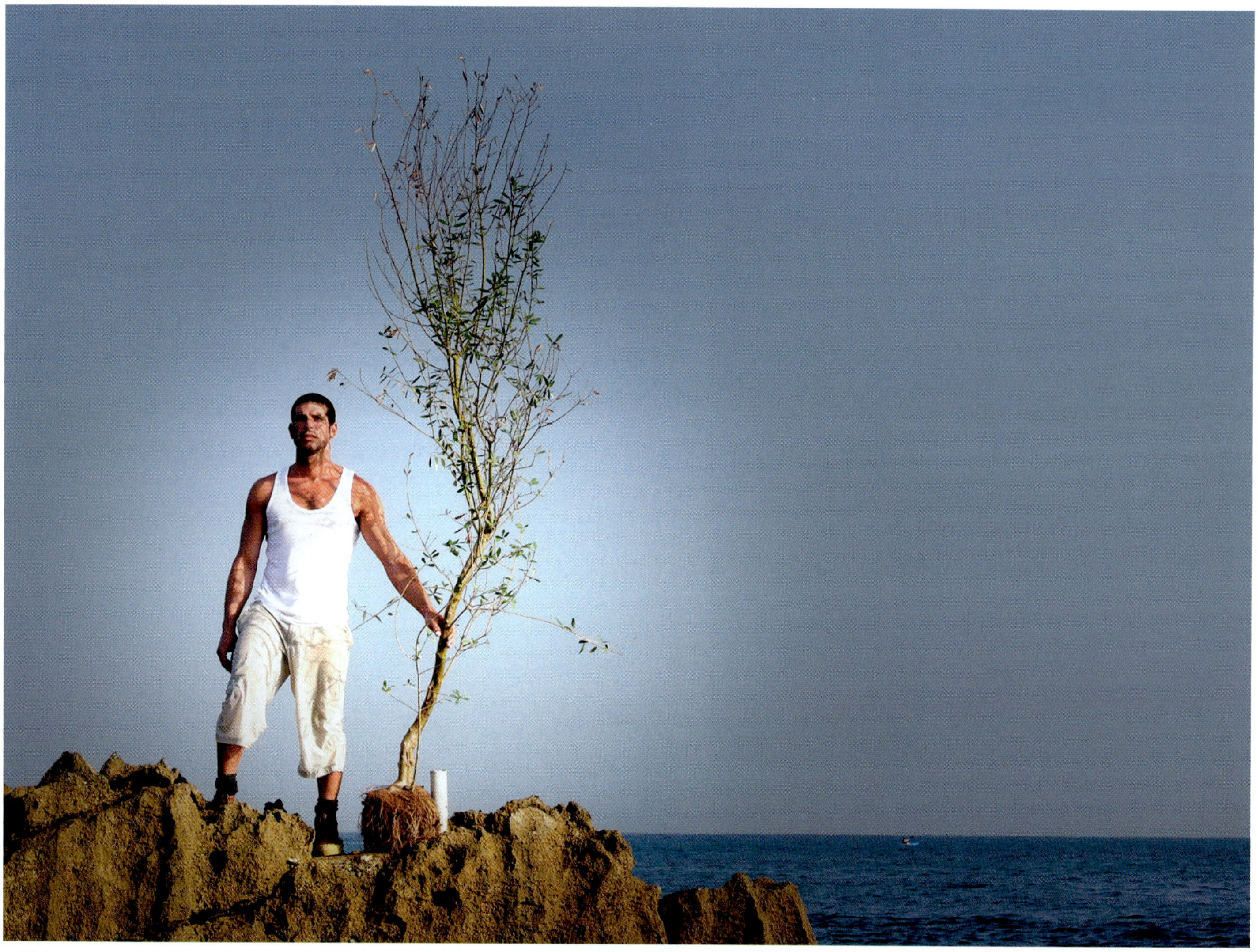

Stills from *A Declaration* 2006 video (color, sound); 7:30 minutes Sound track: Daniel Meir

dual projection on two ten-foot-tall screens that features a color film of teenagers wrestling on one and the English subtitles of their Hebrew dialogue on the other. In *Wild Seeds*, a group of eighteen-year-olds plays a game they invented—"The Evacuation of Gilad's Colony." It starts with "settlers," who intertwine their limbs in a tight human knot. A few other players are the "soldiers," whose objective is to pull people away from the group, one by one. The subtitles of their conversation reveal, for those who don't speak Hebrew, the game's black humor. Their banter is flirtatious, but Bartana inserts a "third voice" into the subtitles that says such things as "We have a plan to conquer this land." and "Soldier, I love you." The ethereal voices of a woman's choir and lingering shots of arms and legs pulling and pushing give the film a mournful and violent resonance. The nationalist anthem and playful anger of the teenagers prompt us to realize that this is a reenactment of the forceful removal of Jewish settlers by the Israeli army, in much the same way that other childhood games re-create historical tragedies (such as "Ring around the Rosie" or "Romans and the Christians"). Filmed in the stunning mountainous landscape of the Nofei Prat Settlement in the West Bank, the young men and women are actually dissidents who intend to dodge their country's mandatory draft. As one commentator has identified, they are "wild seeds" in the context of Genesis 26:3–4 and its promise of the holy land to the Jewish people: "Sojourn in this land, and I will be with thee, and will bless thee; for unto thee, and unto thy seed, I will give all these countries, and I will perform the oath which I sware unto Abraham thy father; And I will make thy seed to multiply as the stars of heaven, and will give unto thy seed all these countries; and in thy seed shall all the nations of the earth be blessed."[2]

RH

1. Yael Bartana, interview with Galit Eilat, in *Yael Bartana Videos & Photographs*, Charles Esche and Esra Sarigedik Oktem, eds. (Eindhoven, the Netherlands: Van Abbemuseum; Rotterdam: Veenman Publishers/Gijs Stork, 2006), 41.

2. See Charles Esche, "Yael Bartana," in *9th International Istanbul Biennial*, exh. cat. (Istanbul: Istanbul Foundation for Culture and Arts, 2005), 215.

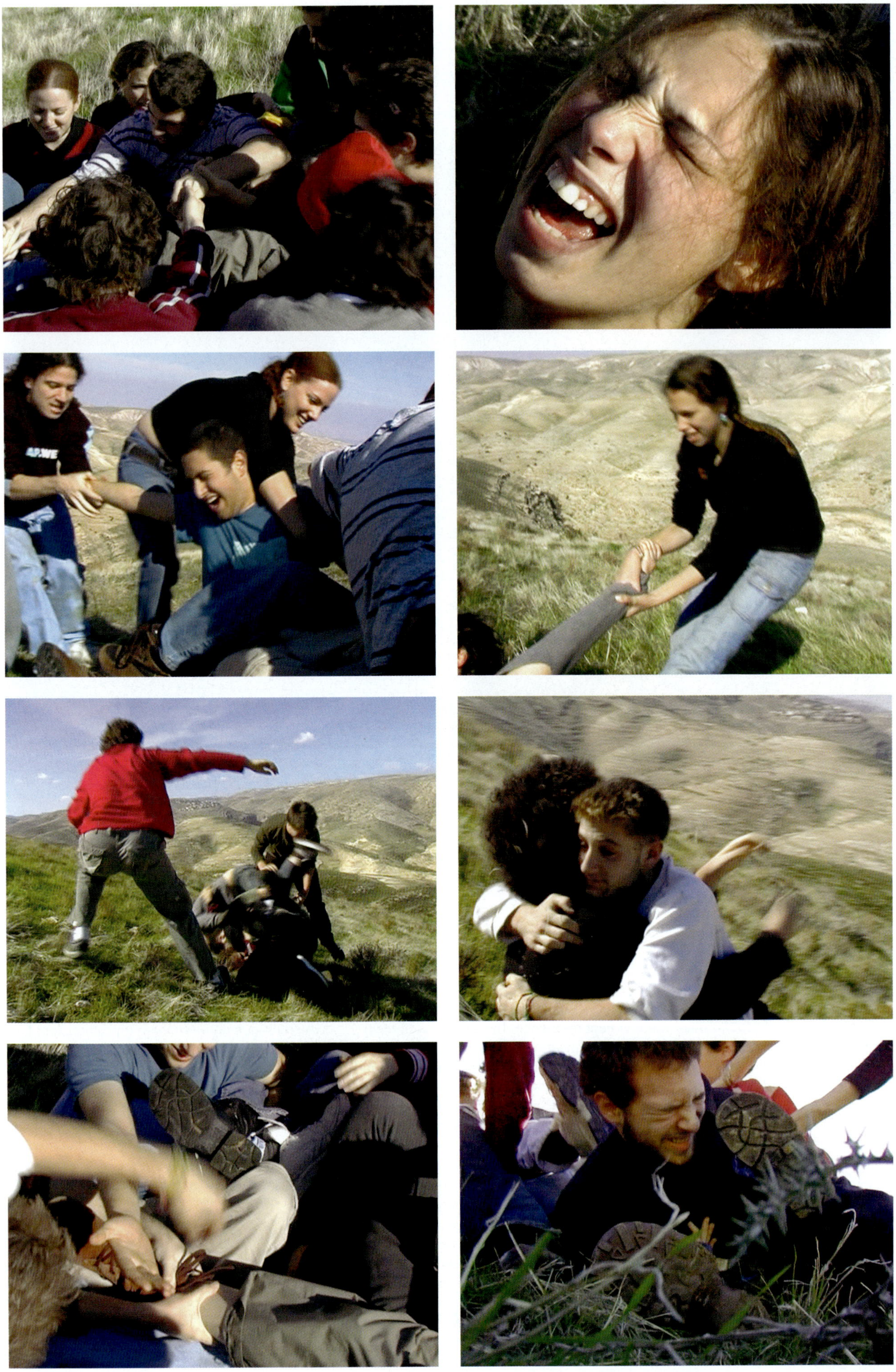

above and following pages: Stills from *Wild Seeds* 2005 two-channel video (color, sound); 4 minutes Sound track: Daniel Meir

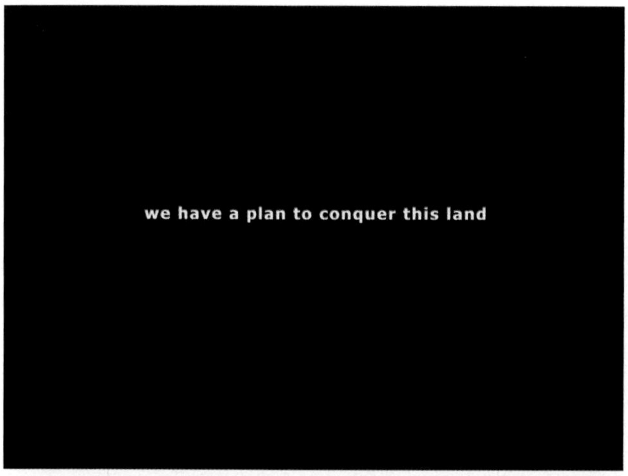
we have a plan to conquer this land

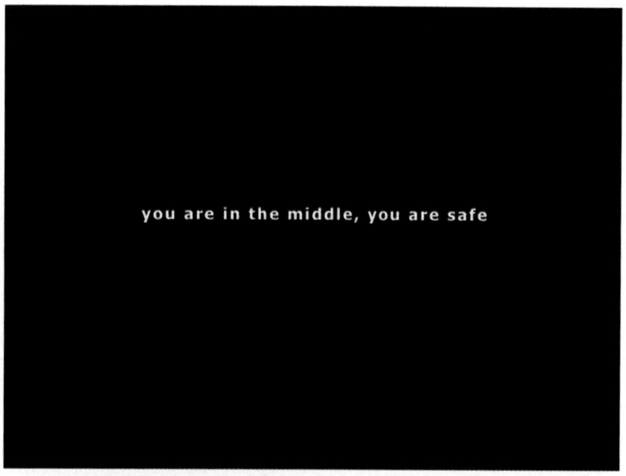
you are in the middle, you are safe

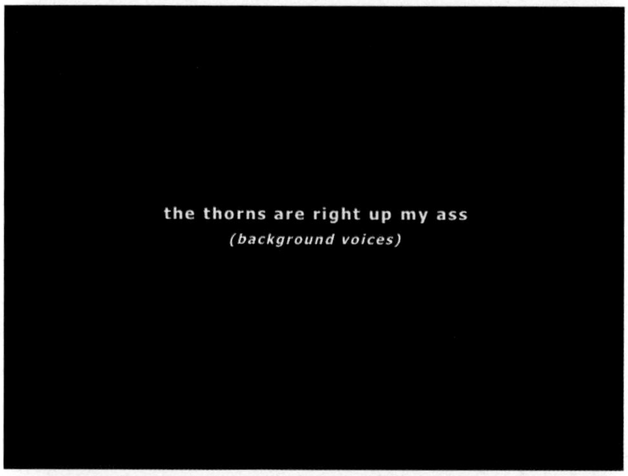
the thorns are right up my ass
(background voices)

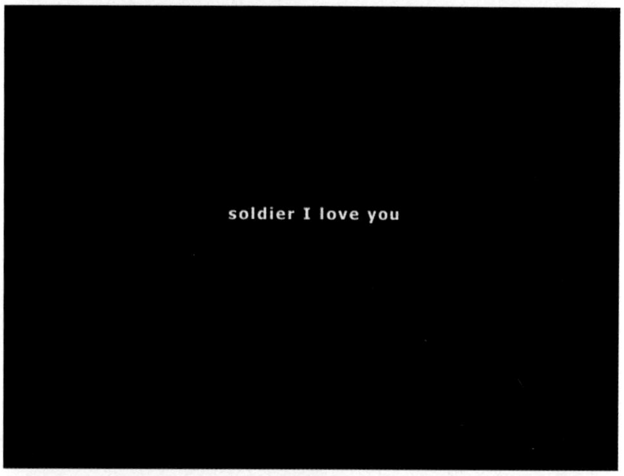
soldier I love you

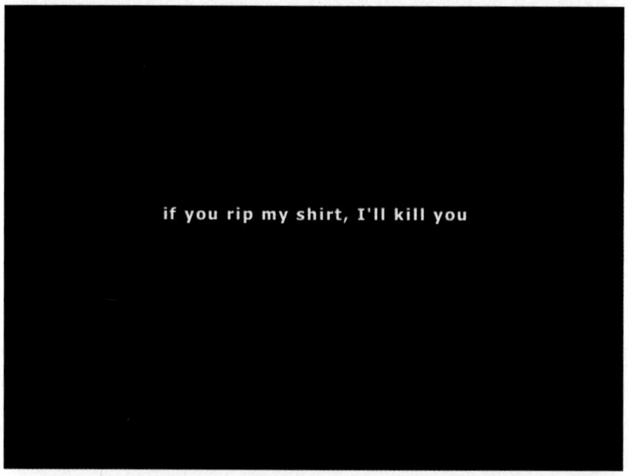
if you rip my shirt, I'll kill you

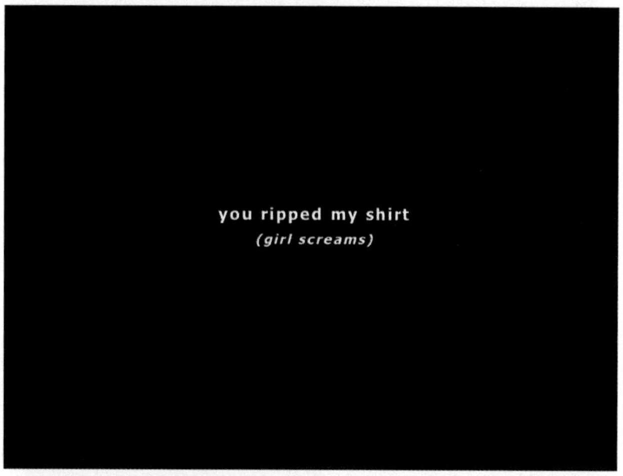
you ripped my shirt
(girl screams)

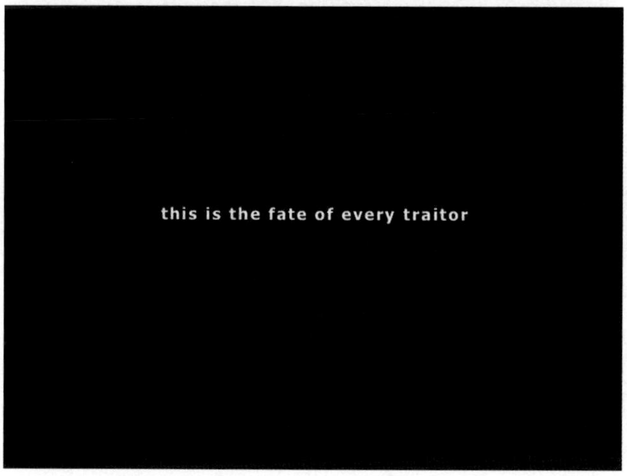
this is the fate of every traitor

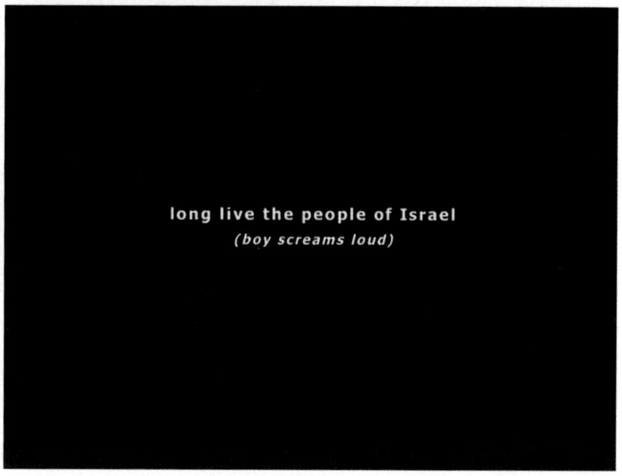
long live the people of Israel
(boy screams loud)

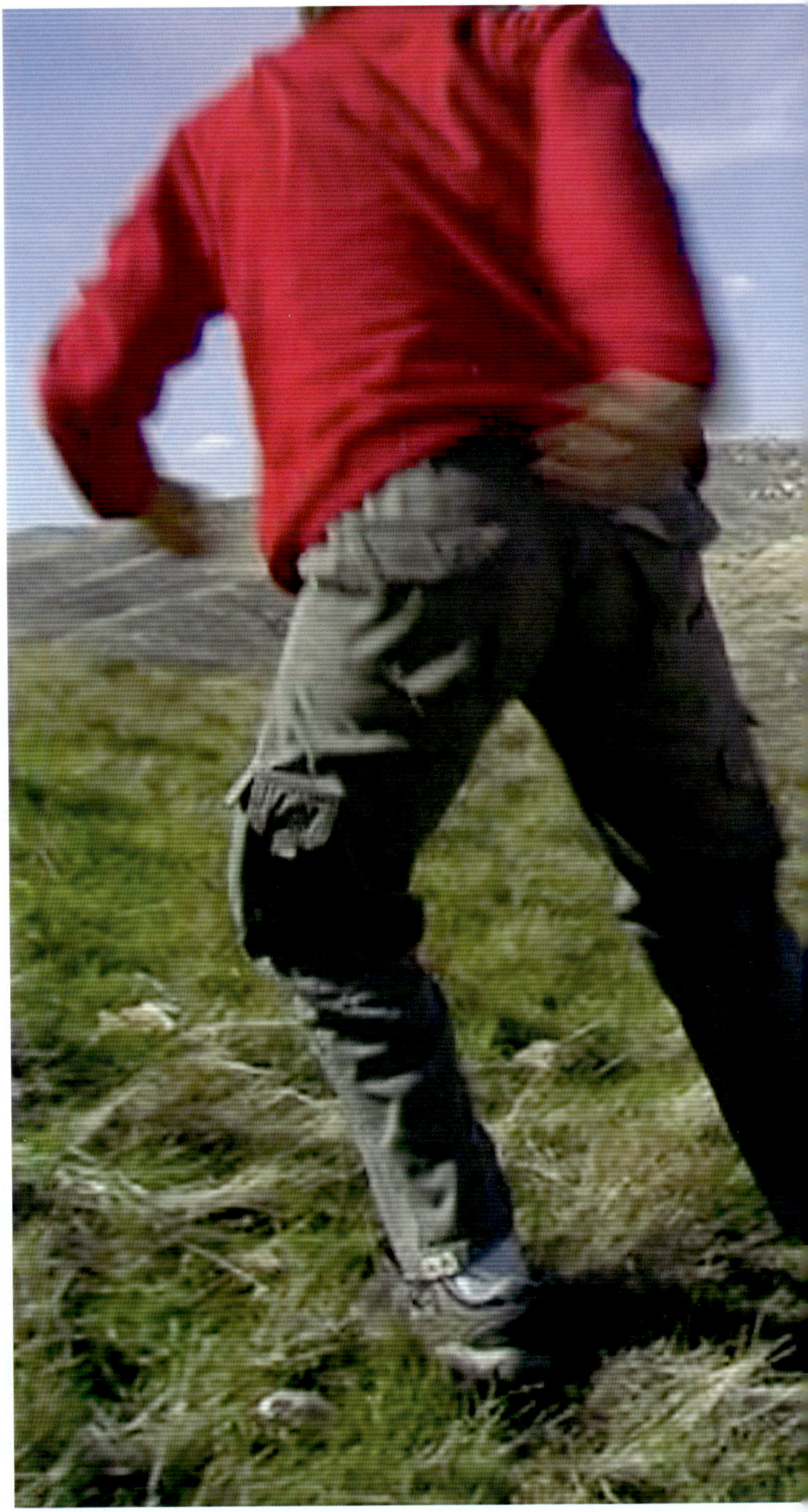

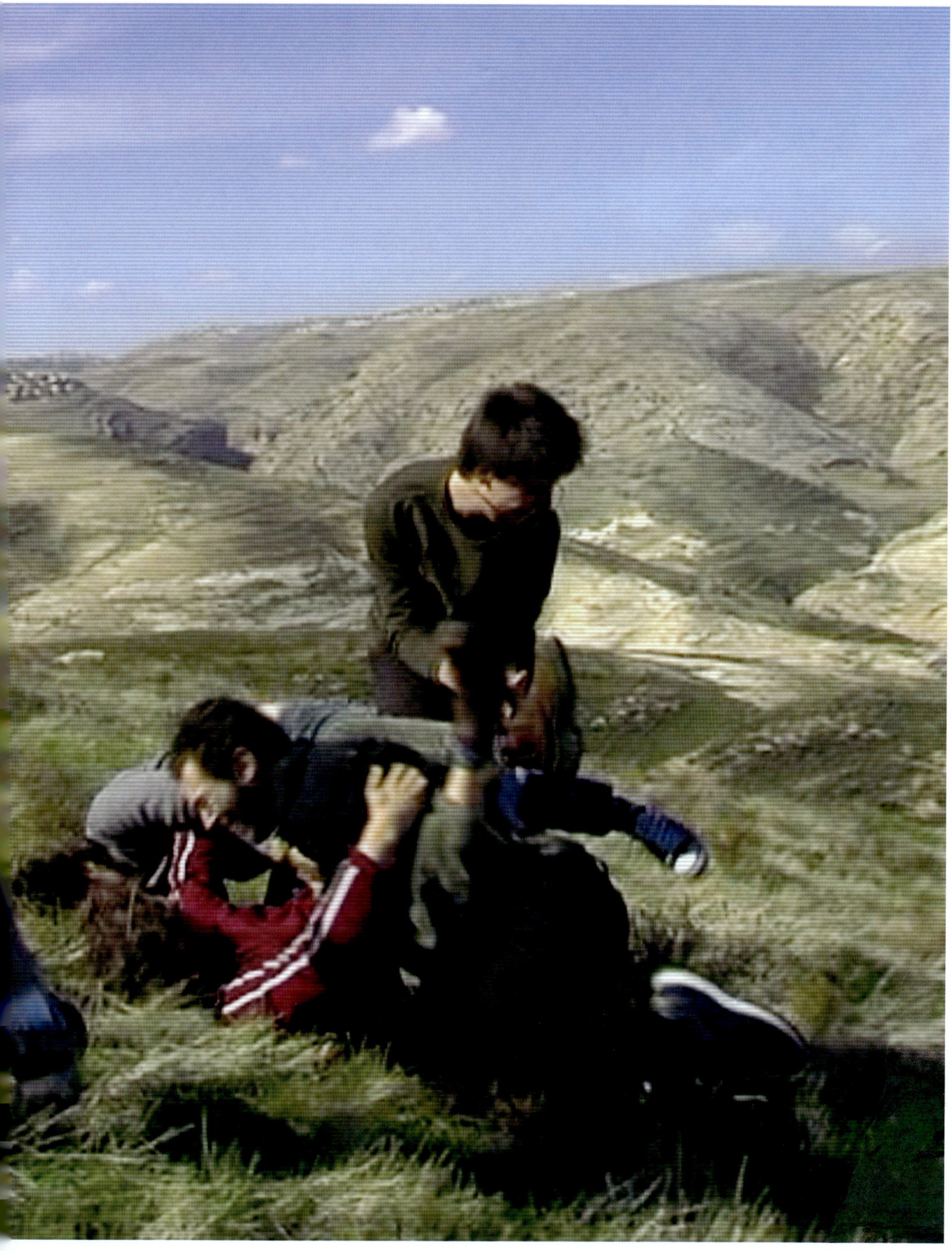

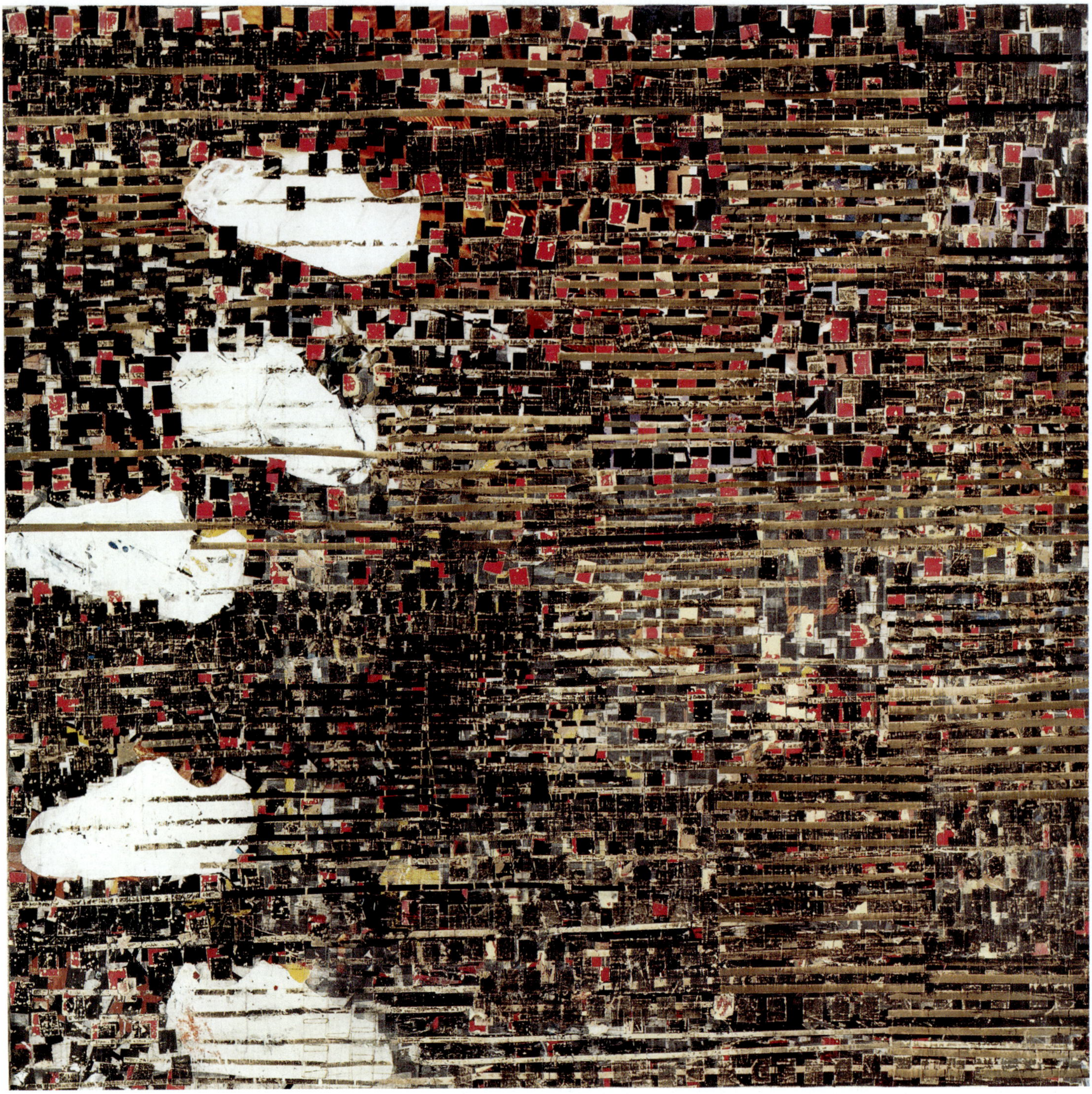

Analog 2004 oil, paper on canvas

ABSTRACTION AND THE BODY: MARK BRADFORD

Born in the United States, 1961. Lives and works in Los Angeles.

In the past few years, Mark Bradford has built up a remarkable body of painting situated at the intersection of an astute understanding of art history, perceptive psycho-geographical experience, and conviction in handiwork and manual labor. His works may be more correctly described as collages, but their heroic scale and ambitious exploration of abstraction are more akin to classical problems of painting. Earlier on, he utilized "endpapers"—translucent, paper squares used during the process of wrapping hair for a permanent wave treatment—on his canvases, which gave them a push-pull optical effect while also pointing to his personal history (he comes from a line of hairdressers). On a formal level, the endpapers, often overlapping like scales of a fish, let colorful layers underneath show through and reinterpret the grid, that historically weighted method of modernist abstraction.

Bradford's collage paintings are firmly rooted in his experience of Los Angeles, where he was born and continues to live as a self-described "postmodern flaneur." The classic image of the flaneur, which was coined by Charles Baudelaire in the 1860s and may be translated as "idle man about town," is the bourgeois dandy strolling the grand boulevards of the modernized Paris of Baron Haussmann and observing the new modern city and its unfolding cultures.[1] Bradford's twenty-first-century flanerie takes place in the Southern Californian metropolis, marked by its peculiar logic of organization and operation: a city in which pedestrianism and public transportation have been systematically excised, replaced by a domineering automobile culture; a site of unrivaled ethnic and cultural diversity, with endless streams of both legal and undocumented immigrants constantly changing its demography; and a stunningly vast, sun-baked desert landscape of racial and class stratifications and of the extremely complex symbiotic coexistence of formal and informal economies.

If Bradford updates the relationship between the artist and his city as defined in the Parisian modernism of the nineteenth century, it is with another group of artists, *affichistes*, that he finds closer formalistic affinities. Raymond Hains and Jacques de la Villeglé, the two best-known of this company, met in 1949 and worked primarily in Paris in the 1950s. Using a method they termed *décollage*, they took wheat-pasted posters from the streets and tore and lacerated them to reveal the successive layers of images that had accumulated. While Bradford, like his predecessors, procures many of his substrates from the streets, he also combines their reductive process with additive methodologies. His vast pictorial frames—measuring at least six-by-six feet and sometimes reaching more than fifteen feet wide—often incorporate a generous list of materials, such as brilliant color papers and mason's strings. He not only collages the different sorts and hues of paper materials but varies their shapes and surfaces by cutting, tearing, soaking, and sanding them, creating wide ranges of gradation and texture. The resulting two-dimensional works, such as *Los Moscos* (2004) and *Potable Water* (2005), evoke an aerial view or map of a city, with simultaneous suggestions of movement and settlement, system and chaos, fixity and fluidity. Certain recognizable images and words may surface through the dense layers, and they sometimes materialize through erasure, as in the case of the torn-out, ghostly reverse silhouettes of basketball shoes in *Analog* (2004). If the economy of tagging is an undeniable part of the artist's method of production, his paintings also embody a sense of constant regeneration that opposes and complements the mechanism of vandalism.

Perhaps the most legible and figurative of Bradford's paintings, *Ridin' Dirty* (2006), consists of an enormous grid of seventy-eight merchant posters that had been put up by local businesses in Los Angeles. Unlike professional posters designed to seduce viewers with catchy words and images, these homespun advertisements simply offer telephone numbers and services ranging from "traffic school," "security guard," "Indian hair," and "shoe sale" to "divorce/custody" and "cash." The artist traces the contours of the block types with mason's strings, singeing some of the posters to produce negative images of the originals, or bleaching and sanding them to leave ghostly residues. Composed in a tight congregation, they become a screen of economies that informally—and perhaps illegally—support everyday urban lives, their collective scale dignifying them into reality and legitimacy.

Bradford's painting involves highly physical processes. And the body and its labor, both conceptually alluded to and materialized in his work, can be a way to understand the artist's exploration of other mediums, such as video. In *Practice* (2003), Bradford is dribbling a ball while wearing the L.A. Lakers' yellow-and-purple jersey top and, instead of shorts, a flowing hoop skirt. This self-imposed bodily stricture awkwardly impedes his efforts, but after some tripping and tumbling, the dogged performer shoots a basket at the end of the short three-minute video. *Niagara* (2005) also focuses on a single subject, but here, unlike *Practice*, the camera is stationary. It shows one man in the artist's neighborhood walking down a street, unabashedly and even defiantly swinging his hips à la Marilyn Monroe in the 1953 film of the same title. Taken together, the videos are crystallized close-up images of individuals who perform and embody their subjectivities beyond the perimeters of standard gender and race identity—specifically, African American masculinity—that are stringently upheld in an urban setting. These are a couple of the many bodies that are not only alluded to, but in fact populate Bradford's growing lexicon of abstraction.

DC

1. See Charles Baudelaire's description of the flaneur in "The Painter of Modern Life," in *The Painter of Modern Life and Other Essays*, Jonathon Mayne, trans. and ed. (London: Phaidon, 1995). Bradford also names a 2005 painting, *Grace and Measure*, after a phrase borrowed from another poem by Baudelaire, "*L'invitation au voyage*" "Invitation to a Voyage," collected in *Les Fleur du mal* (first published in 1857). The original phrase reads, "*Là, tout n'est qu'ordre et beauté,/Luxe, calme et volupté.*" (There'll be nothing but beauty, wealth, and pleasure/With all things in order and measure.) The most thorough and critical account of flanerie and Impressionism and their relationship with the emergent modern city of Paris is found in the canonical art-historical study by T. J. Clark, *The Painting of Modern Life: Paris in the Art of Manet and His Followers* (Princeton, New Jersey: Princeton University Press, 1986).

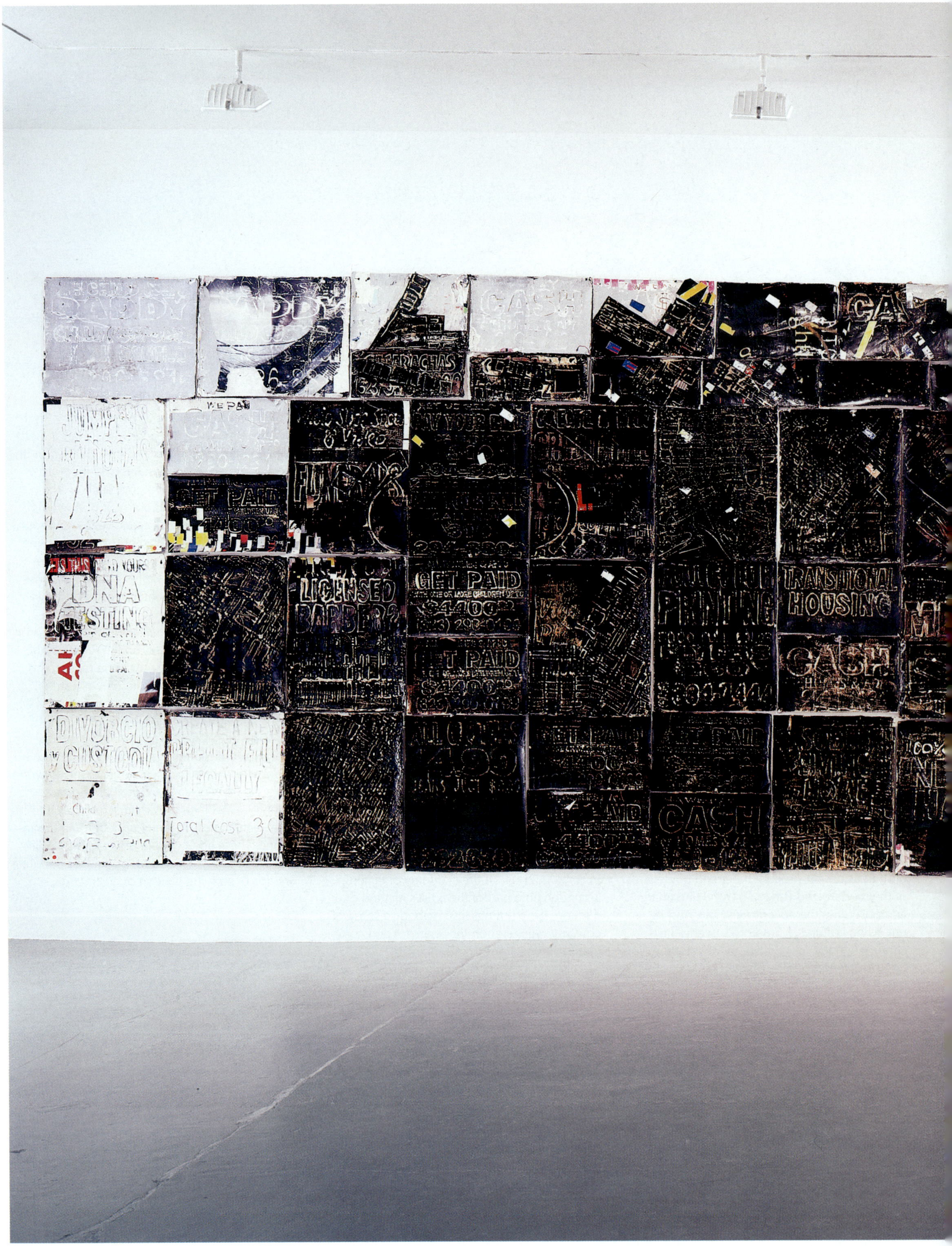

Ridin' Dirty 2006 mixed-media collage on paper

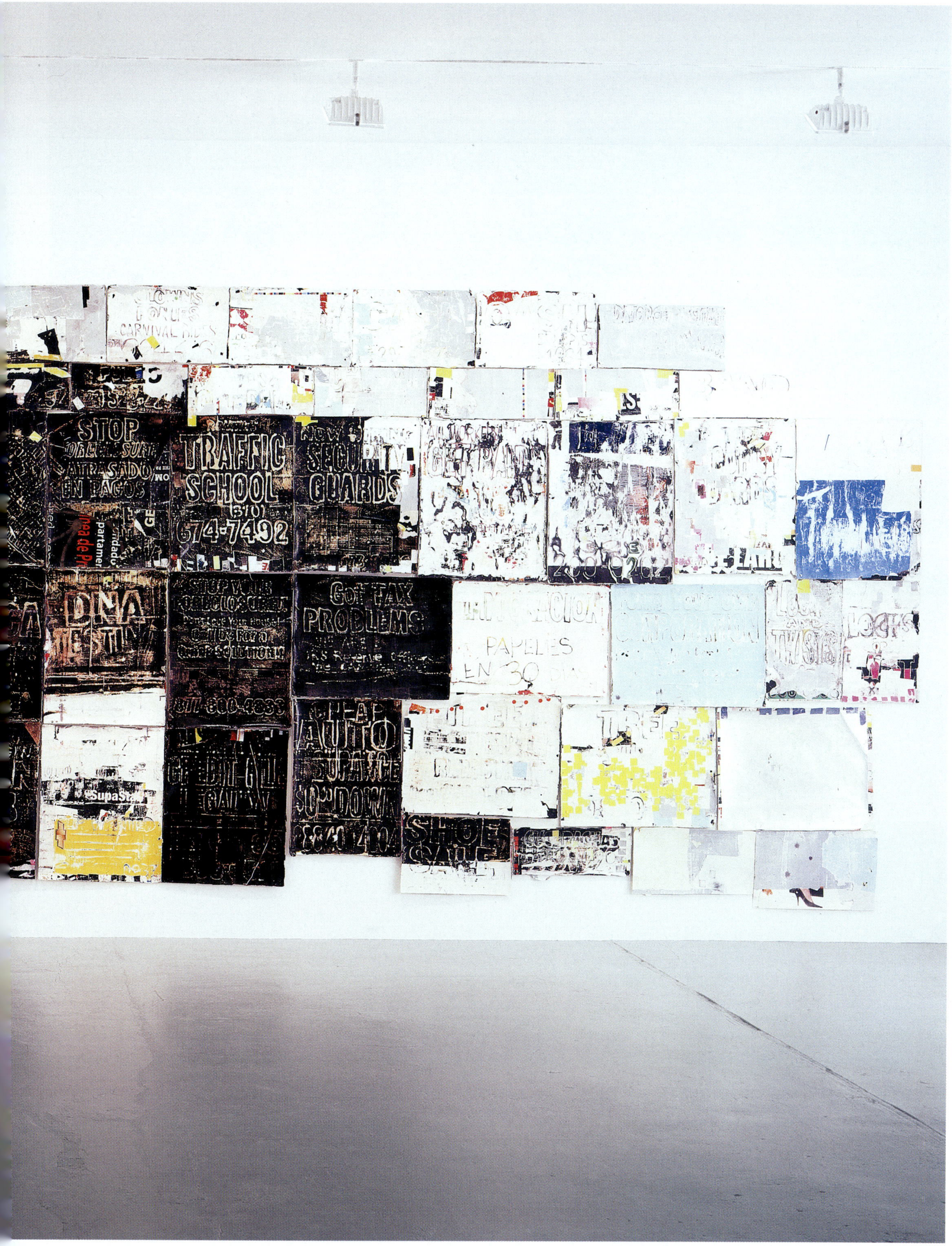
CARNIVAL RIDES
STOP
ATRASADO
EN PAGOS
TRAFFIC
SCHOOL
674-7492
SECURITY
GUARDS
DNA
Got TAX
PROBLEMS
PAPELES
EN 30
877-800-4833
CHEAP
AUTO
SHOES

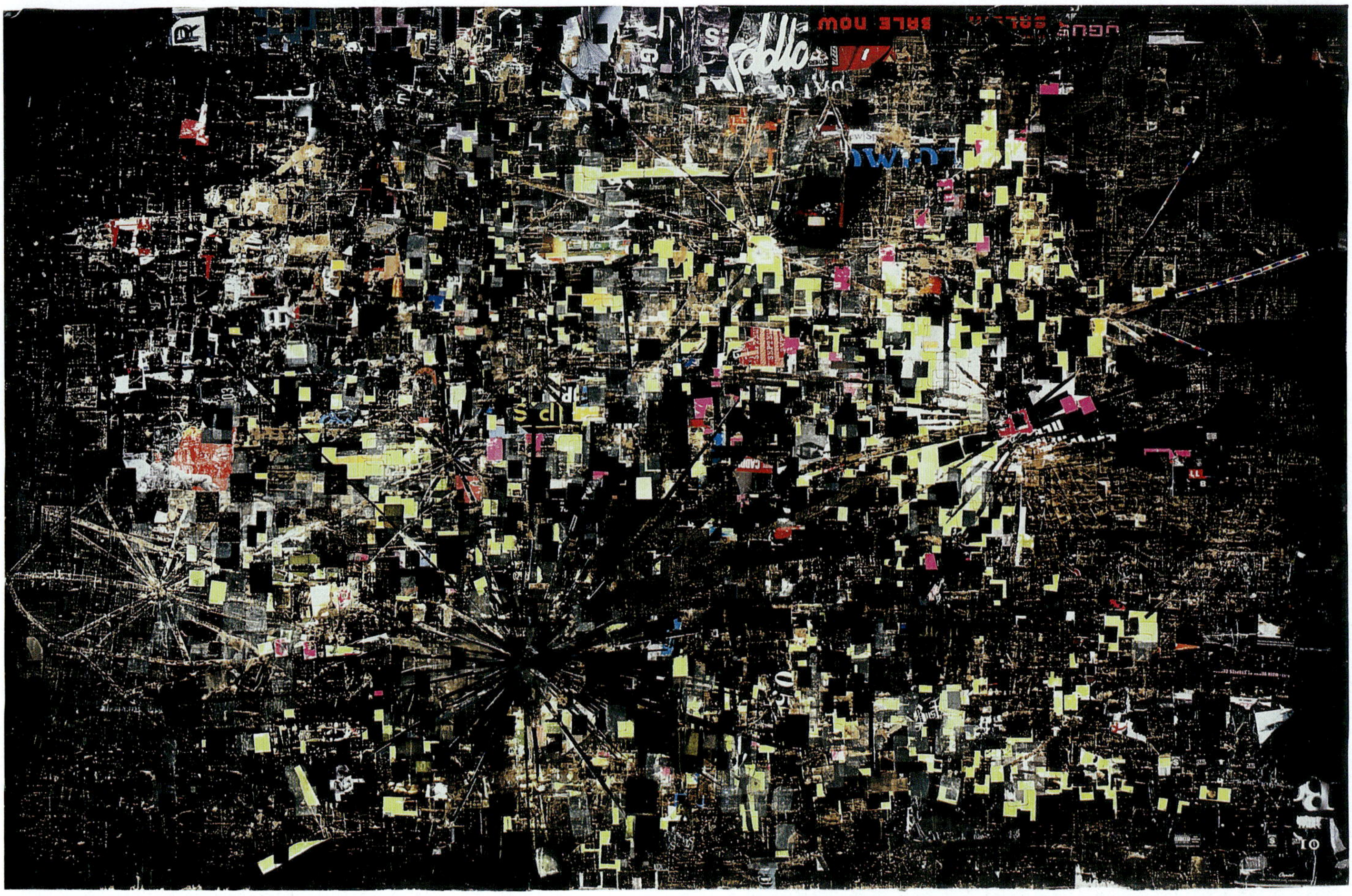

Los Moscos 2004 mixed-media collage on canvas

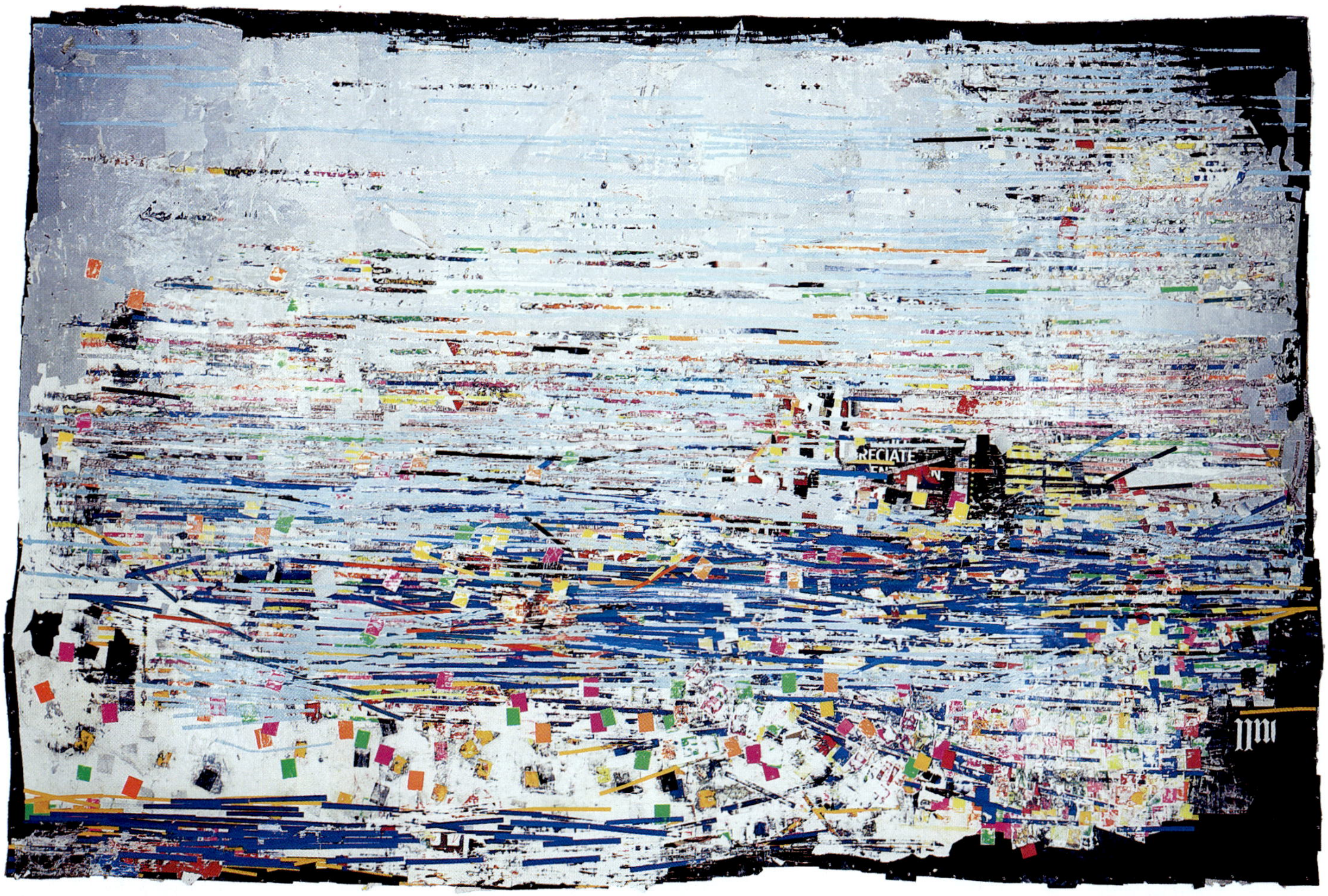

Potable Water 2005 mixed-media collage on canvas

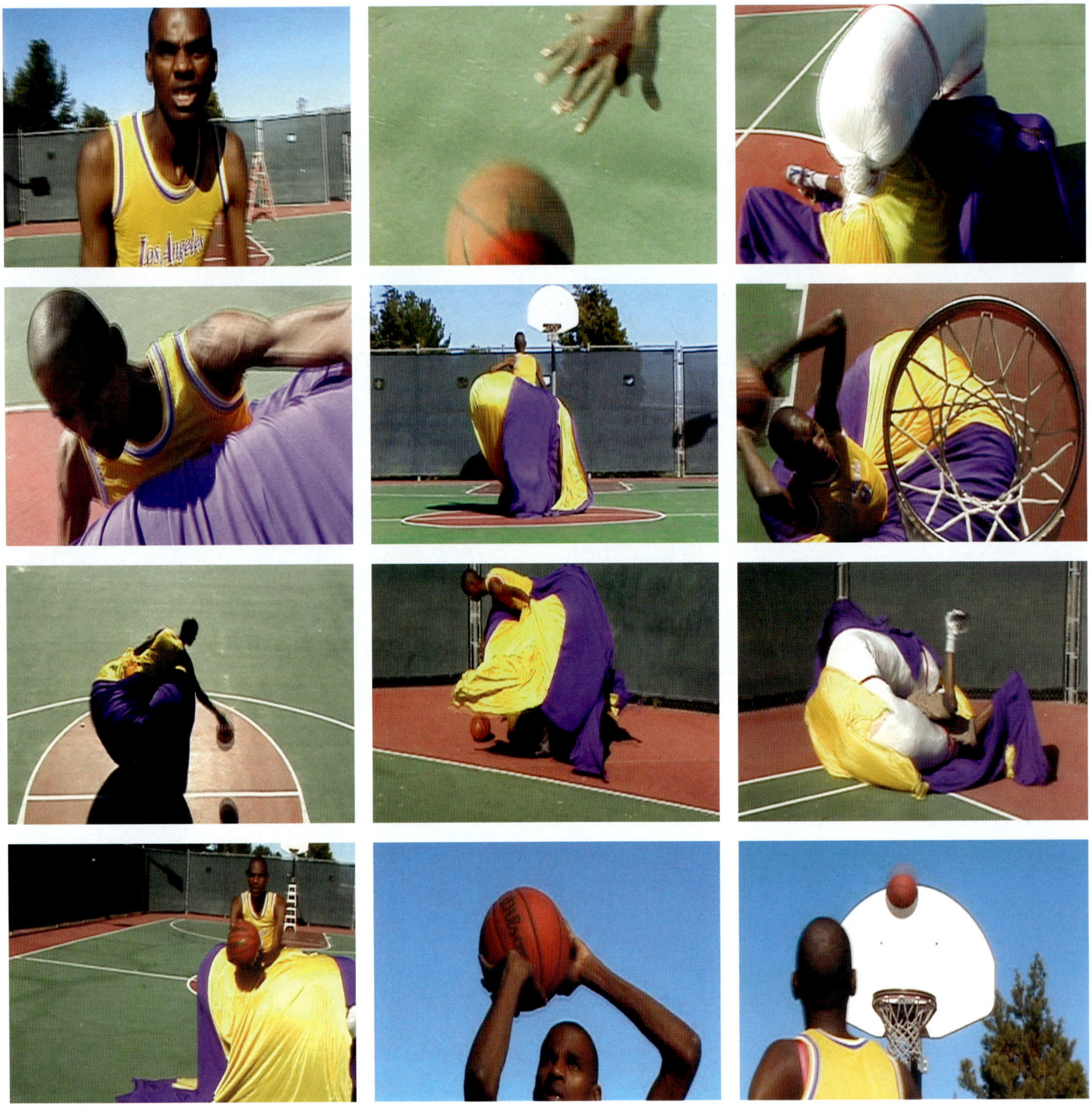

Stills from *Practice* 2003 video transferred to DVD (color, sound); 2:46 minutes (loop)

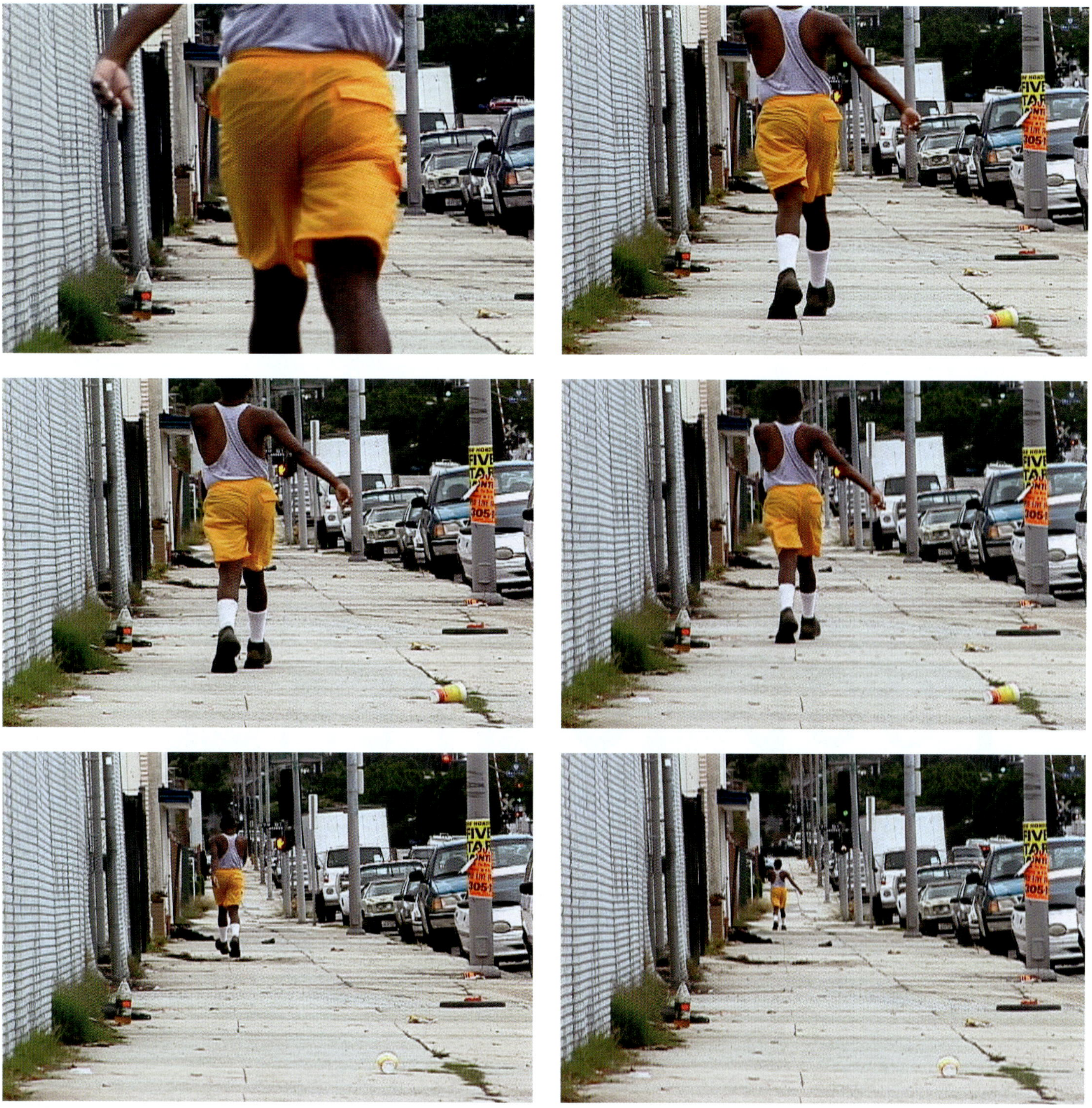

Stills from *Niagara* 2005 video transferred to DVD (color, sound); 3:17 minutes (loop)

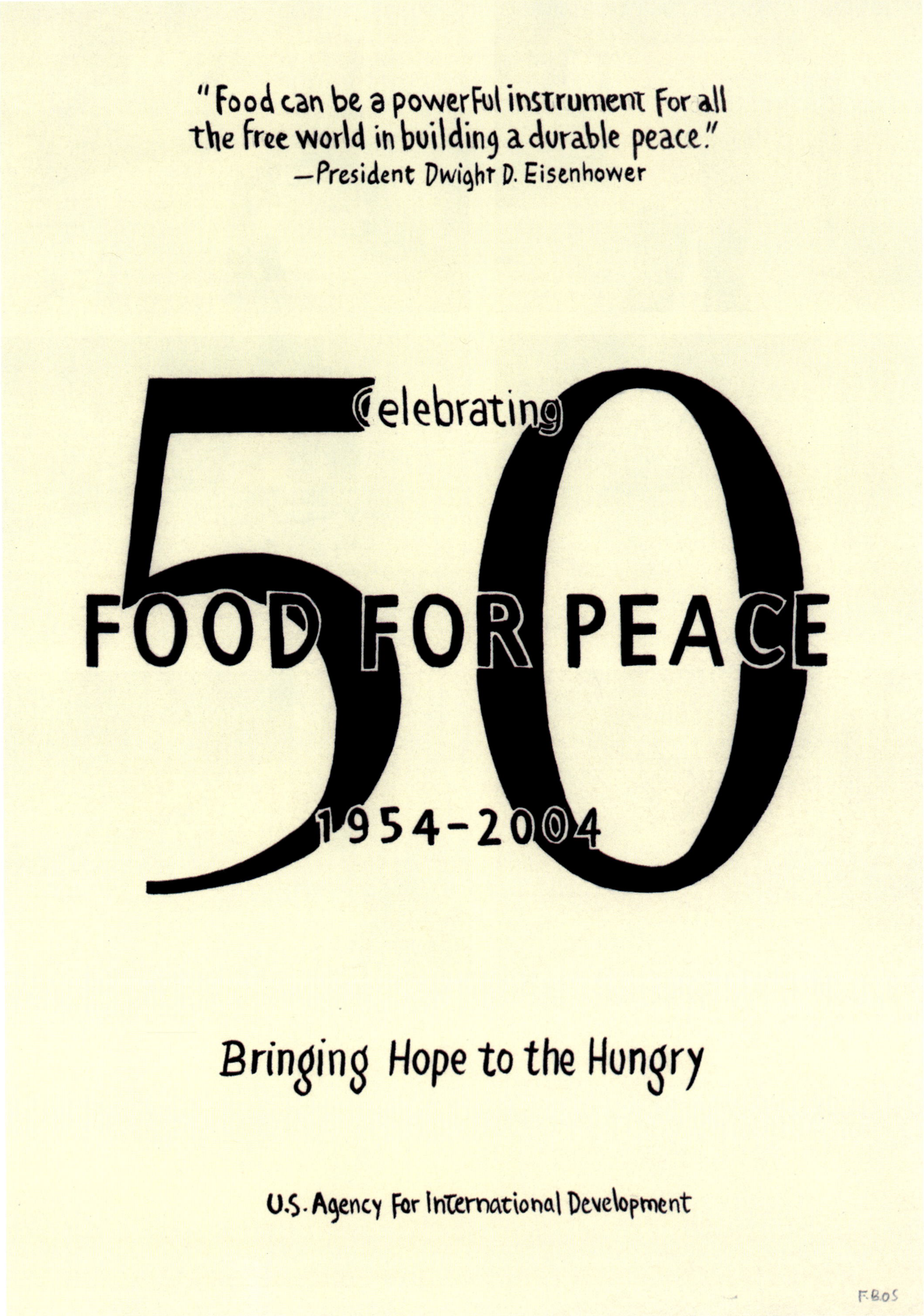

Selection from *Work in Progress* 2005–2006 ink on paper; series of 80

FERNANDO BRYCE'S IDEOLOGICAL NETS

Born in Peru, 1965. Lives and works in Berlin. Fernando Bryce is best known for his uniform, obsessively detailed series of black and gray ink drawings that confront the viewer with their ironic ideological connections and the unsettling Machiavellian nature of power. The question of how to organize and analyze history has become increasingly central in Bryce's practice, which initially centered on painting in the studio of Peruvian artist Leslie Lee and continued in Europe with theory courses at the University of Paris and four years at the École nationale supérieure des beaux-arts studying with artist Christian Boltanski. In the early 1990s, he moved to Berlin and shifted his focus from the accumulative process of painting on canvas to the spontaneity and precariousness of India ink on paper.

The images and texts in Bryce's work range from impeccable duplicates of original documents to arbitrary details isolated on a blank page and often accompanied with a quote or caption. These source materials — culled from discontinued periodicals, reels of microfilm, and publicly available archives — are extremely wide-ranging, including passport head shots, stamped contracts, signed letters, magazine covers, tourist pamphlets, weekly newsletters, photographs, fashion advertisements, newspaper clippings, annual reports, cartoon illustrations, governmental receipts, and inventories. These intentionally chosen objets trouvés are systematically compiled and carefully studied in a process the artist has described as a "method of mimetic analysis" in which he selects documents related to specific events (the Cuban revolution, the Spanish Civil War, the bombing of Hiroshima) or figures he reveres (literary critic Walter Benjamin, Marxist theorist Leon Trotsky, former Chilean president Salvador Allende), and pairs them with other figures related to the subject of investigation and related memorabilia. Through this process of association, Bryce excavates items of contention from the pit of history and uses them to sketch out a past that more closely reaches our immediate present.

In the series *Work in Progress* (2005–2006), the artist replicates front covers, text, and images assembled from annual reports and strategic plans published by a variety of food aid agencies from the United States, the United Kingdom, France, and Germany and from organizations such as the World Bank, the UN World Food Programme (WFP), and the Food and Agriculture Organization (FAO). Bryce's hand-painted facsimiles transcribe, word-for-word, excerpts from official reports, correspondence authored by world leaders, and promotional materials complete with logos. They also replicate the documents' accompanying photographs in which subjects are often shown enjoying the "generosity" of their Western benefactors. Food, however, brings the issue of global inequities to the fore as it exposes the expediency of the "compassion and generosity" of wealthier nations whose current aid budgets amount to half of their totals from 1960.[1] Bryce's poignant work reveals the explicit entrepreneurial motivations behind such humanitarian programs: similar to the colonial endeavors of the recent past, the driving force is not to establish sustainable agricultural systems that ensure the ability of underdeveloped nations to grow their own food independently, but rather to merely provide short-term solutions that keep them dependent.

Bryce's obsession with history leads him to take the conventional order of the archive in order to dissect it and expose the iconography of power and domination. Like a historian, he dips into the ink of language to reconstruct the ideological narrative and interrogate the unsavory interests it disguises. Grouping events loaded with contemporary resonance, he weaves together distant terrains of words and images, turning his drawings into what he calls "iconographic nets" that collect subjective, political, and cultural meanings.

YR

1. Elizabeth Becker, "Number of Hungry Rising, U.N. Says," *New York Times* (May 29, 2007).

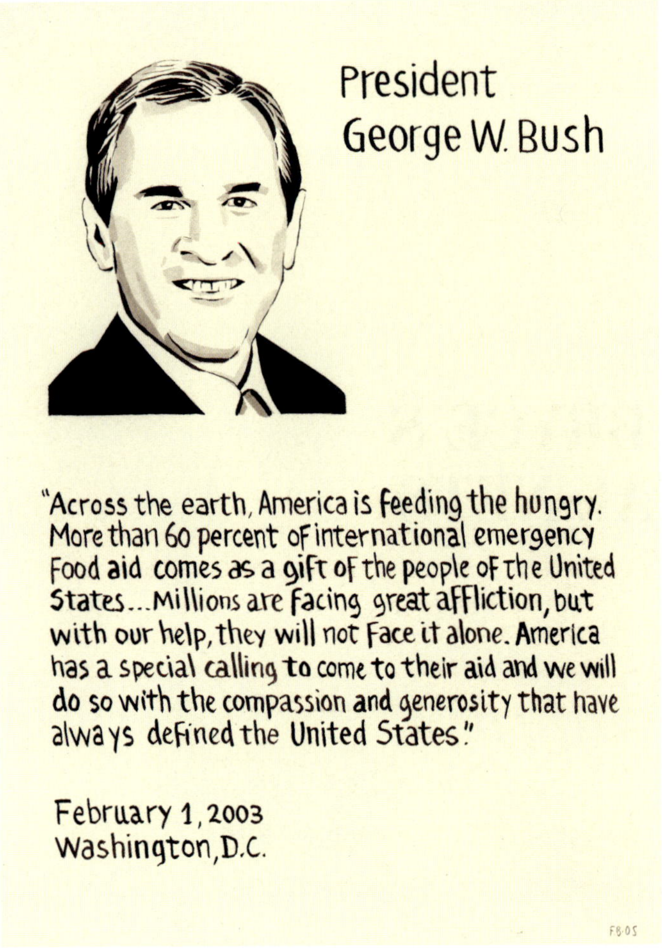

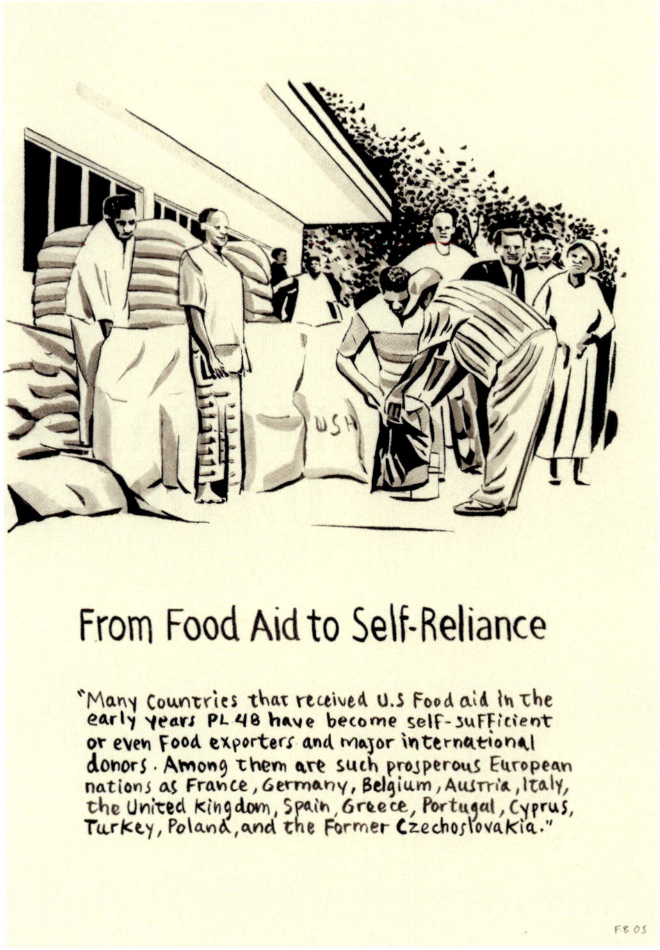

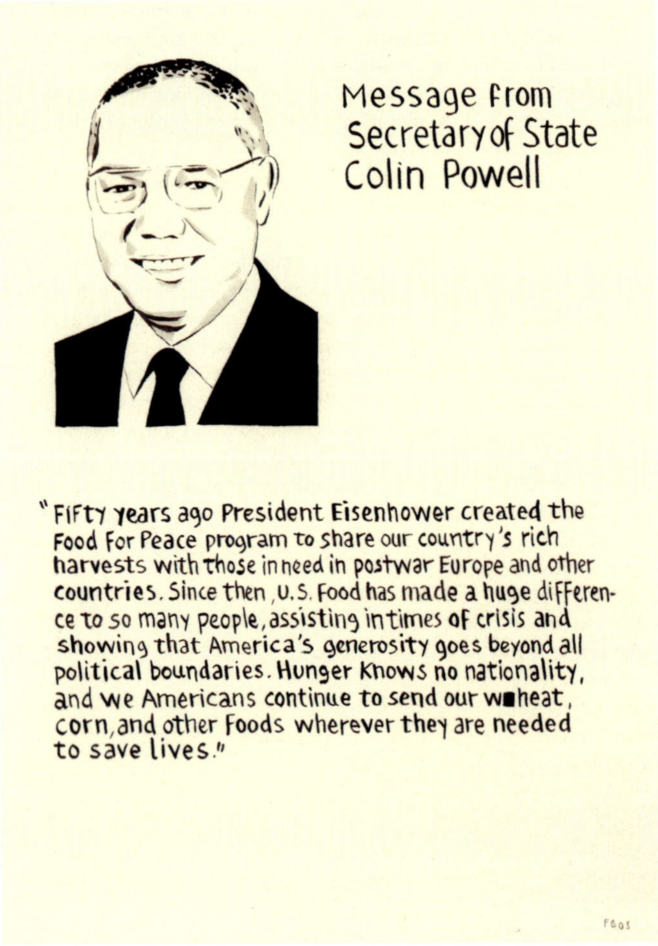

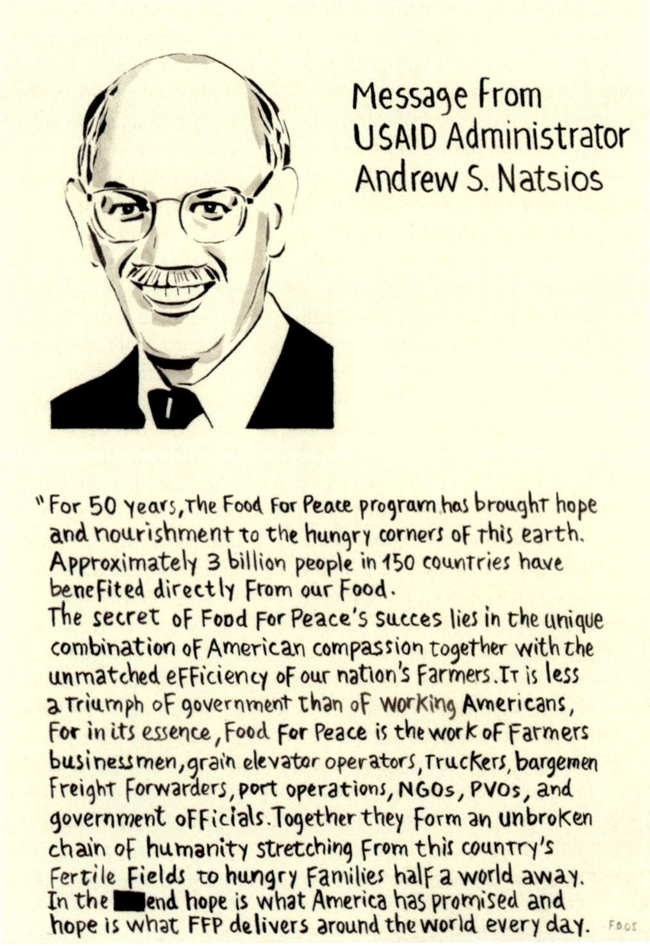

Selections from *Work in Progress* 2005–2006 ink on paper; series of 80

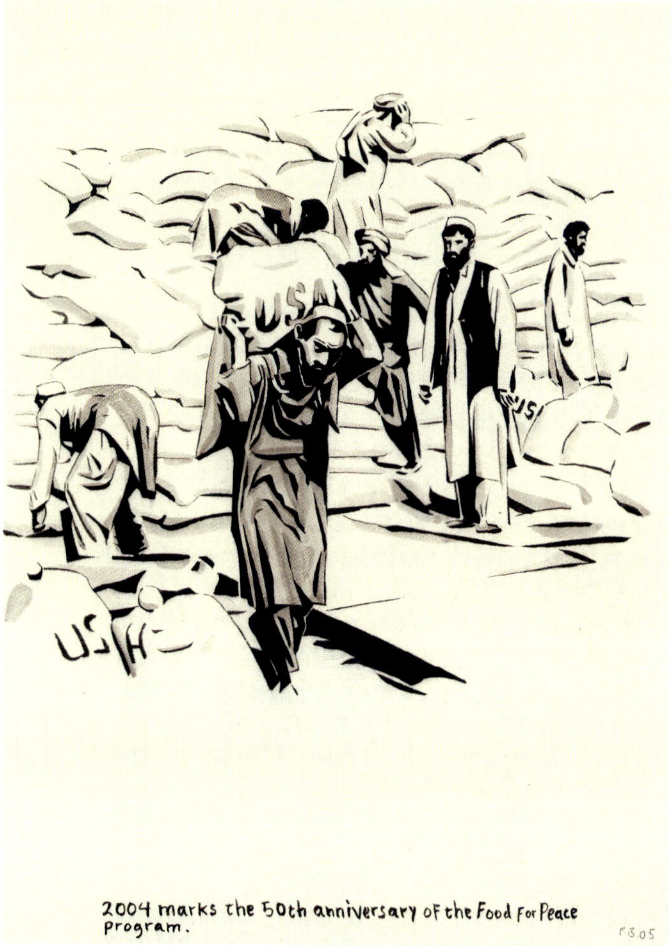
USA
USA
USA
2004 marks the 50th anniversary of the Food For Peace program.
F.B. 05

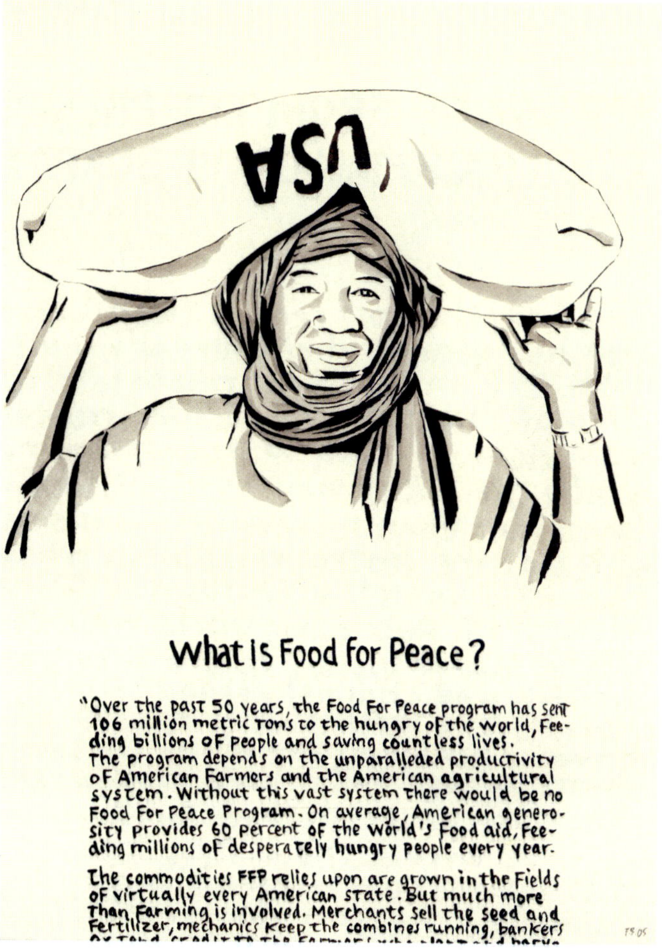
USA
What is Food for Peace?
"Over the past 50 years, the Food For Peace program has sent 106 million metric tons to the hungry of the world, Feeding billions of people and saving countless lives.
The program depends on the unparalleded productivity of American Farmers and the American agricultural system. Without this vast system there would be no Food For Peace Program. On average, American generosity provides 60 percent of the World's Food aid, Feeding millions of desperately hungry people every year.
The commodities FFP relies upon are grown in the Fields of virtually every American state. But much more than Farming is involved. Merchants sell the seed and Fertilizer, mechanics keep the combines running, bankers
F.B. 05

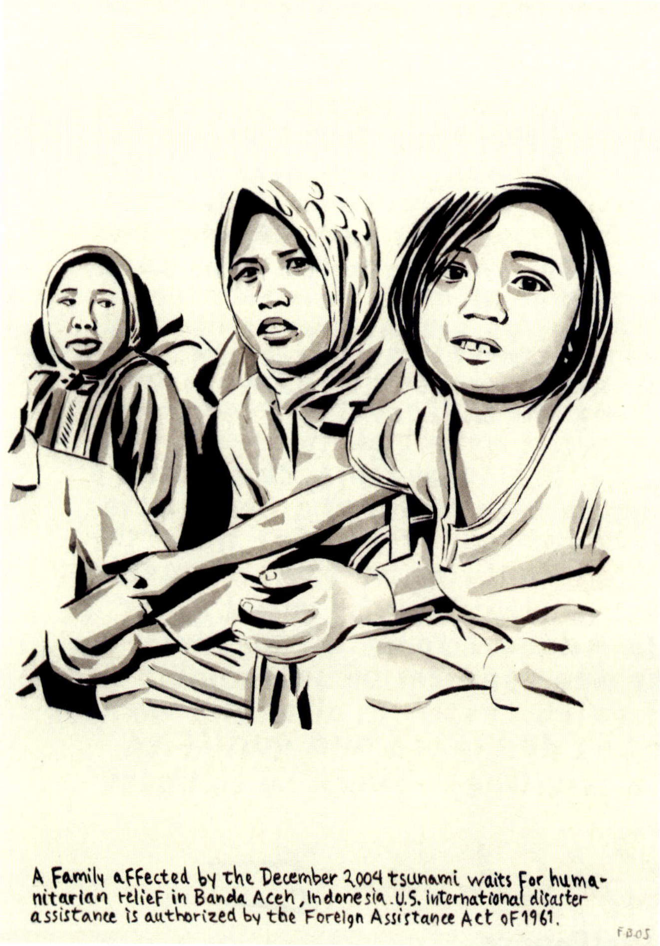
A Family affected by the December 2004 tsunami waits for humanitarian relief in Banda Aceh, Indonesia. U.S. international disaster assistance is authorized by the Foreign Assistance Act of 1961.
F.B. 05

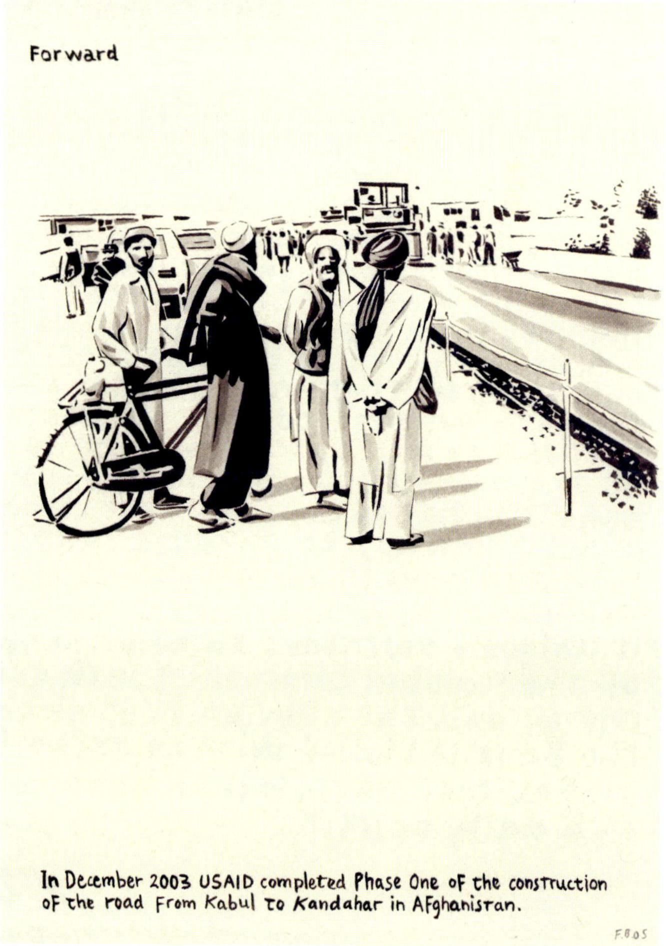
Forward
In December 2003 USAID completed Phase One of the construction of the road from Kabul to Kandahar in Afghanistan.
F.B. 05

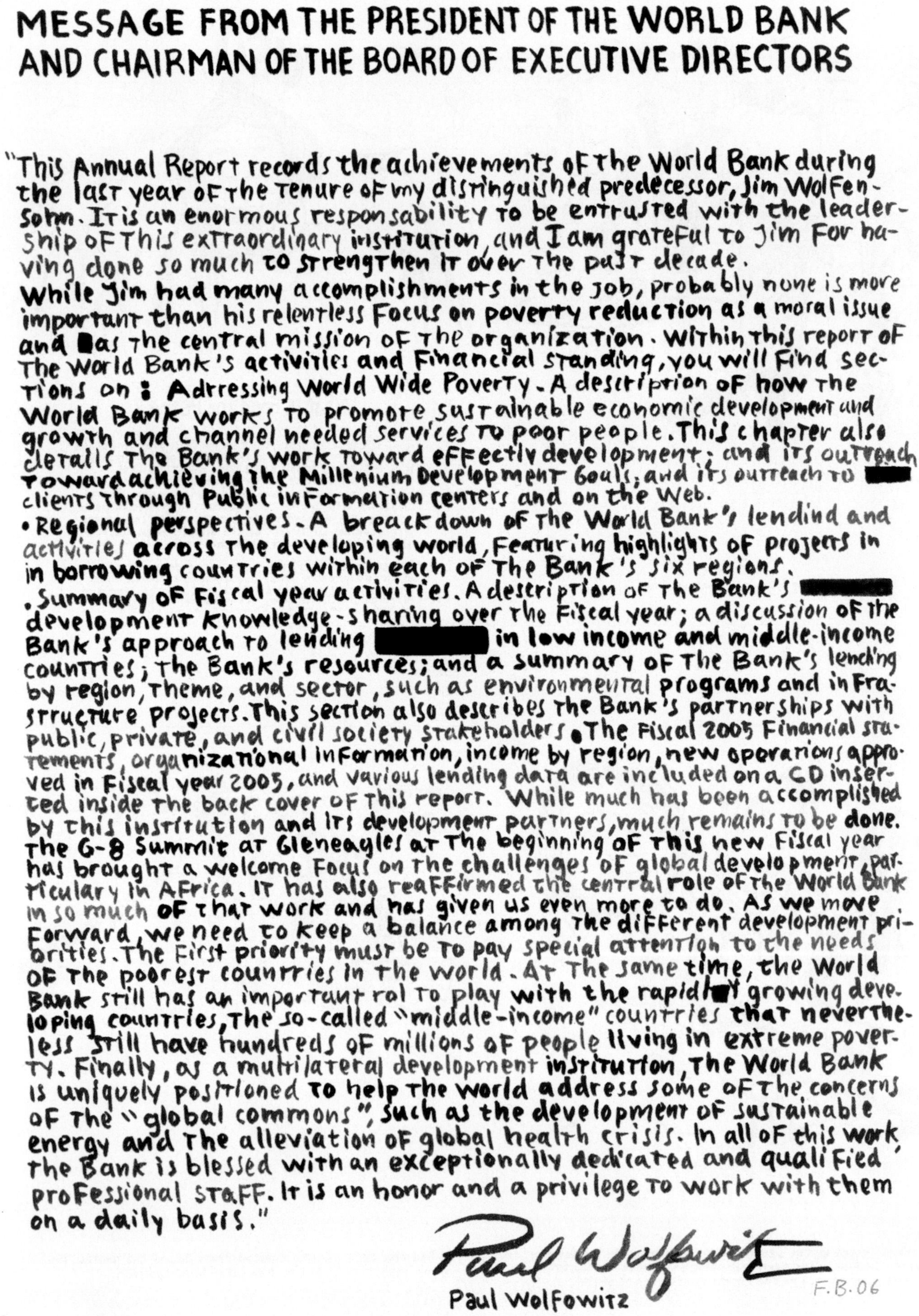

MESSAGE FROM THE PRESIDENT OF THE WORLD BANK AND CHAIRMAN OF THE BOARD OF EXECUTIVE DIRECTORS

"This Annual Report records the achievements of the World Bank during the last year of the tenure of my distinguished predecessor, Jim Wolfensohn. It is an enormous responsability to be entrusted with the leadership of this extraordinary institution, and I am grateful to Jim for having done so much to strengthen it over the past decade.

While Jim had many accomplishments in the job, probably none is more important than his relentless focus on poverty reduction as a moral issue and [redacted] as the central mission of the organization. Within this report of the World Bank's activities and financial standing, you will find sections on: Adrressing World Wide Poverty. A description of how the World Bank works to promote sustainable economic development and growth and channel needed services to poor people. This chapter also details the Bank's work toward effectiv development; and its outreach toward achieving the Millenium Development Goals; and its outreach to [redacted] clients through public information centers and on the Web.

• Regional perspectives. A breackdown of the World Bank's lendind and activities across the developing world, featuring highlights of projects in in borrowing countries within each of the Bank's six regions.

. Summary of fiscal year activities. A description of the Bank's [redacted] development knowledge-sharing over the fiscal year; a discussion of the Bank's approach to lending [redacted] in low income and middle-income countries; the Bank's resources; and a summary of the Bank's lending by region, theme, and sector, such as environmental programs and infrastructure projects. This section also describes the Bank's partnerships with public, private, and civil society stakeholders. • The fiscal 2005 financial statements, organizational information, income by region, new operations approved in fiscal year 2005, and various lending data are included on a CD inserted inside the back cover of this report. While much has been accomplished by this institution and its development partners, much remains to be done. The G-8 Summit at Gleneagles at the beginning of this new fiscal year has brought a welcome focus on the challenges of global development, particulary in Africa. It has also reaffirmed the central role of the World Bank in so much of that work and has given us even more to do. As we move forward, we need to keep a balance among the different development priorities. The first priority must be to pay special attention to the needs of the poorest countries in the world. At the same time, the World Bank still has an important rol to play with the rapidl[redacted] growing developing countries, the so-called "middle-income" countries that nevertheless still have hundreds of millions of people living in extreme poverty. Finally, as a multilateral development institution, the World Bank is uniquely positioned to help the world address some of the concerns of the "global commons", such as the development of sustainable energy and the alleviation of global health crisis. In all of this work, the Bank is blessed with an exceptionally dedicated and qualified professional staff. It is an honor and a privilege to work with them on a daily basis."

Paul Wolfowitz

Paul Wolfowitz

F.B.06

Selections from *Work in Progress* 2005–2006 ink on paper; series of 80

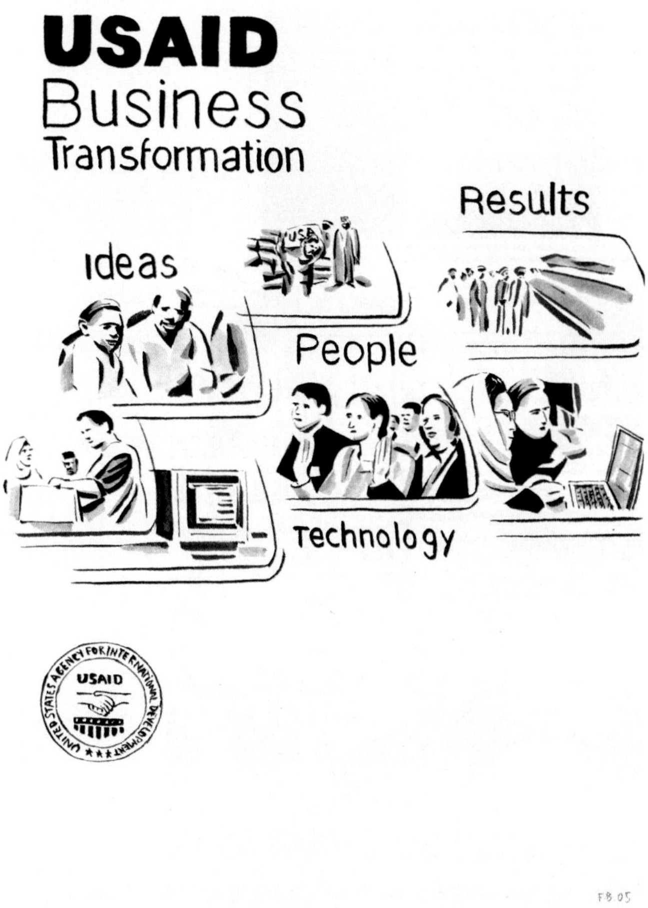
USAID
Business
Transformation
Results
Ideas
People
Technology
USAID
F.B.05

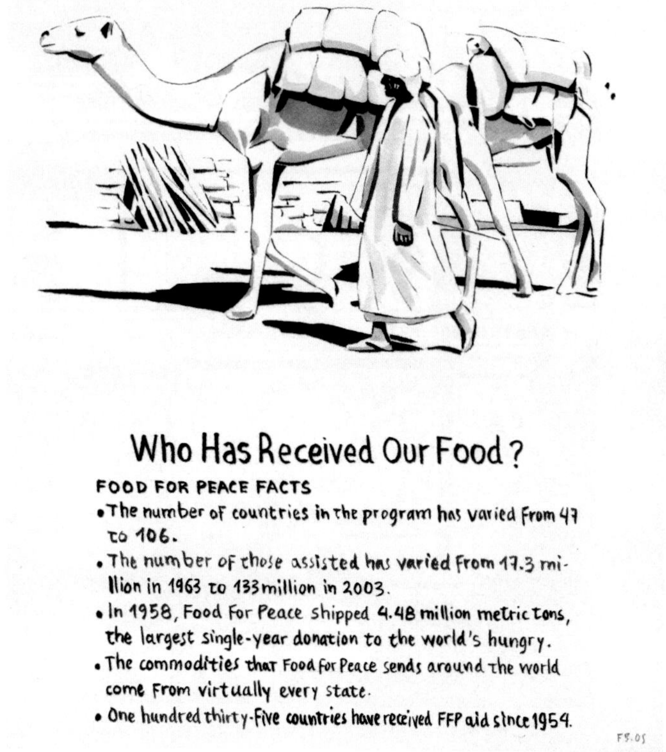
Who Has Received Our Food?
FOOD FOR PEACE FACTS
• The number of countries in the program has varied from 47 to 106.
• The number of those assisted has varied from 17.3 million in 1963 to 133million in 2003.
• In 1958, Food For Peace shipped 4.48 million metric tons, the largest single-year donation to the world's hungry.
• The commodities that Food for Peace sends around the world come from virtually every state.
• One hundred thirty-five countries have received FFP aid since 1954.
F.B.05

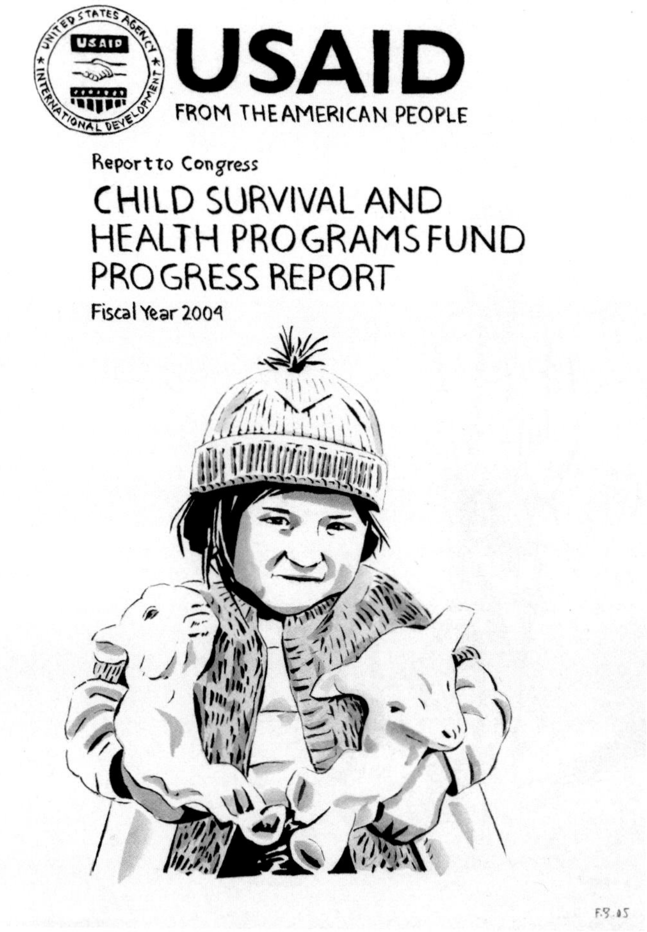
USAID
USAID
FROM THE AMERICAN PEOPLE
Report to Congress
CHILD SURVIVAL AND
HEALTH PROGRAMS FUND
PROGRESS REPORT
Fiscal Year 2004
F.B.05

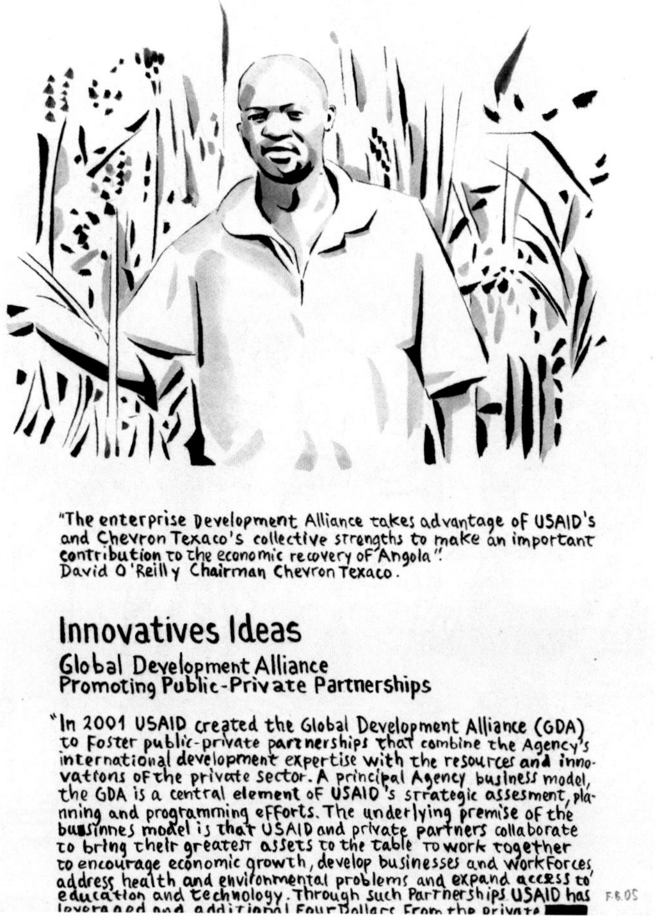
"The enterprise Development Alliance takes advantage of USAID's and Chevron Texaco's collective strengths to make an important contribution to the economic recovery of Angola".
David O'Reilly Chairman Chevron Texaco.
Innovatives Ideas
Global Development Alliance
Promoting Public-Private Partnerships
"In 2001 USAID created the Global Development Alliance (GDA) to foster public-private partnerships that combine the Agency's international development expertise with the resources and innovations of the private sector. A principal Agency business model, the GDA is a central element of USAID's strategic assesment, planning and programming efforts. The underlying premise of the bussinnes model is that USAID and private partners collaborate to bring their greatest assets to the table to work together to encourage economic growth, develop businesses and workforces, address health and environmental problems and expand access to education and technology. Through such Partnerships USAID has
F.B.05

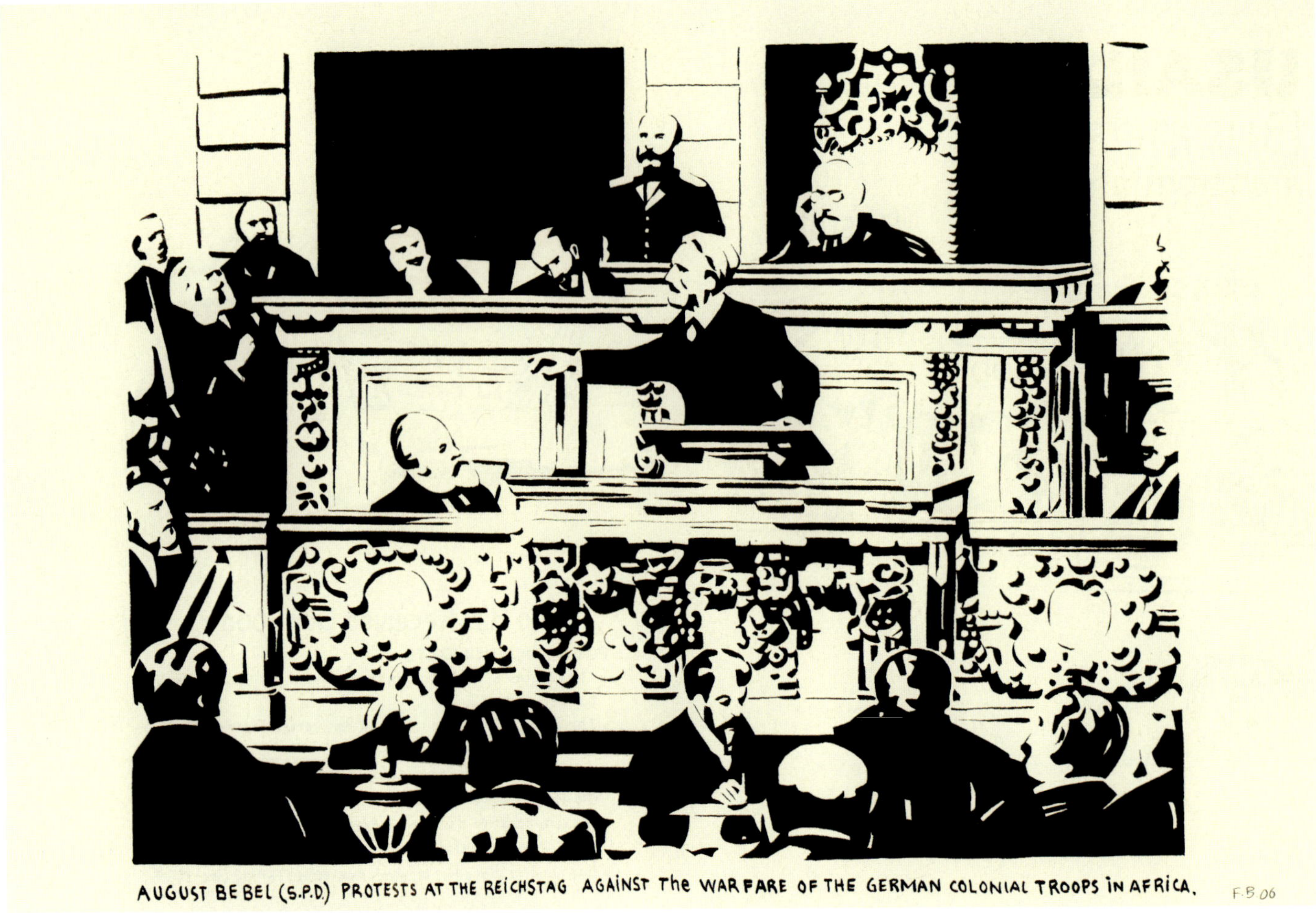

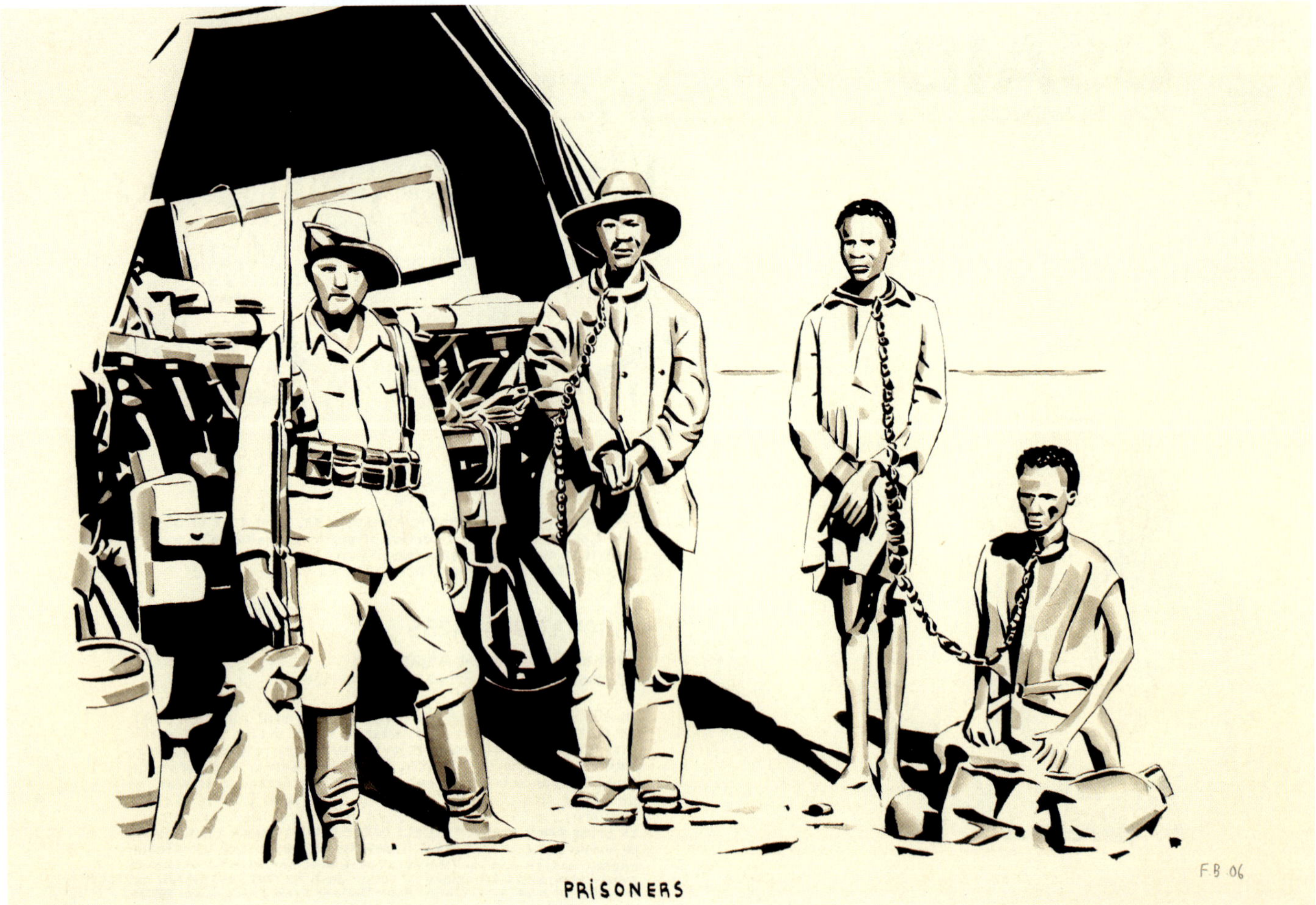

Selections from *Kolonial Post* 2006 ink on paper; series of 111

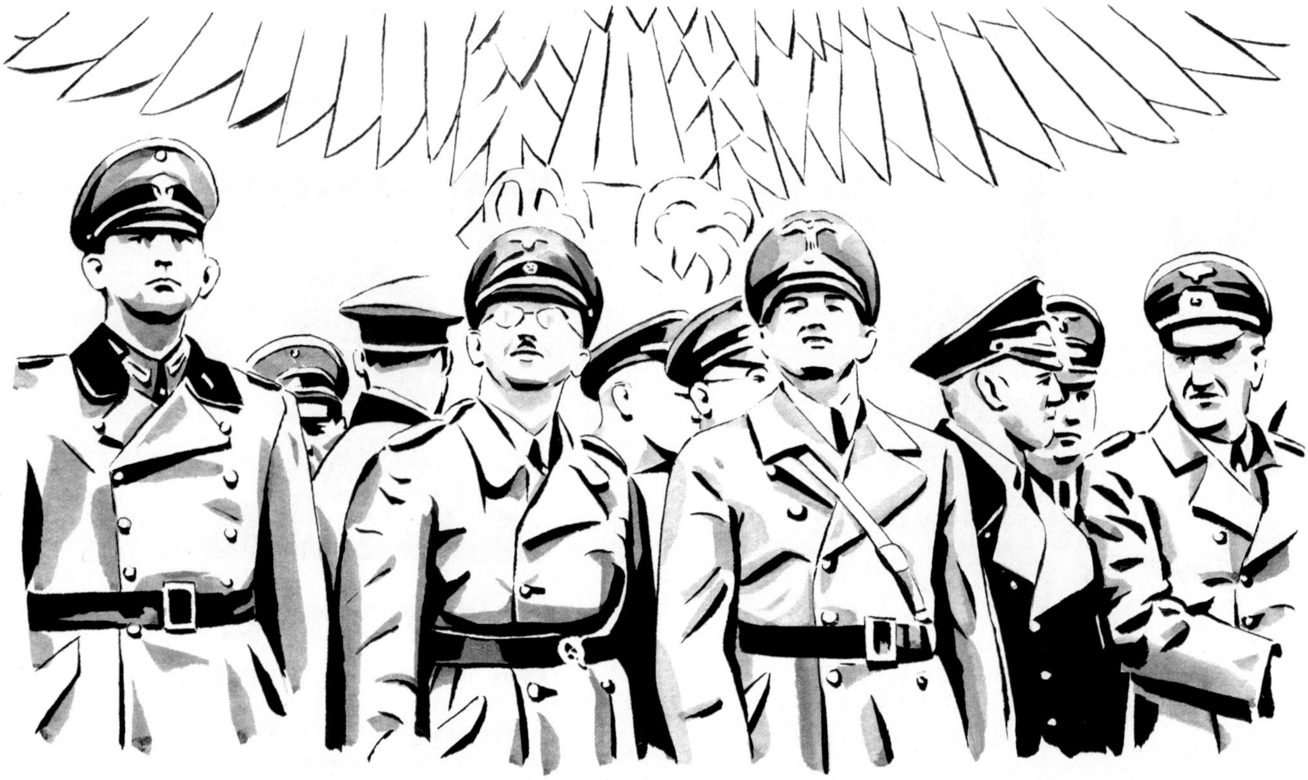

First anniversary of the German Generalgouvernement in Poland.

FB 06

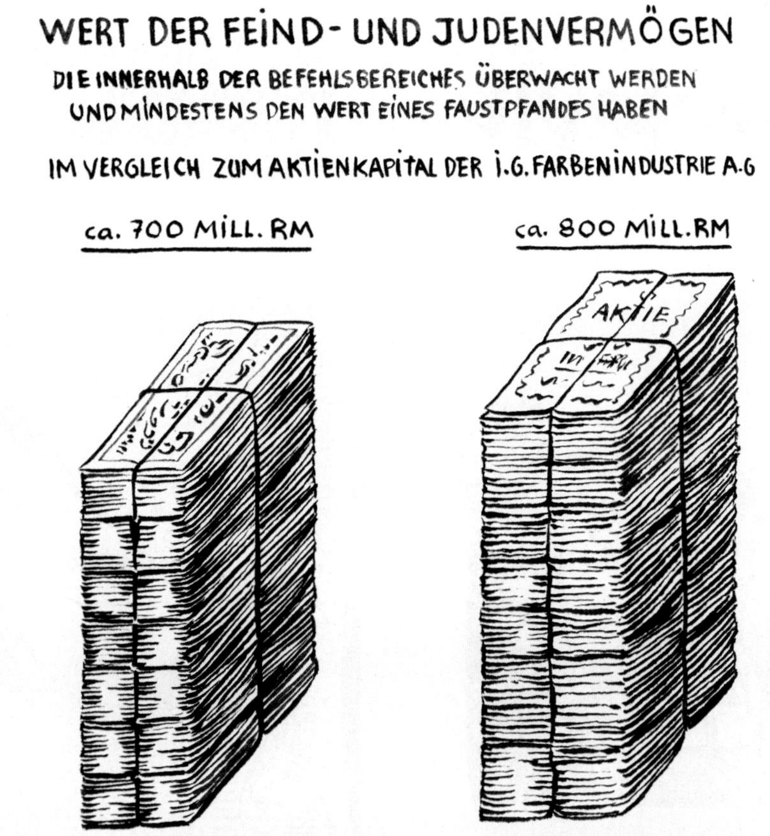

FB 06

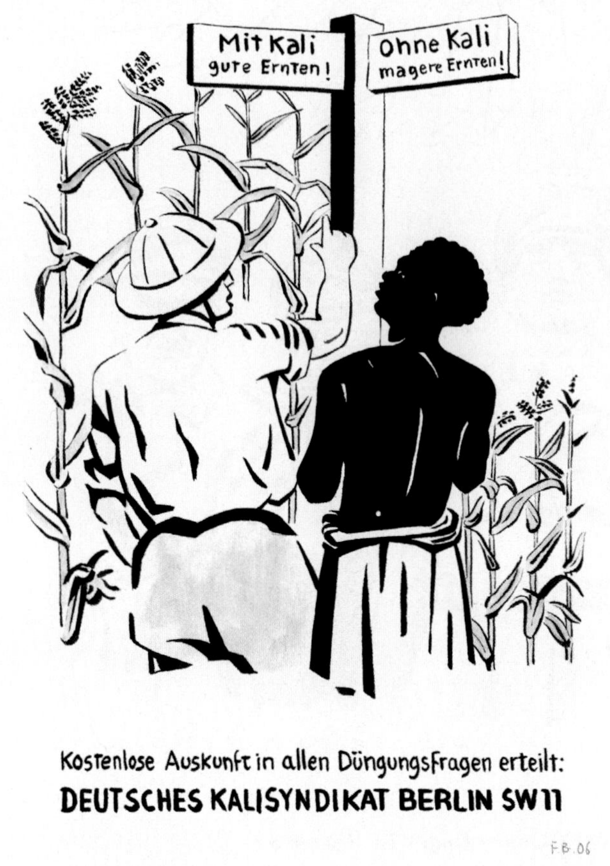

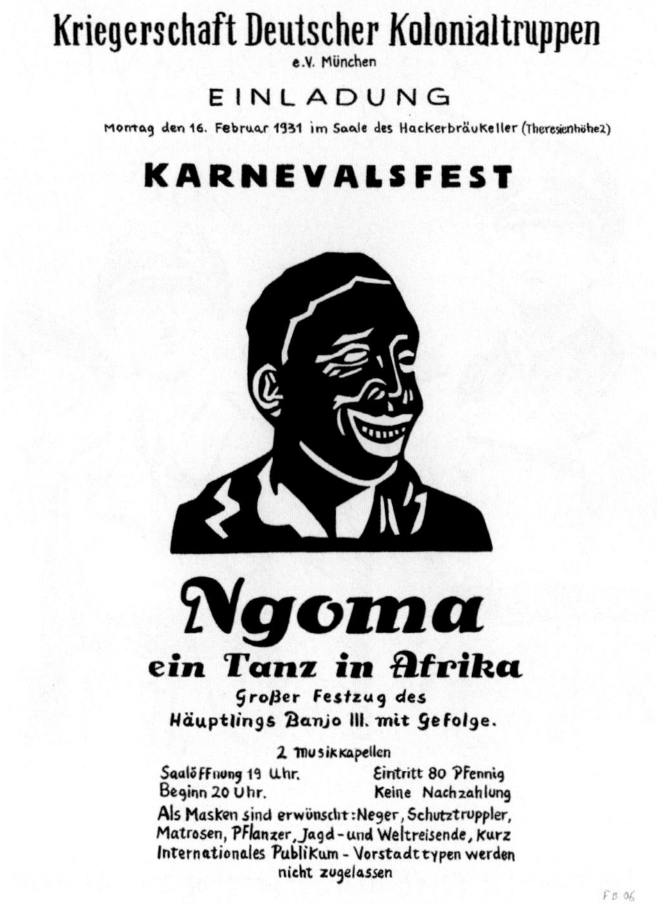

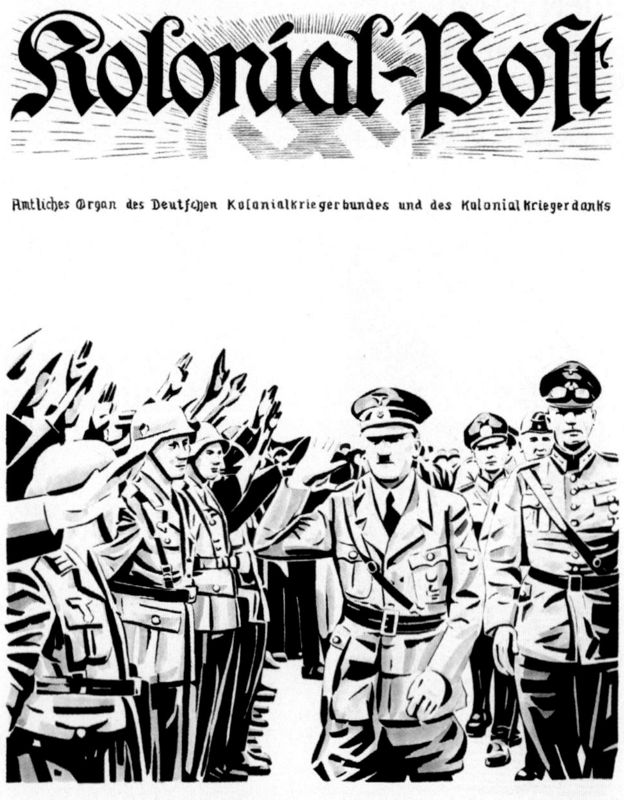

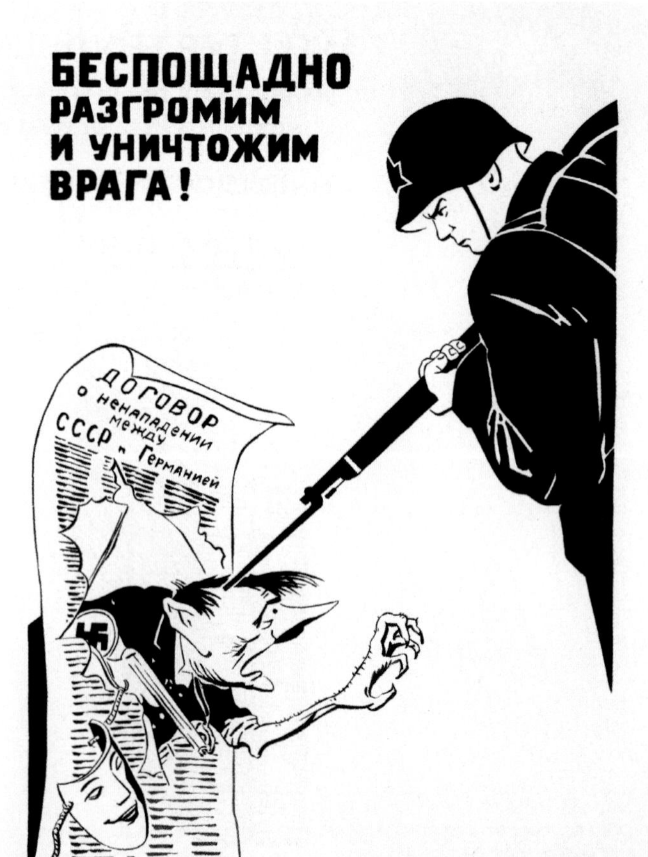

Selections from *Kolonial Post* 2006 ink on paper; series of 111

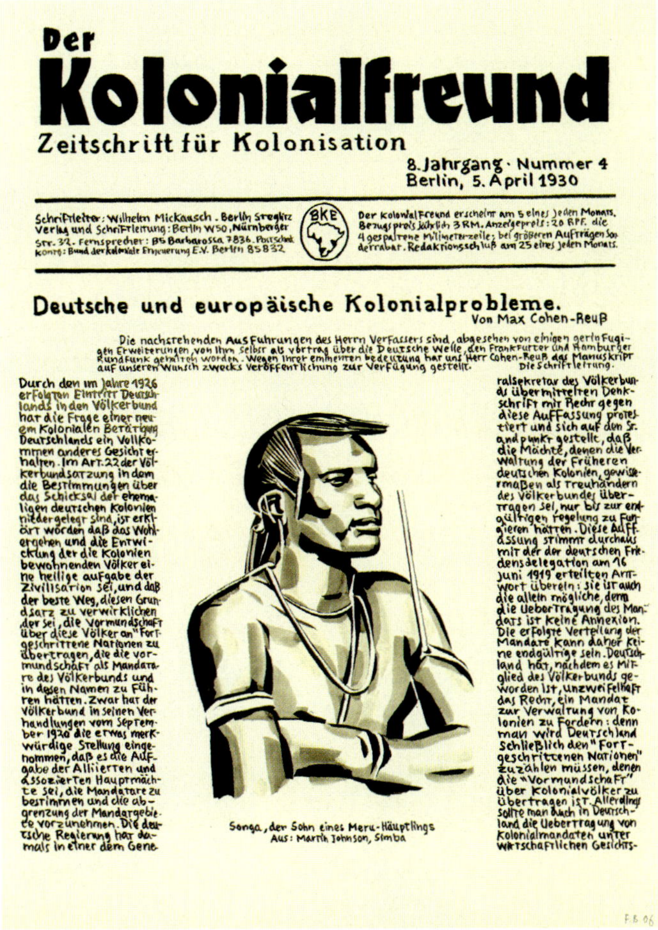

Der
Kolonialfreund
Zeitschrift für Kolonisation

8. Jahrgang · Nummer 4
Berlin, 5. April 1930

Schriftleiter: Wilhelm Mickausch . Berlin Steglitz Verlag und Schriftleitung: Berlin W50, Nürnberger Str. 32. Fernsprecher: B5 Barbarossa 7836. Postscheckkonto: Bund der kolonialen Erneuerung E.V. Berlin 85832

BKE

Der Kolonialfreund erscheint am 5 eines jeden Monats. Bezugspreis jährlich 3 RM. Anzeigepreis: 20 RPF. die 4gespaltene Milimeterzeile; bei größeren Aufträgen Sonderrabat. Redaktionsschluß am 25 eines jeden Monats.

Deutsche und europäische Kolonialprobleme.
Von Max Cohen-Reuß

Die nachstehenden Ausführungen des Herrn Verfassers sind, abgesehen von einigen geringfügigen Erweiterungen, von ihm selbst als Vortrag über die Deutsche Welle, den Frankfurter und Hamburger Rundfunk gehalten worden. Wegen ihrer eminenten Bedeutung hat uns Herr Cohen-Reuß das Manuskript auf unseren Wunsch zwecks Veröffentlichung zur Verfügung gestellt. Die Schriftleitung.

Durch den im Jahre 1926 erfolgten Eintritt Deutschlands in den Völkerbund hat die Frage einer neuem kolonialen Betätigung Deutschlands ein vollkommen anderes Gesicht erhalten. Im Art. 22 der Völkerbundsatzung in dem die Bestimmungen über das Schicksal der ehemaligen deutschen Kolonien niedergelegt sind, ist erklärt worden daß das Wohlergehen und die Entwicklung der die Kolonien bewohnenden Völker eine heilige aufgabe der Zivilisation sei, und daß der beste Weg, diesen Grundsatz zu verwirklichen der sei, die Vormundschaft über diese Völker an "Fortgeschrittene Nationen zu übertragen, die die Vormundschaft als Mandatare des Völkerbunds und in dessen Namen zu führen hätten. Zwar hat der Völkerbund in seinen Verhandlungen vom September 1920 die etwas merkwürdige Stellung eingenommen, daß es die Aufgabe der Alliierten und assoziierten Hauptmächte sei, die Mandatare zu bestimmen und die abgrenzung der Mandatgebiete vorzunehmen. Die deutsche Regierung hat damals in einer dem Generalsekretar des Völkerbundes übermittelten Denkschrift mit Recht gegen diese Auffassung protestiert und sich auf den Standpunkt gestellt, daß die Mächte, denen die Verwaltung der früheren deutschen Kolonien, gewissermaßen als Treuhändern des Völkerbundes übertragen sei, nur bis zur endgültigen regelung zu fungieren hätten. Diese Auffassung stimmt durchaus mit der der deutschen Friedensdelegation am 16 Juni 1919 erteilten Antwort überein: sie ist auch die allein mögliche, denn die Uebertragung des Mandats ist keine Annexion. Die erfolgte Verteilung der Mandate kann daher keine endgültige sein. Deutschland hat, nachdem es Mitglied des Völkerbunds geworden ist, unzweifelhaft das Recht, ein Mandat zur Verwaltung von Kolonien zu fordern: denn man wird Deutschland schließlich den "Fortgeschrittenen Nationen" zuzählen müssen, denen die "Vormundschaft" über Kolonialvölker zu übertragen ist. Allerdings sollte man auch in Deutschland die Uebertragung von Kolonialmandaten unter wirtschaftlichen Gesichts-

Songa, der Sohn eines Meru-Häuptlings
Aus: Martin Johnson, Simba

F.B. 06

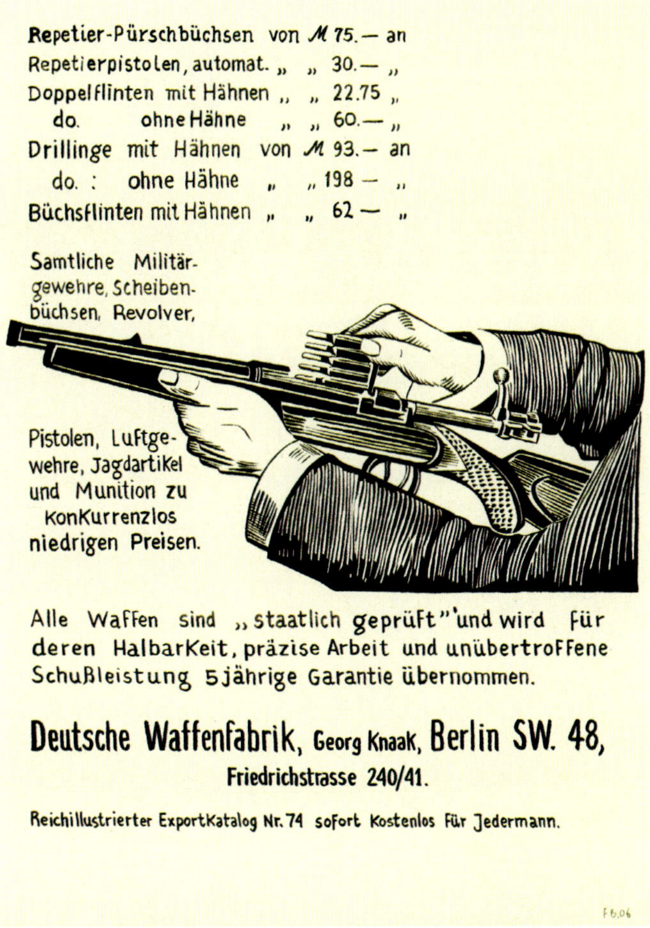

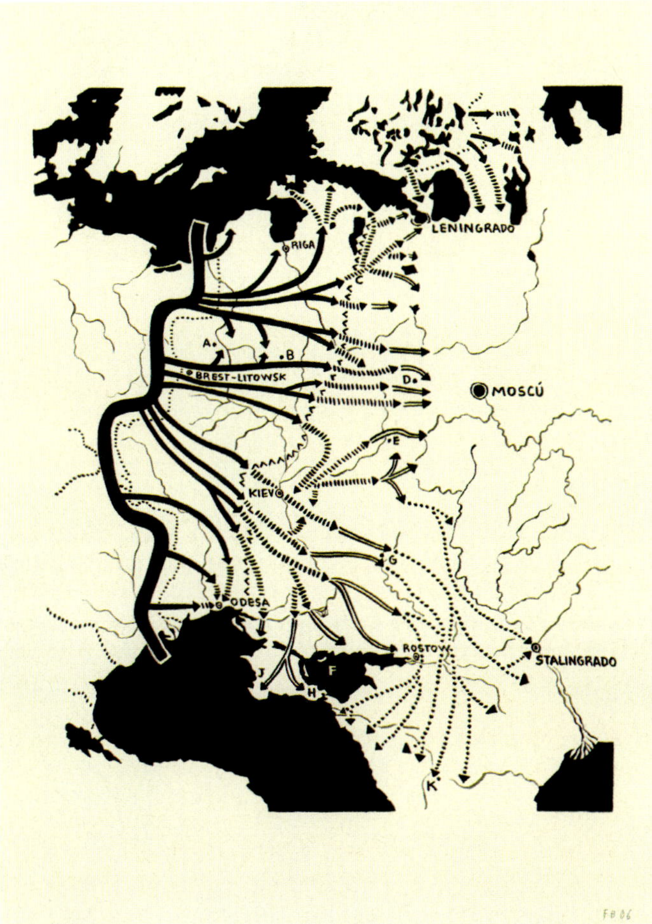

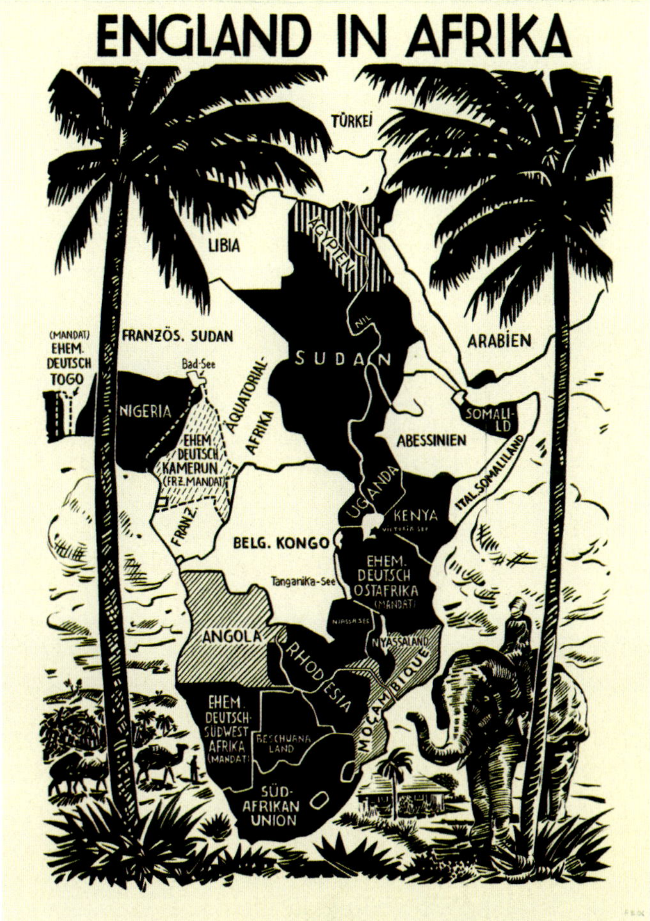

Brave New Worlds April 19, 2007

MOCKUS' BOGOTÁ: ART AS PUBLIC POLICY

JOSÉ ROCA

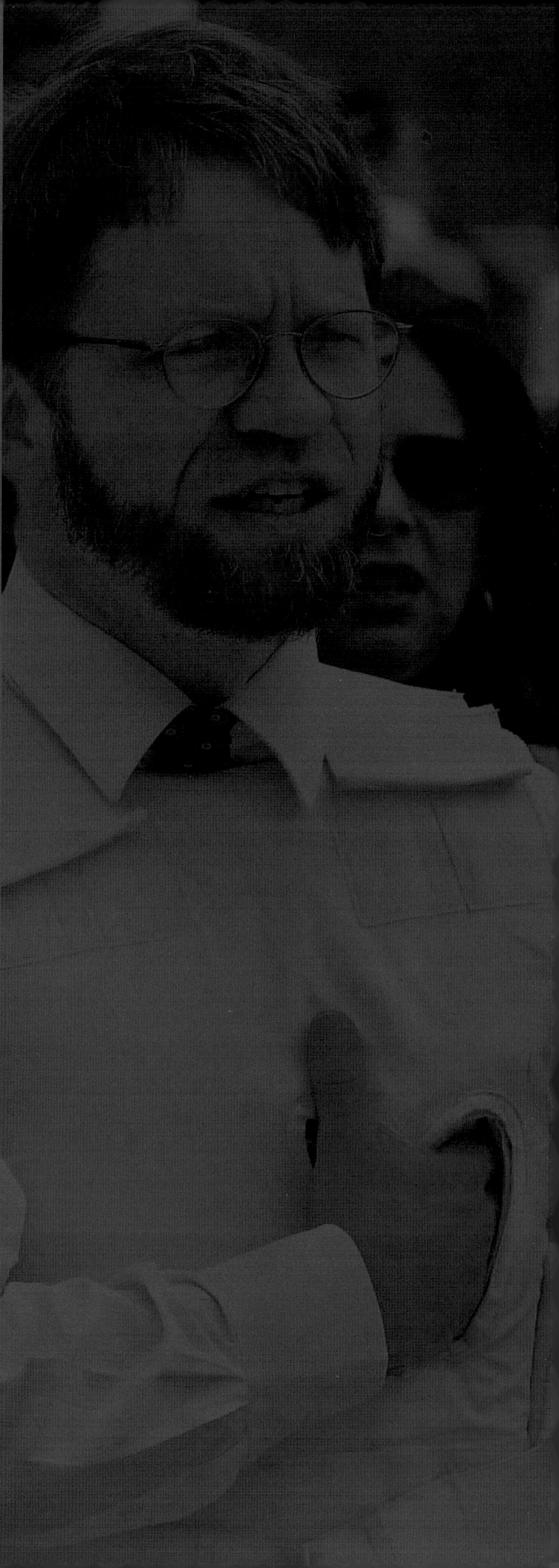

Belonging to a city entails a responsibility toward it. This responsibility evolves from domestic space and opens up toward collective space. Everybody takes care of their house, their front yard, their sidewalk; the range of this "area of empathy" enlarges according to the sense of belonging.[1] Private space is almost always well kept because it belongs—in legal terms—to someone. But what happens to public space? Since ownership is abstract—it belongs to "the public"—only a strong sense of belonging, what could be termed "affective ownership," encourages the dwellers of a city to maintain it or to actively take part in the decisions and policies that shape it. If a concerned and involved public does not control the space that is perceived as collective in terms of use and ownership (which would be public space proper), there will be no social pressure on the state to maintain its proper functioning. Of course, the claim for ownership is a rhetorical one, for as Claude Lefort has remarked, "[Public space] has the virtue of belonging to no one, of being large enough to accommodate only those who recognize one another within it and who give it a meaning."[2]

Indifference or despair vis-à-vis urban malfunction paves the way to privatization of public space and public services. The logic is that if a sewage system or a park is run or maintained by a private company, it will work better because it is in their best interest to do well in order to keep their contracts. In fact, however, quite the opposite occurs: the need to make a big profit puts the interests of the public second. If the infrastructure that should be conceived as a public service is given over to private companies, it begins to respond only to the logic of capital and not to the prevalence of public interest. Services become precarious. In a malfunctioning public system, people turn to the spaces they legally own. Detached and distanced from a city they don't relate to in affective terms, they concentrate only on spaces they can claim as theirs—leaving the rest as residual space. If urban space is perceived as a no-man's-land, it becomes a wasteland. Democratic public space is where the meaning and unity of the social is constituted (or put at risk); therefore, a democracy cannot allow public space to deteriorate to the point that it becomes privately run or owned, the most basic reason being that it undermines its very legitimacy.

This is what happened in Bogotá, Colombia, a city that had reached a critical situation in the mid-nineties. Gated communities, malls, doorman-guarded buildings and condominiums—the architecture of fear—flourished on the argument that they provided the security the state could not guarantee. But soon public spaces were also appropriated following the same logic, and people started closing off streets and public parks, and building sentry boxes right on the sidewalks in order to protect themselves. In regard to public space, democracy gave way to autocracy under the indifferent gaze of the government.

In this context, the inhabitants of Bogotá had lost any hope that Bogotá would develop into an organized city. The indifference of most to the fate of the city stemmed from the fact that very few people considered Bogotá theirs. There was no sense of belonging, no local pride. And with scarce funds, if people don't actively participate in the collective building of the city, there is no way the local government can put in place an effective development policy. Was it possible to reverse this situation? And how could it be done with a small budget in a city of 7.5 million people that was riddled with all the problems of a large metropolis?

This was the main issue with which Antanas Mockus, former mayor of Bogotá, was confronted when he took office in 1995. But who is Antanas Mockus and why was he elected? In order to provide a minimum context, we should go back some years and explore Mockus' background and character, because he is no ordinary politician. Precisely because of this he was able to carry out one of the most innovative and effective social and urban transformations in the recent history of Latin American cities.[3]

The son of Lithuanian immigrants, Mockus studied mathematics and philosophy, and went to work as a professor at the Universidad Nacional in Bogotá. The Universidad Nacional, the main public university in Colombia, is a heavily politicized environment with all the problems typical of public education in Latin America. It is also a privileged space for discussion and the development of ideas.

With the intention of changing the educational system, which had grown static and stale, Mockus involved himself in the movement for curricular change. His clarity of vision impressed the secretary of education, who nominated him to be the dean of the university. Once elected, Mockus initiated many reforms, including letting students pay whatever they felt they could afford (everyone had three options, ranging from very cheap to the tuition normally paid in a private university; many freely chose to pay the highest fee). He also insisted on the necessity to foster research and elevate the level of university instructors.

Mockus' antics garnered him media attention: he did not want to use the cars and chauffeurs that usually come with this kind of job, opting instead to ride a bicycle to work. He always spoke what he thought was the truth, no matter the circumstances; his discourse was symbolic yet very practical, and he was able to engage in profound discussions with the students and teachers at a level usually not found in education bureaucrats.

On one occasion, Mockus was speaking in front of a large auditorium. It was impossible for him to be heard, however, because so many groups were shouting political slogans, drowning out the lecture. Mockus resorted to a gesture (akin to the unexpected actions seen in Luis Buñuel's films) and, taking his pants off, showed his naked behind to the auditorium. The effect was immediate: taken by surprise, people stopped shouting and he was able to continue. The gesture, he said at the time, should be understood "as a part of the resources which an artist can use." His mooning was caught on tape and sent to the local news. This produced a public outcry regarding "the dignity that the dean of the most important public university should observe." The pressure was so strong that Mockus was forced to resign.

Mockus lost his job, but at the same time he gained national notoriety. The press suddenly became interested in what he had to say. This wide exposure led him to think he could take his theories on education to a political arena. He ran for mayor of Bogotá (the second most important job in Colombia after the presidency). He chose a simple strategy: only speak the truth, and never promise anything he would not be in position to fulfill. He spent a ridiculously low amount of money on his campaign—around three thousand dollars, much of which was spent in buying and giving away pirinolas, a very popular game of chance in Colombia.[4] The pirinola is basically a plastic top with seven facets, each one with an inscription: pon uno (put one); pon dos (put two); pierde turno (lose turn); todos ponen (everyone has to put); and todos toman (everybody takes), etc. His message: In such a complex city with a budget that does not cover the expenses of what has to be done, only if "todos ponen," then "todos toman"—only if everyone is willing to give something to the city, can everybody reap the benefits.

It was a simple, even dumb campaign, but it attracted the attention of the press and the public at large. He was running against candidates who had strong political support and money to spend on billboards, newspaper, radio, and TV ads. Mockus had none of that, but he was able to have an equivalent exposure in the form of free press. With this simple strategy he was able to win the election. As Ana María Cuenca states, "The tops sought to communicate through a ludic object the parting philosophy of what came to be known as the program of Cultura Ciudadana (Culture of Citizenship) and the essence of Mockus' promise to the residents of Bogotá: that everybody would obtain the benefits of citizenship in a democracy as long as everybody fulfilled his or her responsibilities. These toys and the message attached to them thus became the first demonstration—almost a preview—of the unusual pedagogical policies that Mockus would later enact after his first successful bid for the mayoralty of Bogotá in 1994, and which would transform the way Bogotanos perceived their city, their laws, and their obligations as citizens."[5]

After the surprise of Mockus' win came a strong sense of anticipation on the part of the public: what was this university teacher—with no previous political experience whatsoever—going to do as mayor of a city of 7.5 million residents (roughly one fifth of the population of the country), with problems that ranged from infrastructure, roads, housing, and public services to corruption, high crime rates, and mounting poverty? Once again, Mockus' strategy was to resort to a language of symbols, always ripe with humor and self-satire.

As journalist María Cristina Caballero observes: "People were desperate for a change, for a moral leader of some sort. The eccentric Mockus, who communicates through symbols, humor, and metaphors, filled the role. When many hated the disordered and disorderly city of Bogotá, he wore a Superman costume and acted as a superhero called 'Supercitizen.' People laughed at Mockus' antics, but the laughter began to break the ice of their extreme skepticism."[6]

As an experienced teacher, he believed that the only way to change habits was through education, so his program was centered in what he called Culture of Citizenship: only if we understand what living in a community entails can we expect things to function with a precarious budget and political situation.[7] The following examples demonstrate his ideas in action:

× Upon winning office, Mockus decided to marry Adriana, his longtime companion. They married at a circus inside the tiger cage and rode off as newlyweds on top of an elephant. This was an ironic commentary—by means of action—upon the "media circus" associated with news reporting in the age of reality television.

× People in Bogotá crossed the street where they wanted, almost never at the intersections. This has caused a lot of accidents (after gunfire, traffic accidents were the major cause of death in the city). Mockus hired mimes to mimic people's actions, thus highlighting the absurd nature of what they were doing, putting their lives at risk. The mimes kindly and humorously coaxed pedestrians to cross through the demarcated areas. Onlookers learned from example.

× Mockus and his team had star-shaped yellow outlines painted on the exact spots where fifteen hundred pedestrians had been killed by cars. In some places there were virtual constellations dispersed on the asphalt. This acted as a visual geography of the incidence of traffic accidents, and gave a tangible dimension to what was until then just statistics. Suddenly, one began to realize the dangers of jaywalking as well as the responsibilities drivers have toward the community at large. The program reduced traffic deaths dramatically.[8]

× In Bogotá many drivers park in prohibited areas and do not respect traffic lights or signals. Mockus appropriated an element from soccer, which is very popular in Colombia. In soccer, when a player commits a severe fault, the referee shows him a red card that signifies he is expelled from the game. Mockus had thousands of large plastic cards made, with a red side and a white side, "thumbs down" on the former and "thumbs up" on the latter. Whenever someone did something illegal or improper, people took out their red cards and showed them to the transgressor, referee-style. The idea was to subject wrongdoers to a public form of sanction—albeit gentler than a fine or a ticket. This strategy functioned well, making people collectively aware of proper and improper behavior, and symbolically empowering citizens to show their disapproval (or approval, in the case of good actions that were rewarded with a "white card").

× Mockus also launched a "Night for Women" and asked the city's men to stay home in the evening and care for the children; seven hundred thousand women went out on the first of three nights that Mockus dedicated to them.[9]

× Arms are a major problem in Bogotá, especially in the slums and poorer neighborhoods. Mockus started a program in which arms were exchanged for toys; surprisingly, the program—that was conceived more as a symbolic move—proved extremely successful.

× When there was a water shortage, Mockus appeared on TV programs taking a shower and turning off the water as he soaped, asking his fellow citizens to do the same. In just two months, people were using 14 percent less water—a savings that increased when people realized how much money they were also saving because of economic incentives approved by Mockus. Water use is now 40 percent less than before the shortage.[10]

× Mockus mobilized people to protest against violence and terrorist attacks. He invented a "vaccine against violence," asking people to draw on balloons the faces of those who had hurt them, which they then popped. About fifty thousand people participated in this campaign.[11] He also enacted what he called "symbolic violence," showing that expressing anger and confrontation does not have to end in a tragic way.[12]

× These and many other actions signified a reduction in mortality of nearly 50 percent, a figure that could be measured statistically. It was thus possible to know how many people did NOT die the previous year. Taking advantage of the fact that, for sanitary reasons, part of the cemetery had to be emptied and the corpses taken elsewhere, Mockus decided to appropriate the image of the empty crypts as a symbol. His motto became: "Let's keep them empty."

On the Day of the Dead, Mockus invited an equivalent number of people to the cemetery, and in a kind of artistic performance invited them to crawl into the empty crypts. When they came out, they filled a vast space. The physical evidence of all these spared lives made everyone reflect on the uniqueness of life, and on the fact that a city and those who govern it are responsible toward the public that elected them.

In a country where the public perceives politicians as people who, through corruption and obscure maneuvers, are only trying to benefit themselves or their friends, a character such as Antanas Mockus gave hope that maybe the country can find an effective way out of the crisis. It also showed that (strangely enough—at least in classical political doctrine) this could be achieved using humor and satire as a way of establishing effective communication.

Antanas Mockus views his unorthodox actions as a means to address a public that has become suspicious of traditional, party-dictated politics: "Contemporary politics aims at constructing a public that, instead of taking sides, constitutes itself as a judge that judges action by action."[13] And he explicitly speaks about using art as the vehicle because of art's alleged capacity to function at a nonrational level.[14] We can see in this a theoretical framework behind Mockus' actions. Within this framework are the ideas of Nobel Prize-winning economist Douglass North, who has done research on the tension between formal and informal rules; Jon Elster's analysis of the limitations of the model of rational selection; and Jürgen Habermas' work on how dialogue creates social capital. Mockus is aware of the limits of strategic reason, which is the preferred line of action in governance under capitalism. Strategic reason privileges results over processes, promotes efficacy and efficiency, rationalizes fear, and establishes a logic of action that takes into consideration the worst-case scenario and acts accordingly (preventively).

Mockus is skeptical about the social outcome of the strategic rationale—adjusting one's moves according to the intelligent calculation of the moves of the adversary. In the micro-politics of a city, this can result in the proliferation of strategies of self-protection (for example, the removal of individuals or areas perceived as dangerous). In state politics, we are all very aware of what preemptive action can entail. So Mockus seeks to deconstruct strategic reason, and one of the tactics he has found useful to do this is to resort to art. His reasoning is purely instrumental and incorporates concepts taken from very diverse sources,[15] "because we want to elicit controlled emotions; because culture can be transformed creatively; because art liberates the individual . . . because each citizen can be an artist; because to exercise politics should be aesthetic."[16]

The actions of Mockus might not be essentially different in the formal definition from works in public spaces done by artists (although it could be argued that the latter usually have a more developed visual sophistication), but it's the instrumentalism of the artistic gesture that seems to set them apart. While all of the works created by artists clearly express their intention of establishing a field for an open discussion, art-as-policy knows that it fulfills a precise role within a plan to govern the city: it is clearly a political tool. The way this strategy works, though, is not clear—at least in classical political terms. And this, paradoxically, might posit Mockus' actions back in the realm of artistic practice proper. Mockus has said that one of the effects of art is to defamiliarize the normative practices and refresh perception in a way that allows people to revisit their own ideas.[17] In this sense, he is aware of the potential of art to destabilize rational discourse.

One of the quintessential graffiti slogans during the revolution of May 1968 was "L'Imagination au pouvoir!" (All power to imagination!). But many political leaders formed on the tenets of the Left, once they got into power, discarded the transformational possibilities of creative thought. In a critical assessment of Mockus' theoretical framework, it has been remarked that "the paradoxical thing about May 1968 is that the agents of the upheavals did not think that someday, when they grew up, they would need a theory of imagination from power. Mockus is one of the few young people from '68 who, upon achieving power, has maintained coherence between his world view and his actions. Because his role as a governor is not simply to question status quo but to generate one; it is not to put an end to institutions, but to reinforce them. And it is precisely there that Mockus is left without a theory. Sociologists do not have an answer for what he does. . . . [As] to the question of how Habermas/Mockus integrates art into his scheme of communicative action, Habermockus has no answer. What is curious about this . . . is that Mockus himself (not Mockus the Theoretician, but the practical Antanas Mockus, former major of Bogotá) uses art in his governing practice. His practice surpasses theory. His theory of the public sphere [does not explain] how his 'magic' (precisely) works. Because it is not simply a discursive and communicative action, nor totally rational; it is artistic, performative."[18]

To conclude, I would like to quote both Chantal Mouffe and Antanas Mockus on the political dimension of art. Mouffe has written, with regard to collective identity and politics: "What makes people act politically is what I've called 'passions.' Collective identifications have to do with desire, with fantasies, with everything that is precisely not interests or the rational. Instead of thinking about politics as a place where we should all get together and try to find the rational solution—this is not what politics is about at all—politics needs to speak to people about their passions in order to mobilize them towards democratic designs."[19] Likewise, in discussing his art and politics, Antanas Mockus states: "I think that sincere communication and what it entails can limit in a certain way the outburst of strategic reason. Nevertheless, I think that . . . the radicalization of interests, which is a feature of the strategic rationale . . . in some cases can only be contained by the radicalization of dis-interests that is the main feature of art."[20] ■

This text is adapted from the paper "Symbolic Actions as Public Policy: The Case of Bogotá," commissioned by Prefix Institute of Contemporary Art, Toronto, 2006, and reproduced with permission from the author and Prefix Institute of Contemporary Art.

NOTES

1 It is important to bear in mind that the notions of public and private are mediated by the notions of use and ownership. For example, an urban square is public in terms of use and ownership: it is public in the deeper sense of the term. But a shopping mall is used by the public although it is privately owned: is it properly "public"? Most governmental buildings are owned "by the public," but their use is restricted to the point that they become a private space. People in gated communities and condominiums have their own "public" space in the form of lawns, playgrounds, sidewalks, and roads, and thus take actions to maintain, protect, and embellish it.

2 Claude Lefort, Democracy and Political Theory (Minneapolis: University of Minnesota Press, 1988), 41.

3 For more information on Antanas Mockus, see: María Cristina Caballero, "Academic turns city into a social experiment: Mayor Mockus of Bogotá and his spectacularly applied theory," Harvard University Gazette (March 11, 2004), http://www.news.harvard.edu/gazette/2004/03.11/01-mockus.html; and Antanas Mockus, "Ampliación de los modos de hacer política," paper presented at the colloquium Democracy in Latin America: A renewal of the political personnel?, at the Center for International Studies and Research (CERI) (December 2-3, 2004; archived May 2005), http://www.ceri-sciencespo.com/archive/mai05/artam.pdf.

4 María Victoria Uribe, "Bogotá en los noventa, un escenario de intervención," Pensar la ciudad, Fabio Giraldo and Fernando Viviescas, eds. (Bogotá: Tercer Mundo Editores, 1996), 399. Mockus stated in an interview that he spent less than 6 million pesos, which at that time was equal to approximately three thousand U.S. dollars. Although in another document (the aforementioned "Ampliación de los modos de hacer política," 5), this amount is estimated as twelve thousand U.S. dollars.

5 Ana Maria Cuenca, "Cultura Ciudadana, Orçamento Participativo and the New Citizenship in Bogotá and Porto Alegre: 'A tale of two cities'," paper for Graduate Student Colloquium in Urban Studies, University of Texas, Austin (April 6, 2002), http://www.utexas.edu/academic/uip/research/docstuds/coll/cuenca.pdf, 5-6.

6 Caballero, "Mayor Mockus of Bogotá."

7 On this subject Mockus has said, "Many things in Bogotá can be made better by means of education, if we understand Cultura Ciudadana as the antidote to the culture of the shortcut." Antanas Mockus, interview with Maria Isabel Silva, in Conversaciones con Bogotá 1945-2005 (Bogotá: Lonja de Propiedad Raíz de Bogotá, 2005), 131. Translated by the author.

8 Caballero. Mockus sees the reduction of homicides from eighty per one hundred thousand inhabitants in 1993 to twenty-two per one hundred thousand inhabitants in 2003 as a major achievement, noting also that traffic fatalities dropped by more than half in the same time period, from an average of thirteen hundred per year to about six hundred.

9 Ibid.

10 Ibid.

11 Ibid.

12 During a debate with Noemí Sanín and Horacio Serpa, political candidates for the presidency, Mockus infamously threw a glass of water in Serpa's face to prove that violence need not be lethal.

13 Mockus, 14. All excerpts from this text translated by the author.

14 Mockus ran for president in 2005, and he posited art at the center of his discourse: "The campaign as art, the party as art, government as art, Colombia as art." Taken from a brief text sent to the author by Mockus' campaign office, January 5, 2006. Translated by the author.

15 The work of such artists as Joseph Beuys and his "every man is an artist" as well as concepts from Christian thought and Western philosophy are among Mockus' influences.

16 Antanas Mockus, quoted in an e-mail sent to the author by Mockus' assistant, 2006.

17 Mockus, 4.

18 Javier Castro quoted in Mockus, 18-19.

19 Chantal Mouffe, et al., "Every Form of Art Has a Political Dimension," in Grey Room 2 (Winter 2001): 123.

20 Mockus, 1. The quote reads: "Pienso que la comunicación sincera y sus exigencias limitan de cierta manera el desmadre de la razón estratégica. Sin embargo, sugiero al final que la radicalización del interés, propia de la racionalidad estratégica, y la concomitante cristalización de un nosotros parcial y crispado, en algunos casos tal vez sólo puedan ser contenidas por la radicalización del desinterés propio del arte." Translated by the author.

IMAGE

page 70 Mayor of Bogotá Antanas Mockus shows off a flak jacket he designed with a heart-shaped hole, a symbol of his protest against the threats made by rebels, during an inauguration at the Millennium Park in Bogotá, Colombia, July 3, 2002.

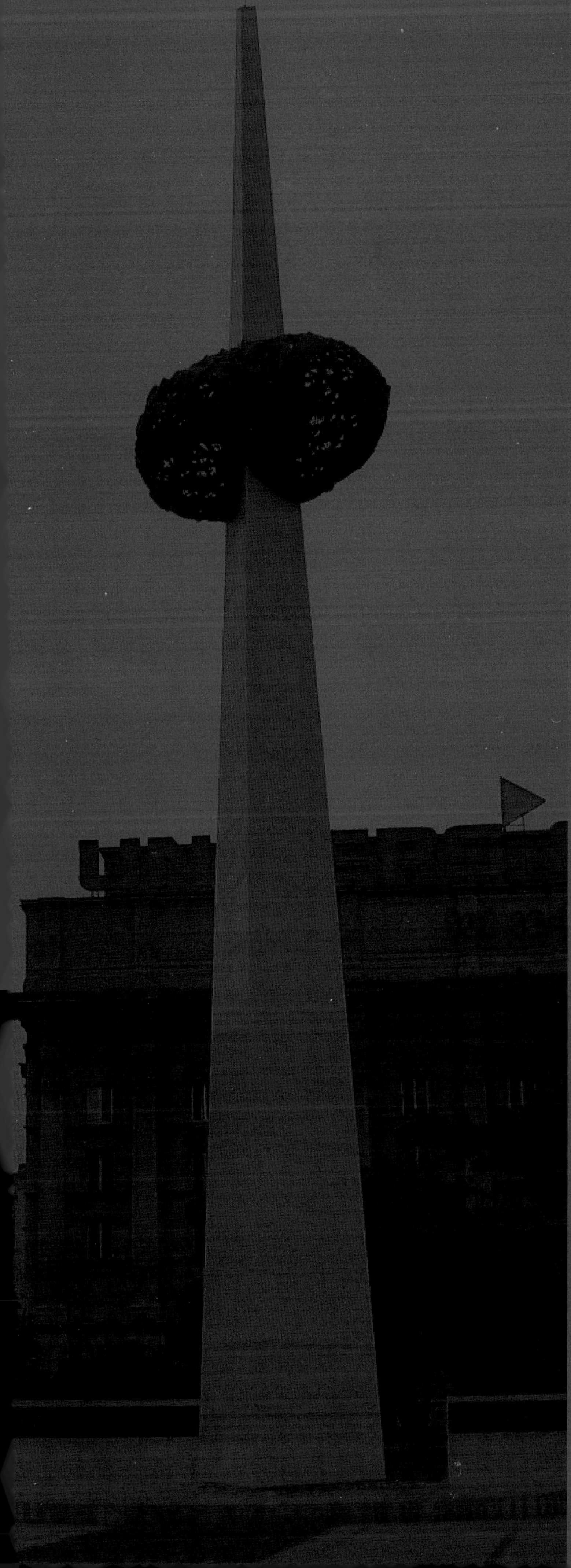

REPORT FROM BUCHAREST, ROMANIA

Brave New Worlds April 16, 2017

MONUMENTAL BACKLASH

MIHNEA MIRCAN

During the past ten years, Romania has been making remarkably cheap cars, cheap computers, and lots and lots of monuments. Booming economic growth and the fits and starts of a colossal societal transformation, to-ing and fro-ing between a past that grows more disorienting and images of a future that contradict the very ideas of nationhood retrieved from that past, have gone in tandem with the unrestrained production of monuments. Spanning the ten years after the country's accession to the European Union in 2007, this monumental saga—although some might call it a tragedy, equipped with its hubris and anticlimax—has brought politics and the arts into an interplay so intricate it might remind the scholar of the Renaissance, while to the cynic it might suggest a profoundly self-defeating conspiracy. Untangling these many misalliances will require not only the acumen of historians and sociologists, but also their labors, since one critic calculated a baffling total of two hundred fifty-three monuments, an impressive data bank that could translate into a clinically rigorous diagnosis for the slowly nascent Romanian democracy.

The monument frenzy has been alternately described as "the understandable need for public meaning and collective solace in times of global insecurity," "reinventing the tradition of great builders of the nation," or as "the shallow scenography of absent solidarity" and "props for emulation around the country's belated renewal," as an art-historical enigma and "retrofuturism in reverse." In spite of the ideological differences that underscore these claims, all political forces and cultural actors in the country have had their share in the "transformation of the cityscape into a wedding cake," as one artist remarked to me while we took part in one of the countless commissions that convened throughout 2008 to validate monument projects. He confessed that he was there to "change something from within," and I had been invited to "survey and report"—a somewhat pompous Foucauldian twist coming from the ex-electronic musician turned activist turned minister of culture. Even if there was indeed a lot to question and punish as far as the proceedings were concerned, the acrid report that followed had only a minor effect: it added the term "citycake" to Bucharest lingo.

This unusual celebration, which seemed to many an allegorical procession looking for the key to the allegory, has brought millions of tourists to Romania—the recent breed of political tourists who find their exotic delights in social contrast and forms of inequity, for whom corrupt political constructions, still abundant in the world, are sources of delectation and replace the box-ticking of museums and sights. They go where what we used to call globalization, and now refer to as normalization, stumbles upon the patriarchal and the authoritarian, where frauds are luxuriant and epochs have collapsed—to places that look like veritable cross sections through the history of the past two centuries. Their much less numerous predecessors had been lured to Romania by another object resulting from the sublime aspirations of politics, the melancholic disaster that is the House of the People in Bucharest, second only to the Pentagon in size but vastly surpassing any other recent construction in its megalomaniac disregard of scale and necessity. In the decade following 2007, the grotesque crown jewel of a city that aimed to become a tourist destination has been replaced by monuments, a less systematic but equally burdensome plan to imbue Bucharest with a new identity.

And tourists came to see the cities of Romania gridlocked by networks of signs or symbols of the recent and distant past, by a utopian or simply confused future, by statues to local legends and grandiose epitaphs to Romanian patriots. Taken to the level of state policy and suggesting a Marshall Plan for the memosphere, this uninhibited symbolic activity of excavating the country for the relics of social meaning, of fabricating a heroic background against which any political maneuver becomes unquestionable, resulted in a dense map of landmarks and obstructions in an often delirious enactment of history—made visible, interrogated rhetorically, repeated, and defeated. Monuments provide an almost theatrical background for Romania's manifold struggles; the country detaching itself with difficulty from an obsolete forma mentis and trying to sketch its future in a homogeneous world of liberal exchange.

Romania's public art—whether monuments that gesticulate toward a poorly defined social sphere, attempting to cover deep-seated dysfunctions and instigate processes of "healing" and "rejuvenation," or memorials that incorporate bits of history, suspicious in their unequivocal patriotic resonance—looked to many like an exercise in groundlessness. The fervor to exhibit motivation, to show causality unfolding and defining an absolute past has always been the business of monuments. But this recent cautionary tale shows that questions are seldom muted by stones, that groundlessness finds a way of showing through granite or metal. The source of these reverberating questions can be traced, according to actors and witnesses that infrequently concur, to December 2007. It was then that Romania, a fresh EU member, was preparing to commemorate the 1989 Revolution, and a 'til-then muted resentment sparked an ample controversy: there were vociferous requests that the extant "Monument for the Heroes of the Revolution" be demolished. A singularly unsightly thing—looking like a contraption devised by Los Angeles artist Paul McCarthy on a less glorious day and seemingly unaware that it could evoke anything but obscene associations instead of the story of sacrifice it aspired to embody—this monument had emerged from the haze of the Revolution, in itself the founding enigma of post-Communist Romania. (To get a sense of this vast mystery, just imagine buying a DVD that contains only abundant bonuses, making-of features, and contradictory interviews, but no film.) Contention surrounding the Revolution monument grew into a larger debate about the management of history and national values. The plans of the Orthodox Church to build a mammoth Cathedral of National Redemption, seeking to match the escalations of Communist architecture; competing definitions of Europe and Romania's role in it; the somewhat unconsummated fall of Communism that resulted both in palpable freedom and moral anarchy; political disengagement and the progressive polarization of the country; a lost sense of collective purpose and growing social emergencies; urban disarticulation allowing the city to fall prey to unscrupulous entrepreneurial architecture—these were some of the arguments brought into passionate play. They were complemented by the tortuous problem of national identity, a question whose avatars, unsatisfactory answers, and Sisyphean inevitability accompany the modernity and postmodernities of Romanian culture. Here the reporter is forced to either operate an implausible jump cut or make recourse to the Marxist "qualitative jump," as the scenario through which these questions and tensions crystallized into a surge of public art commissions remains unclear.

Critical mass was achieved when a political party proposed a competition for a monument to Constantin Brancusi and no one found the change of topic unreasonable. Brancusi, or Brâncuşi, whose Endless Column (1938) in Tîrgu Jiu withstood a few onslaughts of misguided restoration, and whose non-Frenchness seems the main argument in local art history, was a significant choice. Politicians and cultural bureaucrats joined hands to again proclaim his nationality, bringing as unnecessary proof an impressive collection of rural decorative sculpture and paraphernalia supposed to look exactly like Brancusi's mature work or destined to be purified of earthly residue at his hand. The second step could have led to nothing else but a monument that symbolically reclaimed the lost hero. Hastily inaugurated in March 2008, it was a horizontal and thick baroque accumulation of Brancusian motifs, suggesting a rudimentary garden architecture that earned the nickname "art historian's Disneyland."

A frenzy of construction with both public and private money followed, blending incompatible aesthetic and political criteria, providing equal opportunities for artists to propose the projects they would never have dared propose and for businessmen to launder important sums of money. In his Posthumous Papers of a Living Author, Robert Musil argues that "there is nothing as invisible as a monument." Romania's legions of monuments tried to focus attention on the need for social change, but they also evinced the foundation of paradoxes on which they were built. All the things monuments are supposed to ignore or silence echoed in the many holes breached by the construction sites. These beacons of promise were often inadvertently misread, their intentions misinterpreted. All the things monuments are supposed to ignore or silence are echoed in the many holes breached by the construction sites. There were numerous instances of misused monuments, whose "stories" became erased or eroded almost as expeditiously as they were manufactured, leaving behind a landscape of accelerating ruins.

A jollier picture was painted in the survey organized in 2012 at Guggenheim Bucharest, where Romania's new monumentality was hailed as a singular episode, and its typology was diffidently outlined. Traditional monuments, elaborate settings for the symbolic preservation of a dead body or a historical idea, were understandably allotted less space in the installation. More oblique points were given the foreground, generally pertaining to what is known elsewhere as "counter-monuments," those that enact a doubt toward the very pretensions and legitimacy of the monumental. There was a profusion of plans, models, and statements for monuments, built or not, that were supposed to disappear or did, quickly or gradually, which registered the feelings of the community instead of subjecting it to an inevitably authoritarian message; there were dots to be rearranged in collective games, monuments constructed through subjective response, and slabs of corrugated iron that sank into the ground; there were spheres and heaps, monuments mobile, underground, or hidden from sight — all boasting resistance and reluctance to become affiliated politically.

Also on show in the garden of the museum was a monument to justice — a glass labyrinth, its ambiguity not lost to media reports. There was a playful "world's smallest monument" in homage to Jacques Derrida, and one that hovered above the ground in magnetic equilibrium. An isolated room was reserved for the comparatively few international contributions, among them the proposal of British artist Jake Chapman, whose giant plastic model for an "Angel of History" was indebted to Goya's wartime disasters. Other pieces presented or documented in the show were metaphorically impermanent and interactive; they repudiated traditional representation and provoked the viewer to negotiate and share the task of remembering. "Communism never happened," read a gigantic text installed on the wall facing the entrance in the museum, and the strength of that statement threatened to defeat the purpose of the show. A monument to property, aimed at registering the transformation undergone by the country after Communist expropriations and their judicial reparation, consisting of a vacant plot of land in the very center of Bucharest that no one owned or could buy (big enough to attract attention, small enough not to encumber the dizzying real estate developments around it) was revealed as a plagiarism of a proposal made by a Belgian architect for a European monument in Brussels, a similarly extraterritorial site where borders were made visible in their dual action of separating and making contact.

The Guggenheim show helped an entire generation of Romanian artists gain international recognition and join the sprawling circuit of biennials and art fairs. One of them returned briefly to the country to sign the death certificate of monuments in Romania. His "Monument to Anti-Communist Dissidence," dismissed as "a stage for rehearsing the post-Communist syndrome," opened a few months ago with a remarkably unattended ceremony. It is a five-hundred-square-meter hall, a minimally inflected container that would feel like a refuge were it not imbued with a frightful sense of nothingness. The viewer is struck by the cavernous scale and feel of the place, and by the dramatic contrast between the quasi-hermetic appearance of the granite exterior and the belittling expanse of emptiness inside. On a few scattered benches are books written before and after 1989. The stage seems set for a revelation, and hints are dispensed immoderately that something bordering on the sublime is about to happen. Another historical cycle has come to an end, and monuments can resume for a while the function assigned them by Musil—that of deflecting attention. Then this monument will be destroyed and replaced. ■

IMAGE

page 75 The Monument for the Heroes of the Revolution in Bucharest, also known as the Memorial of Rebirth

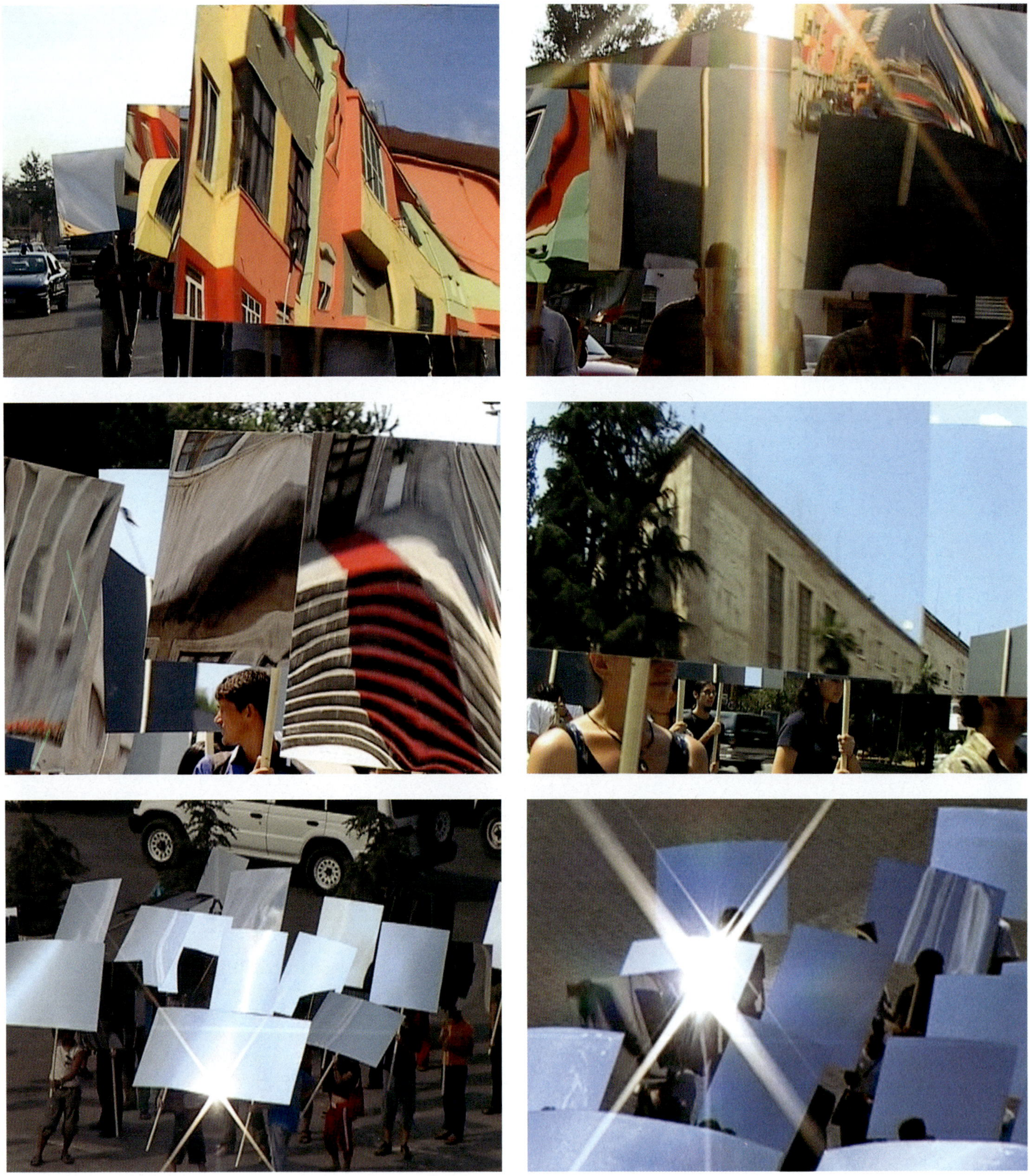

Stills from *The Landscape is Changing* 2003 video (color, sound); 22 minutes

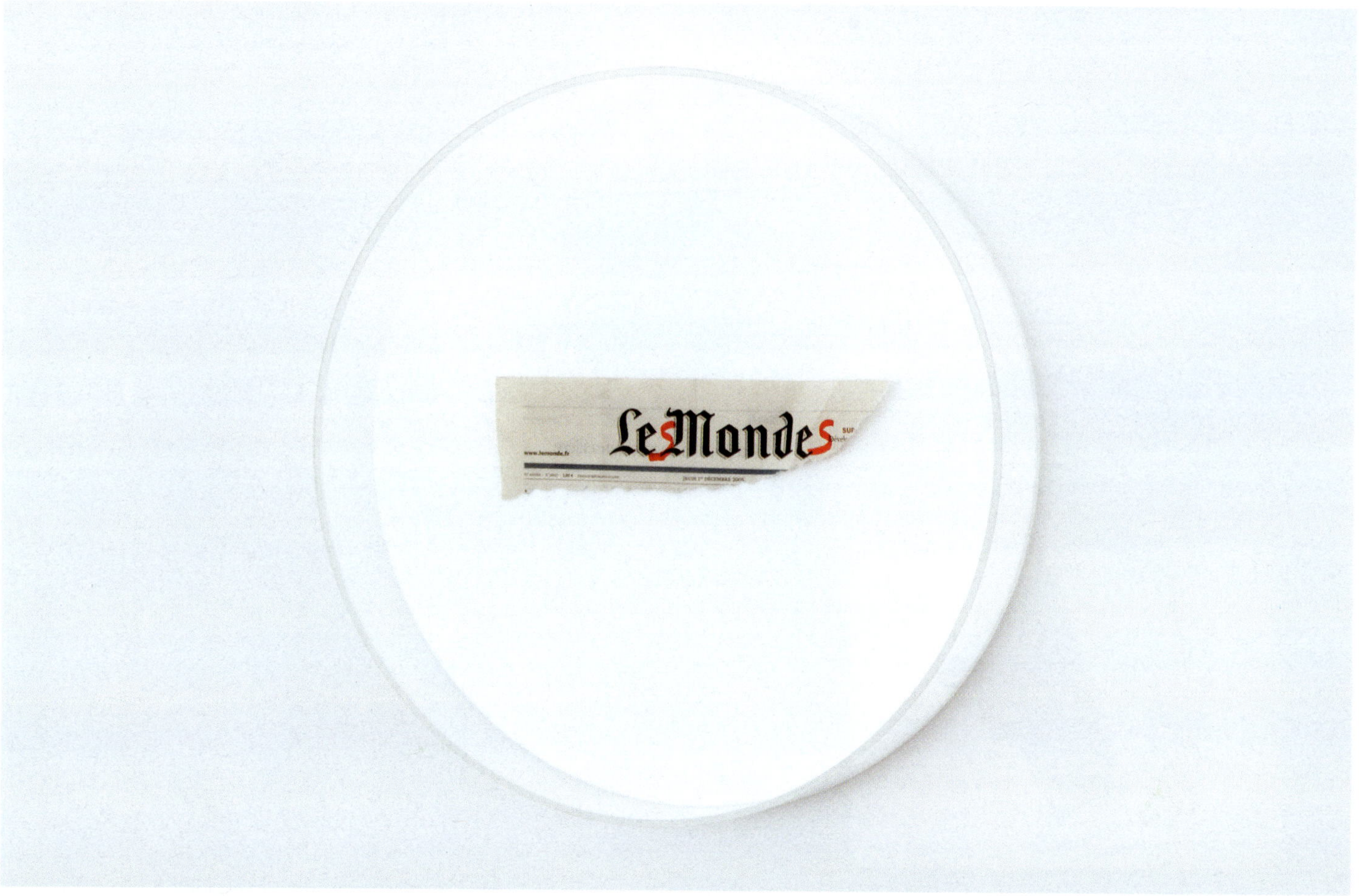

No title 2005 newspaper, felt-tip pen ink, plexiglass box

THE SILENT MARCH OF MIRCEA CANTOR

Born in Romania, 1977. Lives and works in Paris and Cluj-Napoca.

Mircea Cantor's practice is guided by the desire, as the artist has said, "to break free and to go somewhere" visually and experientially.[1] Working with such mediums as 16mm film, video, photography, sculpture, painting, and multiples, he sets up quotidian scenarios where subtle fantasies materialize and viewers contemplate a world of a different order: for example, matchsticks have two heads, kernels of corn are made of crystal, or a wolf and a deer coexist in harmony. For his video piece *The Landscape is Changing* (2003), he arranged a silent march through a city by two dozen young men and women carrying mirrors instead of protest placards and enacting an open-ended campaign of dissent. As their demonstration proceeded through traffic-filled streets, neighborhood sidewalks, and civic plazas, the small crowd under the artist's instructions deliberately stopped at particular points and held their mirrors out toward their surroundings, transforming architecture, vehicles, and pedestrians into fields of abstract reflections and light displays that resembled some sort of celestial bodies announcing a prophecy. Freed from the conventional tactics of political slogans, banners, and graphic imagery, Cantor's demonstration is an exhibition of shifting, reflective, and distorting surfaces, of speedy changes and uncertain destinies taking place in the world after the fall of Communism.

In his black-and-white 16mm film installation *Shadow for a While* (2007), he returns to the notion of protest and dissent through the classic symbol of a burning flag—a gesture of rejection and discontent with a specific set of principles: the flag as a symbol of patriotism, individualism, and ultimately, difference. The imagery consists of repeated shots of the cast shadow of an anonymous flag hanging from a wooden pole as it burns from one corner until both cloth and pole disappear into the void. As in an act of magic, the source of the fire remains invisible to the viewer, which turns the self-combustion into a natural metamorphosis independent of human will. Here lies the optimism of Cantor's ode to equality; as each and every flag along with its accompanying pole is dismantled—the icons of sectarian differences—national and ideological boundaries are rendered obsolete. A world in which flags are not necessary implies a world of inclusion, where ideals and beliefs are in a constant state of flux, unrestrained transformation, and reinvention.

The political dimension in Cantor's work is centered in the transient nature of change as he gives visual forms to philosophical and spiritual counterparts, treating the surface of materials as well as images as a stage upon which questions are projected, enacted, and contemplated. In his images, objects, and occasional interventions, he sets out to work formally and conceptually with the boundaries of social and political ambiguities of representation, playfully camouflaging intentional encounters of the readymade with the arbitrariness of chance to invite viewers to ponder a world of displaced meanings and possibly utopian aspirations.

YR

1. Thomas Boutoux, "Overture: Mircea Cantor," *Flash Art* 36, no. 229 (March–April 2003): 103.

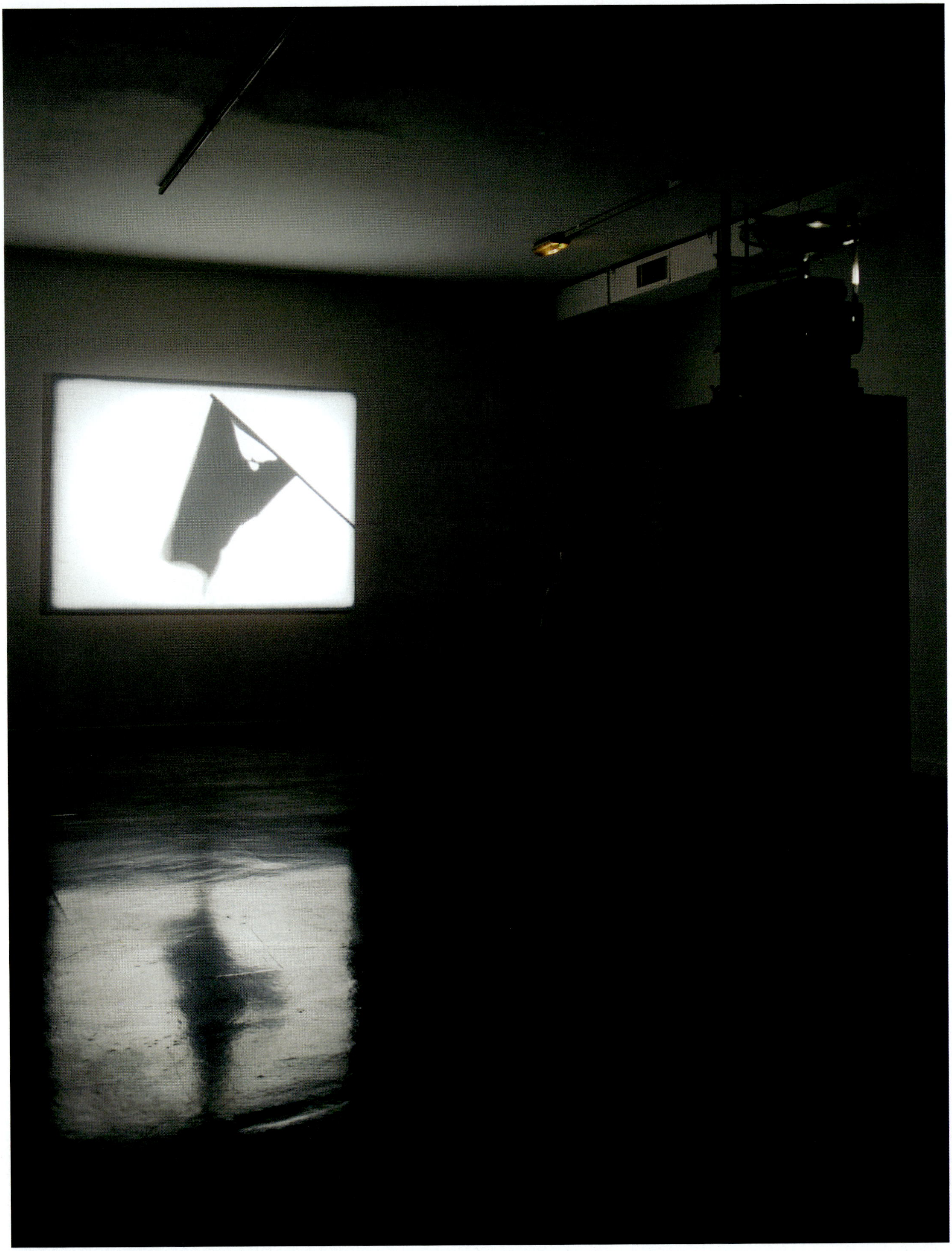

Shadow for a While 2007 16mm film (black and white, silent); 2 minutes Installation view at FRAC Champagne-Ardenne, Reims, France, 2007

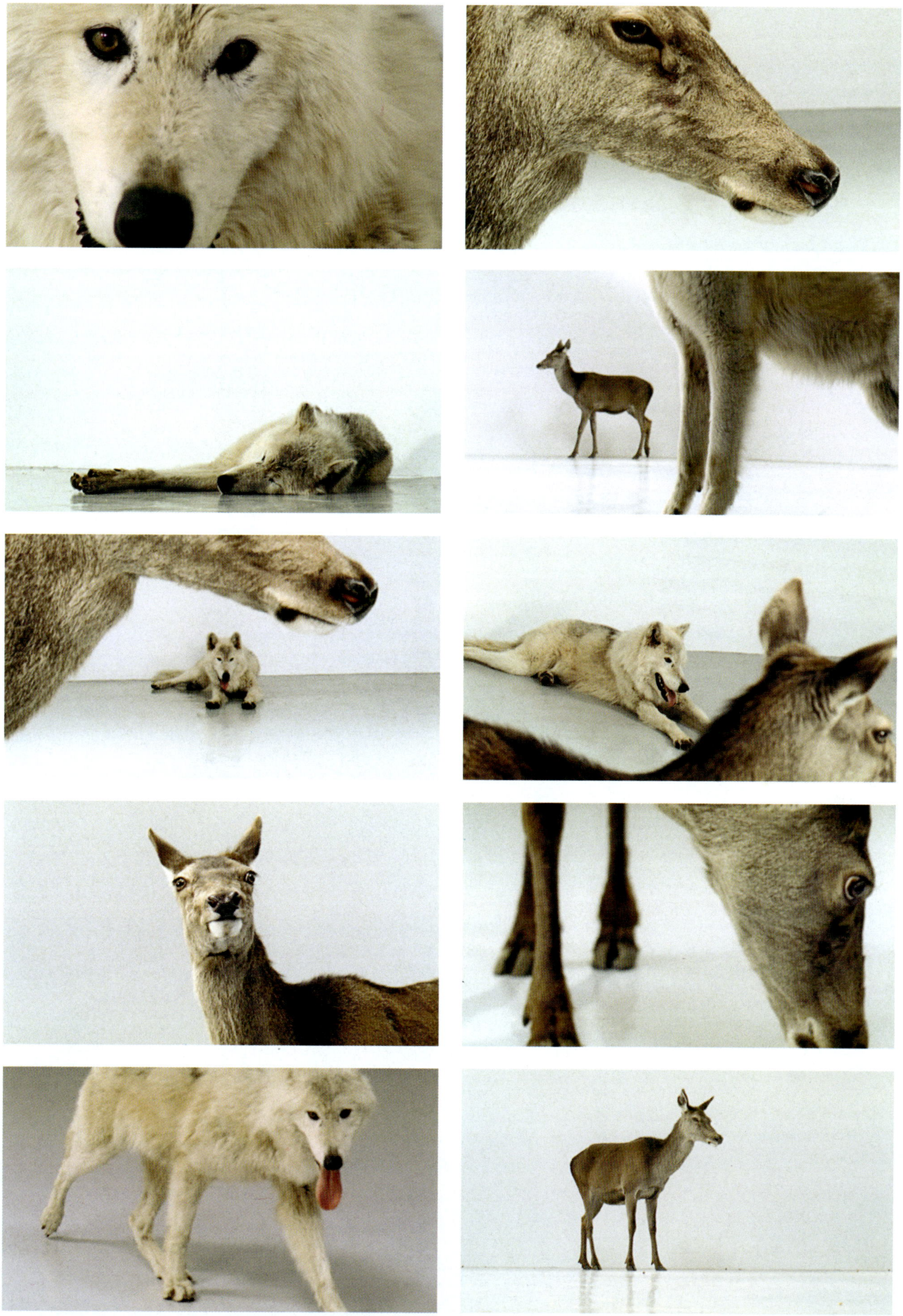

Stills from *Deeparture* 2005 16mm film transferred to DVD (color, silent); 2:43 minutes

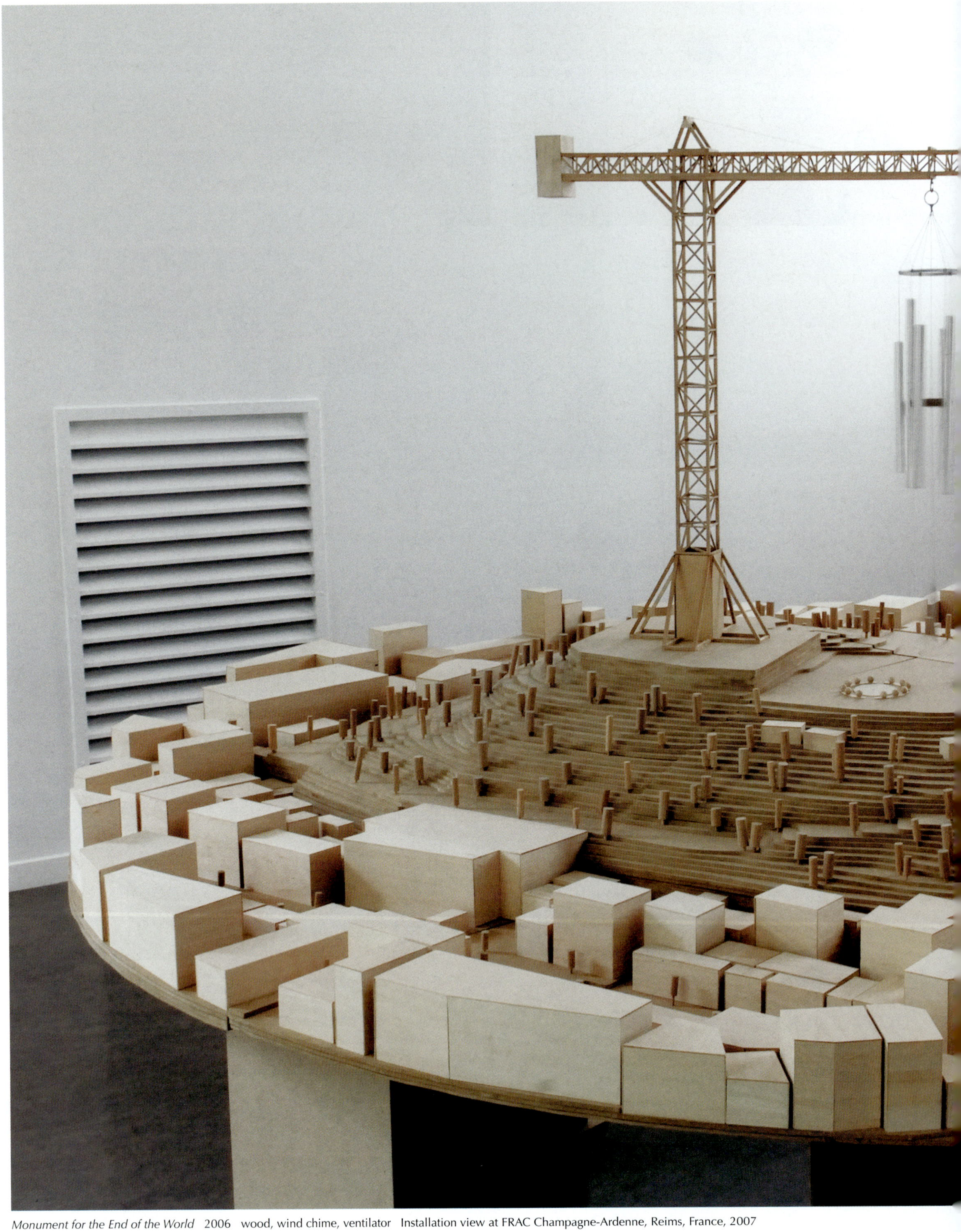

Monument for the End of the World 2006 wood, wind chime, ventilator Installation view at FRAC Champagne-Ardenne, Reims, France, 2007

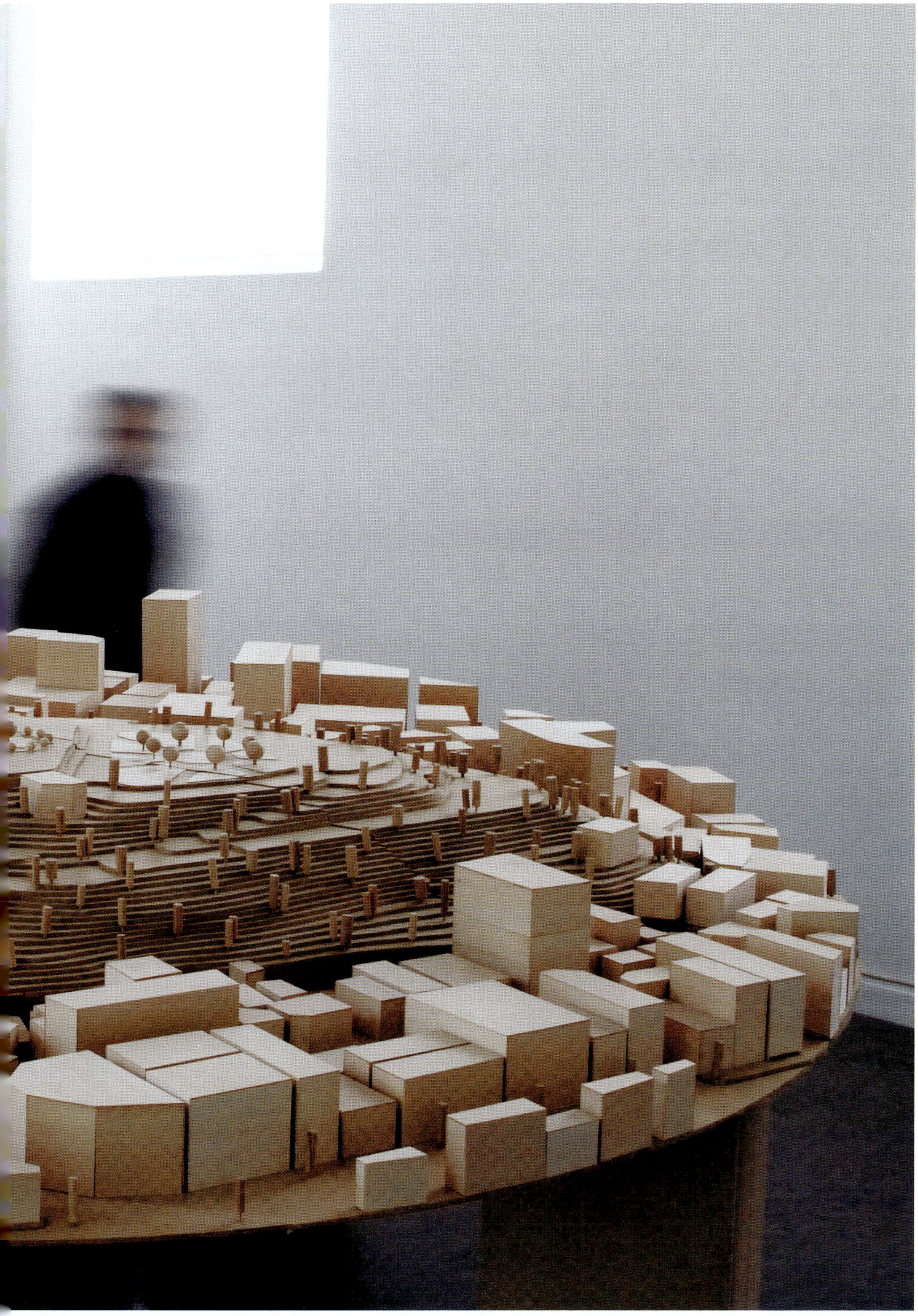

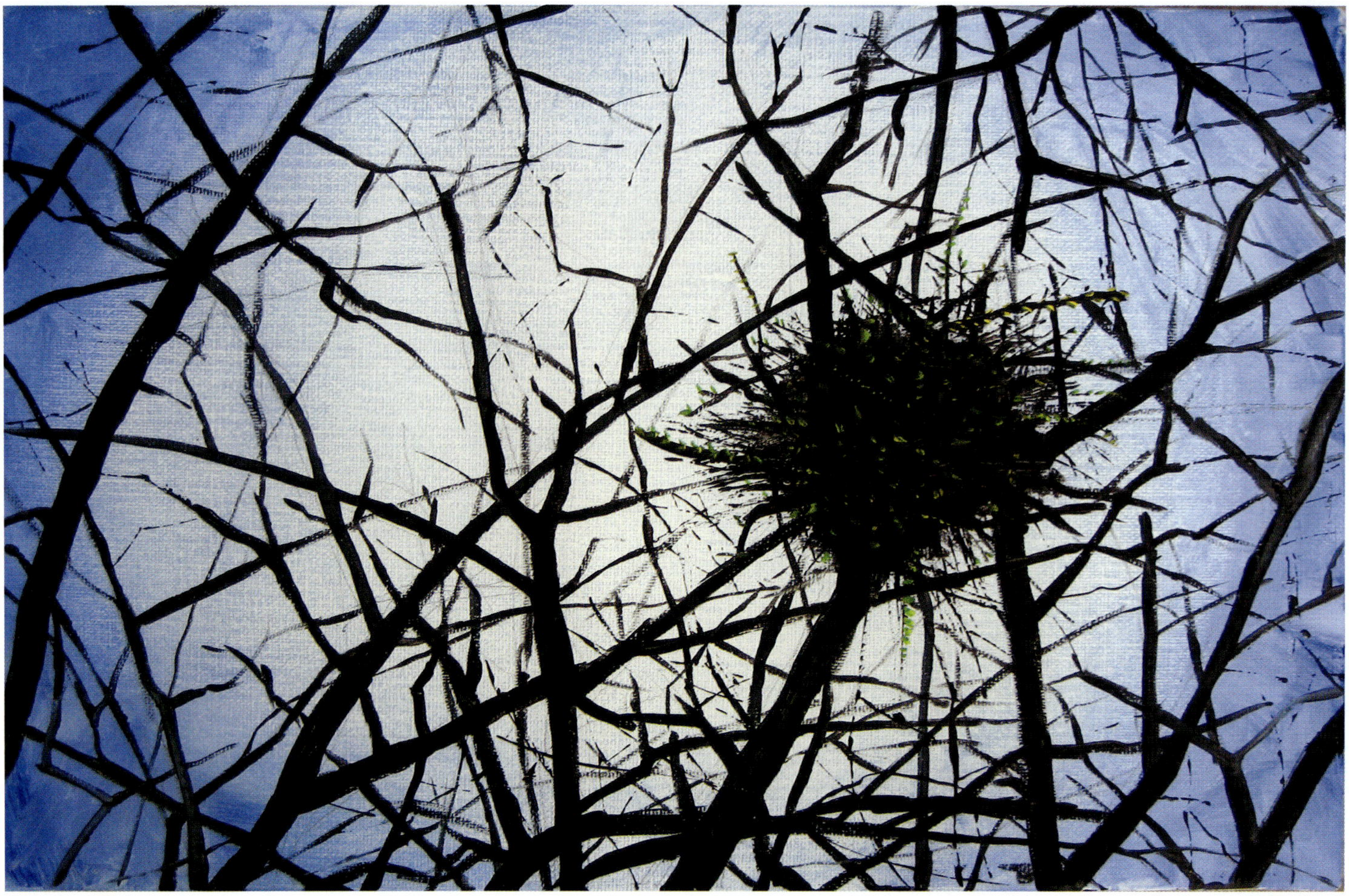

The Spring 2007 oil on canvas

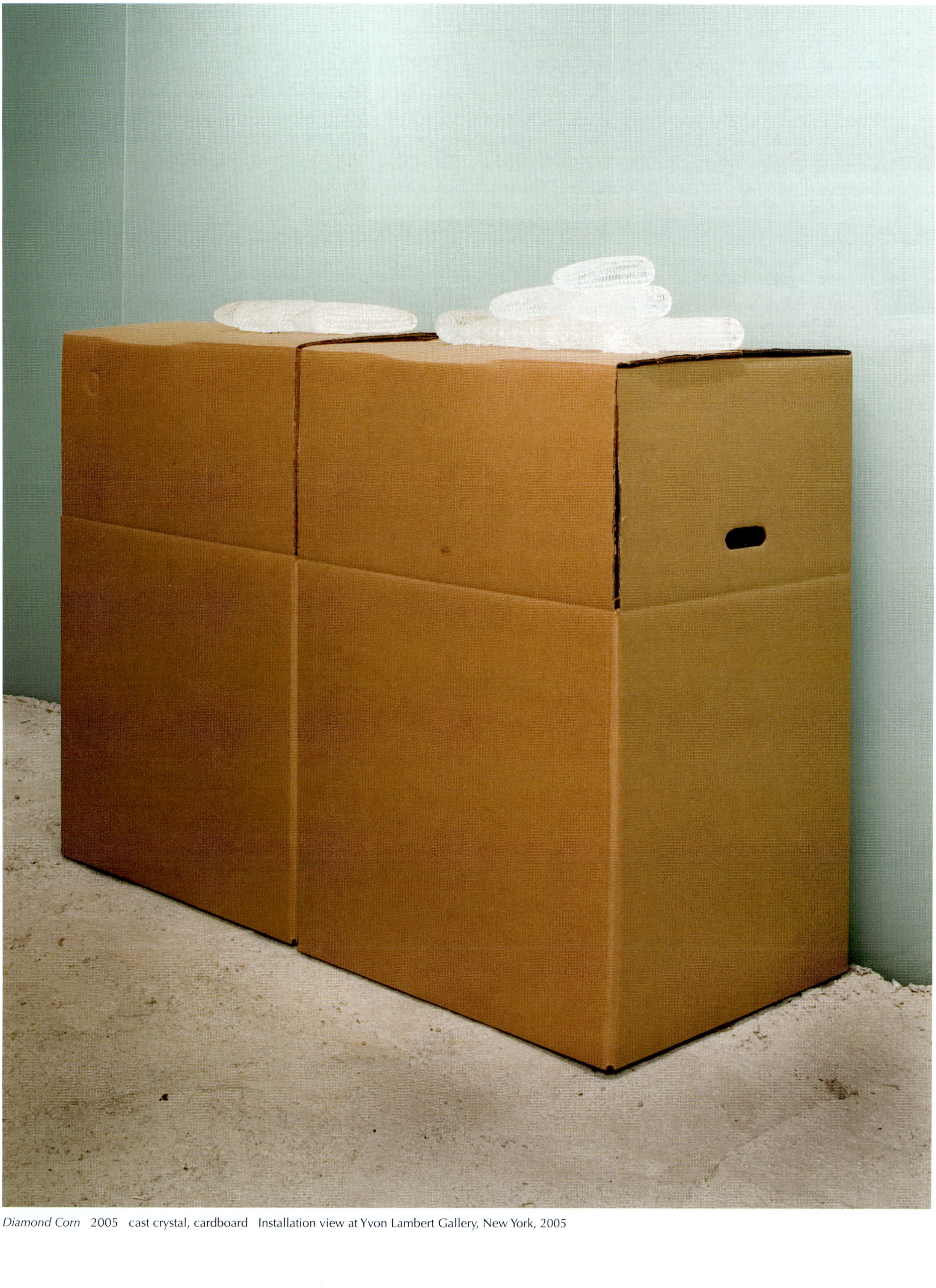

Diamond Corn 2005 cast crystal, cardboard Installation view at Yvon Lambert Gallery, New York, 2005

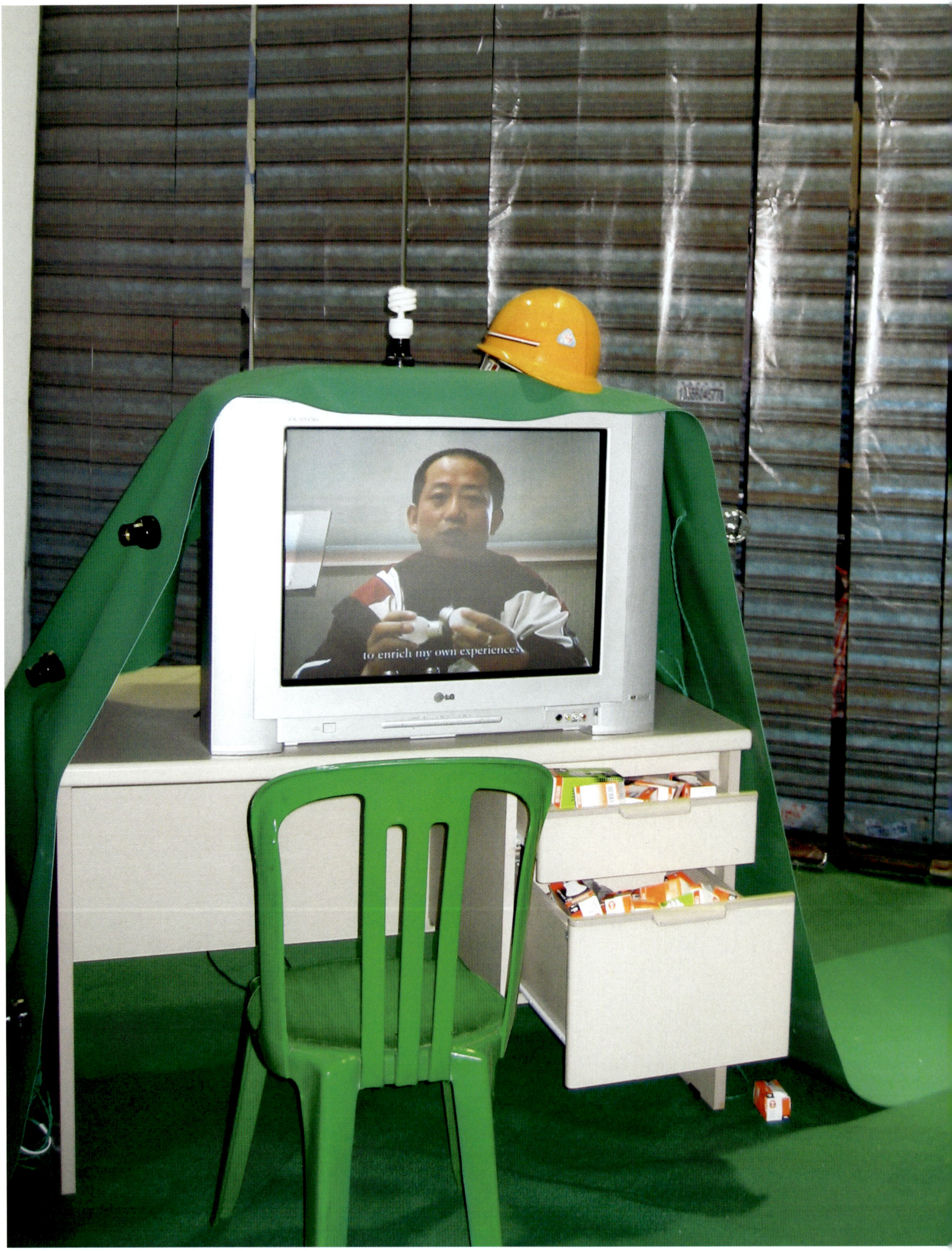

Whose Utopia 2006–2007 multimedia installation, video (color, sound); 20 minutes Installation view at Busan Biennale, South Korea, 2006

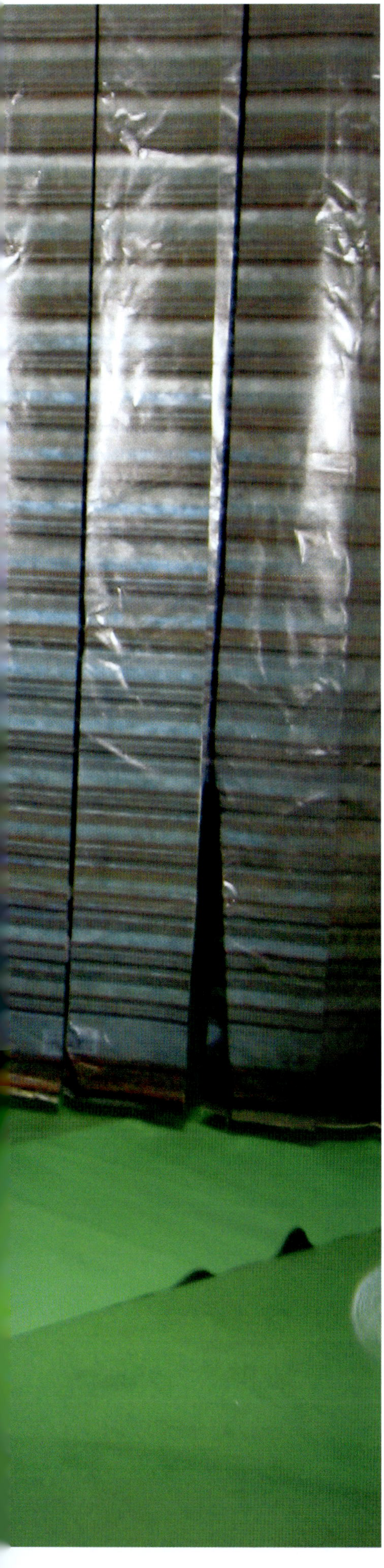

A SCREEN OF FANTASY: CAO FEI

Born in China, 1978. Lives and works in Beijing. One of the most remarkable talents in the generation of Chinese artists coming of age in the new century, Cao Fei has built an incredible body of work in the past few years. Armed with a digital video camera and a fluid sense of intermeshed reality and fantasy, Cao is a hawk-eyed anthropologist and documentarian of the ground shifting beneath her feet as well as new cultures in the making around her. While her projects are anchored to the cultural manifestations and personal stories of particular urban locales in China, her images and narratives resonate far beyond their borders. She explores the seams and structures of the documentary form, deftly expanding the perimeter of the genre through varying types and degrees of theatrical enactment.

COSPlayers (2004), arguably the artist's best-known work to date, features a group of adolescents from Guangzhou dressed as fantastic characters—warriors and assassins—inspired by Japanese animation and computer games. A growing subcultural phenomenon that originated in Japan, "cosplay" (short for "costume play") quickly spread to neighboring Asian countries and eventually gained popularity throughout the world. In the video, the teenagers pose on top of a high-rise, sprint across a grassy meadow, and stage mayhem on a soccer field, on a riverbank, and in an office building—all against the backdrop of one of the world's largest and fastest-growing megalopolises. The scenario progresses from a series of still portraits to sharply edited action sequences, then comes suddenly to a slow, touching denouement: the morning after a night of virtual battles, the teens return to their everyday lives as the city awakens to another working day. Cao's highly cinematic video condenses an entire narrative arc—albeit without spoken words—into a mere eight minutes. As much as her frenetic and colorful piece renders the almost surreal current-day Chinese city as a theater of mega-capitalism and hyper-urbanism, it is also a portrait of boredom and alienation, desire and imagination. In Cao's view, the charismatic characters embodied by these teenagers, whom she calls "New New Human Beings," fill the void left by the towering father figures of Communist China—Mao Zedong and Deng Xiaoping. In fact, the artist has a particular interest in and intimate relationship with the hero worship that so preoccupied the minds of China's older generation; her own father is a sculptor trained in the Socialist Realism school who has created many public statues of the country's leaders. She explored this topic in another video, *Father* (2005).

The exhibition *Brave New Worlds* presents one of Cao's most recent video works, *Whose Utopia* (2006–2007). She spent half a year filming at OSRAM China Lighting Ltd., a factory located in the Pearl River Delta (PRD), an area that includes Guangzhou and the other rapidly growing cities of Shenzhen and Zhuhai, all in close proximity to Hong Kong. The PRD is now one of China's—in fact, the world's—most thriving economic zones as well as a massive manufacturing center. Enormous numbers of people seeking better job opportunities are moving there from all over the country. The artist began the project by engaging workers with a series of questions about their motivations for relocation, their current situation, and their aspirations for the future. Based on the responses, Cao selected a number of subjects and organized performances with them for the video. A hybrid documentary and fantasy feature, *Whose Utopia* flip-flops between images of rote assembly-line labor and dream-like sequences of different styles of dance and music performances. The factory becomes another stage, a model of industrial production oiled and run not only by manual labor but also by the dreams of individuals.

In recent years, Cao has been presenting her videos in three-dimensional installations that function as theaters and conjure simulated experiences. *Whose Utopia* is enfolded into an environment in which a room in the dormitory where the artist's collaborators live is re-created, complete with a metal bunk bed, laundry hanging on the clothesline, and cheap posters that serve as the primary means of aesthetic enhancement as well as a screen of fantasy. Cao's mini-theater invites viewers into an empathetic space where they are gently asked to ponder productivity, humanity, and individuality.

DC

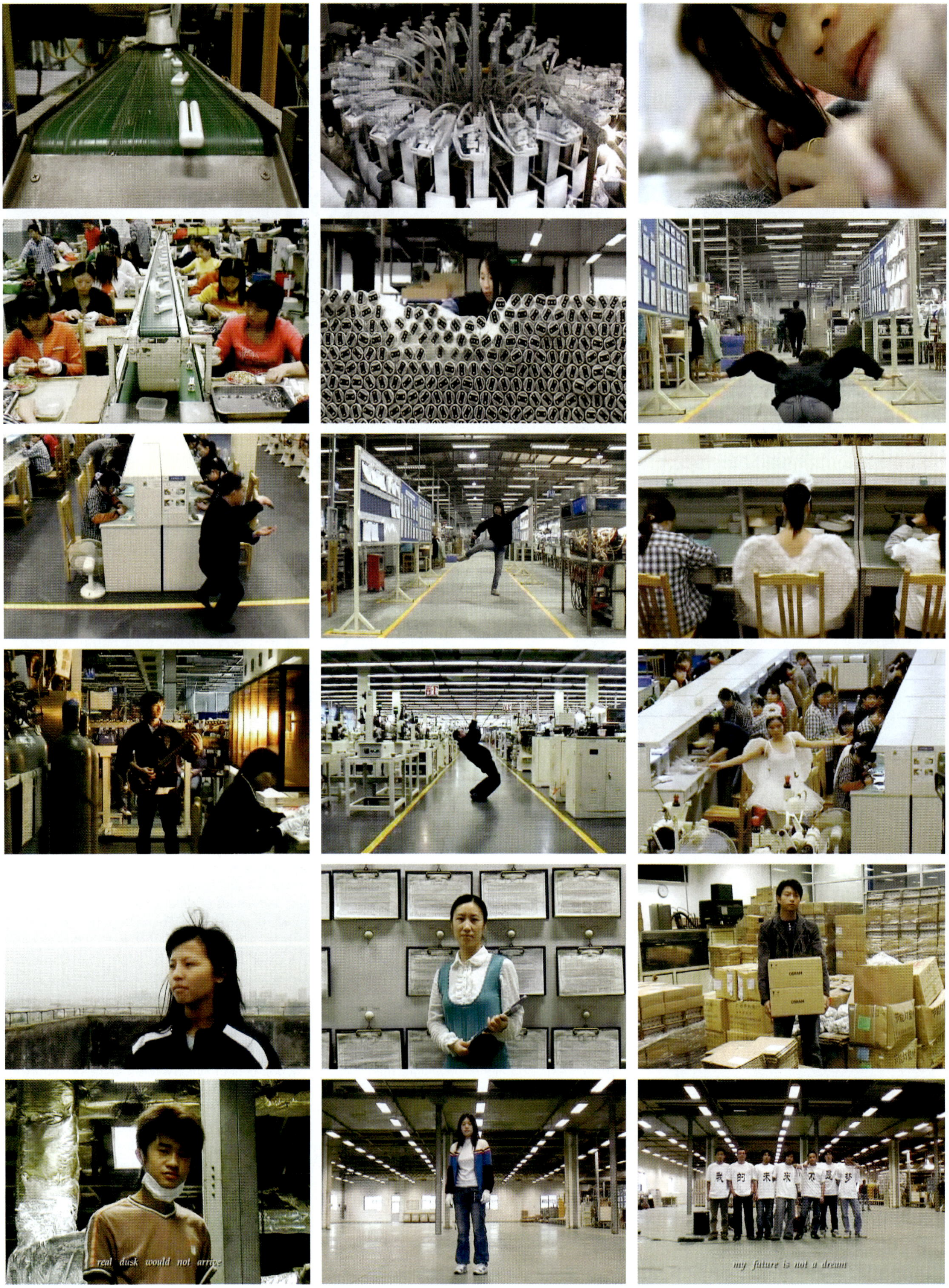

Stills from *Whose Utopia* 2006–2007 multimedia installation, video (color, sound); 20 minutes

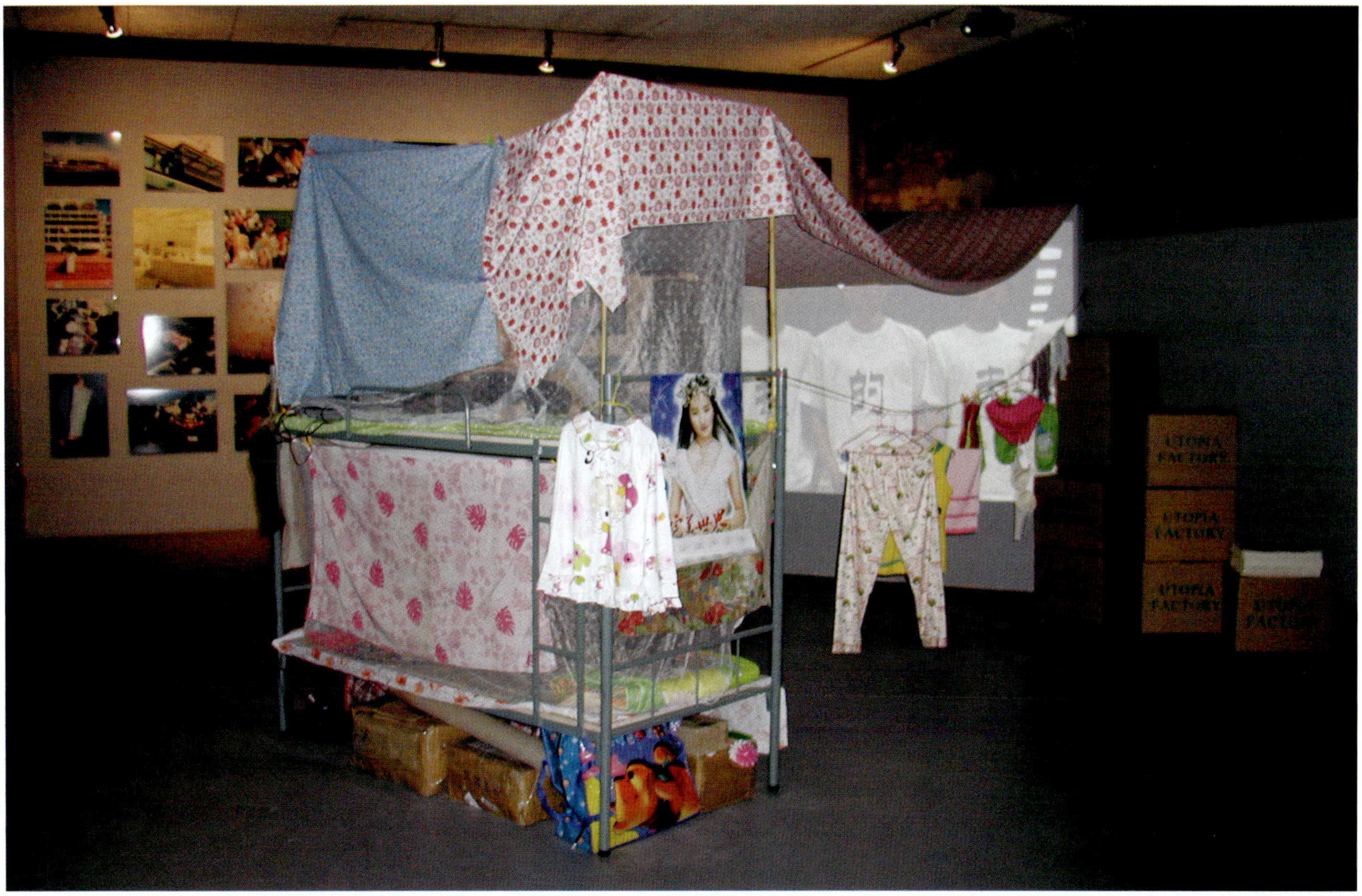

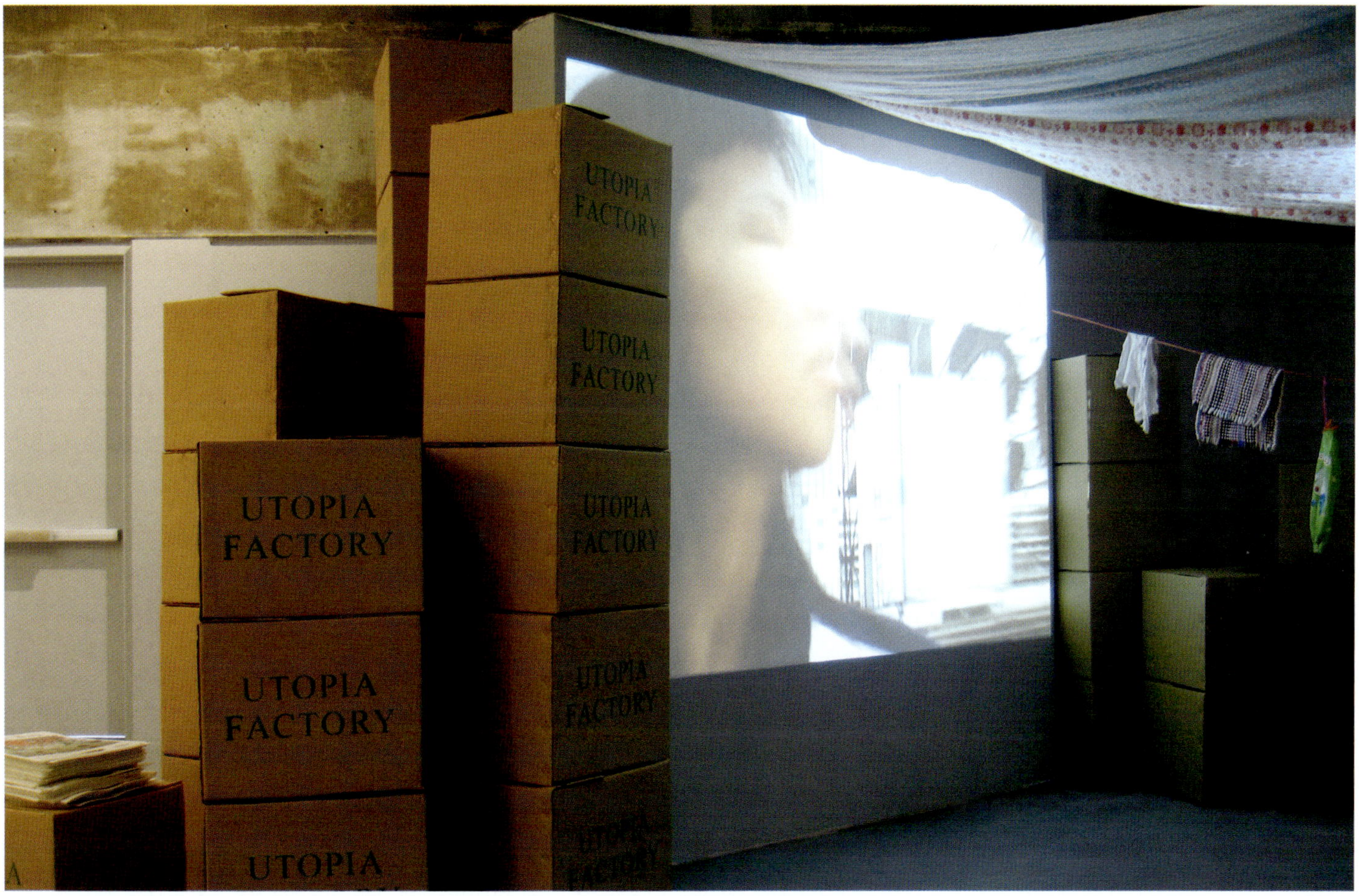

Whose Utopia 2006–2007 Installation views at San Francisco Art Institute, Walter & McBean Galleries, 2007

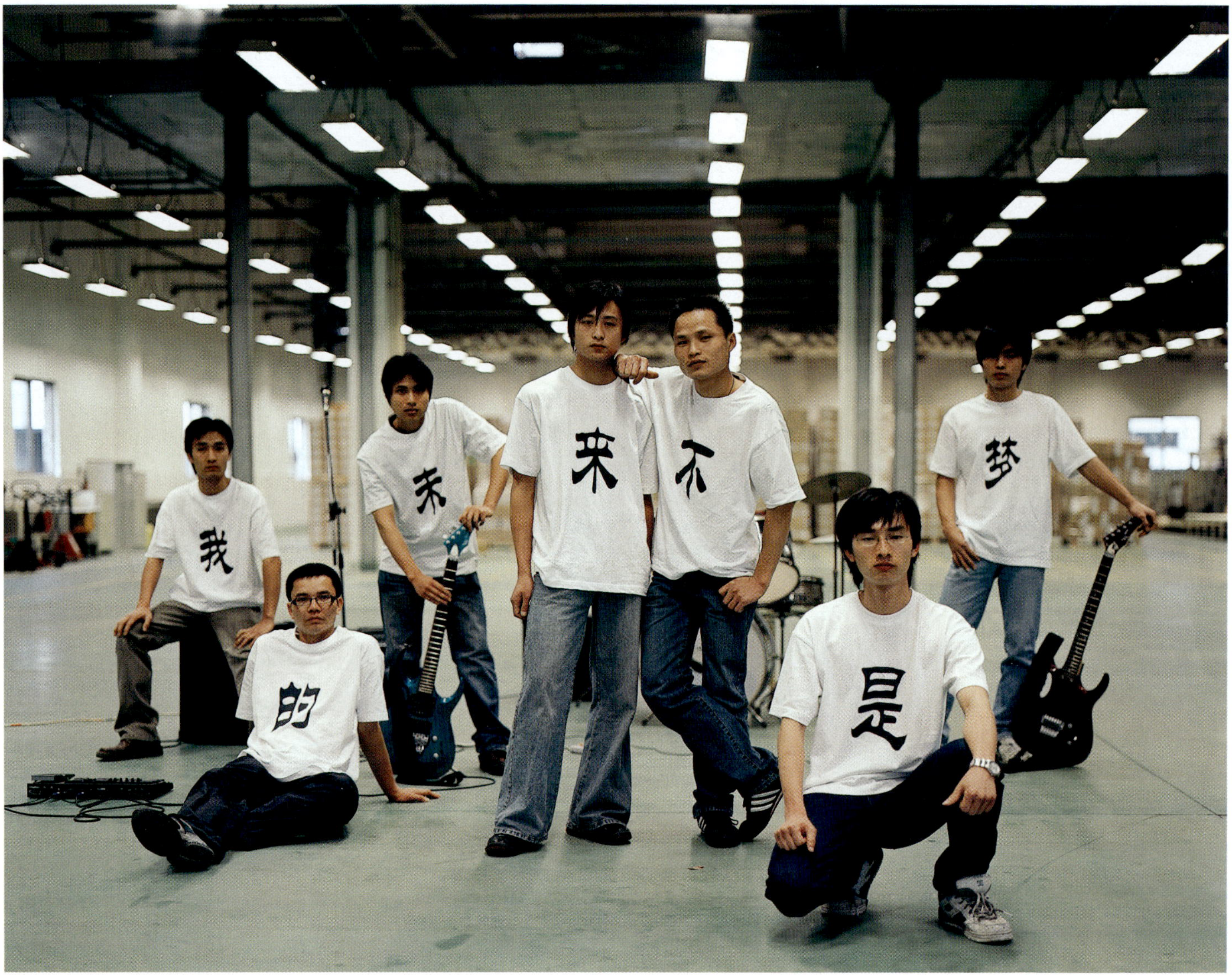

Production stills from *Whose Utopia* 2006 digital chromogenic prints

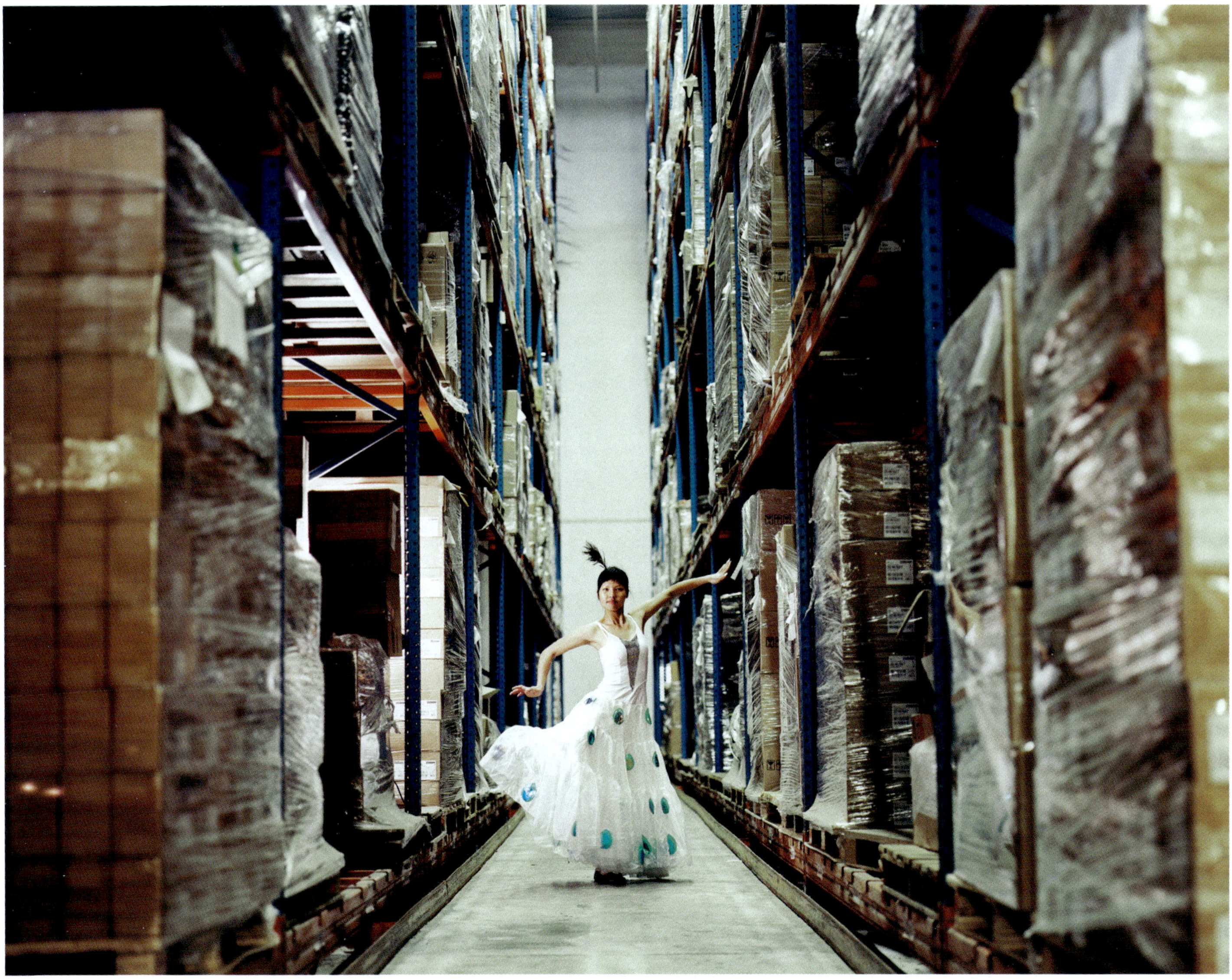

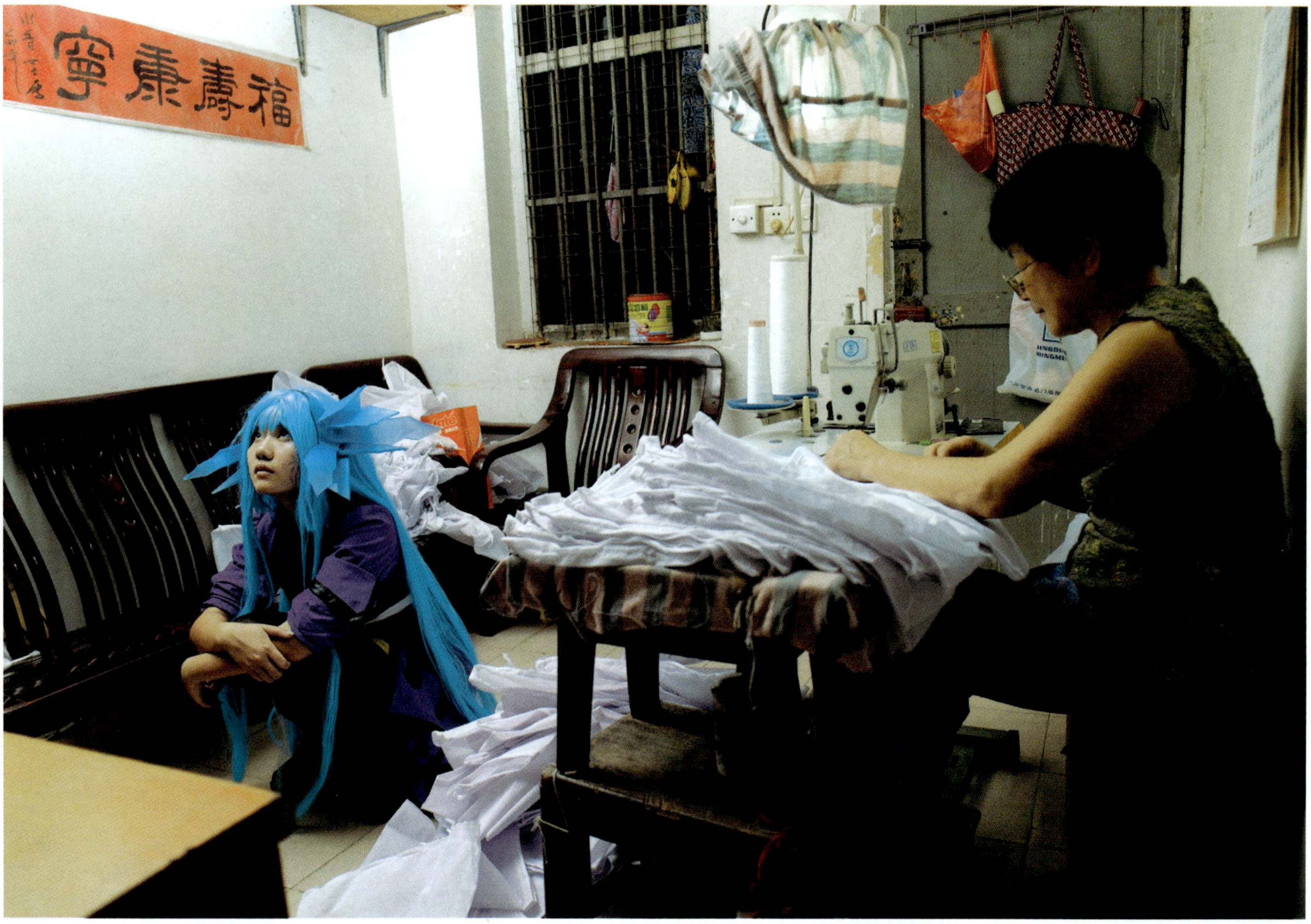

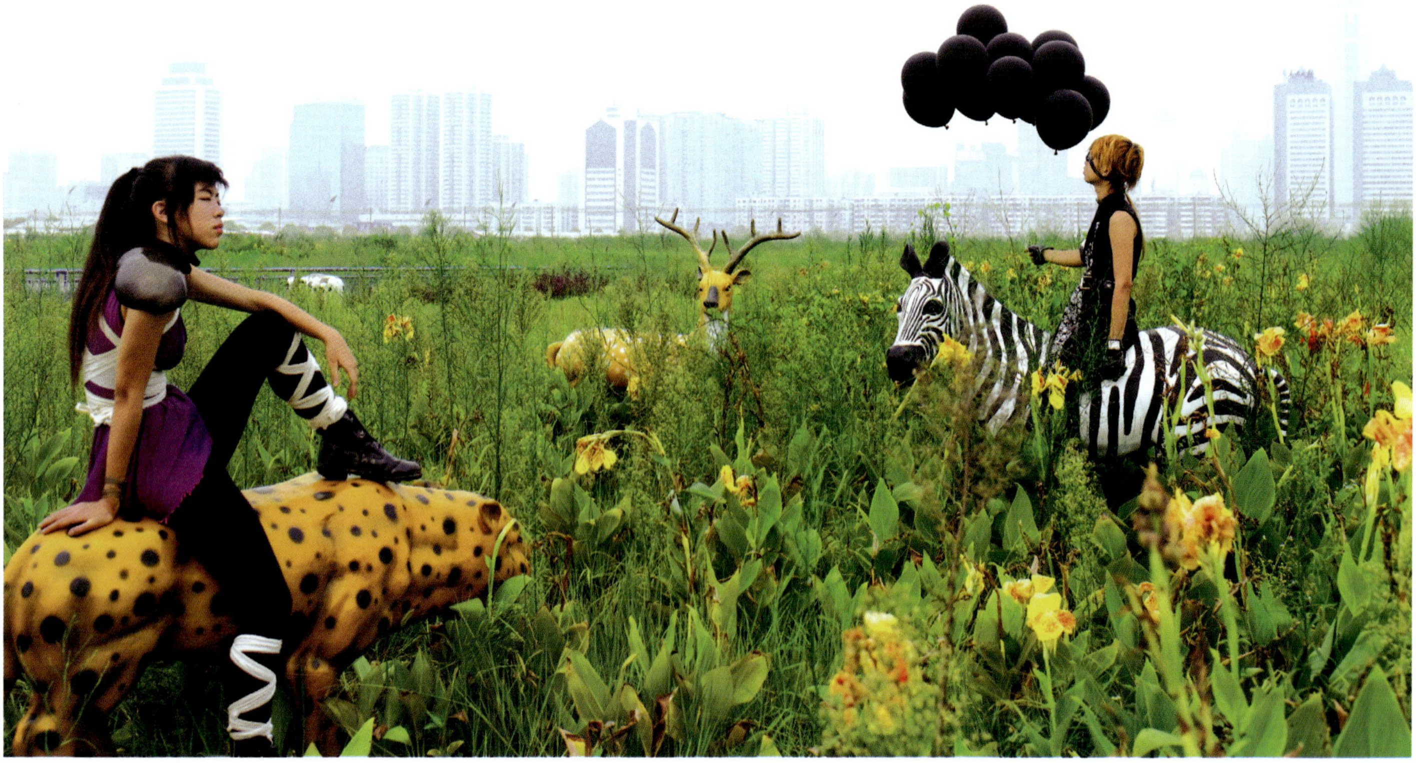

top to bottom: *Yammy at Home* and *Mirage* Production stills from *COSPlayers* 2004 digital chromogenic prints

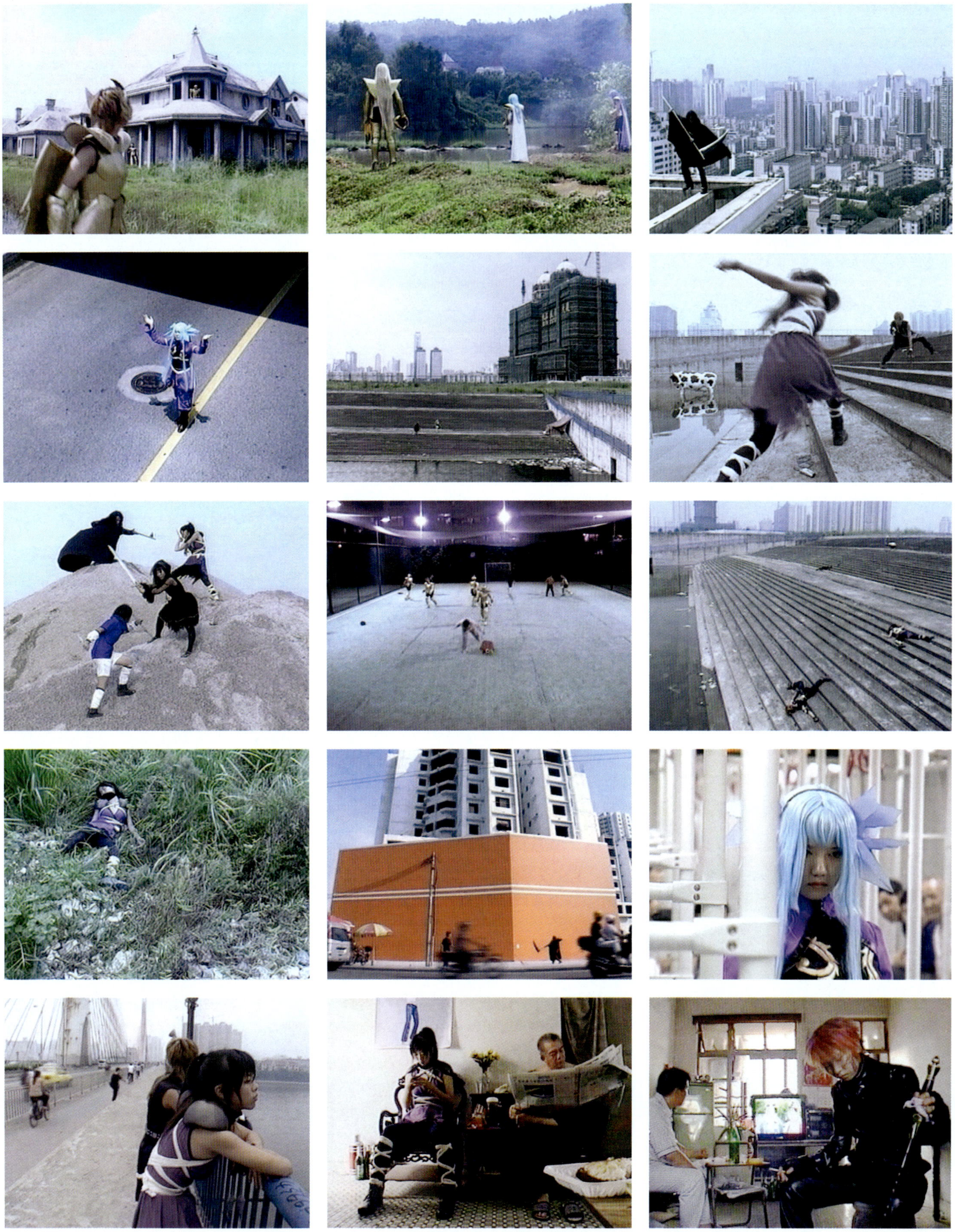

Stills from *COSPlayers* 2004 DVD (color, sound); 8:07 minutes

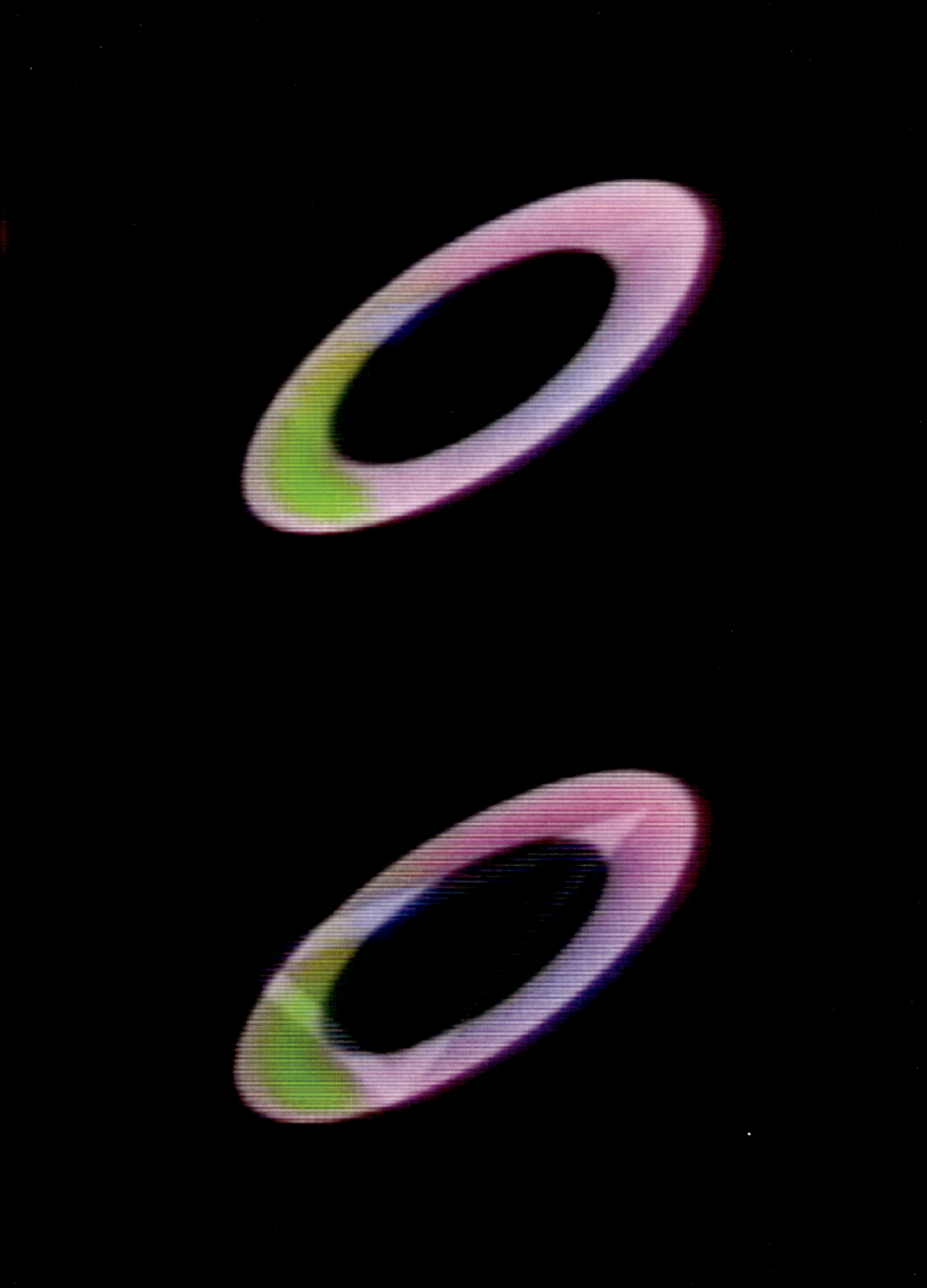

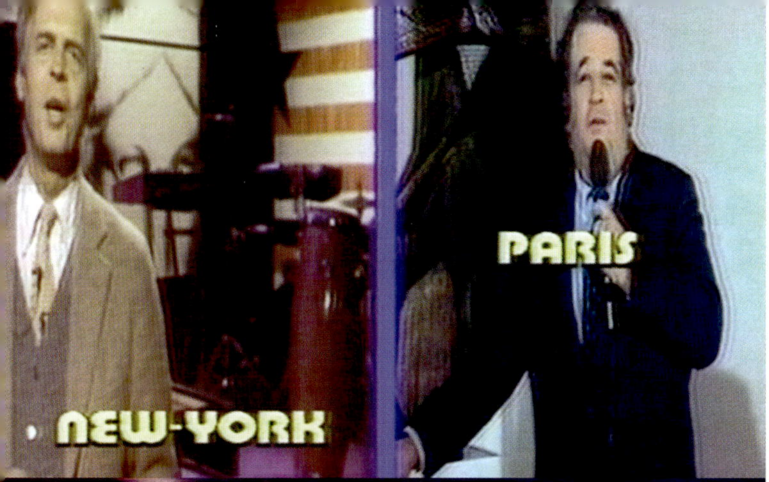

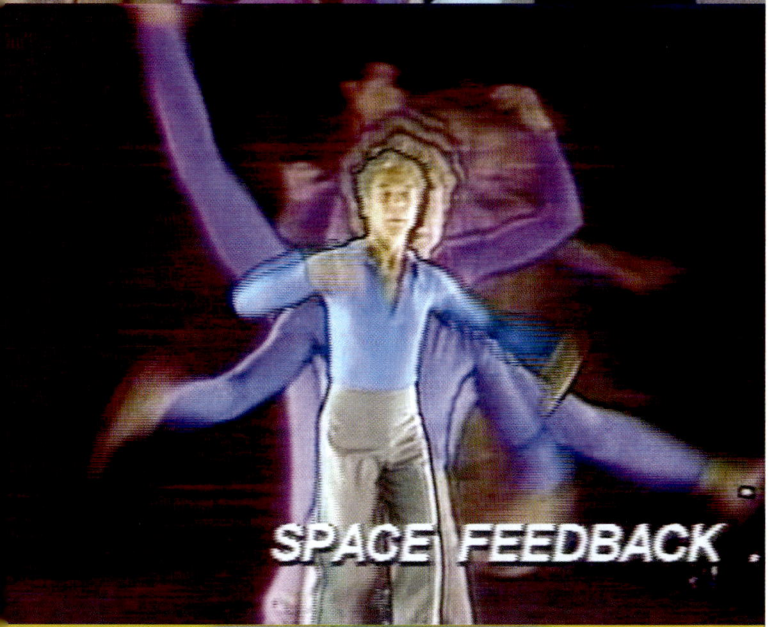

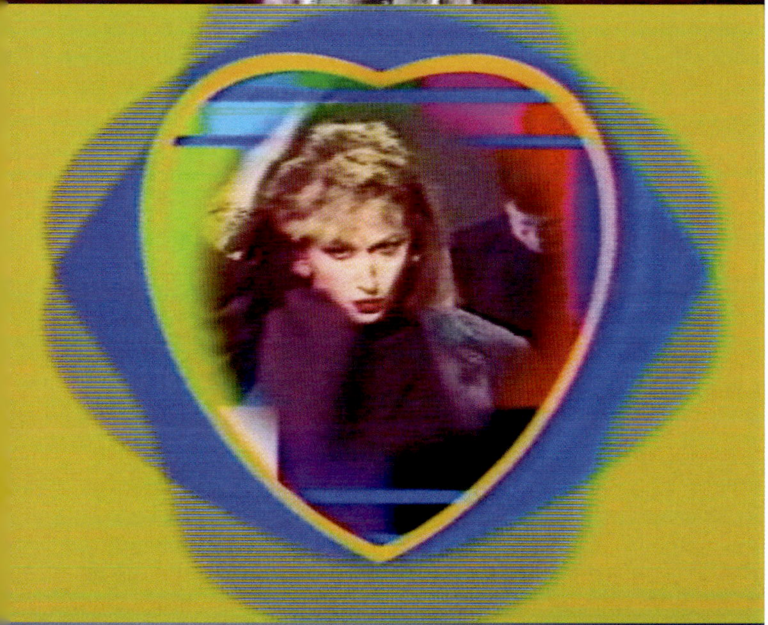

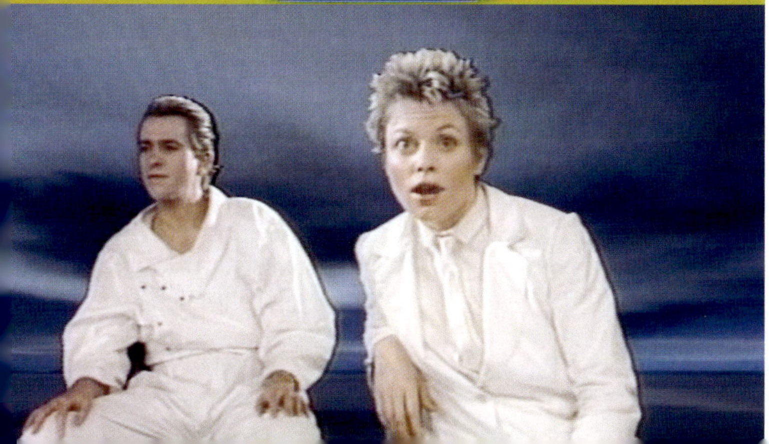

GOODLY CREATURES, BEAUTEOUS MANKIND, O BRAVE NEW WORLDS

§

DORYUN CHONG

1. GOOD MORNING, WORLD!

Let me begin with a small recollection. A boy of school age living in a small industrial city in the southeastern part of South Korea is staying up late, way past his bedtime, to watch a satellite broadcast in the early morning of a New Year's day. It's 1984. A brand new year. The broadcast is that of "video artist" Nam June Paik's *Good Morning, Mr. Orwell*. He learns that the title refers to the British author of a 1948 book titled *Nineteen Eighty-Four*. He hasn't yet read the book, which is just being released in his language, but has read another book by Mr. Orwell, *Animal Farm*. The speaking animal characters in the story reminded him not only of Aesop's fables, but also of a propaganda animation film he saw on school field trips to movie theaters, which depicted North Korean Communists as wolves with a pig as their leader. He doesn't remember much of what he thought of *Good Morning, Mr. Orwell* now. There were "Americans" (for him, all fair-skinned foreigners were Americans) playing music, dancing, and doing other incomprehensible things; there was one particular dancer swirling across the screen, trailed by his own ghostly reflections and colorful, synthesizer-generated shadows. In retrospect, the dancer might have been Merce Cunningham, but he didn't know that at the time. If he remembers little of the program itself, he remembers feeling that he *needed* to see this broadcast, as he heard in the weeks leading up to the day that it was created by a famous Korean artist who lived overseas, that it was shot into homes all over the world simultaneously on the airwaves, and that it was an event the likes of which had never been seen. He didn't really even know what an artist is or does.

Some years later, when the boy had grown up and was living and studying in the United States, he would sometimes recall this experience. He would also recall visiting, when he was a little older, the newly opened National Museum of Contemporary Art just outside Seoul on a balmy late-spring day and seeing Paik's *The More the Better*, a monumental video sculpture installed in the building's entrance atrium. While the art in the museum didn't much affect his bored and anxious adolescent mind, the scale and novelty of this artwork, consisting of some one thousand TV monitors of varying sizes,[1] certainly impressed him. Now that the boy has grown up and found himself involved in the business of contemporary art, he understands a few things about that experience. *Good Morning, Mr. Orwell*, the first international satellite broadcast "installation," was a historically and art-historically momentous event. The live broadcast was simultaneously transmitted from New York and Paris and connected with broadcasters in Germany and South Korea, with prerecorded footage and live feeds. It featured well-known artists such as John Cage, Joseph Beuys, Laurie Anderson, Philip Glass, Allen Ginsberg, and Peter Gabriel. The reference to George Orwell was intended as Paik's optimistic rebuttal to the author's dystopian view of the future, where the television is an instrument of control in the hands of Big Brother, the ruler of a totalitarian regime.[2]

Even after the boy gained a pretty sound historical and intellectual understanding of the work, the thought of Paik would keep coming back to remind him of those early personal experiences. When he saw an artificial waterfall with a zigzagging laser beam—titled *Jacob's Ladder*—installed in the monumental atrium at the Solomon R. Guggenheim Museum in New York on the occasion of the artist's 2000 retrospective, and when on his first trip to Washington, D.C. he saw *TV Flag* (1985–1996), another giant video sculpture of many TV monitors flashing images of past U.S. presidents, he would, without fail, recall that particular early morning in his childhood. Now he works for an American museum of contemporary art, with one of the most iconic works by Paik in its collection, *TV Cello* from 1971, which he built for his frequent collaborator, Charlotte Moorman, and which regularly appears in textbooks of contemporary art. He also thinks often about the moniker "father of video art" given to the artist, who just passed away in 2006 after such an illustrious career. How did a man born in 1932 in an impoverished country with no sovereignty (Korea was Japan's colony from 1910 until 1945) manage to become the vanguard of the most technologically advanced art? How did he become a friend, disciple, and peer to such famous names in twentieth-century art as Cage and Beuys? How did he have the audacity to claim that a president of the United States stole his idea?[3]

Befitting his many proleptic visions, Paik was also the artist who best realized the famous declaration of Marshall McLuhan, the eminent scholar of modern-day and future communications: "The new electronic interdependence re-creates the world in the image of a global village."[4] To this sanguine prediction French theorist Guy Debord countered, "Villages, unlike towns, have always been ruled by conformism, isolation, petty surveillance, boredom and repetitive malicious gossip about the same families. Which is a precise enough description of the global spectacle's present vulgarity."[5] The boy, now an adult, tends to have more intellectual sympathy with the latter's critique. Even so, he would always think of the experience of watching *Good Morning, Mr. Orwell* as the moment when he realized that there was a much wider world out there—beyond the little industrial city in the small country under a virulently nationalist, anti-Communist military regime—to which he could be connected under the umbrella of the idea of the globe. That may also very well have been the moment when he came to be "in sync" with the world, which is now contemporary for him.

2. A (RECENT) HISTORY OF NUMBERS

It is perhaps our intractable habit that we cannot think of history without breaking points or turning points (or is that a particularly modern habit?), a claim that becomes especially trenchant when looking back on the past few years of our lives. There was, of course, arguably the mother of all possible breaks in recent history: September 11, 2001, the day America irrevocably lost its sense of security. In its immediate wake, the momentous disaster echoed another date—December 7, 1941—when Japan attacked Pearl Harbor and which President Franklin Roosevelt, addressing the shocked nation, christened "a date which will live in infamy." The phrase is now literally etched in stone in the World War II Memorial in Washington, D.C., and the more recent disaster will soon have its own soaring monument. As if by a numerological or astrological coincidence, if not by morbidly and maliciously calculating minds, 9/11 has been followed by other numerical sequences: 11/3 (the March 11, 2004 Madrid bombing) and 7/7 (the July 7, 2005 London bombing). Lest we forget, as they are not as often recited, we must invoke a couple other numbers/dates: October 7, 2001, the day when the U.S. invasion of Afghanistan began, and March 20, 2003, the commencement of the U.S.-led war in Iraq. In the growing forest of numbers to remember and commemorate in our contemporary history, how many of us remembered the ten-year anniversaries of the Srebrenica massacre (July 1995), the largest mass murder in Europe since World War II,[6] and the Rwandan genocide (April to July 1994)?[7]

Certain nations are "enemies" or "rogue nations," it seems, because they refuse to see those important breaks that define the dominant view of history. North Korea, thus, is behind the times, still staunchly and aberrantly Communist even after the worldwide collapse almost two decades ago of the primary alternate ideology of the twentieth century. Those who hold this view might say that even China has "opened up" and done away with its Communist revolution, and see where it is now. The border between China and North Korea, then, may be seen as a temporal fault line that separates the rapidly evolving economy that's a hybrid of state planning and free market from a Communist industrialization that came to a halt quite some time ago. Even more starkly, in the 2.5 mile-wide and 155 mile-long demilitarized zone between the two Koreas, time has stood still since 1953, when the civil war ended not in a peacc treaty but a truce that is still to be resolved.[8]

In contrast, different places in the world have leapfrogged to contemporaneity in the last few years. For instance, the "Orange Revolution" in Ukraine (November 2004 to January 2005) has transformed the country's political landscape as well as its relationship to its bigger, more powerful neighbor. In Romania, history might be said to begin in 1989 with its revolution that toppled the long-standing Communist dictatorship. If American international diplomacy is allegedly oriented toward spreading liberal democracy and economic liberalism, we may claim that there have been a number of "successful" cases of nations leaping across the great fissures of evolutionary development in recent years.[9] At the same time, whereas the inclusion in an expanding supranational organization such as the European Union has served new members such as Romania well in their "advancement," the previously bright future for the proposed unified body politic also seems to grow dimmer every year.[10] The Netherlands, itself a longtime vision of liberalism, at least from where I stand, seems to be breaking apart at the seams.[11] And Turkey continues to be the main sticking point in debates around the identity of Europe: can a nation be Islamic and secular and European all at the same time, especially as the West is presenting a far from united front of opinion vis-à-vis that most enigmatic and troubling of "other" civilizations?

Historical reversals and temporal cycles, for some, could be as politically significant as progress and advancement are. Palestinian intifadas—the first in 1987 and the second since 2000—and the state's revanchist policy are attempts to turn back the clock on what it sees as unjust territorial and political usurpation by another state. While Iran's 1979 revolution, which ousted the West-friendly monarchy and installed a theocratic regime, would seem to the West to have derailed the country's progress, this value judgment may be fundamentally misplaced when the state's self-perception lies on an entirely different trajectory. The new leftist populism emerging of late in several South American nations has grown into a veritable multinational revolution against,

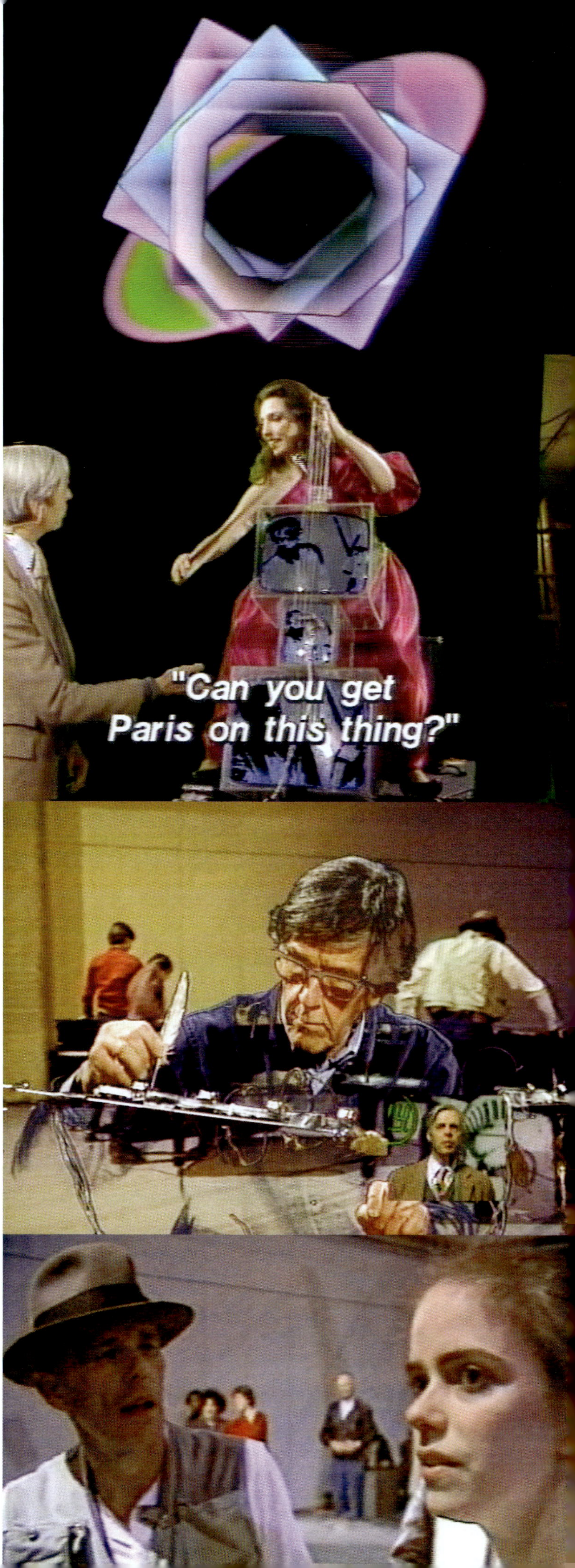

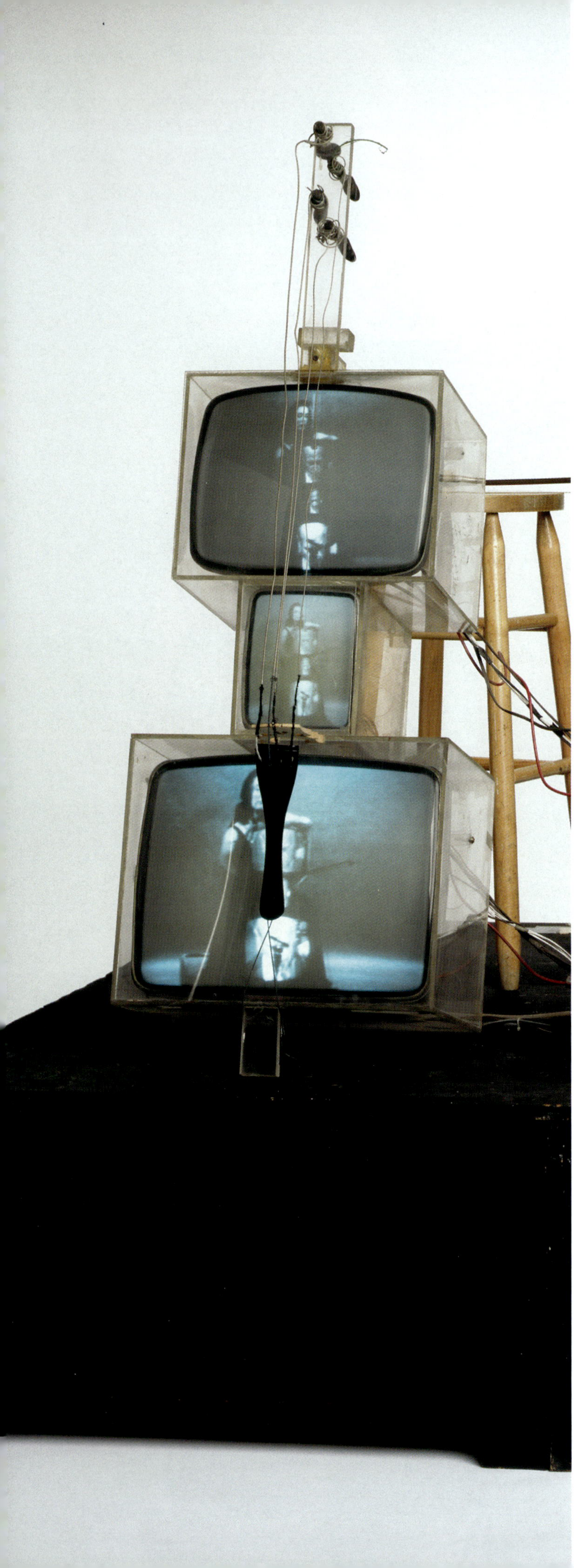

among other things, neo-imperialist structuring of the world's political economy since the end of the Cold War; for them, this revolution is much less a slide in historical progress than a way of making and writing a new history on their own terms. The inadequacy of linear historiography and the existence of multiple modernities may be widely accepted notions by now, but a new paradigm that can account for multiple notions of history is yet to be formulated. Since the late 1980s, the government, policymakers, and intellectual circles in the United States have been grasping for an effective interpretative framework on the world in flux: the first Bush administration's post–Cold War "New World Order" has been replaced by the "Era of Globalization," the "End of History," and the "Clash of Civilizations," each coinage serving less to explicate the world than to reveal the inadequacy of its egocentric purview.[12]

While we are myopically pondering the state of the world and the seemingly endless series of hostilities and political disasters, an unusually high number of natural catastrophes at the same time have reminded us of the indifference of the forces of nature and the coexisting temporalities that operate on wholly different scales. Massive earthquakes—with the largest casualties in Turkey (1999), Iran (2003), and Kashmir (2005)—that killed hundreds of thousands were all but overshadowed by the even more devastating Asian tsunami in December 2004 and Hurricane Katrina in August 2005. If the seismic movements of the tectonic plates that cause earthquakes and tsunamis move in one geological time frame, we are hearing the ticking of another giant clock of climatic changes a little more loudly. Not only are the melting polar ice caps raising sea levels worldwide, but also Darfur, "today's worst humanitarian disaster,"[13] which is usually described as a racially and religiously motivated conflict, may have been caused by a chain of events started by changes in sea temperature.[14] How might we even begin to grasp the significance of political events when they may be connected to far more expansive time frames of human making as well as to that of natural, planetary, even cosmic dimensions that stretch forward and backward infinitely?

This is not to say that our customary way of thinking about history is irrelevant. Rather, while we have collectively embraced the idea of the "globe" (and its corollaries, "global," "globalization," etc.), which has fashioned the world into a unified—homogenized, even—concept through "time-space compression," the world is still a composite of many places, well-known and still distant, and of numerous intersecting, coexisting temporalities.[15]

3. TERRAE INCOGNITAE

O, wonder!
How many goodly creatures are there here!
How beauteous mankind is!
O brave new world,
That hath such people in't!

—William Shakespeare, *The Tempest*, act 5, scene 1

Set in the twenty-fourth century, Aldous Huxley's 1932 novel *Brave New World* limns a society in which humanity is permanently happy thanks to the elimination of warfare and poverty as well as sexual reproduction and all familial structures and relations. Human lives are mass-produced, quality-controlled, and maintained and recycled in a system based on Henry Ford's assembly-line industrial production (in fact, "Ford" has replaced "God" in this society as the supreme spiritual being and as the most common exclamation). In the "World State," a unified government ruling over the entire planet under the motto of "Community, Identity, Stability," citizens daily consume *soma*, a psychotropic substance that eradicates any negative or distressing emotions and ensures perpetual bliss and satisfaction. While Huxley seems to have intended his vision of the future to be dystopian, the hedonistic society resembles our own contemporary vision of utopia as well, especially in light of certain human inventions and interventions that are taking place today. Preceding the more ruthlessly dark vision of the future in Orwell's *Nineteen Eighty-Four* by more than a decade, Huxley's future is perhaps more insidiously devastating because its society is equipped with more thoroughly debilitating machinations of social engineering.

Huxley's book borrows its title from Miranda's speech in the final act of Shakespeare's play *The Tempest*. And lines from the speech are uttered several times in Huxley's novel by John "the Savage," the only known human being born of viviparous reproduction in this future society and one of very few to know of the existence of Shakespeare. Born and raised in a reservation in New Mexico, the Savage is brought to London and becomes a cause célèbre amongst people who have never seen such an "uncivilized" human, but he soon withdraws from his newfound fame and life. As the novel moves toward its fateful denouement, Miranda's words, each time he utters them, take on bleaker and more ironic overtones. The gradual narrative turn from the ambiguously dystopian to the darkly tragic can be said to lie in this technique of repetitively employing the well-known literary precedent.

One may very well see Huxley's early twentieth-century vision of the future and Shakespeare's early seventeenth-century image of a distant place located in an ambiguous past as literary bookends to the history of European imperialism, its "discovery" and understanding of the "world." While *The Tempest* is apparently set on an island in the Mediterranean Sea, it has been suggested that the locale exhibits many features of the Caribbean. Prospero—the Milanese sorcerer, Miranda's father, and the master of the island—had been overthrown by Antonio, his brother, aided by Alonso, the King of Naples, before drifting to the island. The play revolves around Prospero's partly chance/partly machinated plot to right the injustice done to him and his authority when his deposers are shipwrecked in his newfound territory. Prospero's effort to reassert and redefine virtuous kingship through revenge is challenged, if to little effect, by his slave, Caliban, a barbaric and deformed monster who is native to the island and views himself as the rightful master of the pied-à-terre. Based on the particular power relationship between Prospero and Caliban and the description of the latter as a dark-skinned savage, some scholars have read *The Tempest* as a fable and commentary on colonization.[16] Indeed, in Shakespeare's time there were a number of circulating accounts of sea voyages to the "New World," and there is evidence of the playwright's explicit knowledge and use of Montaigne's essay "On Cannibals," in which the French Renaissance writer praises the society of Caribbean natives. The name of Caliban is itself believed to derive from the spelling of "Carib(be)an" and/or is an anagram of "cannibal," thus clearly referencing the New World.[17]

While suggesting a historical trajectory through these two literary examples cannot but be Eurocentric, a more powerful metaphorical possibility lies in the notion that the world is the utmost subject of knowing—and unknowing—for all humankind. Through many historical stages of mapping and developing it, we have perhaps come to know the world and then un-know the world; the world on the verge of "discovery" and the world continuing to evolve and then even fall off the grid constitute the selfsame and never-same terra incognita. While the face of authority over the world changes from Prospero to Ford, it is the two savages—Caliban and John—who are agents of political consciousness occupying the moral center; they are the ones who maintain a sense of outrage through shackles of enslavement and through the haze of collective amnesia and unwillingness to see the world out there. On the one hand, they are tragic victims of both knowing and un-knowing too much of the world, and on the other hand, they possess a clarity of vision lost on others who are blinded by power and revenge or lost in pleasure and apathy.

In *Brave New World*, John the Savage refuses to take *soma*, in spite of the others' constant urging and its promise of eliminating the pain and suffering that stems from his not being part of the new world. It is a gesture of refusal to be blinded by the illusion that everyone else has embraced. Certain commentaries on Shakespeare's play have focused on its overt concern with its nature as a play. That is, while conjuring a distant, exotic island, *The Tempest*, with its many invocations of sorcery, also makes explicit the theatrical illusionism it utilizes. Thus, in act 4, scene 1, Prospero, about to extricate the marooned Europeans, states that the whole world is an illusion: "like the baseless fabric of this vision . . . the great globe itself . . . shall dissolve."[18] While "globe" may be a poetic equivalent of or perhaps a merely seventeenth-century synonym for "world," I would also like to see it as a suggestion of how the world will always be there even when the *notion* of the globe dissolves. The world, in all its political and economic, material, and psychological dimensions, continues to be one big terra incognita, with innumerable terrae incognitae in it, to be discovered with all sense of indignation and wonderment, curiosity and solemnity. And it may be none other than the savages, *only* the savages, who will guide us through it.

4. HOW TO PUT A WINDOW, OR A GRID, ON THE WORLD

The world gives us many possible "worlds." It can comprise seven continents, five oceans, and almost two hundred nations; it may be the stage of endless bloodshed, conflicts, and wars, if it were to be constructed based on reports by the mass media; or it may be an optimistic sphere of unity, mutual trust, and good will. Starting with the premise that an important tendency in contemporary art is a collective effort to find artistic manifestations of political consciousness about the world, the exhibition *Brave New Worlds* brings together an exemplary group of artists who are exploring, with especially sharpened consciousness, different possible forms of knowing and experiencing this world. These artists' approaches to their subjects are akin to what we may think of as reporters' and documentarians' relationships to theirs. In a sense, a number of the artists in *Brave New Worlds* have built on a tendency in contemporary art since the early 1990s that has been termed an "ethnographic turn," which has enabled artists to "work *horizontally* (in a synchronic movement from social issue to issue, from political debate to debate) rather than *vertically* (in a diachronic engagement with the disciplinary forms of a given genre or medium)."[19] But unlike their immediate predecessors who themselves followed on the heels of the art of the 1960s and 1970s, the "sitings" and "mappings" of their investigations reach beyond the institution—the museum, most prominently—and different notions of otherness into a realm of mutually implicated geopolitics and psycho-geography.[20] Importantly, these efforts are firmly rooted in the awareness that one cannot know the whole world or even approximate the experience in any fundamental way. In the systems of knowledge and ranges of experience presented and suggested in the works by these artists, times are multiple, malleable, and flexible, and histories are always necessarily contingent. If the Renaissance perspective was a means of imposing an order onto the world as it was concurrently "expanding," the purviews of the artists in this exhibition are ones that are inevitably fractured and incomplete.

Yto Barrada and **Banu Cennetoğlu** explore in their photographic works locations of transitional existence. Tangier, Morocco, is the jumping-off point for illegal migrants from North Africa and beyond to cross the Strait of Gibraltar into Spain, thus wider Europe. It is also the place where Barrada has chosen to live and work. In *A Life Full of Holes: The Strait Project*, Barrada's camera captures diverse lives of labor and leisure, individual complexity and many-sided sociality—that are much more than the mere image of illegal migration. Cennetoğlu's site in *False Witness* is located on the other side—i.e., the Asylum Seeker Registration Center in Ter Apel, the Netherlands. Without explicitly identifying the physical situation and political/human implications of the institution, the project re-creates the spatio-psychological experience by displaying the photos of the center in a darkened, narrow corridor. If migration is often understood via a simplified push-pull theory of political economy, these two artists and their projects suggest lives and realities that are far more multidimensional.

Zwelethu Mthethwa's generously scaled photographs capture workers in a sugarcane field near Cape Town, South Africa. Classically posed and composed, these portraits are dignified images of everyday labor and ownership in a land that for the most part is synonymous with crises such as AIDS, crime, and poverty. **Artur Żmijewski** and **Cao Fei**, both working in video, also provide narratives about conditions of labor in a changing world, but their methodologies couldn't differ more starkly from one another. Unlike his earlier works, for which he hired actors to reenact psychologically jarring situations, Żmijewski in *Danuta*, *Dorota*, and *Halina* turns his matter-of-fact, affectless camera upon three middle-aged, working-class women whose lives are nothing if not utterly mundane. The lens follows them for a twenty-four-hour period, from their workplaces to their kitchens and even into their bedrooms, with no direction or intervention. What emerges is a portrait of everydayness that is graceful in all its honest ordinariness. Cao's *Whose Utopia*, on the other hand, skillfully interweaves documentary with fantasy. The video first shows workers engaged in their rote assembly-line work in a German-owned lightbulb factory in southern China, then unexpectedly presents some of them as self-absorbed, even ecstatic performers while still in the factory. If Barrada and Cennetoğlu's portraits conjure images of stability and stagnancy in sites defined by migration, Mthethwa, Żmijewski, and Cao's subjects are those "stuck" in ruts, apparently, while environments outside their immediate proximities are radically transforming.

In her double-projection video *Wild Seeds*, **Yael Bartana** has a group of teenagers, divided into two groups, play a game on a mountainside: while one group tries to hold itself as a unit, the other attempts to break it apart, all having an apparently jolly time. The texts spelling out the players' utterances, however, reveal that they are reenacting the forceful removal of Israeli settlers from redrawn Palestinian territories. **Erik van Lieshout**, in contrast, is always at the center of his "documentaries." He reveals most private dimensions of his life—from his sexual preferences to emotional vulnerabilities and social prejudices—and, with the same openness and guile, he elicits from others what had perhaps better remain unexposed (such as an elderly woman's lingering sympathy for fascism). In his new "American trilogy," the artist finds himself in an unfamiliar setting, and in his attempt to form his own view beyond stereotypical images of the land of his fantasies and nightmares, he turns his videos into the most extended self-examination to date.

Some works in *Brave New Worlds* plumb archival sources to resurrect the past in order to highlight its irrevocable interrelation with present and future. At the same time, the authority of the archive itself is rendered unreliable, contributing to one of the more general questions raised in this exhibition: is our knowledge of the world fair and just? In his quest to meticulously document civil wars and incursions in his native Lebanon, **Walid Raad**—sometimes working with the Atlas Group, a fictional entity—has employed various means of documentation, such as photography, video, and text, with results that willfully disregard and blur the boundaries between truth and fiction. In his recent photographic series, *Let's Be Honest, The Weather Helped*, Raad exhibits black-and-white photographs of urban sites, covered with colorful sticker dots. The images allegedly record the places where the artist collected bullets as an adolescent living in Beirut, with colors matching the seventeen countries that continue to supply ammunitions to militias and armies fighting in Lebanon. If Raad's "documents" turn the photographic ability to witness and record on its head, **Fernando Bryce** exploits the tension between the act of seemingly perfect copying and the subjectivity and fallibility of the drawing hand in his method of "mimetic analysis." He extensively researches historical sources and salvages them copying them by hand, thereby introducing a relationship that is both collusive and contradictory between the subjective context and the pristine, a perfect grid presentation that commands archival authority. **Gimhongsok** investigates in his work myriad possibilities of (mis)understanding inherent in the rhetoric of nationalism, economic transaction, and cultural difference. He conjures sculptural objects that sometimes claim monumental historical significance with deadpan seriousness. *Mao Met Nixon*, for instance, consists of a simple cubic object that, according to an accompanying textual panel, holds the air from a room in the White House, where a thus-far-unknown meeting between Richard Nixon and Mao Zedong took place. Together, these "archivists/historians" proffer a whole spectrum of believability and fictiveness about the world.

In many ways, these artists' attempts at truth-telling are only meaningful because of their unflagging awareness of treacheries inherent in facts, records, and documents. **Sean Snyder**, an avid archivist-cum-cartographer, has explored and brought to light many historically neglected and geopolitically charged sites—from Skopje, Macedonia, to Pyongyang, North Korea. In one recent project that interrogates the media and representation, he finds a surprisingly limited range of iconography shared by the U.S. Department of Defense and Jihadi media material, both found and accessed on the Internet. In one Jihadi propaganda video, he identifies a particular Sony video camera, which is equipped with a Carl Zeiss lens. Taking a cue from this identification, he juxtaposes images of a raw optical glass from the Zeiss factory archive in Jena, Germany, in several different resolutions with the actual object and photographs of the video camera. Thus, his investigation also contemplates the questions of accessibility of information, limitation of visual technology, and transparency (or nontransparency) of so-called truth as well as undeniable interconnectedness in the world.

The strange coexistence and mutual construction of the material world and phantasmagoria in Snyder's work are echoed, rather unexpectedly, in the works of **Mark Bradford** and **Haegue Yang**. Bradford's painting simultaneously incorporates and is structured by the grid, one of the most art-historically weighted means of abstraction. A longtime observer of the shifting ethnic, commercial, and legal landscapes of urban Los Angeles, where he was born and continues to live and work, Bradford makes his painting a realm of visual translations and material accumulations of his psychogeographic experience. In Yang's video trilogy—*Unfolding Places*, *Restrained Courage*, and *Squandering Negative Spaces*—the artist is everywhere and nowhere. The footage is derived from many different places in the world—Seoul, London, São Paulo, among others—but they rarely register as distinctive territories. The sequence of images in each video is accompanied by a voice-over, but with no apparent logical or narrative interrelation. If there is a unifying principle, it is the artist's sustained contemplation of lostness in the world. Yang shows these images and voices in an environment constructed with commercially available industrial products—such as blinds, lights, a humidifier, a scent machine. In this installation, these objects that generate perceptual experiences both constitute her psychological landscape and stand in perhaps as equal members of a community to which she longs to be a part.

In a sense, all these strategies of *visual* art question their own ability to see and discern. Photographer **Noguchi Rika** has explored in her many photographic series geographically, culturally, and psychically distant places—from a rocket-launching station to the depths of the ocean. While the sites are not all inherently extraordinary or fascinating—or even if they are—Noguchi unfailingly finds ways to infuse all her images with a deep sense of poetry and makes them mysterious, even spiritual. In the series *The Sun*, the artist offers the viewer images taken from many different sites, but the locations hardly matter. Each picture registers a bright spot that blinded the photographer's own eye as well as her camera's eye, turning the proverbial philosophical questions associated with the medium—about seeing, witnessing, and knowing—into mute suggestions of an almost religious, ecstatic experience of un-knowing.

5.

In closing, let us return to the boy who was awed and bemused by moving images he had never seen before. He now likes to think of himself as a diligent reader who's always curious about the world. At times, however, he feels exhausted and even dejected by information overload, as if the innumerable words and images falling off newspaper pages and TV screens every day were like a thicket of trees hiding the sun. He wonders how one might regain the sense of wonder about the world he once possessed, even with the awareness of all its tragedies and disasters. How might we, indeed, see again "how many goodly creatures are there here" and "how beauteous mankind is"?

How might we learn to make the best of both the reality and the illusion of the globe without ever losing the conviction of having our feet firmly planted on a piece of land—and of that piece of land being connected to numerous other territories beyond many literal, arbitrary fault lines? How might we learn to be a "savage" equipped with a sharply-honed sense of right and wrong, of justice and outrage, who knows that all of these moral structures and value systems are fatally and hopefully unstable? How we might answer such questions is not clear. But it is because we do and should ask them that there are, and always will be, many brave new worlds. ■

NOTES

1. The number of television monitors in the work—1,003—refers to the date, October 3, which is Foundation Day, or literally, "Heaven's Opening Day" in South Korea. Korean mythology tells of the founding of the nation by a sky god.

2. The video was shown in the Unites States on public television and is said to have reached more than 25 million people all over the world.

3. Paik coined the phrase "electronic superhighway" in "Media Planning for Post-Industrial Society: The 21st Century Is Now Only 26 Years Away," a 1974 Rockefeller Foundation–commissioned report on telecommunications of the future. In it, Paik predicted that the electronic superhighway would "become our springboard for new and surprising human endeavors." Two decades later, when "information superhighway" was used by President Clinton and became a widely used phrase, Paik commented, "Bill Clinton stole my idea." See "Video Artist Nam June Paik Dies at 74," obituary, *International Herald Tribune* (January 30, 2006).

4. Marshall McLuhan, *The Gutenberg Galaxy* (London: Routledge & Kegan Paul, 1962), 31.

5. Guy Debord, *Comments on the Society of the Spectacle*, trans. Malcolm Imrie (London: Verso, 1998, originally published in French, 1967), 33.

6. The Srebrenica Massacre refers to the killing of an estimated eight thousand Bosniak males by the Army of Republika Srpska (VRS) and a Serbian paramilitary unit. The United Nations had previously declared Srebrenica a UN-protected "safe area" but did not prevent the massacre, even though four hundred armed Dutch peacekeepers were present in the area at the time. In April 2004, the Appeals Chamber of the International Criminal Tribunal for the former Yugoslavia in the Hague ruled that the massacre was an act of genocide. The ruling was confirmed subsequently by the International Court of Justice.

7. The Rwandan Genocide was the 1994 mass extermination of hundreds of thousands of ethnic Tutsis and moderate Hutu sympathizers in Rwanda and was the largest atrocity during the Rwandan Civil War. This genocide was mostly carried out by two extremist Hutu militia groups during a period of about one hundred days from April 6 through mid-July 1994. Over half a million Tutsis and thousands of moderate Hutus were killed, while some reports estimated the number of victims to be between eight hundred thousand and one million. During the violence, despite wide media coverage, most countries, including France, Belgium, and the United States, declined to intervene in the atrocity, while Canada continued to lead the UN peacekeeping force in Rwanda, the United Nations Assistance Mission for Rwanda (UNAMIR). However, the UN did not authorize UNAMIR to interfere or use force to prevent or halt the killing.

8. But could the image of a North Korea in a time warp really be true? Just as I'm writing these words, the *New York Times* reports that the Bush administration allowed Ethiopia to purchase arms from North Korea in a scenario in which the enforcer of the order of global economy is actively facilitating black-market transactions that it purportedly curtails. See "North Koreans Arm Ethiopians as U.S. Assents," *New York Times* (April 8, 2007).

9. The case of Spain is one such example. See Max Andrews and Mariana Cánepa Luna's correspondent essay from Barcelona in this catalogue, 43–45.

10. Of late, there have been a spate of books that prophesy the rise of the EU and the waning of the United States, such as T. R. Reid, *The United States of Europe: The New Superpower and the End of American Supremacy* (New York: Penguin, 2005) and Mark Leonard, *Why Europe Will Run the 21st Century* (New York: PublicAffairs, 2006). At the same time, *The Economist*, in a recent special report on the European Union, casts a sobering look at the challenges facing the EU on the 50th anniversary of its signing of the Treaty of Rome, the historic first step toward European integration. The article enumerates three main problems with the yet-to-be-ratified draft constitution, "popular disenchantment with the project" (i.e., the European integration), and poorly performing economy. See "Fit at 50?" *The Economist* (March 17–23, 2007): 3, 4, 6.

11. In his book *Murder in Amsterdam: The Death of Theo van Gogh and the Limits of Tolerance* (New York: Penguin Press HC, 2006), Ian Buruma discusses the failure of liberalism, mounting xenophobia, and unresolved historical legacy in the Netherlands through the lens of the murders of the country's two prominent figures: controversial politician Pim Fortuyn and filmmaker and cultural commentator van Gogh.

12. In his 1992 book *The End of History and the Last Man* (New York: Free Press, 1992), Francis Fukuyama argued that with the end of the Cold War, the progression of human history would come to an end with the triumph and installation of Western-style free-market democracy throughout the world. While seemingly sharing the basic model of evolution with Marx's historical materialism, Fukuyama's thesis is the polar opposite of Marx's conclusion—that human society goes through successive stages of development until it reaches the final state of classlessness, i.e., communism. Around the same time, Samuel P. Huntington predicted that the end of the age of ideology would give rise to new conflicts based on cultural differences. His thesis, originally formulated in an article in the journal *Foreign Affairs*, was later expanded in his 1996 book *The Clash of Civilizations and the Remaking of World Order* (New York: Simon & Schuster, 2003; first edition, 1996).

13. See "Sudan Facing Worst Humanitarian Disaster in the World" by James Elder, UNICEF Communications Officer in Darfur, Sudan, http://www.democracynow.org/article.pl?sid=04/06/23/140223, accessed April 2007.

14. Stephan Faris, "The Real Roots of Darfur," *Atlantic Monthly* (April 2007): 67–69.

15. Coined by geographer David Harvey, "time-space compression" is a term that describes "processes that... revolutionize the object qualities of space and time." See Harvey, *The Condition of Postmodernity: An Inquiry into the Origins of Cultural Change* (London: Blackwell Publishing Limited, 1991), 240.

16. The relationship of dependency between Prospero and Caliban has been interpreted by the French psychoanalyst Octave Mannoni (1899–1989) as a paradigm of the "psychology of colonization." Mannoni believed that it is naturally ingrained in the psyche of the black person to look up to the whites for protection, and that the former lacks any flare for freedom or liberation. He also argued that this psychological situation was already in place in the form of traditional oracles even before the "white man" came to Africa. Later writers—most notably Aimé Césaire and Frantz Fanon—passionately critiqued Mannoni's overreliance on the simplified notion of native psychology and the social, historical perpetuation of the idea of "dependency."

17. Shakespeare uses Montaigne's essay "On Cannibals" in *The Tempest*, notably at the point when Gonzalo tries to cheer up King Alonso by describing the ideal commonwealth he would institute on the island (act 2, scene 1).

18. The full verse reads: "These our actors,/As I foretold you, were all spirits and/Are melted into air, into thin air:/And, like the baseless fabric of this vision,/The cloud-capp'd towers, the gorgeous palaces,/The solemn temples, the great globe itself,/Yea, all which it inherit, shall dissolve/And, like this insubstantial pageant faded,/Leave not a rack behind." The "great globe" here has also been interpreted as a reference to the Globe Theater, the venue for most of Shakespeare's plays. In such readings, these lines are seen as making reference to the literary images and motifs of magic and illusion that dominate *The Tempest*, as well as to the very theatrical conceit of conjuring a far-off place and a realm of spirits.

19. Hal Foster, *The Return of the Real* (Cambridge, Massachusetts: MIT Press, 1996), 199.

20. One of the most important accomplishments of Minimalism in the 1960s may be the shifting of artistic discourse and concern to the holistic, spatial, and phenomenological experience of art objects and also the spaces in which they are sited. Conceptual Art, in turn, opened up and then legitimated the institutions that presented art and produced its discourse as the sites of art-making itself. It is this expansion of purview, which has been enabled by successive artistic movements and tendencies since the 1960s, I argue, that allows today's artists to take on the world per se as a viable, and even most pressing, subject for contemporary art.

IMAGES

pages 94, 95, 97 Nam June Paik Stills from *Good Morning Mr. Orwell* 1984 video (color, sound); 38 minutes

page 98 Nam June Paik *TV Cello* 1971 video tubes, TV chassis, plexiglass boxes, electronics, wiring, wood base, fan stool, photograph

page 103 Nam June Paik *66-76-89* 1990 103 television cabinets, 32 video monitors, 4 laser disc players, steel

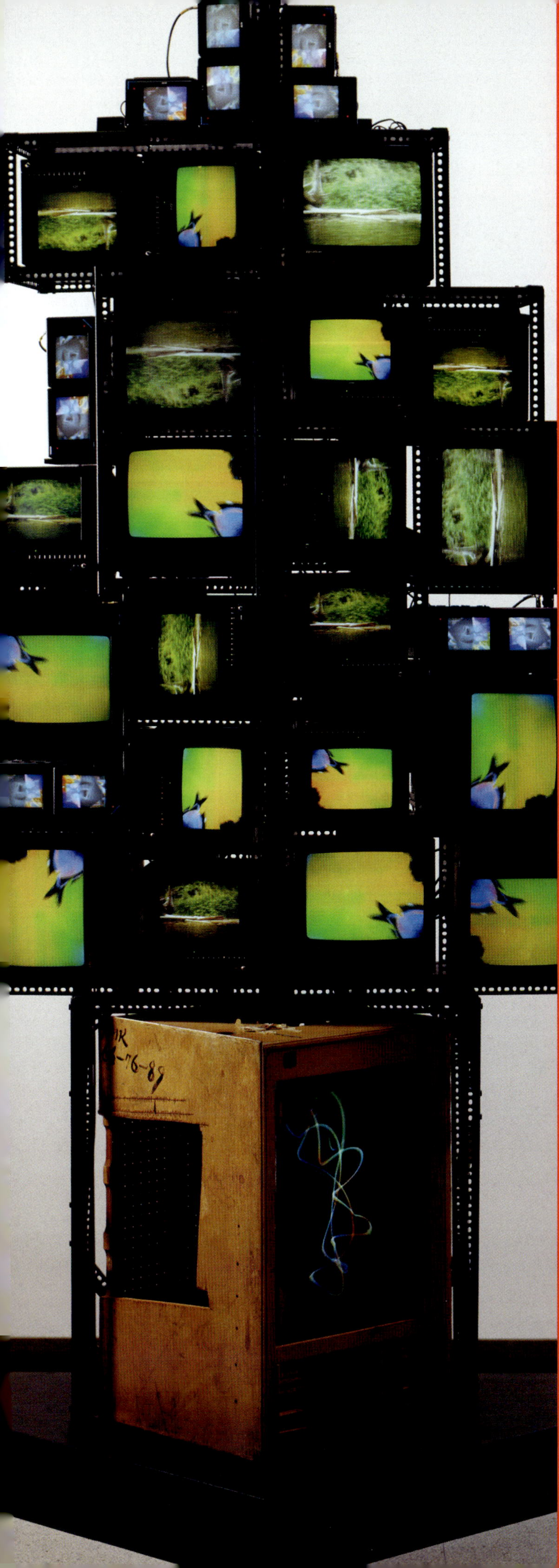

Brave New Worlds April 26, 2007

MAPPING A NEW TERRAIN

TONE HANSEN

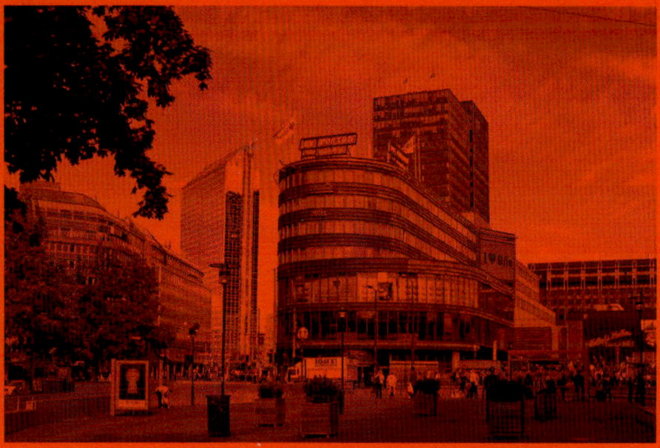

Writing a correspondent letter from Norway is bound to be a faltering business when one imagines the other stories and realities that will appear parallel to it. Norwegians can seem totally naïve seen from outside: We are all socialized into a social democracy, providing a contract between the citizen and the state so strong that we prefer to talk about a welfare society rather than a welfare state. "The welfare society is more than simply a political construct. It is more than social engineering. It is a reflection of how we see ourselves as a society,"[1] writes Victor D. Norman, the former conservative Norwegian Minister of Labor. Neither Norman nor members of the extreme right, populist Progress Party would ever admit that the consequences of their ideology would mean a dismantling of the state as we know it; they do everything to appear as social democrats, while efficiently and successfully concealing their neoliberal goals.

Thomas Hylland Eriksen, a professor of social anthropology at the University of Oslo, points to three fundamental dilemmas facing Norway when it comes to outsourcing today: 1.) The limits of solidarity—we don't want to do the dirty jobs, nor do we want to share our benefits with workers from abroad. In the coming years, Norway will need one hundred thirty thousand workers in health care; one heavily discussed solution to the problem is to import a skilled workforce from the so-called Third World. Another suggestion is to establish nursery schools in Africa in order to educate labor for Norwegian hospitals. The welfare state is being deterritorialized; 2.) The borders of a country are harder to define in a transnational time where, for instance, Norwegians expect the same social benefits and protection anywhere in the world. A large colony of Norwegian émigrés on the sunny coast of Málaga, Spain, opens their own schools, hospitals, and cafés, expecting the staff to speak Norwegian when working for Norwegians; and 3.) We have everything, but that's all we have: happiness is connected with hope. More than ever, a future-oriented, collective project is needed.[2] That is, if we desire a common national identity at all.

Outsourcing
Here we can add a fourth dilemma to the list. Until the early nineties, Norway's approach to reforms in the public sector had been very cautious. With the introduction of the New Public Management reform strategy in the eighties, these processes gained accelerating momentum. New Public Management comprises a shopping basket of reform solutions based on the outsourcing of previously public tasks, the parceling and deacquisition of public property and enterprises, and the subjection of unprofitable tasks to competition. There are many examples of long chains of interlinked cases of outsourcing of entities providing public services. In Norway, as many as seventy state administrative bodies have had their affiliation to government changed to external outsourcing. In short, business activities that are viewed as profitable are outsourced from state administrative bodies in order to make money, while the welfare services and cultural institutions are being outsourced in order to save money.

There are many differences between the reforms in government-owned companies and those in cultural institutions, but some shared characteristics are striking. So-called corporate-rational modes of operation have been implemented en masse, and new identities have been created for these institutions/companies. New needs for a comprehensive identity have resulted in a great number of new logo programs and presentation forms. The objective of such incentives is to create a "corporate identity" that applies both internally and externally. Norway has a mixed economy, where state and private interests blend. One would think this would discourage private investors, but that is not the case. The Norwegian economy is booming.

And here is a fifth dilemma: Outsourcing does not stop there. The huge petroleum and pension funds are invested and salted down in foreign investments, making Norway one of the most influential investors on the international market. It has become an imperialist country, with half the population, one way or another, living on benefits from the welfare state and with the foreign workforce doing the heavy work. This is also one of the reasons why Norway sees a need to reconfigure its national identity abroad. We are no longer one of the poorest countries in Europe; we are one of the richest. The need to build a nation state and to create a new identity—as was necessary in 1905 to differentiate Norway from Denmark and Sweden, and also to some extent in 1945 in order to build a modern society after the war—has been an issue for the previous shifting governments. How to advertise this nouveau riche country?

Peace Industry
Lack of obvious, common "Norwegian" values might be another reason for the former conservative government to set up a committee to develop a strategy to address the country's bad reputation, or its lack of reputation, abroad. Omdømmeutvalget, the governmental committee dealing with the perception of Norway abroad, delivered a report in 2004 outlining its strategy to market Norway as a country where culture, nature, peace, and innovation are tightly interwoven, and as a contrast to the international uproar caused by the Mohammed cartoons printed in newspapers both in Denmark and Norway.[3] The need to create consensus and peace is a problematic aspect of the social democracy, and this issue has been frequently discussed in light of the report. Peace and financial investments go hand in hand, and we should agree upon a set of values to be represented abroad. The strategy of Norway as a peace-giving country had its humble beginnings in the nineties when the efforts were mainly run by private organizations. Today peace has gained a privileged position in foreign diplomacy. As a country outside of the EU, Norway can claim neutrality. The newspaper Dagens Næringsliv goes as far as calling the Norwegian peace effort a "peace industry"; the country has been involved in peace negotiations with varying results in the Philippines, Colombia, Ache Province in Sumatra, Burundi, Guatemala, Haiti, Cyprus, Palestine, Sudan, and Uganda.

The expensive Nobel Peace Center was established in Norway in 2004 to educate and inform the public about peace negotiations all over the world and also to function as a tourist attraction. Half of its financing comes from the state, and half from sponsors such as Hydro, Telenor, Orkla, and Höeg—international investors in telecom, shipping, oil, and gas. When it comes to sponsor interest, nothing can beat a peace center. What better cause can you find in order to strengthen your profile internationally as well as at home? The Nobel Peace Center is as soft and harmless as any administrative agency. There is a constant lack of little else being produced other than a shell of a peace ideology, the content of which is hard to grasp. Their Internet pages are witness to this. It is like visiting a museum's Web site on which nothing is on display except the usual information about the shop, facilities rental, sponsors, and restaurants. The future is still white, bright, and safe at home. The conflict is outsourced.

Everything at an Arm's-Length Distance
When talking about the country's art policies and institutions, one must keep in mind that in Norway almost all institutions and support systems and artist grants are state-financed (there are exceptions, but they are of minor influence). The sociopolitical background for the Norwegian production of art is therefore ambivalent, and most support systems—with the exception of the newly established Office for Contemporary Art (OCA)—prevent Norwegian

art from becoming more than a domestic affair. On the one hand, the state is tightening its grip on institutions through content incentives and a larger expectation of culture's instrumental function in society when it comes to inclusion and education. On the other hand, there is the usual demand for more external income and larger visitor numbers. This might seem somewhat paradoxical, but often state interest in art is instrumental, and the argument for the role of art in society often equals requests for large numbers of visitors and spectacular events as well as a focus on both national heritage and cultural diversity, and so on.

The question is, to what extent have recent changes within society also influenced artistic production and arts institutions? And how does the art world respond to recent changes? Is the rigid and consensus-seeking structure of the social democracy capable of providing space for a multitude of voices, or do we need to find ways of altering the democratic ideal in order to maintain the new and heterogeneous situation that we are facing? This is a difficult and perhaps provocative yet important set of questions to ask today, since art institutions seem to be the among the first to adapt to new "rules of the game" in order to secure funding rather than oppose such changes. This might be the case because the possible dynamic between art and politics has not been examined recently—there is simply too much to lose. The art market is not the big bad wolf in Norway; it still has a minor influence on art production. A new class of cultural bureaucrats with ambitions of their own, many lacking professional artistic knowledge, is rapidly gaining power within the state-supported art institutions. This bureaucracy has proved to be far more obedient to state interests (and therefore also commercial interests) than the traditional skilled cultural worker.

This (quite local) situation for cultural institutions has come about as a result of a major museum reform program that has changed the landscape significantly. The reform plan merges art and cultural museums into larger units to create better, stronger, and more coherent professional communities that, in theory, are intended to be independent bodies with a greater degree of self-governance. However, self-governance is a debatable term in this context since the reform program is controlled and supported by a relatively new bureaucratic body, the Norwegian Archive, Library and Museum Authority (ABM-Utvikling), founded January 1, 2003. The ABM-Utvikling is an outsourced, bureaucratic organ made in order to outsource and merge museums and libraries. The agency has so far reduced the number of museums from two hundred seventy state-supported institutions to ninety-seven private foundations still financed by the state. Do you get it? There is no way the state is giving up either its support or its control over the institutions, but they have, to a larger degree, created a longer arm's-length distance between the government and the museums. This makes the governmental bureaucracy smaller, and the merged museums significantly more bureaucratic.

For example, the National Museum for Art, Architecture and Design was established in Oslo in 2003 as the result of the consolidation of five independent institutions into a single private foundation as part of museum reform. The National Museum of Art comprises the former Norwegian Museum of Architecture, the former Museum of Decorative Arts and Design, the former Museum of Contemporary Art, and the former National Gallery. Today, these names only exist as designations of the actual buildings; the old logos have been removed, and new job descriptions and titles have been implemented as well as a new hierarchical structure that leaves much responsibility to the single director. These processes can be characterized as outsourcing and merger in one single operation. All systems have expenses, and synergy effects might very well appear as a result within larger units, but imagine: Oslo is the largest city in Norway with five hundred thousand inhabitants. We had five independent institutions located around town—now we have one.

Heterogeneity?

This is an important fact, as we are facing a multifaceted cultural situation that is not reflected in the large, state-run cultural institutions' programs that tend to include diversity only as an exotic exception. One reason might be that social democracy is based on a homogeneous, unifying identity. One country, one people, one flag. As a cure, Norway is now copying the Swedes, and 2008 has been set to be the year of diversity. A white woman in her fifties has been hired as the director. These questions are: how do we identify diversity: and is a year of celebration enough? This is one of the most important questions to ask now, as the social democratic system must be improved in order to meet with today's heterogeneous realities. Statistics tell one side of reality: the immigrant population in Norway constitutes 8.3 percent, or three hundred eighty-six thousand people, from more than two hundred countries. Oslo has the largest group, comprising 23 percent of the population.[4] Diversity is not a single phenomenon/group, but rather an exchange among individuals/identities occurring at the micro-level below the radar of the political system. This issue is not only relevant in terms of the multiparty political system's division of the population into identifiable groups and shopping centers' construction of fictitious identities to attract moneyed groups and tourists, but also with regard to museums being required to reflect diversity as if it were a homogeneous entity.

Institutions, whether cultural or others, that are designed to create a representative image of the nation's cultural capital, internally and externally, produce hierarchies. While inclusion into these is attractive, their very existence also causes exclusion. When nations dedicate a year to a cause, it might be taken into consideration that diversity comes about on a small-scale exchange.

At the same time, it is welcome news that in the recent debate on the meaning of the terms "culture" and "diversity," the Cultural Committee of the Norwegian Parliament recently voted down the Progressive Party's proposal for the creation of a national artistic canon. The rationale was that such a canon would be an obstacle to diversity. The canon lives on inside us at any rate, programmed by the culture in which we live, but it should not be followed slavishly. Artistic and cultural canons can easily come across as parodic, since they refer to a culture that has never been homogeneous or belonged to a national state. "Politics are international . . . art is transnational," says Jan Brockmann, former director of the Museum of Contemporary Art.[5] The same holds true for diversity. ■

NOTES

1. Victor D. Norman, "Crumbling from Within?: The Microfoundations of Welfare States," in Art of Welfare, Marta Kuzma and Peter Osborne, eds. (Oslo: Office for Contemporary Art, 2006), 96.

2. Thomas Hylland Eriksen, "We Have Everything, But That's All We Have; Outsourcing the Welfare States," in Art of Welfare, 96.

3. "Nyskapende i samspill med naturen" ("Innovative in Tune with Nature"), final report by Omdømmeutvalget, http://odin.dep.no/filarkiv/275674/Nyskapende_i_samspill_internett.pdf, accessed April 2007.

4. Statistisk sentralbyrå (Statistic Norway), http://www.ssb.no/, accessed April 2007.

5. See "The First Director of the Museum," in Tone Hansen, Megamonstermuseum: How to Imagine a Museum of Today? (Oslo: Torpedo Press, 2007), 221 (in Norwegian).

IMAGES

page 103 City square near Madou Plaza, the European Commission's headquarters in Brussels, Belgium, 2006

page 107 Page from the New York Times, May 4, 2007

vould like to see more political
age in the news pages. "I might
nore emphasis on Washington,"
aid. He's not a huge fan of the
day Journal begun in 2005, but
ould continue it and look at con-
ng its Pursuits section into a
y weekend magazine to com-
with The New York Times Sun-
Magazine.
d while he's no technology geek,
so said he regularly reads the
's technology columnist, Wal-
Mossberg, although he added: "I

He insists he won't meddle in the journalism or slash-and-burn the staff. "We're not coming in with a bunch of cost-cutters," he said, but added: "I'm not saying it's going to be a holiday camp for everybody."

In an interview in his eighth-floor office in Midtown Manhattan yesterday, Mr. Murdoch, who occasionally glanced at his notes on a yellow tablet, waxed on about his plans to in-

Continued on Page 6

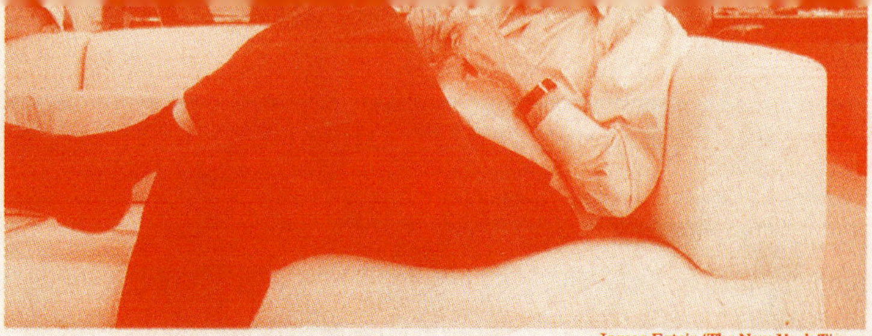

James Estrin/The New York Times

"I'm sometimes frustrated by the long stories," Rupert Murdoch says.

confider
deals, in
of the T
The ju
fiz Muh
who wo
gy bank
accused
banker
about de
publicly
The
traded
counts
himself.
well-kno
Pakista
the part
million,
The
crimina
late yest
ed State
hattan
change C
Mr. N
who live
rested
Suisse
Park in
returnin
trip to P
close to t
He wa
reau of
Lower
emerged
white sh
a federa

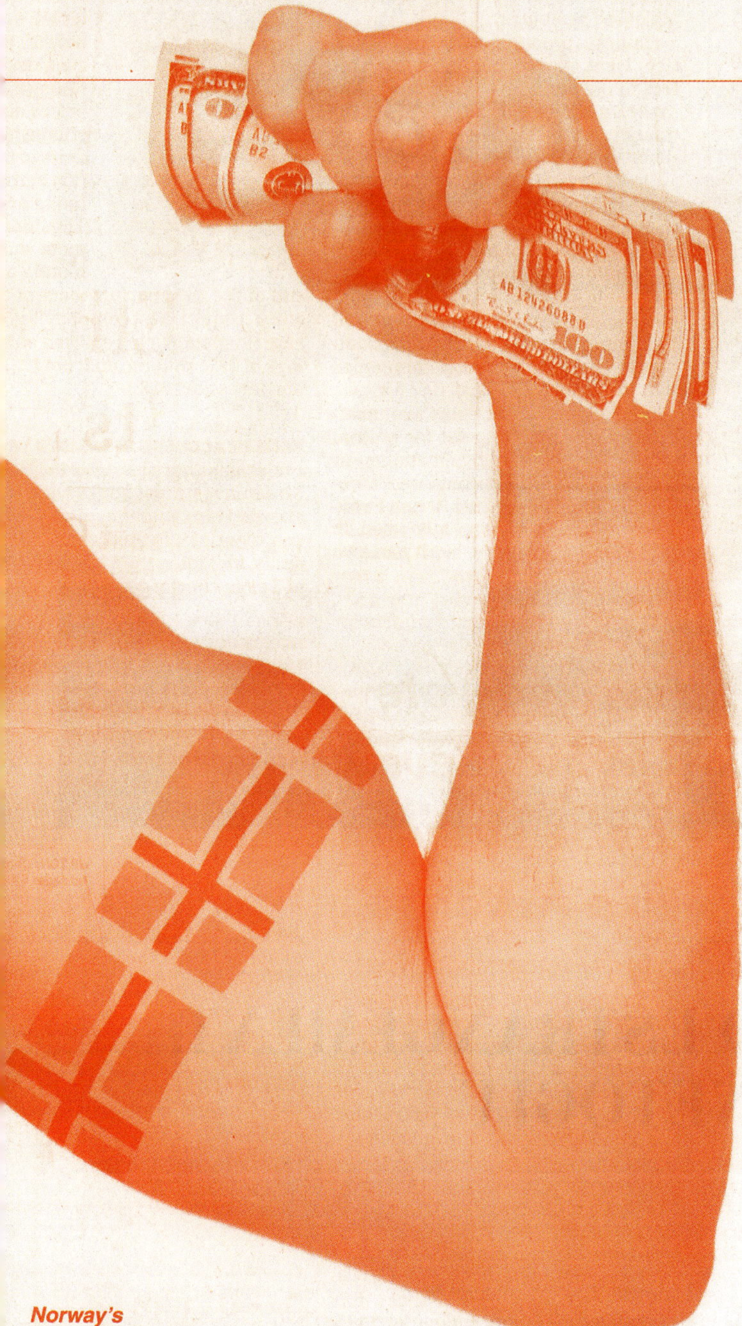

Norway Backs Its Ethics With Its Cash

Investing Vast Oil Profits, It Snubs Foreign Companies On Moral Grounds

By MARK LANDLER

OSLO — For a people whose deep national pride is in bestowing the Nobel Peace Prize, Norwegians are developing a reputation for throwing some sharp elbows.

And they are doing so in an unexpected way: by pulling investments out of Wal-Mart and other big companies like Boeing and Lockheed Martin for what they say are ethical failings.

Norway has amassed a fortune of more than $300 billion over the last decade, thanks to its profits from oil exports. Yet few countries are more ambivalent about their vast wealth than this modest, socially conscious society of less than five million people.

So rather than managing their monstrous nest egg simply for the best returns, the reluctant billionaires of Norway are using the money to advance an ambitious ethical code they established in 2004 for their oil reserve, known as the Government Pension Fund.

Norway's investment choices have become a focus of attention in the last nine months over the exclusion of Wal-Mart, the American retailer whose big-box stores do not exist in this pristine country.

Public pension funds on both sides of the Atlantic commonly avoid investing in certain companies on social or ethical grounds. But it is rare for a sovereign state to make such judgments, and rarer still for one to do it in the pointed, public way that Norway has.

Among the first companies to run afoul of Norway's standards were makers of cluster bombs and nuclear weapons or related components — a list that includes General Dynamics and Northrop Grumman, in addition to Boeing and Lockheed Martin.

Then last June, Norway added Wal-Mart Stores to its blacklist, alleging that the retailer was guilty of tolerating child-labor violations by its suppliers in the developing world and obstructing unions at home. The fund sold off more

Continued on Page 4

Norway's Government Pension Fund cites the following ethical concerns for not investing in these companies:

CLUSTER WEAPONS OR RELATED PRODUCTION
Alliant Techsystems *U.S.*
General Dynamics *U.S.*
L-3 Communications Holdings *U.S.*
Lockheed Martin *U.S.*
Poongsan Corp. *South Korea*
Raytheon *U.S.*
Thales *France*

ENVIRONMENTAL DAMAGE
Freeport McMoRan Copper and Gold *U.S.*
DRD Gold *South Africa*

HUMAN RIGHTS
Wal-Mart Stores, Wal-Mart de Mexico *U.S.*

LAND MINES
Singapore Technologies Engineering *Singapore*

NUCLEAR WEAPONS OR RELATED PRODUCTION
BAE Systems *Britain*
Boeing *U.S.*
EADS, EADS Finance *European consortium*
Finmeccanica *Italy*
Honeywell International *U.S.*
Northrop Grumman *U.S.*
Safran *France*
United Technologies *U.S.*

Illustration by The New York Times

Nex
Fro
Cos

By
The lo
tha Stew
tends in
furniture
and even
Now th
tic is tur
to perha
all: groc
Beginn
name —
a line of
zen food
largest w
The pa
day, coul
art's app
ils that
fore enco
After a
spoil in th
Ms. S
from sou
syndicate
ducing a
exactly i
So why
zen dinne
One ob
to impr
pointing
Costco w
first-qua
showed a
wider tha
same qua
Althou

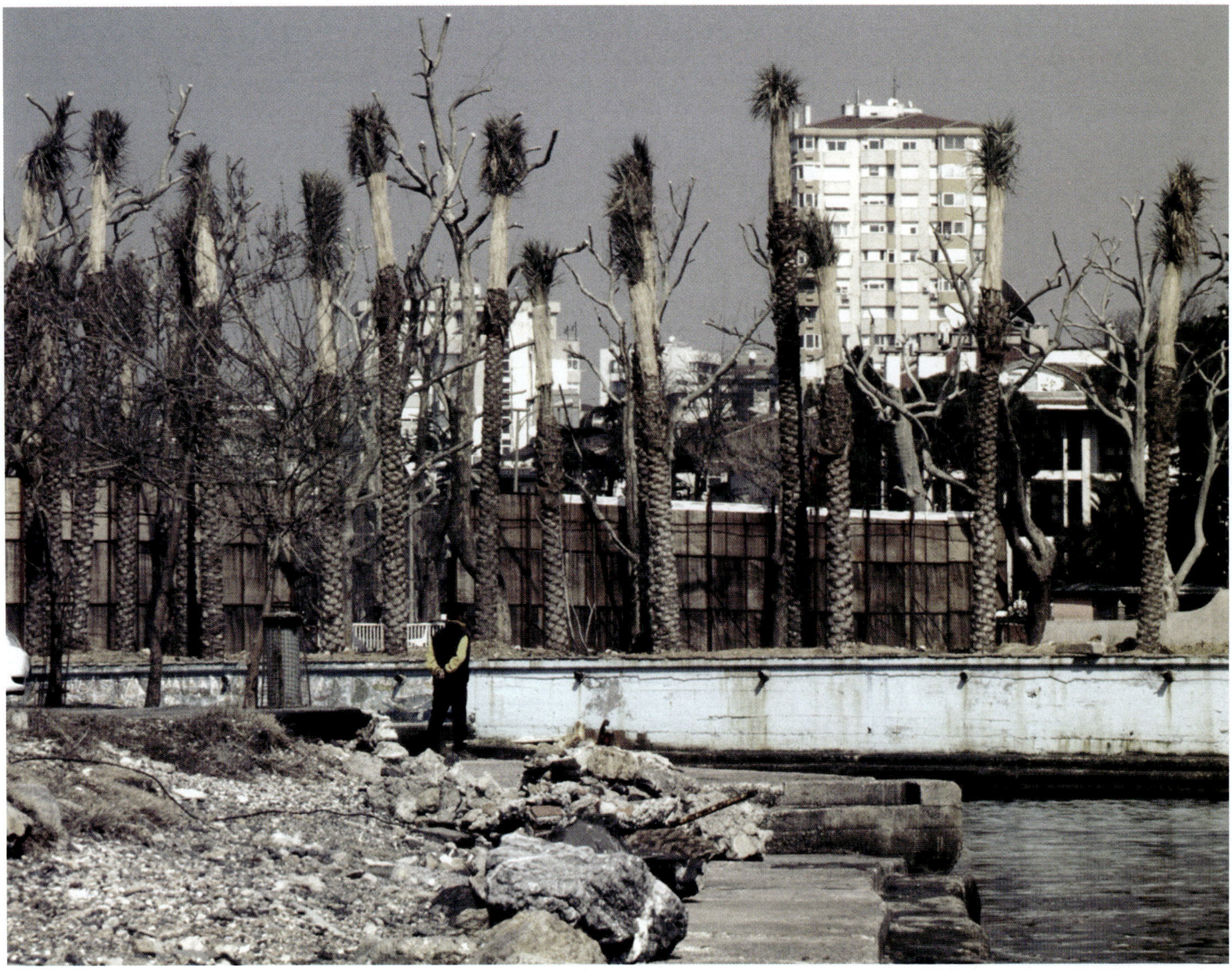

Stills from *Are There Any Palm Trees in Grozny?* 2005 video (color, silent)

DISPLACEMENT AND ESTRANGEMENT: BANU CENNETOĞLU

Born in Turkey, 1970. Lives and works in Istanbul.

The spaces that Banu Cennetoğlu photographs have a restrictive quality to them. Her explorations of displacement and estrangement have taken her into environments of intense mental and physical isolation infused with psychological weight—detention centers, refugee camps, and abandoned buildings. The ambiguity that arises from her images adds to the mysterious nature of the sites as if confirming the deviant purpose of their social and political role in the construction of "order" and the enforcement of the law. In her artist's book *False Witness* (2003), she focused on the notion of measuring truth and fairness. The volume opens with a list of phrases compiled from a corpus-based database that presents the word "measure" in a variety of configurations emphasizing its semantic relationship to order, ethics, and justice. Accompanying the text are thirty-two photographs shot over a period of five years that include outdoor sites in France and Ecuador as well as interior views of such places as a registration center for asylum seekers in Ter Apel, the Netherlands. The imagery, which ranges from arid landscapes to carpeted conference rooms to close-up portraits, emanates a sense of impenetrability and is occasionally obstructed by natural or man-made barriers that demark terrain between inside and outside, alluding to the vulnerable state of the immigrant or refugee.

The span of Cennetoğlu's work goes beyond the discipline of photography into the realm of sculpture and printed matter, where she adapts methods from the fields of psychology and architecture to stage her own system of examination and interrogation. In recent years, she has sometimes displayed her photographs in cramped, dimly lit corridors that echo the claustrophobic ambiance of a prison cell, a hallway in a governmental building, or a secret passage. Taking control of the viewer's gaze and

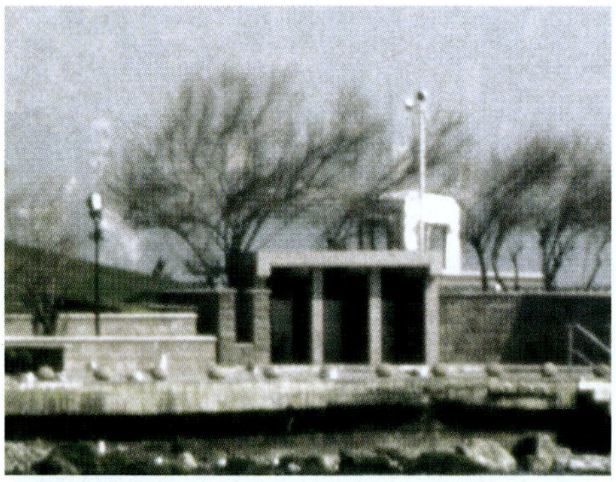
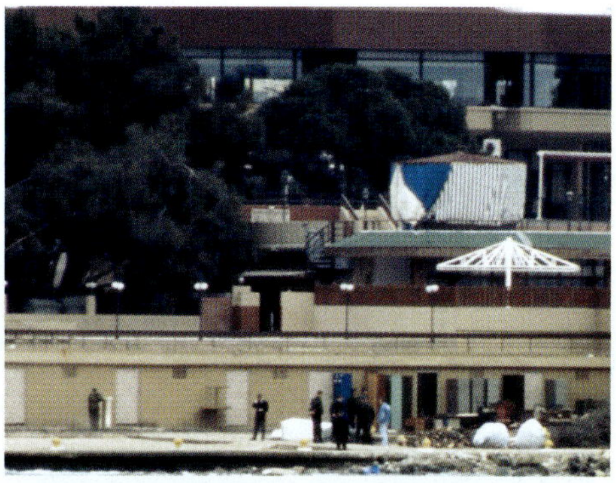
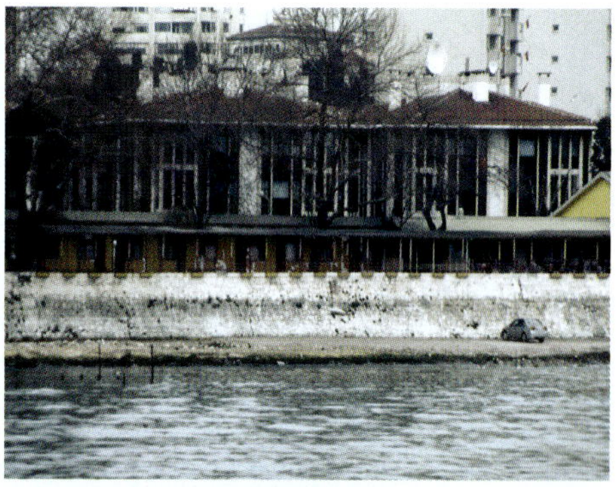
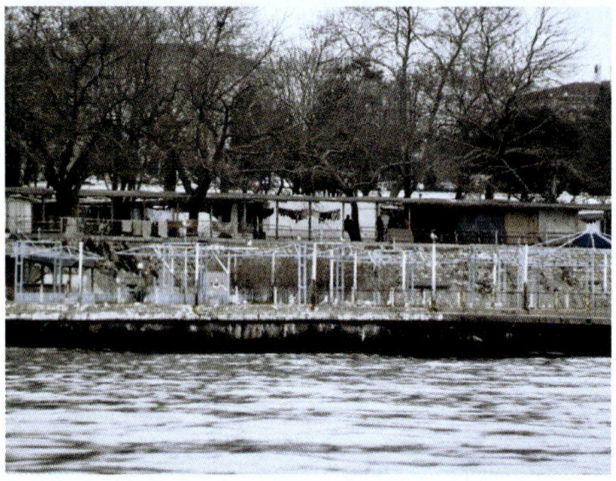
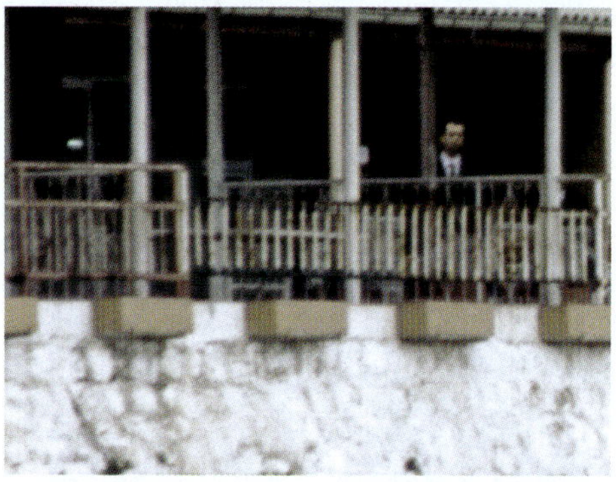
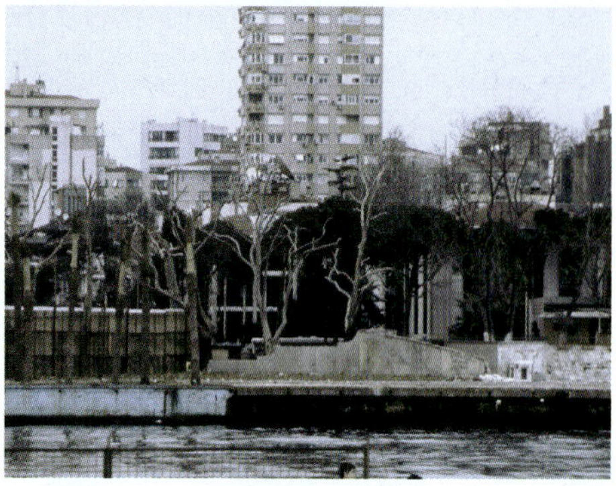
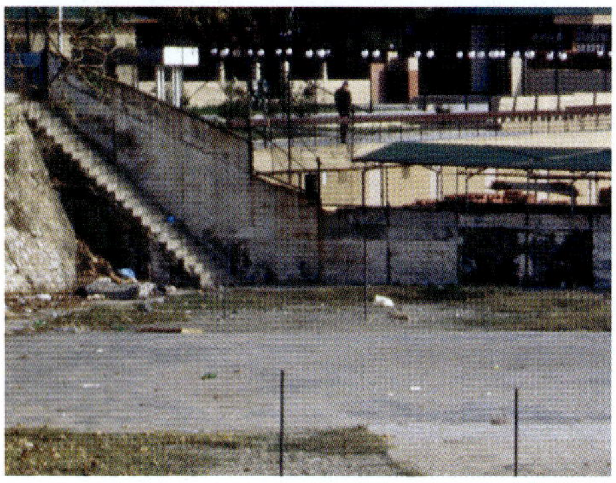
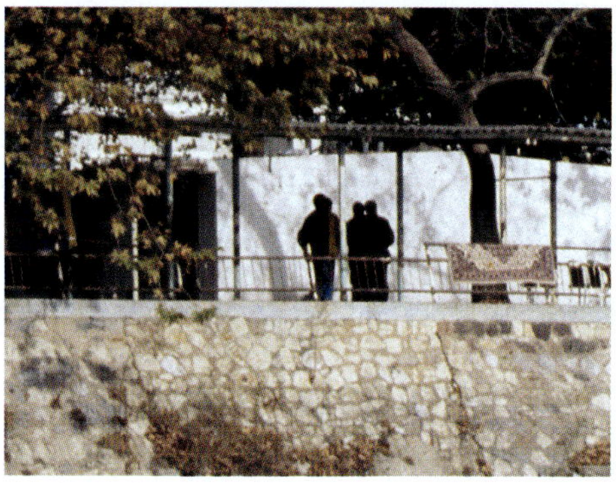
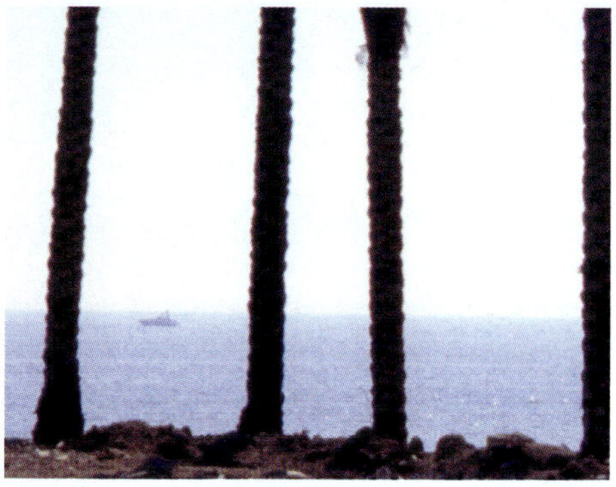

movement, she reaffirms the emotional and physical restraints of her subjects and reproduces their sense of vulnerability for the spectator. Stripped of any illusion of individuality, spectators must abandon their sense of autonomy and coexist in harmony with the people standing on either side of them within this artificial limbo. This play of power repeats in the installation *Determined Barbara* (2002–2004), which consists of thirty-two photographs from Banja Luka (the de facto capital of and largest city in the newly formed Republic of Srpska) and the Glamoc Valley in Bosnia and Herzegovina. From these images emerge desolate roads and off-limits sites that symbolize the displacement of the region's prewar residents whose villages have been used as training grounds for NATO's Stabilization Force (SFOR) since 1998. In an ironic twist of fate, these people—most of whom are farmers—have been denied the right to return to their land and have thus become refugees in their own country by the direct intervention of the agencies who were there to protect them. Less concerned with providing a clear narrative, Cennetoğlu constructs an experience aimed at measuring a state of mind that takes the problems of distance and apathy to their origins as each visitor is forced to walk through the unsettling hallway and negotiate a way out. As the artist has said, her work "raises questions about photography and especially the production and distribution of information."[1]

YR

1. Antonia and Miriam Garcia Castro Perier, "Art has the power of its undefinability," in *Cultures & Conflicts Sociologie Politique de l'international*, http://www.conflicts.org/document1865.html.

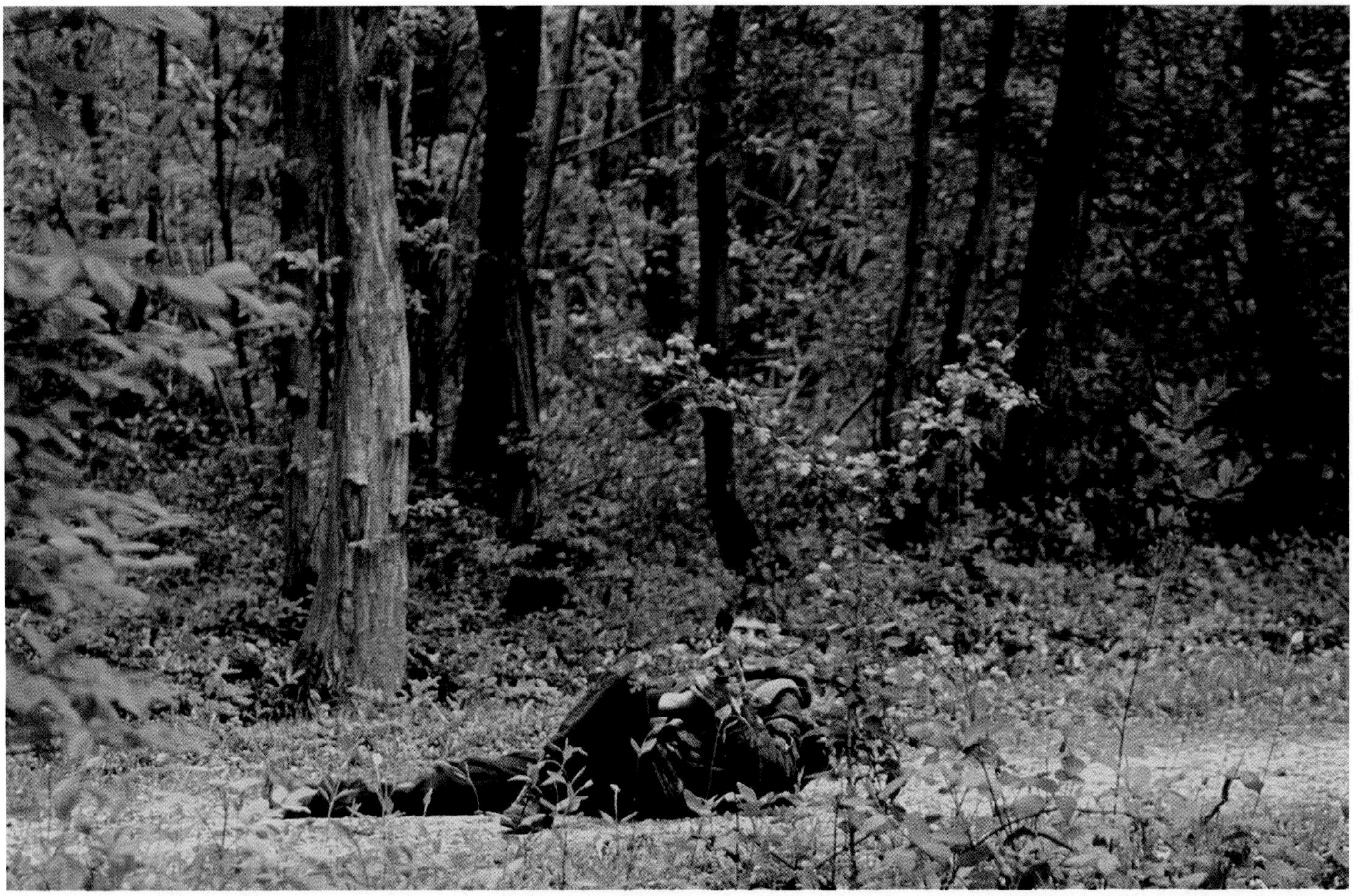

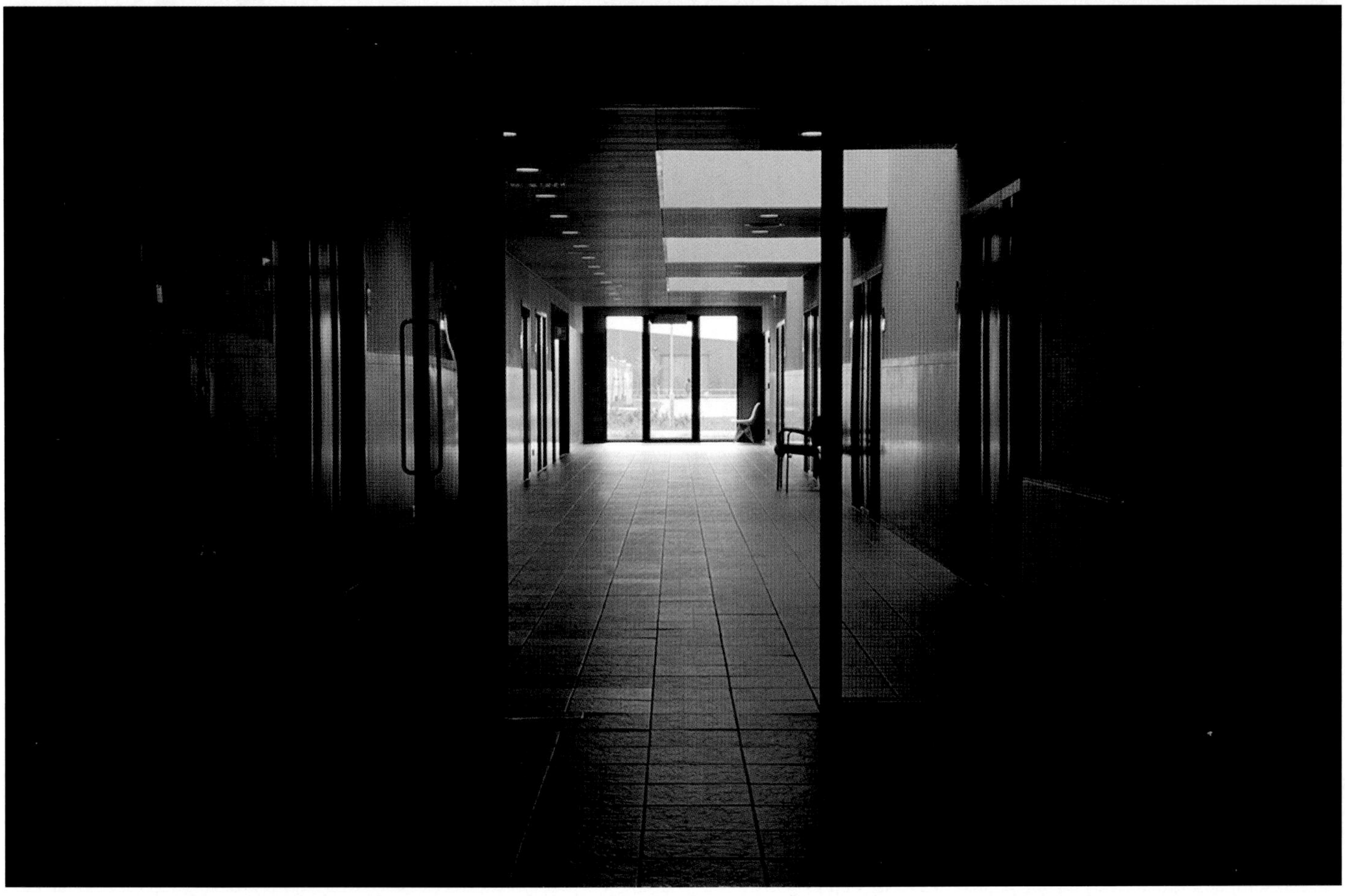

Selections from the book *False Witness* 2003 offset prints

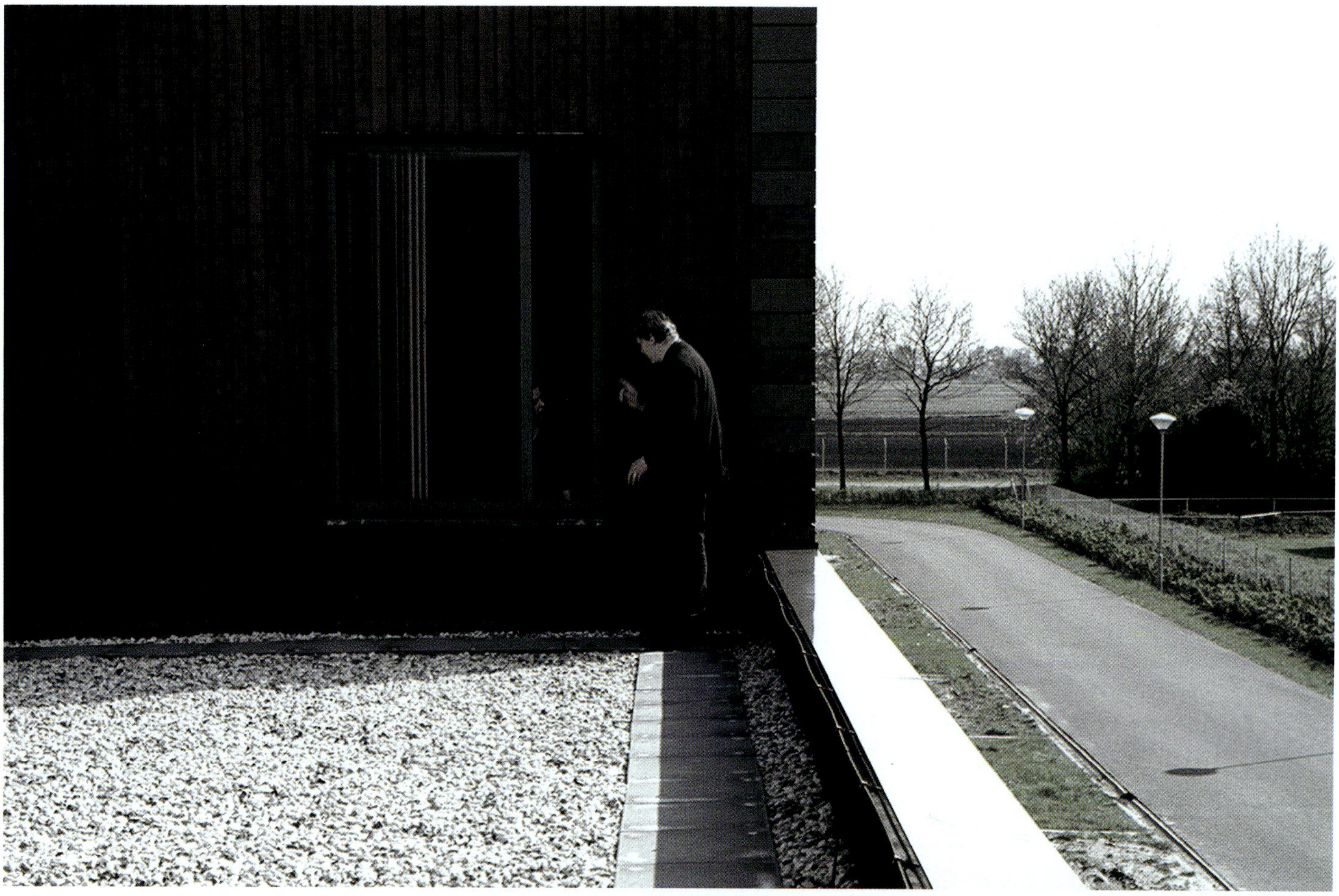

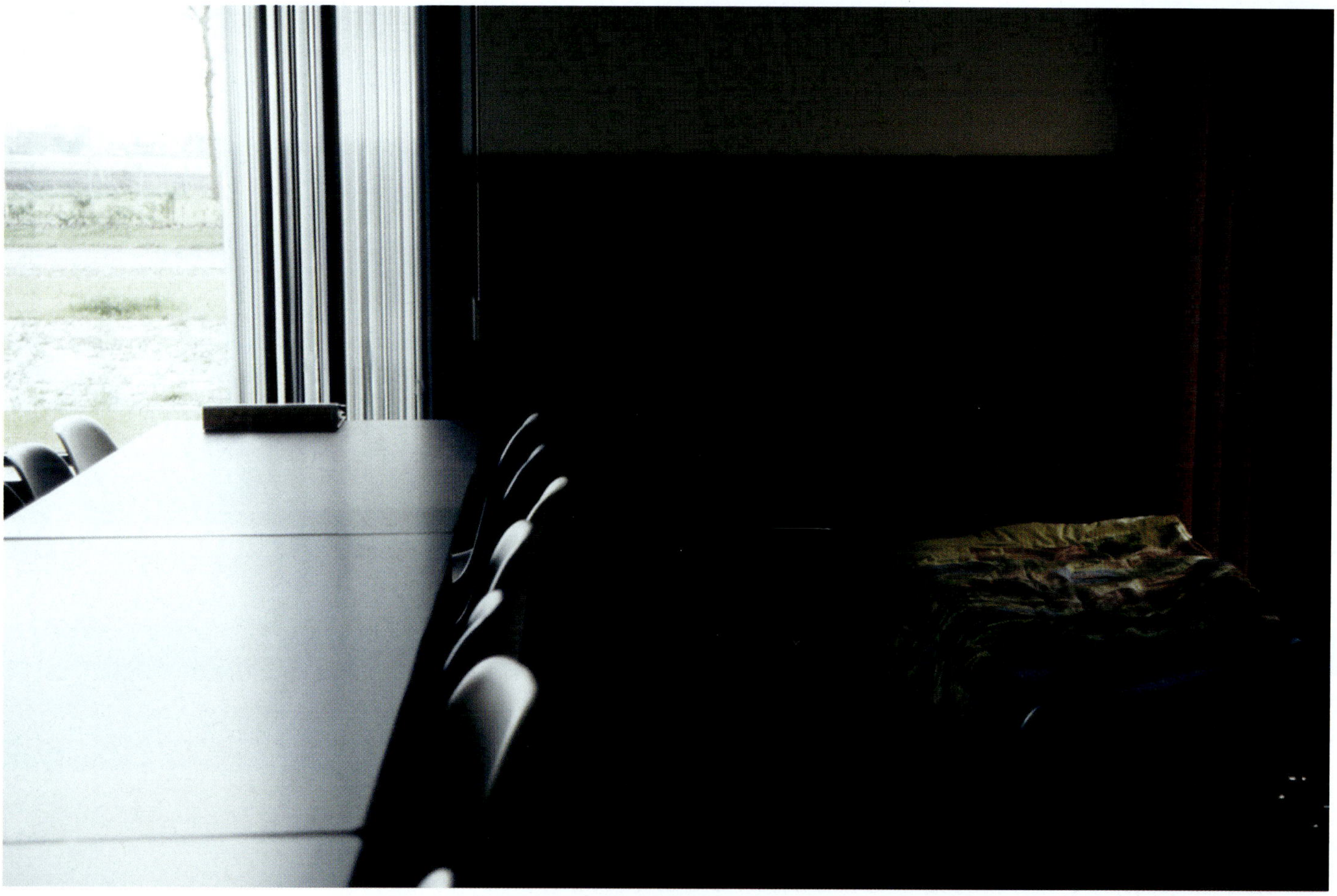

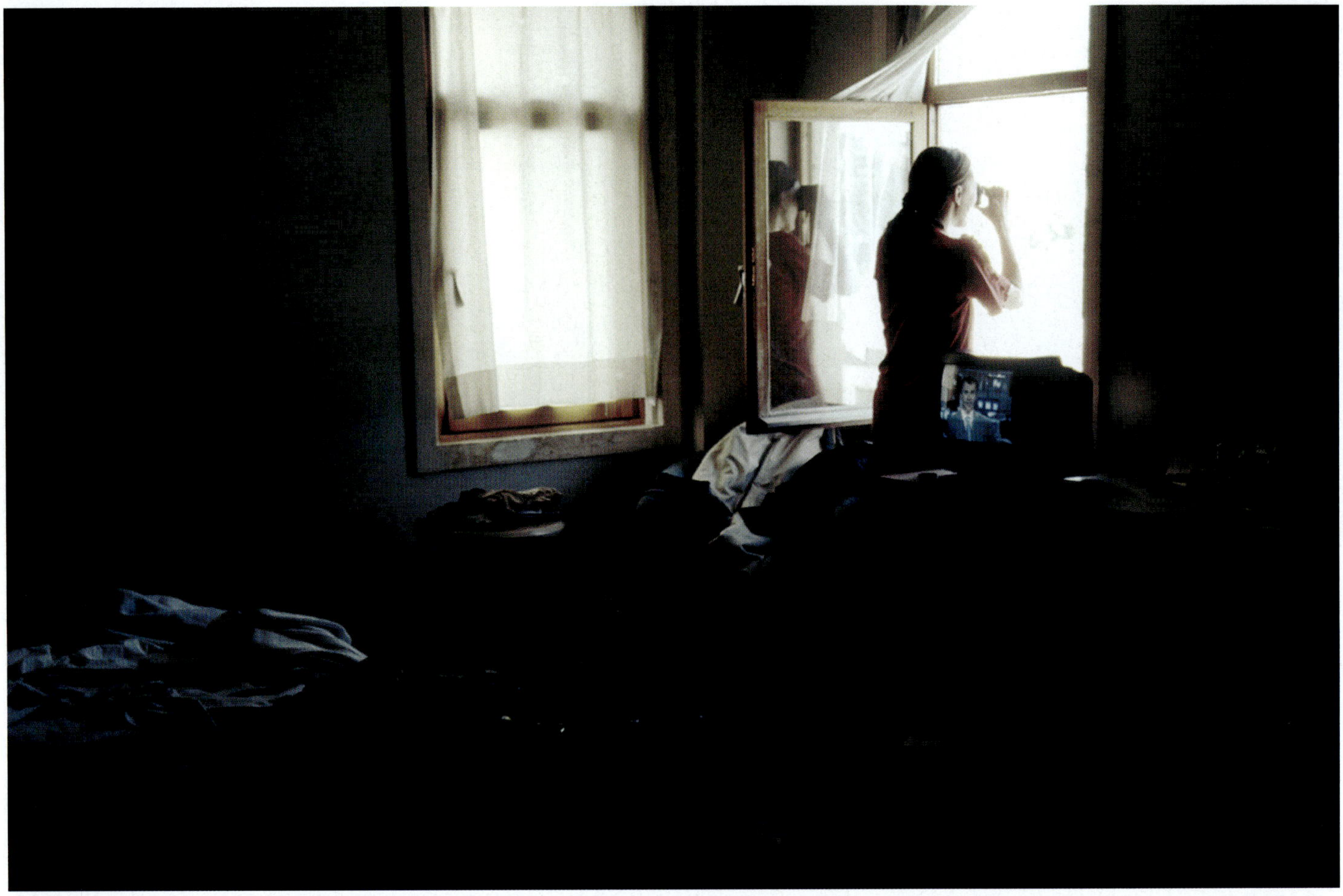

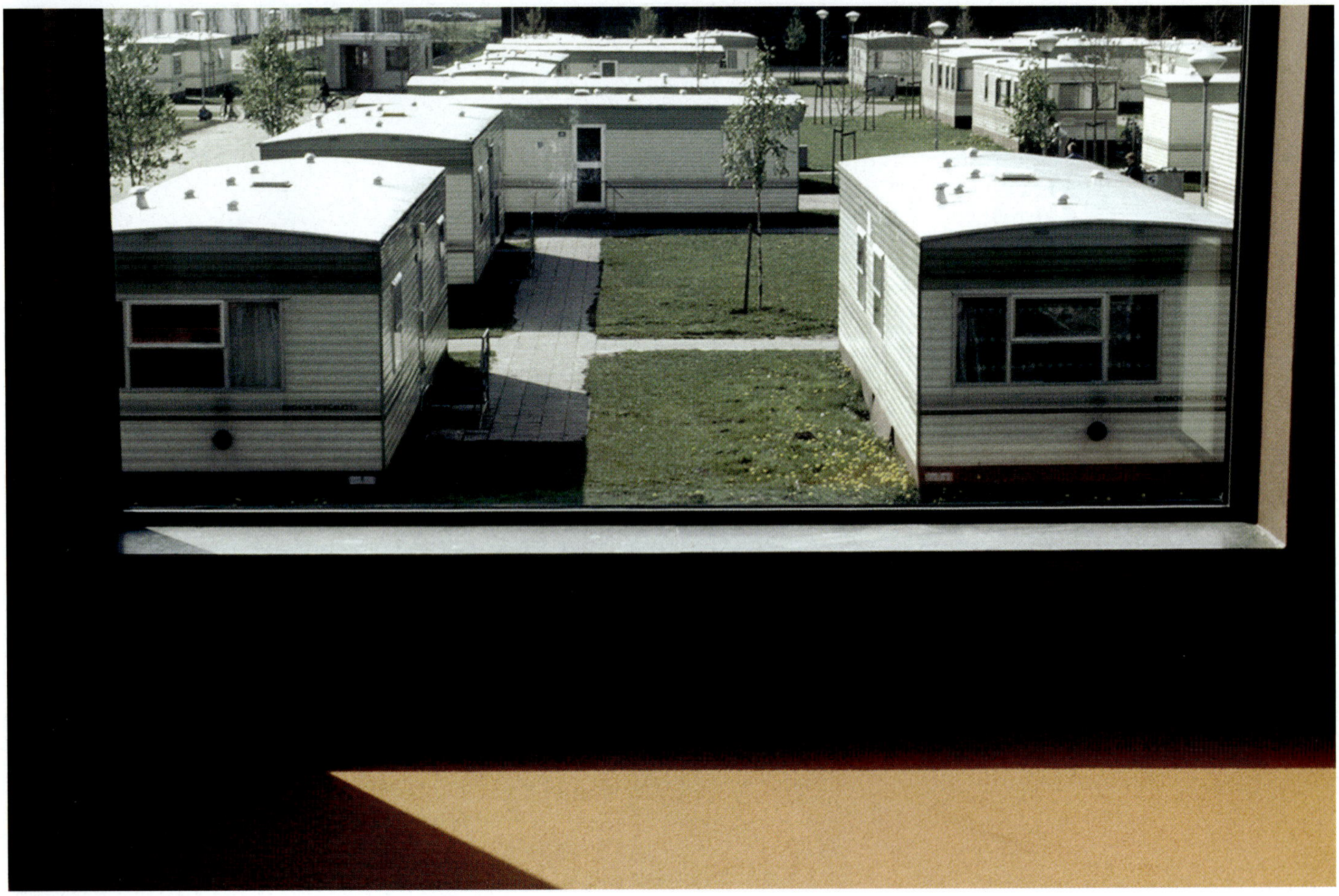

Selections from the book *False Witness* 2003 offset prints

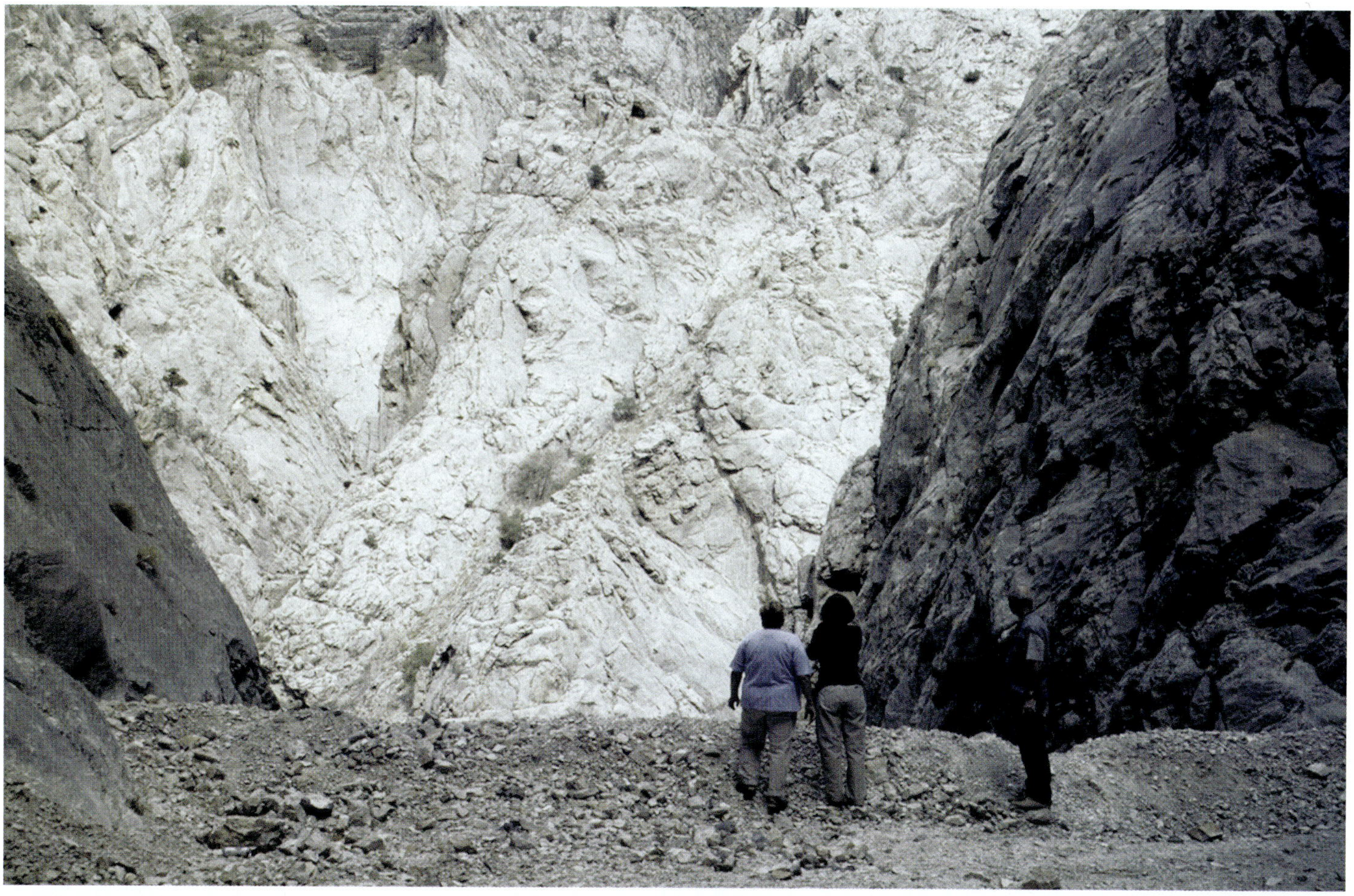

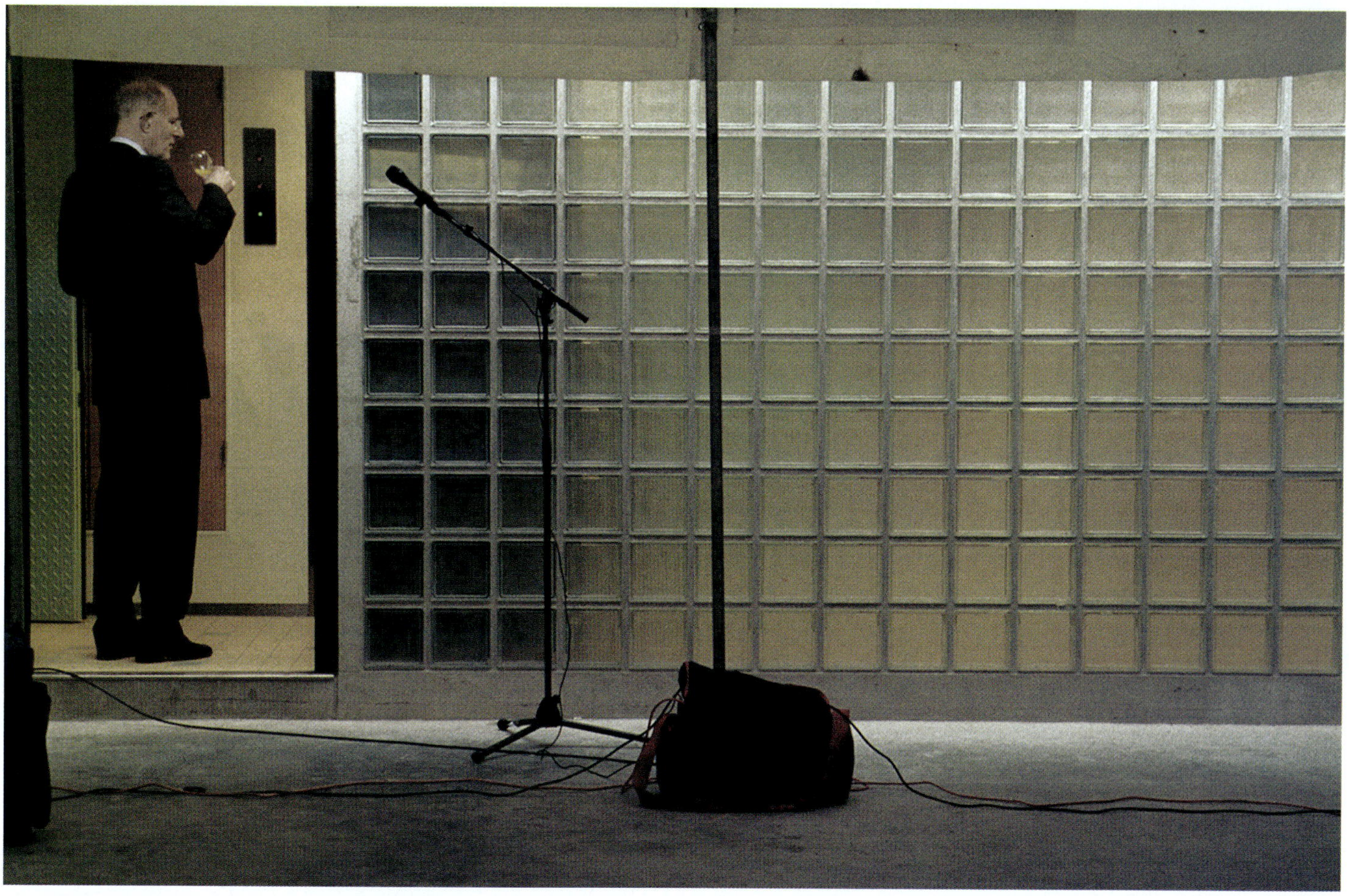

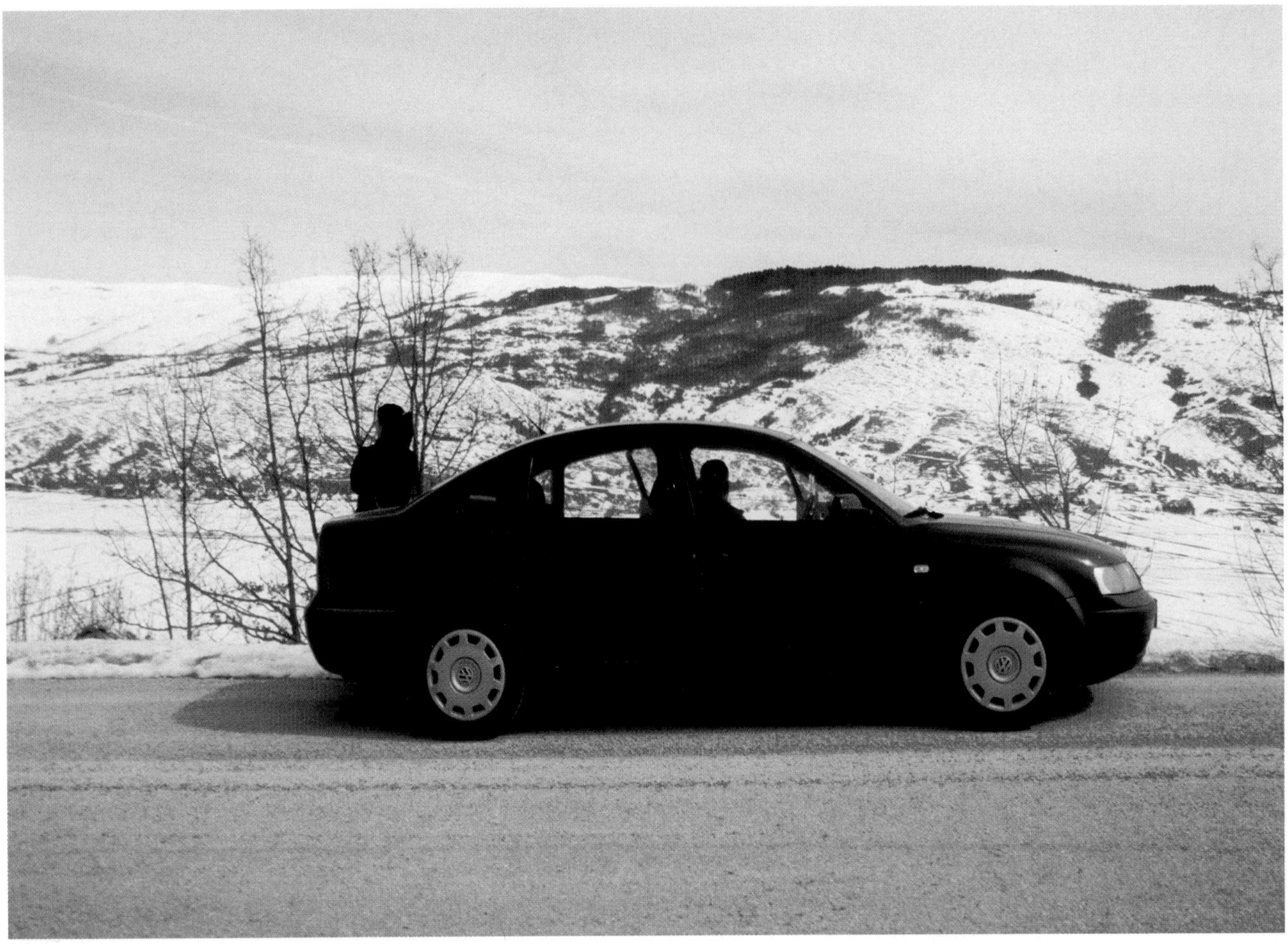

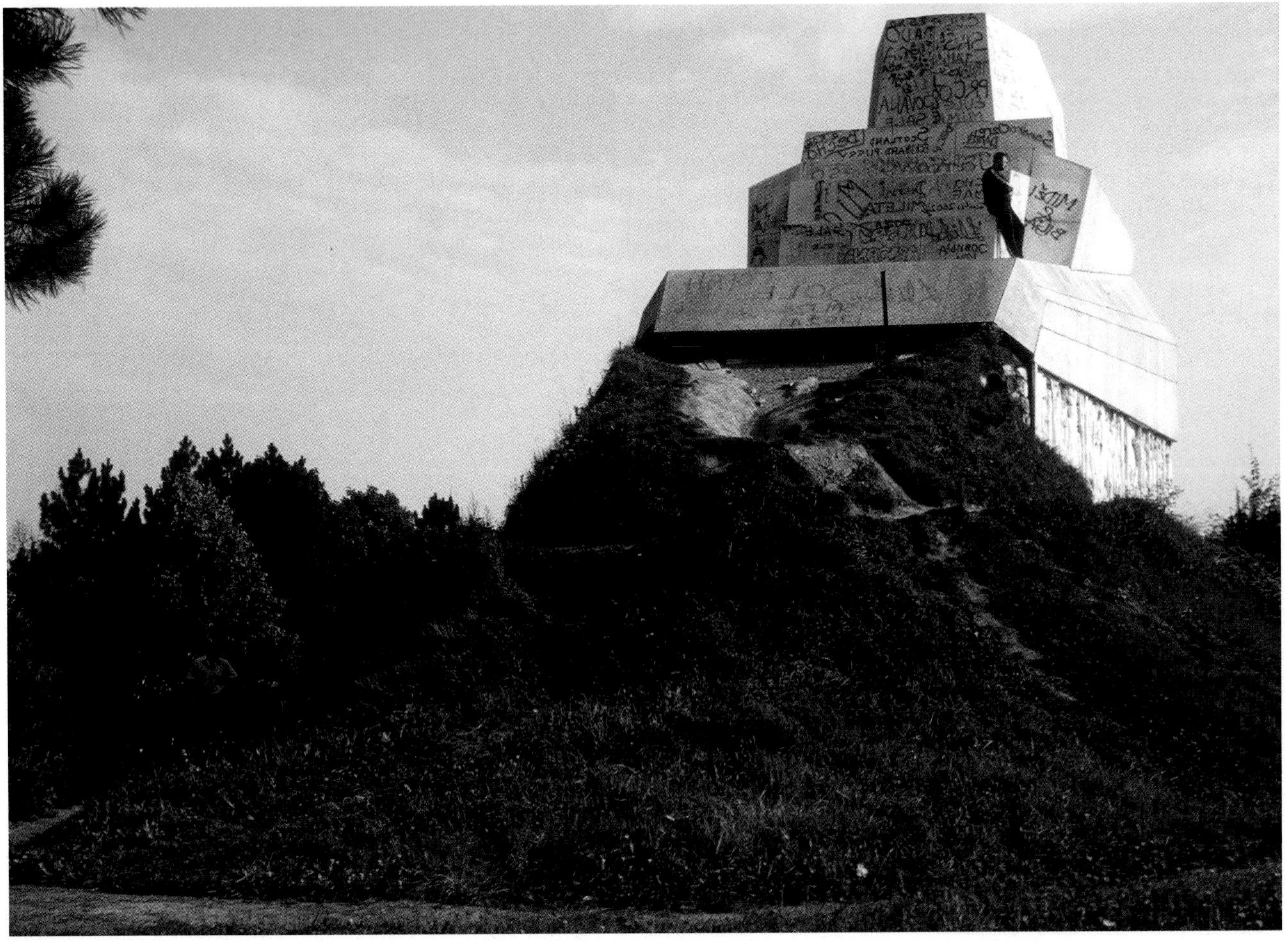

Selections from *Determined Barbara* 2002–2004 ink-jet prints on paper; series of 32

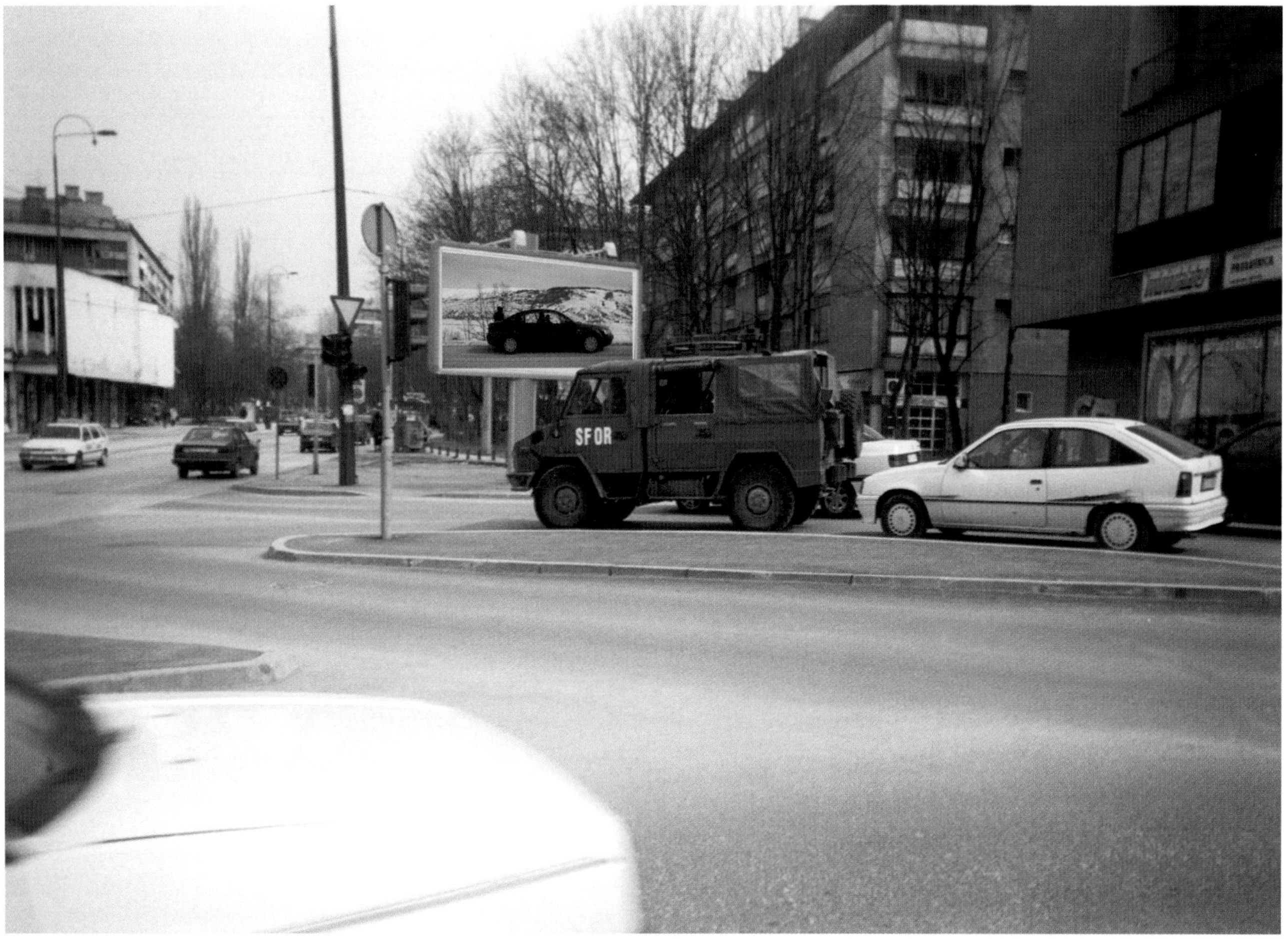
SFOR

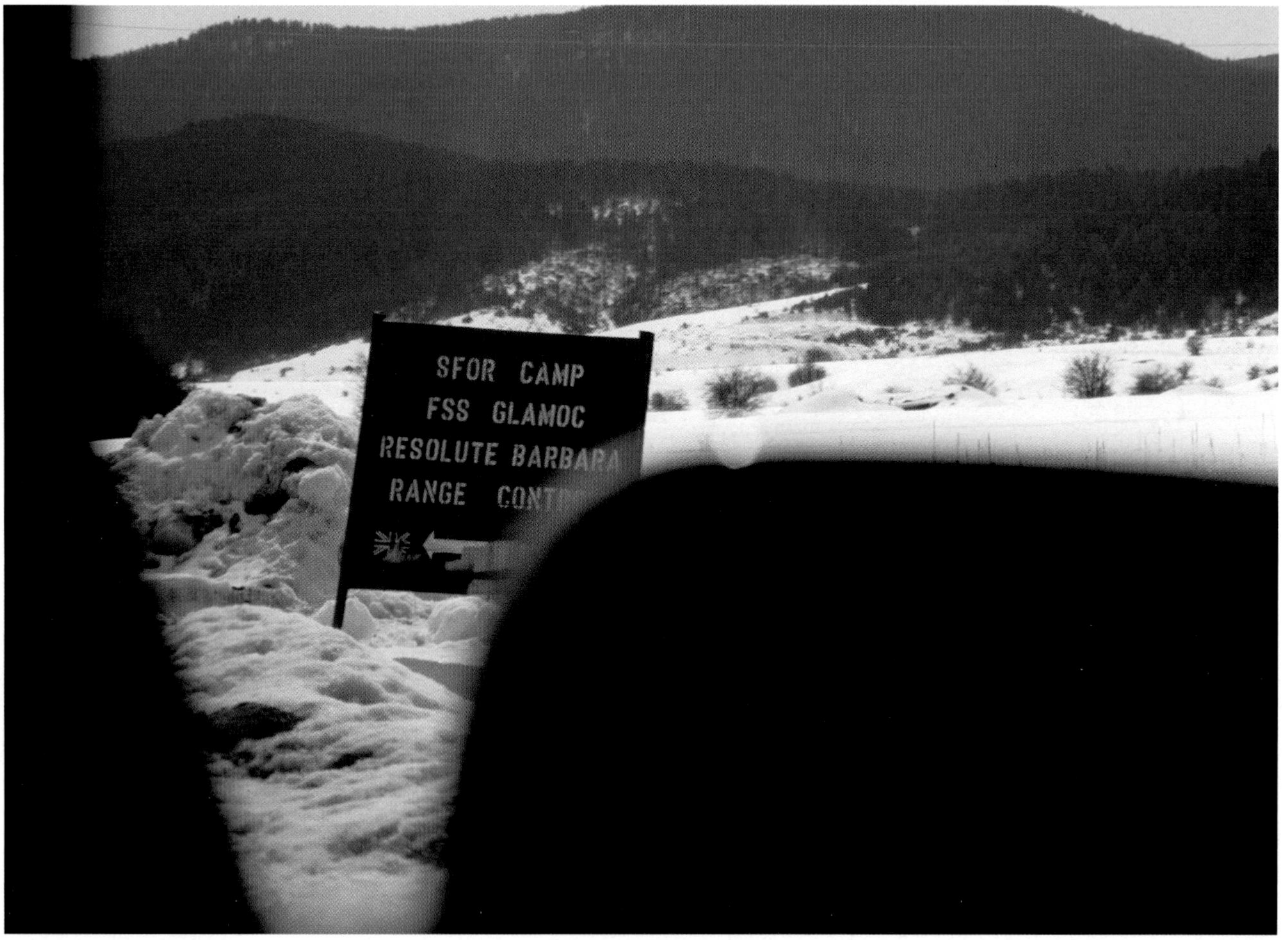
SFOR CAMP
FSS GLAMOC
RESOLUTE BARBARA
RANGE

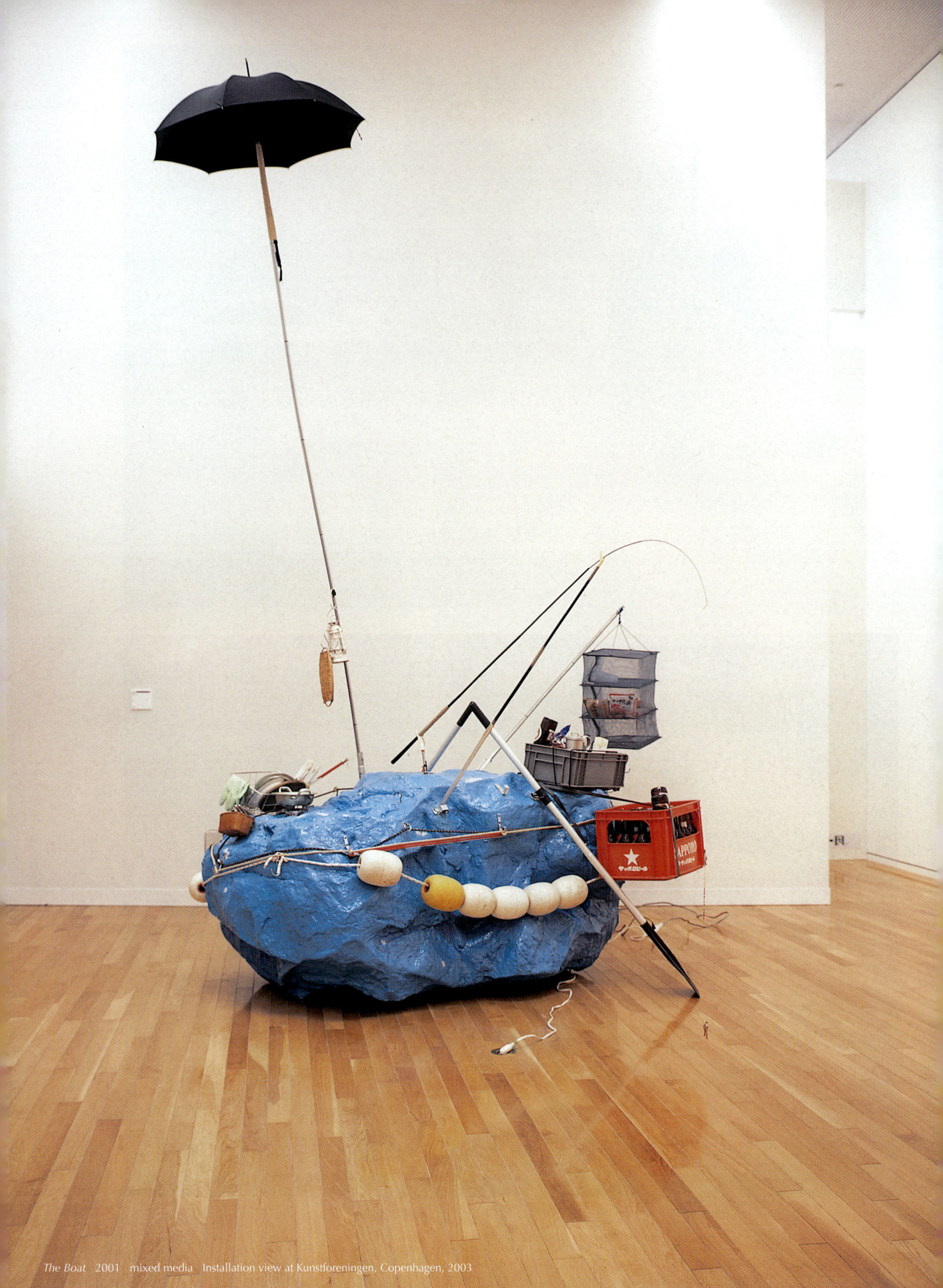

The Boat 2001 mixed media Installation view at Kunstforeningen, Copenhagen, 2003

GIMHONGSOK'S CHEATING ART

Born in South Korea, 1964. Lives and works in Seoul.

"*Traduttore, Traditore.*" This famous Italian adage, which is customarily translated as "A translator is a traitor," could very well describe Gimhongsok's abiding artistic concern and working methodology. His practice, which freely crosses between text-based work and image- and object-making, mines the lacunae and incommensurabilities that occur in transfers between languages, cultures, and contexts. There also is a generous dose of the artist's humor—sometimes verging on acerbic cynicism—arising from thinking processes and scenarios that unfold in surreal and even absurdist ways. Many of his projects are developed through translation or interpretation: "My attempts often generate another kind of communicative practice, which confuses the initial intention and eventually causes further alienation. I am not inclined to resolve such confusion and alienation, nor do I desire to know the reason why it happened."[1] Translation is also the method he employs to unpack the state of confusion that plagues and defines the culture and society in which he lives. The work of Gimhongsok, who was trained at Seoul National University in South Korea and the Kunstakademie in Düsseldorf, Germany, can then be seen as generally addressing, or at least departing from, the peculiar nature of his own country, whose modern identity has been shaped by many conflicting forces: its hybrid spiritual and cultural landscape; its delayed start on modernization; and its sudden catapult to the forefront of technology, industry, and global economy.

Gimhongsok's *G5* (2004) is a video of five people singing, one at a time, the national anthems of the United States, England, France, Russia, and Japan, with lyrics translated into Korean. While each of the performers—some trained singers, others not—carries out the task with due seriousness, the overall effect is one of strange suspension between the identifiable and the foreign. The title of the work derives from the so-called Group of Eight (G8).[2] While the name G8 is for many a synonym for the injustices and inequalities brought on by globalization, Gimhongsok's "Group of Five" makes a more specific reference to the foreign powers that have been particularly influential and instrumental in Korea's modern history via their roles in Christianization, colonization, and Cold War–era conflict and containment. The artist also frequently invents historical narratives that are wholly fallacious but whose deadpan deliveries often confound viewers into believing them. An example in this taxonomy that the artist calls "Cheating Art" is found in *Mao Met Nixon* (2004), which tells of a fictional meeting between Mao Zedong and Richard Nixon that secretly took place in the White House following the well-publicized historical visit by the American president to China in 1972. A text panel describes the event with the impassive authority of a history book while claiming that the accompanying wood and glass cube—the only one remaining of two containers made to "hold" the conversation that transpired at the time—has passed through various hands, from the CIA to a private collection in Hong Kong, before arriving in this display.

The artist's contribution to the present exhibition includes *Mao Met Nixon* along with two works that together exemplify his wide-ranging practice, which evades any stylistic characterization. *This Is Coyote* (2006) consists of a human-scale puppet of Wile E. Coyote, the Road Runner's perpetually unfortunate Looney Tunes adversary, sitting atop a round white pedestal painted with English and Korean inscriptions. The text conjures a narrative regarding a nonexistent but completely plausible Korean defector in Japan and an alleged arrangement of labor and compensation made between him and the artist. The question of economic transactions in art-making is further explored in *The Boat*, a constantly evolving and transmogrifying sculpture. Originally created in 2001, the large blue boulder equipped with a pair of oars and a string of buoys accumulates different local products—foodstuffs and other items pertinent to each locale—as it travels from one exhibition venue to the next. These objects are purchased with the production budgets given to the artist by museums, and after each show is complete, they are distributed and consumed by staff members and workers at the site. In this way, *The Boat* operates as a reminder of the temporary financial arrangement that underpins such cultural productions as an exhibition. In a broader sense, the work highlights ways that such relationships simultaneously resemble and deviate from typical social and commercial transactions. But perhaps most importantly, it is a contemplation on the meaning of being an artist and the act of making sculpture in today's world.

DC

1. Gimhongsok, artist's statement, in *Gwangju Biennale 2006: Fever Variations I*, exh. cat. (Seoul: Designhouse Co. Ltd., 2006), 245.

2. The G8 countries are the United States, the United Kingdom, France, Germany, Canada, Russia, Japan, and Italy—the nations that dominate the majority of the world's wealth and also are the strongest militarily and politically.

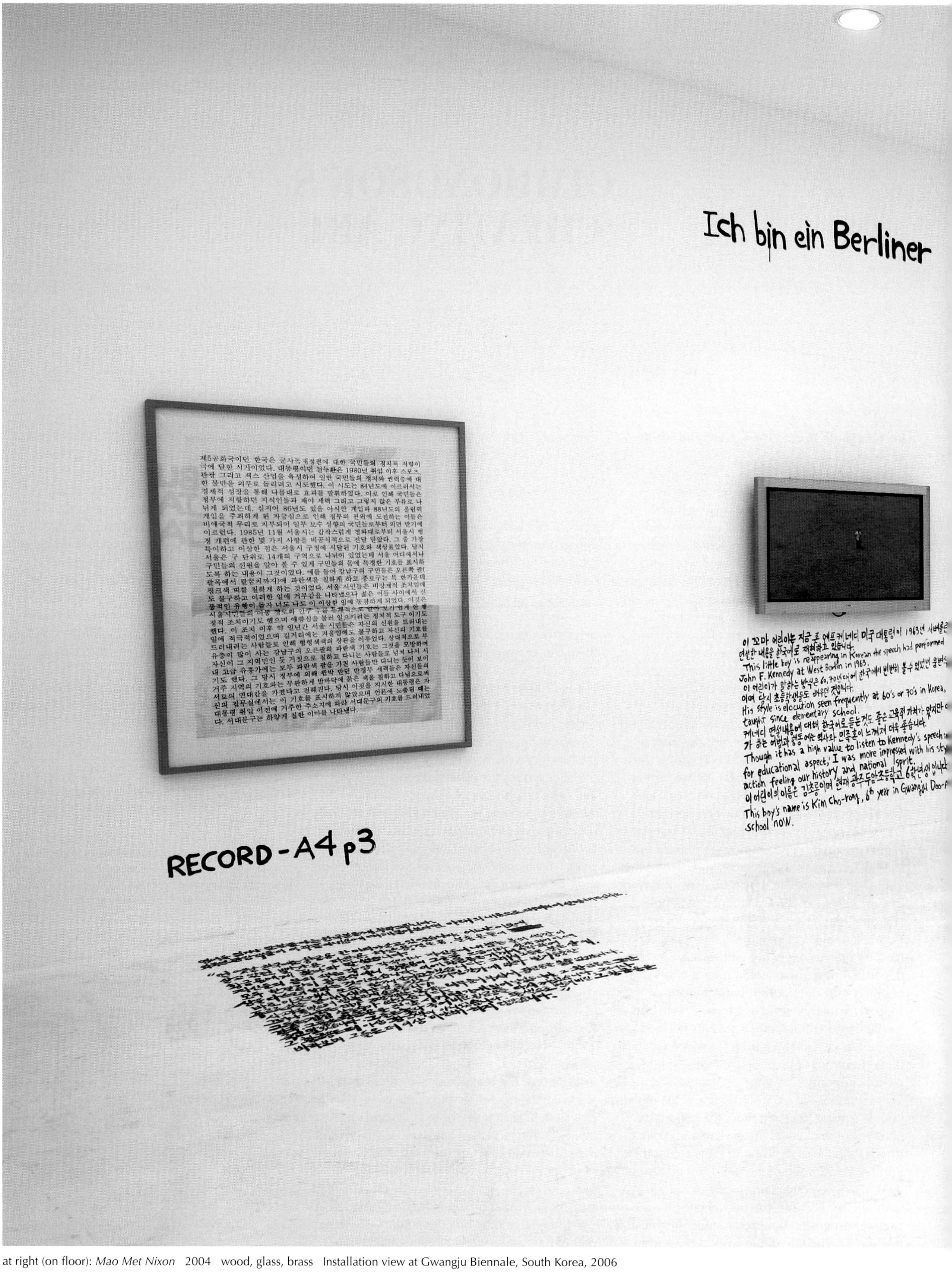

at right (on floor): *Mao Met Nixon* 2004 wood, glass, brass Installation view at Gwangju Biennale, South Korea, 2006

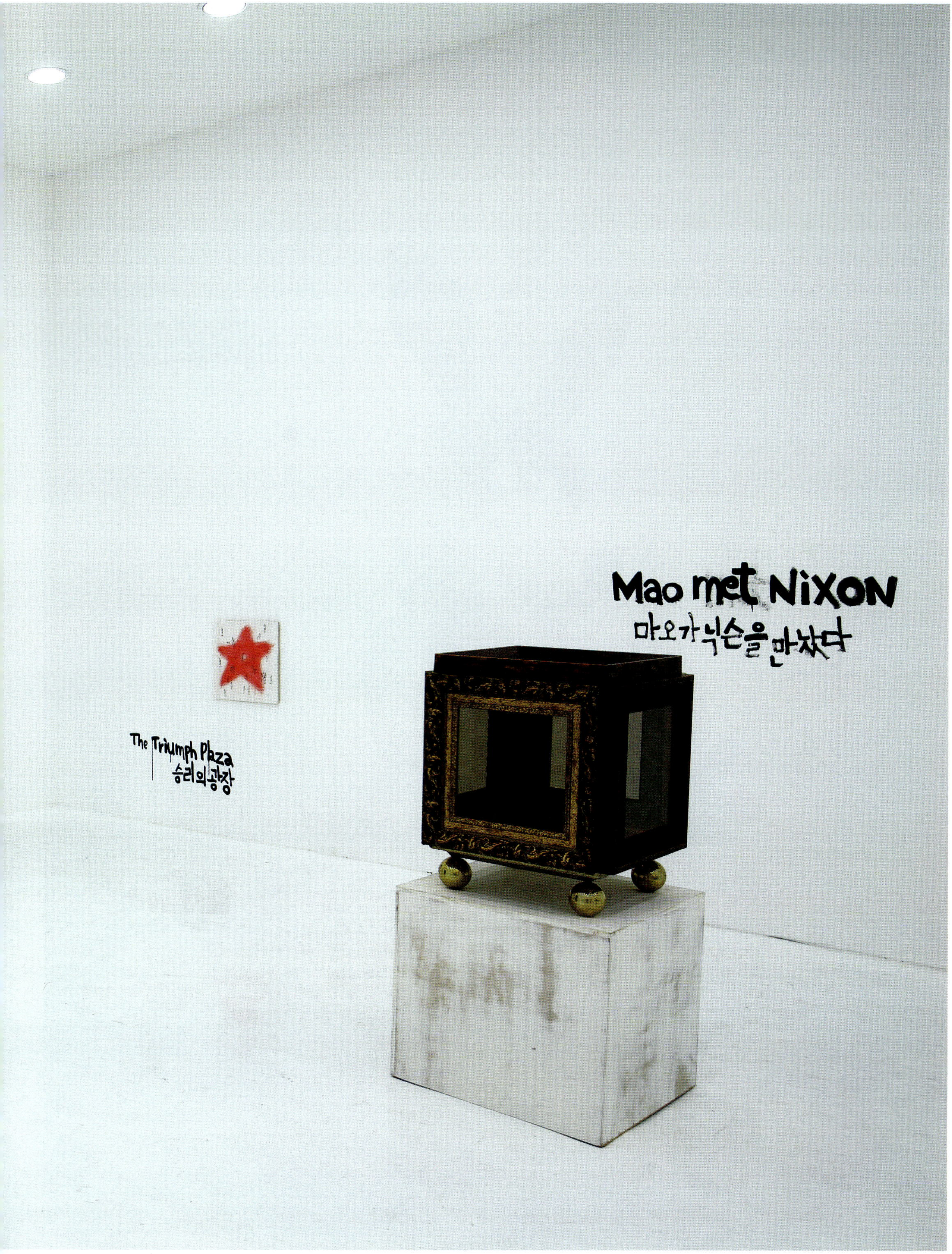
Mao met NiXON
마오가닉슨을만났다
The Triumph Plaza
승리의광장

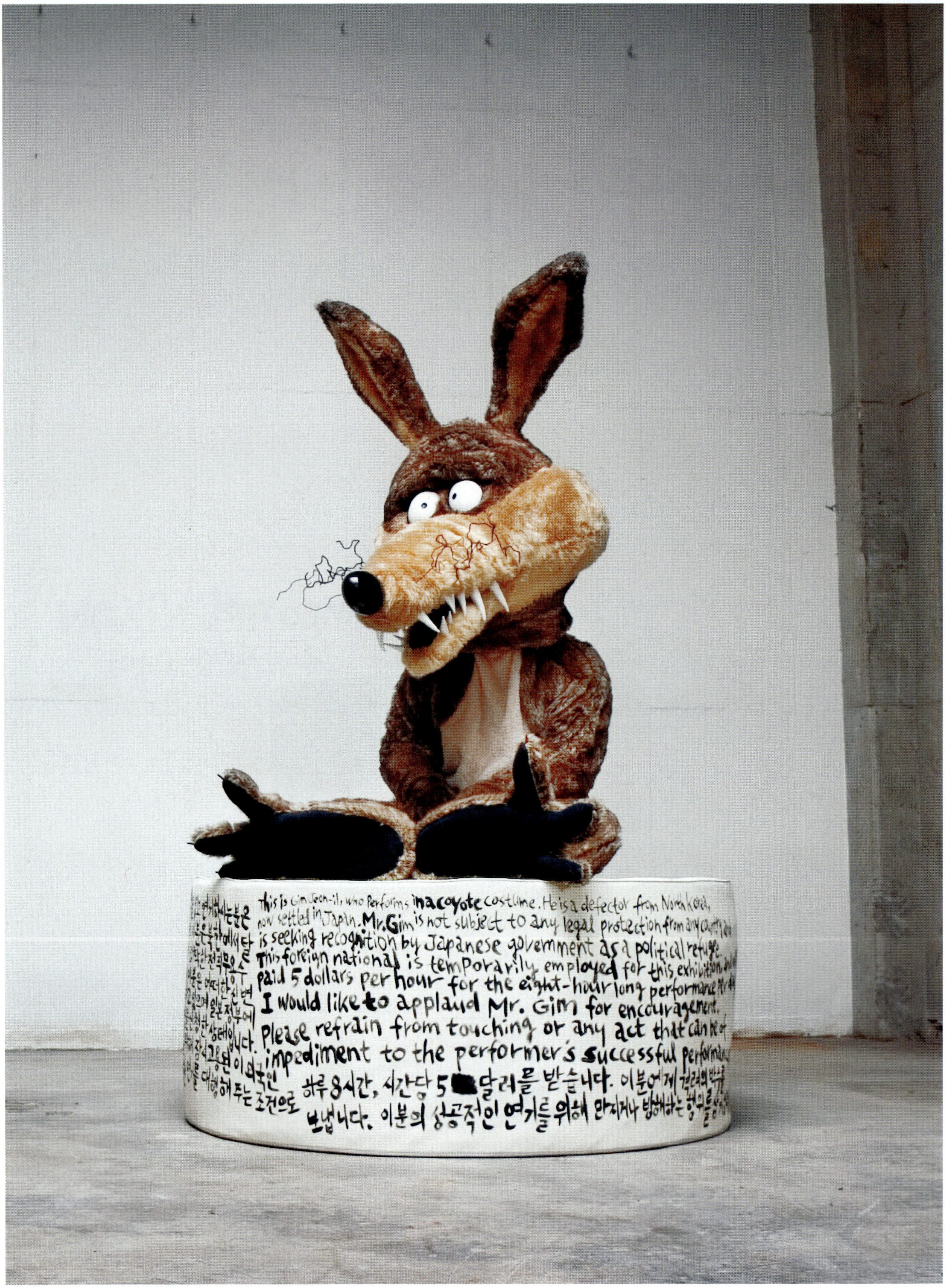

This Is Coyote 2006 foam rubber, fabric

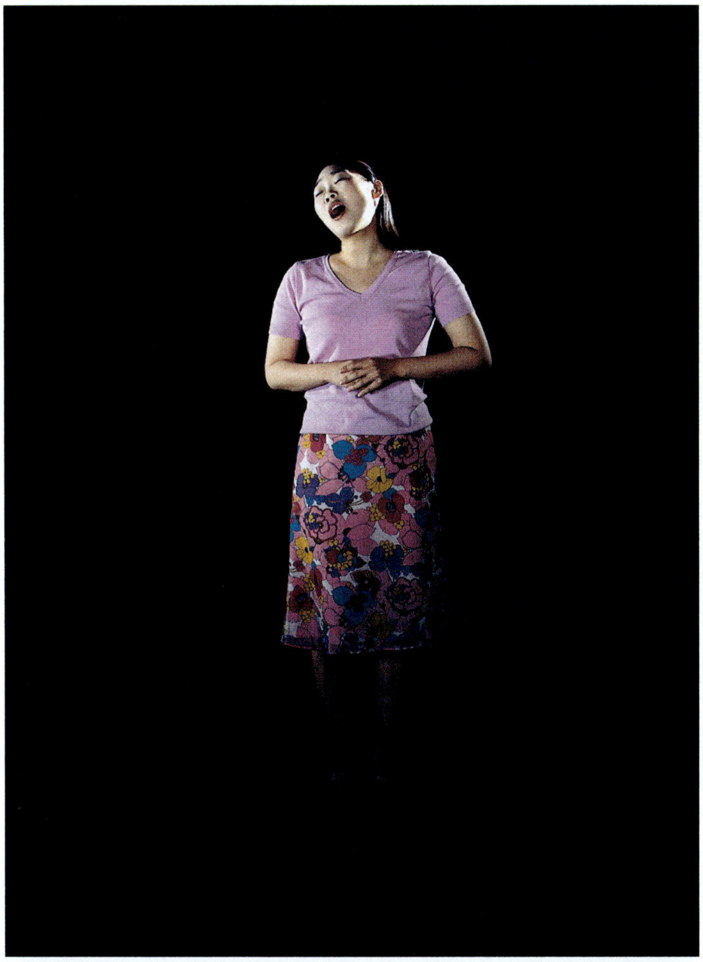

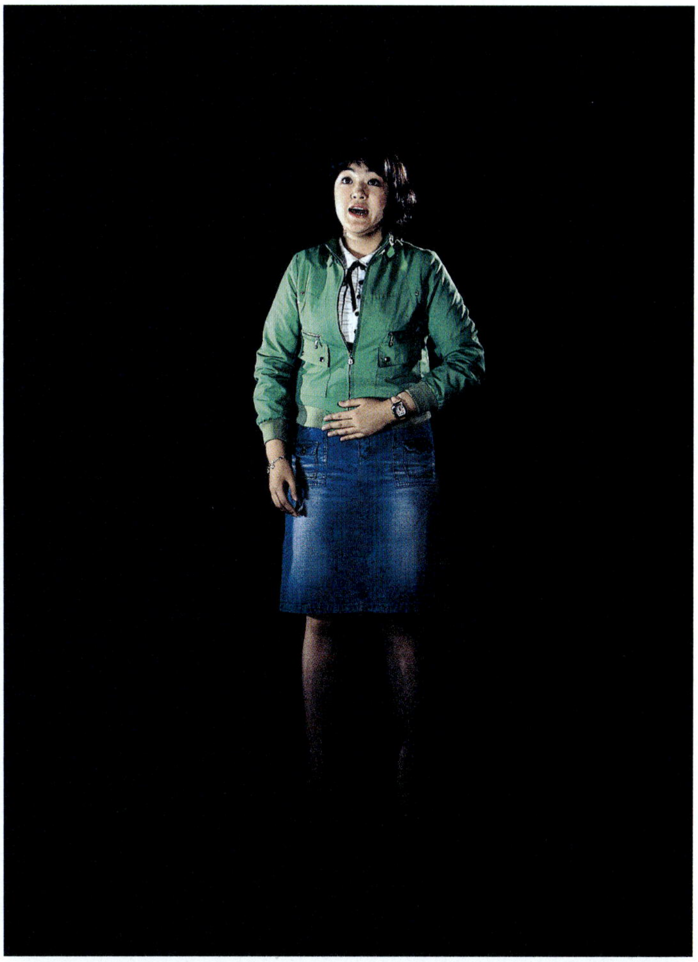

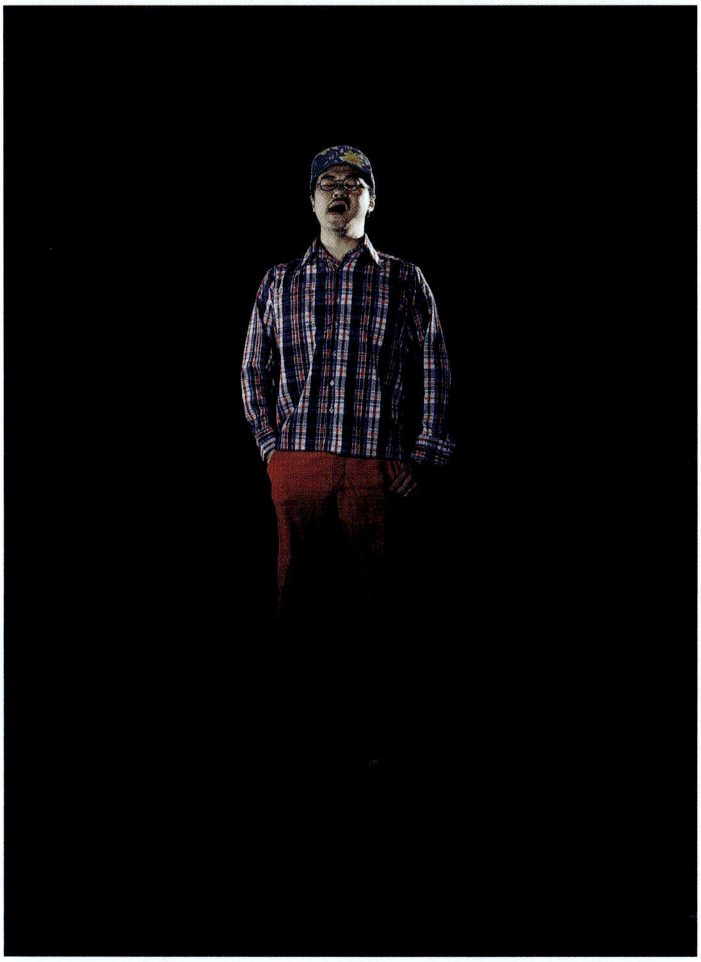

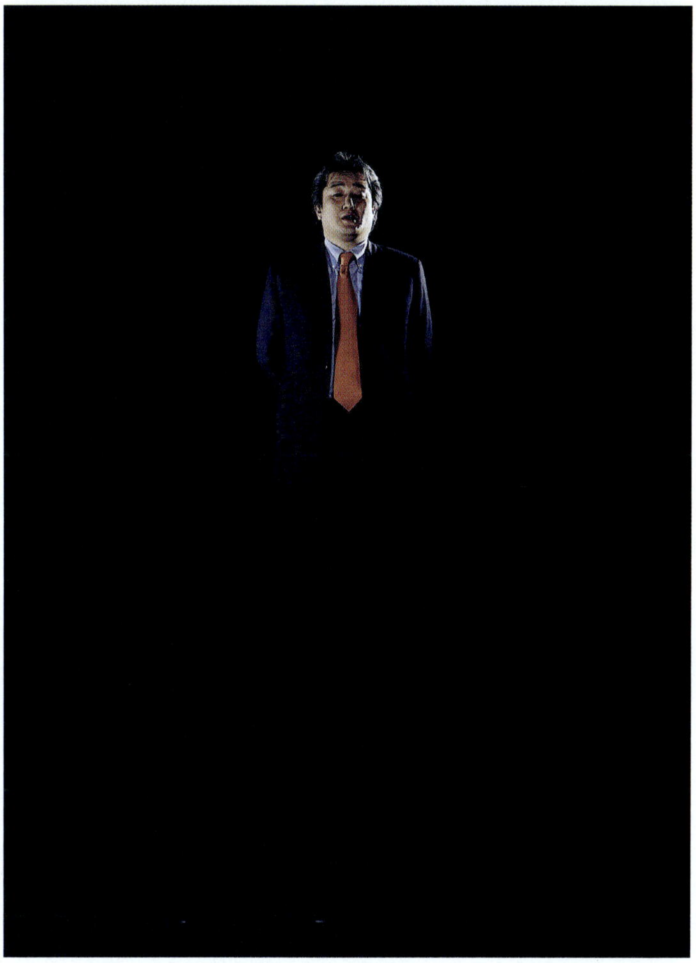

Stills from *G5* 2004 16mm film transferred to DVD (color, sound); 17:14 minutes

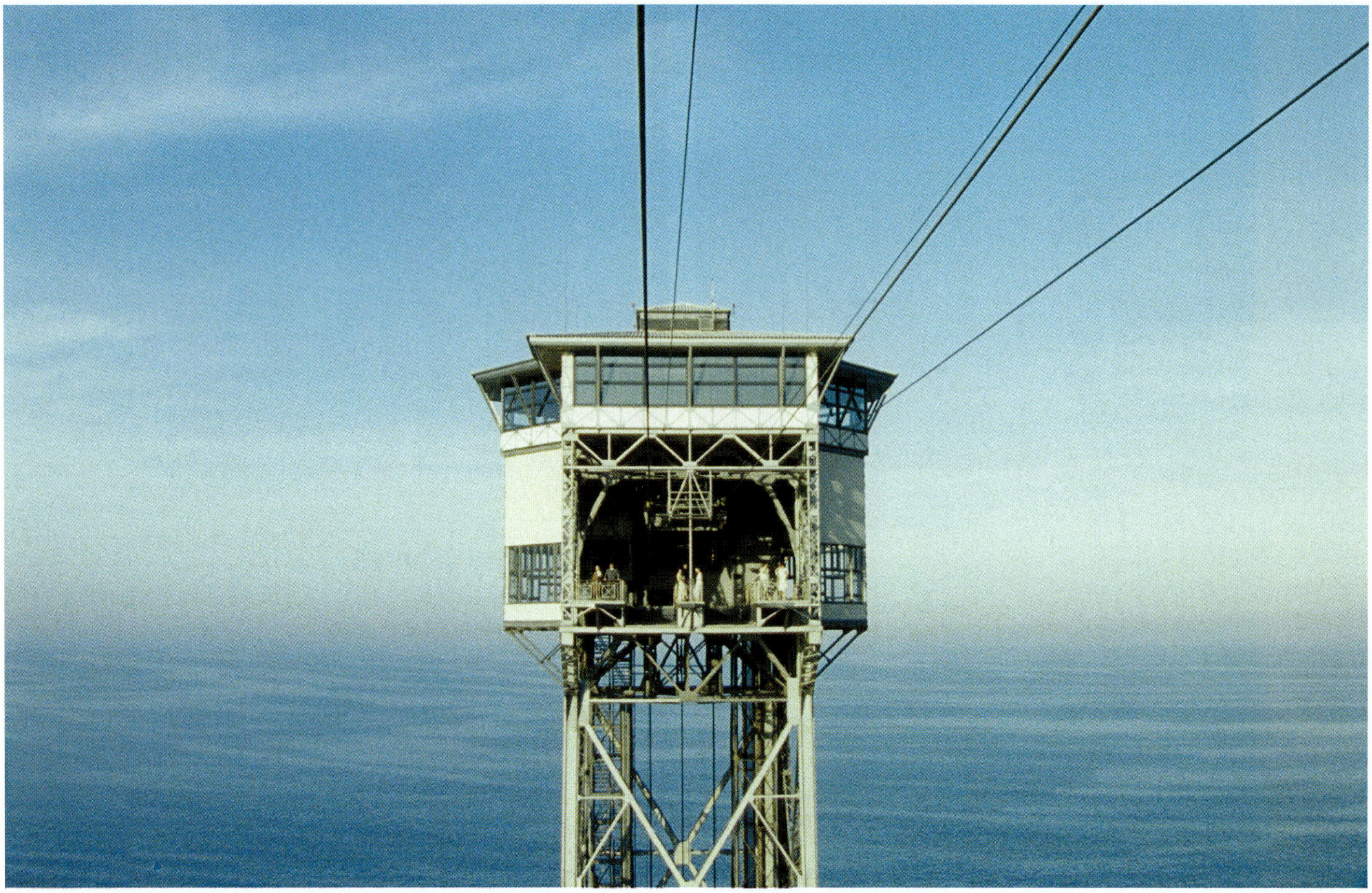

Stills from *Time Lines* 2005 35mm film (color, sound); 17:05 minutes

PHENOMENOLOGY OF SEEING: RUNA ISLAM

Born in Bangladesh, 1970. Lives and works in London.

Filmmaker Runa Islam thrives in the relative freedom of a gallery context, which allows her to walk the line between entertainment and treatise, fantasy and documentary. By carefully crafting a cinematic experience of subtle contradictions, Islam's work embraces a paradoxical perspective that allows for free associations, emotional resonances, and ontological debates that ultimately leave her films radically open-ended. "When I use film within a fine arts context," the artist has said, "I don't need to work from the 'storytelling' basis and am free to exercise the medium as an investigative instrument." **1** Thus, she uses the "logic" of film—the cinematic building blocks of camera work, character-building, editing, and plot—to study what these conventions typically overlook: marginalized, intuitive, and unexpected moments.

Islam's undergraduate and graduate studies in art history and philosophy have informed the theoretical basis of her work, as has her two-year residency at the Rijksakademie van beeldende kunsten in Amsterdam studying under artist/filmmakers such as Dan Graham and Joan Jonas. During her residency, she made a group of 16mm films that examined the phenomenology of seeing, including *Turn (Gaze of Orpheus)* (1998), in which a woman slowly rotates toward the viewer over the course of fifty seconds, only to shoot them an intense stare a split second before the film cuts off and loops over again; *Tuin* (1998), a deconstructive re-creation of the 360-degree revolving tracking shot that Fassbinder invented for *Martha* (1973); and *Stare Out (Blink)* (1998), which features a woman's face shown in negative so that when the screen occasionally flashes white, her positive image appears.

Two double-screen projections, *Parallel* (2001) and *Director's Cut (Fool for Love)* (2001), were created following her stay in Amsterdam. Soon after, her work grew more explicitly narrative, scripted, and staged in *Rapid Eye Movement* (2002) and *Scale (1/16 inch=1 foot)* (2003), which used the larger-aspect ratio of Super 16mm film. *Be the First to See What You See as You See It* (2004) studies the gaze with all of its psychological and theoretical resonances. It revisits an early motion study of a man smashing a vase, possibly the first test film in a Vinten slow-motion camera. This time, however, instead of depicting the violent result of masculine strength, a female protagonist gently tips fine china onto the ground, where we see the dishes slowly shatter. In *First Day of Spring* (2005), Islam slowly tracks across a group of Bangladeshi rickshaw drivers whom she paid to relax while being filmed. Thus, the dichotomy of labor and leisure is twisted around, and the director works so the drivers don't have to.

Time Lines (2005) is Islam's first project using 35mm film, an elaborate process typically reserved for commercial motion pictures. The film is set in two Barcelona tourist destinations: the century-old Tibidabo amusement park, famous for the ride that lifts its passengers to the highest point in the city; and the cable car that runs from a castle on Montjuïc Mountain to a tower near the coast. A feeling of nostalgia for a time in which these amusements were state-of-the-art is the central paradox on which the artwork is based. Islam has said of her inspiration, "I started thinking about what was the intended effect of these vehicles of the early twentieth century. It's not just about panoramas. . . . They are all motifs of how we can't fly but got fascinated trying." **2** Like other artists in the exhibition *Brave New Worlds*, Islam reflects on the past to unpack the present, focusing especially on ways that tourism and movies form our historical imagination. *Time Lines* also examines the peculiar relationship between time and film, as an index of light that allows us to see what was recorded in the past, a way to depict motion by sequencing through distinct frames, and a storytelling device that can make a two-hour feature or a seventeen-minute work seem like a lifetime.

RH

1. Runa Islam, interview with Rebecca Fortnum, in *Contemporary British Women Artists in Their Own Words* (New York and London: I. B. Taurus & Co. Ltd., 2007), 132.

2. Serena Davies, "A Cable Car Named Desire," *Telegraph*, United Kingdom (December 10, 2005): Arts section, 7.

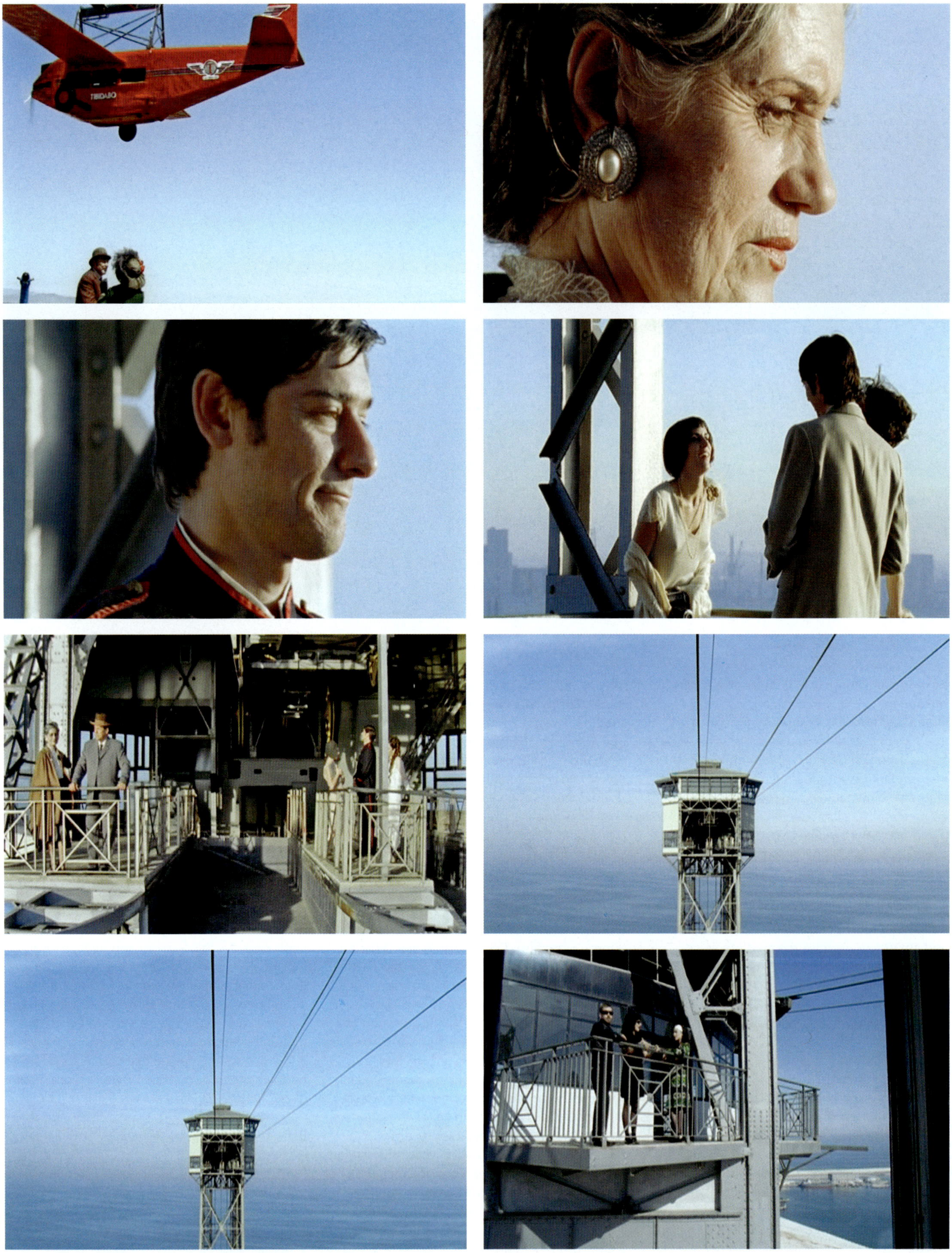

Stills from *Time Lines* 2005 35mm film (color, sound); 17:05 minutes

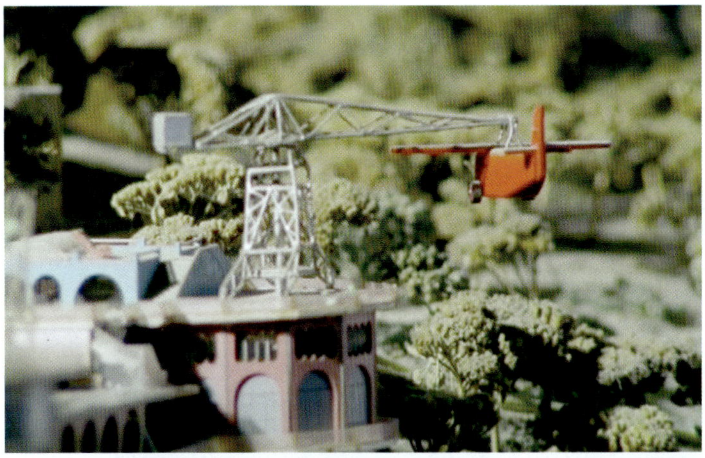
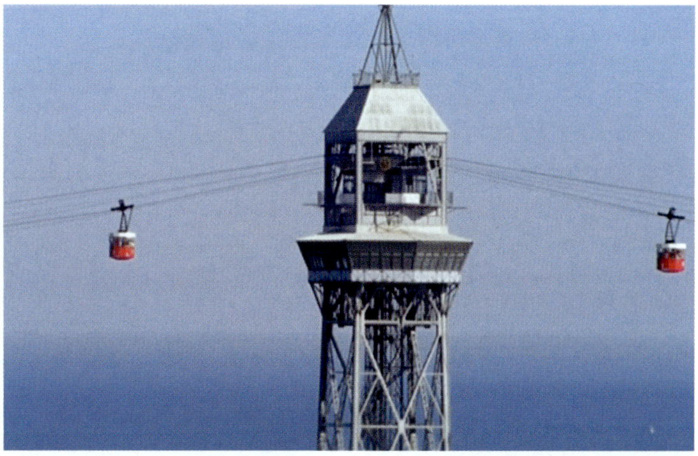
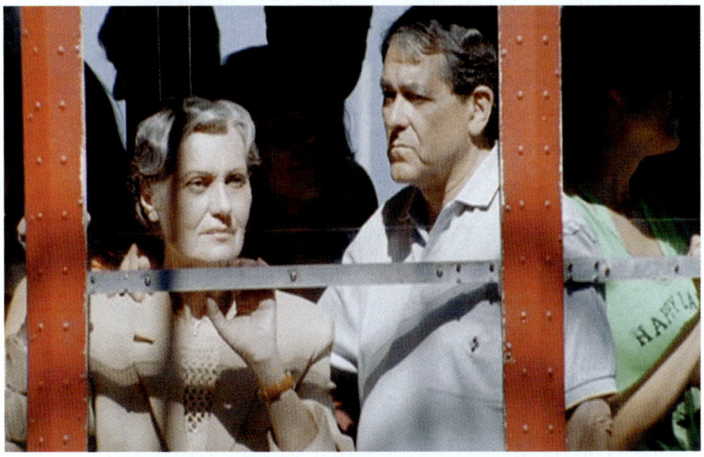
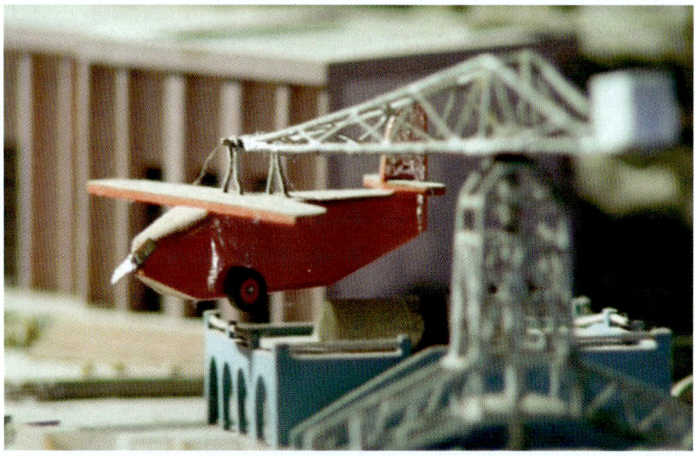
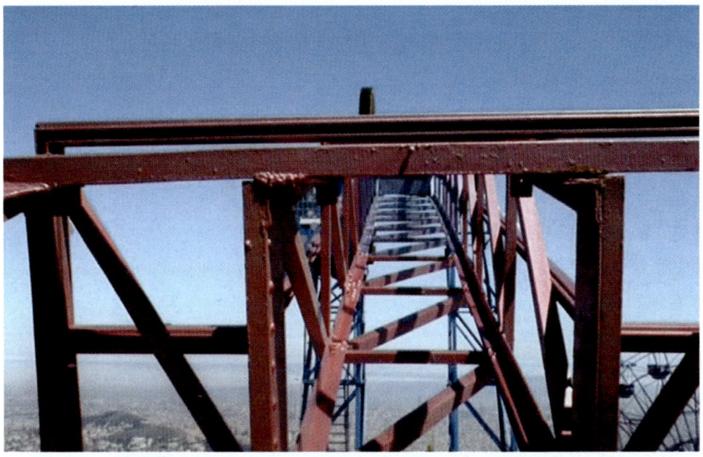
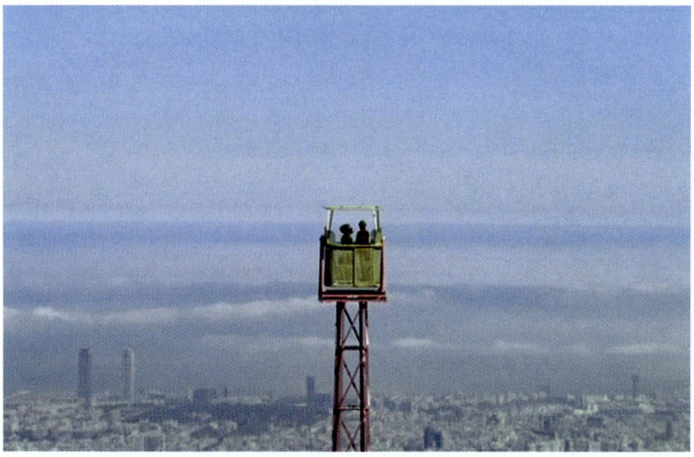
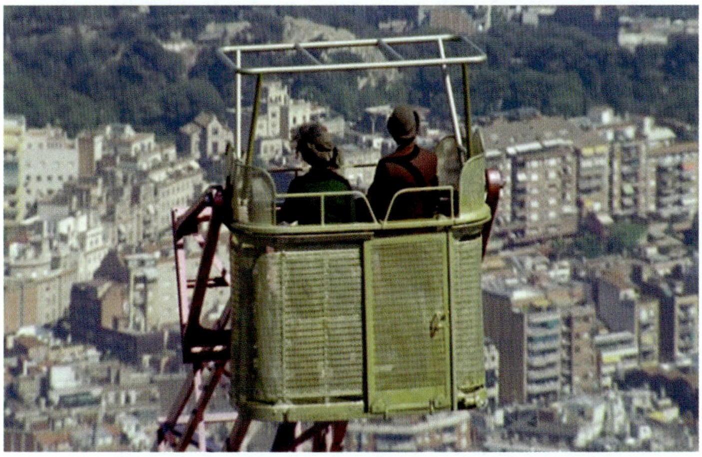
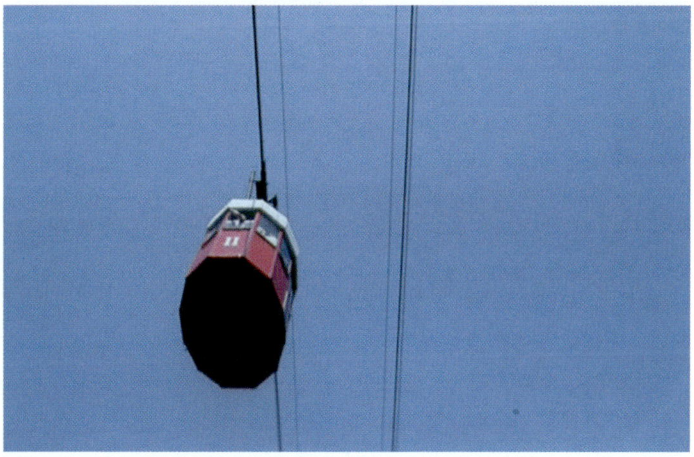

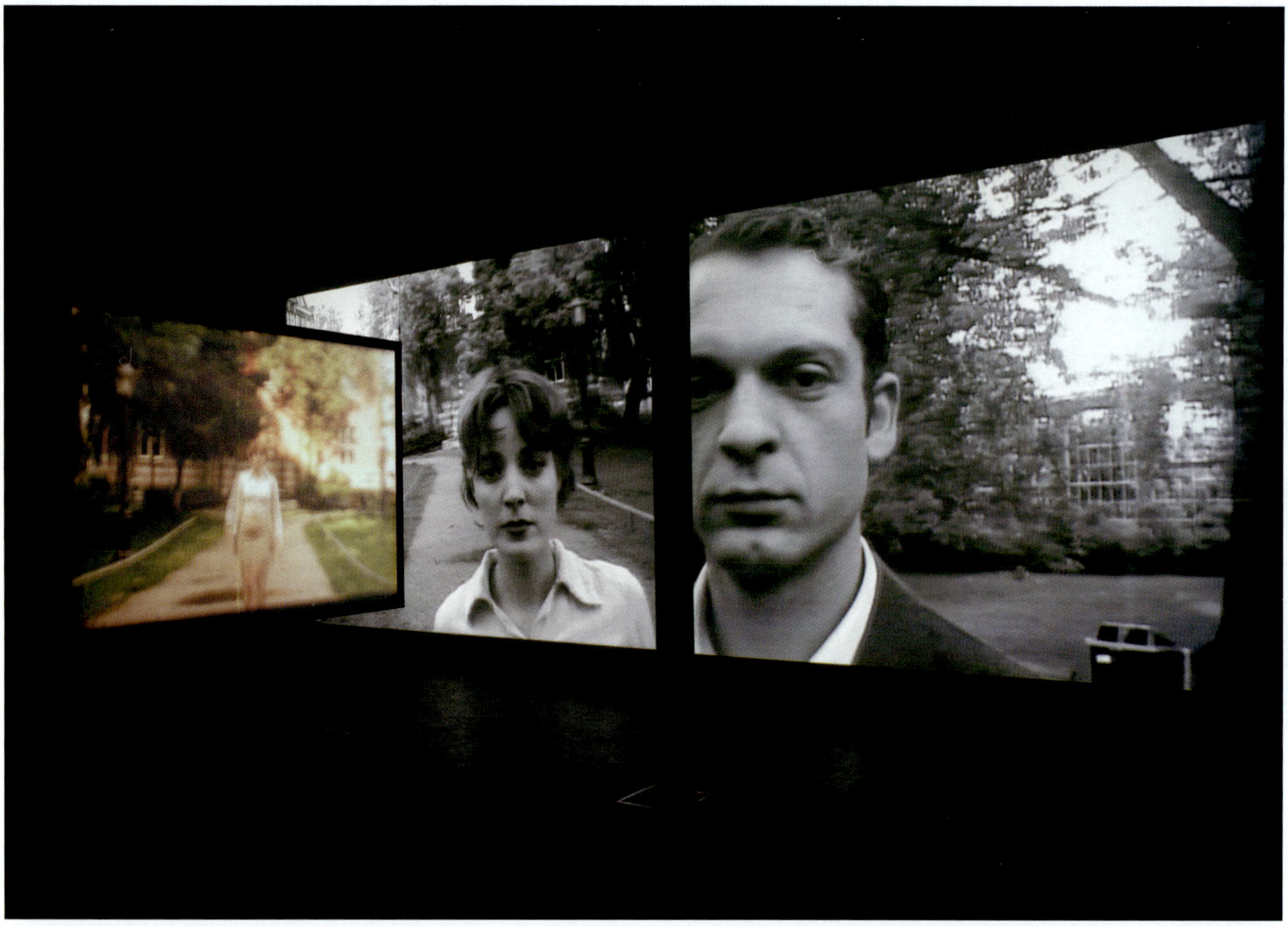

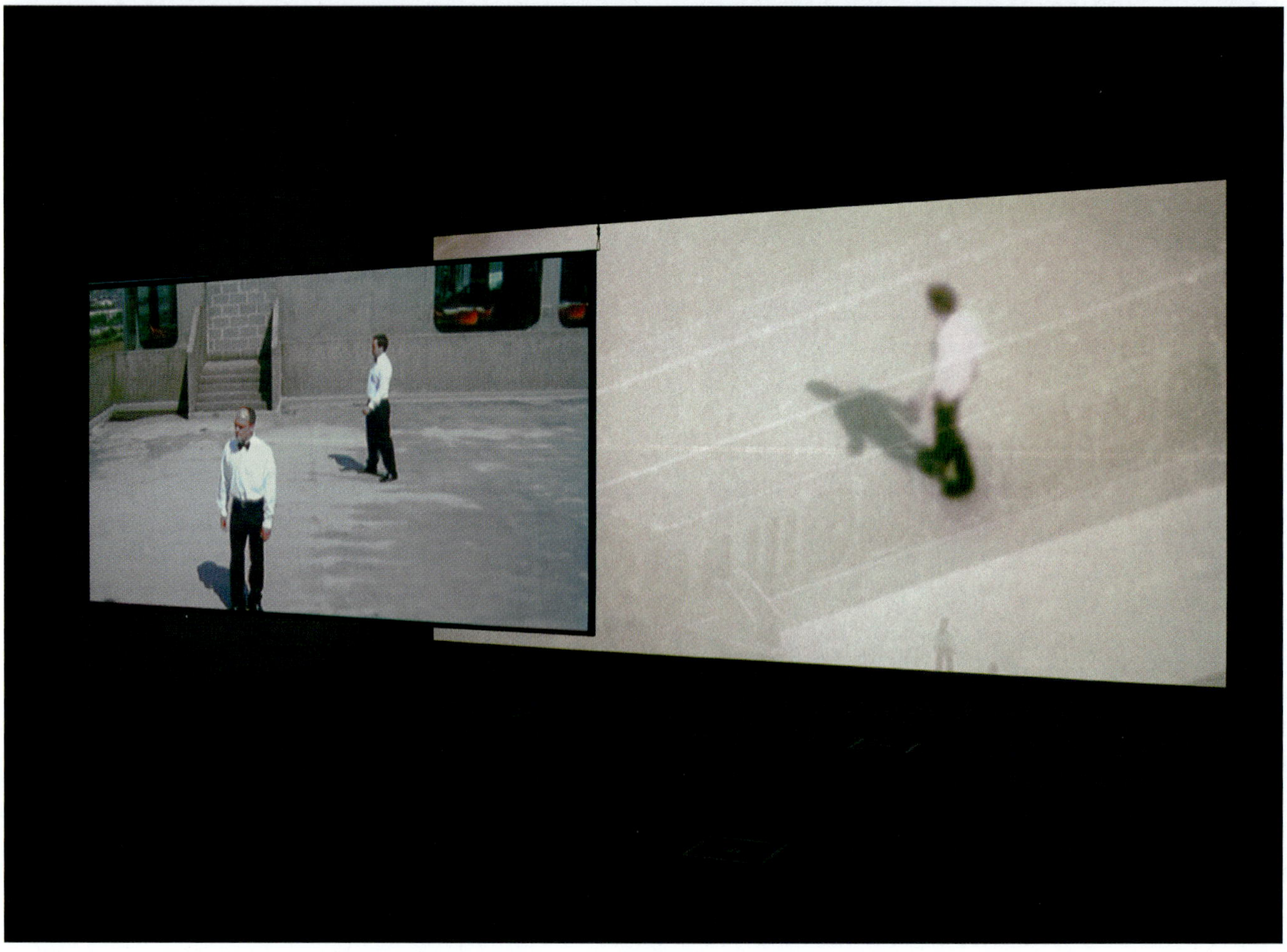

top: *Tuin* 1998 16mm film, video (triple projection, color, sound); 6 minutes bottom: *Scale 1/16 inch=1 foot* 2003 DVD (dual projection, color, sound); 16:51 minutes

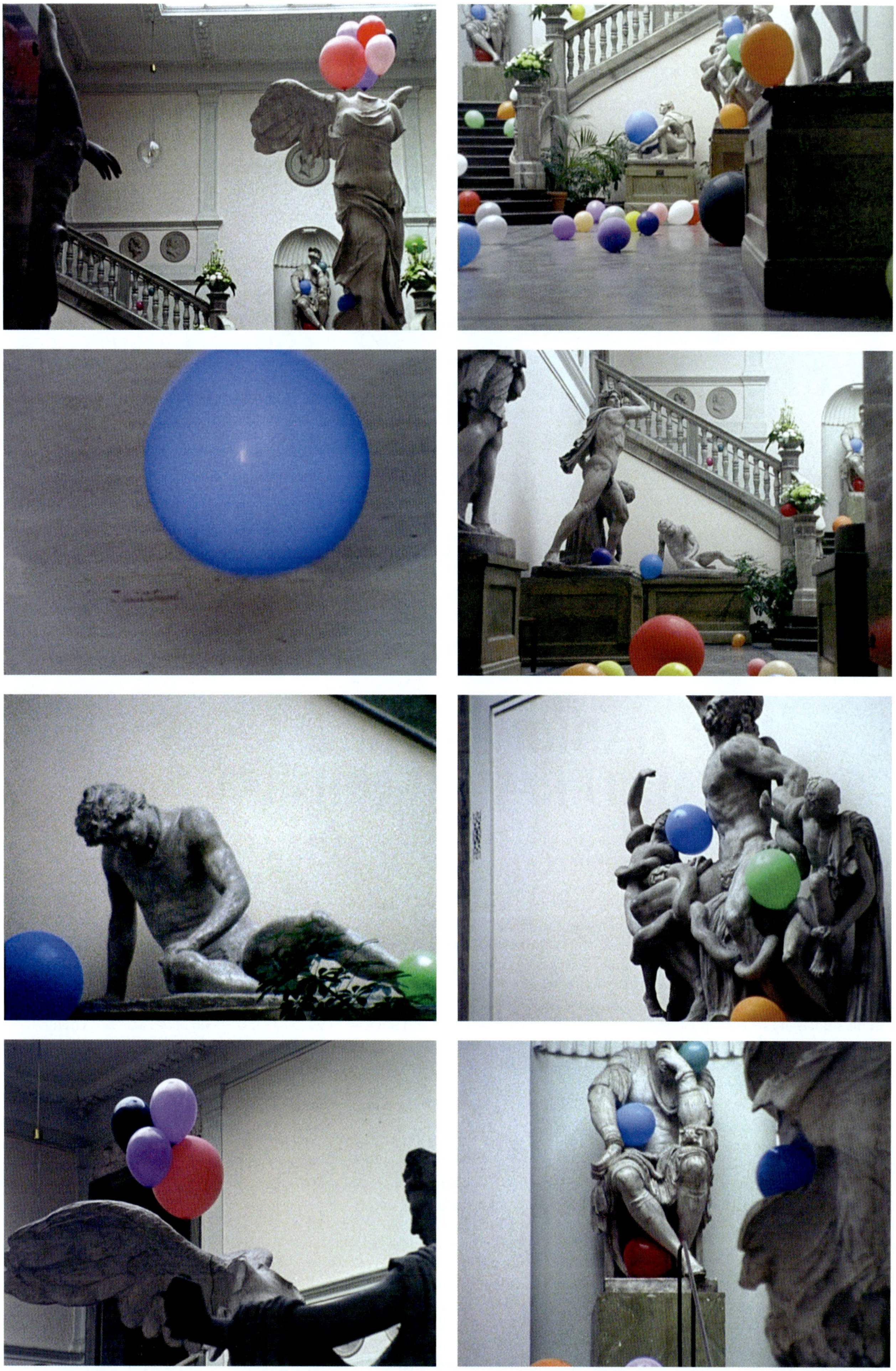

Stills from *What Is a Thought Experiment, Anyhow?* 2007 two-channel 16mm film (color, sound); 17:05 minutes

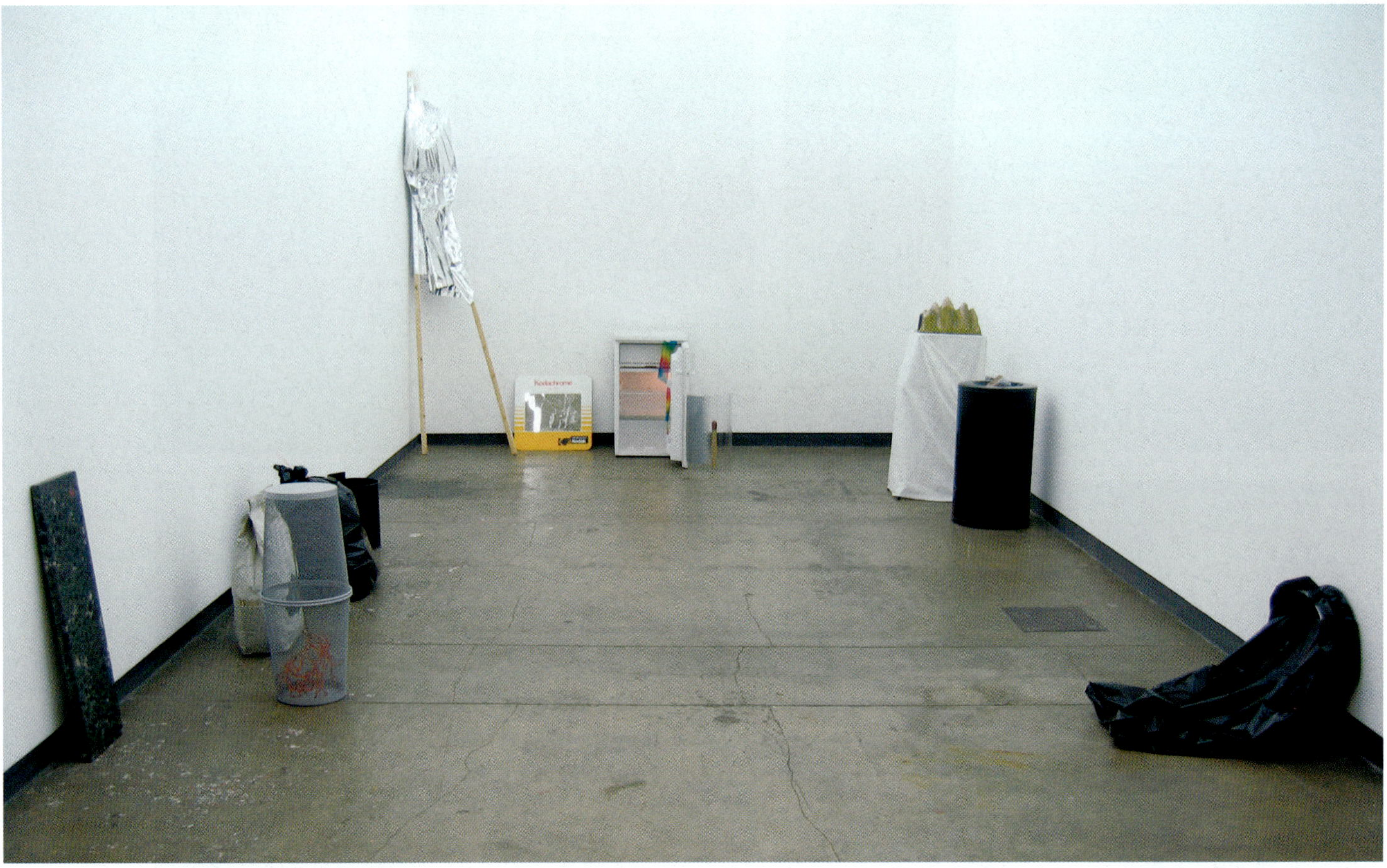

Dato duro, dato blanco, dato ciego 2006 Installation view at Galleria Franco Noero, Turin, 2006

GABRIEL KURI: THE MATERIAL ARCHIVIST

Born in Mexico, 1970. Lives and works in Brussels and Mexico City.

The work of Gabriel Kuri is a careful investigation into the physical and semantic weight of materials and their sculptural and allegorical abilities to sustain, shape, and accumulate meaning. He began his studies at Escuela Nacional de Artes Plásticas in Mexico City, spent four years working in the studio of sculptor Gabriel Orozco, and in 1993 moved to London to attend Goldsmith's College, where he studied with Liam Gillick. Over the past two decades, he has concentrated on making sculptures, collages, photographs, and environments that zealously rummage through the detritus of material consumption. Both his objects and images are often the residue of monetary exchanges and consumed goods that Kuri collects on a daily basis. Displayed on the bare floor, on a working table, on top of piled newspapers or cardboard boxes, they speak to his conscious rejection of the conventional museum use of wooden pedestals, frames, and vitrines. His arrangements and references appear to emerge from the debris left by an imaginary consumer who creates new forms from domestic and mundane habits, such as wrapping fruit with sheets of newspaper to accelerate the ripening process. Kuri is a material archivist who extracts visual and linguistic value from tracking systems (calendars, bulletin boards, expiration dates), greetings and phrases from retail supplies (plastic bags, sales receipts), and meaning from trivial marketing mechanisms (discount flyers, coupons, lottery tickets) that constitute daily life in the twenty-first century.

In his group of floor pieces entitled *Overlapping Statistic* (2007), he resorts to multiple groupings of objects, both found and fabricated, and pairs malleable and firm materials such as weatherproof roofing rolls, newspaper, and canned goods with their counterparts—plexiglass, Styrofoam, foam board, aluminum, and glass—to construct theorems that predict internal relationships. The work continues his study of material contradictions, as he has described: "Turning something upside down, or wronging it, is often the way to understand more deeply how it works." Stroked with a touch of humor and self-parody, Kuri's spatial and sculptural accumulations combine the social tone of Conceptual Art with the poetry of Arte Povera to construct a material abstraction. In *Overlapping Statistic (Blind Olives Eyelid)* (2007), for example, a box of facial tissues showing a closed eye sustains the elevation of a translucent surface on which a jar of green olives acts as a counterweight for a second surface that could possibly collapse. The fragility of the balancing act is offset by the necessity for equilibrium generated by the weight of the content in the can and jar. Some surfaces appear to get closer while others keep their distance; together, they demand a different understanding of their partnerships, their equal weight and indispensable roles.

YR

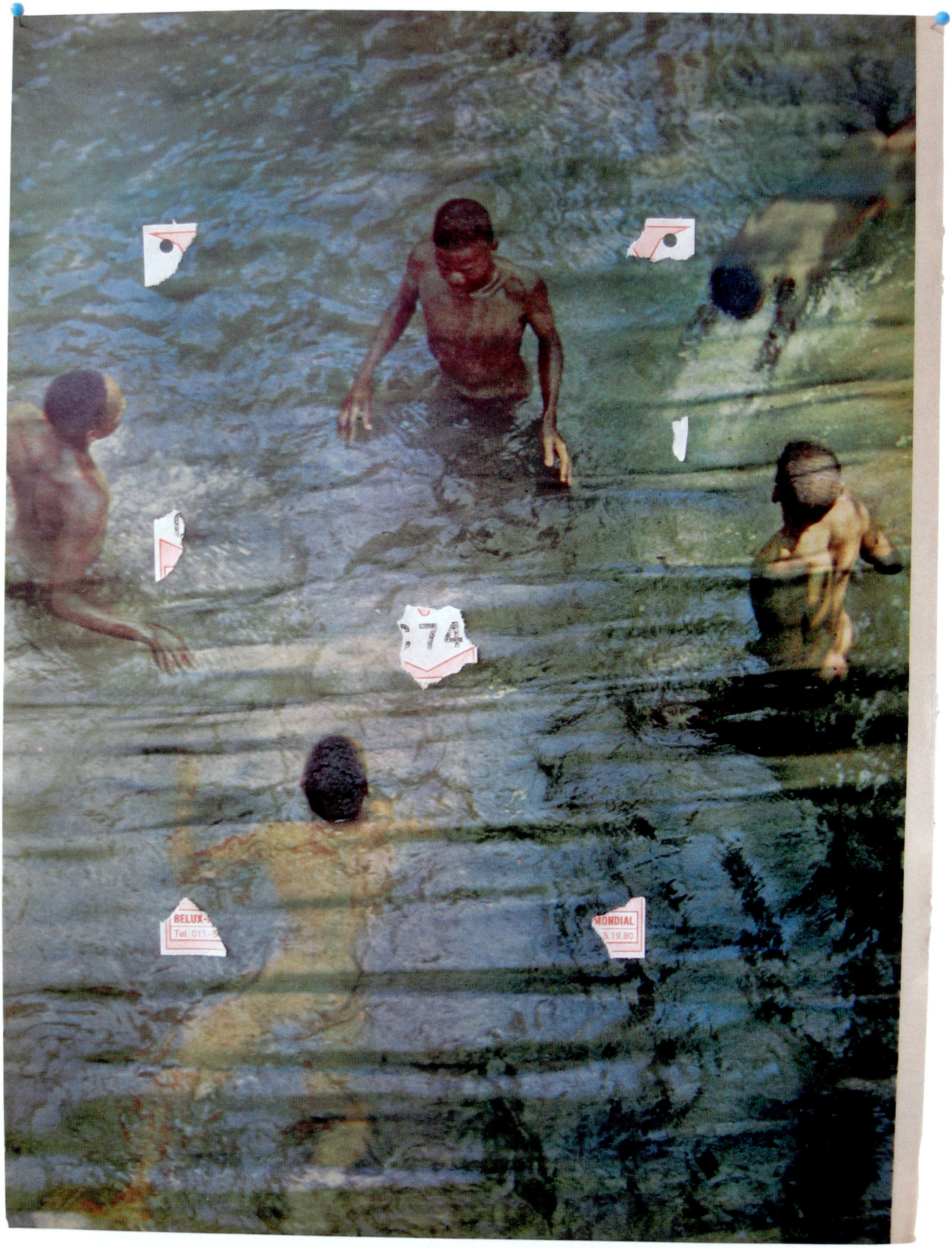

C74 2007 ticket stub on magazine page

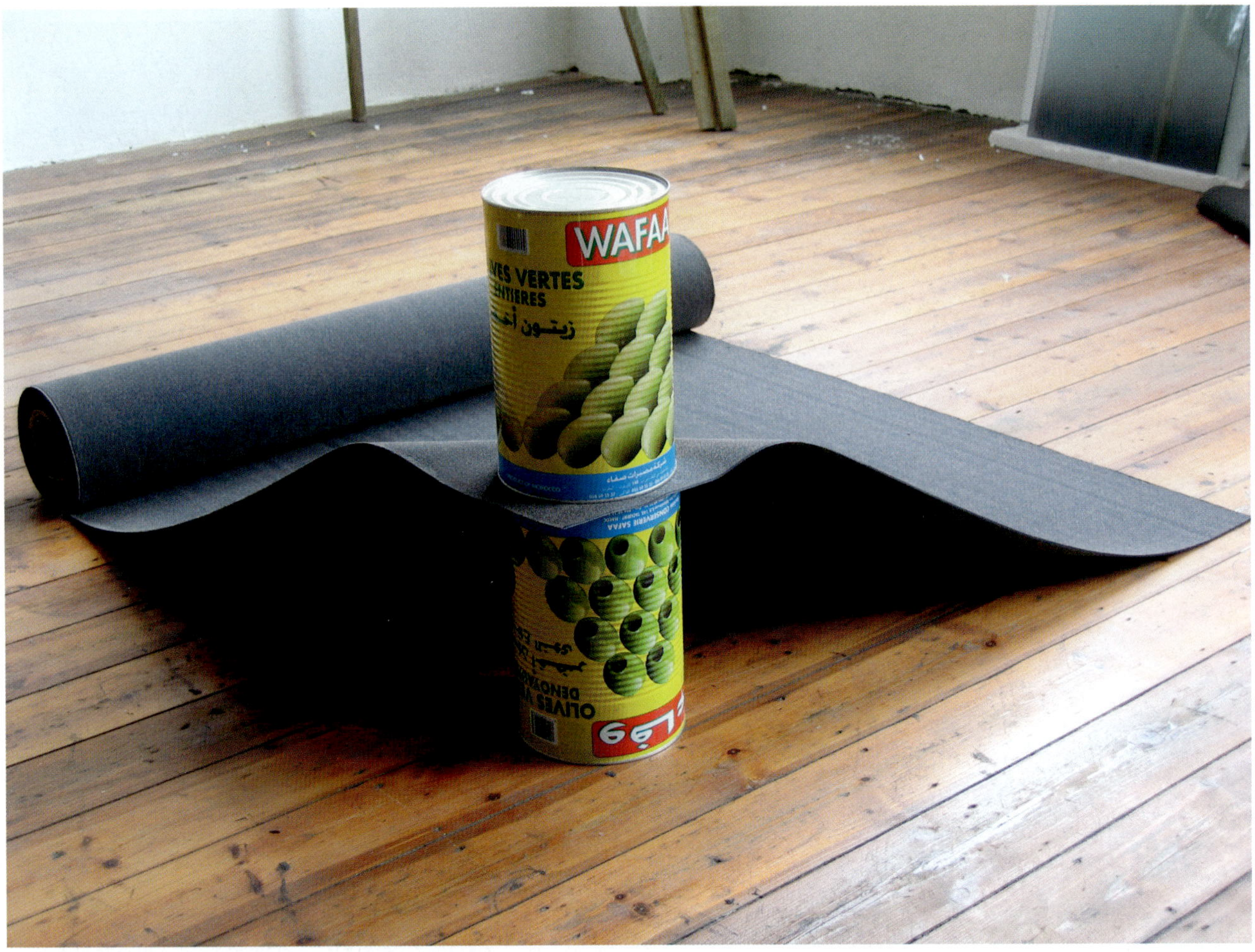

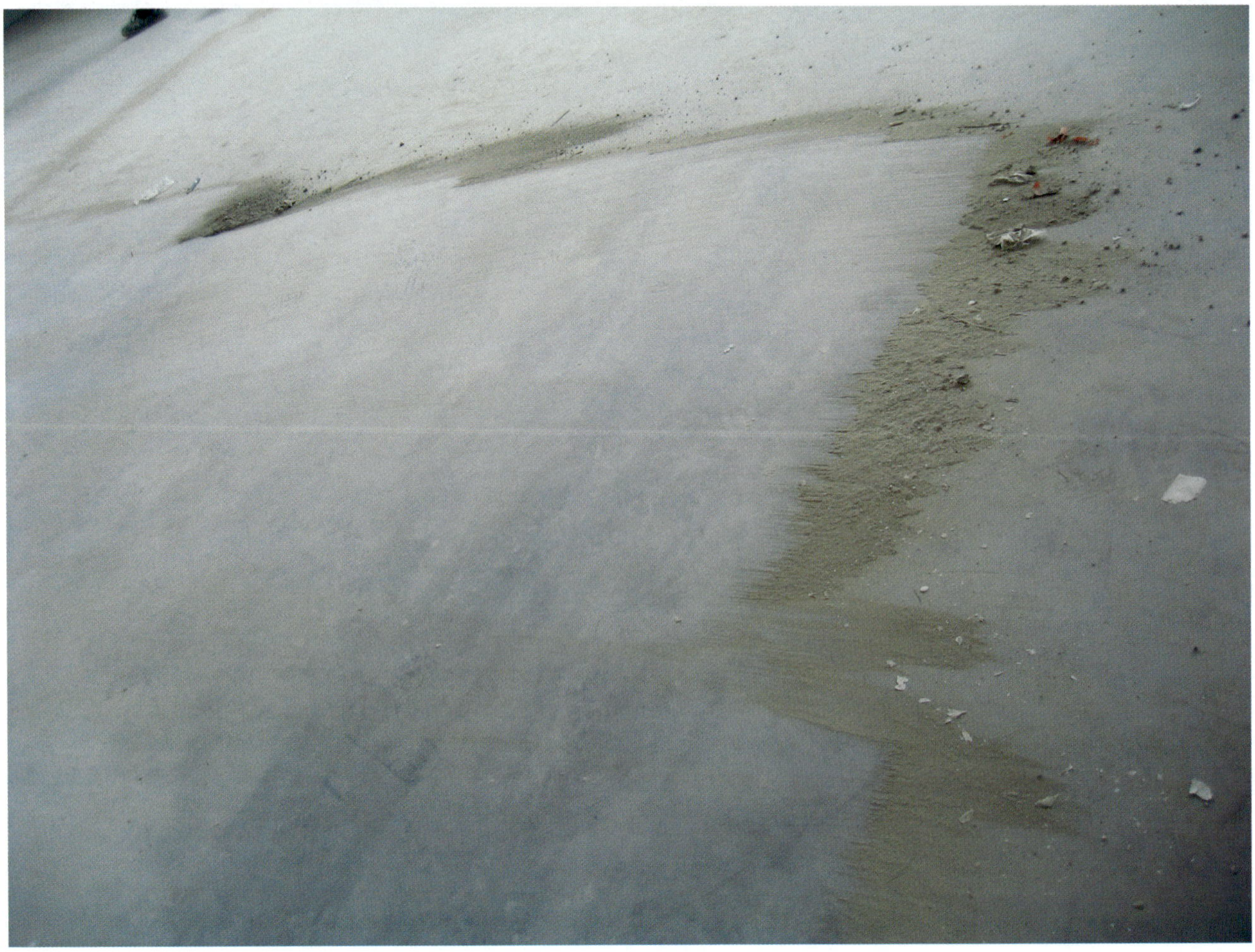

top: *Untitled Olive Void* 2007 2 cans of olives (one whole, one pitted), weatherproof roofing roll bottom: Study for *Dust at Wiels* 2007

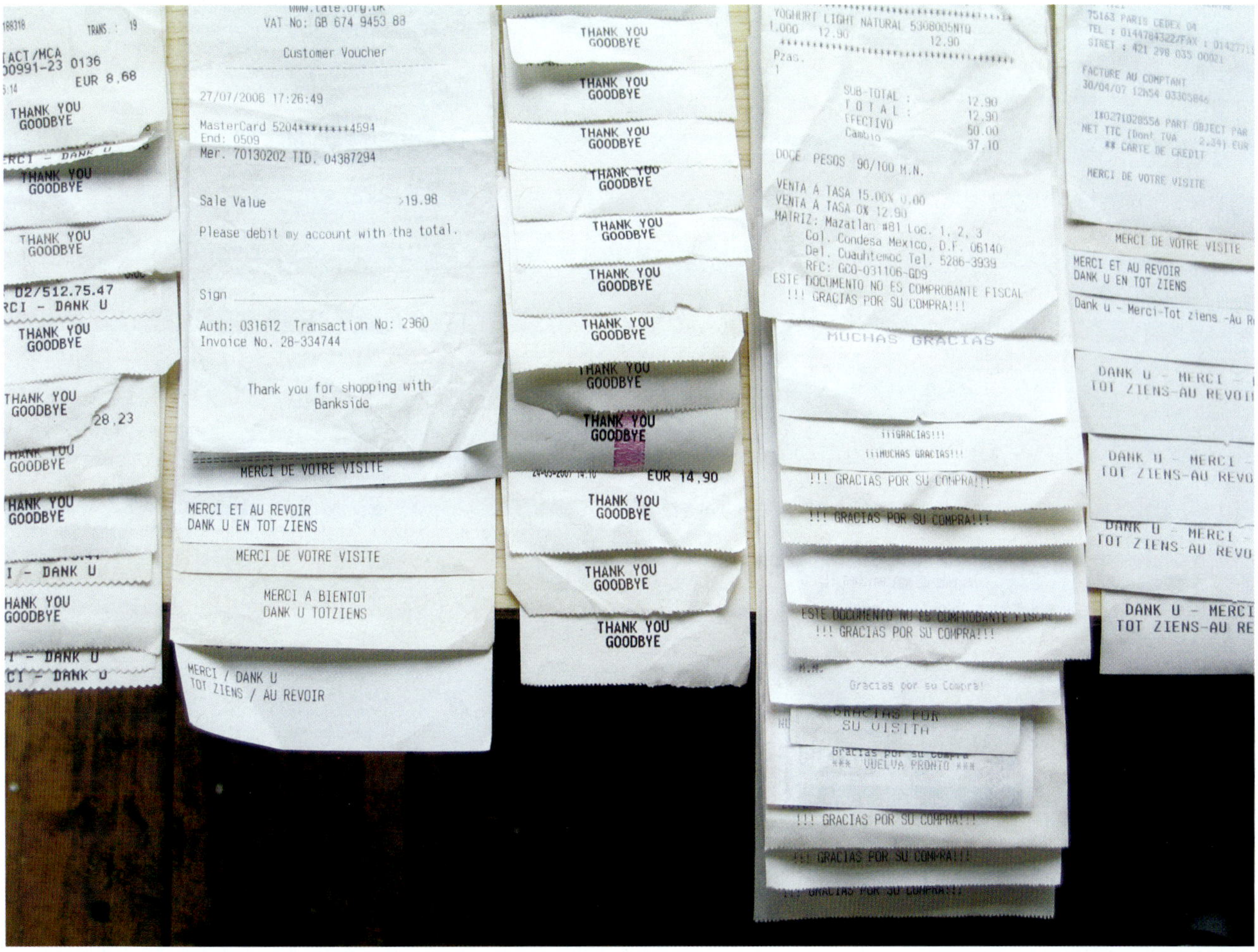

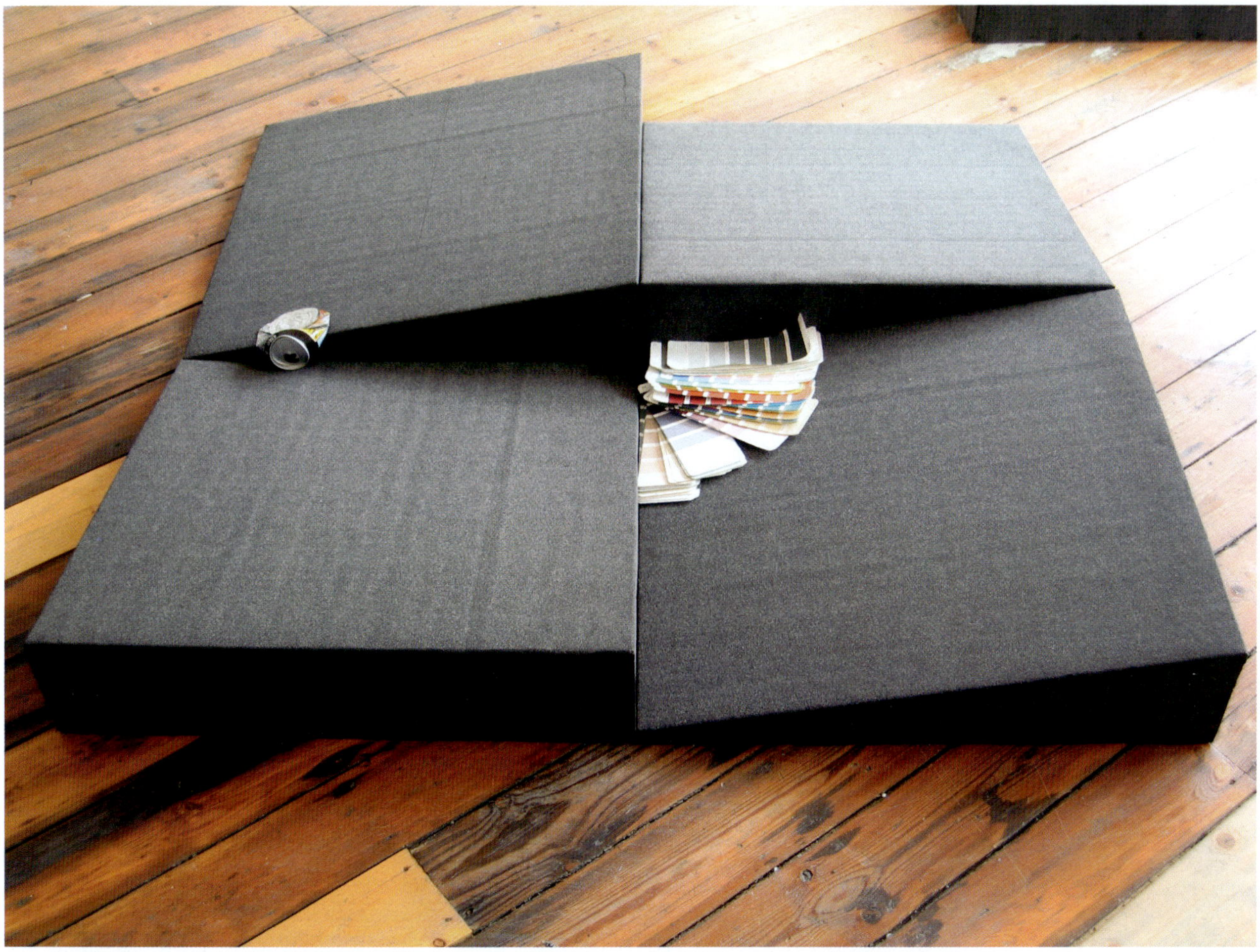

top: *Thank You Stacks* 2007 (detail of work in progress) bottom: Study for *Slanted Concentric Statistic (Color Chart and Crushed Can)* 2007 plywood, weatherproof roofing roll, color chart, aluminum can

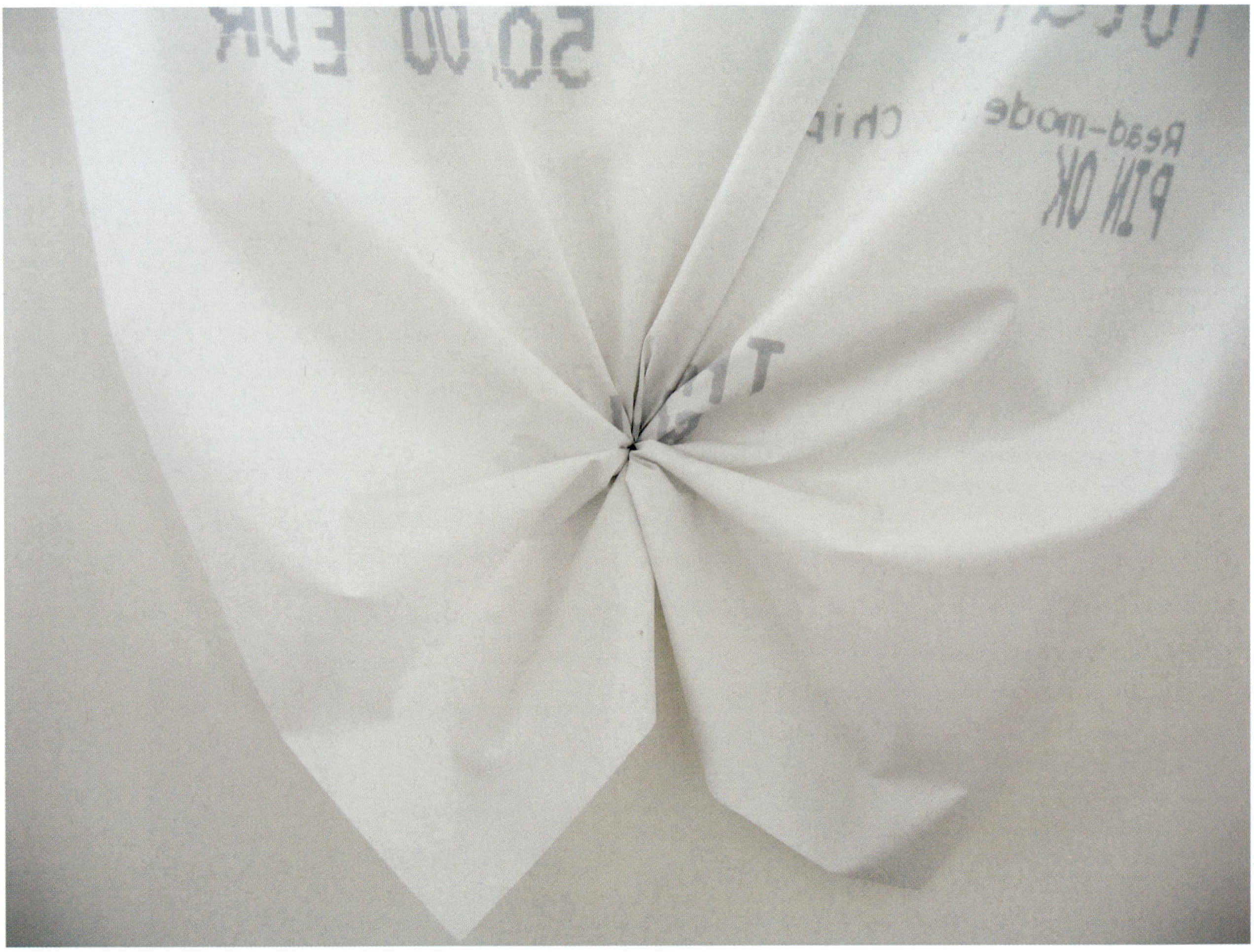

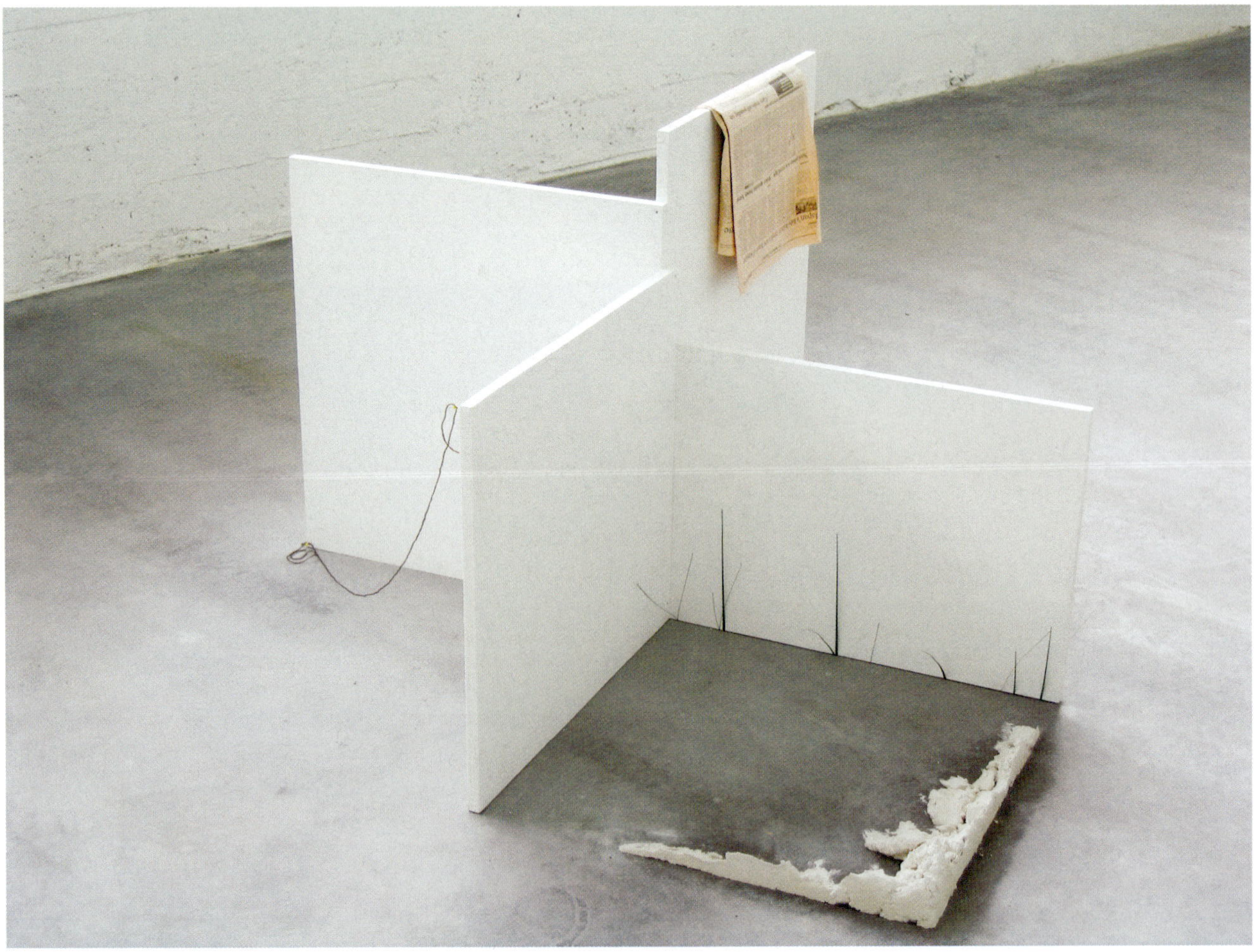

top: *Speculation* 2007 (detail) printed nylon banner bottom: *Speculation* 2007 painted plywood, plaster, string, pushpins, financial newspaper

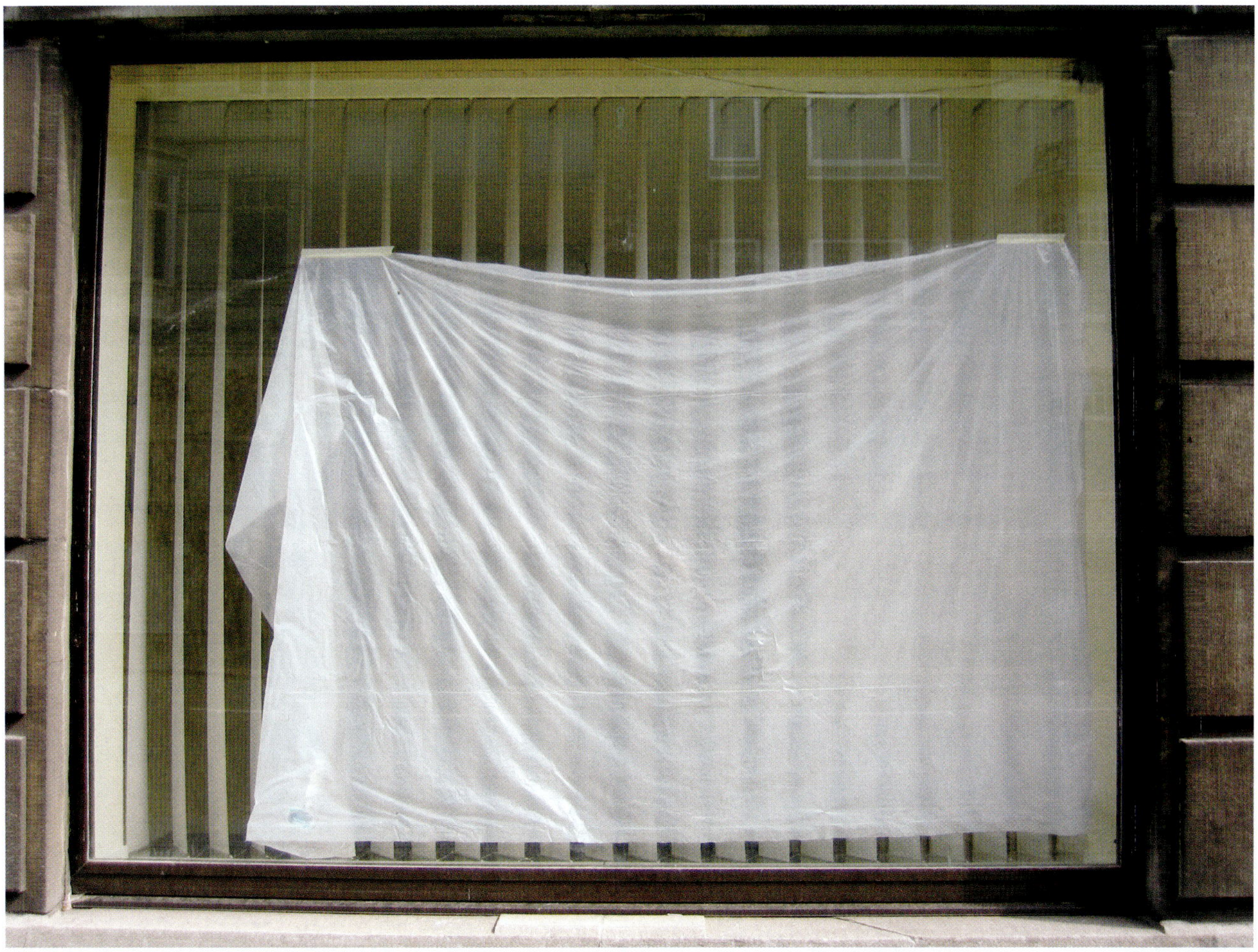

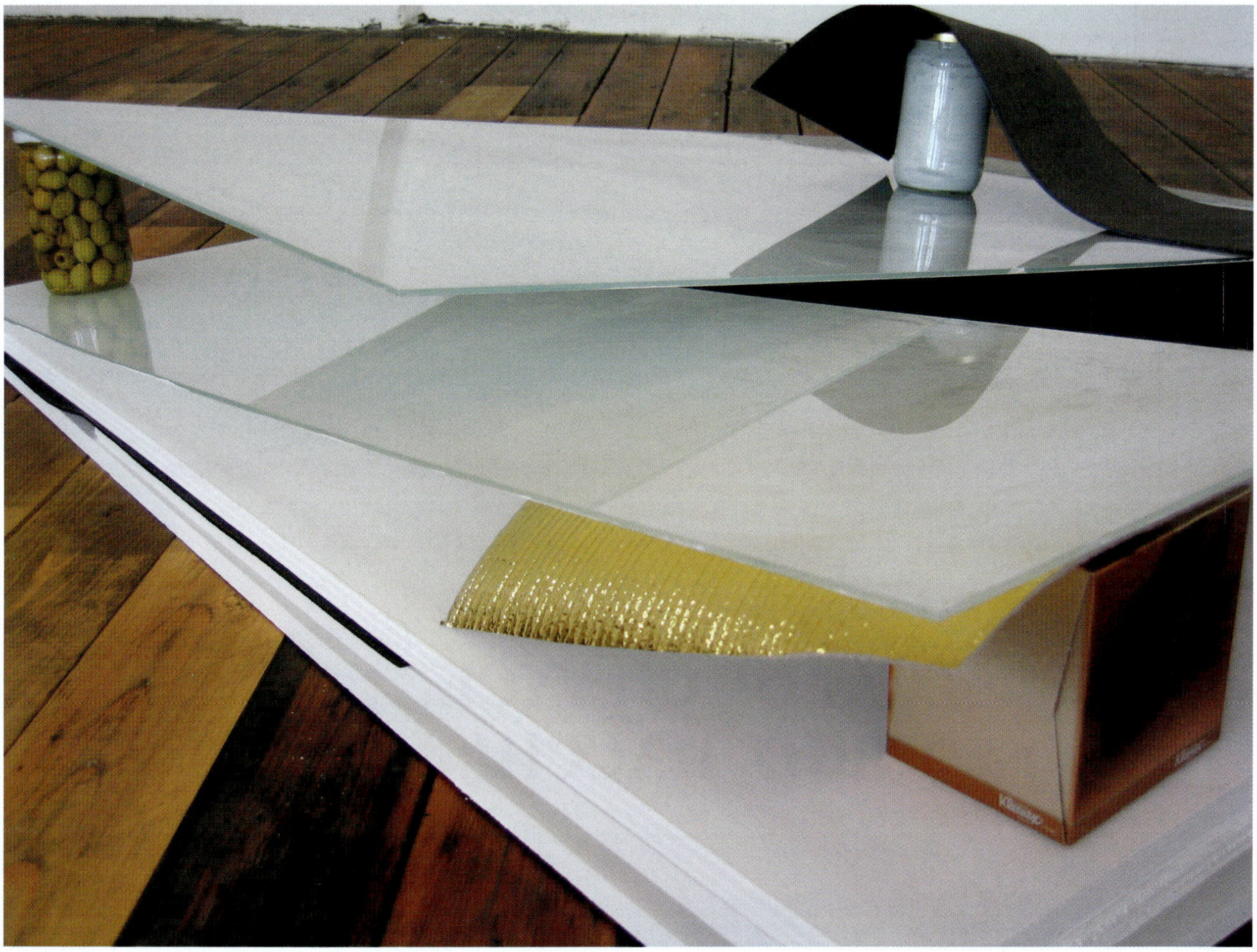

top: Study for *Hard Soft Blind* 2006 bottom: *Overlapping Statistic (Blind Olives Eyelid)* 2007 painted plywood, weatherproof roofing roll, painted glass, tissue box, painted jar, isolating roll

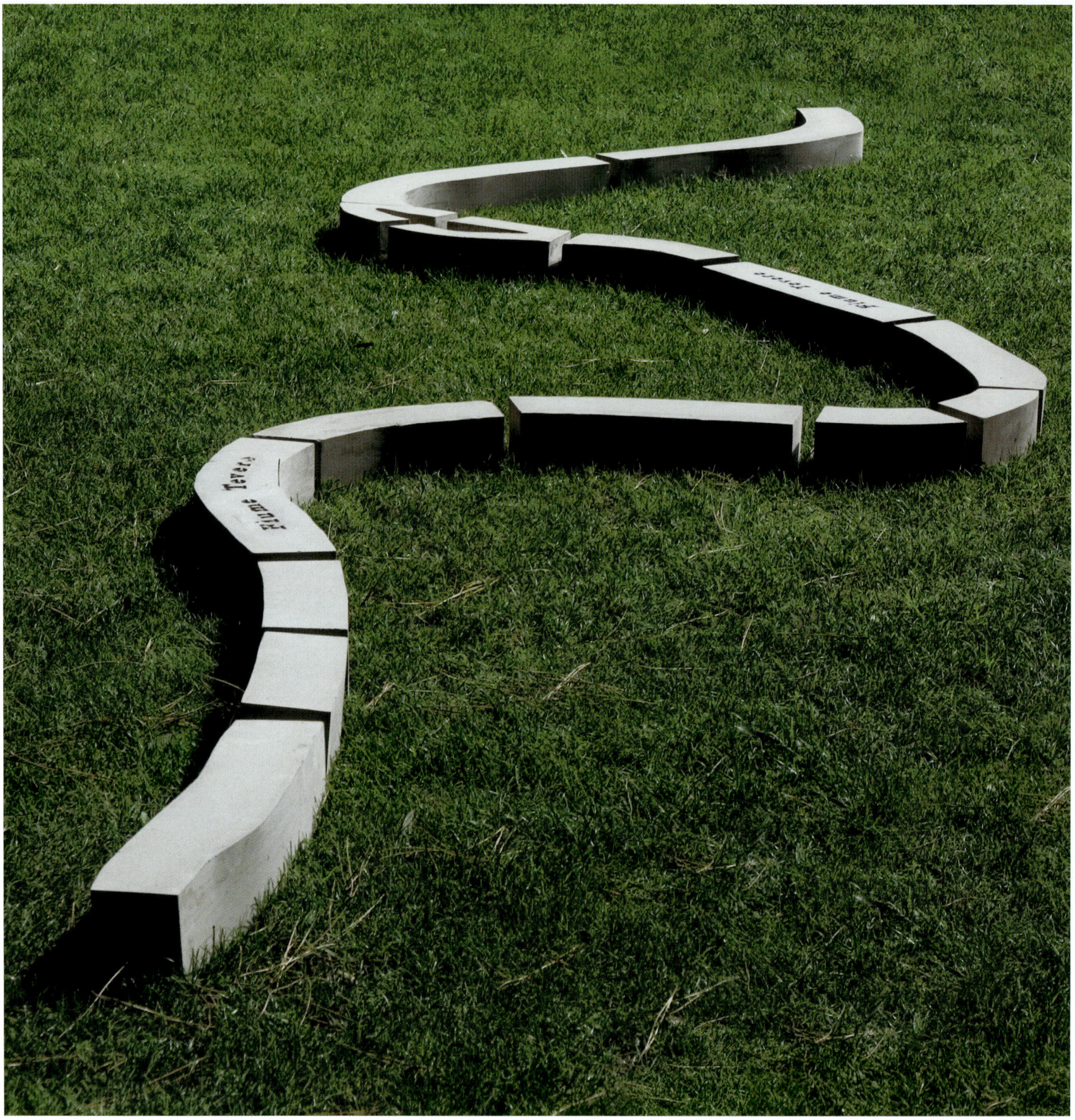

Tevere 2006 concrete

MAPS OF CHANCE: JORGE MACCHI

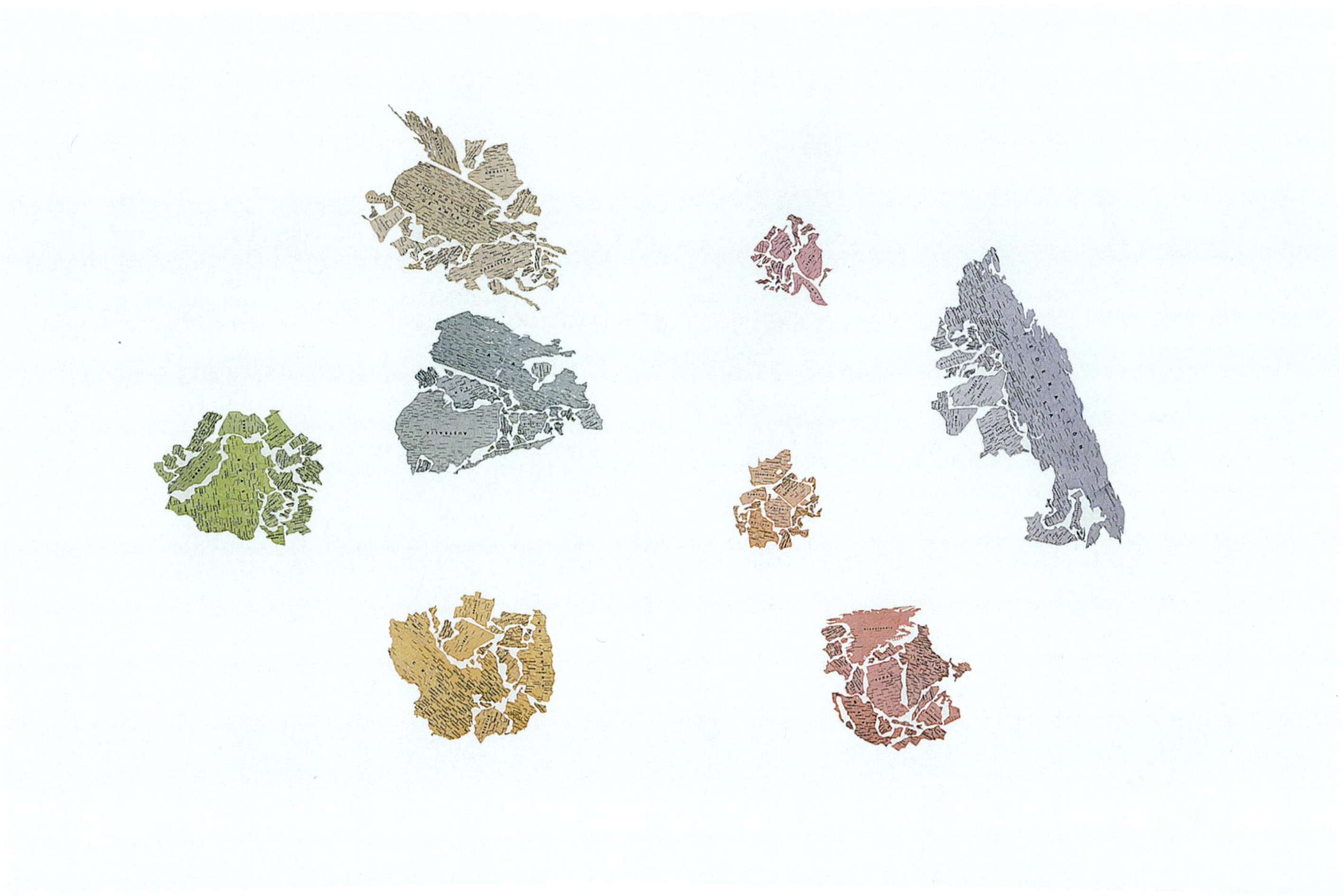

Nuevo Mundo 2006 paper collage

Born in Argentina, 1963. Lives and works in Buenos Aires.

Since the 1990s, Jorge Macchi has been creating meticulous works through tracing, cutting, fragmenting, and rearranging lines and shapes on surfaces ranging from newspaper pages to maps to sheets of music. His works heighten an awareness of the structures that organize language, geography, and sound. The notion of location is fundamentally linked to these material references, as they often invoke mental and physical trajectories, the meeting of parallel tracks, or the overlapping of isolated sites. By following the established order, and cutting along the edges of meridians and latitude lines in *Untitled* (2006), Macchi bestows pictorial value on an everyday, functional object. The result is a delicate grid system of subtractions, spared from excesses in slightly absurdist extreme because only fractions of words, coastlines of countries, and dots of oceans remain in this network of thin horizontal and vertical lines. Reducing the atlas to its barest elements, he returns the map to its original organizing principle and transforms it into a three-dimensional net, a mass of lines that hang in midair, sagging with its own weight. "I am interested in how the paper acquires a sculptural aspect when the information it conveyed disappears," he explains.[1]

Trained as a painter at the Escuela Nacional de Bellas Artes de Buenos Aires, Macchi has developed a multidisciplinary practice that ranges from collages to paper sculptures, video to light and sound installation. His tendency toward absence and invisibility stems from a desire to trace but also to humorously misrepresent and fictionalize the schematic system of representation and interpretation of the world. In *Liliput* (2007), for example, the artist proceeds to conceive a map of the area where Gulliver's fictional island might be located by throwing together cutout chunks of islands on paper and letting gravity and chance determine their location on the blank "ocean." Measuring the edge from one piece of paper to the next, he invented a table of relative distances and glued each shape to the fateful site of its landing. A map of chance, Macchi's collage invites us on a pilgrimage to distant lands and acts as an oracle to be invoked by those overwhelmed with wanderlust; it places a particular emphasis on "throwing" into existence a new geography to be imagined and potentially explored. As he has done with many of his works, he scatters familiar references or common objects—street networks, newspaper headlines, obituaries, musical annotations—to draw upon existential themes such as birth, transformation, and death and to rearrange their symbolic meanings.

Macchi's work also presents a world view that contests current systems of information classification systems and fictionalizes relationships, differences, and distances by setting forth a critical engagement with the printed order. His suggestive gestures—fragile perforations, careful removals, and intentional fragmentations—take on abstract forms beyond claims of accuracy, moving toward a new topography of transient spaces.

YR

1. Jorge Macchi, interview with Carla Zaccagnini, in Lisette Lagnado and Adriano Pedrosa, eds., *27a. Bienal de São Paulo Guia*, exh. pub. (São Paulo: Fundação Bienal de São Paulo, 2006), 36.

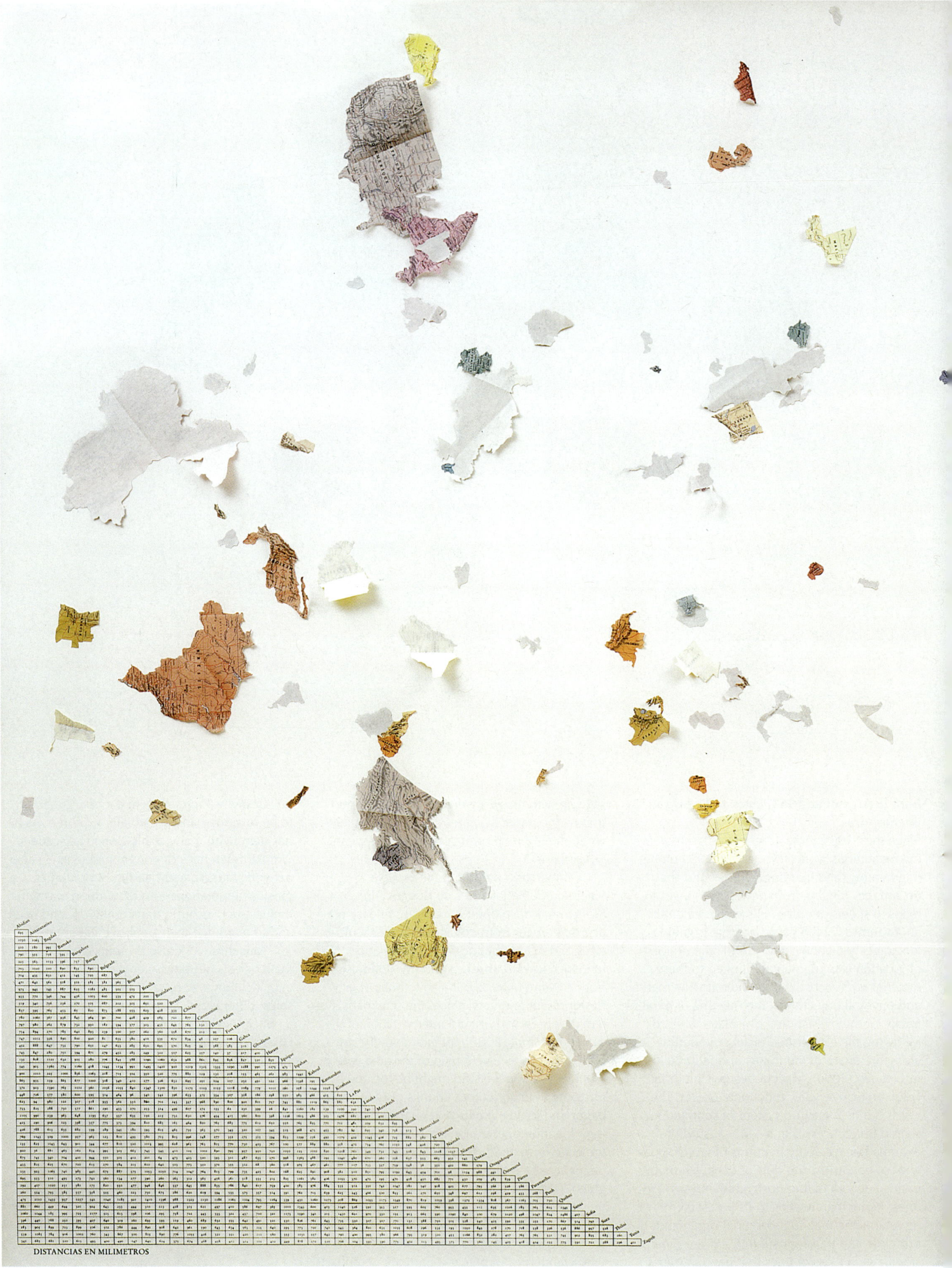

Liliput 2007 paper collage

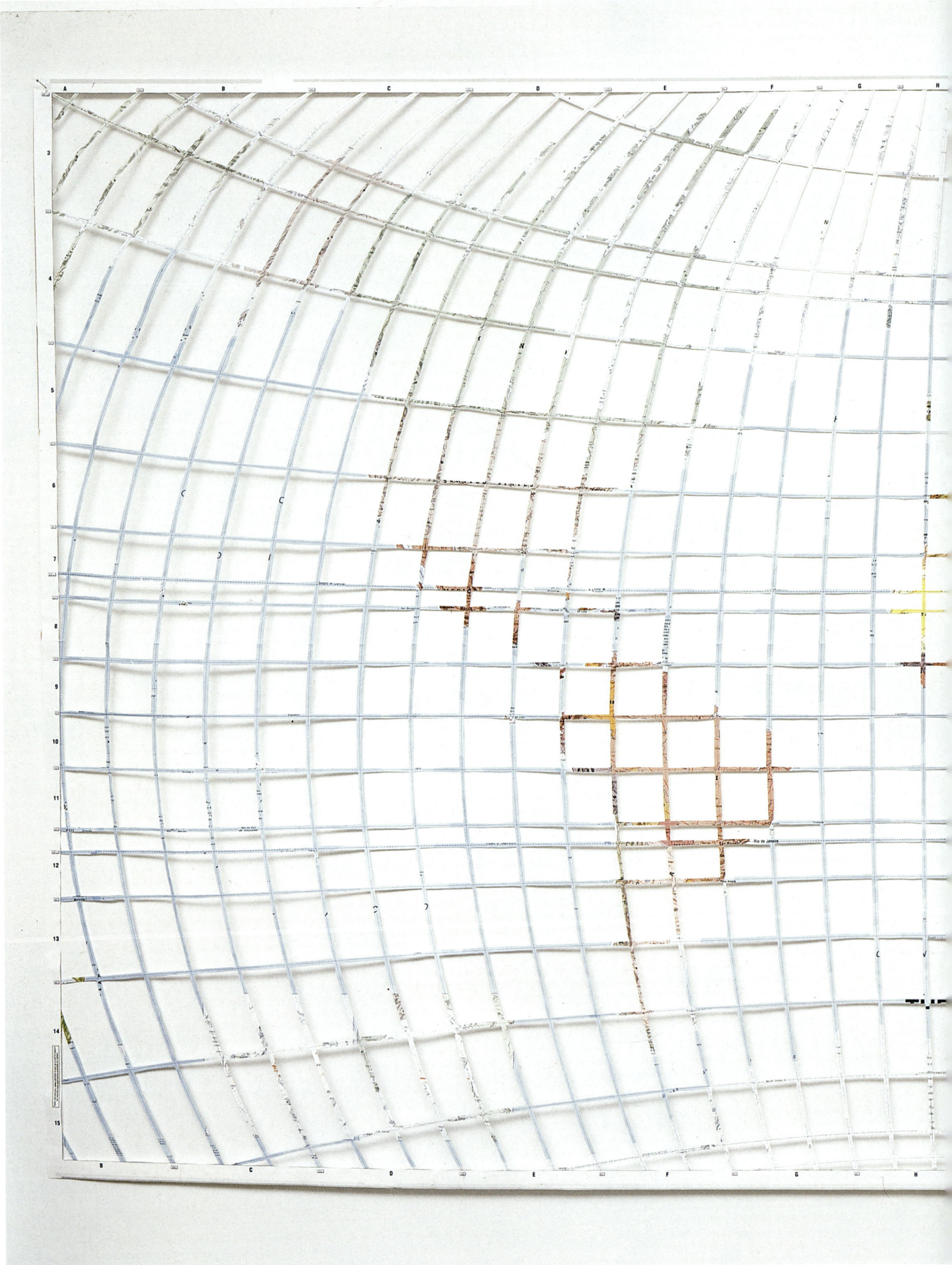

Untitled 2006 paper

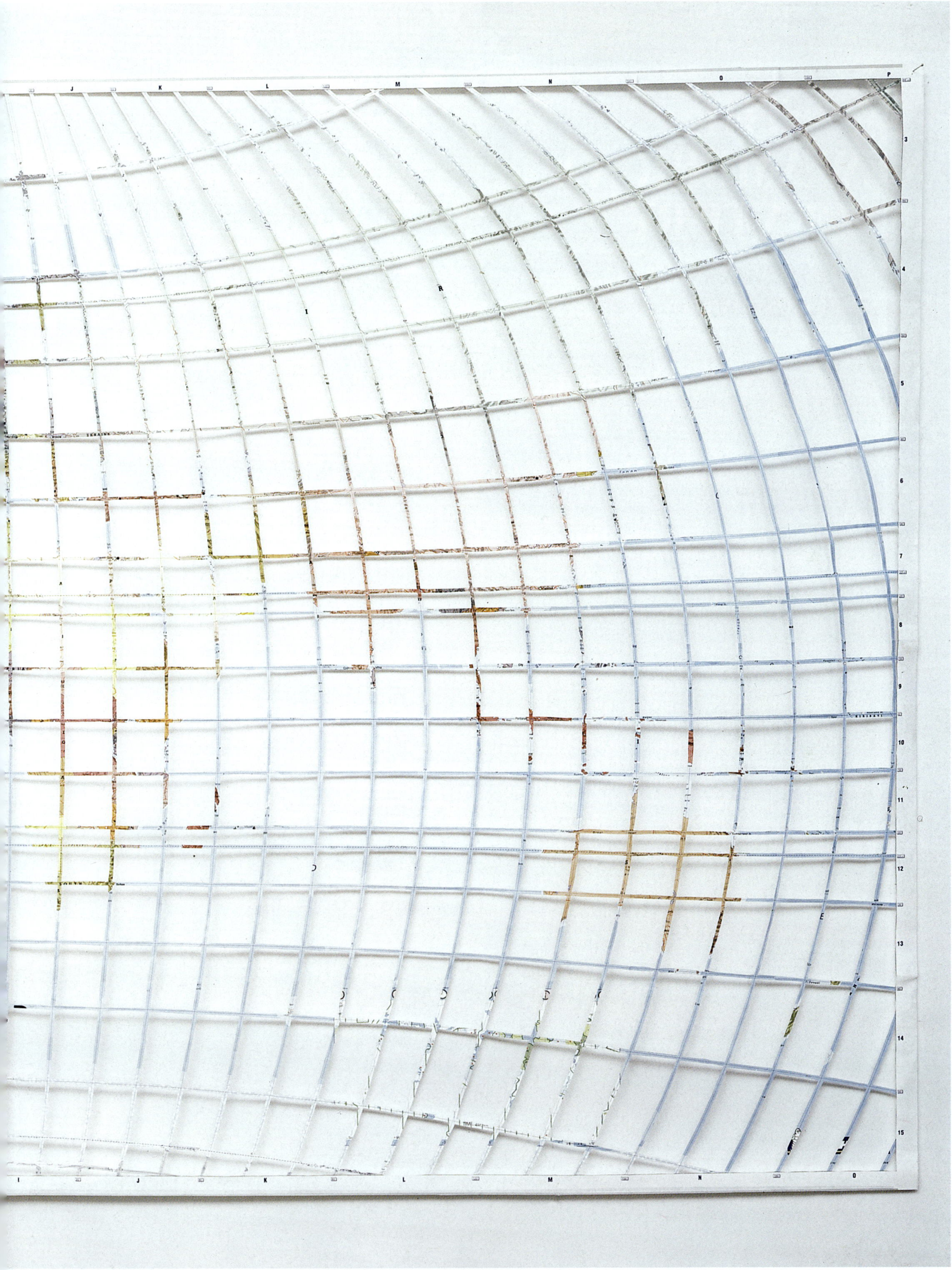

THE NEW AMERICAN CENTURY

ARUNDHATI ROY

n January 2003 thousands of us from across the world gathered n Porto Alegre in Brazil and declared—reiterated—that "Another Vorld Is Possible." A few thousand miles north, in Washington, George W. Bush and his aides were thinking the same thing.

Our project was the World Social Forum. Theirs—to further vhat many call the Project for the New American Century.

In the great cities of Europe and America, where a few years ago these things would only have been whispered, now people are openly talking about the good side of imperialism and the need for a strong empire to police an unruly world. The new missionaries want order at the cost of justice. Discipline at the cost of dignity. And ascendancy at any price. Occasionally some of us are invited to "debate" the issue on "neutral" platforms provided by the corporate media. Debating imperialism is a bit like debating the pros and cons of rape. What can we say? That we really miss it?

In any case, New Imperialism is already upon us. It's a remodeled, streamlined version of what we once knew. For the first time in history, a single empire with an arsenal of weapons that could obliterate the world in an afternoon has complete, unipolar, economic and military hegemony.

t uses different weapons to break open different markets. There sn't a country on God's earth that is not caught in the cross-hairs of the American cruise missile and the IMF checkbook. Argentina's he model if you want to be the poster boy of neoliberal capitalsm, Iraq if you're the black sheep. Poor countries that are geopolitically of strategic value to Empire, or have a "market" of any size, or infrastructure that can be privatized, or, God forbid, natural resources of value—oil, gold, diamonds, cobalt, coal—must do as they're told or become military targets. Those with the greatest reserves of natural wealth are most at risk. Unless they surrender their resources willingly to the corporate machine, civil unrest vill be fomented or war will be waged.

In this new age of empire, when nothing is as it appears o be, executives of concerned companies are allowed to influence foreign policy decisions. The Center for Public Integrity in Washington found that at least nine out of the thirty members of he Bush Administration's Defense Policy Board were connected o companies that were awarded military contracts for $76 billion between 2001 and 2002. George Shultz, former Secretary of State, was chairman of the Committee for the Liberation of Iraq. He is also on the board of directors of the Bechtel Group. When asked about a conflict of interest in the case of war in Iraq he said, "I don't know that Bechtel would particularly benefit from t. But if there's work to be done, Bechtel is the type of company

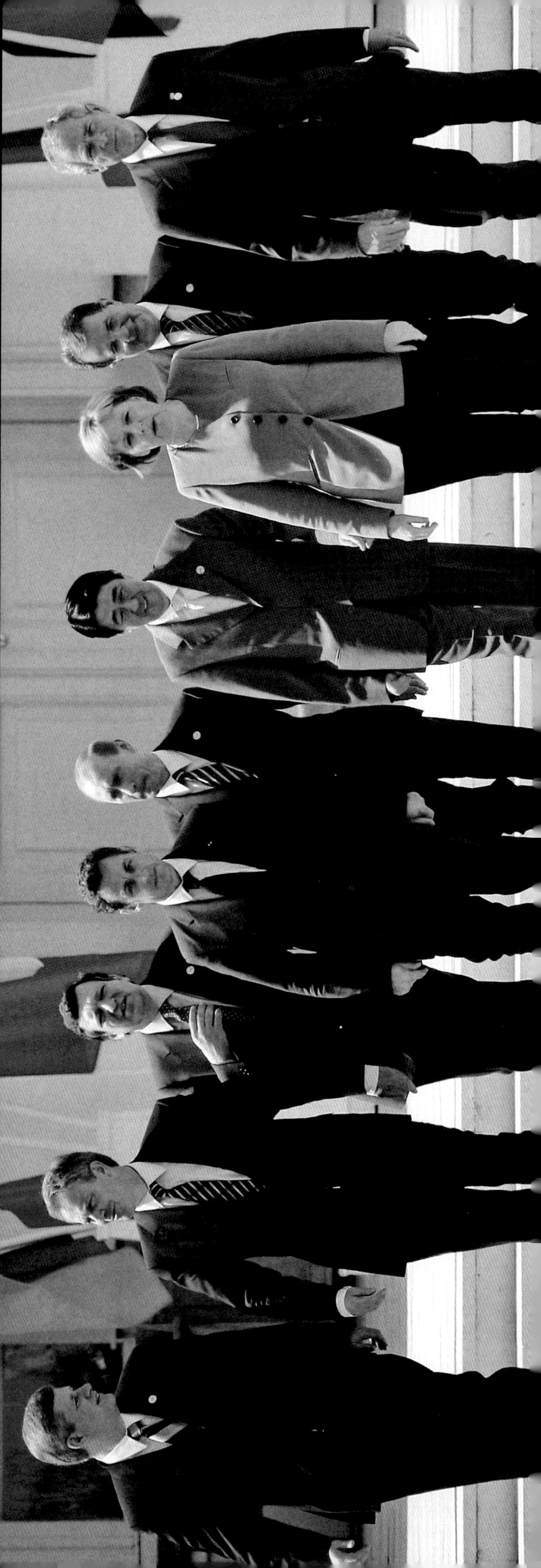

that could do it. But nobody looks at it as something you benefit from." In April 2003, Bechtel signed a $680 million contract for reconstruction.

This brutal blueprint has been used over and over again across Latin America, in Africa and in Central and Southeast Asia. It has cost millions of lives.

It goes without saying that every war the Empire wages becomes a Just War. This, in large part, is due to the role of the corporate media. It's important to understand that the corporate media don't just support the neoliberal project. They *are* the neoliberal project. This is not a moral position they have chosen to take; it's structural. It's intrinsic to the economics of how the mass media work.

Most nations have adequately hideous family secrets. So it isn't often necessary for the media to lie. It's all in the editing—what's emphasized and what's ignored. Say, for example, India was chosen as the target for a righteous war. The fact that about 80,000 people have been killed in Kashmir since 1989, most of them Muslim, most of them by Indian security forces (making the average death toll about 6,000 a year); the fact that in February and March of 2002 more than 2,000 Muslims were murdered on the streets of Gujarat, that women were gang-raped and children were burned alive and 150,000 driven from their homes while the police and administration watched and sometimes actively participated; the fact that no one has been punished for these crimes and the government that oversaw them was re-elected . . . all of this would make perfect headlines in international newspapers in the run-up to war.

Next thing we know, our cities will be leveled by cruise missiles, our villages fenced in with razor wire, US soldiers will patrol our streets, and Narendra Modi, Pravin Togadia or any of our popular bigots will, like Saddam Hussein, be in US custody having their hair checked for lice and the fillings in their teeth examined on prime-time TV.

But as long as our "markets" are open, as long as corporations like Enron, Bechtel, Halliburton and Arthur Andersen are given a free hand to take over our infrastructure and take away our jobs, our "democratically elected" leaders can fearlessly blur the lines between democracy, majoritarianism and fascism.

Our government's craven willingness to abandon India's proud tradition of being non-aligned, its rush to fight its way to the head of the queue of the Completely Aligned (the fashionable phrase is "natural ally"—India, Israel and the United States are "natural allies"), has given it the leg room to turn into a repressive regime without compromising its legitimacy.

A government's victims are not only those it kills and imprisons. Those who are displaced and dispossessed and sentenced to a lifetime of starvation and deprivation must count among them too. Millions of people have been dispossessed by "development" projects.

In the past fifty-five years, big dams alone have displaced between 33 million and 55 million in India. They have no recourse to justice. In the past two years there have been a series of incidents in which police have opened fire on peaceful protesters, most of them Adivasi and Dalit. When it comes to the poor, and in particular Dalit and Adivasi communities, they get killed for encroaching on forest land, and killed when they're trying to protect forest land from encroachments—by dams, mines, steel plants and other "development" projects. In almost every instance in which the police opened fire, the government's strategy has been to say the firing was provoked by an act of violence. Those who have been fired upon are immediately called militants.

Across the country, thousands of innocent people, including minors, have been arrested under the Prevention of Terrorism Act and are being held in jail indefinitely and without trial.

In the era of the War against Terror, poverty is being slyly conflated with terrorism. In the era of corporate globalization, poverty is a crime. Protesting against further impoverishment is terrorism.

And now our Supreme Court says that going on strike is a crime. Criticizing the court is a crime too, of course. They're sealing the exits.

Like Old Imperialism, New Imperialism relies for its success on a network of agents—corrupt local elites who service Empire. We all know the sordid story of Enron in India. The then-Maharashtra government signed a power purchase agreement that gave Enron profits that amounted to 60 percent of India's entire rural development budget. A single American company was guaranteed a profit equivalent to funds for infrastructural development for about 500 million people!

Unlike in the old days, the New Imperialist doesn't need to trudge around the tropics risking malaria or diarrhea or early death. New Imperialism can be conducted on e-mail. The vulgar, hands-on racism of Old Imperialism is outdated. The cornerstone of New Imperialism is New Racism.

The best allegory for New Racism is the tradition of "turkey pardoning" in the United States. Every year since 1947, the National Turkey Federation has presented the US President with a turkey for Thanksgiving. Every year, in a show of ceremonial magnanimity, the President spares that particular bird (and eats another one). After receiving the presidential pardon, the Chosen One is sent to Frying Pan Park in Virginia to live out its natural life. The rest of the 50 million turkeys raised for Thanksgiving are slaughtered and eaten on Thanksgiving Day. ConAgra Foods, the company that has won the Presidential Turkey contract, says it trains the lucky birds to be sociable, to interact with dignitaries, school children and the press. (Soon they'll even speak English!)

That's how New Racism in the corporate era works. A few carefully bred turkeys—the local elites of various countries, a community of wealthy immigrants, investment bankers, the occasional Colin Powell or Condoleezza Rice, some singers, some writers (like myself)—are given absolution and a pass to Frying Pan Park. The remaining millions lose their jobs, are evicted from their homes, have their water and electricity connections cut, and die of AIDS. Basically they're for the pot. But the Fortunate Fowls in Frying Pan Park are doing fine. Some of them even work for the IMF and the WTO—so who can accuse those organizations of being antiturkey? Some serve as board members on the Turkey Choosing Committee—so who can say that turkeys are against Thanksgiving? They participate in it! Who can say the poor are anti-corporate globalization? There's a stampede to get into Frying Pan Park. So what if most perish on the way?

Leaders of the G8 nations—U.S. President George Bush, Italian Premier Romano Prodi, German Chancellor Angela Merkel, Japanese Premier Shinzo Abe, Russian President Vladimir Putin, French President Nicolas Sarkozy, EU Commission President Jose Manuel Barroso, British Prime Minister Tony Blair, and Canadian Prime Minister Stephen Harper—gather for a summit meeting in Heiligendamm, Germany, June 7, 2007.

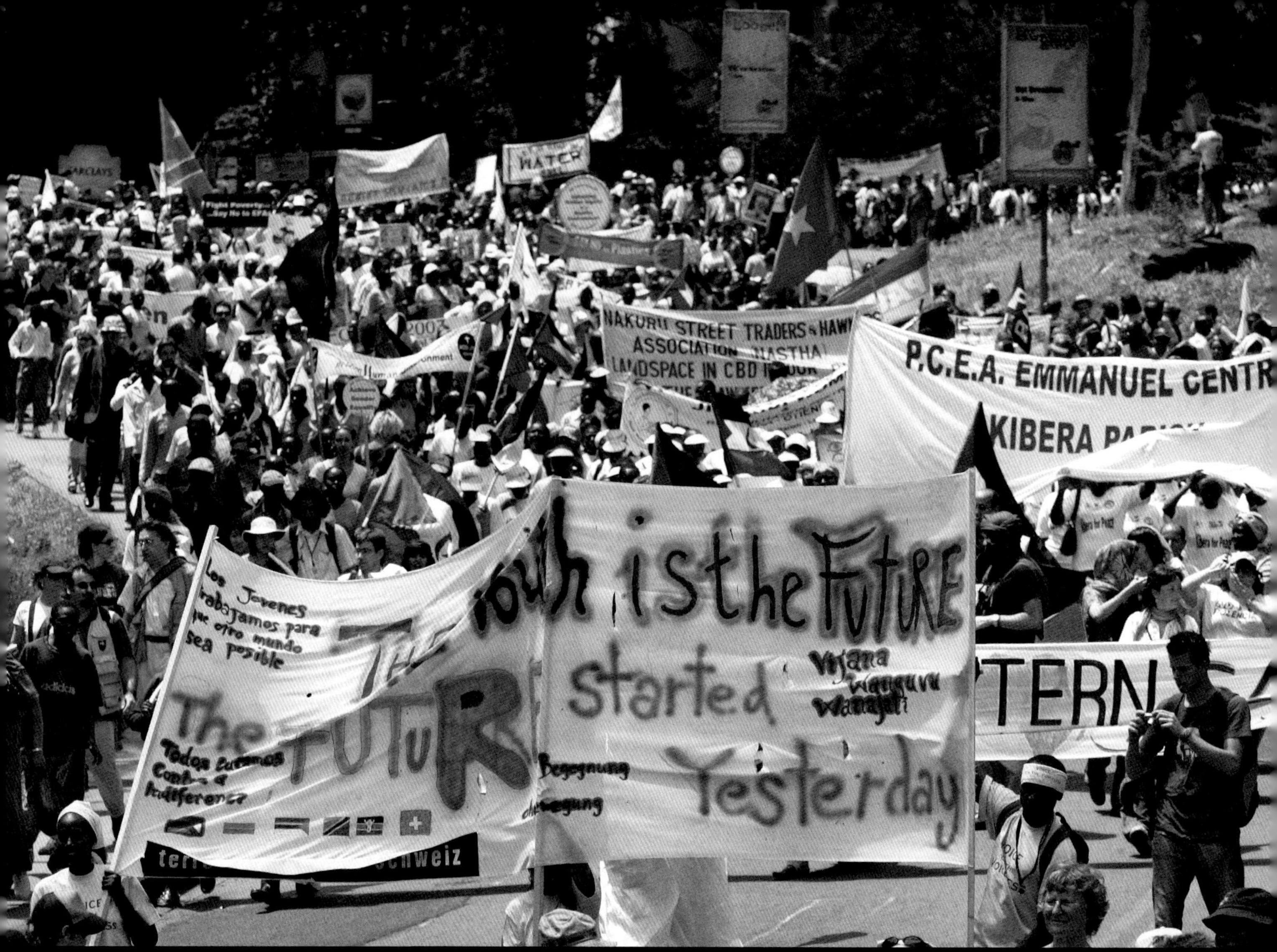

At a march during the opening of the World Social Forum in Nairobi, Kenya, on January 20, 2007, more than 80,000 people gathered, hoping to network with other activists and protest global policies they say hurt the poor.

As part of the project of New Racism we also have New Genocide. New Genocide in this new era of economic interdependence can be facilitated by economic sanctions. New Genocide means creating conditions that lead to mass death without actually going out and killing people. Denis Halliday, who was the UN humanitarian coordinator in Iraq between 1997 and 1998 (after which he resigned in disgust), used the term genocide to describe the sanctions in Iraq. In Iraq the sanctions outdid Saddam Hussein's best efforts by claiming more than half a million children's lives.

In the new era, apartheid as formal policy is antiquated and unnecessary. International instruments of trade and finance oversee a complex system of multilateral trade laws and financial agreements that keep the poor in their bantustans anyway. Its whole purpose is to institutionalize inequity. Why else would it be that the US taxes a garment made by a Bangladeshi manufacturer twenty times more than a garment made in Britain? Why else would it be that countries that grow cocoa beans, like the Ivory Coast and Ghana, are taxed out of the market if they try to turn it into chocolate? Why else would it be that countries that grow 90 percent of the world's cocoa beans produce only 5 percent of the world's chocolate? Why else would it be that rich countries that spend over a billion dollars a day on subsidies to farmers demand that poor countries like India withdraw all agricultural subsidies, including subsidized electricity? Why else would it be that after having been plundered by colonizing regimes for more than half a century, former colonies are steeped in debt to those same regimes and repay them some $382 *billion* a year?

For all these reasons, the derailing of trade agreements at Cancún was crucial for us. Though our governments try to take the credit, we know that it was the result of years of struggle by many millions of people in many, many countries. What Cancún taught us is that in order to inflict real damage and force radical change, it is vital for local resistance movements to make international alliances. From Cancún we learned the importance of globalizing resistance.

No individual nation can stand up to the project of corporate globalization on its own. Time and again we have seen that when it comes to the neoliberal project, the heroes of our times are suddenly diminished. Extraordinary, charismatic men, giants in the opposition, when they seize power and become heads of state, are rendered powerless on the global stage.

I'm thinking here of President Lula of Brazil. Lula was the hero of the World Social Forum last year. This year he's busy implementing IMF guidelines, reducing pension benefits and purging radicals from the Workers' Party. I'm thinking also of the former president of South Africa, Nelson Mandela. Within two years of taking office in 1994, his government genuflected with hardly a caveat to the Market God. It instituted a massive program of privatization and structural adjustment that has left millions of people homeless, jobless and without water and electricity.

Why does this happen? There's little point in beating our breasts and feeling betrayed. Lula and Mandela are, by any reckoning, magnificent men. But the moment they cross the floor from the opposition into government they become hostage to a spectrum of threats—most malevolent among them the threat of capital flight, which can destroy any government overnight. To imagine that a leader's personal charisma and a c.v. of struggle will dent the corporate cartel is to have no understanding of how capitalism works or, for that matter, how power works. Radical change cannot be negotiated by governments; it can only be enforced by people.

At the World Social Forum some of the best minds in the world come together to exchange ideas about what is happening around us. These conversations refine our vision of the kind of world we're fighting for. It is a vital process that must not be undermined. However, if all our energies are diverted into this process at the cost of real political action, then the WSF, which has played such a crucial role in the movement for global justice, runs the risk of becoming an asset to our enemies. What we need to discuss urgently is strategies of resistance. We need to aim at real targets, wage real battles and inflict real damage. Gandhi's salt march was not just political theater. When, in a simple act of defiance, thousands of Indians marched to the sea and made their own salt, they broke the salt tax laws. It was a direct strike at the economic underpinning of the British Empire. It was real. While our movement has won some important victories, we must not allow nonviolent resistance to atrophy into ineffectual, feel-good, political theater. It is a very precious weapon that must be constantly honed and reimagined. It cannot be allowed to become a mere spectacle, a photo opportunity for the media.

It was wonderful that on February 15 last year, in a spectacular display of public morality, 10 million people on five continents marched against the war on Iraq. It was wonderful, but it was not enough. February 15 was a weekend. Nobody had to so much as miss a day of work. Holiday protests don't stop wars. George Bush knows that. The confidence with which he disregarded overwhelming public opinion should be a lesson to us all. Bush believes that Iraq can be occupied and colonized as Afghanistan has been, as Tibet has been, as Chechnya is being, as East Timor once was and Palestine still is. He thinks that all he has to do is hunker down and wait until a crisis-driven media, having picked this crisis to the bone, drops it and moves on. Soon the carcass will slip off the bestseller charts, and all of us outraged folks will lose interest. Or so he hopes.

This movement of ours needs a major, global victory. It's not good enough to be right. Sometimes, if only in order to test our resolve, it's important to win something. In order to win something, we need to agree on something. That something does not need to be an overarching preordained ideology into which we force-fit our delightfully factious, argumentative selves. It does not need to be an unquestioning allegiance to one or another form of resistance to the exclusion of everything else. It could be a minimum agenda.

If all of us are indeed against imperialism and against the project of neoliberalism, then let's turn our gaze on Iraq. Iraq is the inevitable culmination of both. Plenty of antiwar activists have retreated in confusion since the capture of Saddam Hussein. Isn't the world better off without Saddam Hussein? they ask timidly.

Let's look this thing in the eye once and for all. To applaud the US Army's capture of Saddam Hussein, and therefore in retrospect justify its invasion and occupation of Iraq, is like deifying Jack the Ripper for disemboweling the Boston Strangler. And that after a quarter-century partnership in which the Ripping and Strangling was a joint enterprise. It's an in-house quarrel. They're business partners who fell out over a dirty deal. Jack's the CEO.

So if we are against imperialism, shall we agree that we are against the US occupation and that we believe the United States must withdraw from Iraq and pay reparations to the Iraqi people for the damage that the war has inflicted?

How do we begin to mount our resistance? Let's start with something really small. The issue is not about *supporting* the resistance in Iraq against the occupation or discussing who exactly constitutes the resistance. (Are they old killer Baathists, are they Islamic fundamentalists?)

We have to *become* the global resistance to the occupation.

Our resistance has to begin with a refusal to accept the legitimacy of the US occupation of Iraq. It means acting to make it materially impossible for Empire to achieve its aims. It means soldiers should refuse to fight, reservists should refuse to serve, workers should refuse to load ships and aircraft with weapons. It certainly means that in countries like India and Pakistan we must block the US government's plans to have Indian and Pakistani soldiers sent to Iraq to clean up after them.

I suggest we choose by some means two of the major corporations that are profiting from the destruction of Iraq. We could then list every project they are involved in. We could locate their offices in every city and every country across the world. We could go after them. We could shut them down. It's a question of bringing our collective wisdom and experience of past struggles to bear on a single target. It's a question of the desire to win.

The Project for the New American Century seeks to perpetuate inequity and establish American hegemony at any price, even if it's apocalyptic. The World Social Forum demands justice and survival.

For these reasons, we must consider ourselves at war. ■

Arundhati Roy is a political activist and author whose books include *The God of Small Things*, which won the 1997 Booker Prize, *An Ordinary Person's Guide to Empire*, and *War Talk*. Roy received the Lannan Foundation's Prize for Cultural Freedom in 2002. This text, adapted from her January 16 speech to the opening plenary of the World Social Forum in Mumbai, is reprinted by permission from the author, ©2004 by Arundhati Roy. First printed as "The New American Century," *The Nation* 278, no. 5 (February 9, 2004): 11–14. See also Arundhati Roy, "Do Turkeys Enjoy Thanksgiving?," in *An Ordinary Person's Guide to Empire* (Cambridge, Massachusetts: South End Press, 2004), 83–94.

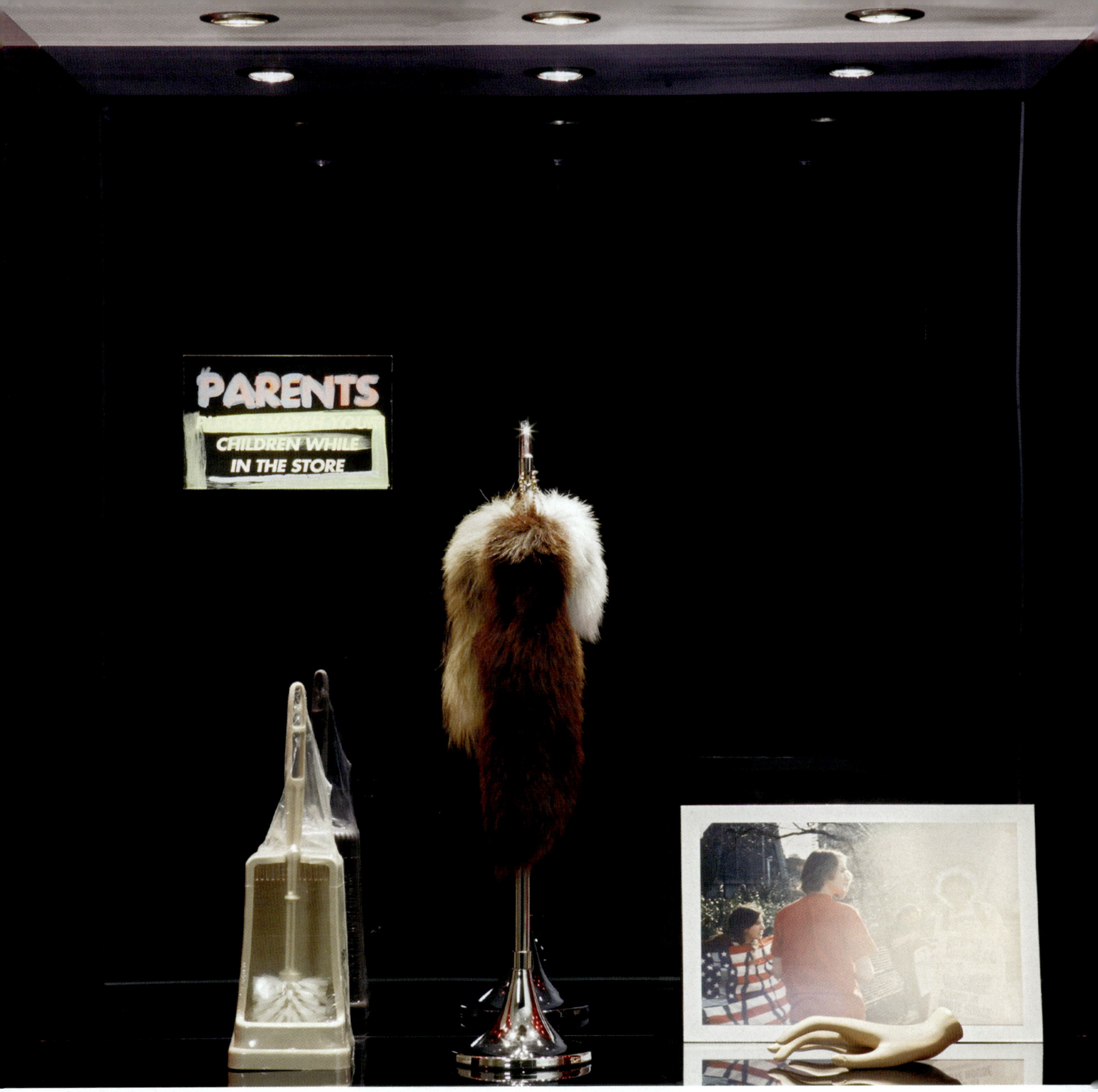

SATIRE AND A CYNICAL SMILE: JOSEPHINE MECKSEPER

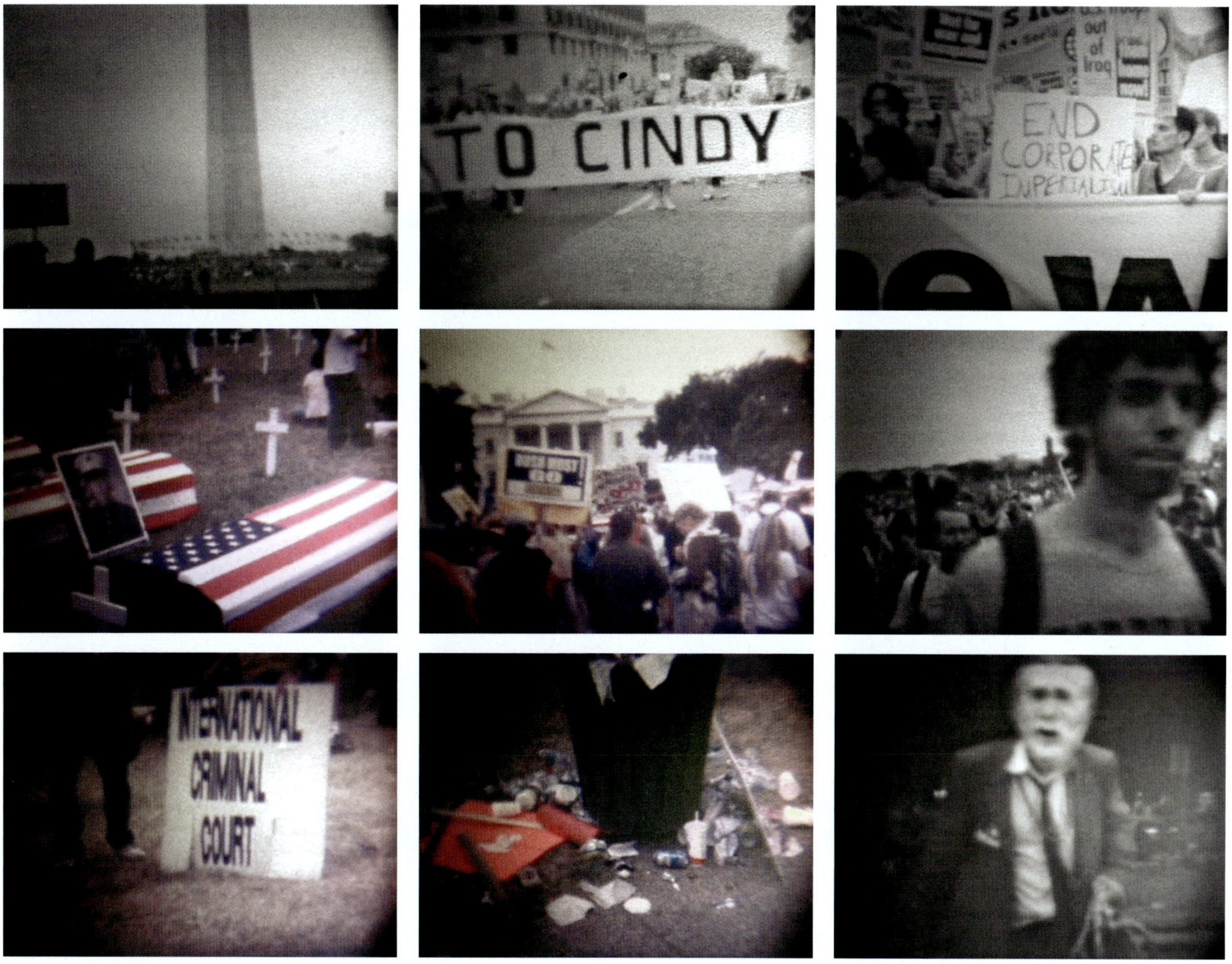

left: *The Children's Crusade* 2006 (detail) mixed media in display window above: Stills from *March on Washington to End the War on Iraq, 9/24/05* 2006 Super 8 film and video transferred to DVD (black and white/color, silent); 8:50 minutes

Born in Germany, 1964. Lives and works in New York.

Josephine Meckseper's artwork evokes the empty simulacra that cultural theorist Jean Baudrillard warned about in his essays on nightmarish capitalism. He saw the "cynical smile" of Pop Art in particular as "one of the obligatory signs of consumption; it no longer indicates a humor, a critical distance."[1] Meckseper wears a cool smile with her slick display cases and shelves, photographs that look like fashion magazine spreads, and silent films of political protests that render the social movements of this generation into clichés of the previous. By using commercial displays to comment on the complicity between protest, performance, and profit, the artist herself embraces both criticism of and collusion with consumerism, an ambiguous and complicated position. But the antiwar street marches that she depicts inherently undermine any dichotomy between cynicism and commercialism, for they reference, albeit distantly, the very real consequences of the Iraq war.

Meckseper studied art in Berlin and in 1990 left her homeland for the United States to complete her MFA at the California Institute of Arts. There she began making films and soon after, in 1994, started publishing her own magazine, *FAT*, a quirky collage of tabloid news, photos, and essays on art and culture. In 2001, Meckseper started constructing shelves of brightly colored acrylic or plexiglass that display commercially manufactured knick-knacks along with her photographs. As she continued to expand her practice, the shelves became only one element of her gallery installations, which by 2004 also included textiles, wallpaper, vitrines, and shoes.

The Children's Crusade (2006) is a window onto a set of carefully arranged objects. Somewhere between department store display case and museum vitrine, the box encases a hodgepodge of items—from a toilet brush in its stand sealed in plastic to a chromogenic print of a 2003 antiwar demonstration in New York's Washington Square Park. Taped to the glass on the front of the vitrine is a sign on which the words "PARENTS PLEASE WATCH YOUR CHILDREN WHILE IN THE STORE" can be made out through the gouache painted on the placard's plastic surface. The posted message refers back to the work's title, which in turn alludes to the medieval legend of a band of Northern European children who left for the Near East to convert Muslims but were sold into slavery when they reached the coast of the Mediterranean Sea.

Shown near *The Children's Crusade* in the exhibition *Brave New Worlds* is a film that documents a 2005 protest on the National Mall, *March on Washington to End the War on Iraq, 9/24/05* (2006). The fuzzy focus and scratches on the footage give it a vintage feel, which is echoed in the Cold War–motif wallpaper that is also part of the installation. These artworks mine the gray area in which street protests become catwalks, articles of clothing make political statements, and leftist proclamations operate like advertising slogans. Meckseper's melding of commercial design and leftist symbols presents an ideological paradox of progressive politics and profit-making that hits close to home for many liberal Americans.

RH

1. Jean Baudrillard, "Pop—An Art of Consumption," trans. Paul Foss, in Paul Taylor, ed., *Post-Pop Art* (Cambridge, Massachusetts: MIT Press, 1989), 33–44. Baudrillard predicted a world taken over by the endless commercial reproduction of images that manifest our desires rather than a meaningful connection with the real world.

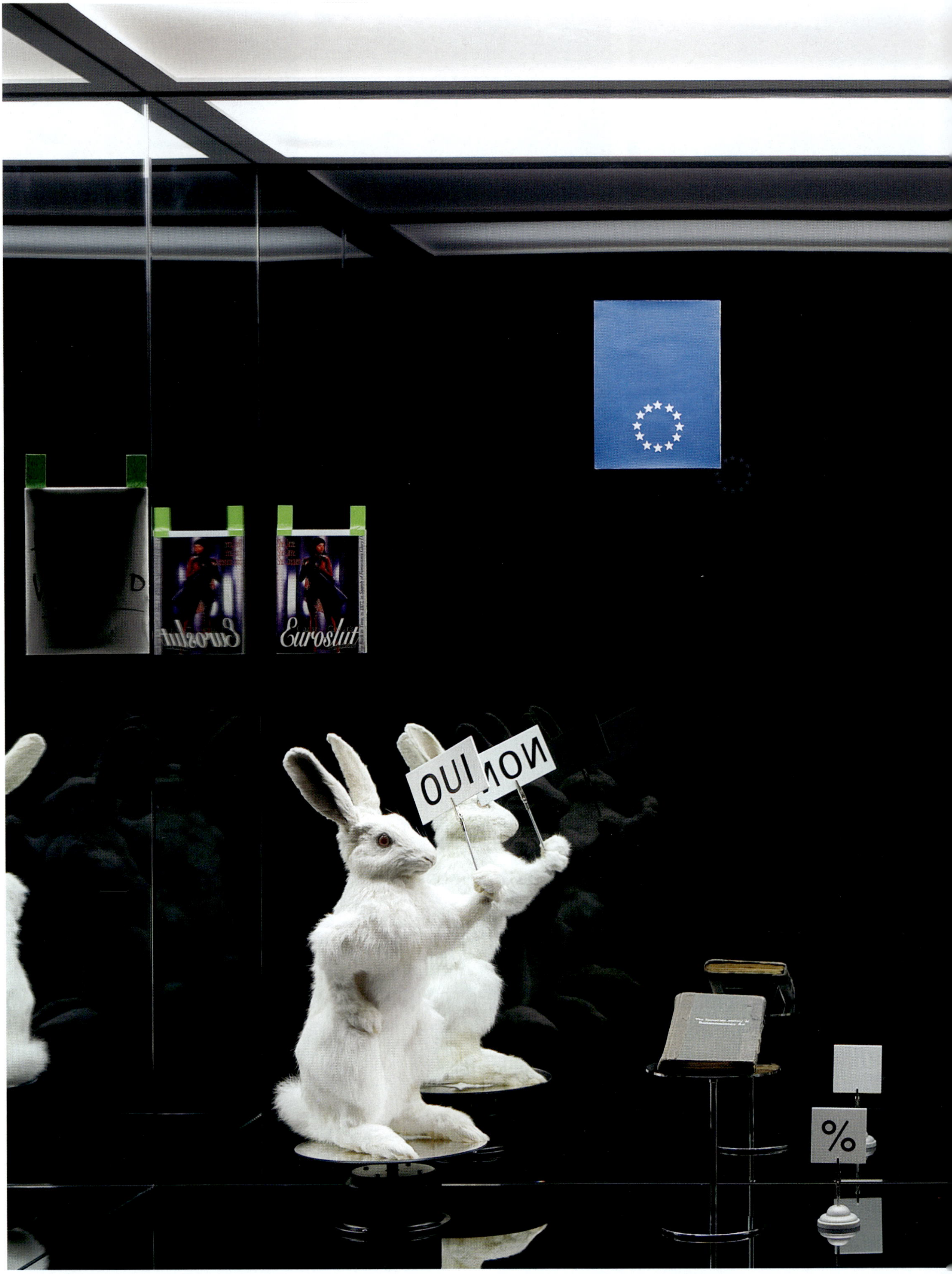

The Complete History of Postcontemporary Art I 2005 (detail) mixed media in display window following pages: *Untitled (Cold War)* 2006 wallpaper of color photographs

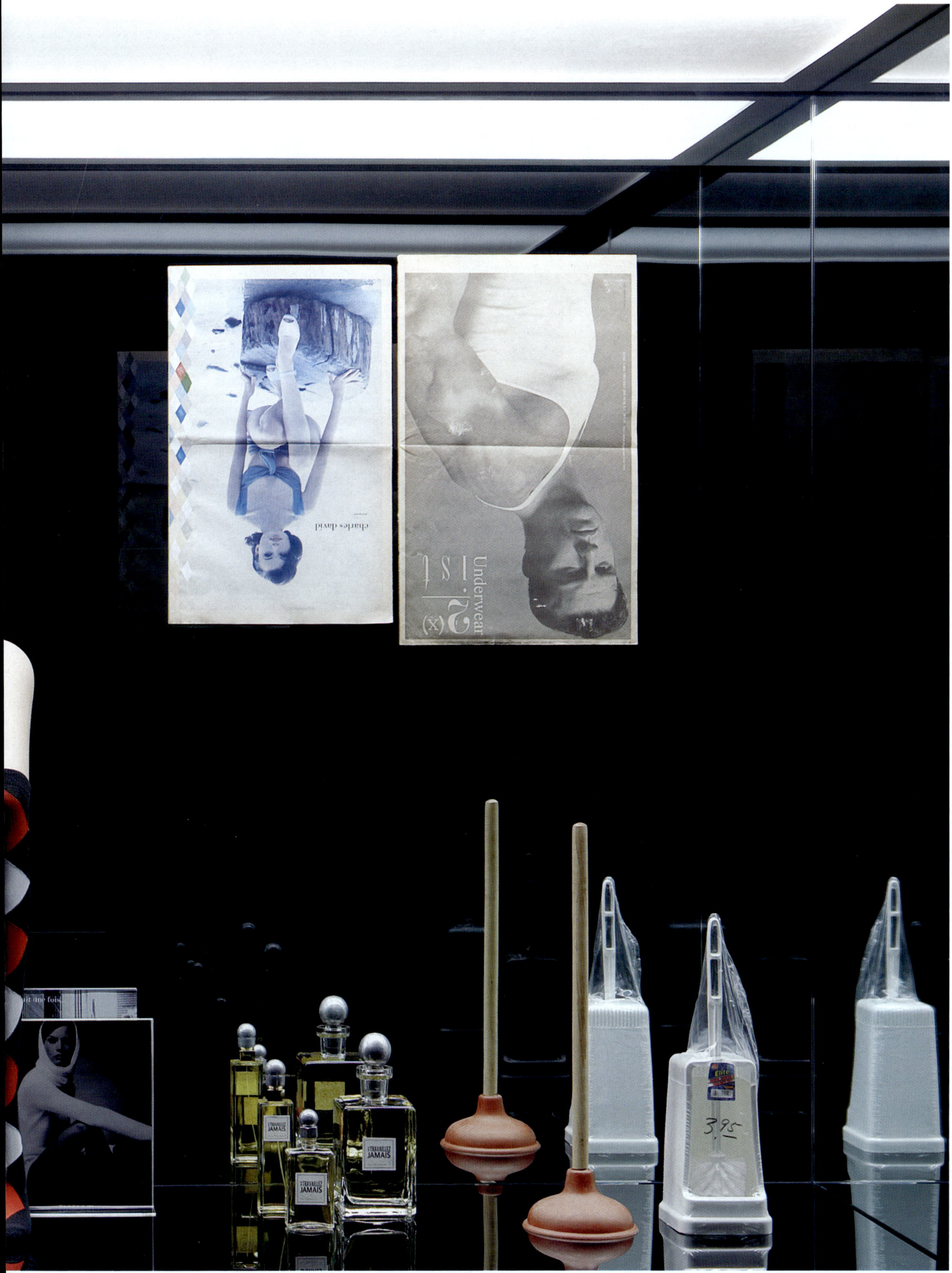
charles david
Underwear
TRAVAILLEZ
JAMAIS
3.95

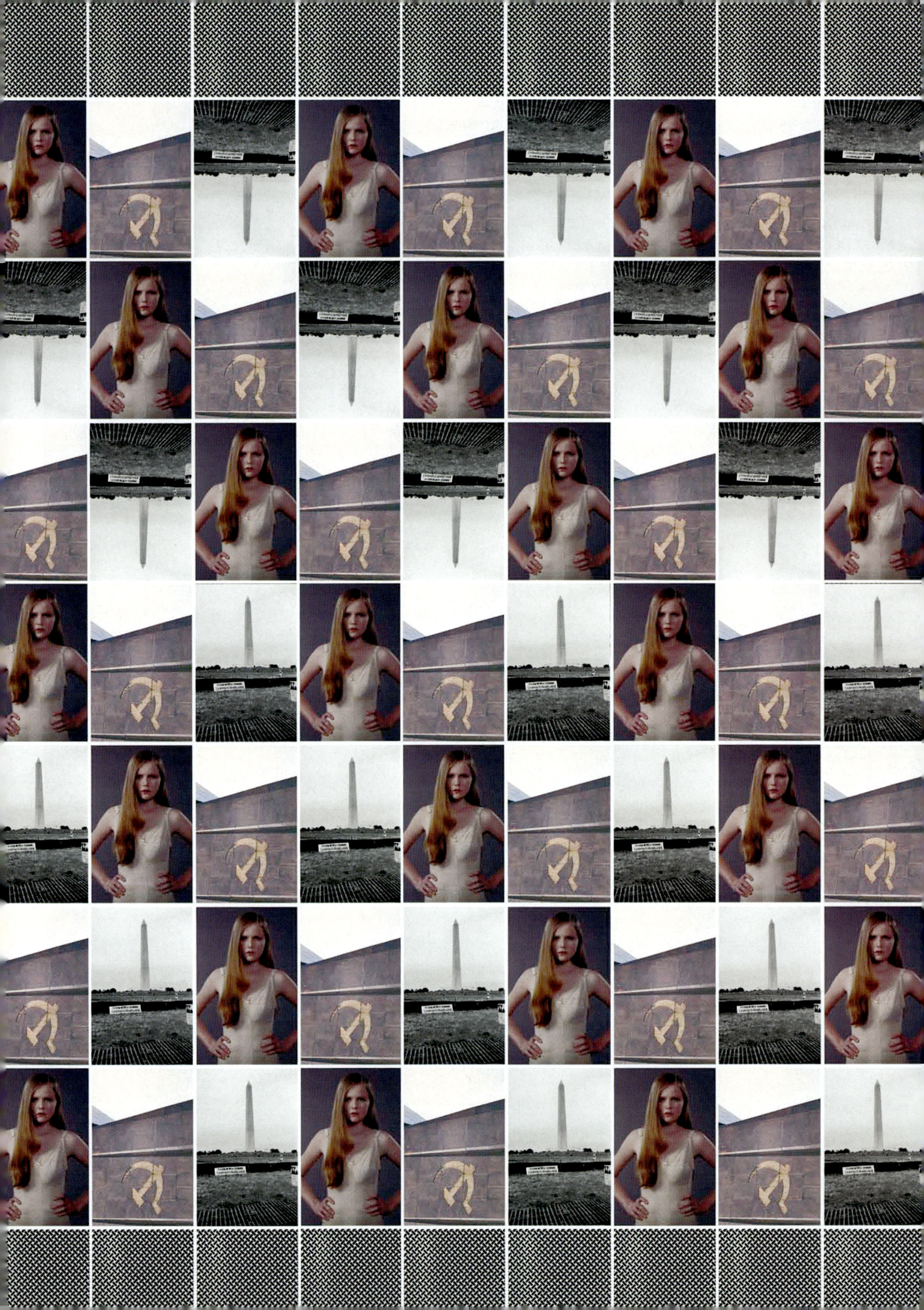

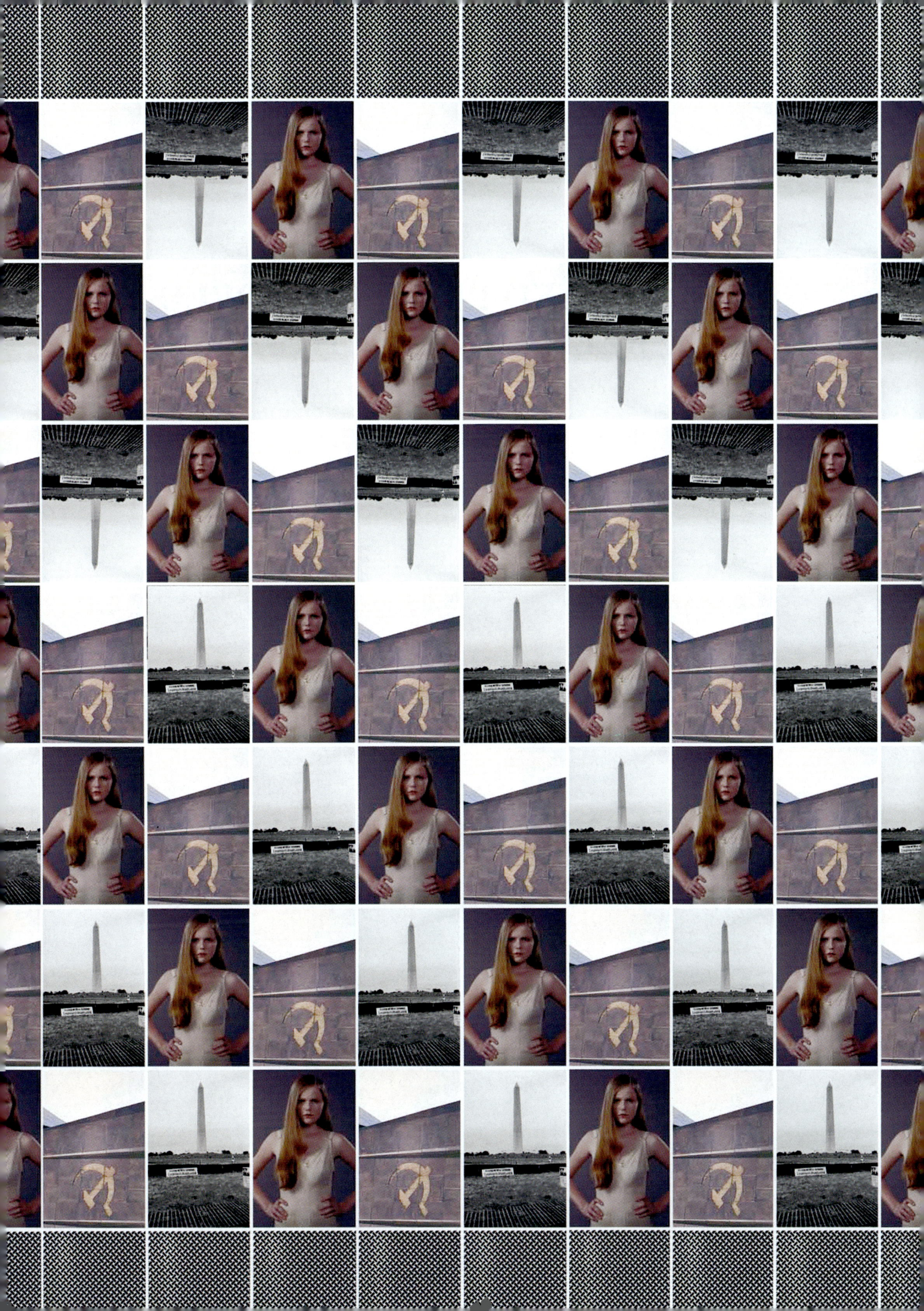

RESPECT AND PRIDE RESTORED: ZWELETHU MTHETHWA

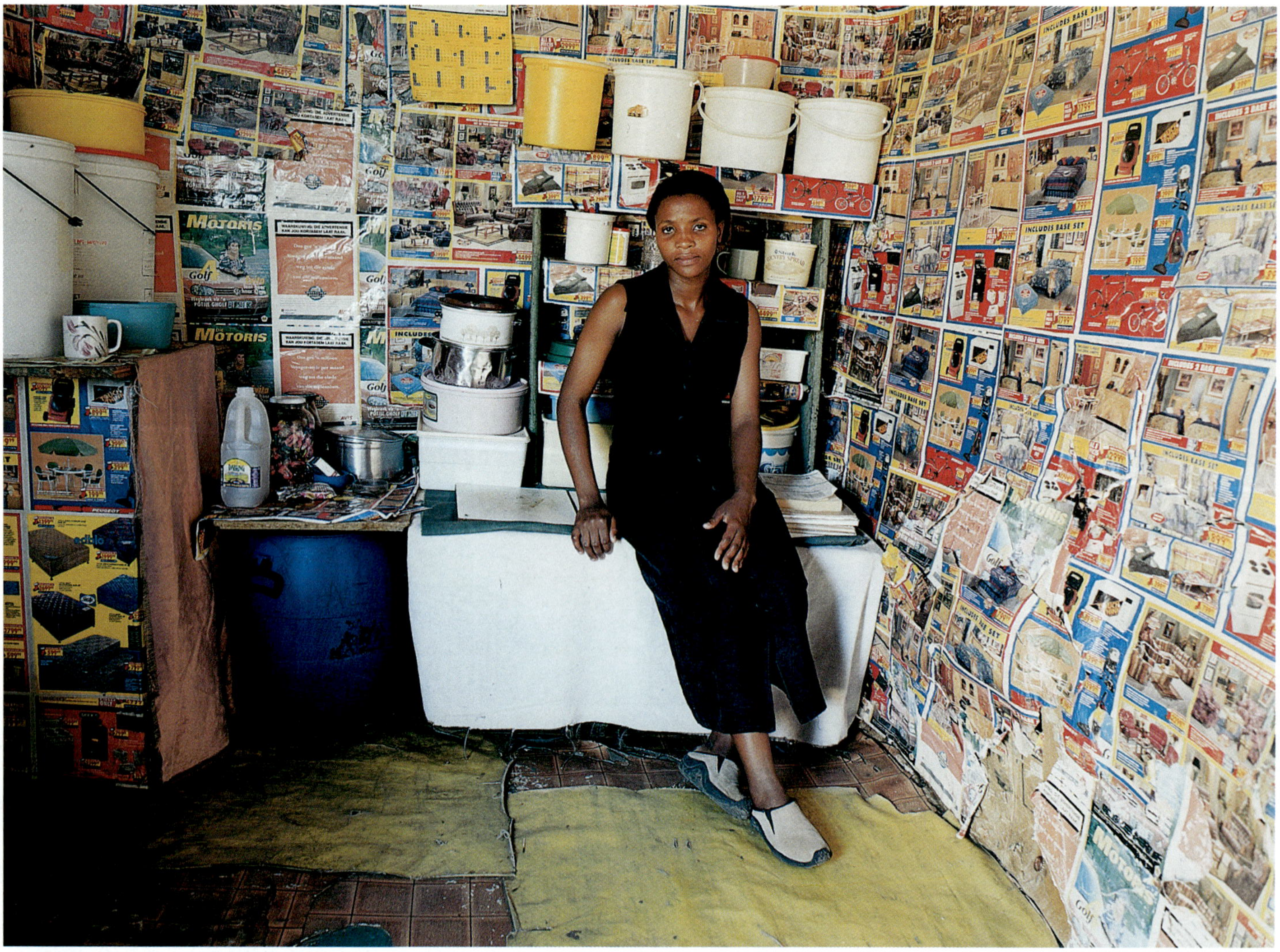

Untitled 2000 chromogenic print

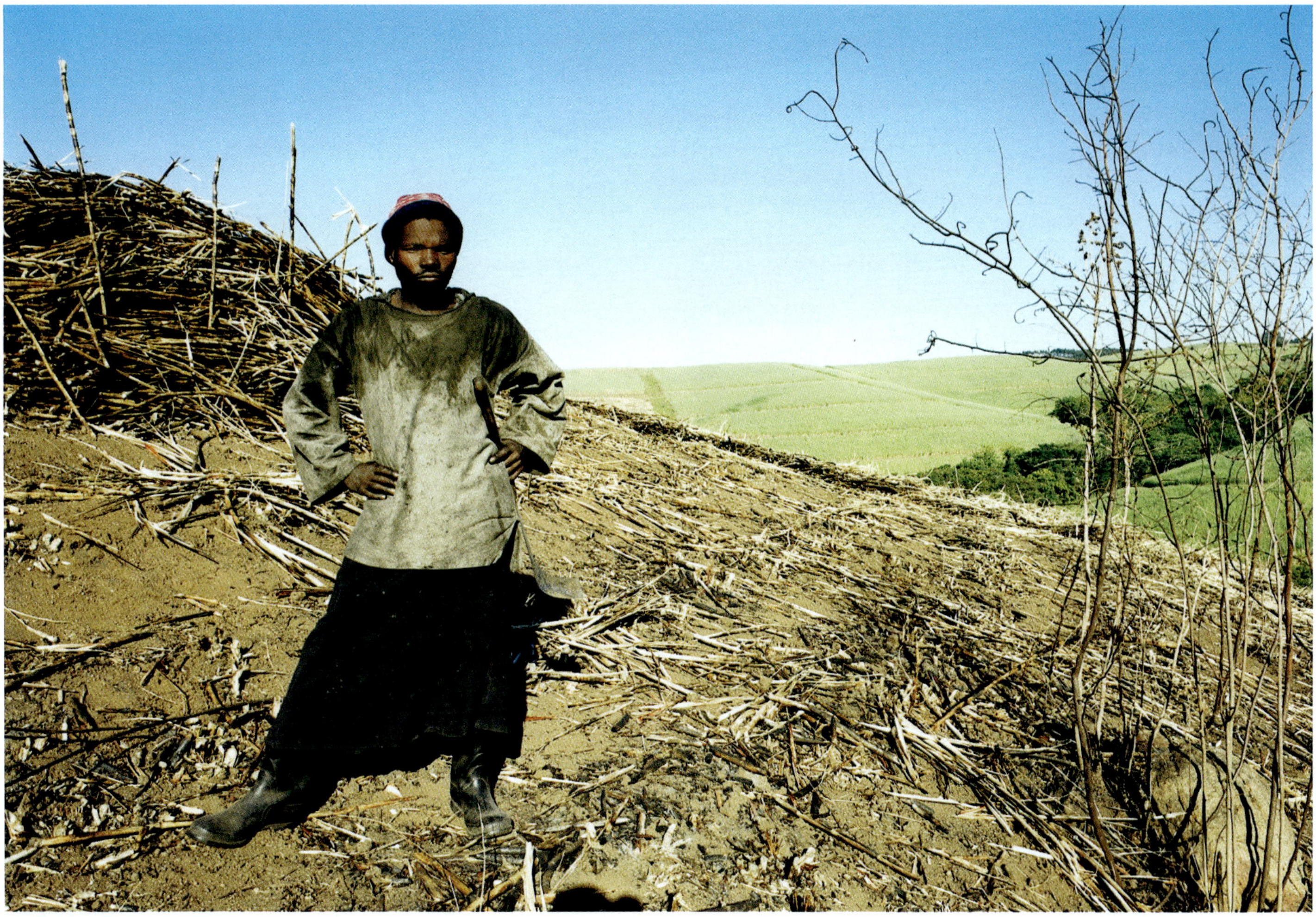

Untitled 2004 chromogenic print

Born in South Africa, 1960. Lives and works in Cape Town.

Zwelethu Mthethwa's large-scale, richly colored photographic portraits of South African laborers and residents of the Paarl shantytown near Cape Town evidence their subjects' hard work and impoverished lives in vivid detail. But the figures' confident stance and self-determined presentation emphasize the strength of their character over their economic circumstances. Images of Africans as hungry, violent, and diseased are all too common, and Mthethwa has intentionally set out to counteract negative portrayals of his country and continent. Instead of taking pictures that illustrate a tragic story or political purpose, the artist works in collaboration with the people and communities he photographs to allow them to dictate the terms by which they wish to be seen. "I do not believe poverty is equal to degradation," the artist has asserted. "I think . . . [my] photographs preserve and show a humane-ness of the occupants in their private spaces. They restore their pride and affirm their ownership."[1]

Mthethwa was born in 1960 into apartheid South Africa. Like many successful black South African artists of his generation, he took a circuitous path of chance and circumstance to become a professional photographer. As a teenager, he attended the South African Institute of Race Relations' Abangani Open School in Durban, which was one of the few schools where blacks could take fine arts courses. His tutors encouraged him to apply to the Michaelis School of Fine Art at the University of Cape Town to get the best education, but black students could not attend unless they wanted to study a subject that was unavailable at black universities. Mthethwa applied to the Michaelis because photography was only taught there. After graduating, he received a Fulbright Scholarship to pursue a master's degree in imaging arts at the Rochester Institute of Technology, New York, which he received in 1989. In 1994, he was appointed one of the first black lecturers at his South African alma mater, and in 1999, he left teaching to devote himself full time to his artwork.

In the artist's first major photographic series, images of interior scenes from 2000 and sugarcane workers from 2004, Mthethwa used two visual strategies to "restore respect and dignity" to his subjects—a large format and bright colors.[2] The image size allows for an incredible amount of detail. It is possible to read the newspapers decorating the houses, see every clean cut on the reeds of sugarcane, and observe the wrinkles and calluses on the protagonists' skin. In the manner of a photojournalist, the artist tells a story with these minutiae, but he presents them on a large scale like a painter of the eighteenth-century French salon. As with neoclassical paintings, the scale of the photographs connotes importance and power reserved in the Western tradition for royalty and the very wealthy. Vibrant pigments have a similarly dignified connotation for Mthethwa and are a distinctive characteristic of his art. For him, vivid colors signify a uniquely African aesthetic but also, metaphorically, a rich and energetic life. The formal qualities of the artist's work therefore perfectly complement his political message. Like other prominent fine-art photographers thriving around the Cape Town area, including Guy Tillim and Tracey Derrick, Mthethwa is following the dream laid out in his childhood by the anti-apartheid and Pan-African movements to reclaim African self-images in the face of oppression and degradation.

RH

1. Zwelethu Mthethwa, interview with Bongi Dhlomo, "Zwelethu Mthethwa Talks about His Photographs," in Frank Herreman, ed., *Liberated Voices: Contemporary Art from South Africa*, exh. cat., The Museum for African Art, New York (New York: Prestel, 1999), 75.

2. Zwelethu Mthethwa, in Ashraf Jamal, "A feature on an artist in the public eye: Zwelethu Mthethwa," Art Throb, http://www.artthrob.co.za/99apr/artbio.htm.

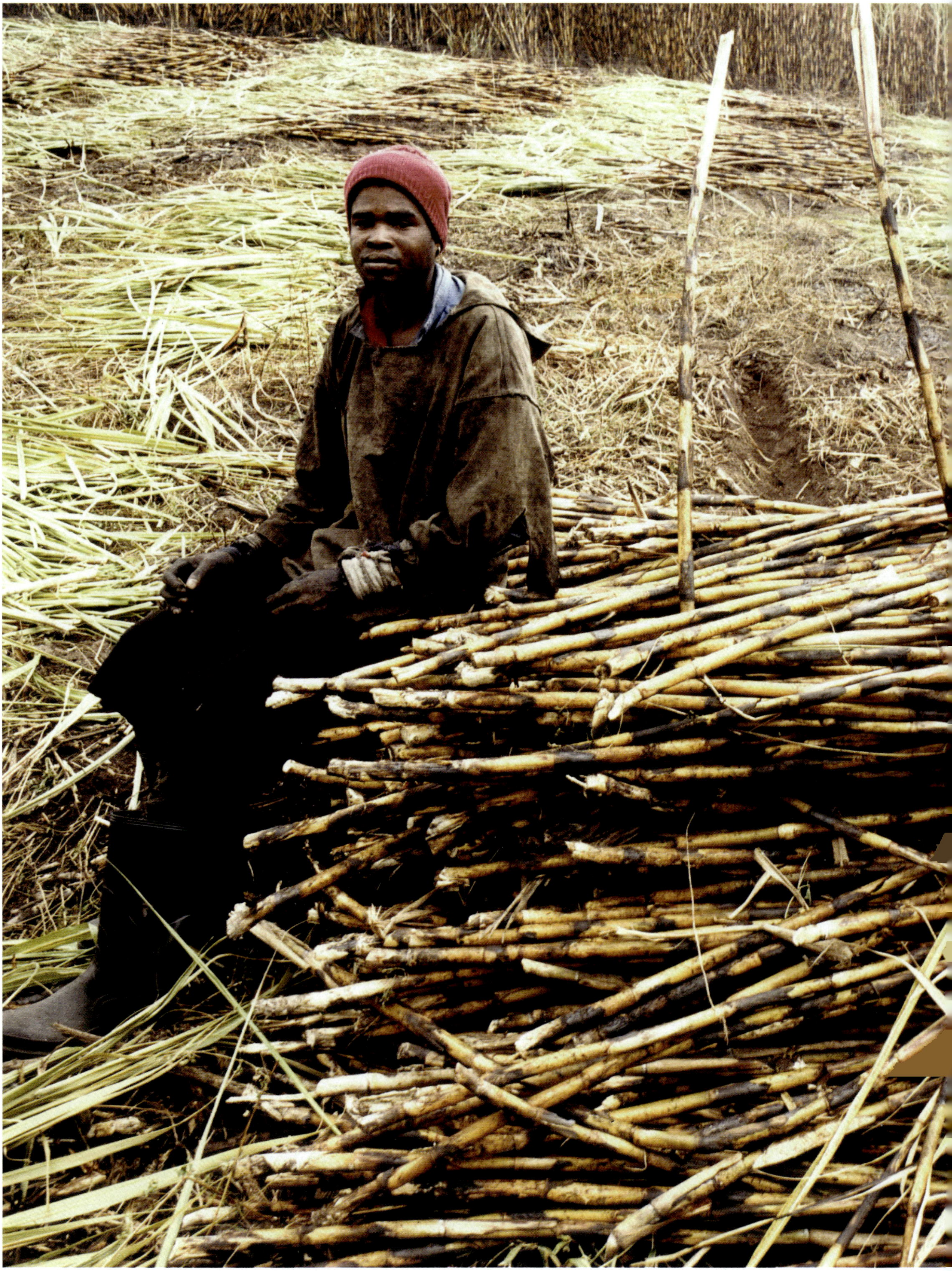

Untitled 2004 chromogenic print

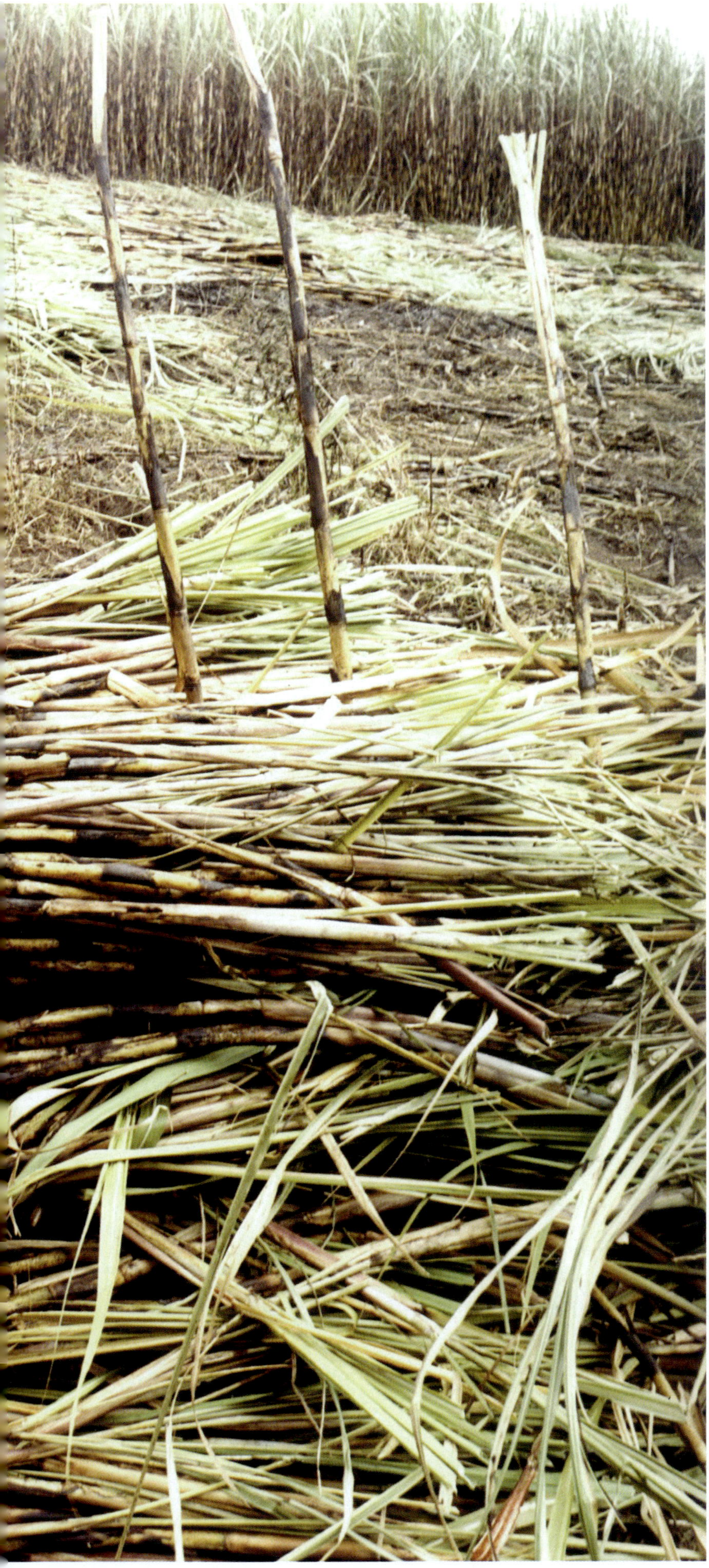

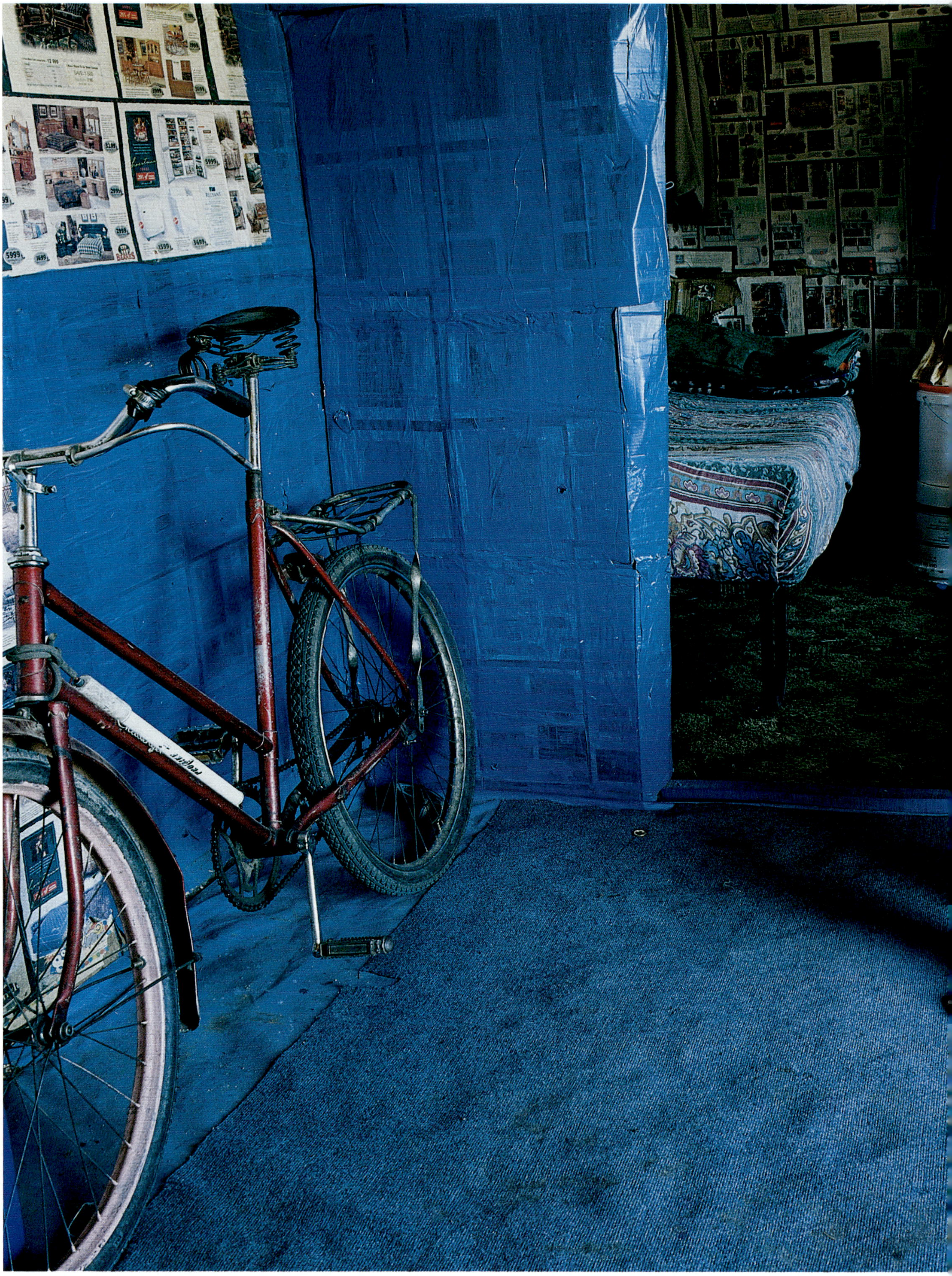

Untitled 2000 chromogenic print

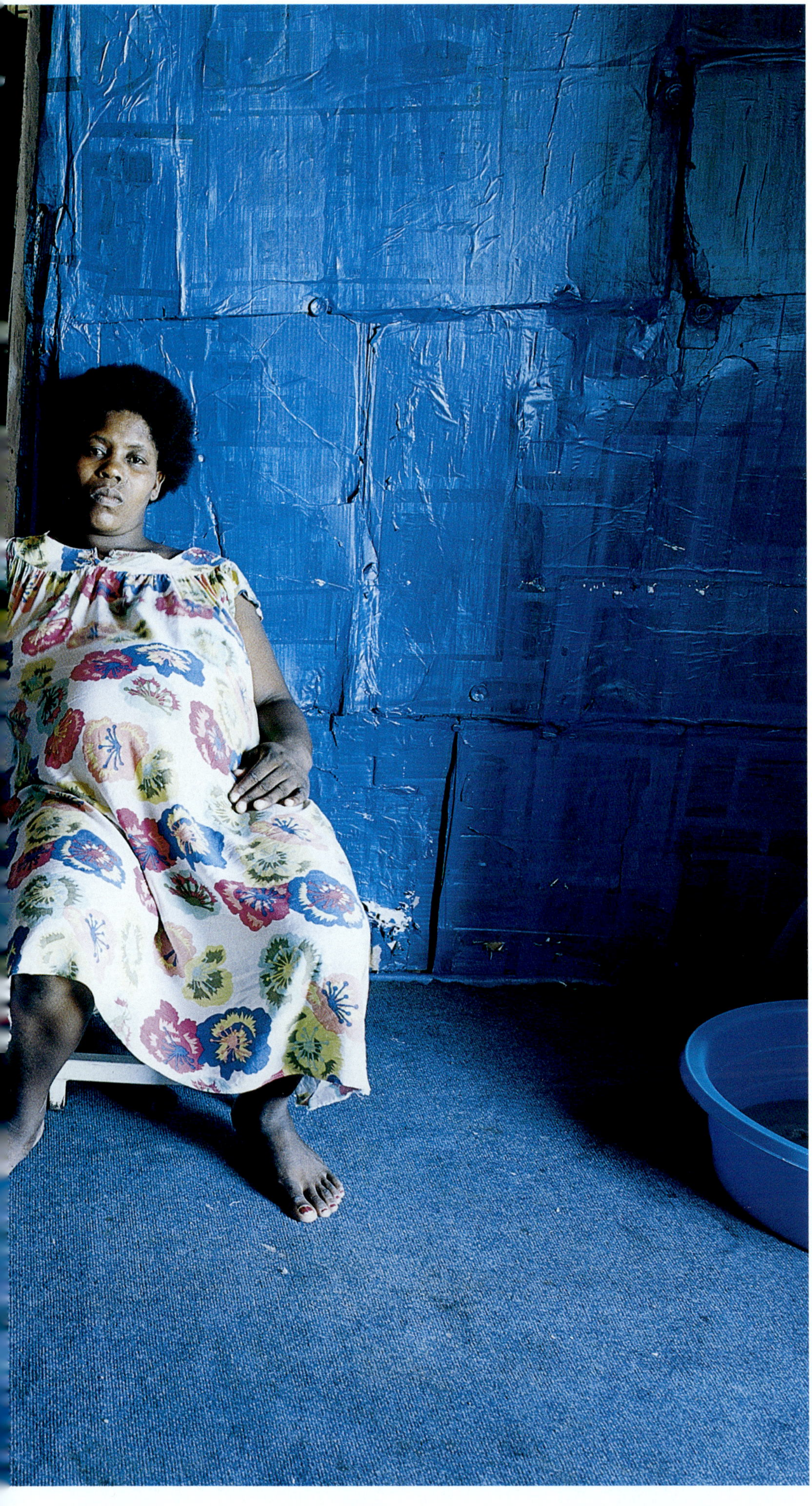

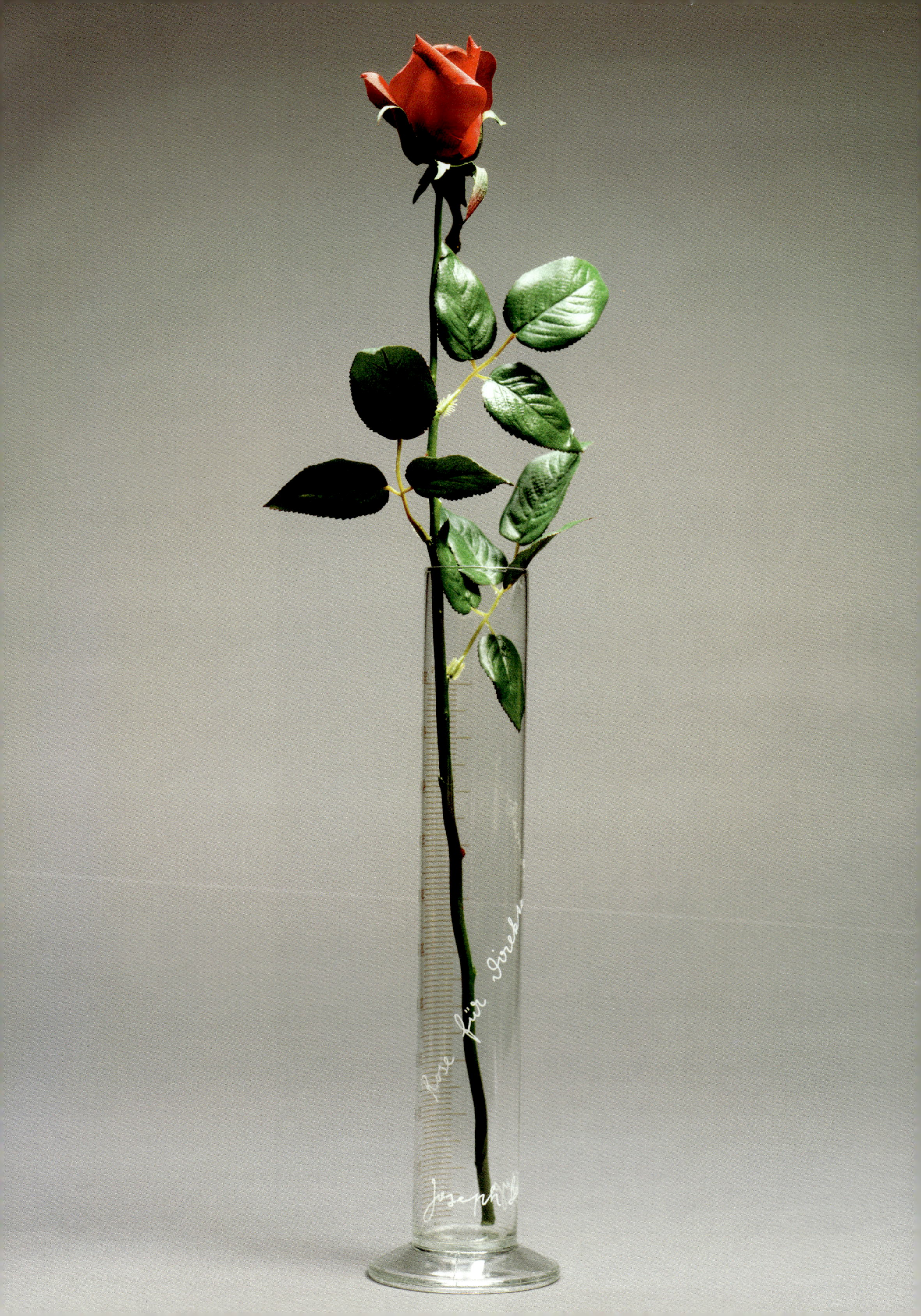
Rose für
Joseph

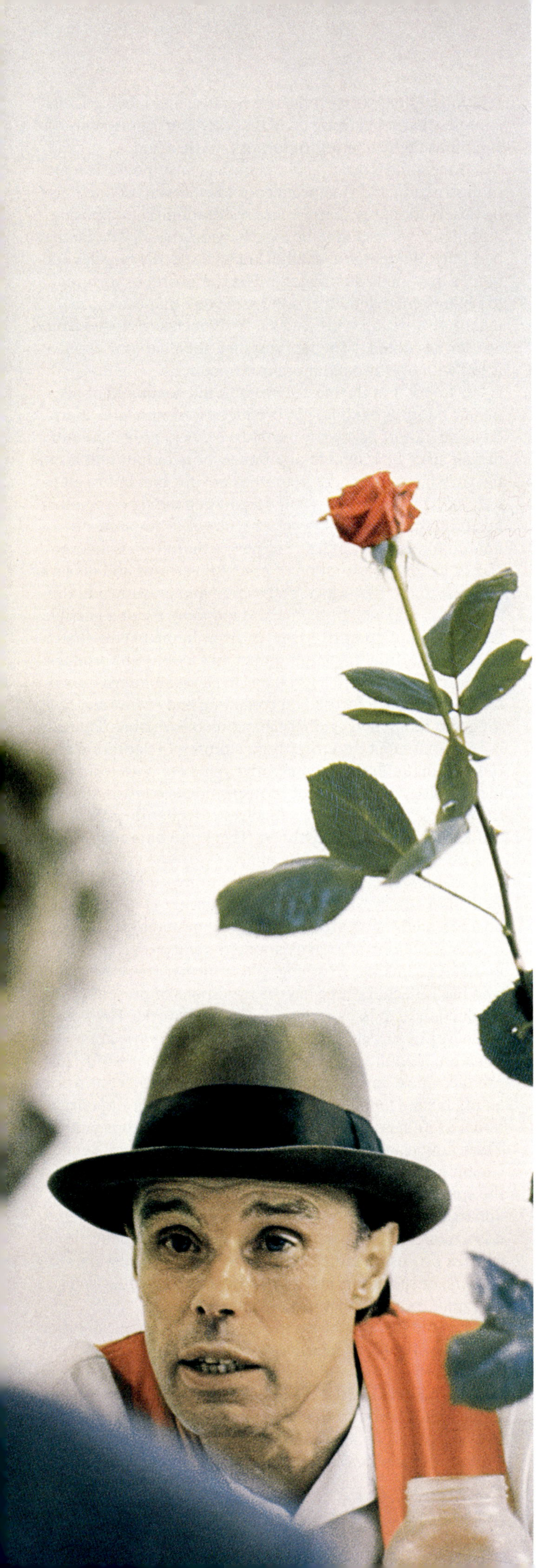

A ROSE FOR BRAVE NEW WORLDS

§

YASMIL RAYMOND

The act of creation knows no fear. The worst thing that can happen to a work of art, book, script, composition, or film is to be physically destroyed. But even then, the ghost of art is brave and very stubborn, and it won't ever cease to recite the names of its destroyers so that history can memorize them. Artists are mortal but the product—the fruits (or wreckage) of their labor—is not. This might be obvious to many, but it has taken me twelve years to understand the meaning of Hippocrates' dictum "ars longa, vita brevis" (art is long, life is short)—a Latin text that circled the insignia on my public school uniform in Puerto Rico.

What does art have to do with courage? And, conversely, what does courage have to do with art? Courage and fear are two poles around which human behavior revolves. Bourgeois society seems to be dependent on a consensus of ideas, opinions, and beliefs, and it insists that minority groups camouflage their individualities, flatten their differences, and unify within the masses. This is the mask of intolerance. Tolerance, on the other hand, is integral to the nature of art; there is no such thing as a work of art destroying another in order to assert its place. Art exists on a simple principle of courage, of having the nerve to be different, unpopular, or even disliked.

Contrary to the general consensus, the quest for peace is not some dreamy utopian ideal but a real-life pursuit of conditions that allow for diversity. Peace is the conduct of tolerance, a principle intricately connected to the practice of nonviolence, which we must keep articulating and enacting. Edward Said left us with a persuasive argument before his death in 2003 when he said, "Peace cannot exist without equality; this is an intellectual value desperately in need of reiteration, demonstration, and reinforcement." [1] In taking up this enormous challenge, he proposed a practice and conduct that seeks to expand borders: "It takes a good deal more courage, work, and knowledge to dissolve words like 'war' and 'peace' into their elements. . . . The intellectual is perhaps a kind of countermemory, with its own counterdiscourse that will not allow conscience to look away or fall asleep." [2]

I owe my first thoughts about art to an image of an artist who had fallen asleep on his work table, an etching about the size of my hand that became a source of inspiration and questioning. The print turned out to be Francisco Goya's well-known *El sueño de la razón produce monstruos* (*The sleep of reason begets monsters*) (1797–1798). [3] This modest work of immense force would resurface with regularity in my experience of art and has shaped a great part of what I understand as the promise of art, the process of transformation driven by a desire to change. This belief was reinforced later through my experience of the work of Joseph Beuys, who considered this quality of art to be determined internally in much the same way that a rose manifests itself by transforming its buds into blossoms from within (a point I shall return to later). [4]

We might say that Goya's etching of the artist exhausted by his own labor is an allegory of the internal logic of the creative process. The ambition, however, lies in the caption, which equates reason with imagination. At stake here is not the eternal sleep of reason, since we know that the artist will eventually awaken, but, to paraphrase Jorge Luis Borges, the "splendid irony" of artistic production, the tension between consciousness and invention, irreverence and attention. [5] In a sense, Goya volunteered to render a picture of the relationship between productive impulse and inevitable discontent, that revitalizing cycle that drives artistic activity and summons the will to return to work, to try again.

To assume a constructive stance against the futile logic of destruction and violence means to embrace production by observation, re-creation, and restoration. The opposing arguments here seem to be exactly symmetrical. The human hand that detonates dynamite, launches deadly missiles and bombs, that pulls the trigger, raises the sword, or tortures the blindfolded detainee, is the same one that can make, invent, restore, and reconstruct. As French sociologist Bruno Latour has noted, "The idol smasher, the mediator breaker is left with only two polar opposites: either he (I guess it is fair to put it in the masculine) is in full command of his hands, but then what he has produced is 'simply' the 'mere' consequence of his own force and weakness projected into matter since he is unable to produce more output that his input; in which case, there is another way for him but to alternate between *hubris* [sic] and despair depending on whether he emphasizes his infinite creative power or his absurdly limited forces." [6] A practice of peace, therefore, is an exercise of hands, a restoration of preexisting forms and ideals in contrast to the rhetoric of destruction and erasure, and this awareness may well be a crucial standpoint, if not a possible voice, of contemporary artistic practice in the twenty-first century. It is from the latter model that a different productive force in visual arts has taken shape on an international scale—a practice focused on compiling and redrawing, revisiting and remapping, gathering and reconstructing. There is an autonomous argument for a culture of restoration and renewal that affirms a regenerative reality in both form and methodology. A position of introspection is consistent with the experience of art, which involves a deliberate process of self-consciousness and selfhood. This is the unpretentiousness and compelling promise of art.

In this context, it feels necessary to revisit Walter Benjamin's essay "The Author as Producer" (1934), in which he advocated for an artistic activity calibrated by its own logic of creation and organization, its ability to serve as a model for thinking. "Nothing will be further from the author who has reflected deeply on the conditions of present-day production than to expect, or desire, such works. His work will never be merely work on products but always, at the same time, on the means of production. In other words, his products must have, over and above their character as works, an organizing function, and in no way must their organizational usefulness be confined to their value as propaganda. Their political tendency alone is not enough." [7] Unlike the violent tactics of interrogation, intimidation, and isolation, the creative process is anchored in a dialectical process of understanding between reasoning and producing; ultimately, it is a model of conversation and change by experience in which a process of empowerment occurs, when viewers, readers, or spectators are transformed into artists, writers, and creators, as Benjamin had imagined.

I would like to address the art included in the exhibition *Brave New Worlds* by focusing on the artistic process—the different routes and activities employed by the artists function as, in Said's words, "a kind of countermemory, with its own counterdiscourse that will not allow conscience to look away or fall asleep." [8] The different models of creation present in the group's various practices invite viewers to reflect on the political dimensions of what it means to recuperate, reconstruct, and restore the world by conceiving of multiple living environments that could coexist in harmony. These models affirm a different notion of making—one that insists on reclaiming, reinterpreting, and repeating, and one that is less concerned with claims of revolution and radicalism or with raising robust obelisks. As a result, their art proposes a discourse of renewal that aims to create the new by means of salvaging the discarded, compiling the dismissed, and re-enacting the experienced, to give just three examples. Here, the working model is not based on the triumphant mastery of matter or technology or the manufacture of resilient products, but on the self-critical and materially precarious position of permanent reexamination that counters the nihilism of globalization.

In the spirit of this undertaking, artists such as **Mark Bradford**, **Fernando Bryce**, **Runa Islam**, **Jorge Macchi**, **Zwelethu Mthethwa**, **Noguchi Rika**, **Dan Perjovschi**, and **Tomás Saraceno** have integrated the act of repetition and replication into their practice. The recurrence of forms or methods of production affirm a return. In their working process, repetition often materializes in the act of compiling (Bradford), copying and retracing (Bryce and Macchi), and redrawing (Perjovschi). Similarly, the recurring form (Saraceno), site (Mthethwa), movement (Islam), or subject (Noguchi) is accomplished by means of the artist's voluntary return to it. To repeat is to interrupt randomness and in the process assert a clarification, consciously reducing speedy results in favor of revisions, rearrangements, and experimentation. To repeat is to establish recognition of and intimacy with the unfamiliar while producing a variety of continuities and uniqueness rather than sameness. To repeat is to know. It is on this premise that the consistent formal and conceptual logic of their practice is revealed, summarizing graphically or visually its process.

There are multiple influential examples of repetition as poetic construction. It seems appropriate, in particular, to cite the work of On Kawara, an artist who has tested the authenticity of art with the discipline and patience of a timekeeper. In New York on January 4, 1966, he began his *TODAY* series, for which he completes at least one painting from beginning to end in one day. (If he doesn't finish, he destroys the piece.) This endeavor, which takes between eight or nine hours, starts with stretching and priming the canvas and covering the surface with a background color.[9] Replacing the expected image with language, he paints in the middle of the canvas—always in white and in a sans serif typeface—the date in the language of the country in which the painting was made. At the end of the process, he makes a final entry in the artist inventory and in his monthly calendar of production, and then the canvas is stored in a handmade cardboard box that holds a folded page from that day's newspaper.[10] The notion of repetition in Kawara's practice is redemptive, as the work produced in the present simultaneously promises the possibility of the next piece, a promise that can only be kept by the artist's willful act of reiteration.

A different production principle is present in the works by **Armando Andrade Tudela**, **Yto Barrada**, **Yael Bartana**, **Mircea Cantor**, **Banu Cennetoğlu**, **Haegue Yang**, **Erik van Lieshout**, and **Artur Żmijewski**. Their practice, one could say, often consists of retracing and performing formal and conceptual journeys into a variety of ideological landscapes.

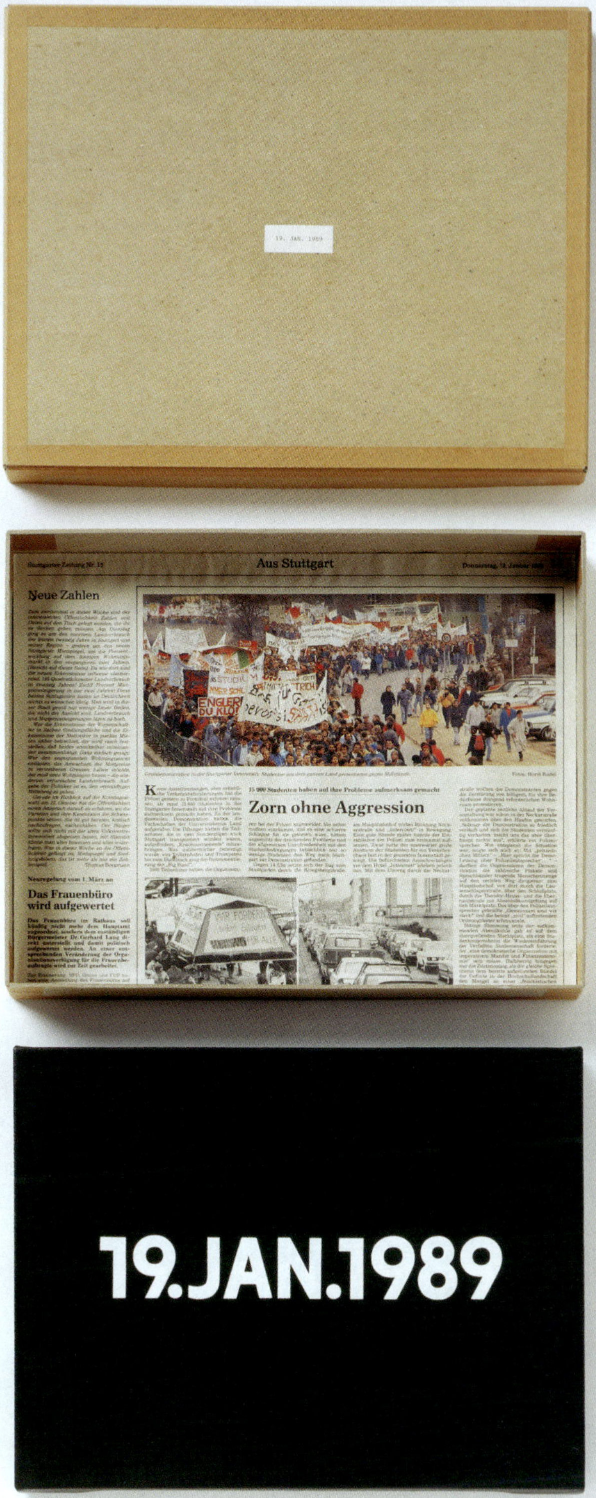

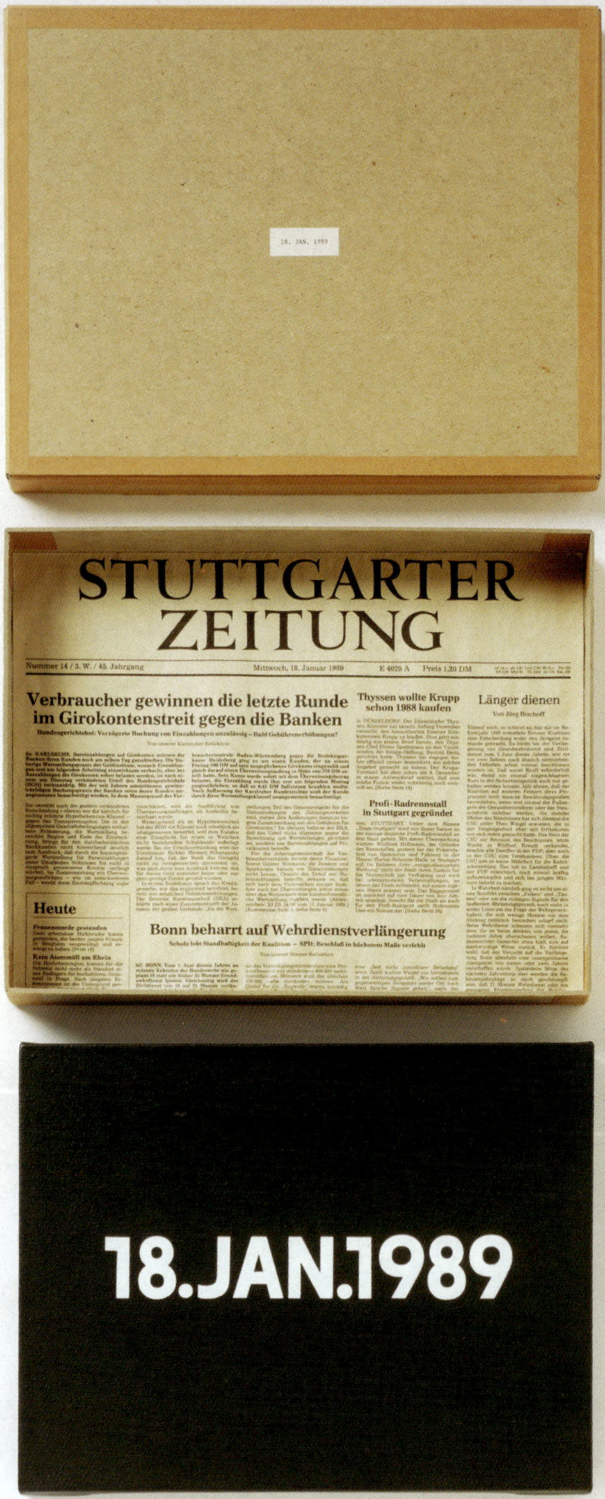

Their working method involves arranging intentional encounters with specific sites that embody the utopian excesses of the past (Andrade and Cantor) or the overwhelming reality of the present (Barrada and Bartana). In other instances the landscape is treated as a still life (Cennetoğlu and Yang) or, on the contrary, a human portrait is rendered as a landscape (van Lieshout and Żmijewski). As a whole, their still or moving images treat the act of looking as a revision rather than a discovery, as a form of interpretation that transforms the mechanical lens of the camera into an exploratory eye, as that of a traveler who intuitively retraces surfaces by remapping political subjectivities and social crossroads. The state of contemplation evoked by such images and movements is a parable of perception in which the subject matter is always at arm's length, never too distant or too close, making the process of recording accountable to what is chronicled. Hence, the act of making becomes an act of observation and documentation aimed at recalling the past, while reclaiming a place in the present.

This process of enacting and retracing recalls the work of Chantal Akerman, in particular her installation *Bordering on Fiction: Chantal Akerman's "D'Est."* In 1990, the artist traveled with a film crew across Germany, Poland, and Russia, capturing the surroundings at a measured, uniform distance, pace, and height. By this method, she reenacted the transitory state of those she observed, crossed landscapes of people, flattened details, and frustrated any voyeuristic desires toward her subjects. The allure of a journey, for Akerman, is a visualization of inertia—her camera aims a straight line across fields, bus stops, and waiting rooms at train stations in order to trace the parallel between her nearly motionless subjects and the political and economic inertia of the post-Soviet turmoil. In *Bordering on Fiction*, the viewer is invited to walk through a labyrinth of television monitors placed on pedestals at eye level that show fragments of the journey that leads to a 16mm film projection and a sound installation in adjacent rooms. This transitory experience built on movement and time gives an account of the methodology employed by the artist, one infused with an awareness of speed and distance toward her subjects and the landscape; it also asks the viewer to contemplate the piece by physically mimicking the pace of the artist's experience.

Meanwhile, the process of tracing and collage present in the practice of **Cao Fei**, **Gimhongsok**, **Gabriel Kuri**, **Josephine Meckseper**, **Lia Perjovschi**, **Walid Raad**, **Sean Snyder,** and **Zheng Guogu** is characterized by activities such as gathering, recuperating, and reclaiming images and objects that range from novel appliances to everyday gadgets to news footage to relics of past ideologies. Recalling the methods of collectors, the artists pay meticulous attention to the order and arrangement of their findings, which are often enclosed in glass cases or frames, alluding to the careful placement of a still life composition or a museum display. Others prefer an easy assortment of items on display in the fashion of a flea market or the encyclopedic categorization of a cabinet of curiosity. In each case, found images or objects are rescued items, mementos or keepsakes that assume myriad forms—an explorer's inventory (Gimhongsok and Perjovschi), a dubious archive (Raad), a phantasmagoria of images (Snyder and Zheng), a reliquary of revolutionary and also consumerist memorabilia (Meckseper), a compendia of monetary transactions (Kuri), or a fantasy factory (Cao). In their transference of meanings, the material trace is recaptured from the peril of silence and revived as quotations, fables, or proverbs from not one but various worlds.

Certainly, there are many precedents in recent art history leading to this method of making by inserting, combining, and gathering to bring attention to the object's potential poetic expressions. I'd like to point, however, to a modest example by Beuys: his multiple *Rose für direkte Demokratie* (*Rose for Direct Democracy*), first conceived in 1972 as part of his contribution to the international exhibition *documenta 5* in Kassel, Germany, for which the artist set up a temporary information office, where for one hundred days he answered questions and discussed a variety of topics with visitors. On a table near the artist's station was a laboratory beaker that served as a vase for a single long-stemmed rose. Beuys considered the rose to be "a very simple and clear example and image of this evolutionary process with its revolutionary goal," and he added, "because a rose is itself a revolution in regard to its genesis. The blossom doesn't come about with a jerk, but only as the result of an organic process of growth in which the petals are already contained in the green leaves and develop out of them." [11] One of the uses of Beuys' method today, in fact, is his principle of collecting: batteries of energy, blankets of warmth, scribbled chalkboards, and rescued vessels all become, through his invested signification, declarations of solidarity and optimism.

There is no singular directive as such in this exhibition, but rather a multiplicity of crossroads, shared spaces, and also distances among the works and the artists who created them. In contrast to a campaign of intolerance and strategies of destruction enacted on a daily basis in the world, art insists on being a conduit for recognition, an instrument for realization that operates from a principle of inclusion, reliance, coexistence, and equality. "The exemplary character of production," says Benjamin, is not only "to induce other producers to produce," but also its ability "to put an improved apparatus at their disposal. And this apparatus is better the more consumers it is able to turn into producers—that is, readers or spectators into collaborators." [12] Like several of their contemporaries, the artists in this exhibition are improving the "apparatus" of art from within by reexamining recognizable orders, fracturing the fences of exclusion, and repurposing broken beakers to hold new blossoms.

The exhibition *Brave New Worlds* is a handwritten map consisting of a variety of destinations, bewildering walks, labyrinthine routes, secret detours, and fantastical climbs. It employs three approaches—how to know, how to experience, and how to imagine the world—as guiding arrows on the brave journey ahead in the coming decades. The works on view contain a constellation of worlds—places where teenagers fake violence and workers take their leisure, sites defined by borderlines and high-minded architectural goals, collections of emptied maps and maps of ideological traps—all simultaneously rotating on their own axes as they also navigate alongside each other. In this sense, the exhibition starts off from the model of the universe—one that contains different spheres, spaces within spaces of artistic reflection, and forms of transmission that connect each other to different geographies and conditions. The experience is not defined by its accuracy but by the points of recognition that allow the eye and the mind to understand the unfamiliar and direct the body courageously toward it. ■

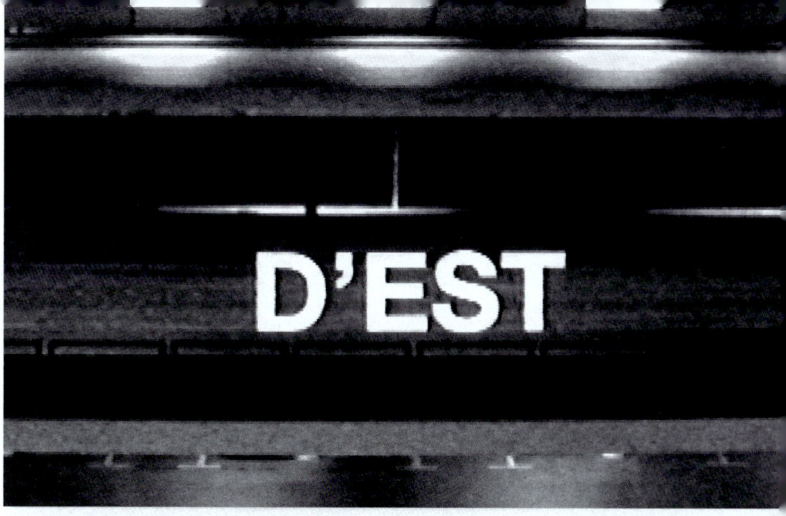

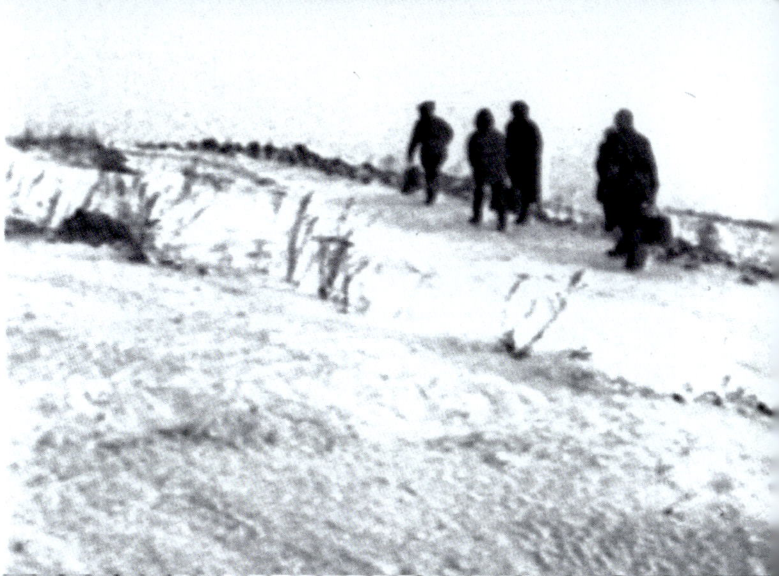

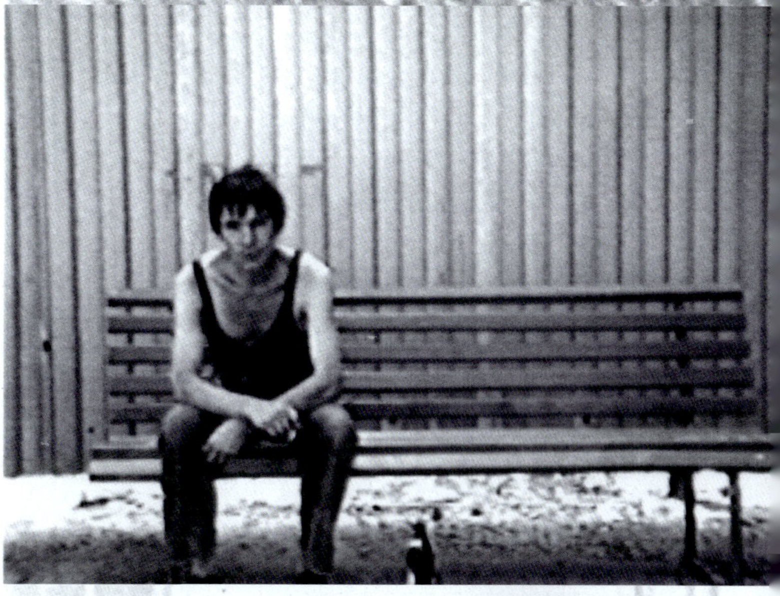

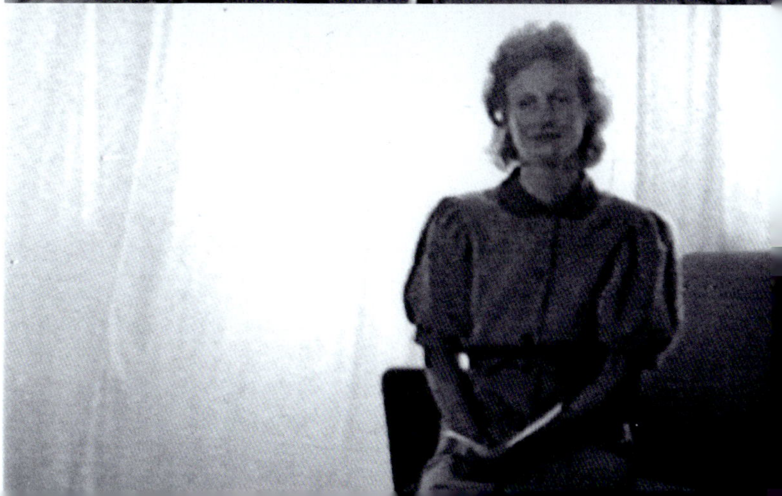

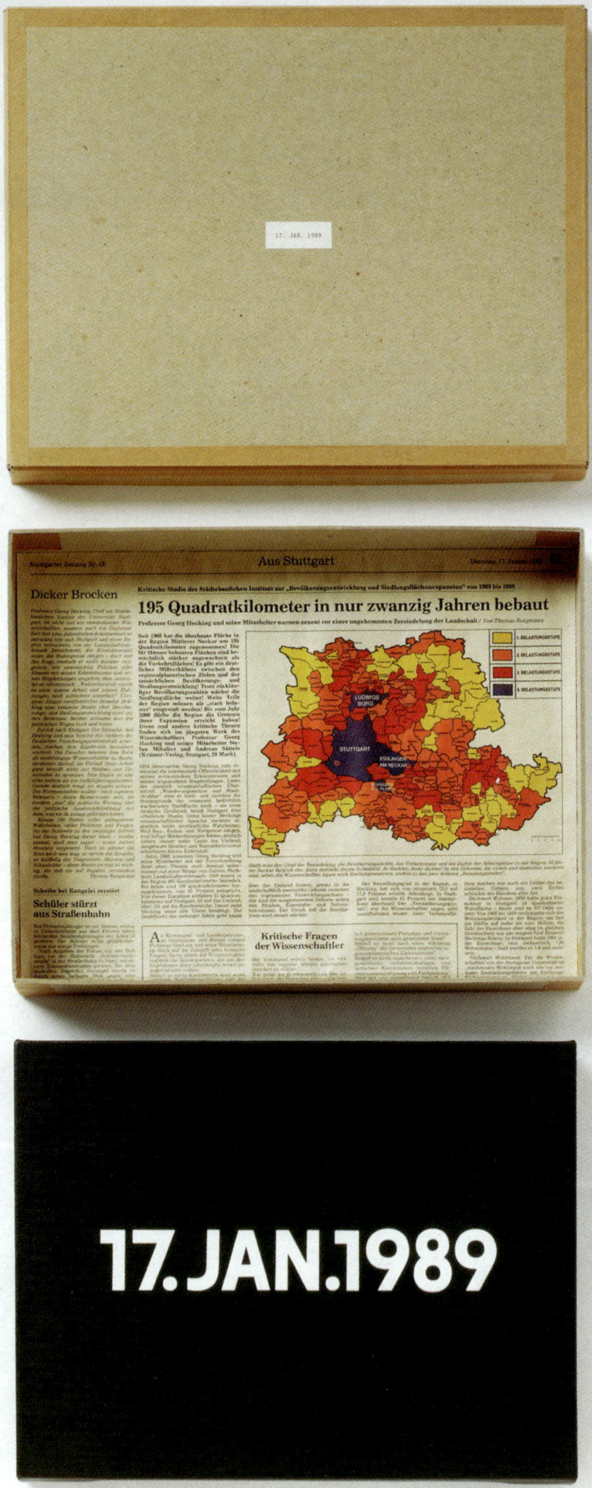

NOTES

1. Edward Said, *Humanism and Democratic Criticism* (New York: Columbia University Press, 2004), 142.

2. Ibid., 143.

3. This etching with aquatint was number forty-three in a portfolio of eighty prints entitled *Caprichos* (*Caprices*) Goya made between 1793 and 1796.

4. Caroline Tisdall, *Joseph Beuys* (New York: The Solomon R. Guggenheim Foundation, 1979), 273.

5. This expression is borrowed from the opening paragraph of Jorge Luis Borges' "Poem of the Gifts," which he quotes in his essay to accentuate the irony of his appointment as the director of the national library. Jorge Luis Borges, "Blindness," in *Selected Non-Fictions*, Eliot Weinberger, ed. (New York: Penguin, 1999), 475.

6. Bruno Latour, "What Is Iconoclash? Or Is There a World Beyond the Image Wars?" in *Iconoclash: Beyond Image Wars in Science, Art and Religion*, exh. cat. (Cambridge, Massachusetts: MIT Press, 2002), 22–23.

7. Walter Benjamin, "The Author as Producer," in *Reflections: Essays, Aphorisms* (New York: Schocken, 1986), 233.

8. Said, 143.

9. Jonathan Watkins, "Where 'I Don't Know' Is the Right Answer," in *On Kawara* (London: Phaidon Press, 2002), 82.

10. Elizabeth Carpenter, "On Kawara," in *Bits & Pieces Put Together to Present a Semblance of a Whole* (Minneapolis: Walker Art Center, 2005), 311.

11. Veit Loers, "Von der Rose zum Boxkempf," in *Joseph Beuys: documenta. Arbeit*, Museum Fridericianum Kassel, exh. cat. (Stuttgart: Edition Cantz, 1993); 113. Translated by Rachel Hooper.

12. Benjamin, 233.

IMAGES

page 156 Joseph Beuys *Rose für direkte Demokratie* (*Rose for Direct Democracy*) 1973 glass graduated cylinder with inscription, rose

page 157 Joseph Beuys *ohne die Rose tun wir's nicht* (*We Won't Do It without the Rose*) 1972 (detail) offset lithograph on paper, ink

pages 159–160, 162 On Kawara *TODAY* series 1989 acrylic on canvas, paperboard box, newspaper

pages 161, 163 Chantal Akerman Stills from *Bordering on Fiction: Chantal Akerman's "D'Est"* 1993/1995 25-channel video installation, 16mm film (color, sound)

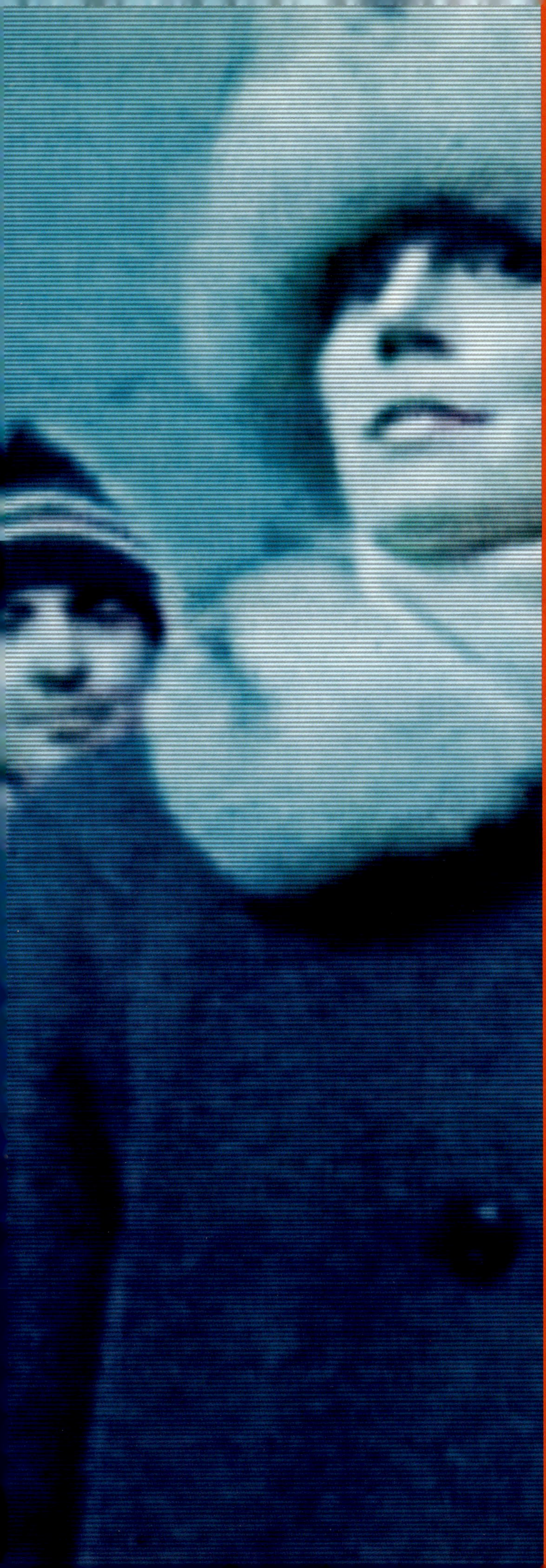

REPORT FROM SANTIAGO, CHILE

Brave New Worlds April 23, 2007

NOTES FROM CHILE: UTOPIA AND MELANCHOLIA

CECILIA BRUNSON

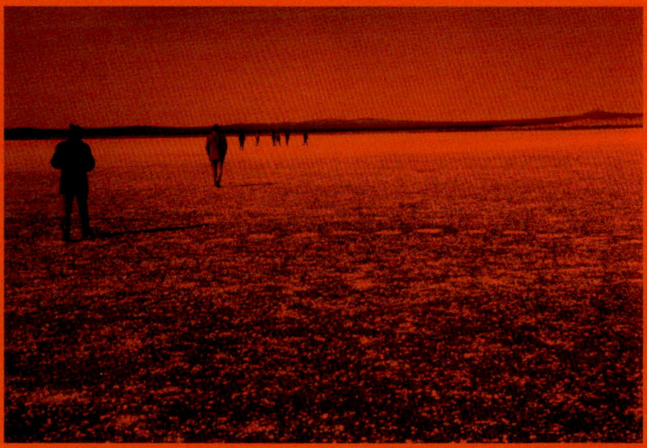

For imagination is always melancholic.
—Soren Kierkegaard, Either/Or (1843)

There is one creative experience in Chile that is worth narrating; it helps us consider how the present is crossed by past events such as doubts, problems, and attitudes that question the way modern thought is articulated in contemporary life. It happened in 1952, when Chilean architect Alberto Cruz, together with Argentine poet Godofredo Iommi, revamped the curriculum at the Escuela de Arquitectura (School of Architecture) in Universidad Católica de Valparaíso, setting forth a new way for understanding and teaching the profession of architecture, one different and separate from all other architectural or artistic trends that existed at that time in Chile or anywhere else.[1]

Cruz and Iommi worked together to create an educational forum in which architecture and poetry would meet. The Institute of Architecture was a kind of creative laboratory where architects, poets, and artists gathered. Architecture should be a collective exercise. It was worthless to have a good teacher: one had to have a working group. Study, research, creative action, interdisciplinary dialogue—especially the relationship between architecture and poetry—coexisted as one. The founding group lived communally and favored collective work. Together, they undertook a constant search for what could be a distinct type of architecture, unique to the country and its circumstances. This creative position and the group's point of view led its members to rethink its relationship with the American continent. Although elements of the Bauhaus are evident in the foundations of its pedagogical model, the Institute had a different understanding of the ideas it had inherited from the historical avant-garde in the First World, especially because it focused on researching its American context.

The Institute started to develop a unique concept of the origin and destiny of America, which grew out of the theories of Mexican historian Edmundo O'Gorman, who argued that it was not discovered, but "found."[2] Iommi suggested that it is therefore a gift that deserves to be known beyond its borders, its shores, and its oceans. It was necessary to navigate toward its core, to descend inland. Thus emerged the idea of a journey through America—a great voyage that would attempt to conquer it anew, from the perspective of the American being, a discovery of the homeland in the new world—recovering a trail and bringing a connection back to South America and the origin of its territory and its people.

In 1965, the Valparaíso group began its first journey together with six foreign colleagues.[3] Its objective was to explore the inside of the continent from Cape Horn, the southernmost point in Chile, to Santa Cruz de la Sierra in Bolivia, where the Pampas end and the jungle begins, and which the group named Capital Poética de América (America's Poetic Capital). The group wanted the trip to be, on the one hand, a public statement on the American condition as a gift to the modern world. On the other hand, it was an attempt to unveil its inner mysteries through poetic acts, improvised artistic works, and sculptural signs executed on the landscape, which slowly attested to the destiny and identity of their journey through the continent. The search was named Amereida. As Iommi and Cruz point out, the word Amereida resulted from an interpretation of The Aeneid, the poem by Virgil that is the foundational myth of the Latin condition of Roman culture, which is defined by language and by inhabiting a specific location rather than by a sense of nationality. It is a poem of Latinity and longing for the homeland, because the Latin condition does not correspond to nationality—in terms of geographical location—but rather to a status obtained simply by belonging to a culture. We can therefore conclude that the first Amereida voyage was the starting point of a search for a new Aeneid for the Americas.[4]

After three months of travel, on September 13, the Amereida was officially concluded and its participants returned to Chile. It must be pointed out that the group failed to reach its destination since its path was blocked by another revolution, that of Che Guevara, who had launched a guerrilla war in Bolivia. Thus, the poetic discovery of the continent was an unfinished task and the group had to return to Chile, after having gained much ground and opening up a great deal of what they called the Mar Interior (Inner Sea) of America.

The notion of the Inner Sea underscores the importance of the great void that exists in the continent; because our colonization took place on the seashores, we are people on the edges, lured by the coast, and therefore the interior has been forgotten, uncared for, and abandoned. Amereida therefore proposes that since America was found by chance, and nothing is known of its origin, it is necessary to find out what to do with this gift and find its destiny and identity. The group—which is also the Institute of Architecture—tried to shape that destiny.

Five years after the Amereida voyage, in 1970, the Institute responded to the challenges and ideas that resulted from that wandering and engaged in the construction of a city that followed the principles developed during the trip and set forth in the poem Amereida.[5] Ciudad Abierta (the Open City) is located on the edges, in Ritoque, along the Pacific coast of Chile. It was intended as a city in a metaphorical sense, and it is open because of the uncertain future faced by its physical environment, constructed on sand dunes. In fact, over time, the grouping of edifices were transformed by the terrain. The city grew around meeting places such as a chapel, a cemetery, and inns, all intended to unite life, study, and work. There have been attempts to look for precedents or influences for it. It has been said, for example, that it resembles Frank Lloyd Wright's Taliesin West, but the truth is that Ciudad Abierta is a response to a landscape, a geography, and a foundation that develops from questions about the American being, from doing something unique and original. Today, it is still a laboratory for reflection and action, where professors and students gather to put to work on the dunes—the knowledge they have acquired in the classroom—posing a fundamental question as to what constitutes a "city" in a landscape.[6]

Since the Amereida in 1965 and the founding of Ciudad Abierta in 1972, the ideas of the Valparaíso group moved away from historical centers and, like a root, turned toward a return to the origin, toward the local. The poetic acts that the group performed in relation to the land made it possible for an aesthetic avant-garde to develop in Chile in the 1970s whose activities, rather than a recycling of the heroic deeds of the historical avant-garde, were something unique and original. We should not forget that André Breton and the Surrealists had put into practice the "wandering travel" but this was the first time that such a poetics of space was implemented on such a grand scale.

Before closing, I would like to stop at a sculpture located in the Ciudad Abierta cemetery and titled El Pozo (The Well) (1976), by artist Claudio Girola (1923–1994), one of the founders of the Valparaíso School. The piece, which began as a poetic act, was built by the collective. Conceived as a sculpture within the landscape, El Pozo is actually a hole in the ground made up of the sandy natural terrain, stone, and soil that viewers can enter and stroll through. Being in a hole usually means having a restricted view, but Girola reverts that notion by creating a game of depth and special expansion: viewers descend through a narrow path, but as they walk, the interior view becomes broader. The sculpture acts as a source of feedback between the terrain and depth of space. It is neither a monument nor a commemorative piece; instead, it is a sculpture that questions the relationship of man to the environment with his own identity and location. It is a sculptural proposition that reflects on the limits between a living entity that passes through it and death, between fullness and a void, between edge and interior. This sculpture is like an allegory that recovers something that was threatening to disappear—revealing, through a sculptural exploration, an immediate present.

My hypothesis is as follows: In Chile today, in the artistic and academic arenas, there is a notable lack of declarations of principle—even more so, of utopian principles—such as those upheld by the Escuela de Arquitectura in the 1950s. Because of powerful global, political, and economic changes during which Chile has chosen to go along with the challenges posed by globalization and the marketplace, there is a great sense of loss, of something having disappeared or about to disappear. Although most of the world at this time considers great and well-intentioned actions of art a thing of the past, we are living in the present, a time of reflection and sensibility. If I am not mistaken, I dare say we are living at a time of little risk, because the historical avant-garde—which risked it all in order to bring about utopian change—is a thing of the past.

In his inspiring 1917 essay "Mourning and Melancholia," Sigmund Freud states that the goal of the mourning process is to loosen, to sever the ties to the abstract ideal (the lost object). Those who are unable to achieve this tend toward melancholia. If that is the case, I run the risk of engaging in nihilism by thinking that utopian ideals should not be lost. It is worth remembering, bringing back to the surface, and rediscovering the moving courage of these ideals—perhaps with the hope of one day having the ability to take a chance, not in order to achieve personal salvation, but rather a common good. ■

Translated by Fernando Feliu-Moggi.

NOTES

1 The architects who emigrated with Alberto Cruz from Santiago to Viña del Mar were Arturo Baeza, Jaime Bellalta, Fabio Cruz, Miguel Eyquem, José Vial, painter Francisco Méndez, and Argentine sculptor Claudio Girola.

2 Edmundo O'Gorman, La Invención de América Mexico City, Mexico Fondo de Cultura Económica, 1992; originally published in 1958), 53.

3 The members of this first expedition were Panamanian poet Edi Simonds, French poet Michel Deguy, Briton Jonathan Boulting, French philosopher Francois Fedier, designer Henry Tronquoy, and Argentine painter Jorge Pérez Román. The group from Valparaíso consisted of architects Alberto and Fabio Cruz, Argentine poet Godofredo Iommi, and sculptor Claudio Girola.

4 See Ann M. Pendleton-Jullian. The Road That Is Not a Road and the Open City, Ritoque, Chile (Cambridge, Massachusetts: MIT Press, 1996). Together with this book, see the detailed study by Sara Browne Cruz, Habitar es construir lo gratuito: Refundación de la Escuela de Arquitectura de la Universidad Católica de Valparaíso, unpublished master's thesis, Universidad Finis Terra, Santiago, Chile, 2003.

5 It should be explained that the idea of Amereida developed from Godofredo Iommi's stay in Paris. In 1962, before the first voyage, Godofredo Iommi sent a poem to Chile from Europe titled "Amereida." In it he set forth the theory that the American condition is a gift to the modern world. After the first voyage, in 1965, the poem was published in a volume that also included the group's anonymous writings about its theories on America. The book later became the pedagogical foundation for the Escuela de Arquitectura de Valparaíso.

6 It should be pointed out that this experience of wandering travel was a vision that eventually came to mean, after the 1970s, that each generation of students in the Escuela de Arquitectura had to undertake, with other class members, a new "voyage" for the discovery of America.

IMAGE

page 163 Amereida Journey, Puelches, Argentina, 1965

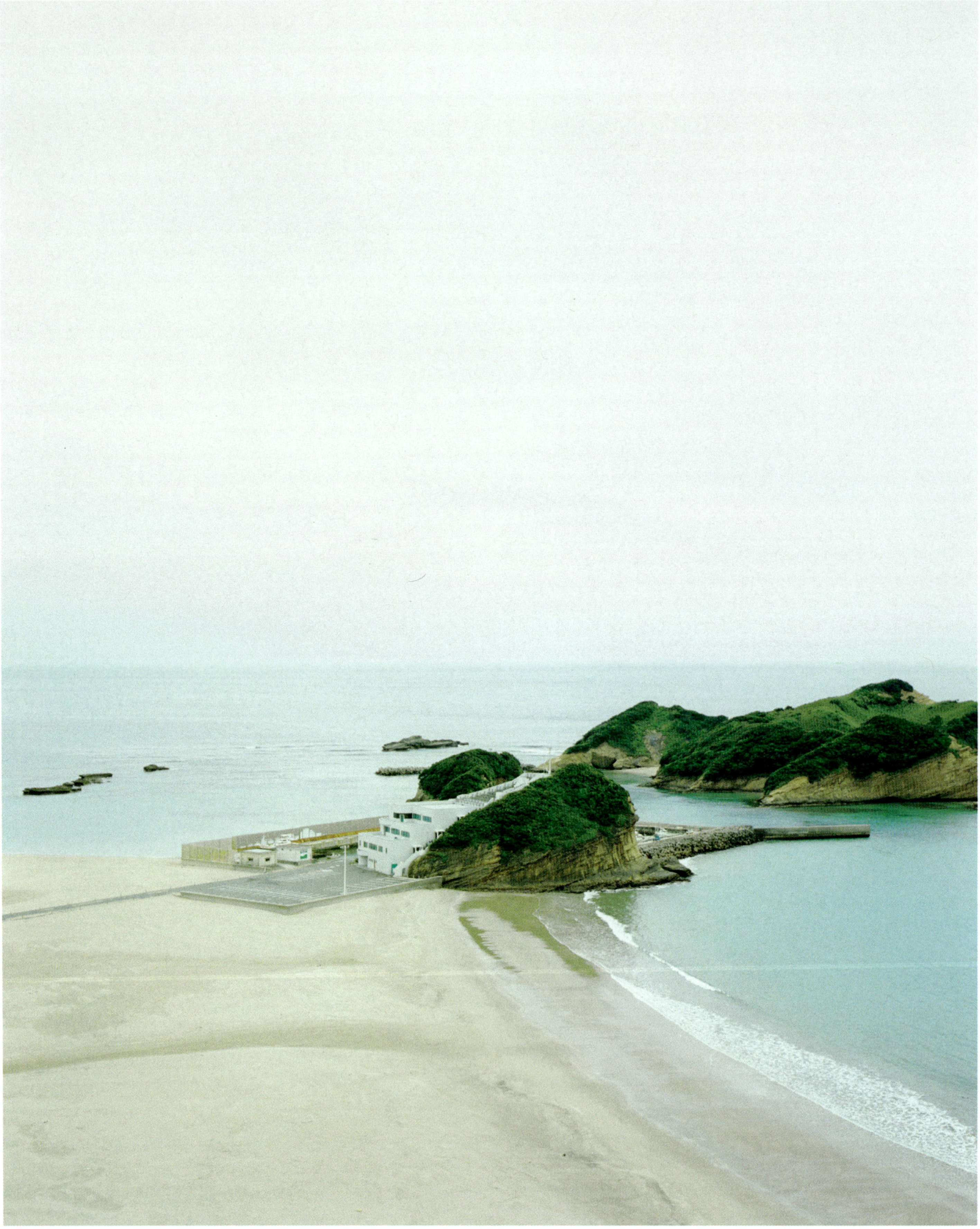

#7 from *Rocket Hill*   2001   chromogenic print

THE QUIET AWE OF NOGUCHI RIKA

Born in Japan, 1971. Lives and works in Berlin. One word that may best describe Noguchi Rika's photography is awe—the quiet awe of seeing the world. And the world here is not one of physical realities so much as it is a realm of impressions, elastic time, and serene atmospherics. It could even be said that the photographer's world is unabashedly Romantic. Her images often seem to be imbued with mists and mirages, or the ether of mystery. For her early series *A Prime* (begun 1997),[1] Noguchi climbed Mount Fuji and captured the slopes of the tallest mountain in Japan emerging against a sea of clouds and a pastel blue sky. Some of the pictures feature evidence of human presence: antlike climbers appear as almost extraneous detail. Her photographs have invited comparisons with the paintings of Caspar David Friedrich, a name synonymous with nineteenth-century German Romanticism. But while she may share his fundamental interest in transcendent realms, her imagery does not suggest a sense of awe about the sublime vastness of nature—and sublimated fear and trembling toward it—in the way that his paintings do. The awe in Noguchi's work does not possess the kind of religious cast in Friedrichian landscapes, either, but rather seems akin to pure curiosity.

That is not to say that Noguchi's approach to nature is devoid of questions about its interrelationship with human intervention. In fact, for a number of her series, she intentionally trekked to distant places where landscapes bear marks of irrevocable transformation via science and technology, capital and industry. *Rocket Hill* (begun 2001) consists of large vertical images of the Tanegashima Space Center, a rocket-launching facility that belongs to the Japan Aerospace Exploration Agency, and its surroundings at the southern tip of Kyushu Island. Some images were taken from afar, rendering the utterly functional structures of the space center not as obnoxious intrusions in pristine nature but almost as part of the landscape. Even when Noguchi's camera lens is in closer proximity to the soaring hangars and towers, which then nearly fill the entire frame, there is little sense of the menace of technology, or admiration for it. She matter-of-factly approaches this subject, potentially fraught with many political and philosophical implications, and uses her genuine inquisitiveness not as a tool of interrogation but as a gentle framing device.

If in *Rocket Hill* the artist observes humanity's vertical aspirations from a decidedly earthbound position, in *Color of the Planet* (begun 2004) she went in the other direction, diving into the deep sea off Yonaguni, the westernmost island in the Japanese archipelago. It became well-known in the mid-1980s when massive structures were discovered on its surrounding seabed, setting off debates about whether they were created by a prehistoric civilization or by natural geological processes. Taking the straightforward approach of documentary photography in the style of *National Geographic*, the artist captures this eerie underwater landscape of subtle gradations of blue in her horizontally expansive shots. Her pictures are not concerned with the archaeology-versus-geology question but instead become abstract meditations on the sea and its paradoxical impressions of enormity and intimacy. And as she dove toward the center of the Earth, her images, as the title suggests, lead us to think about what gives the planet its particular color when seen from outer space.

Noguchi does not use digital manipulation or enhancement in her images, as contemporary photographers are increasingly wont to do, and there is little technical trickery involved in general. If there is a certain uncanny and otherworldly quality to her work, it arises from her encounters with the subjects; she is deeply curious about them, but at the same time, her fascination with each subject avoids an anthropological, exoticist, or fabulist investment. In one commentator's words, Noguchi is "interested instead in the idea of confrontations of strangers in a strange world, and identifying with them."[2] Her recent works exemplify her continuing fascination with the strangeness permeating the world. *In the Desert* (2006–2007) is a series of calm portraits of camels and their caretakers in their environs in Sharjah, the United Arab Emirates, and the pictures, with their washed-out, subtle palettes, depict the subjects in neither abject nor particularly extraordinary ways. Closer to home, *Marabu*—also the name of a large African stork that Noguchi found in a Berlin zoo—is depicted coming in and out of focus in the lush, hazy greenery. The artist seems to view this displaced, peculiar-looking creature and the desert dwellers as alien beings, but not without suggesting that the image-maker is herself equally alien to the photographed subjects.

The Sun (begun 2005), her recent series featured in the present exhibition, consists of modestly scaled pictures taken in various locations—their exact identities are neither clear nor critical. In the pictures, the sun is seen as bursting circles of light, oozing through windows, silhouetting or being eclipsed by a person, reflecting on a shiny surface, erupting between and beside buildings, and bathing a riverside like a J. M. W. Turner painting. Violating the cardinal rule of picture-taking—not to point the camera at any direct source of light—Noguchi embraces that most quintessential symbol of vitality and spirituality and instills it with the affecting lyricism that characterizes all her works. Early in her career, she said, "I will continue to shoot photos. For the sake of the 99% of the riddles that dominate daily life."[3]
Her oeuvre has been one abiding exploration of little enigmas in our phenomenal world. In *The Sun*, she turns her gaze directly at the very source of all phenomena.

DC

1. The artist considers many of her series ongoing. When this is the case, the dates are indicated accordingly.

2. Jonathan Watkins, "Somebodies," in *The Planet: Noguchi Rika*, exh. cat. (Tokyo: Hara Museum of Contemporary Art; Birmingham, England: Ikon Gallery, 2004), unpaginated.

3. Noguchi Rika, artist's statement, in *New Cosmos of Photography* 5 (Tokyo: Canon Inc., Cultural Program Operation Dept., 1996), 23. English translation can be found at: http://www.canon.com/scsa/newcosmos/gallery/1996/rika_noguchi/index.html.

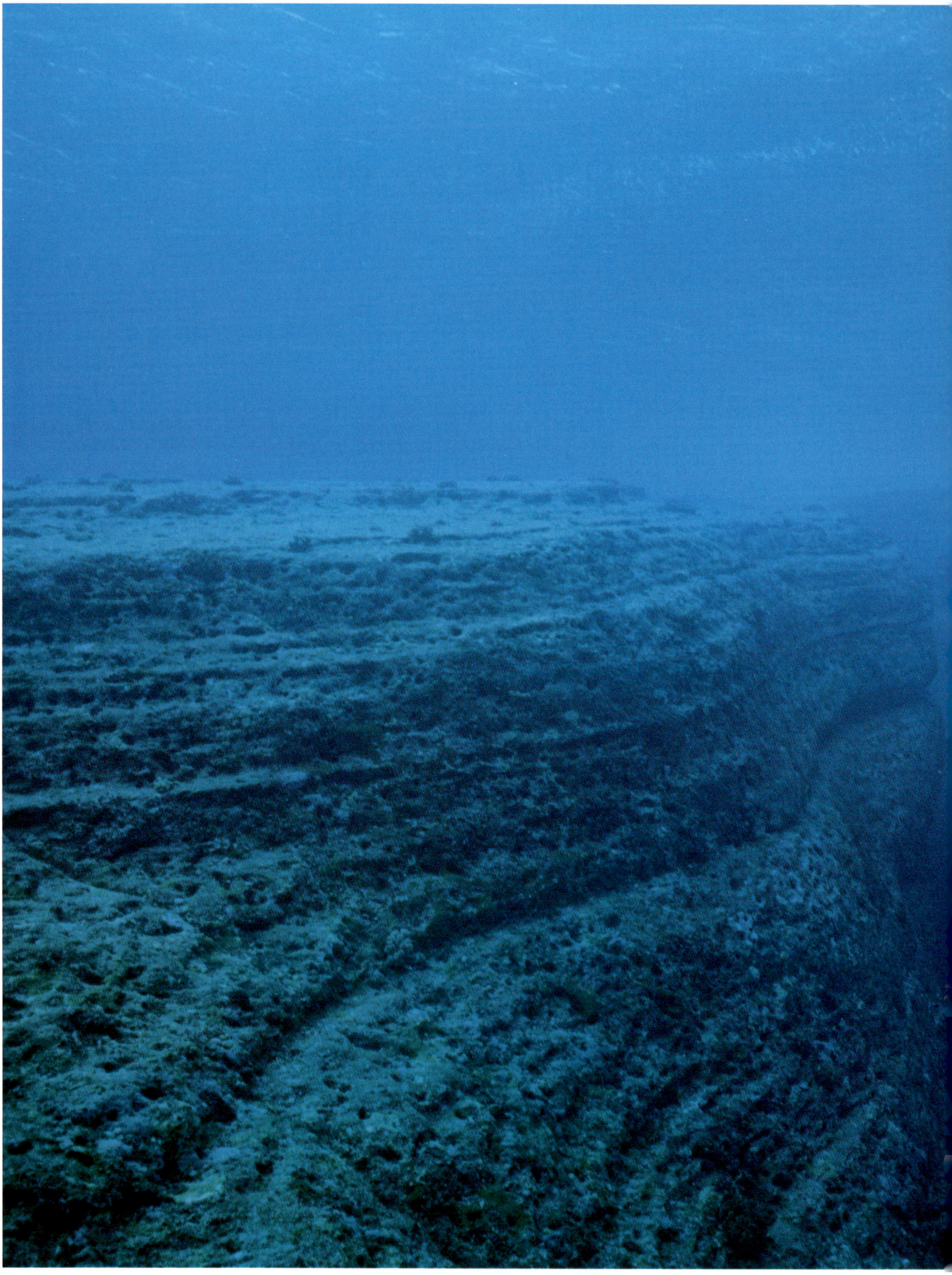

#1 from *Color of the Planet* 2004 chromogenic print

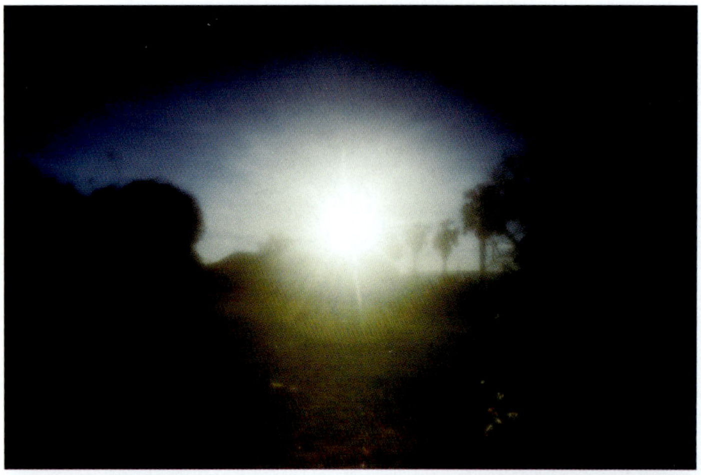
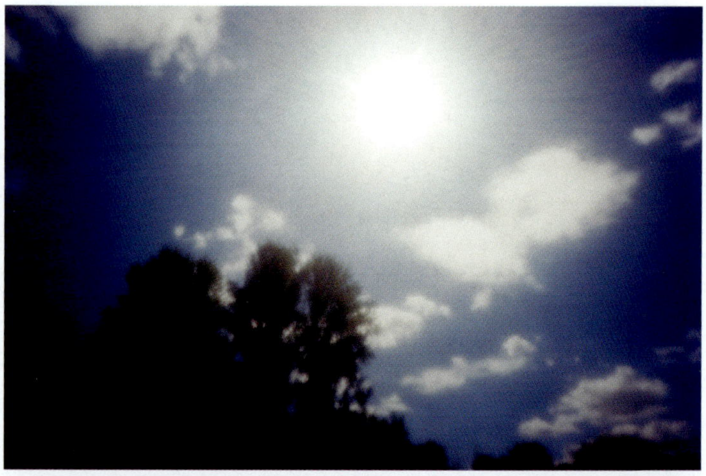
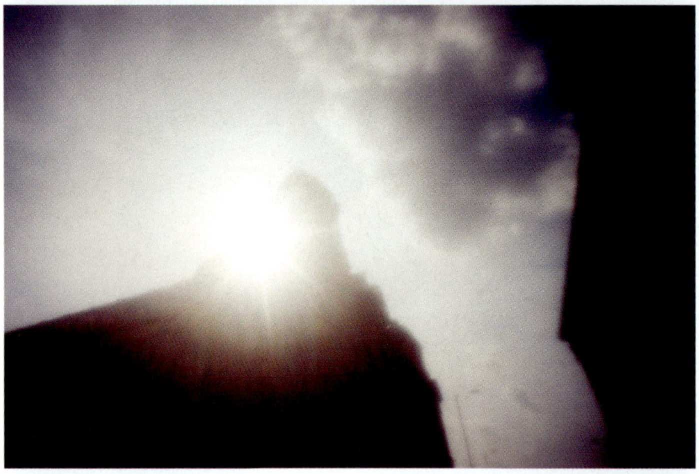
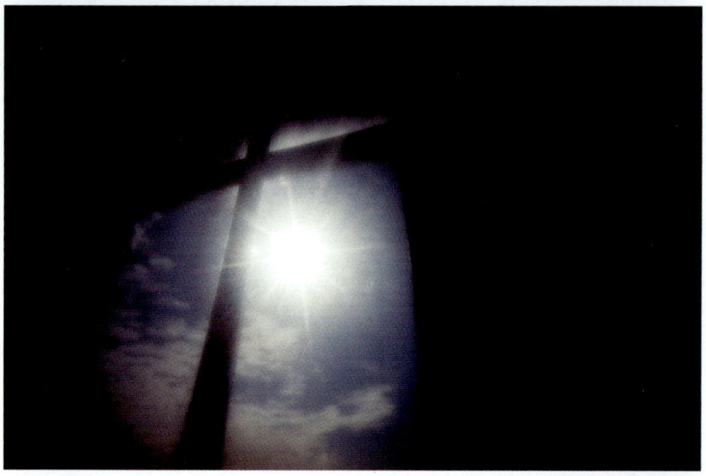
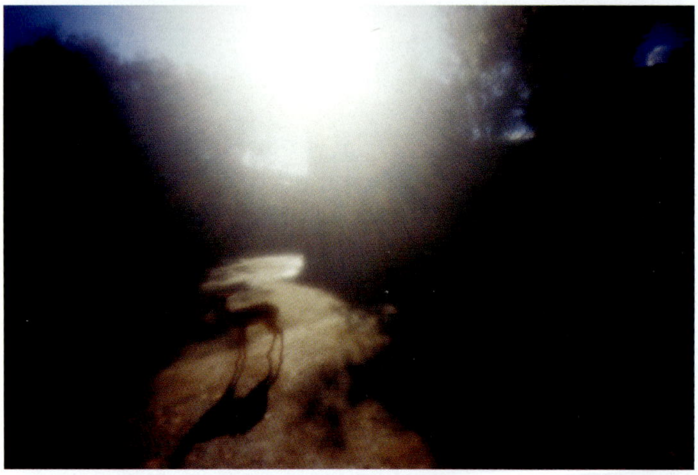
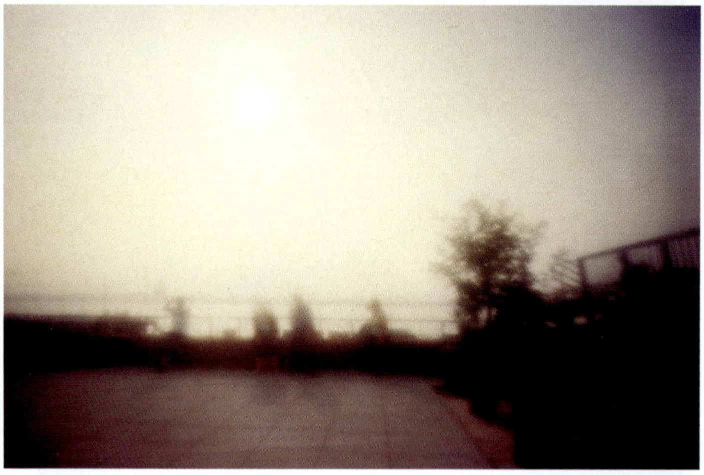
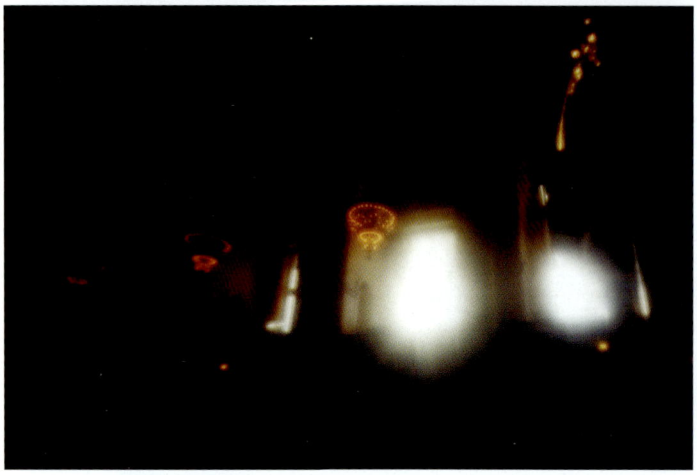
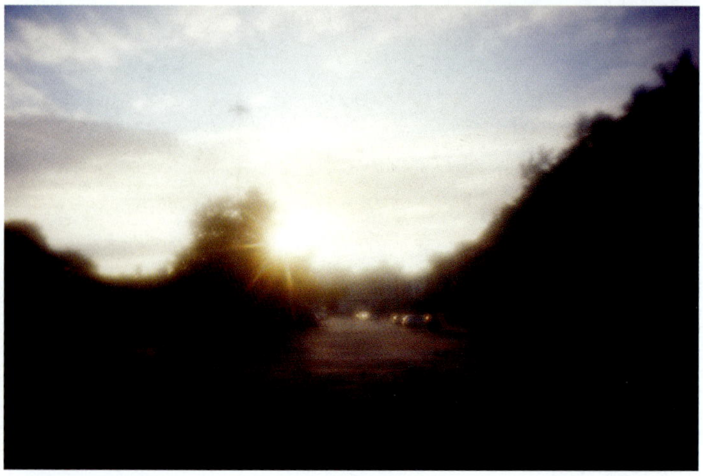

Selections from *The Sun* 2005–2006 chromogenic prints; series of 18

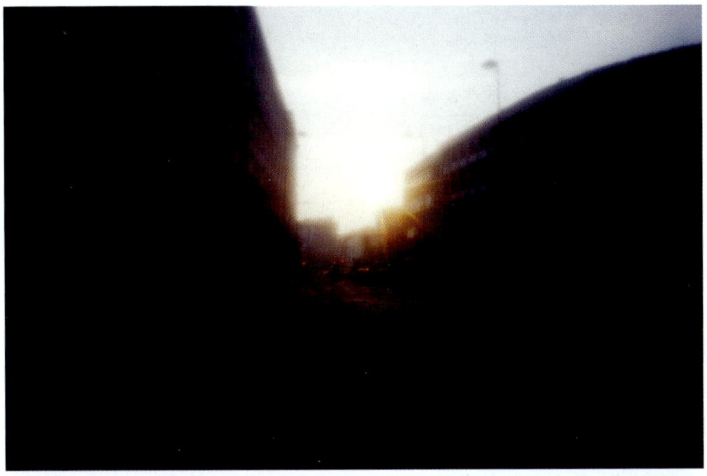
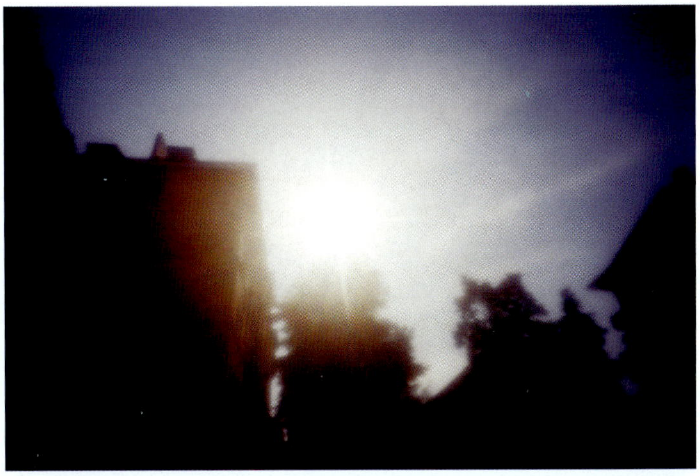
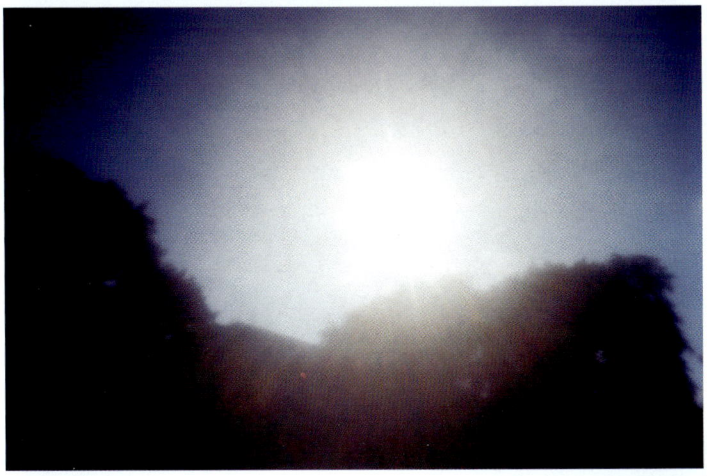
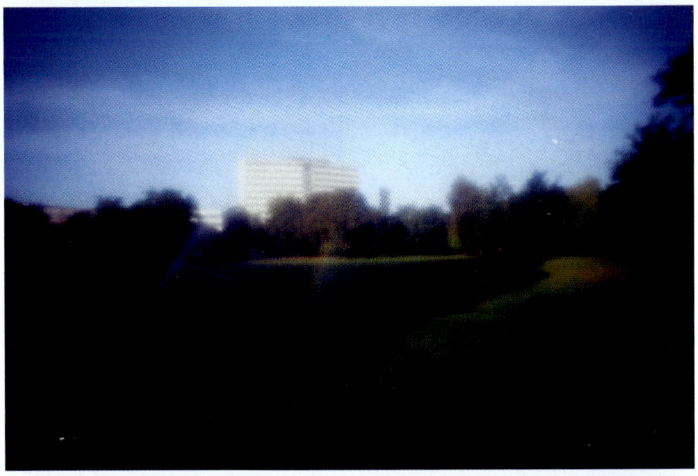
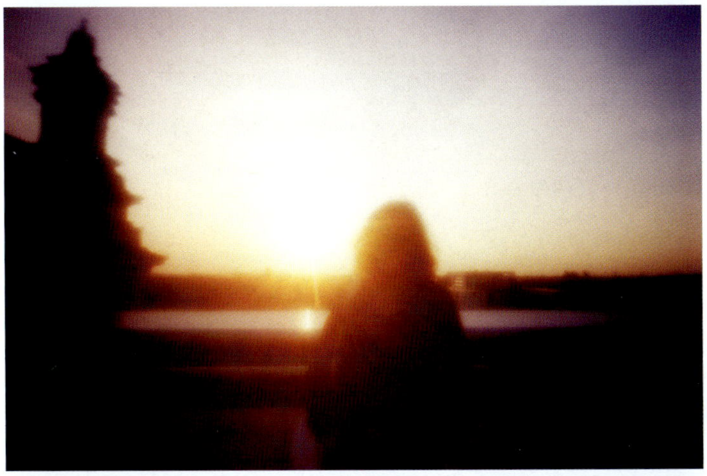

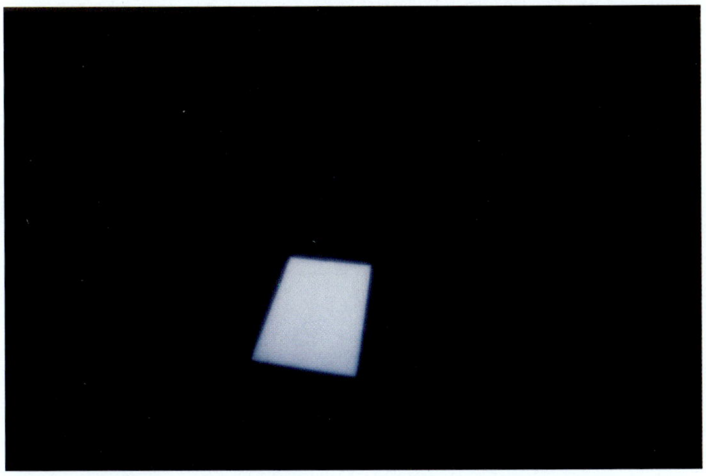

following pages: *#11* from *The Sun* 2006 chromogenic print

DAN PERJOVSCHI STILL LIVES IN BUCHAREST

Born in Romania, 1961. Lives and works in Bucharest.

In 1993, Dan Perjovschi had "Romania" tattooed on his arm during Europe Zone East, the first national performance festival, which was held in Timişoara, the city where the 1989 revolution that toppled Nicolae Ceauşescu's dictatorship began. A decade later in 2003, he had it removed, in three successive sessions, as a performance in the context of the exhibition *In the Gorges of the Balkan* at the Kunsthalle Fridericianum in Kassel, Germany. In that span of time, Romania had gone through an irrevocable transformation from an oppressive Communist regime, where Perjovschi felt like "cattle—marked and owned by someone beyond my reach," toward integration into the European Union and global economy.[1] At the same time, the artist increasingly found himself traveling outside his country, showing his work in many well-known venues of contemporary art throughout Europe and gaining a growing international reputation. While numerous invitations to make his signature in situ temporary wall (and sometimes floor) drawings have taken Perjovschi—just in the past few years—to Venice, Istanbul, and New York, among other places, he continues to be committed to his residence in Bucharest. In fact, his decidedly fixed location has given him a perspective of sustained lucidity on the constantly shape-shifting, relative perimeters of the world around him: "In the early 1990s I was a Central European. In the mid-1990s I was called an eastern European. At the end of the century I was seen as a southeastern European. Today I am called a Balkan artist. But I lived all this time in Bucharest."[2]

Although formally trained in painting at the University of Art George Enescu in Iaşi, Perjovschi quickly abandoned the medium, which he perceived to be too closely tied to oppressive official education and ideology. Instead, he embraced drawing—a form with immediacy and informality that he had always favored as a young student—as his main avenue of expression. His sharply-honed capacity for social observation and disarming wit also brought him to the attention of Bucharest's prominent opposition newspaper, *22*, for which he has worked as illustrator, art director, and editor since 1991. His illustrations for the newspaper often respond to divisions between the elite and the disadvantaged masses in Romania, the feckless and lumbering European Union, and the movements of capital around the world. The United States—the global superpower that has historically maintained a peculiar relationship with Romania—also features prominently.

Perjovschi always carries a small notebook in which he jots down his thoughts and observations in doodles and scribbles. It functions as a databank that stores numerous ideas and thoughts, selections from which he can quickly and spontaneously deploy for specific sites. Before he adopted wall drawing as his signature style, however, he had created two significant works that served as a transition from notebook to wall. *Wonderful World* (1994–1997) consists of letter-sized flip books, each containing about twenty drawings. The artist began the work in Romania and completed it during his extended stays in New York and a teaching stint at Duke University in Durham, North Carolina. *Postcards from America* (1994), a work consisting of five hundred ink and pencil drawings on colored paper mounted on cardboard, was made on a cross-country trip he took during his sojourn in the United States and conveys the excitement he felt during his "first encounter with the enormity and diversity of America."[3] The formats of these pieces allowed Perjovschi to extend his practice of spontaneous observation without compromising his mobility. He now works only by hand and with an ever-expanding repository of ideas and motifs. Once on-site, he uses permanent markers, and sometimes chalk, to create drawings that thoroughly respond to given physical conditions and incorporate his casual ad-lib style with the economy of tagging.

Perjovschi's drawing functions almost like a language with a set vocabulary that constantly adds new constituents to its growing pool and forms combinations of available parts comparable to individual sentences. Certain images and words appear repeatedly, much as basic nouns and verbs do in our everyday speech, but each iteration is different from those that preceded it. And just as certain public speeches and recited poems can be an awakening experience, an encounter with Perjovschi's wall drawings helps viewers see the world with newfound sharpness.

DC

1. Dan Perjovschi, interview with Roxana Marcoci, in "What Happened to Us?," *Projects 85: Dan Perjovschi*, exh. pub. (New York: Museum of Modern Art, 2007), 7.

2. See Dan Perjovschi, "Key Words in the New Europe," in *Das Neue Europa: Kultur des Vermischens und Politik der Repräsentation* (*The New Europe: Culture of Mixing and Politics of Representation*) (Vienna: Generali Foundation, 2005), 139.

3. *Projects 85*, 4.

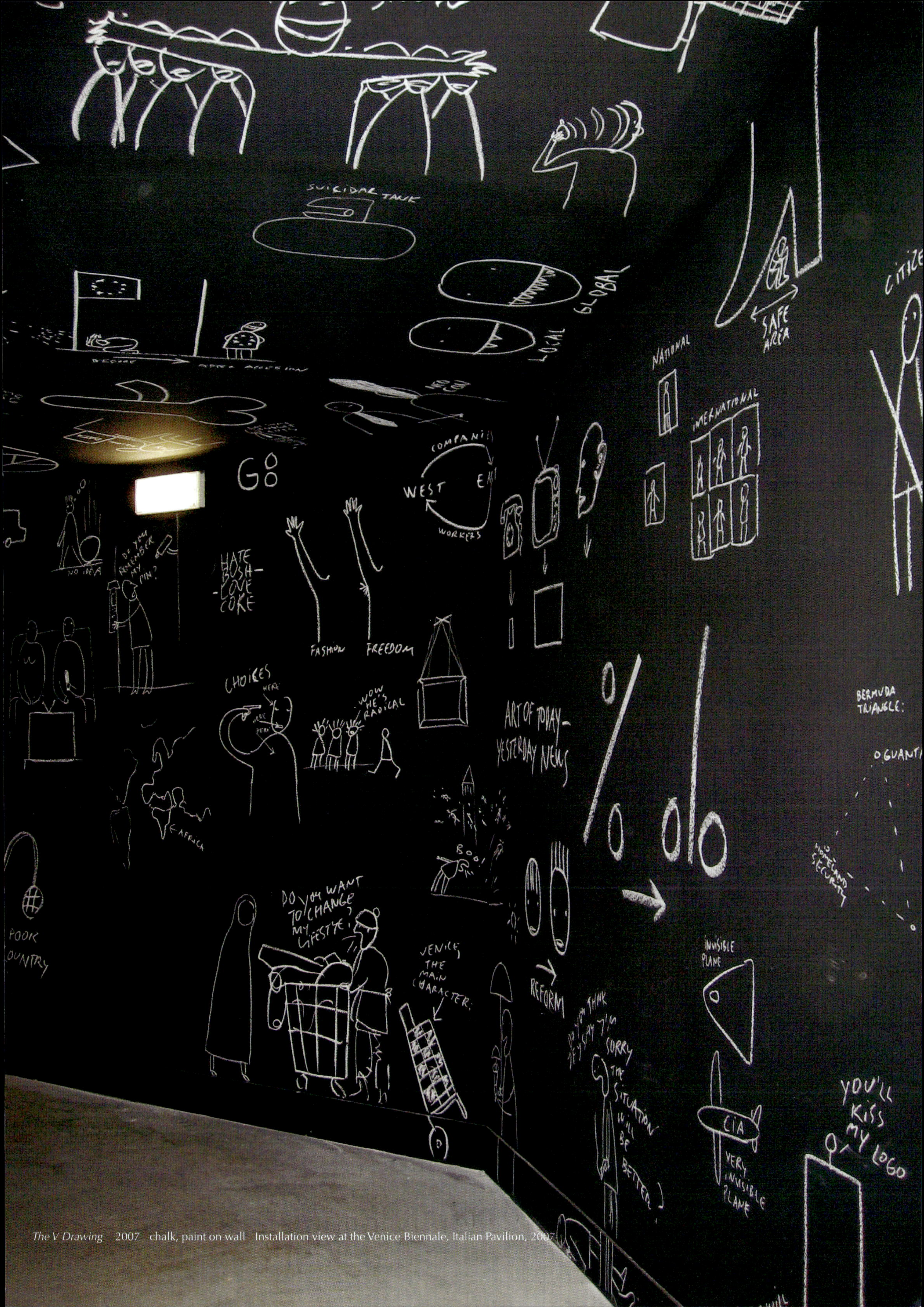

The V Drawing 2007 chalk, paint on wall Installation view at the Venice Biennale, Italian Pavilion, 2007

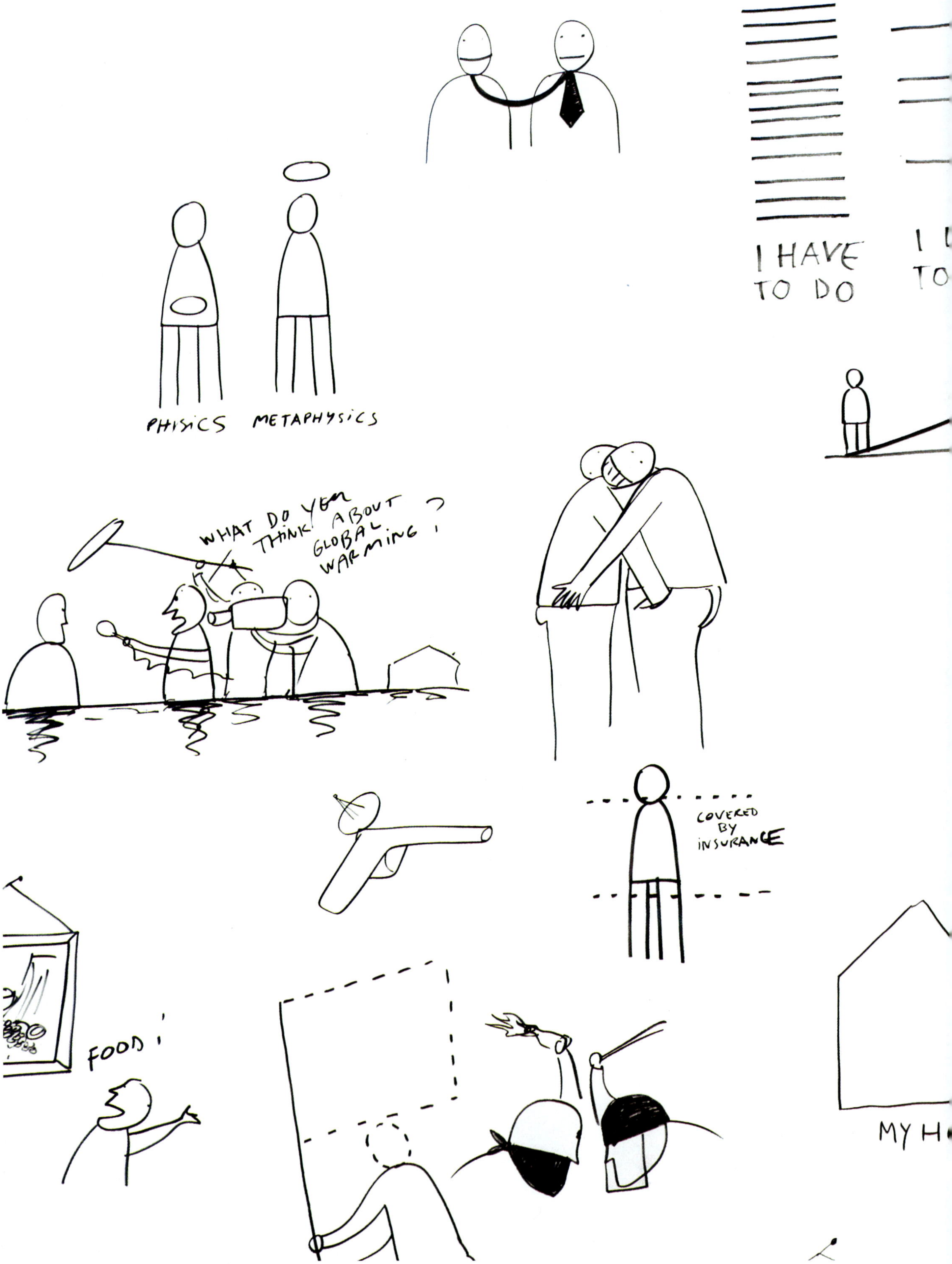

What Happened to Us? 2007 (detail) felt-tip pen ink on painted wall Installation at the Museum of Modern Art, New York, 2007

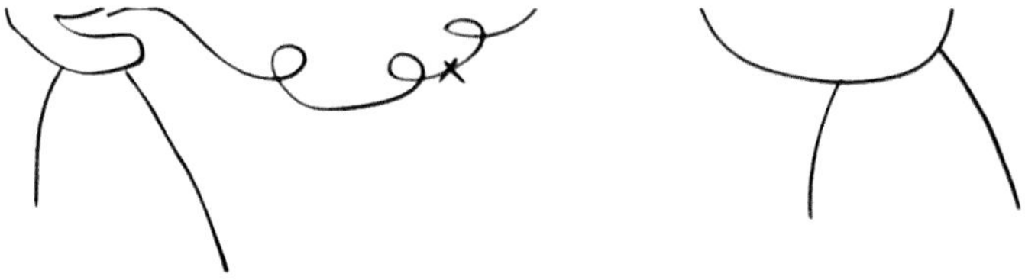

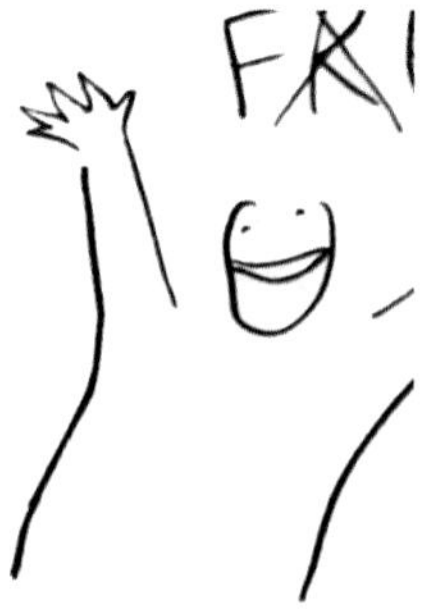

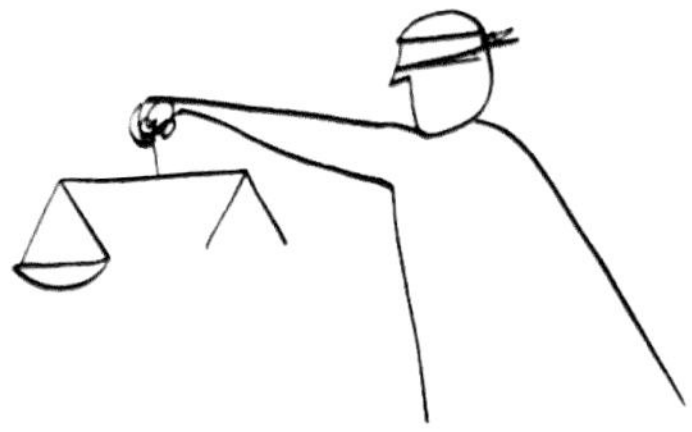

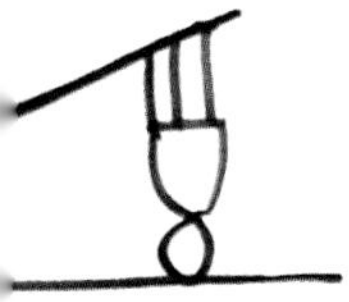

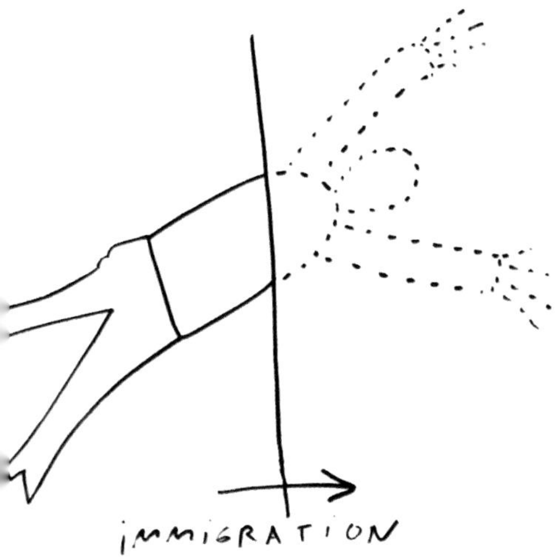
iMMiGRATiON

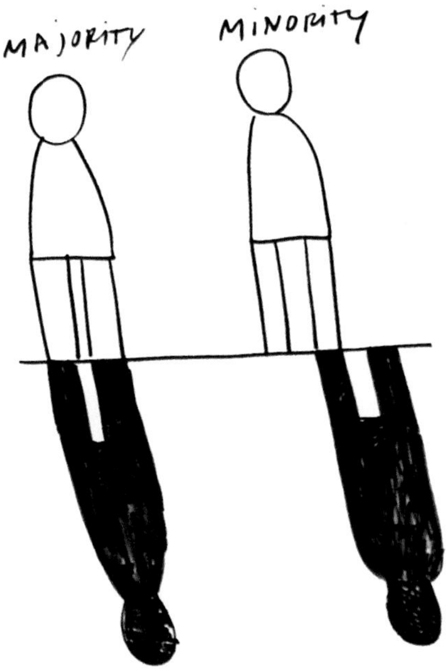
MAJORITY
MINORITY

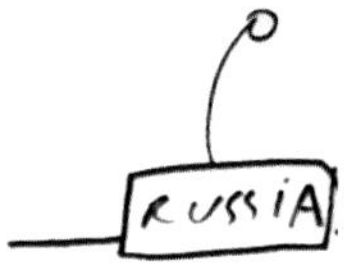
RUSSIA

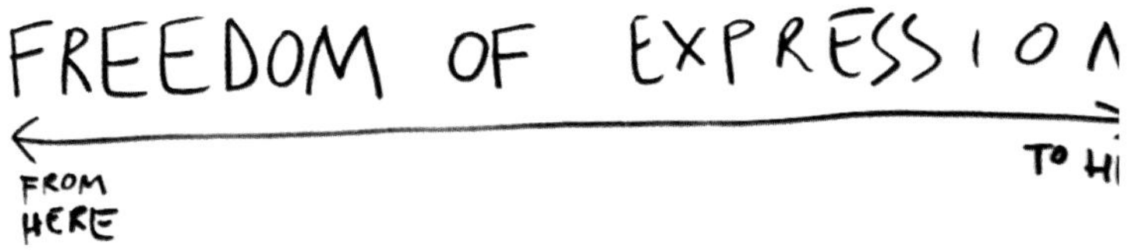
FREEDOM OF EXPRESSIO
FROM HERE
TO H

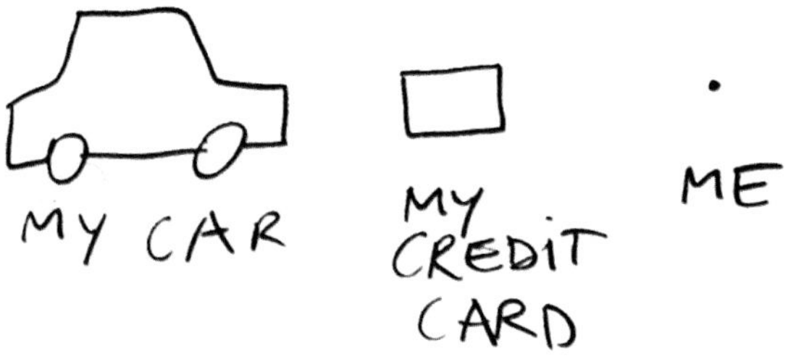
MY CAR
MY CREDIT CARD
ME

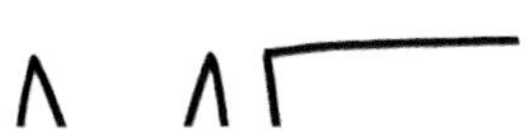

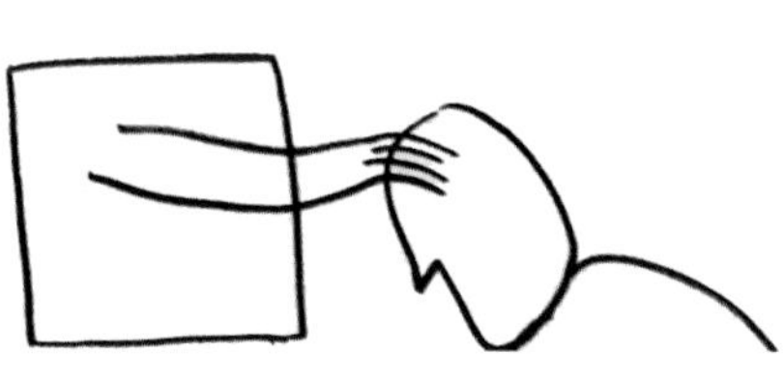

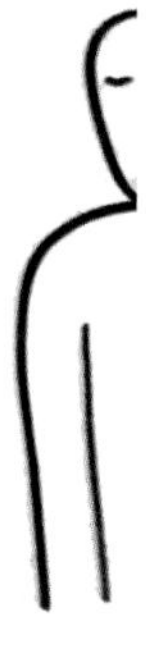

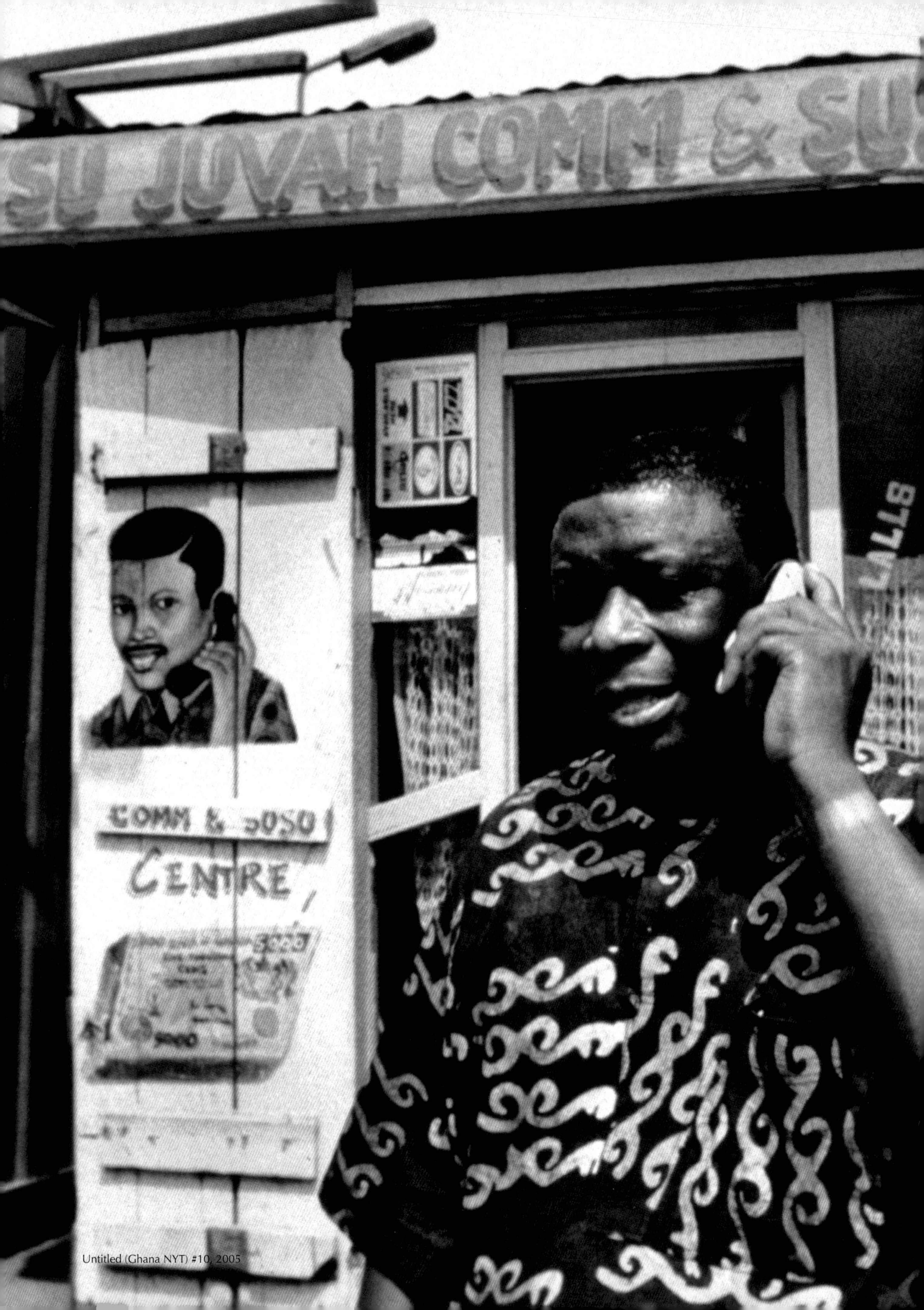

Untitled (Ghana NYT) #10, 2005

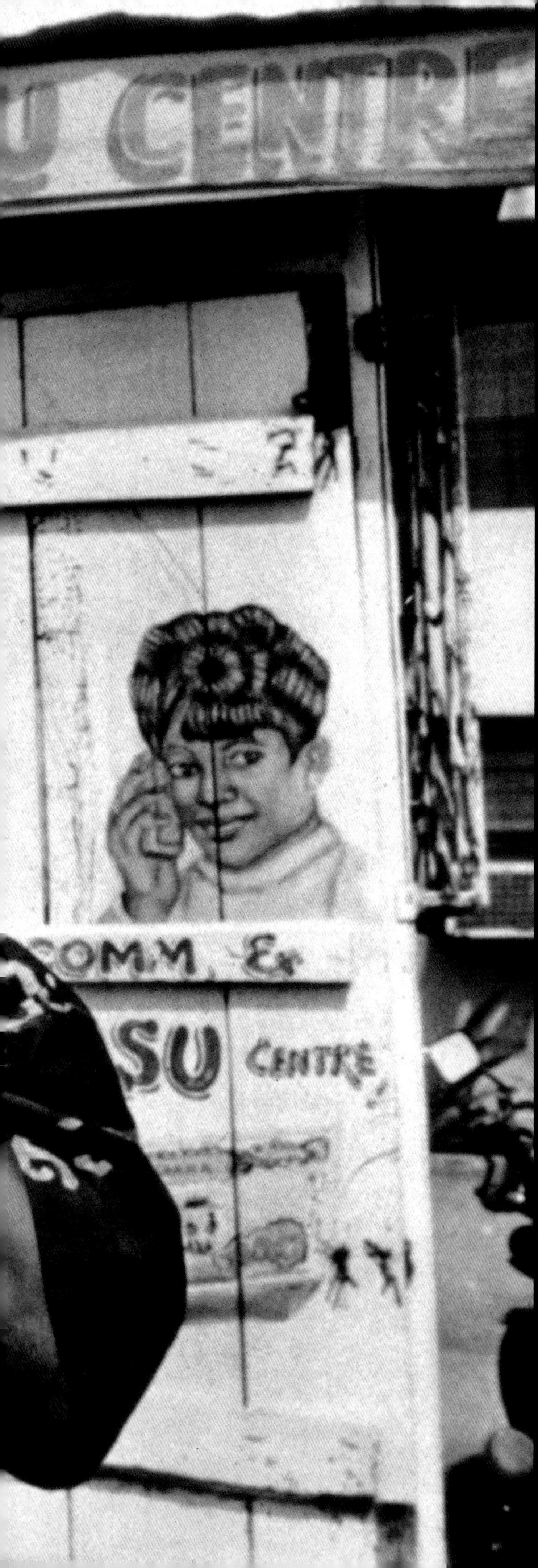

The New York Times Magazine

THE CASE FOR CONTAMINATION

KWAME ANTHONY APPIAH

1.

I'm seated, with my mother, on a palace veranda, cooled by a breeze from the royal garden. Before us, on a dais, is an empty throne, its arms and legs embossed with polished brass, the back and seat covered in black-and-gold silk. In front of the steps to the dais, there are two columns of people, mostly men, facing one another, seated on carved wooden stools, the cloths they wear wrapped around their chests, leaving their shoulders bare. There is a quiet buzz of conversation. Outside in the garden, peacocks screech. At last, the blowing of a ram's horn announces the arrival of the king of Asante, its tones sounding his honorific, *kotoko hene*, "porcupine chief." (Each quill of the porcupine, according to custom, signifies a warrior ready to kill and to die for the kingdom.) Everyone stands until the king has settled on the throne. Then, when we sit, a chorus sings songs in praise of him, which are interspersed with the playing of a flute. It is a Wednesday festival day in Kumasi, the town in Ghana where I grew up.

Unless you're one of a few million Ghanaians, this will probably seem a relatively unfamiliar world, perhaps even an exotic one. You might suppose that this Wednesday festival belongs quaintly to an African past. But before the king arrived, people were taking calls on cellphones, and among those passing the time in quiet conversation were a dozen men in suits, representatives of an insurance company. And the meetings in the office next to the veranda are about contemporary issues: H.I.V./AIDS, the educational needs of 21st-century children, the teaching of science and technology at the local university. When my turn comes to be formally presented, the king asks me about Princeton, where I teach. I ask him when he'll next be in the States. In a few weeks, he says cheerfully. He's got a meeting with the head of the World Bank.

Anywhere you travel in the world—today as always—you can find ceremonies like these, many of them rooted in centuries-old traditions. But you will also find everywhere—and this is something new—many intimate connections with places far away: Washington, Moscow, Mexico City, Beijing. Across the street from us, when we were growing up, there was a large house occupied by a number of families, among them a vast family of boys; one, about my age, was a good friend. He lives in London. His brother lives in Japan, where his wife is from. They have another brother who has been in Spain for a while and a couple more brothers who, last I heard, were in the United States. Some of them still live in Kumasi, one or two in Accra, Ghana's capital. Eddie, who lives in Japan, speaks his wife's language now. He has to. But he was never very comfortable in English, the language of our government and our schools. When he phones me from time to time, he prefers to speak Asante-Twi.

Over the years, the royal palace buildings in Kumasi have expanded. When I was a child, we used to visit the previous king, my great-uncle by marriage, in a small building that the British had allowed his predecessor to build when he returned from exile in the Seychelles to a restored but diminished Asante kingship. That building is now a museum, dwarfed by the enormous house next door—built by his successor, my uncle by marriage—where the current king lives. Next to it is the suite of offices abutting the veranda where we were sitting, recently finished by the present king, my uncle's successor. The British, my mother's people, conquered Asante at the turn of the 20th century; now, at the turn of the 21st, the palace feels as it must have felt in the 19th century: a center of power. The president of Ghana comes from this world, too. He was born across the street from the palace to a member of the royal Oyoko clan. But he belongs to other worlds as well: he went to Oxford University; he's a member of one of the Inns of Court in London; he's a Catholic, with a picture of himself greeting the pope in his sitting room.

What are we to make of this? On Kumasi's Wednesday festival day, I've seen visitors from England and the United States wince at what they regard as the intrusion of modernity on timeless, traditional rituals—more evidence, they think, of a pressure in the modern world toward uniformity. They react like the assistant on the film set who's supposed to check that the extras in a sword-and-sandals movie aren't wearing wristwatches. And such purists are not alone. In the past couple of years, Unesco's members have spent a great deal of time trying to hammer out a convention on the "protection and promotion" of cultural diversity. (It was finally approved at the Unesco General Conference in October 2005.) The drafters worried that "the processes of globalization . . . represent a challenge for cultural diversity, namely in view of risks of imbalances between rich and poor countries." The fear is that the values and images of Western mass culture, like some invasive weed, are threatening to choke out the world's native flora.

The contradictions in this argument aren't hard to find. This same Unesco document is careful to affirm the importance of the free flow of ideas, the freedom of thought and expression and human rights—values that, we know, will become universal only if we make them so. What's really important, then, cultures or people? In a world where Kumasi and New York—and Cairo and Leeds and Istanbul—are being drawn ever closer together, an ethics of globalization has proved elusive.

The right approach, I think, starts by taking individuals—not nations, tribes or "peoples"—as the proper object of moral concern. It doesn't much matter what we call such a creed, but in homage to Diogenes, the fourth-century Greek Cynic and the first philosopher to call himself a "citizen of the world," we could call it cosmopolitan. Cosmopolitans take cultural difference seriously, because they take the choices individual people make seriously. But because cultural difference is not the only thing that concerns them, they suspect that many of globalization's cultural critics are aiming at the wrong targets.

Yes, globalization can produce homogeneity. But globalization is also a threat to homogeneity. You can see this as clearly in Kumasi as anywhere. One thing Kumasi isn't—simply because it's a city—is homogeneous. English, German, Chinese, Syrian, Lebanese, Burkinabe, Ivorian, Nigerian, Indian: I can find you families of each description. I can find you Asante people, whose ancestors have lived in this town for centuries, but also Hausa households that have been around for centuries, too. There are people there from every region of the country as well, speaking scores of languages. But if you travel just a little way outside Kumasi—20 miles, say, in the right direction—and if you drive off the main road down one of the many potholed side roads of red laterite, you won't have difficulty finding villages that are fairly monocultural. The people have mostly been to Kumasi and seen the big, polyglot, diverse world of the city. Where they live, though, there is one everyday language (aside from the English in the government schools) and an agrarian way of life based on some old crops, like yams, and some newer ones, like cocoa, which arrived in the late 19th century as a product for export. They may or may not have electricity. (This close to Kumasi, they probably do.) When people talk of the homogeneity produced by globalization, what they are talking about is this: Even here the villagers will have radios (though the language will be local); you will be able to get a discussion going about Ronaldo, Mike Tyson or Tupac; and you will probably be able to find a bottle of Guinness or Coca-Cola (as well as of Star or Club, Ghana's own fine lagers). But has access to these things made the place more homogeneous or less? And what can you tell about people's souls from the fact that they drink Coca-Cola?

It's true that the enclaves of homogeneity you find these days—in Asante as in Pennsylvania—are less distinctive than they were a century ago, but mostly in good ways. More of them have access to effective medicines. More of them have access to clean drinking water, and more of them have schools. Where, as is still too common, they don't have these things, it's something not to celebrate but to deplore. And whatever loss of difference there has been, they are constantly inventing new forms of difference: new hairstyles, new slang, even, from time to time, new religions. No one could say that the world's villages are becoming anything like the same.

So why do people in these places sometimes feel that their identities are threatened? Because the world, their world, is changing, and some of them don't like it. The pull of the global economy—witness those cocoa trees, whose chocolate is eaten all around the world—created some of the life they now live. If chocolate prices were to collapse again, as they did in the early 1990's, Asante farmers might have to find new crops or new forms of livelihood. That prospect is unsettling for some people (just as it is exciting for others). Missionaries came awhile ago, so many of these villagers will be Christian, even if they have also kept some of the rites from earlier days. But new Pentecostal messengers are challenging the churches they know and condemning the old rites as idolatrous. Again, some like it; some don't.

Above all, relationships are changing. When my father was young, a man in a village would farm some land that a chief had granted him, and his maternal clan (including his younger brothers) would work it with him. When a new house needed building he would organize it. He would also make sure his dependents were fed and clothed, the children educated, marriages and funerals arranged and paid for. He could expect to pass the farm and the responsibilities along to the next generation.

Nowadays, everything is different. Cocoa prices have not kept pace with the cost of living. Gas prices have made the transportation of the crop more expensive. And there are new possibilities for the young in the towns, in other parts of the country and in other parts of the world. Once, perhaps, you could have commanded the young ones to stay. Now they have the right to leave—perhaps to seek work at one of the new data-processing centers down south in the nation's capital—and, anyway, you may not make enough to feed and clothe and educate them all. So the time of the successful farming family is passing, and those who were settled in that way of life are as sad to see it go as American family farmers are whose lands are accumulated by giant agribusinesses. We can sympathize with them. But we cannot force their children to stay in the name of protecting their authentic culture, and we cannot afford to subsidize indefinitely thousands of distinct islands of homogeneity that no longer make economic sense.

Nor should we want to. Human variety matters, cosmopolitans think, because people are entitled to options. What John Stuart Mill said more than a century ago in "On Liberty" about diversity within a society serves just as well as an argument for variety across the globe:

"If it were only that people have diversities of taste, that is reason enough for not attempting to shape them all after one model. But different persons also require different conditions for their spiritual development; and can no more exist healthily in the same moral, than all the variety of plants can exist in the same physical, atmosphere and climate. The same things which are helps to one person towards the cultivation of his higher nature, are hindrances to another. . . . Unless there is a corresponding diversity in their modes of life, they neither obtain their fair share of happiness, nor grow up to the mental, moral, and aesthetic stature of which their nature is capable."

If we want to preserve a wide range of human conditions because it allows free people the best chance to make their own lives, we can't enforce diversity by trapping people within differences they long to escape.

2.

Even if you grant that people shouldn't be compelled to sustain the older cultural practices, you might suppose that cosmopolitans should side with those who are busy around the world "preserving culture" and resisting "cultural imperialism." Yet behind these slogans you often find some curious assumptions. Take "preserving culture." It's one thing to help people sustain arts they want to sustain. I am all for festivals of Welsh bards in Llandudno financed by the Welsh arts council. Long live the Ghana National Cultural Center in Kumasi, where you can go and learn traditional Akan dancing and drumming, especially since its classes are spirited and overflowing. Restore the deteriorating film stock of early Hollywood movies; continue the preservation of Old Norse and early Chinese and Ethiopian manuscripts; record, transcribe and analyze the oral narratives of Malay and Masai and Maori. All these are undeniably valuable.

But preserving culture—in the sense of such cultural artifacts—is different from preserving cultures. And the cultural preservationists often pursue the latter, trying to ensure that the Huli of Papua New Guinea (or even Sikhs in Toronto) maintain their "authentic" ways. What makes a cultural expression authentic, though? Are we to stop the importation of baseball caps into Vietnam so that the Zao will continue to wear their colorful red headdresses? Why not ask the Zao? Shouldn't the choice be theirs?

"They have no real choice," the cultural preservationists say. "We've dumped cheap Western clothes into their markets, and they can no longer afford the silk they used to wear. If they had what they really wanted, they'd still be dressed traditionally." But this is no longer an argument about authenticity. The claim is that they can't afford to do something that they'd really like to do, something that is expressive of an identity they care about and want to sustain. This is a genuine problem, one that afflicts people in many communities: they're too poor to live the life they want to lead. But if they do get richer, and they still run around in T-shirts, that's their choice. Talk of authenticity now just amounts to telling other people what they ought to value in their own traditions.

Not that this is likely to be a problem in the real world. People who can afford it mostly like to put on traditional garb—at least from time to time. I was best man once at a Scottish wedding at which the bridegroom wore a kilt and I wore kente cloth. Andrew Oransay, the islander who piped us up the aisle, whispered in my ear at one point, "Here we all are then, in our tribal gear." In Kumasi, people who can afford them love to put on their kente cloths, especially the most "traditional" ones, woven in colorful silk strips in the town of Bonwire, as they have been for a couple of centuries. (The prices are high in part because demand outside Asante has risen. A fine kente for a man now costs more than the average Ghanaian earns in a year. Is that bad? Not for the people of Bonwire.)

Besides, trying to find some primordially authentic culture can be like peeling an onion. The textiles most people think of as traditional West African cloths are known as Java prints; they arrived in the 19th century with the Javanese batiks sold, and often milled, by the Dutch. The traditional garb of Herero women in Namibia derives from the attire of 19th-century German missionaries, though it is still unmistakably Herero, not least because the fabrics used have a distinctly un-Lutheran range of colors. And so with our kente cloth: the silk was always imported, traded by Europeans, produced in Asia. This tradition was once an innovation. Should we reject it for that reason as untraditional? How far back must one go? Should we condemn the young men and women of the University of Science and Technology, a few miles outside Kumasi, who wear European-style gowns for graduation, lined with kente strips (as they do now at Howard and Morehouse, too)? Cultures are made of continuities and changes, and the identity of a society can survive through these changes. Societies without change aren't authentic; they're just dead.

3.

The preservationists often make their case by invoking the evil of "cultural imperialism." Their underlying picture, in broad strokes, is this: There is a world system of capitalism. It has a center and a periphery. At the center—in Europe and the United States—is a set of multinational corporations. Some of these are in the media business. The products they sell around the world promote the creation of desires that can be fulfilled only by the purchase and use of their products. They do this explicitly through advertising, but more insidiously, they also do so through the messages implicit in movies and in television drama. Herbert Schiller, a leading critic of "media-cultural imperialism," claimed that "it is the imagery and cultural perspectives of the ruling sector in the center that shape and structure consciousness throughout the system at large."

That's the theory, anyway. But the evidence doesn't bear it out. Researchers have actually gone out into the world and explored the responses to the hit television series "Dallas" in Holland and among Israeli Arabs, Moroccan Jewish immigrants, kibbutzniks and new Russian immigrants to Israel. They have examined the actual content of the television media—whose penetration of everyday life far exceeds that of film—in Australia, Brazil, Canada, India and Mexico. They have looked at how American popular culture was taken up by the artists of Sophiatown, in South Africa. They have discussed "Days of Our Lives" and "The Bold and the Beautiful" with Zulu college students from traditional backgrounds.

And one thing they've found is that how people respond to these cultural imports depends on their existing cultural context. When the media scholar Larry Strelitz spoke to students from KwaZulu-Natal, he found that they were anything but passive vessels. One of them, Sipho—a self-described "very, very strong Zulu man"—reported that he had drawn lessons from watching the American soap opera "Days of Our Lives," "especially relationship-wise." It fortified his view that "if a guy can tell a woman that he loves her, she should be able to do the same." What's more, after watching the show, Sipho "realized that I should be allowed to speak to my father. He should be my friend rather than just my father." It seems doubtful that that was the intended message of multinational capitalism's ruling sector.

But Sipho's response also confirmed that cultural consumers are not dupes. They can adapt products to suit their own needs, and they can decide for themselves what they do and do not approve of. Here's Sipho again:

"In terms of our culture, a girl is expected to enter into relationships when she is about 20. In the Western culture, a girl can be exposed to a relationship as early as 15 or 16. That one we shouldn't adopt in our culture. Another thing we shouldn't adopt from the Western culture has to do with the way they treat elderly people. I wouldn't like my family to be sent into an old-age home."

It wouldn't matter whether the "old-age homes" in American soap operas were safe places, full of kindly people. That wouldn't sell the idea to Sipho. Dutch viewers of "Dallas" saw not the pleasures of conspicuous consumption among the superrich—the message that theorists of "cultural imperialism" find in every episode—but a reminder that money and power don't protect you from tragedy. Israeli Arabs saw a program that confirmed that women abused by their husbands should return to their fathers. Mexican telenovelas remind Ghanaian women that, where sex is at issue, men are not to be trusted. If the telenovelas tried to tell them otherwise, they wouldn't believe it.

Talk of cultural imperialism "structuring the consciousnesses" of those in the periphery treats people like Sipho as blank slates on which global capitalism's moving finger writes its message, leaving behind another cultural automaton as it moves on. It is deeply condescending. And it isn't true. In fact, one way that people sometimes respond to the onslaught of ideas from the West is to turn them against their originators. It's no accident that the West's fiercest adversaries among other societies tend to come from among the most Westernized of the group.

Who in Ghana excoriated the British colonizers and built the movement for independence? Not the farmers and the peasants. Not the chiefs. It was the Western-educated bourgeoisie. And when Kwame Nkrumah—who went to college in Pennsylvania and lived in London—created a nationalist mass movement, at its core were soldiers who had returned from fighting a war in the British Army, urban market women who traded Dutch prints, unionists who worked in industries created by colonialism and the so-called veranda boys, who had been to colonial schools, learned English and studied history and geography in textbooks written in England. Who led the resistance to the British Raj? An Indian-born South African lawyer, trained in the British courts, whose name was Gandhi; an Indian named Nehru, who wore Savile Row suits and sent his daughter to an English boarding school; and Muhammad Ali Jinnah, founder of Pakistan, who joined Lincoln's Inn in London and became a barrister at the age of 19. The independence movements of the postwar world that led to the end of Europe's African and Asian empires were driven by the rhetoric that had guided the Allies' own struggle against Germany and Japan: democracy, freedom, equality. This wasn't a conflict between values. It was a conflict of interests couched in terms of the same values.

4.

Sometimes, though, people react to the incursions of the modern world not by appropriating the values espoused by the liberal democracies but by inverting them. One recent result has been a new worldwide fraternity that presents cosmopolitanism with something of a sinister mirror image. Indeed, you could think of its members as counter-cosmopolitans. They believe in human dignity across the nations, and they live their creed. They share these ideals with people in many countries, speaking many languages. As thoroughgoing globalists, they make full use of the World Wide Web. They resist the crass consumerism of modern Western society and deplore its influence in the rest of the world. But they also resist the temptations of the narrow nationalisms of the countries where they were born, along with the humble allegiances of kith and kin. They resist such humdrum loyalties because they get in the way of the one thing that matters: building a community of enlightened men and women across the world. That is one reason they reject traditional religious authorities (though they disapprove, too, of their obscurantism and temporizing). Sometimes they agonize in their discussions about whether they can reverse the world's evils or whether their struggle is hopeless. But mostly they soldier on in their efforts to make the world a better place.

These are not the heirs of Diogenes the Cynic. The community these comrades are building is not a polis; it's what they call the ummah, the global community of Muslims, and it is open to all who share their faith. They are young, global Muslim fundamentalists. The ummah's new globalists consider that they have returned to the fundamentals of Islam; much of what passes for Islam in the world, much of what has passed as Islam for centuries, they think a sham. As the French scholar Olivier Roy has observed, these religionists—his term for them is "neofundamentalists"—wish to cleanse Islam's pristine and universal message from the contingencies of mere history, of local cultures. For them, Roy notes, "globalization is a good opportunity to dissociate Islam from any given culture and to provide a model that could work beyond any culture." They have taken a set of doctrines that once came with a form of life, in other words, and thrown away that form of life.

Now, the vast majority of these fundamentalists are not going to blow anybody up. So they should not be confused with those other Muslims—the "radical neofundamentalists," Roy calls them—who want to turn jihad, interpreted as literal warfare against the West, into the sixth pillar of Islam. Whether to endorse the use of violence is a political decision, even if it is to be justified in religious terms. Nonetheless, the neofundamentalists present a classic challenge to cosmopolitanism, because they, too, offer a moral and, in its way, inclusive universalism.

Unlike cosmopolitanism, of course, it is universalist without being tolerant, and such intolerant universalism has often led to murder. It underlay the French Wars of Religion that bloodied the four decades before the Edict of Nantes of 1598, in which Henry IV of France finally granted to the Protestants in his realm the right to practice their faith. In the Thirty Years' War, which ravaged central Europe until 1648 and the Peace of Westphalia, Protestant and Catholic princes from Austria to Sweden struggled with one another, and hundreds of thousands of Germans died in battle. Millions starved or died of disease as roaming armies pillaged the countryside. The period of religious conflict in the British Isles from the first Bishops' War of 1639 to the end of the English Civil War in 1651, which pitted Protestant armies against the forces of [an Anglican] king, resulted in the deaths of perhaps 10 percent of the population. All these conflicts involved issues beyond sectarian doctrine, of course. Still, many Enlightenment liberals drew the conclusion that enforcing one vision of universal truth could only lead the world back to the blood baths.

Yet tolerance by itself is not what distinguishes the cosmopolitan from the neofundamentalist. There are plenty of things that the heroes of radical Islam are happy to tolerate. They don't care if you eat kebabs or meatballs or kung pao chicken, as long as the meat is halal; your hijab can be silk or linen or viscose. At the same time, there are plenty of things that cosmopolitans wi

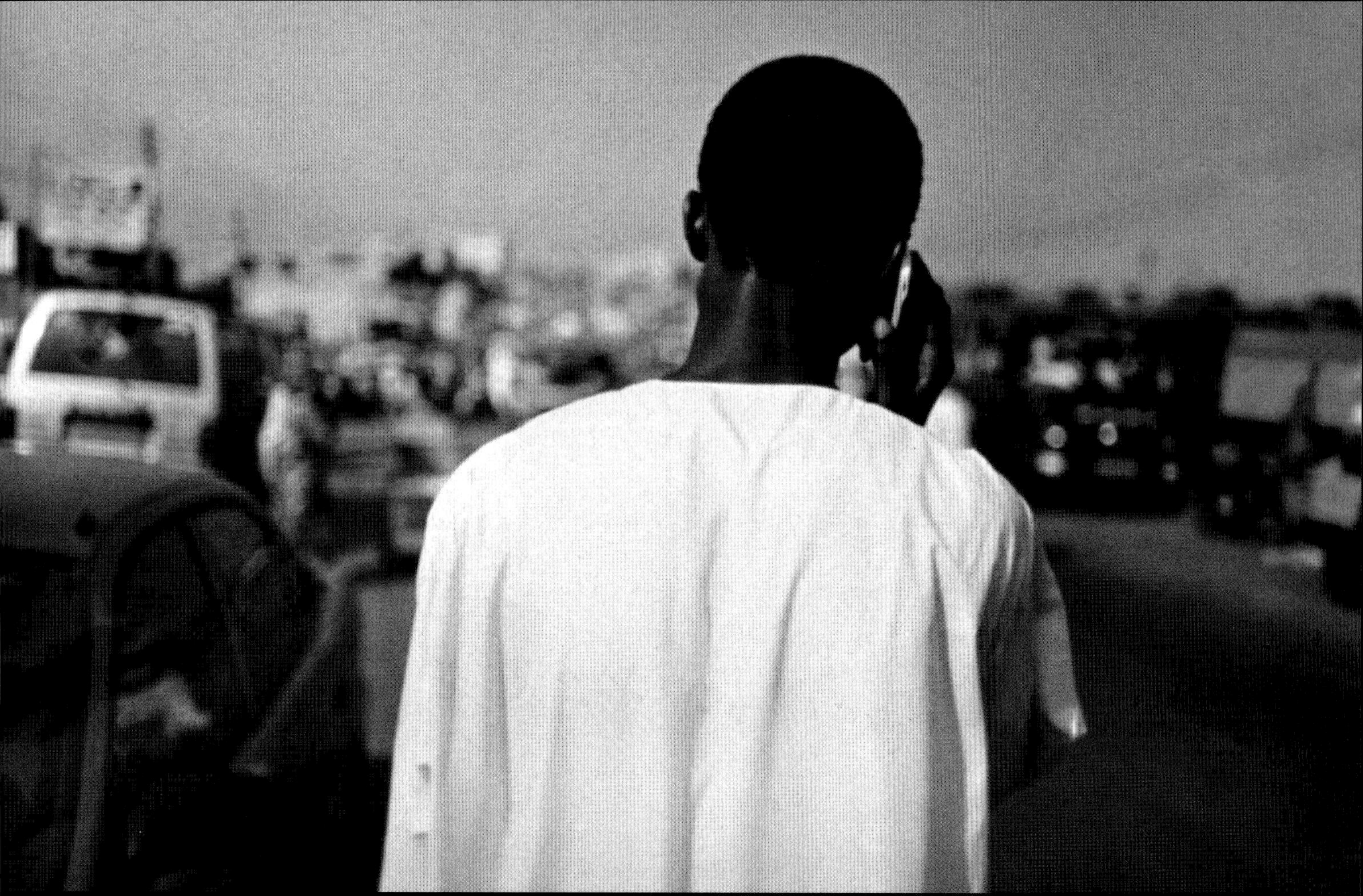

Untitled (Ghana NYT) #11, 2005

not tolerate. We will sometimes want to intervene in other places because what is going on there violates our principles so deeply. We, too, can see moral error. And when it is serious enough—genocide is the least-controversial case—we will not stop with conversation. Toleration has its limits.

Nor can you tell us apart by saying that the neofundamentalists believe in universal truth. Cosmopolitans believe in universal truth, too, though we are less certain that we already have all of it. It is not skepticism about the very idea of truth that guides us; it is realism about how hard the truth is to find. One tenet we hold to, however, is that every human being has obligations to every other. Everybody matters: that is our central idea. And again, it sharply limits the scope of our tolerance.

To say what, in principle, distinguishes the cosmopolitan from competing universalisms, we plainly need to go beyond talk of truth and tolerance. One distinctively cosmopolitan commitment is to pluralism. Cosmopolitans think that there are many values worth living by and that you cannot live by all of them. So we hope and expect that different people and different societies will embody different values. Another aspect of cosmopolitanism is what philosophers call fallibilism—the sense that our knowledge is imperfect, provisional, subject to revision in the face of new evidence.

The neofundamentalist conception of a global ummah, by contrast, admits of local variations—but only in matters that don't matter. These counter-cosmopolitans, like many Christian fundamentalists, do think that there is one right way for all human beings to live; that all the differences must be in the details. If what concerns you is global homogeneity, then this utopia, not the world that capitalism is producing, is the one you should worry about. Still, the universalisms in the name of religion are hardly the only ones that invert the cosmopolitan creed. In the name of universal humanity, you can be the kind of Marxist, like Mao or Pol Pot, who wants to eradicate all religion, just as easily as you can be the Grand Inquisitor supervising an auto-da-fé. All of these men want everyone on their side, so we can share with them the vision in their mirror. "Indeed, I'm a trustworthy adviser to you," Osama bin Laden said in a 2002 "message to the American people." "I invite you to the happiness of this world and the hereafter and to escape your dry, miserable, materialistic life that is without soul. I invite you to Islam, that calls to follow of the path of Allah alone Who has no partners, the path which calls for justice and forbids oppression and crimes." Join us, the counter-cosmopolitans say, and we will all be sisters and brothers. But each of them plans to trample on our differences—to trample us to death, if necessary—if we will not join them. Their motto might as well be the sardonic German saying Und willst du nicht mein Bruder sein, So schlag' ich Dir den Schädel ein. (If you don't want to be my brother, then I'll smash your skull in.)

That liberal pluralists are hostile to certain authoritarian ways of life—that they're intolerant of radical intolerance—is sometimes seen as kind of self-refutation. That's a mistake: you can care about individual freedom and still understand that the contours of that freedom will vary considerably from place to place. But we might as well admit that a concern for individual freedom isn't something that will appeal to every individual. In politics, including cultural politics, there are winners and losers—which is worth remembering when we think about international human rights treaties. When we seek to embody our concern for strangers in human rights law, and when we urge our government to enforce it, we are seeking to change the world of law in every nation on the planet. We have declared slavery a violation of international law. And, in so doing, we have committed ourselves, at a minimum, to the desirability of its eradication everywhere. This is no longer controversial in the capitals of the world. No one defends enslavement. But international treaties define slavery in ways that arguably include debt bondage, and debt bondage is a significant economic institution in parts of South Asia. I hold no brief for debt bondage. Still, we shouldn't be surprised if people whose incomes and style of life depend upon it are angry.

It's the same with the international movements to promote women's equality. We know that many Islamists are deeply disturbed by the way Western men and women behave. We permit women to swim almost naked with strange men, which is our business, but it is hard to keep the news of these acts of immodesty from Muslim women and children or to protect Muslim men from the temptations they inevitably create. As the Internet extends its reach, it will get even harder, and their children, especially their girls, will be tempted to ask for these freedoms, too. Worse, they say, we are now trying to force our conception of how women and men should behave upon them. We speak of women's rights. We make treaties enshrining these rights. And then we want their governments to enforce them.

Like many people in every nation, I support those treaties; I believe that women, like men, should have the vote, should be entitled to work outside their homes, should be protected from the physical abuse of men, including their fathers, brothers and husbands. But I also know that the changes these freedoms would bring will change the balance of power between men and women in everyday life. How do I know this? Because I have lived most of my adult life in the West as it has gone through just such a transition, and I know that the process is not yet complete.

So liberty and diversity may well be at odds, and the tensions between them aren't always easily resolved. But the rhetoric of cultural preservation isn't any help. Again, the contradictions are near to hand. Take another look at that Unesco Convention. It affirms the "principle of equal dignity of and respect for all cultures." (What, all cultures—including those of the K.K.K. and the Taliban?) It also affirms "the importance of culture for social cohesion in general, and in particular its potential for the enhancement of the status and role of women in society." (But doesn't "cohesion" argue for uniformity? And wouldn't enhancing the status and role of women involve changing, rather than preserving, cultures?) In Saudi Arabia, people can watch "Will and Grace" on satellite TV—officially proscribed, but available all the same—knowing that, under Saudi law, Will could be beheaded in a public square. In northern Nigeria, mullahs inveigh against polio vaccination while sentencing adulteresses to death by stoning. In India, thousands of wives are burned to death each year for failing to make their dowry payments. Vive la différence? Please.

5.

Living cultures do not, in any case, evolve from purity into contamination; change is more a gradual transformation from one mixture to a new mixture, a process that usually takes place at some distance from rules and rulers, in the conversations that occur across cultural boundaries. Such conversations are not so much about arguments and values as about the exchange of perspectives. I don't say that we can't change minds, but the reasons we offer in our conversation will seldom do much to persuade others who do not share our fundamental evaluative judgments already. When we make judgments, after all, it's rarely because we have applied well-thought-out principles to a set of facts and deduced an answer. Our efforts to justify what we have done—or what we plan to do—are typically made up after the event, rationalizations of what we have decided intuitively to do. And a good deal of what we intuitively take to be right, we take to be right just because it is what we are used to. That does not mean, however, that we cannot become accustomed to doing things differently.

Consider the practice of foot-binding in China, which persisted for a thousand years—and was largely eradicated within a generation. The anti-foot-binding campaign, in the 1910's and 1920's, did circulate facts about the disadvantages of bound feet, but those couldn't have come as news to most people. Perhaps more effective was the campaign's emphasis that no other country went in for the practice; in the world at large, then, China was "losing face" because of it. (To China's cultural preservationists, of course, the fact that the practice was peculiar to the region was entirely a mark in its favor.) Natural-foot societies were formed, with members forswearing the practice and further pledging that their sons would not marry women with bound feet. As the movement took hold, scorn was heaped on older women with bound feet, and they were forced to endure the agonies of unbinding. What had been beautiful became ugly; ornamentation became disfigurement. The appeal to reason can explain neither the custom nor its abolition.

So, too, with other social trends. Just a couple of generations ago, most people in most of the industrialized world thought that middle-class women would ideally be housewives and mothers. If they had time on their hands, they could engage in charitable work or entertain one another; a few of them might engage in the arts, writing novels, painting, performing in music, theater and dance. But there was little place for them in the "learned professions"—as lawyers or doctors, priests or rabbis; and if they were to be academics, they would teach young women and probably remain unmarried. They were not likely to make their way in politics, except perhaps at the local level. And they were not made welcome in science.

How much of the shift away from these assumptions is a result of arguments? Isn't a significant part of it just the consequence of our getting used to new ways of doing things? The arguments that kept the old pattern in place were not—to put it mildly—terribly good. If the reasons for the old sexist way of doing things had been the problem, the women's movement could have been done in a couple of weeks.

Consider another example: In much of Europe and North America, in places where a generation ago homosexuals were social outcasts and homosexual acts were illegal, lesbian and gay couples are increasingly being recognized by their families, by society and by the law. This is true despite the continued opposition of major religious groups and a significant and persisting undercurrent of social disapproval. Both sides make arguments, some good, most bad. But if you ask the social scientists what has produced this change, they will rightly not start with a story about reasons. They will give you a historical account that concludes with a sort of perspectival shift. The increasing presence of "openly gay" people in social life and in the media has changed our habits. And over the last 30 years or so, instead of thinking about the private activity of gay sex, many Americans and Europeans started thinking about the public category of gay people.

One of the great savants of the postwar era, John von Neumann, liked to say, mischievously, that "in mathematics you don't understand things, you just get used to them." As in mathematical arguments, so in moral ones. Now, I don't deny that all the time, at every stage, people were talking, giving one another reasons to do things: accept their children, stop treating homosexuality as a medical disorder, disagree with their churches, come out. Still, the short version of the story is basically this: People got used to lesbians and gay men.

I am urging that we should learn about people in other places, take an interest in their civilizations, their arguments, their errors, their achievements, not because that will bring us to agreement but because it will help us get used to one another—something we have a powerful need to do in this globalized era. If that is the aim, then the fact that we have all these opportunities for disagreement about values need not put us off. Understanding one another may be hard; it can certainly be interesting. But it doesn't require that we come to agreement.

6.

The ideals of purity and preservation have licensed a great deal of mischief in the past century, but they have never had much to do with lived culture. Ours may be an era of mass migration, but the global spread and hybridization of culture—through travel, trade or conquest—is hardly a recent development. Alexander's empire molded both the states and the sculpture of Egypt and North India; the Mongols and then the Mughals shaped great swaths of Asia; the Bantu migrations populated half the African continent. Islamic states stretch from Morocco to Indonesia; Christianity reached Africa, Europe and Asia within a few centuries of the death of Jesus of Nazareth; Buddhism long ago migrated from India into much of East and Southeast Asia. Jews and people whose ancestors came from many parts of China have long lived in vast diasporas. The traders of the Silk Road changed the style of elite dress in Italy; someone buried Chinese pottery in 15th-century Swahili graves. I have heard it said that the bagpipes started out in Egypt and came to Scotland with the Roman infantry. None of this is modern.

Our guide to what is going on here might as well be a former African slave named Publius Terentius Afer, whom we know as Terence. Terence, born in Carthage, was taken to Rome in the early second century B.C., and his plays—witty, elegant works that are, with Plautus's earlier, less-cultivated works, essentially all we have of Roman comedy—were widely admired among the city's literary elite. Terence's own mode of writing—which involved freely incorporating any number of earlier Greek plays into a single Latin one—was known to Roman littérateurs as "contamination."

It's an evocative term. When people speak for an ideal of cultural purity, sustaining the authentic culture of the Asante or the American family farm, I find myself drawn to contamination as the name for a counterideal. Terence had a notably firm grasp on the range of human variety: "So many men, so many opinions" was a line of his. And it's in his comedy "The Self-Tormentor" that you'll find what may be the golden rule of cosmopolitanism—Homo sum: humani nil a me alienum puto; "I am human: nothing human is alien to me." The context is illuminating. A busybody farmer named Chremes is told by his neighbor to mind his own affairs; the homo sum credo is Chremes's breezy rejoinder. It isn't meant to be an ordinance from on high; it's just the case for gossip. Then again, gossip—the fascination people have for the small doings of other people—has been a powerful force for conversation among cultures.

The ideal of contamination has few exponents more eloquent than Salman Rushdie, who has insisted that the novel that occasioned his fatwa "celebrates hybridity, impurity, intermingling, the transformation that comes of new and unexpected combinations of human beings, cultures, ideas, politics, movies, songs. It rejoices in mongrelisation and fears the absolutism of the Pure. Mélange, hotch-potch, a bit of this and a bit of that is how newness enters the world." No doubt there can be an easy and spurious utopianism of "mixture," as there is of "purity" or "authenticity." And yet the larger human truth is on the side of contamination—that endless process of imitation and revision.

A tenable global ethics has to temper a respect for difference with a respect for the freedom of actual human beings to make their own choices. That's why cosmopolitans don't insist that everyone become cosmopolitan. They know they don't have all the answers. They're humble enough to think that they might learn from strangers; not too humble to think that strangers can't learn from them. Few remember what Chremes says after his "I am human" line, but it is equally suggestive: "If you're right, I'll do what you do. If you're wrong, I'll set you straight." ■

Kwame Anthony Appiah, a philosopher, teaches at Princeton University. His books include *The Ethics of Identity* and *Cosmopolitanism: Ethics in a World of Strangers*, winner of the Council on Foreign Relations' 2007 Arthur Ross Book Award. This essay, adapted from *Cosmopolitanism* (New York: W. W. Norton, 2006), is reprinted by permission from the *New York Times Magazine* (January 1, 2006): 30–52.

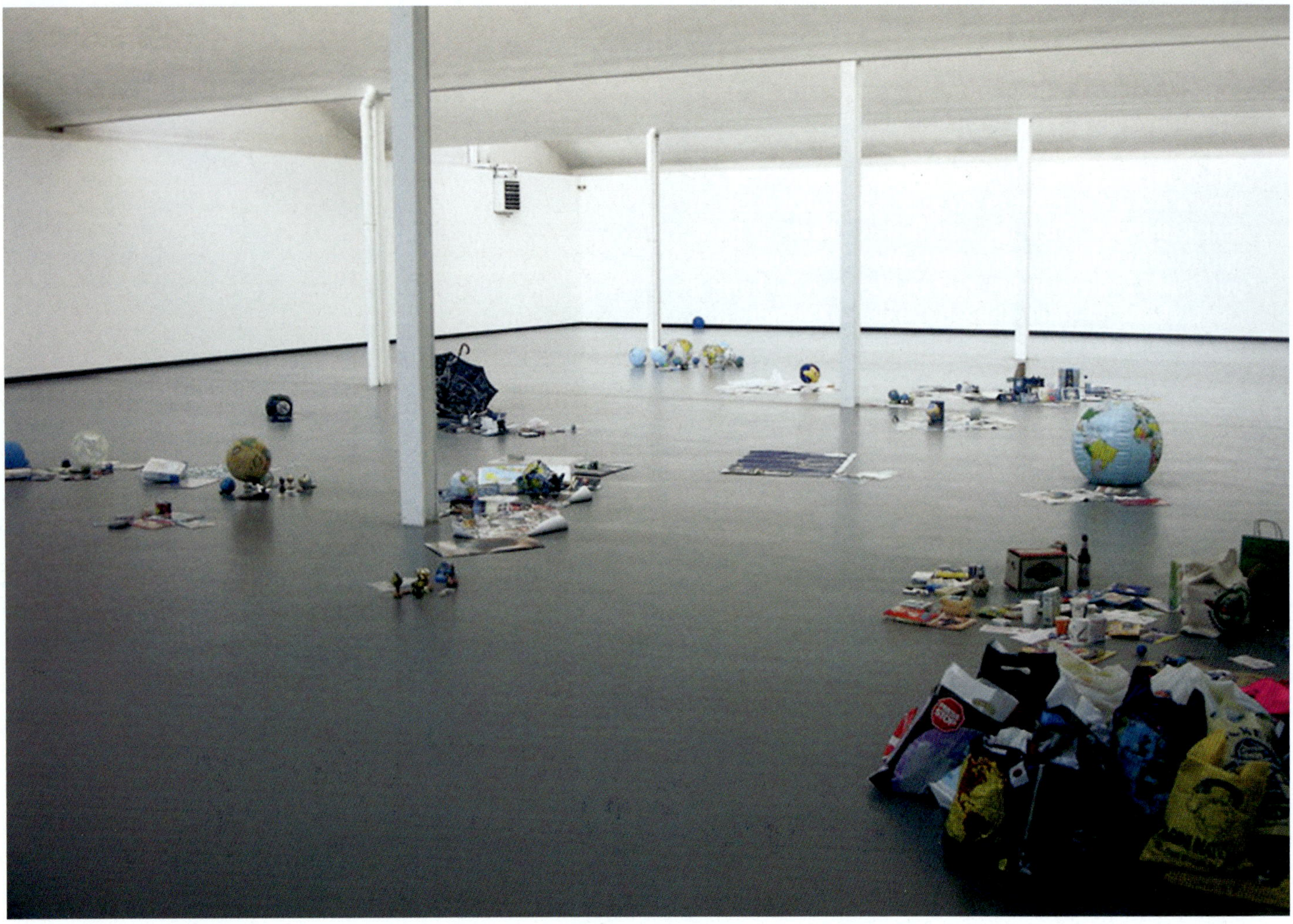

Globe Collection 1990–present Installation view at Göppingen Kunsthalle, Göppingen, Germany, 2003

THE DIZZIDENT: LIA PERJOVSCHI

Born in Romania, 1961. Lives and works in Bucharest.

When the Communist government of Romania fell in 1989 and the oppressive secret police Securitate lost control, the country was flooded with information from outside its borders. Lia Perjovschi was a student at the Art Academy Bucharest at the time and was determined to catch up on knowledge that had previously been denied to her. As travel outside Romania became increasingly possible, she crossed Europe gathering catalogues, books, and news clippings that were eventually incorporated into her ongoing project, the *Contemporary Art Archive/Center for Art Analysis* (*CAA*). The artist has described the *CAA* as a "context in motion" that is constantly reinvented by the artists, curators, and critics who interpret art based on the information they find there. To a large extent, her artistic practice continues to revolve around the activities of the *CAA* as she publishes newspapers, collects objects, and draws conceptual diagrams that present her own view of how history is formed.

In 1985, Perjovschi and her husband, Dan, started hosting open studios in Bucharest where artists could gather and discuss art criticism, the state of Romanian art, and their place in an international artistic context. She entered the Art Academy in 1987, where she made mostly performance and video art. When she studied the history of these mediums, Perjovschi came to realize that what she was attempting to make had already been done elsewhere in the 1960s, so instead her research became her art. Of the motivation behind the *CAA* in particular, the artist says, "In order to create something you need to know what was done, and . . . these materials started to help me understand what I was doing."[1] In 1990, she began accumulating various collections, such as globes and plastic bags, and started to display them in galleries as comprehensive catalogues on the way we see the world. Most of the objects she has collected were bought in museum gift shops, and thus she uses this material culture to show ways that the artworks in those institutions as well as the museums themselves are commodified and marketed. After a stint teaching contemporary art, theory, and practice at Duke University in 1997, her work took an even more ideological turn, and she published her first in an ongoing series of newspapers, a dictionary of contemporary art terms that includes entries such as "avant-garde," "critical theory," and "detective," a word that relates to the artist's current practice and that she defines as "to detect, to

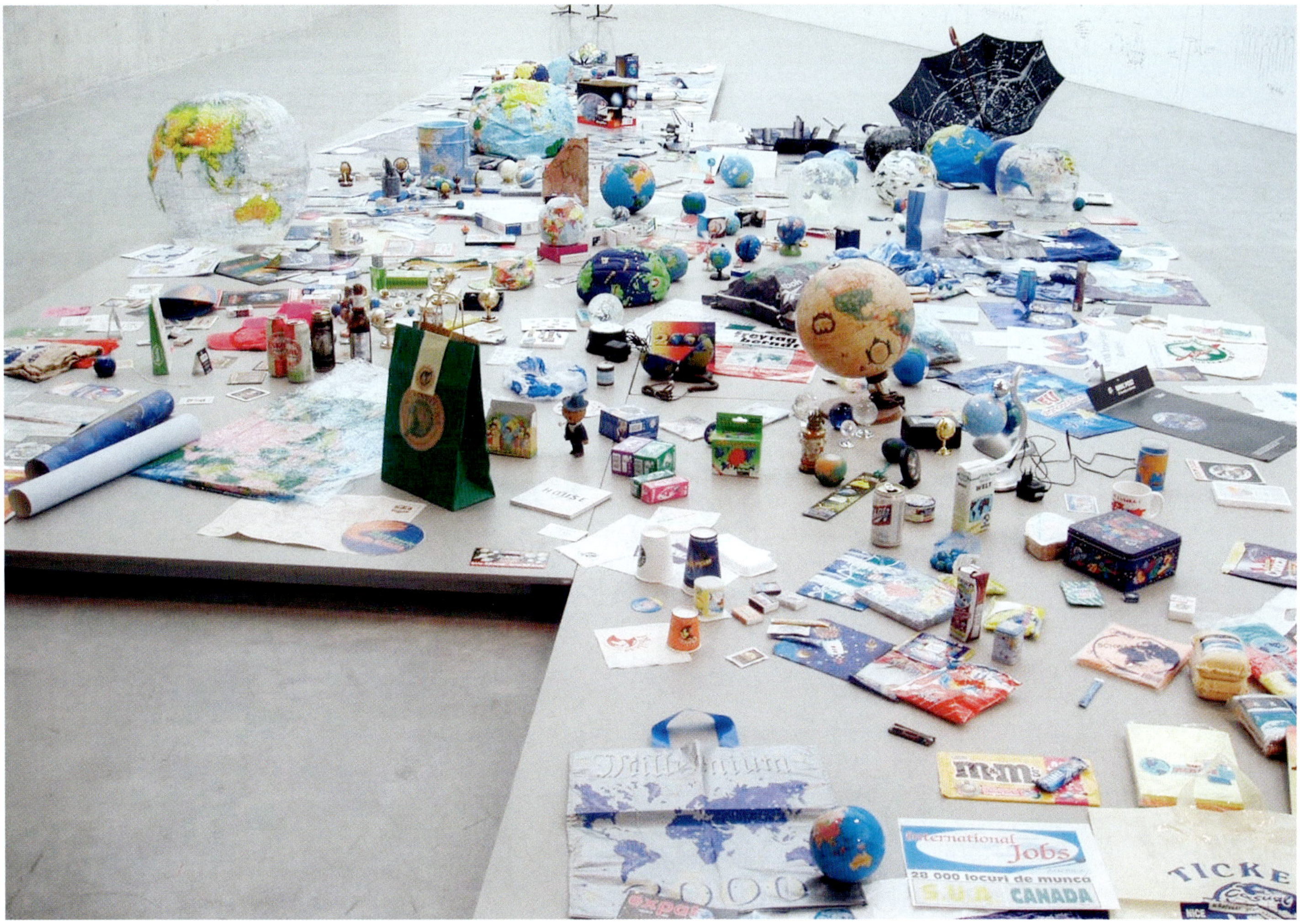

Globe Collection 1990–present Installation view at the Generali Foundation, Vienna, 2003

identify, to determine, organized, research, form of surveillance."[2]

Perjovschi's installation *Knowledge Museum* (1999–present) is an extension of her interest in archives and lexicons. It is a museum within a museum that is divided into seven departments: body, earth, universe, culture, art, science, and knowledge. Each category has a corresponding "mind map," an enlargement of the artist's notes and collages on each topic. The museum objects are only loosely grouped, as the sections of the museum are not mutually exclusive and a walk through the installation is intended to parallel a free-floating yet analytical journey through the recesses of one's brain. The items signal a return to modernist inventions such as Marcel Broodthaers' museums and eclectic nineteenth-century libraries such as Aby Warburg's Kulturwissenschaftliche Bibliothek, for which the scholar obsessively gathered books, images, and cultural artifacts and arranged them as a theoretical history of civilization from pagan antiquity through Renaissance art.

Unlike her forbears, however, Perjovschi does not claim to be searching for a single truth. In fact, she subverts this impulse. In gathering a collection that is all-encompassing, she creates a dizzying context for those who seek to formulate a coherent world view. The only limits put on the collection are the artist's own decisions, experiences, and ultimately arbitrary organization. Her museum-within-a-museum represents, therefore, the current situation for those who yearn for an ever-elusive clarity. She has even taken to calling herself a "dizzident" who strives for a coherent viewpoint but lacks definitive facts from which she can launch an effective critique. By embracing relativism as a central premise of her practice, she creates art from an unabashedly personal point of view. Nonetheless, works such as *Subjective Art History* (1999–2004) lay out her thinking clearly for anyone to learn from and respond to.[3] Through her process, Perjovschi implicitly affirms the possibility of action and change in a bewildering and often confusing world.

RH

1. Lia Perjovschi, interview with Andréa Adcock and Dale Adcock, in *Lia Perjovschi: Chronology*, Andréa and Dale Adcock, eds. (London: Gallery Yujiro, 2006), 9.

2. Lia Perjovschi, *Detective Draft 2005* (Bucharest: Center for Art Analysis, 2005), 15.

3. See Perjovschi's artist project in this catalogue, 245–280.

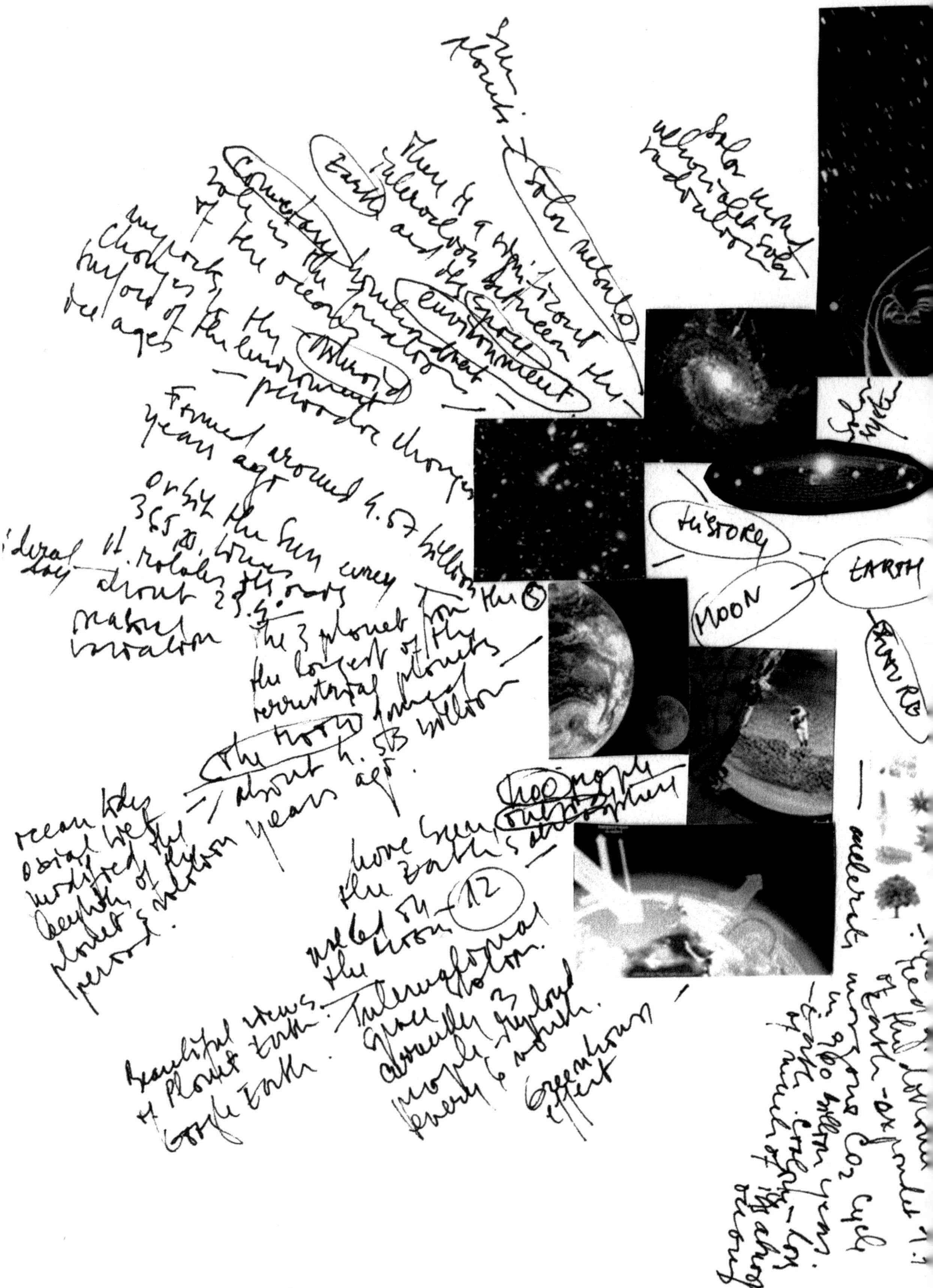

Universe Mind Map 2006 ink on paper manipulated and transferred to ink-jet on paper

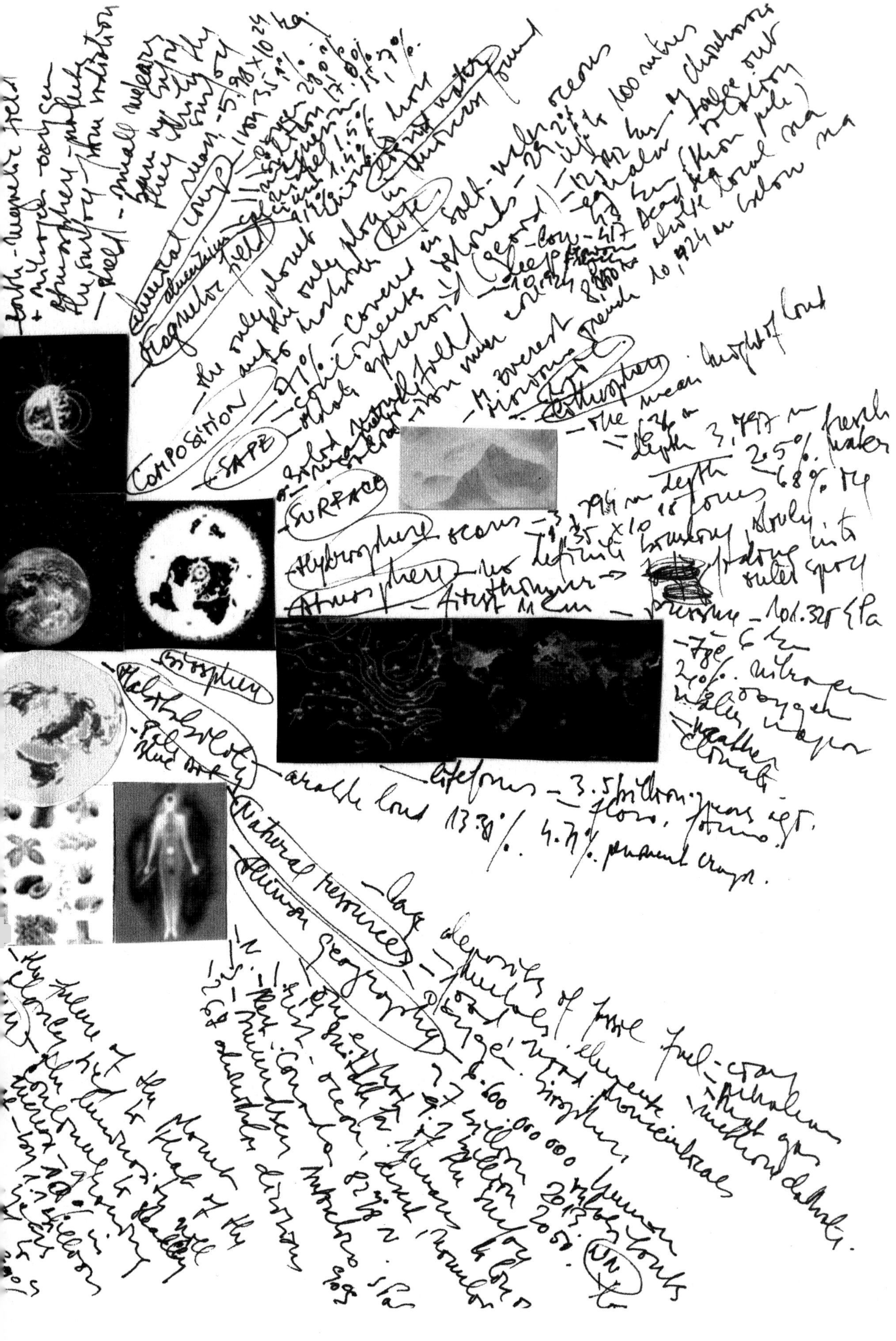
COMPOSITION
SURFACE
Hydrosphere
Atmosphere
Biosphere
Natural resources
Human geography

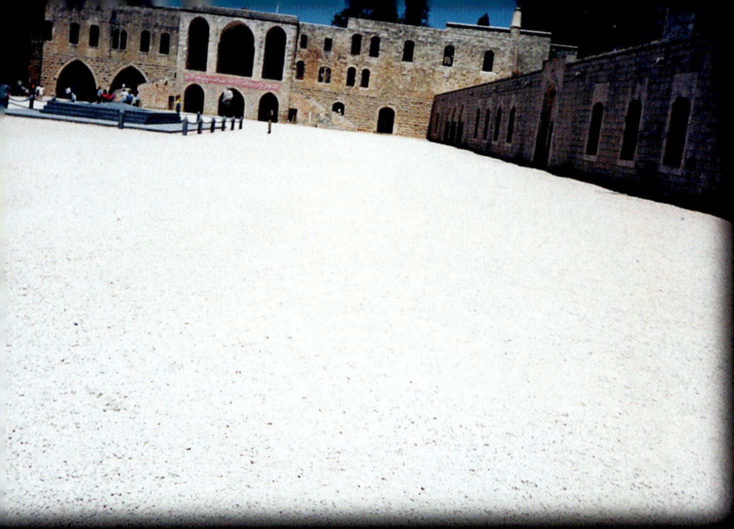

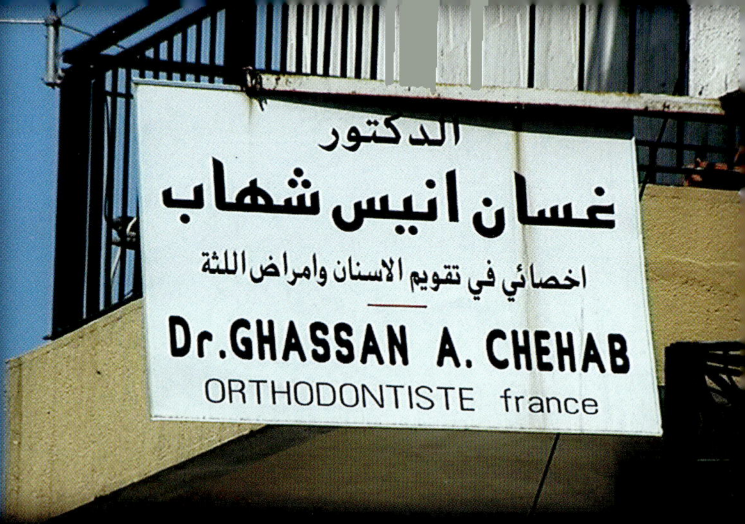
الدكتور
غسان انيس شهاب
اخصائي في تقويم الاسنان وامراض اللثة
Dr.GHASSAN A. CHEHAB
ORTHODONTISTE france

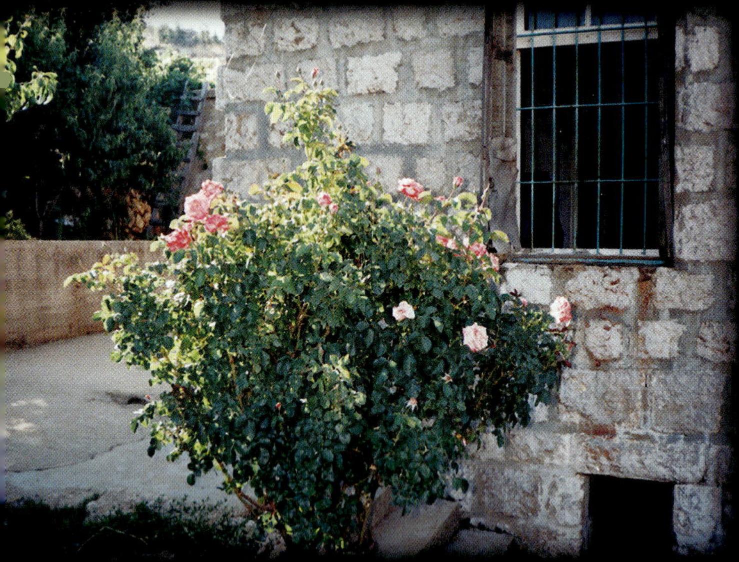

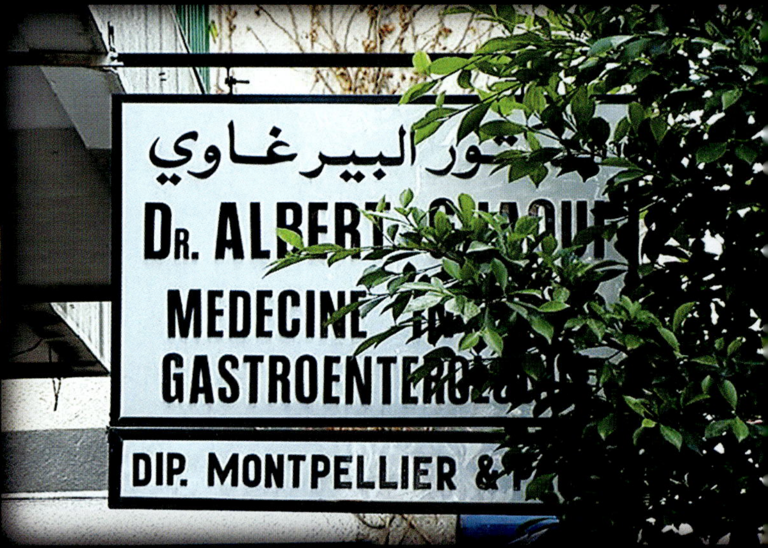
البير غاوي
MEDECINE
DIP. MONTPELLIER &

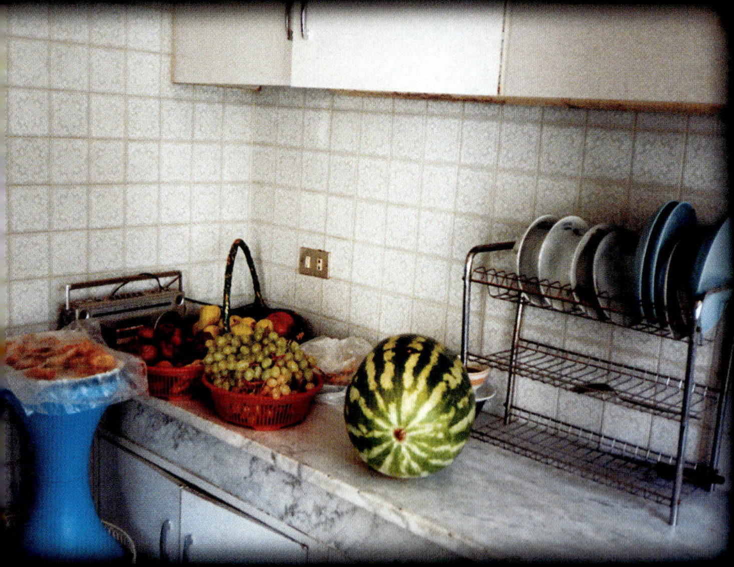

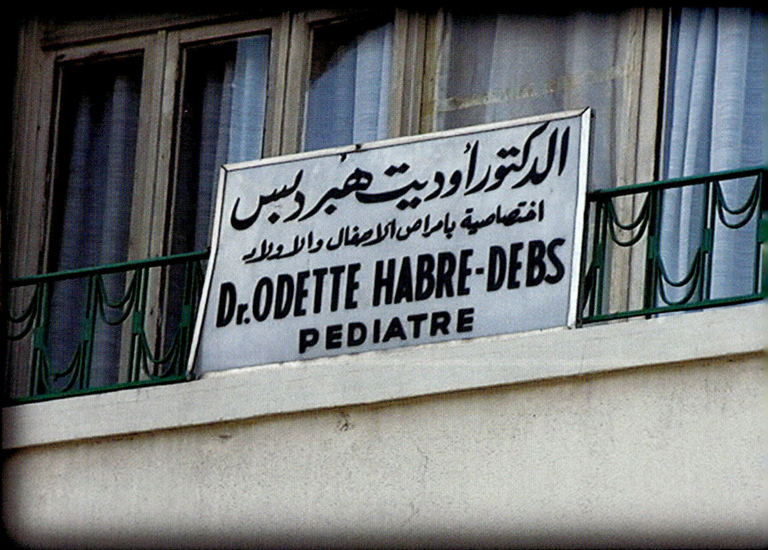
الدكتوراوديت هبر دبس
Dr.ODETTE HABRE-DEBS
PEDIATRE

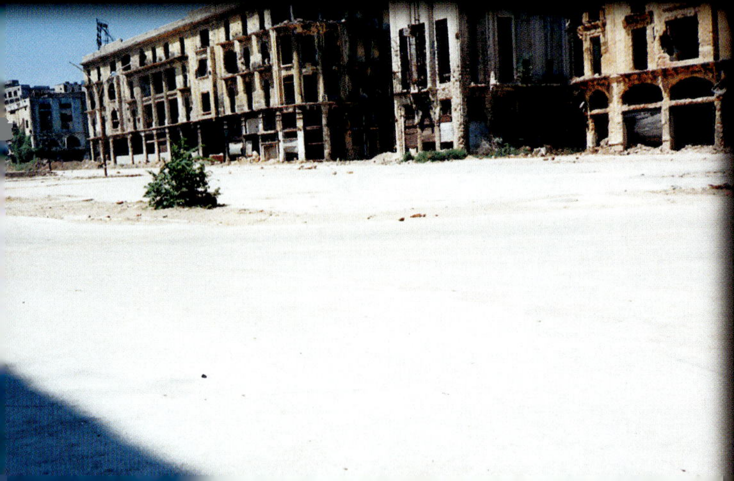

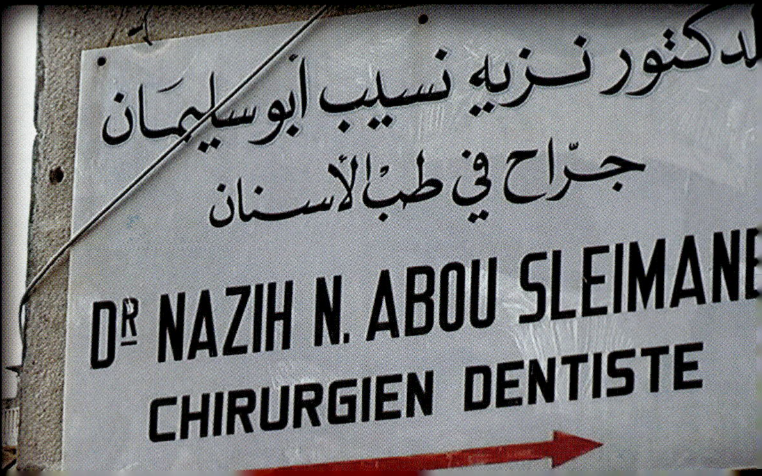
الدكتور نزيه نسيب ابو سليمان
جرّاح في طبّ الأسنان
Dr NAZIH N. ABOU SLEIMANE
CHIRURGIEN DENTISTE

BETWEEN POETICS AND SEVERITY: WALID RAAD

Born in Lebanon, 1967. Lives and works in Beirut and New York.

Since the late 1990s, Walid Raad has been making work about Lebanon. His many projects—photography, video, notebooks, multimedia lectures, writing, Web sites—have all been remembrances of the civil war that ripped through the country from 1975 until 1991. Beyond any logical description or human comprehension, this war involved not only a multitude of militias of different religious affiliations but also many neighboring countries and organizations, creating a scenario of incredibly Byzantine complexity. Raised in Beirut until he immigrated to the United States as a teenager, Raad saw his city and country become embroiled in progressive ruination. Trained in photography and holding a doctoral degree in cultural and visual studies, the artist formed in 1999 the Atlas Group, an organization dedicated to the research and recording of the contemporary history of Lebanon. The group has created an archive of meticulously catalogued documents, with dossiers categorized by provenance: coming from a known individual, found, or generated by the group itself.

The thoroughness of the archive's detailed organization supports its alleged truth-telling and gives credence to the surreal and even ridiculous claims embedded in its many small narratives. For viewers, the effect is akin to the experience of getting caught in a mental tug-of-war between fact and fiction. One category that has been especially productive is a series of documents originating from a certain Dr. Fadl Fakhouri, who is said to have been a prominent historian of the Lebanese wars. From him, we inherit Notebook Volume 38, *Already Been in a Lake of Fire*, pages of his notebook containing cutout photographs of cars that correspond to the "exact make, model, and color of every car that was used as a car bomb in the Lebanese war of 1975 to 1991." Also from this source, we get a different portrait of a time and place and its cultural practice. Dr. Fakhouri's Notebook Volume 72, *Missing Lebanese Wars*, is a compilation of black-and-white photos of jockeys and racehorses about to cross the finish line, with pencil scribbles on the pages. Readers are informed that the historian and his colleagues were "avid gamblers" who got together and bet not on which horse would win, but rather on "precisely when . . . the [racetrack] photographer would expose his frame." Furthermore, he seems to have been something of a flaneur, if a strangely obsessive one, on the streets of Beirut, carrying around a camera and taking pictures of the doctors' and dentists' signs he encountered. The images of the signs were neatly cut out and pasted on pages of another notebook, each grouping organized by a medical discipline, its spare composition seeming mysteriously artful (Notebook Volume 57, *No, Illness Is Neither Here Nor There*).[1]

Who was Dr. Fakhouri? While any astute reader will soon realize that the historian and his records are concocted fictions, each project becomes evidence of the fact that life in the midst of an ongoing war could be much fuller than we would imagine. And that may be the point of the Atlas Group's project. Even as its archive lets us know the impossibility of telling an "official" history of a long-standing disaster like the Lebanese civil war, it also exposes the power of the institution of the archive, which can conjure subjects such as Dr. Fakhouri. This is an especially critical gesture at this point in our shared history, as Lebanon, or the larger Middle East for that matter, remains an abstraction; that part of the world, in the minds of many people, is a mosaic of buildings and streets and bodies torn asunder and represents an utter absence of rationality, modernity, or even worse, life as we understand it. The paradoxical power of Raad and the Atlas Group's work is the way it has managed to produce a poetics of intimacy through the severity of grids and sequences while humanizing subjects it summoned through its own invented mechanism of representation.

In 2004, Raad dissolved the Atlas Group (it was never clear who the other members were), and his more recent work seems to have taken on more personal, intimate tones. *Let's Be Honest, The Weather Helped* (1982–2007), included in the present exhibition, is a series of seventeen photographic prints of what appear to be pages from a scrapbook. It is said that as a teenager in Beirut in the 1970s, Raad was a keen collector of bullets, which he excavated from his urban surroundings. He also photographed the locations and covered the printed pictures with sticker dots, matching their colors and diameters with those of the bullet holes he found. Only later, it is alleged, did the artist come to the realization that the bullets were color-coded by the manufacturers who supplied ammunitions to the armies and militias fighting in Lebanon. As viewers peruse these photographic plates, the implausibility of the claim becomes clear due to, among other clues, the unlikely densities and diameters of some of the color dots. But hidden behind the story of a boy with an interrogative mind is perhaps an even more unlikely yet actual reality: that of an insidious global commerce that continues to drive the devastation of places like Lebanon in our world.

DC

1. All citations are taken from the Atlas Group and Walid Raad, *The Truth Will Be Known When the Last Witness Is Dead: Documents from the Fakhouri File in the Atlas Group Archive* (Köln: Les laboratoires d'Aubervilliers, La Galerie de Noisy-le-Sec, and Verlag der Buchhandlung Walter König, 2004).

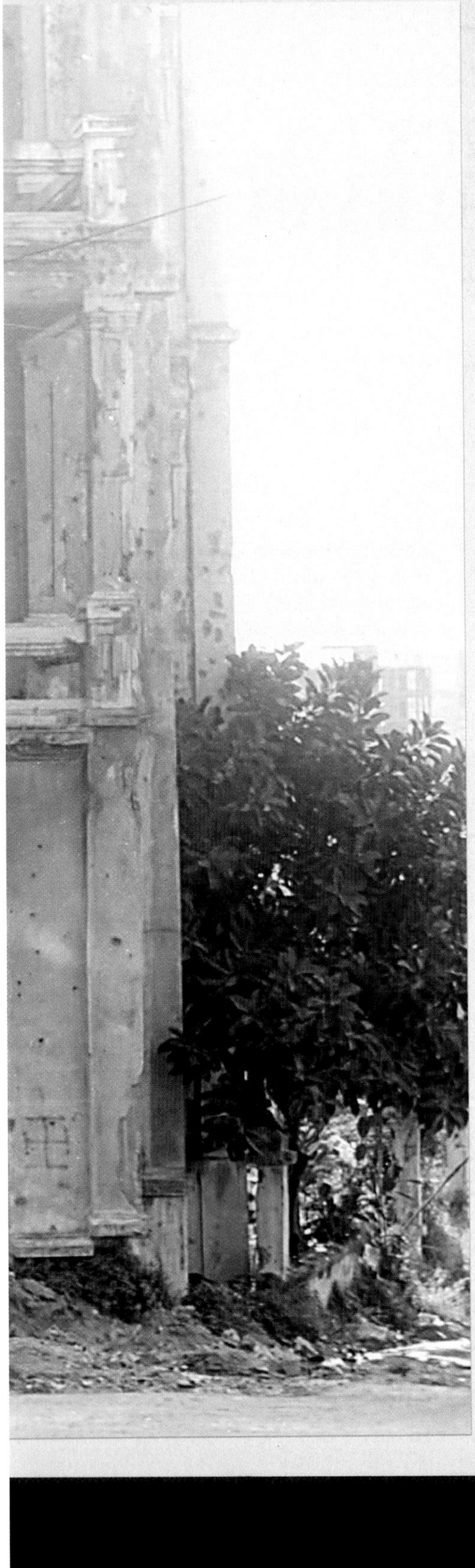

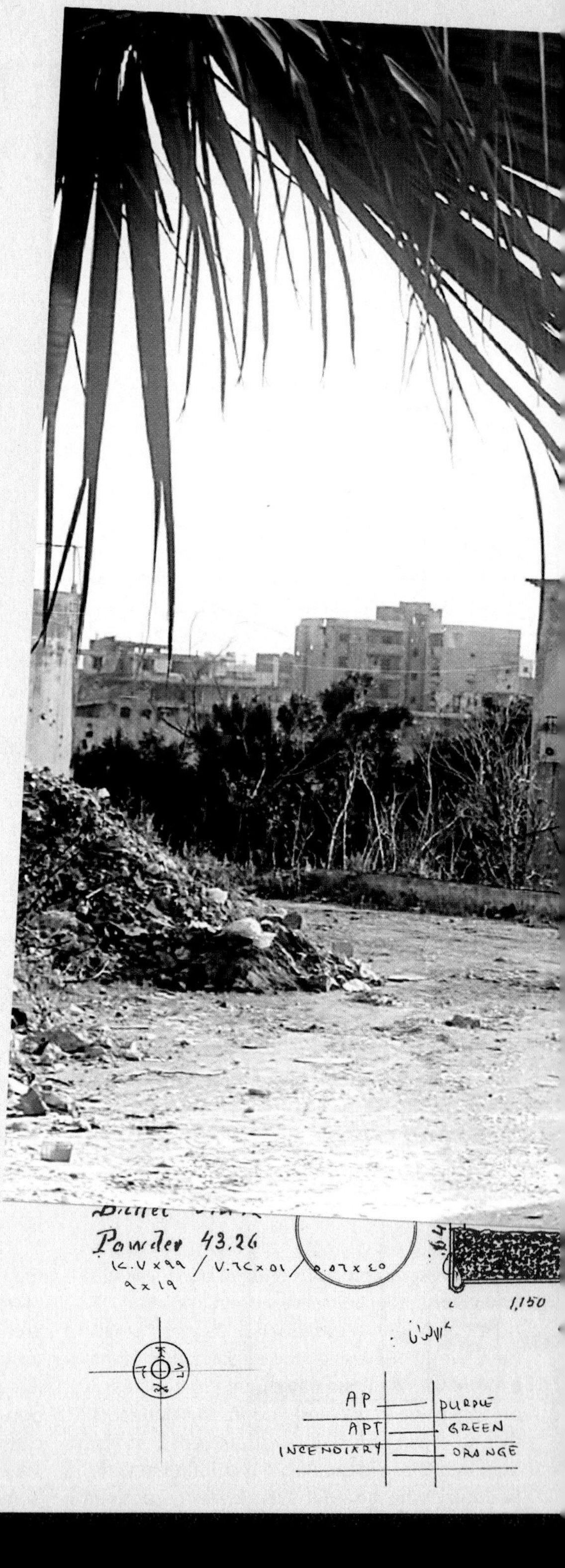

Let's Be Honest, The Weather Helped (Saudi Arabia) 1984–2007 archival color ink-jet print previous page: Stills from *Miraculous beginnings* and *No, illness is neither here nor there* 1993 dual-channel video (color, silent); 1:04 minutes

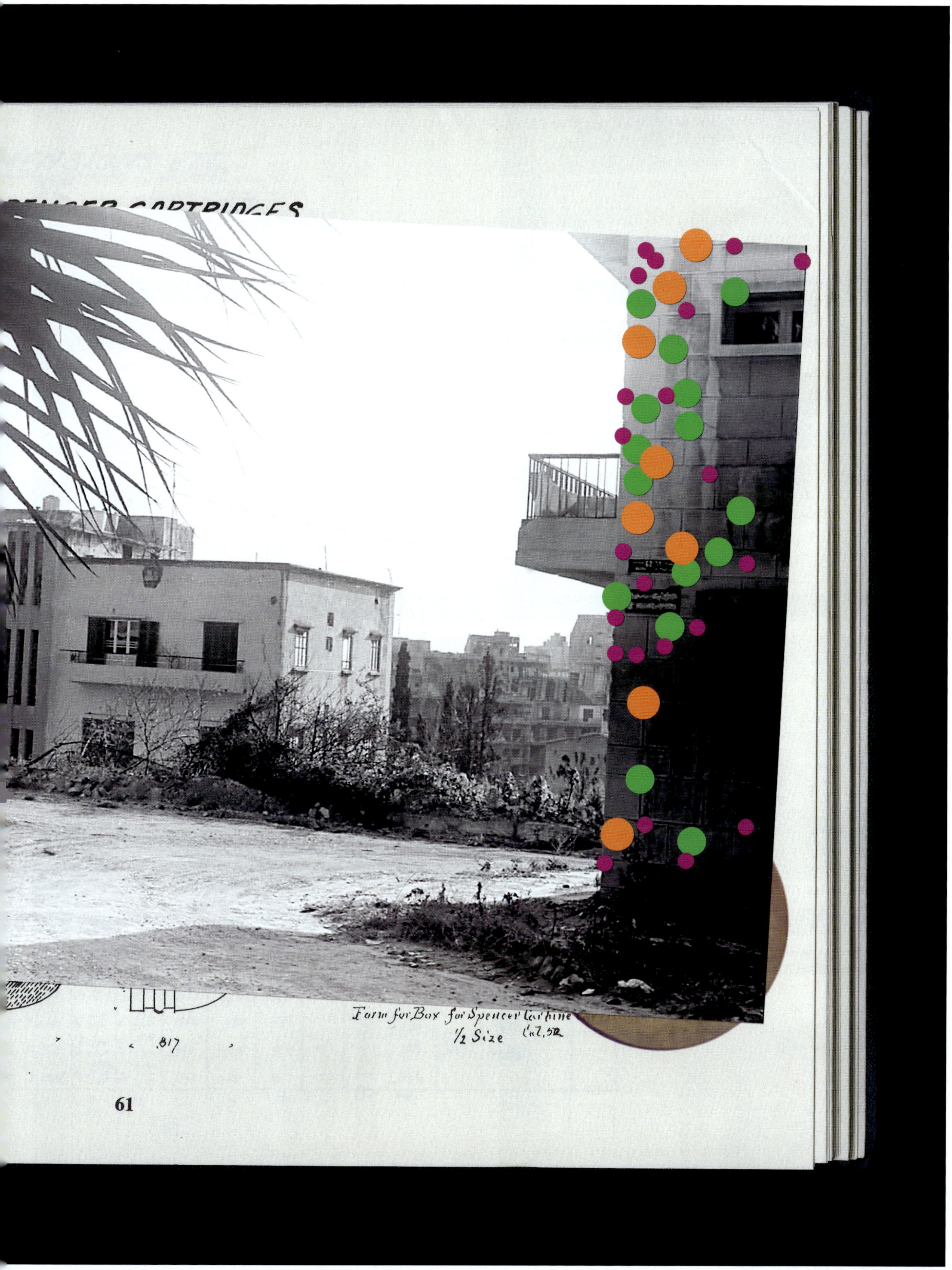
Form for Box for Spencer Carbine
½ Size
61

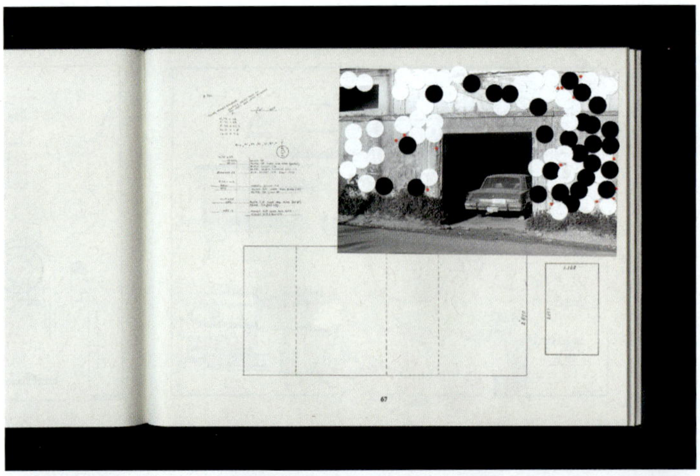
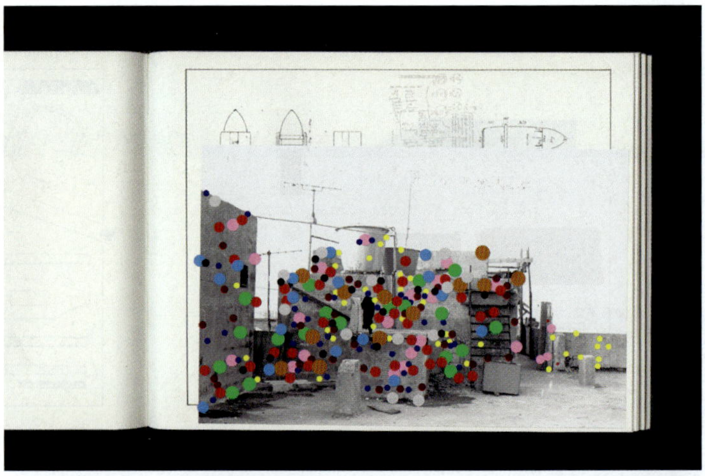
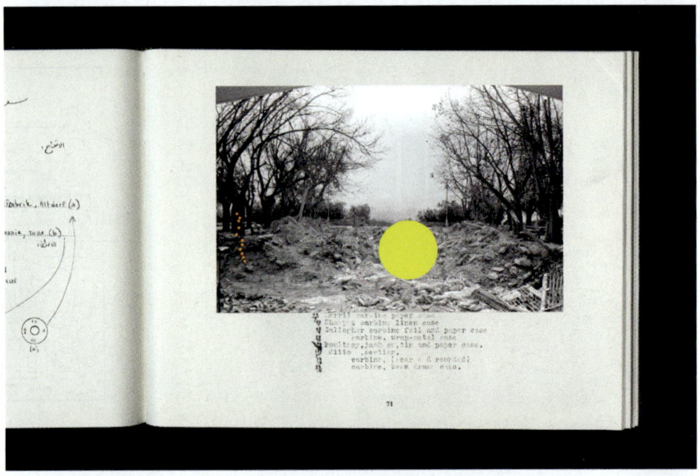
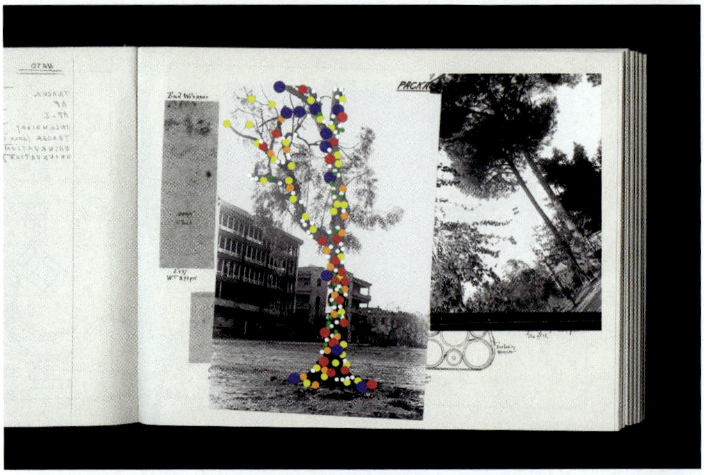
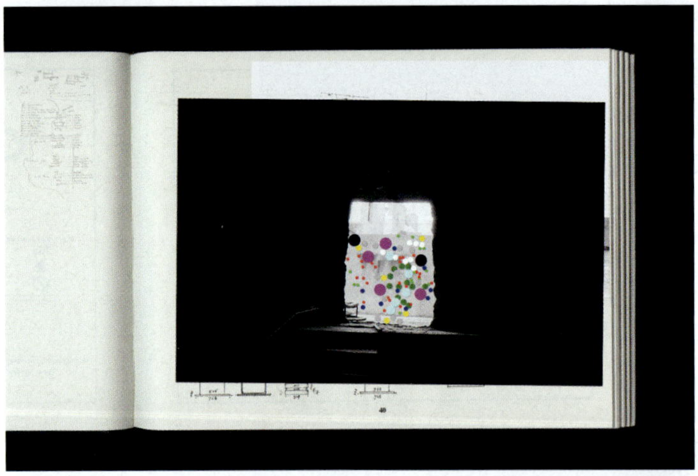
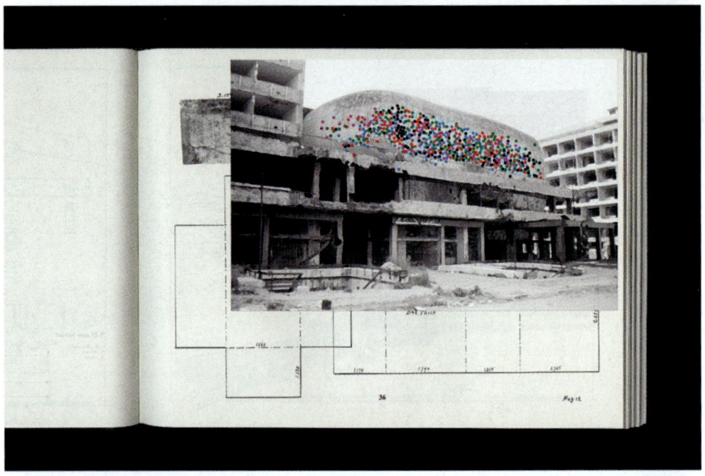
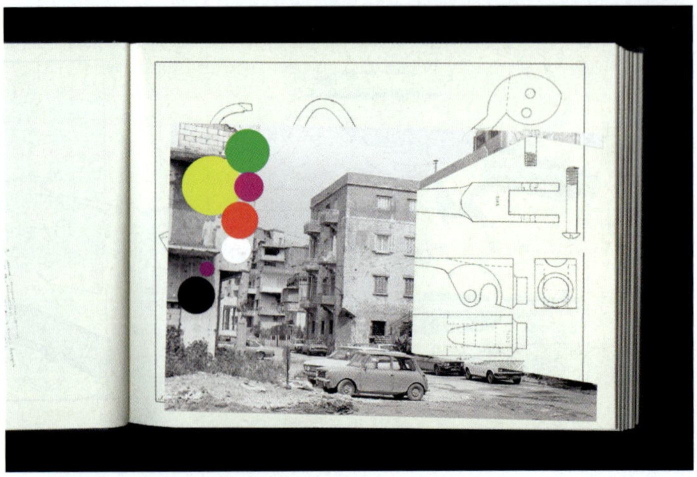
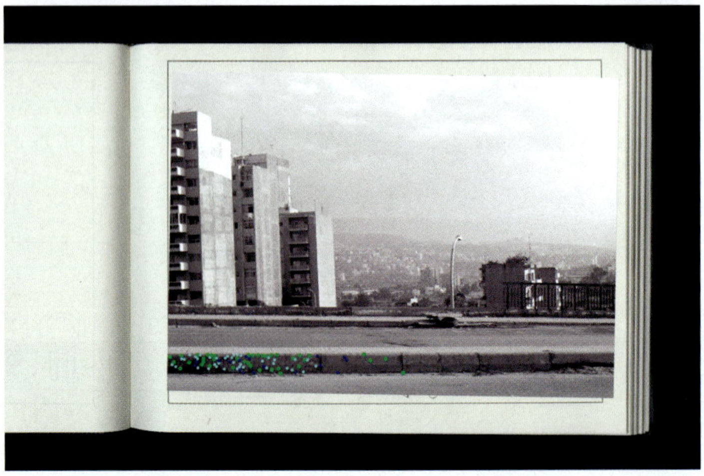

top to bottom, left to right: *Let's Be Honest, The Weather Helped (China, Swiss, U.K., Finland, USA, NATO, Israel, Germany, Greece, Libya, Romania, Iraq, Egypt, Venezuela, Italy, Belgium)* 1984–2007 archival color ink-jet prints

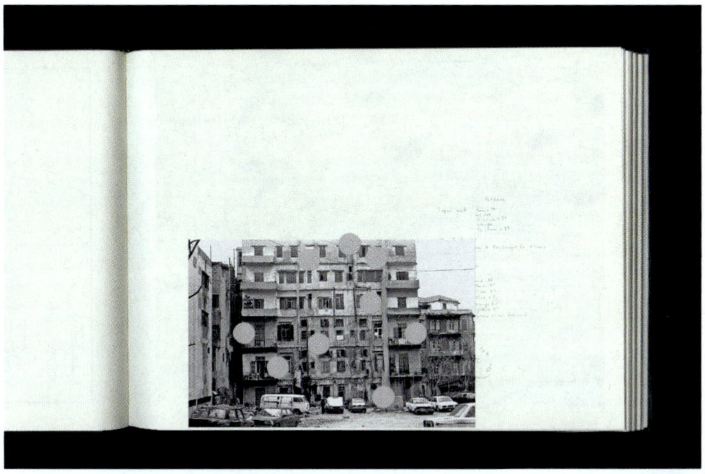
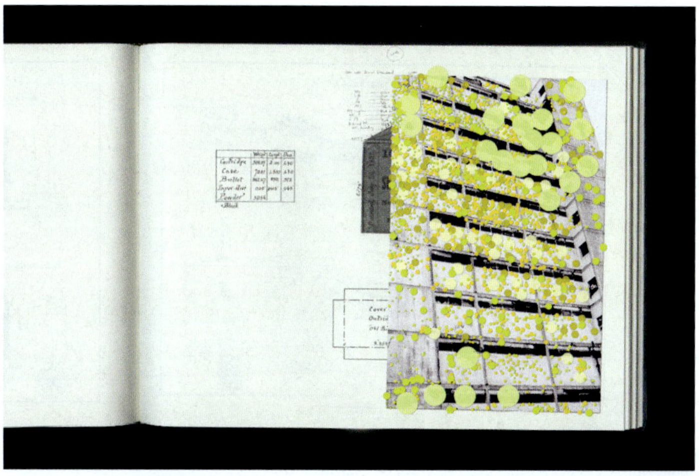
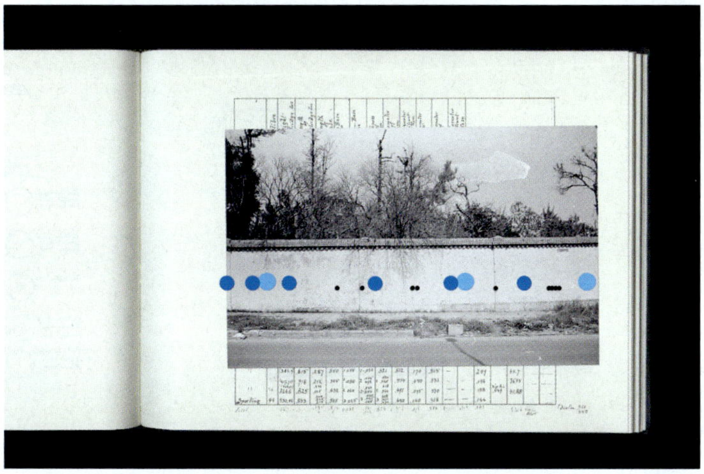
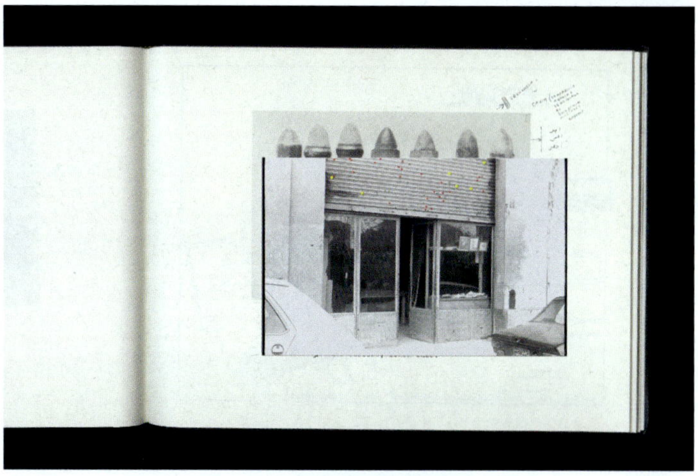
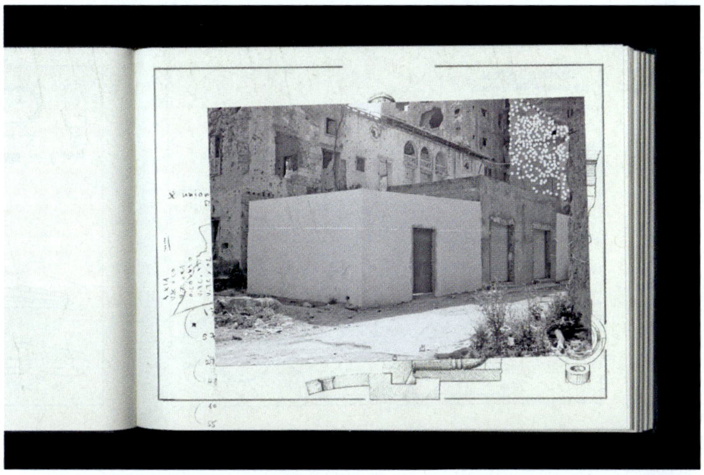
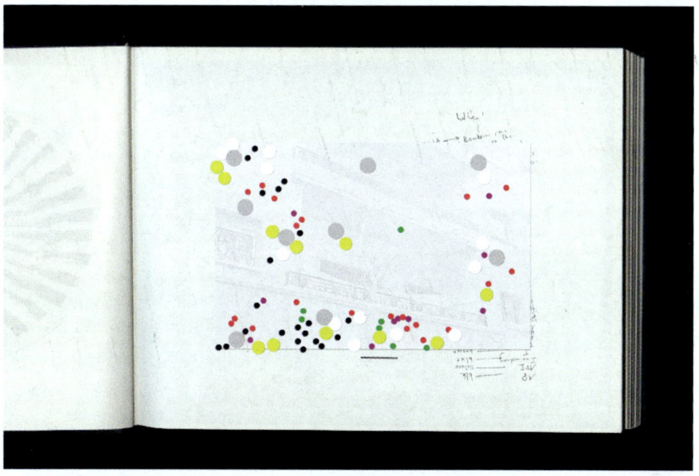
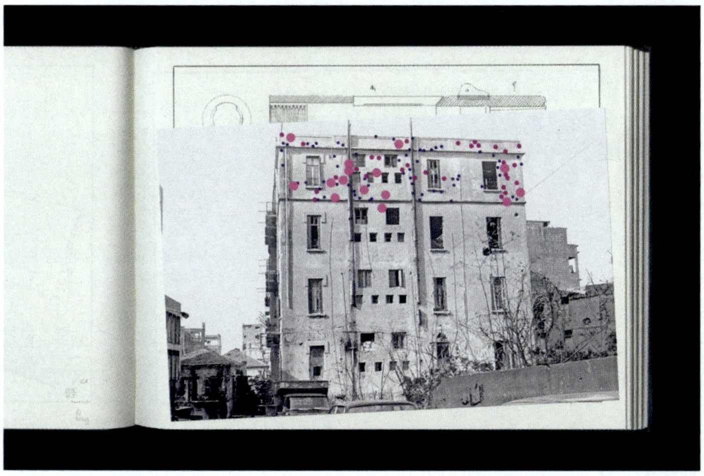
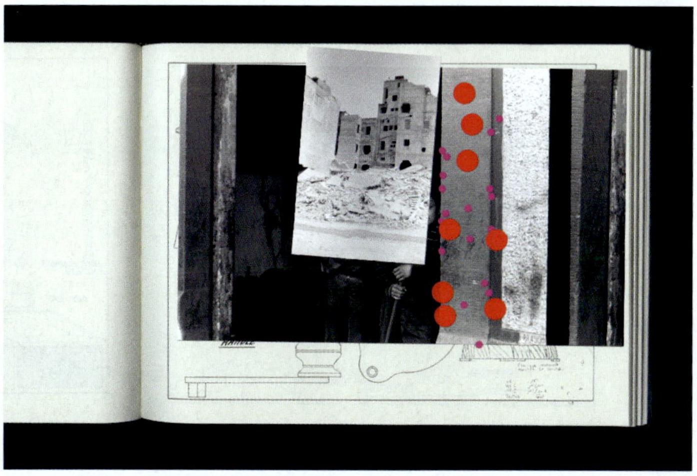

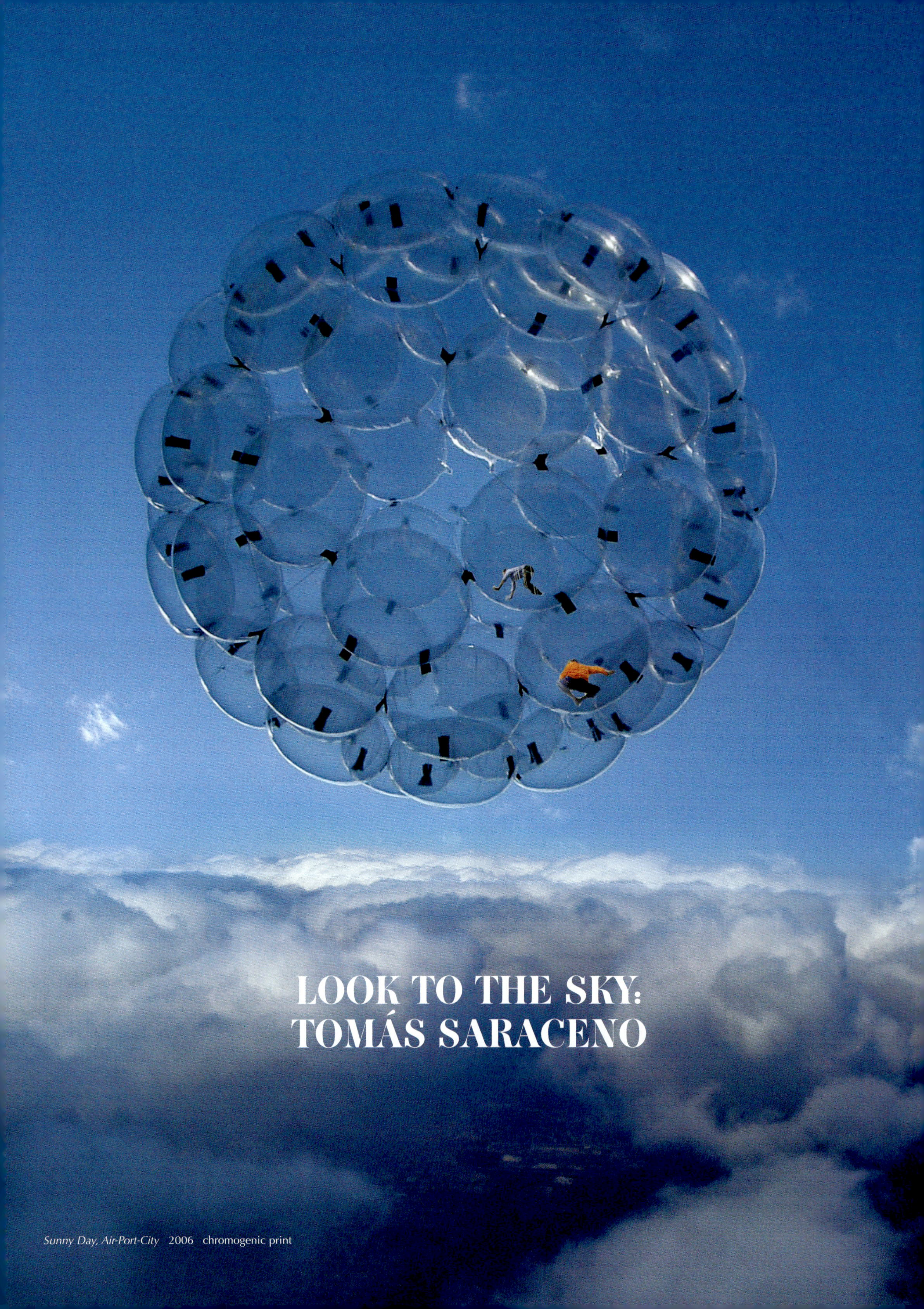

LOOK TO THE SKY: TOMÁS SARACENO

Sunny Day, Air-Port-City 2006 chromogenic print

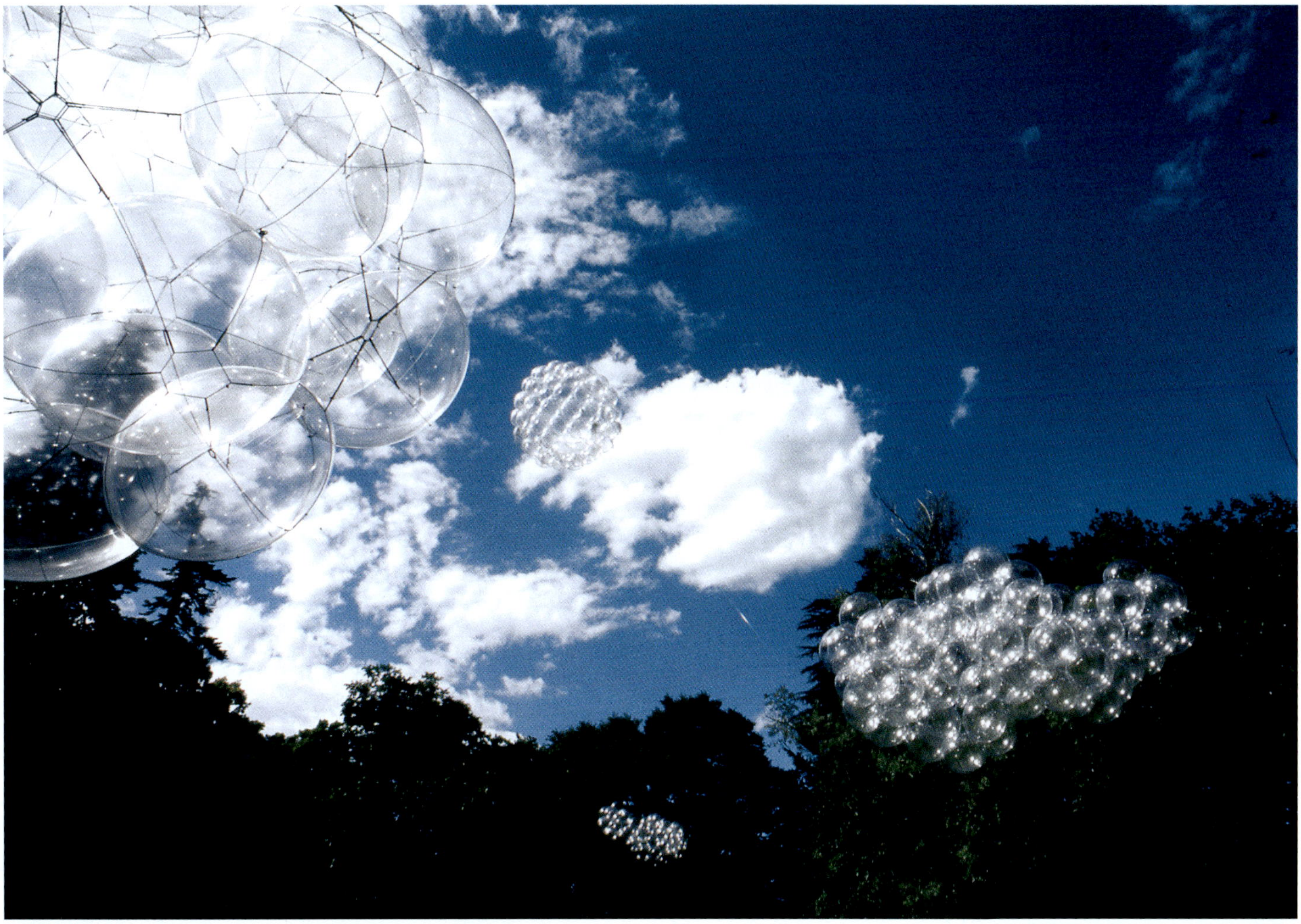

Flying Garden 2006 Installation view at Sudeley Castle, Winchcombe, England, 2006

Born in Argentina, 1973. Lives and works in Frankfurt.

Flying and floating, elevation and suspension are recurring elements in Tomás Saraceno's work, which is characterized by an ambition to lift our attention from the ground to the space above the clouds. Drawing inspiration from his initial training as an architect, he has modeled an artistic practice that applies principles from such disciplines as engineering, physics, and aeronautics. During the past seven years, Saraceno has set out to address questions of self-sustainability, mobility, and coexistence by constructing spaces and vehicles that generate conditions for conversations and collaborations among people. At the heart of his practice is a long-term project entitled *Air-Port-City* (2001–present), which he envisions as a mile-long geodesic balloon that could allow navigation in international air space and provide a living environment free from the demarcations of nationhood and borderlines. Saraceno has been able to physicalize his utopian vision in a series of kinetic sculptures, inflatable spheres, and walk-in environments that float above ground with the use of solar power. His projects take as their starting point the potential shelter offered in the spherical shape of the globe and the ability of the air balloon to frame both a symbolic space where living conditions can be sustained and a physical environment in which viewers experience gravity anew.

An extension of his airborne cities is the series *Flying Garden* (2004–present), a group of floating sculptures that serve as greenhouses in which to grow Spanish moss. Also known as an air plant, a member of the Tillandsia genus, this enigmatic and self-reliant leaf is able to grow without soil by attaching itself to other plants and tree branches and obtaining its necessary nutrients from the air. This ability to be "air-sufficient," as Saraceno puts it, extends to the conceptual spirit of all his projects.[1] Physically and metaphorically, the primary material and medium in his work is air, which provides the conditions for reconciliation between organic and handmade materials. "I'm occupied by the distinction between human beings and nature, and our inabilities to incorporate nature into art," Saraceno says, stressing the importance of coexistence and collaboration as formal and structural premises in his practice, which materialize in the form of colonies of networks that float in space and in the airborne vehicles that act as conduits of messages and traveling energy.[2] Most recently, he has combined the ideas of collectivity and air sufficiency into an ambitious ongoing project entitled *Museo Aerosolar* (2007–present), a solar-powered hot-air balloon made from recycled shopping bags that the artist assembles with the help of local residents at the site where the piece is flown. First conceived in Italy in 2007, the balloon continued to expand as it traveled, acquiring more than twelve thousands bags from its stops in Germany, the United Arab Emirates, and Colombia, where it was last exhibited. After the piece is assembled, it is flown, followed, and rescued in a game between man and nature. Likewise, Saraceno's practice seeks mobility itself—while embracing the balancing act between producing and preserving energy, flying and landing, he follows the tradition of those who have "looked to the sky to escape the reality of earth" and in return invites us to visualize new horizons and aims.[3]

YR

1. Tomás Saraceno, in conversation with Hans Ulrich Obrist and Stefano Boeri, *Domus* 883 (July–August 2005), unpaginated.

2. Maria Kjær Themsen, "Interview: Tomás Saraceno," (June 16, 2007), http://www.kopenhagen.dk/interviews/interviews/interview_tomas_saraceno.

3. Tomás Saraceno, in "Conversation with Tomás Saraceno, Luca Cerizza, and pinksummer" (October 1, 2004), http://www.pinksummer.com/pink2/exb/sar/exb001en.htm.

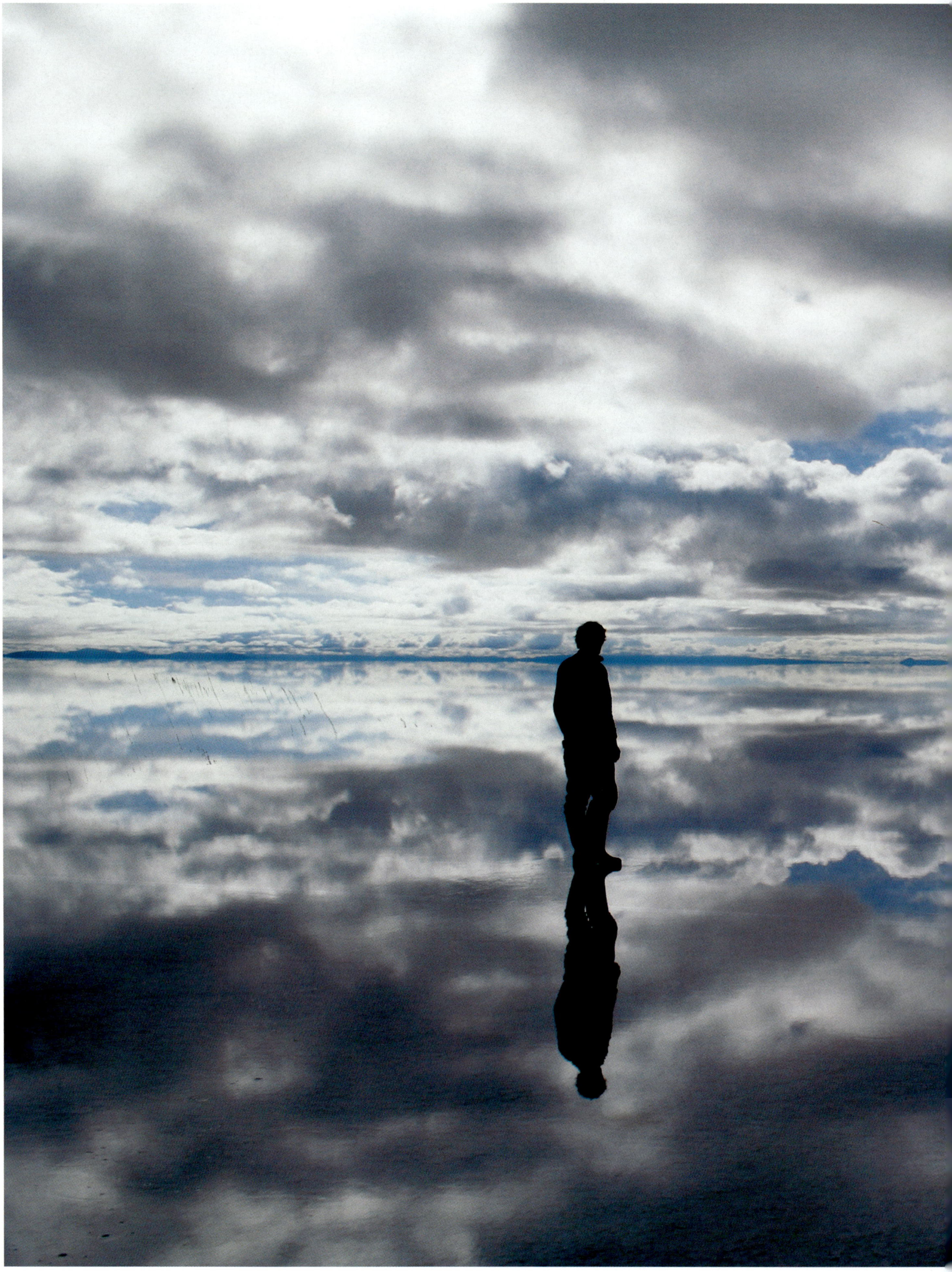

Selection from *Cumulus* 2006 chromogenic print

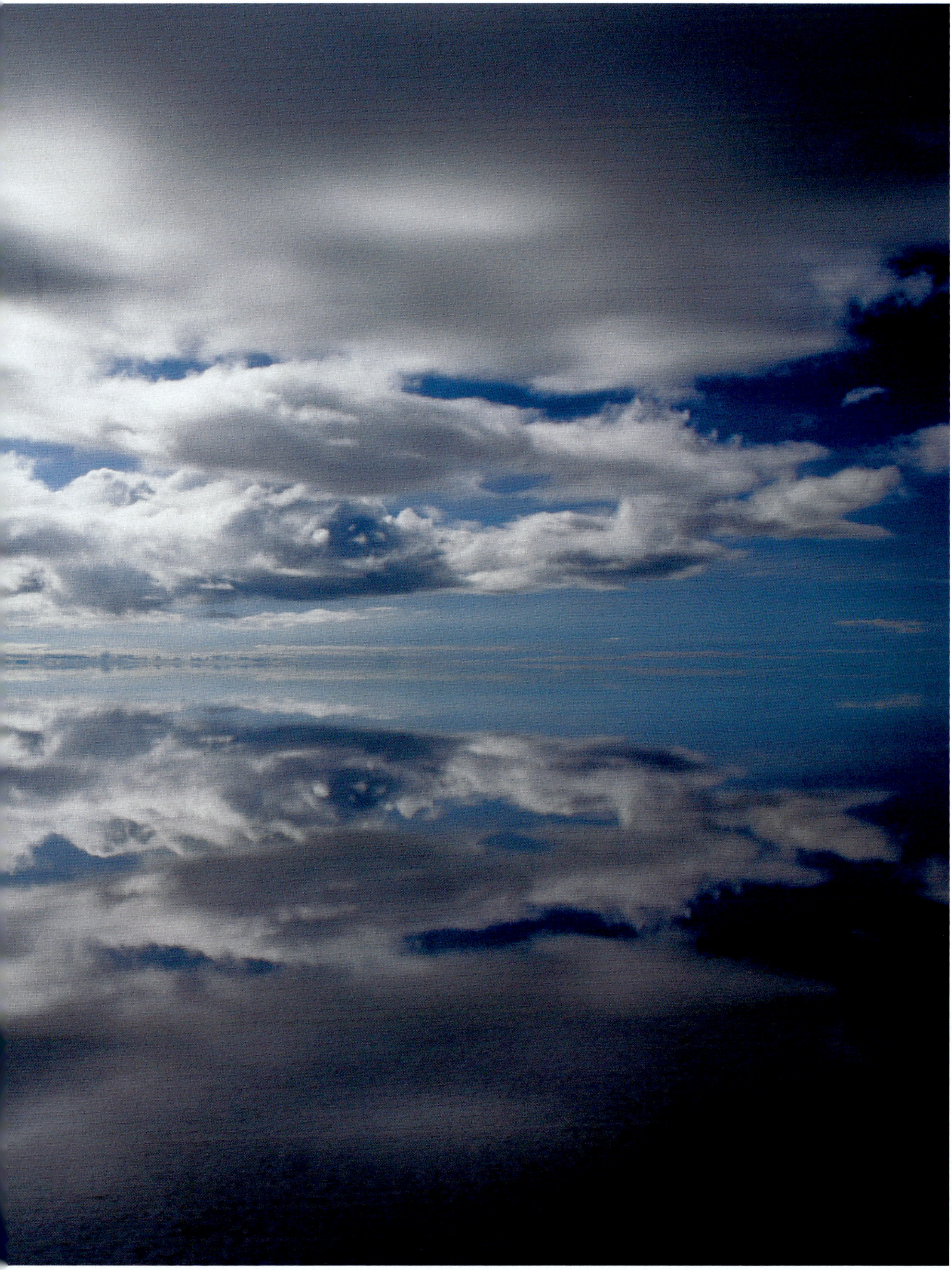

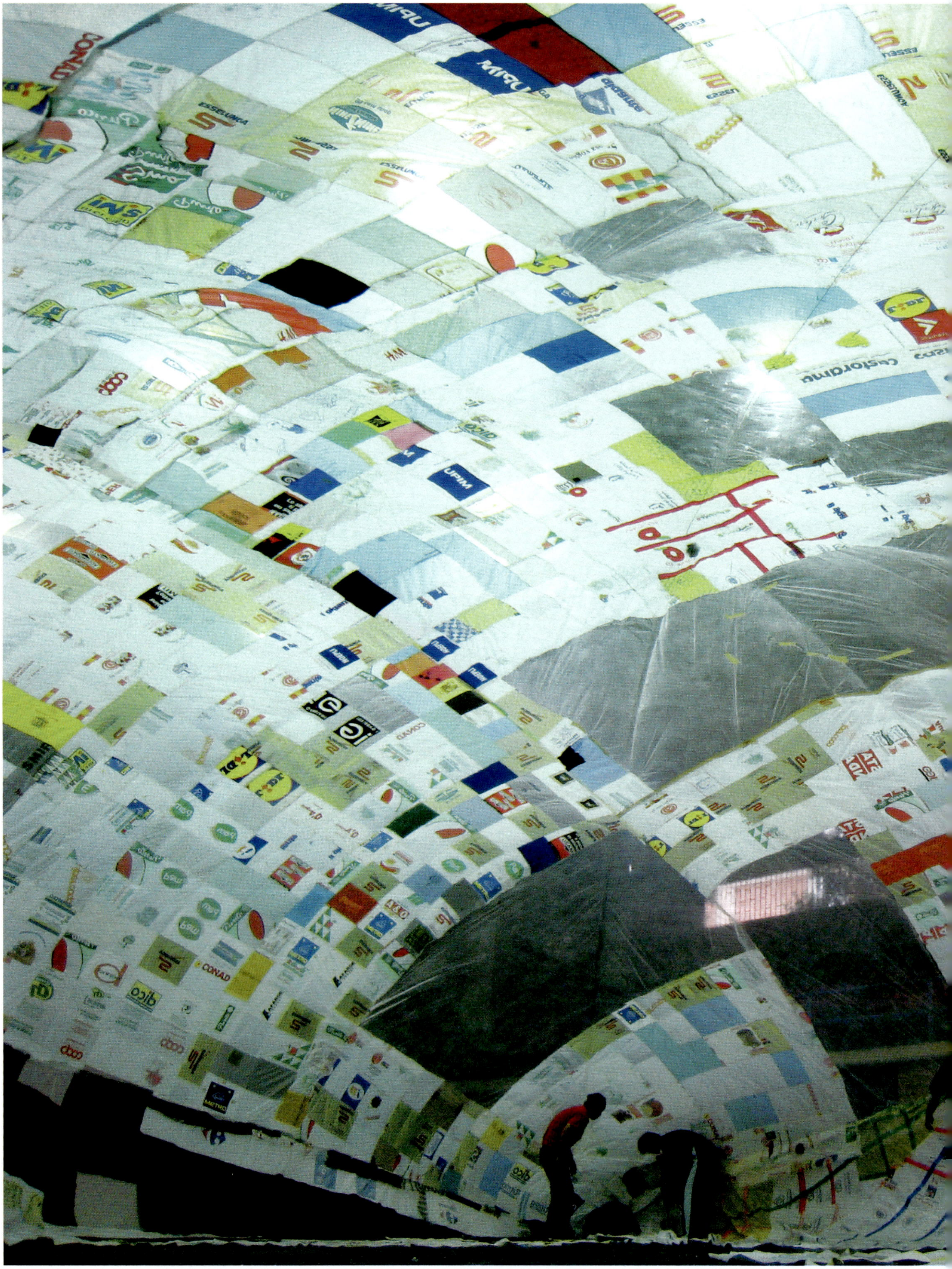

Museo Aerosolar 2007 Installation view at *Encuentro Medellín 2007*, Medellín, Colombia, 2007

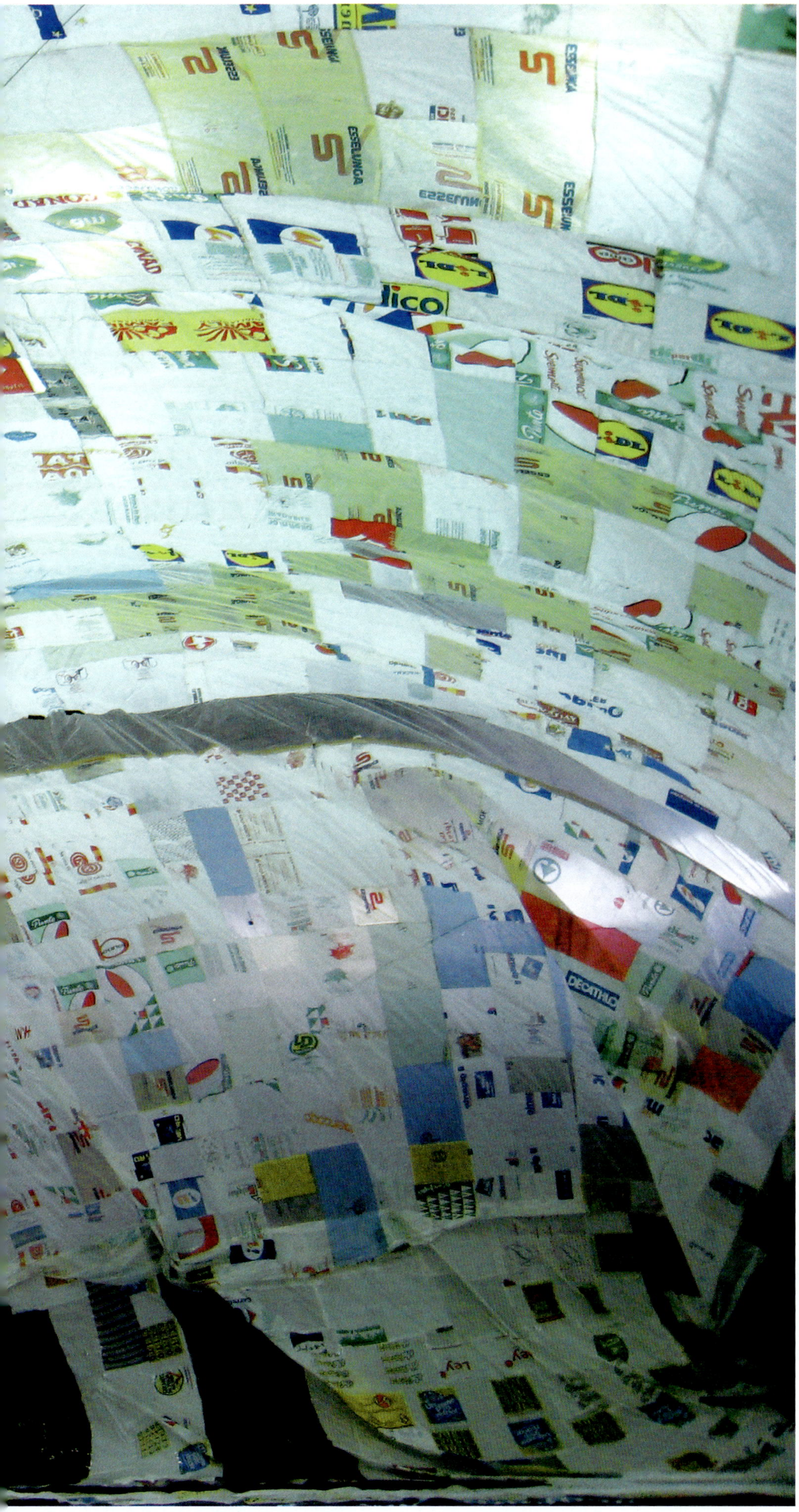

INCREASINGLY UNFAMILIAR: SEAN SNYDER

Born in the United States, 1972. Lives and works in Berlin and Kiev, Ukraine.

The work of Sean Snyder shares ironic commonalities with the Global Positioning System (GPS)—a satellite-based navigational technology that is becoming increasingly commonplace. Based in Europe but reaching many distant corners of the world in his interests and investigations, Snyder has zoomed in to dissect ideological (self-)representations of disparate places, from Paris suburbs to Brasília, from Bucharest to Pyongyang, from Skopje, Macedonia, to the site of Saddam Hussein's capture in Tikrit, Iraq. For each project, the artist conducts thorough research and compiles a massive databank, out of which illuminating networks of references and connections are drawn. He is a collector, cataloguer, and cartographer, but his projects do not manifest themselves in mere displays of the information he has gathered. Often presented in a combination of different imaging and informational mediums—video, photograph, and text—Snyder's "findings" are made through associative processes and are suggested in an open narrative that exploits the mechanism per se of the visual evidence, thus differing from and exceeding what an academic analysis of the same topic would be. As one writer aptly stated, "Many of the connections he makes are based on imaginative associations. Yet every connection is backed up by documentary images or factual research material. The plausibility of every associative link can thus be tested against the material evidence on display." [1] Although the artist's subjectivity may not be clearly evident in his work, Snyder builds in a space of interpretation so viewers can activate the epistemological apparatus that has remained dormant in their minds.

One of the artist's best-known projects to date, *Dallas Southfork in Hermes Land, Slobozia, Romania* (2001) analyzes a surreal recreation of Southfork Ranch, the main setting for the television series *Dallas*, in the Transylvanian hinterland. Built by Ilie Alexandru, a corrupt business tycoon, the replica was constructed based on calculations made from the building's TV appearance. While the original was primarily a set designed specifically for shooting, this version was built as if it were an existing architectural structure. Around this already unlikely relationship of the original (a tool of simulation) and the copy (more real than what it purportedly replicates), Snyder gathers yet more implausible, interlinked facts: *Dallas* was one of the few representations of America available to the Romanian public during the reign of Communist dictator Nicolae Ceauşescu; and Larry Hagman, the actor who played a conniving oil baron in the drama and was something of a role model for Alexandru, has appeared in advertisements for Lukoil, the Russian oil giant. The fact that Ceauşescu's regime, a renegade in the Soviet-led Communist bloc, received the Most Favored Nation status from the United States seems far more improbable and surprising than the intimate relationship between Romania and North Korea, but the latter turned out to be no smaller folly. In *Bucharest/Pyongyang* (2001–2004), Snyder reveals how the Romanian dictator's massive urban renovation—or, destruction, to be more precise—of his capital was inspired by the North Korean program of urban monumentalization in "a kind of competition over monumentality and grandeur." [2] While the People's Palace in Bucharest hypes its status as one of the largest buildings in the world, the soaring behemoth that is the Ryugyong Hotel in

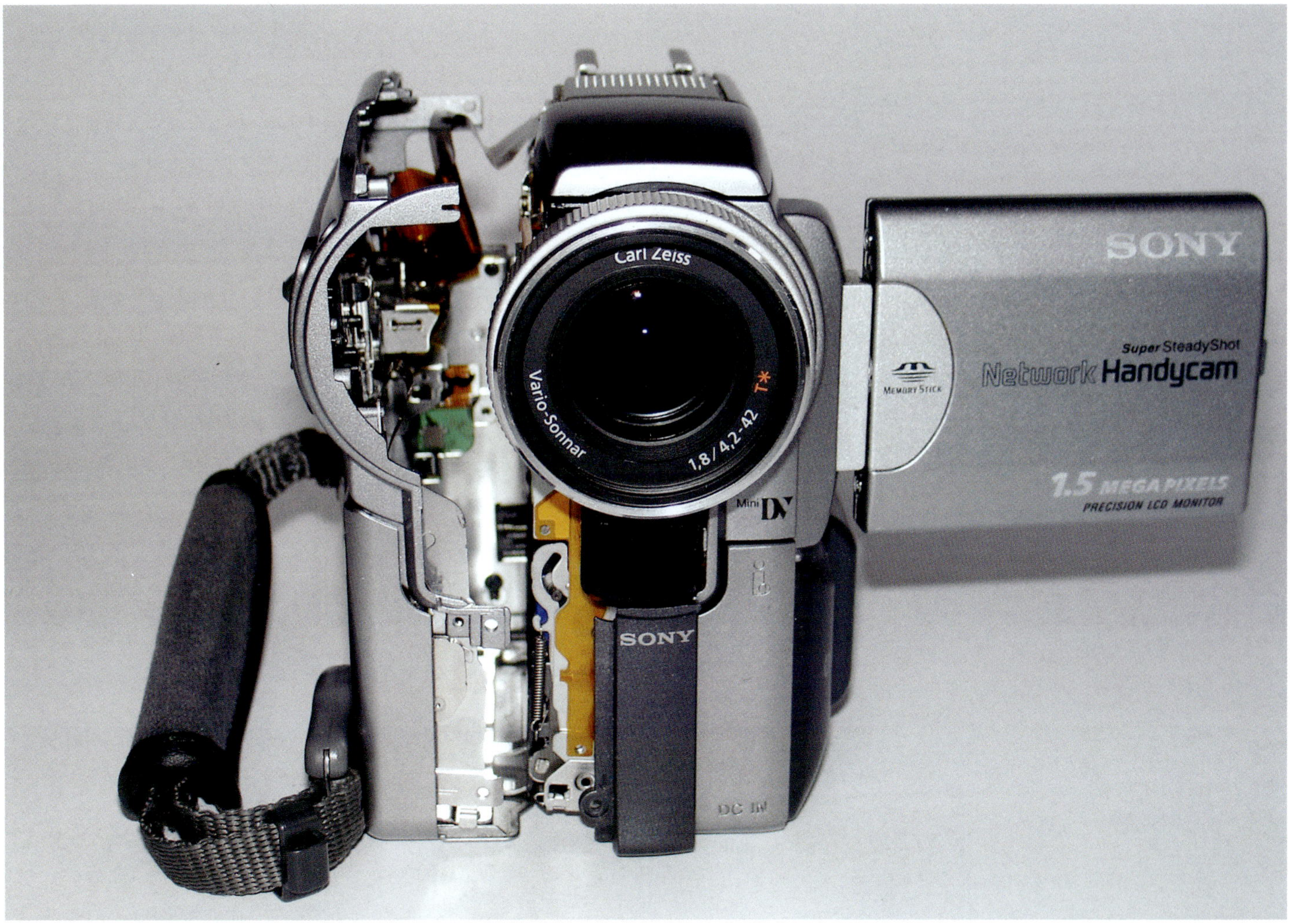

Apparatus, (Sony DCR-PC 120E) 2007 LightJet print

Pyongyang was for a time the ambivalent title holder of the world's tallest hotel—except that it will probably never be completed. Snyder's various investigations of architecture and urbanism are, in a broader sense, a study of the utopian impulse—and its frequent descent into madness and almost-always unfulfilled promise—that are part and parcel of modernity and modernism.

In *Optics.Compression.Propaganda* (2006–2007), Snyder focuses on technologies of representation while still maintaining his methodology of subjective yet meticulous investigation. Less interested in critiquing the alleged truth-telling of the world than considering the operation of mediation and visuality, the project questions, in particular, the shaping and manipulation of political representations as well as the mechanics of such processes. One part of the piece, for instance, contrasts the current visual strategies of the U.S. Department of Defense with those of As-Sahab Media, Al Qaeda's media wing. The work identifies the Sony camera used for a recent As-Sahab release—a model that includes Bluetooth wireless technology and the ability to transmit low-resolution imagery via cellular phone. The camera's high technical caliber rebuts the poor quality "videotape" described by Western media sources in its coverage of the report. Snyder zooms in, frames and reframes, and crops his source images, and in the process reveals the contingencies and limitations inherent in contemporary journalistic production.

Snyder's video *Schema (Television)* (2006–2007), which may be characterized as having a more editorial approach, is a delirious mosaic of footage from television stations around the world amassed via satellite. Starting with test color patterns and news program logos, the video mixes segments of utterly mundane televised entertainment, such as cooking shows and game programs, with the news. While the formats of such entertainment may have become so widespread as to be almost global, the general impression that emerges from this montage is uncanny incomprehensibility. Cultural differences and quirks turn these recognizable forms into bizarre yet compelling anthropological specimens. Snyder interrupts the image flow, and its hypnotic capacity, with short textual insertions scripted in collaboration with Ukrainian film critic/theorist Olga Bryukhovetska. At the beginning of the video, one reads, for instance, "Spellbound from the moment of contact." By the end of the video, however, viewers are brought to ask, "Television: a window to reality, or a screen of desire and fear?" Technology may have allowed us to have the world at our fingertips, but this world turns out to be not so much globally unified as increasingly unfamiliar. And that may very well describe the lesson one learns from Snyder's work in general.

DC

1. Jan Verwoert, "Jump Cut Cities," *Afterall* 7 (2002): 77.

2. Discussion between Raluca Visinescu and Sean Snyder.

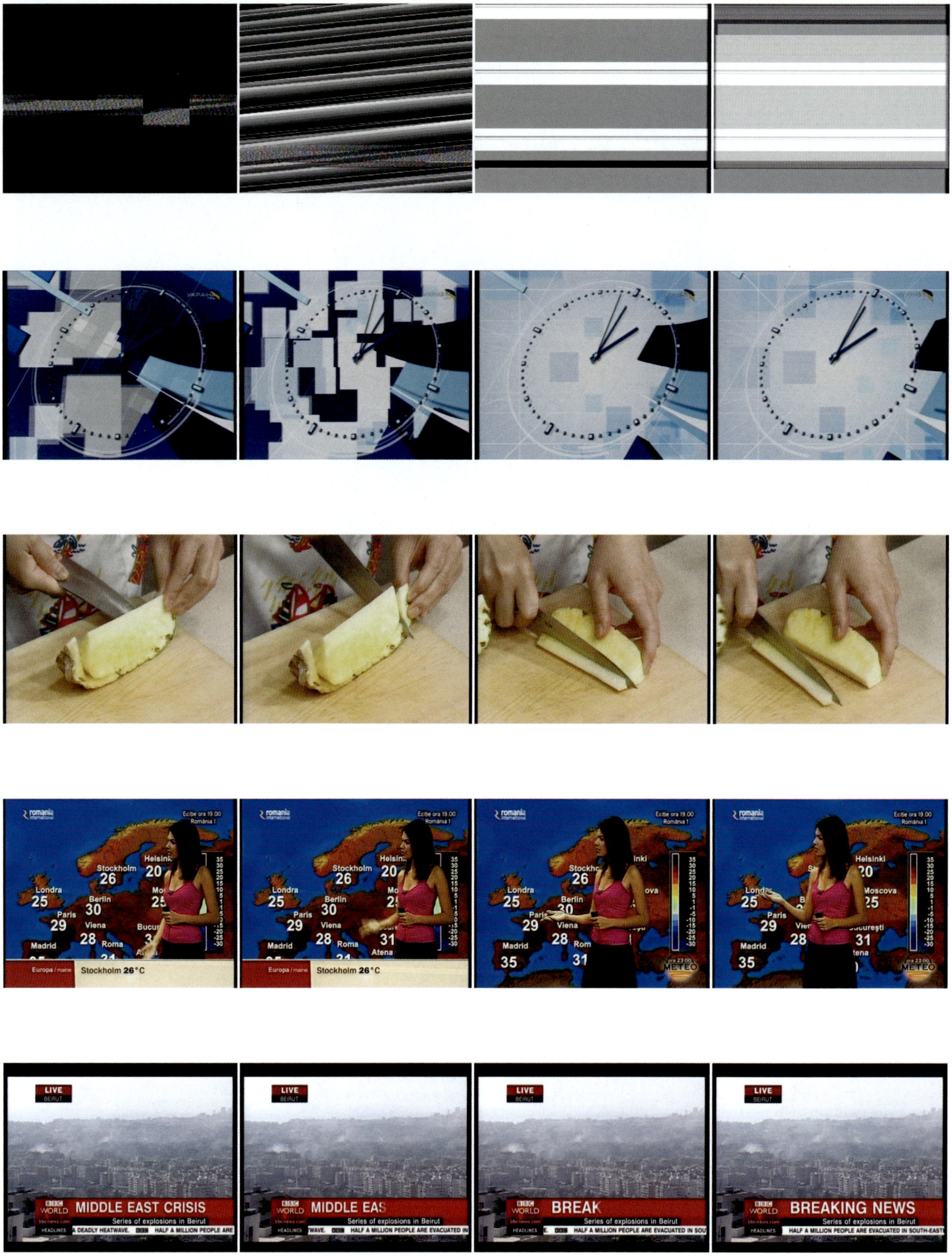

Stills from *Schema (Television)* 2006–2007 rear-projection DVD (color, sound); 7:19 minutes

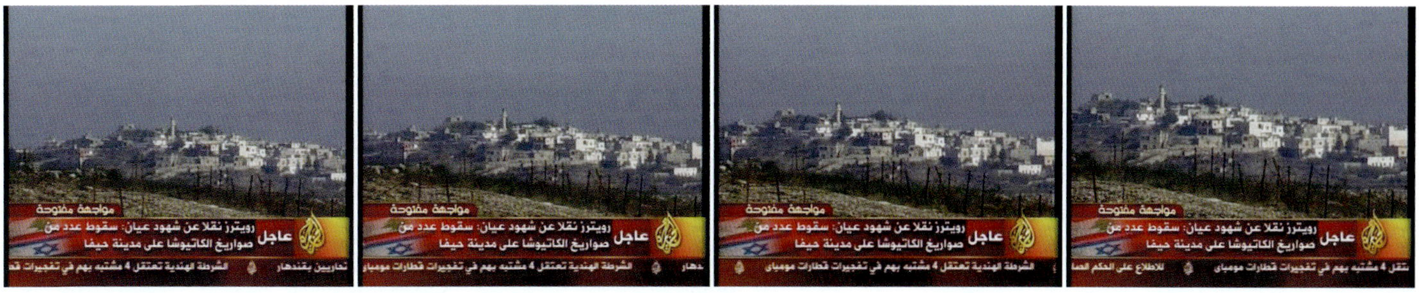
مواجهة مفتوحة
عاجل
رويترز نقلا عن شهود عيان: سقوط عدد من
صواريخ الكاتيوشا على مدينة حيفا

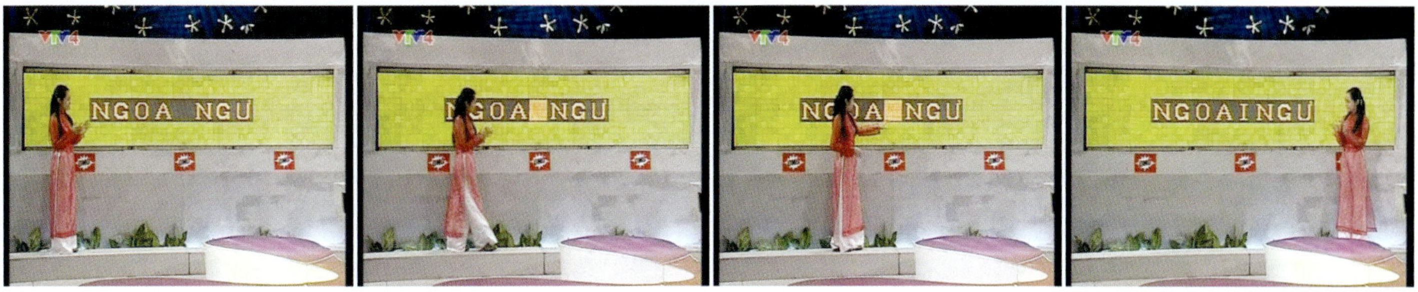
VTV4
NGOAINGU

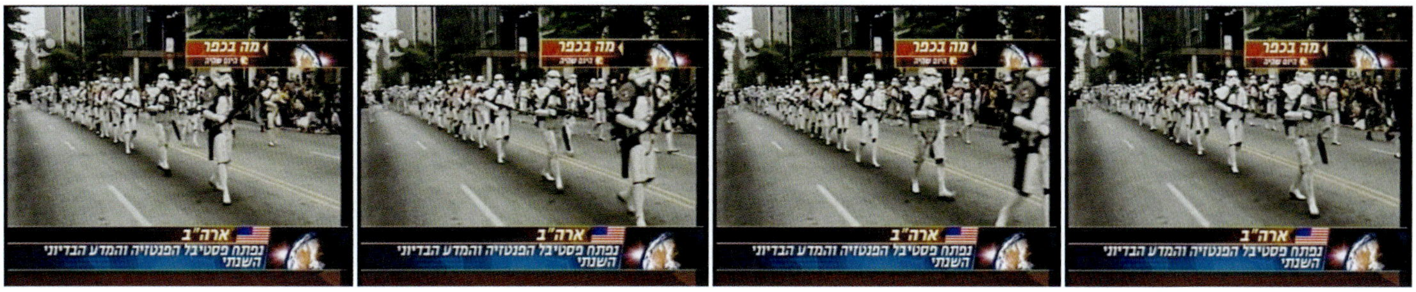
מה בכפר
ארה"ב
נפתח פסטיבל הפנטזיה והמדע הבדיוני
השנתי

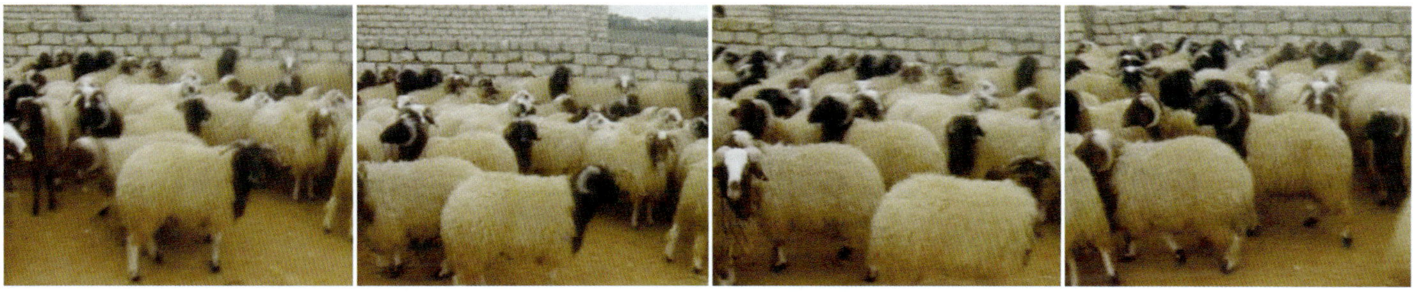

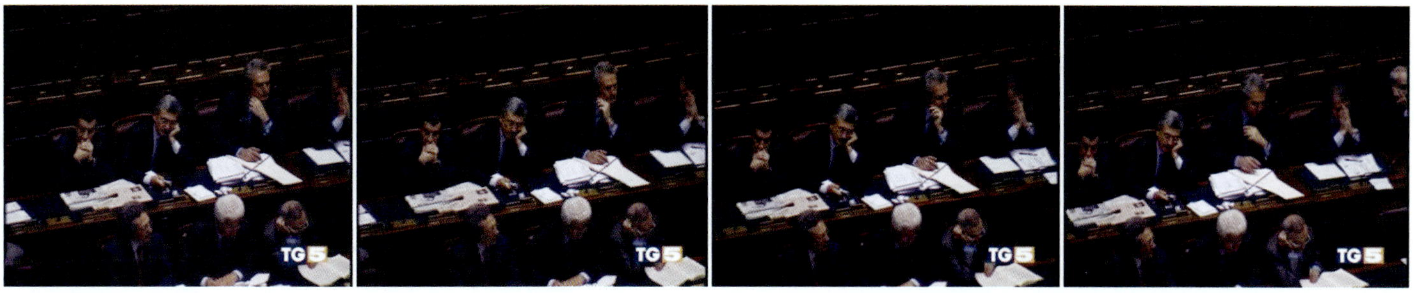
TG5

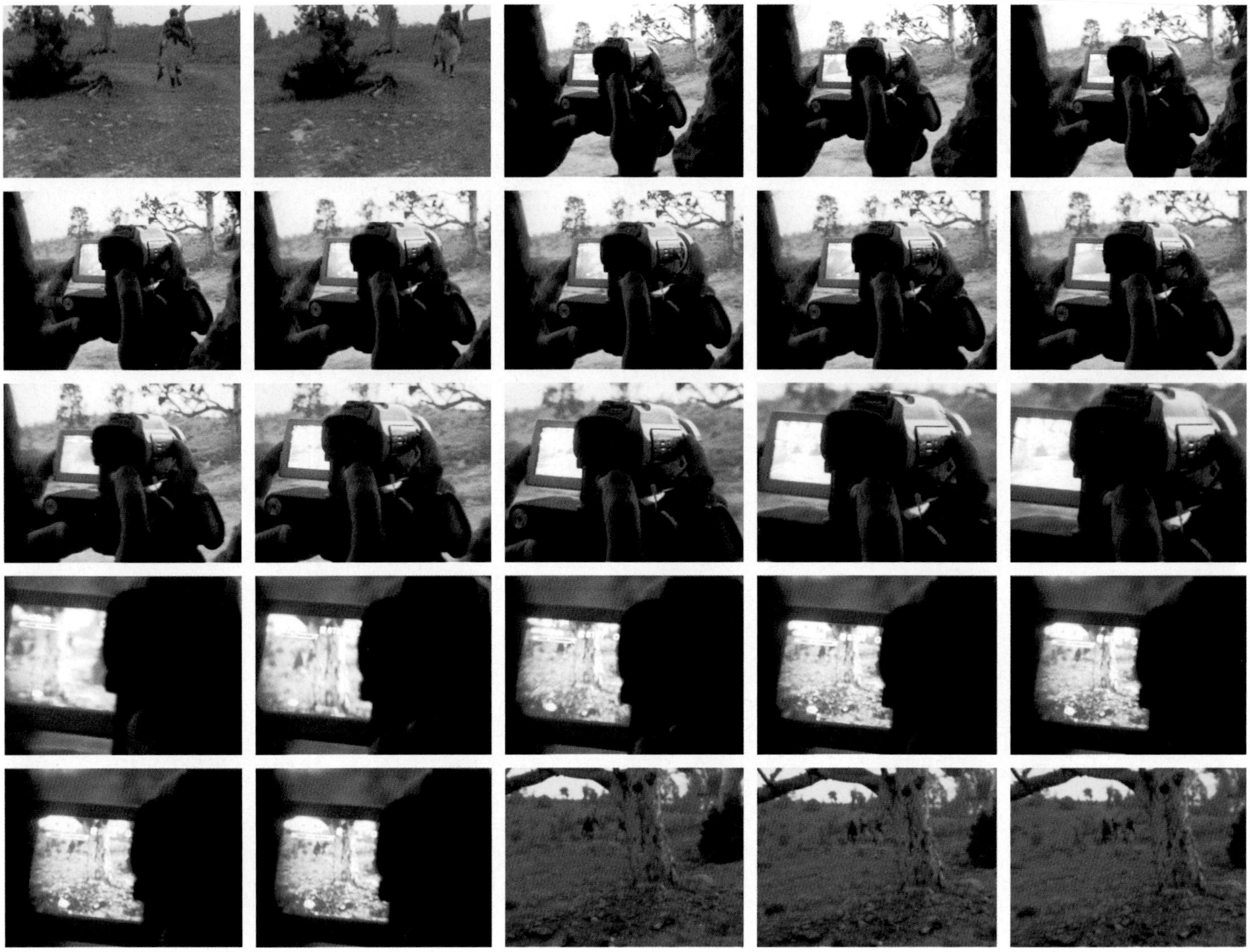

Sequence No. 077, 25 Frames (Al Qaeda/As-Sahab Media) from *Optics.Compression.Propaganda* 2006–2007 LightJet prints

Harb ul Mustadhefeen / Qahr us Saleeb

Source: harbulmustadhefeen.mpg
Production: As-Sahab Media
Date: 2005
Audio/Visual: sound, color
Format: MPEG 1 Muxed, 320 x 240
FPS: 25
Data Size: 598.23 MB
Data Rate: 1378.34 kbits/sec
Duration: 00:59:58:16/25
Size: 320 x 240 pixels

sony.com/press release
Sept 4, 2001

Sony DCR PC-120E
Product Description

This international wireless standard in data transmission lets you e-mail your digital still photos and MPEG e-Movies when you're miles from the nearest PC. You can even surf the Web on the color LCD screen. Your Network-enabled camcorder works with a Bluetooth mobile phone or the Sony BTA-NW1 Bluetooth adaptor, so whenever you want to share your footage with the world, all you need to do is write your e-mail, attach your shots and wait for the reply. So if you thought connectivity was all about cables, think again.

Sequence No. 077, Title (Al Qaeda/As-Sahab Media) from *Optics.Compression.Propaganda* 2006–2007 (detail) LightJet prints

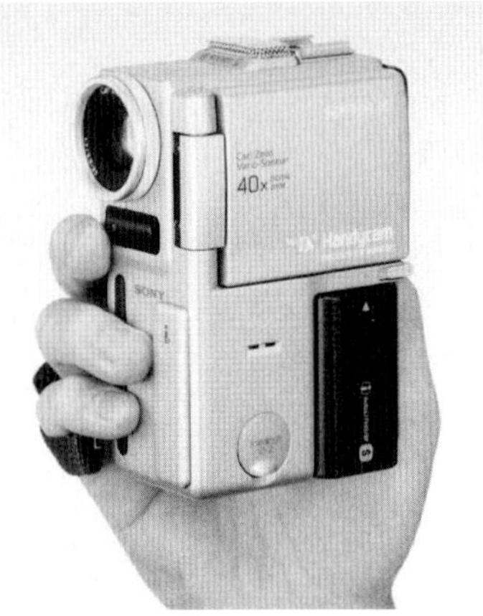

dcr pc1_1.jpg

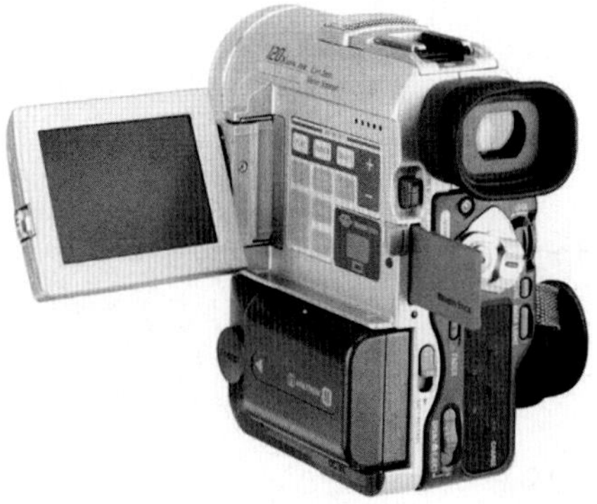

dcr-pc100_3.jpg

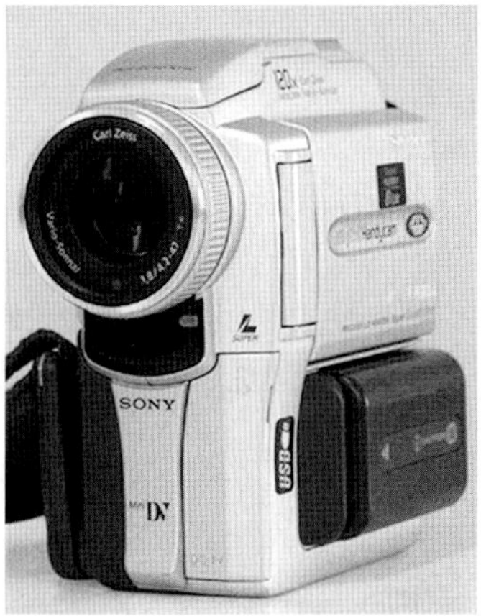

dcr-pc110_2.jpg

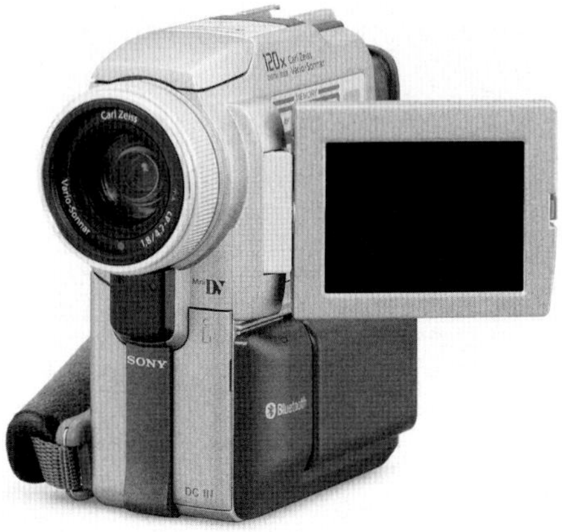

dcr-pc120e_17.jpg

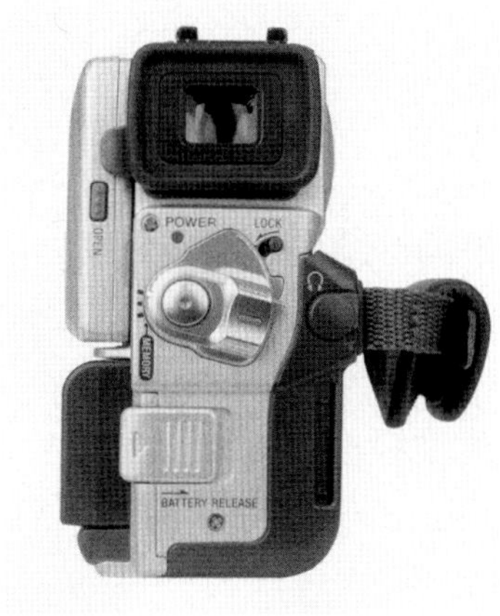

dcr-pc5_1.jpg

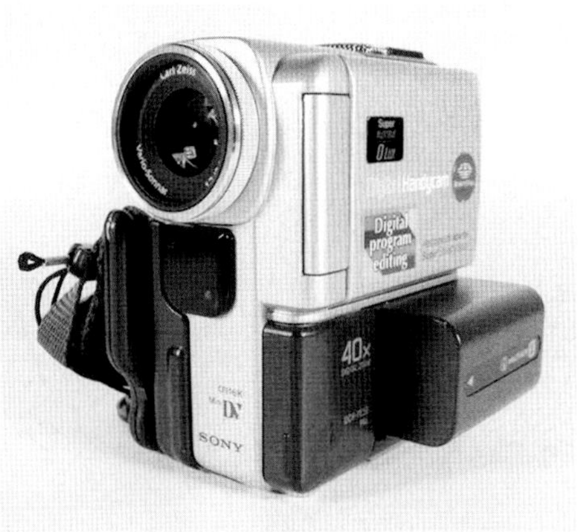

dcr-pc5_2.jpg

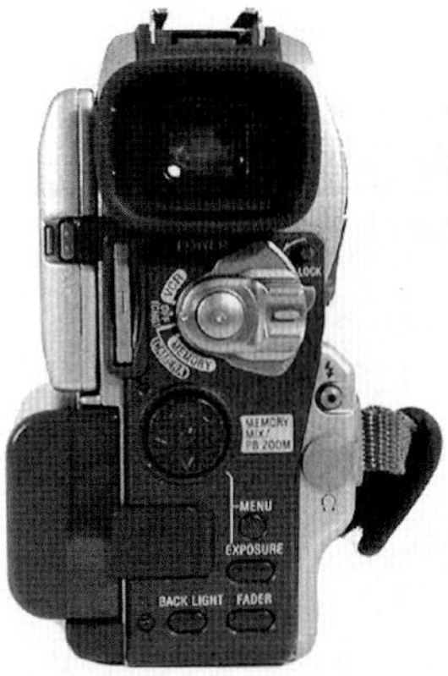

pc115_1.jpg

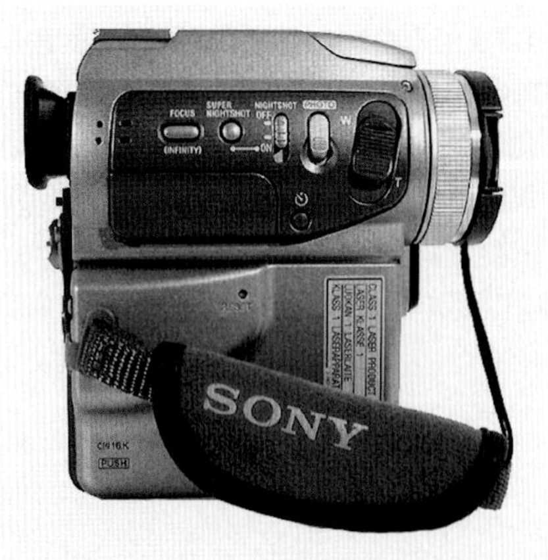

pc115_2.jpg

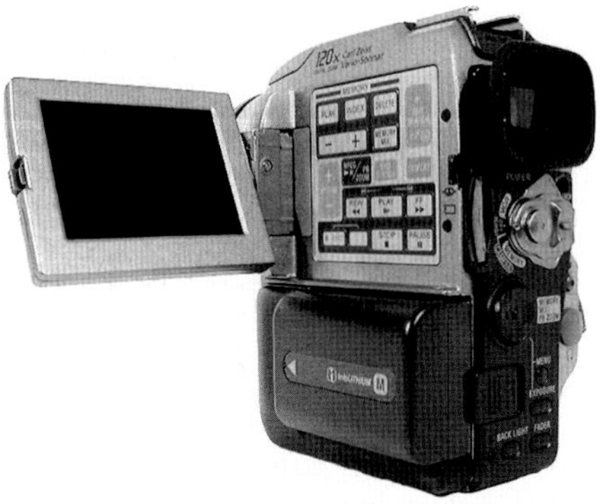

pc115_3.jpg

Sequence No. 077, Title (Al Qaeda/As-Sahab Media) from *Optics.Compression.Propaganda* 2006–2007 (detail) LightJet prints

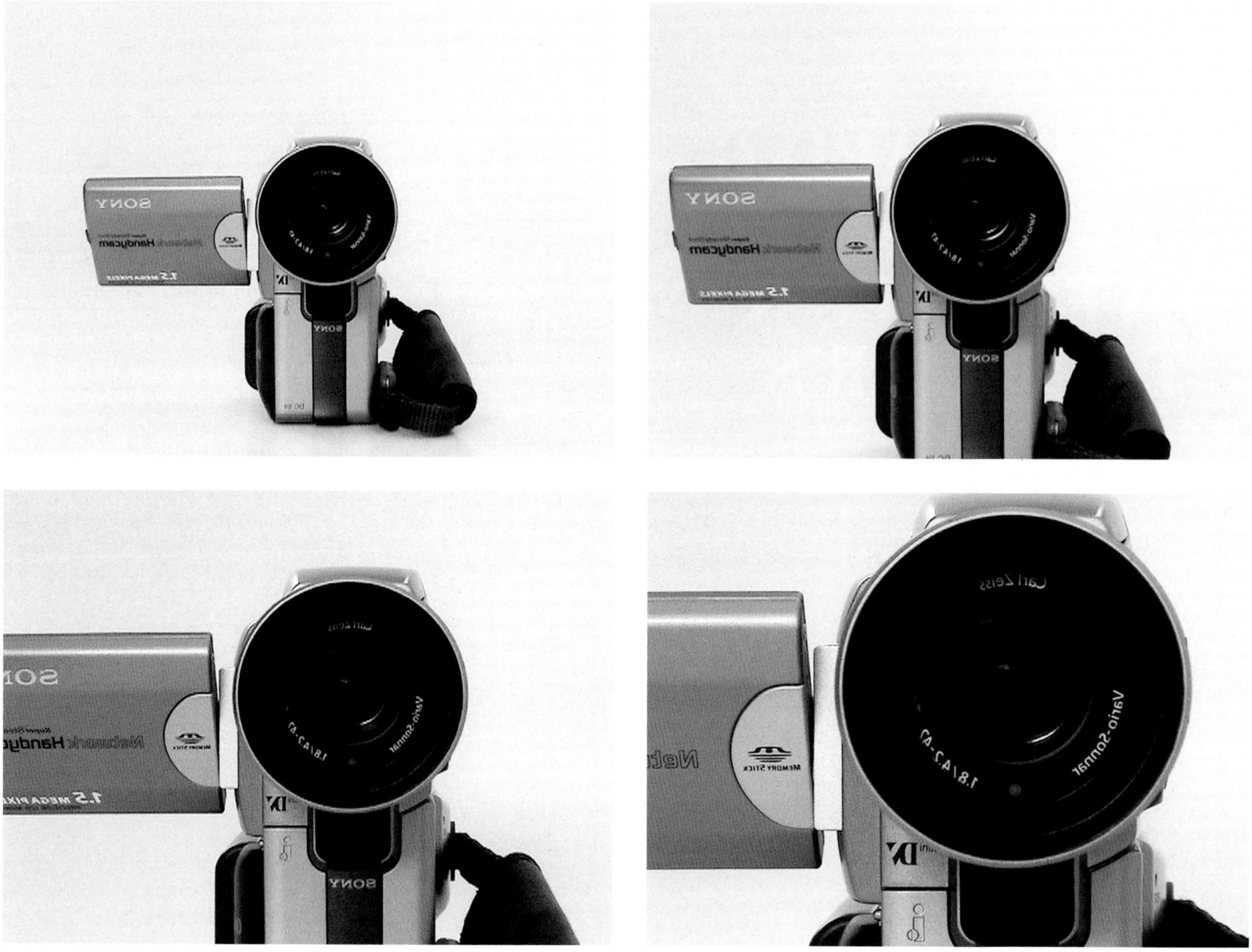

Stills from *Sony DCR-PC 120E, (Disassembled)* 2007 DVD (color, sound); 1 minute

WHEN BEARING WITNESS OVERRIDES A REPORTER'S FEAR

JANINE DI GIOVANNI

The novelist Adam Thorpe, writing in *The Guardian* (U.K.) newspaper, recently reviewed my book, "The Place at the End of the World: Stories from the Frontline." It was a very good review but, as always, when one reads something written about oneself, there are interesting revelations, to say the least.

"War is di Giovanni's staple subject," he writes. "She's covered it in places such as Rwanda, Iraq, Bosnia, Sierra Leone, Chechnya and Afghanistan. She's not quite sure how she's survived, and neither are we." That part made me laugh. I'm afraid it is true.

Later Thorpe writes that in my 18-year career, I have gone to "suicidal lengths" to bear witness to human rights abuse around the world and to bring back the stories of the "small voices." He describes me as "stubbornly brave." I like reading these words, but they embarrass me, too. Stubborn I am, fiercely and annoyingly so. But brave is not something I would call myself.

As a child I was afraid of the dark. I still hold an irrational horror for jungle creatures: spiders, insects, large things with wings. I sometimes sleep with the bathroom light on if I am alone and get up at least five times to make sure all the doors are locked and the windows barred. And once, in a guesthouse in Liberia during the civil war, I was so frightened of what lay outside my door that I barricaded the room with chairs and drugged myself to sleep with a codeine painkiller that a United Nations doctor had slipped me in case of gunshot wounds.

Some of the places that I have been have been very frightening. There are things I will never forget. The early, frozen dawn of a Grozny suburb after Russian forces had taken the city, when I huddled in a potato cellar with an old woman listening to the bombardment and sure I would be dead by daylight. Watching an Ivorian solider slowly raise his gun to my chest after I screamed at him to let me take a wounded man to the hospital in my taxi during the first day of the coup d'etat. The sound of rapid gunfire over a bush in Sierra Leone, where a few seconds before there had been stillness. Then the rush of chaos. My car being surrounded by teenage, drugged soldiers in Freetown who waved RPG's and demanded that I get out so they could rape me. The terrible hollow sound of a bomb being dropped near my base camp in Kosovo and the screams of pain from the people that it hit.

I have been terribly frightened at times, but innermost in my mind was that I would always survive. Why, I am not sure, but I believe it probably has something to do with faith. A friend of mine, a former combat photographer once said, "I never think I will get hurt because my mother loves me too much." It sounds ridiculous, but everyone has their own reason as to why the bullet that hits the guy next to you won't hit you.

I believe the work that I have done over the years is important, and I am proud when I get a letter from an ordinary person, someone in Middle America or Middle England, a housewife or a teacher or a radio technician, who writes and says, "Thank you for your compassion."

But I don't think of myself as courageous. Because courage is meant for the people I leave behind—the civilians who could not cross the frontlines of Sarajevo to leave the debilitating medieval siege. The young boy in Mogadishu who helped me find my way through the maze of clan warfare and who told me how one day, walking down the street with his brother, he heard the whiz of a bullet, then found his brother dead on the ground next to him. Or even that old woman in the potato cellar in Grozny, who got up from the cellar at one point to make us tea on a camp stove.

I went to lots of terrible places. I got marched in the woods by Serb paramilitaries with a gun pointed at my back. I got stuck in dangerous places in Africa. I slept a terrible sleep on a door frame in East Timor and waited for an assault from rebels with machetes. But eventually—and sometimes it took weeks and even months—I got out, I went home, I took a hot shower, I ate a good meal. I went to the cinema, I slept in a real bed with clean sheets. The people who befriended me, who shared their rice, who made me laugh, who helped me find water to wash, did not. They stayed behind.

That is always the guilt of the reporter who covers conflict. You survive, someone else does not. And why? And why is it that I was born in a comfortable suburban American hospital and had good shoes and music lessons, and someone else was born in Srebrenica and was of fighting age in 1995, so therefore is probably dead? These are the things I think about when I go to sleep at night, and because of that I do know that I have something that is known as compassion.

But courage is reserved for other people.

Courage was my father bravely and doggedly fighting cancer, saying right up until the very end, "I'm not going to let cancer kill me!" And trying to be brave so that we would not falter.

Courage is Lotti Latrous, a wealthy Swiss woman who gave up her entire life, including her family, to sleep on the floor of a hut and nurse Ivorians dying of AIDS who had been left to die in the street.

Courage is Felicia Langer, an Israeli Jewish woman who inspired me to do the work I do now, who for many years was one of the few Jewish lawyers defending Palestinians in military court. The cost she paid to defend the enemy was being constantly worried about her own personal security.

Courage is the Kosovar Serbs who hid Kosovar Albanians in their homes during the NATO bombing in 1999.

Courage is the mothers of Srebrenica who saw their menfolk walk into the forest in July 1995 to defend their town against a brutal onslaught—and never return.

Was it Hemingway who described courage as grace under pressure? I am not sure. But when I think of that, courage is not me, a clunky reporter clutching a notebook and treading on people's lives, trying to get them to open up their souls.

Grace under pressure is Gordana Knezevic, a Bosnian of Serb origin who managed not only to bring out a newspaper every day of the siege—the embattled and wonderful Sarajevo daily Oslobodjenje—but to raise her children in the back room of her

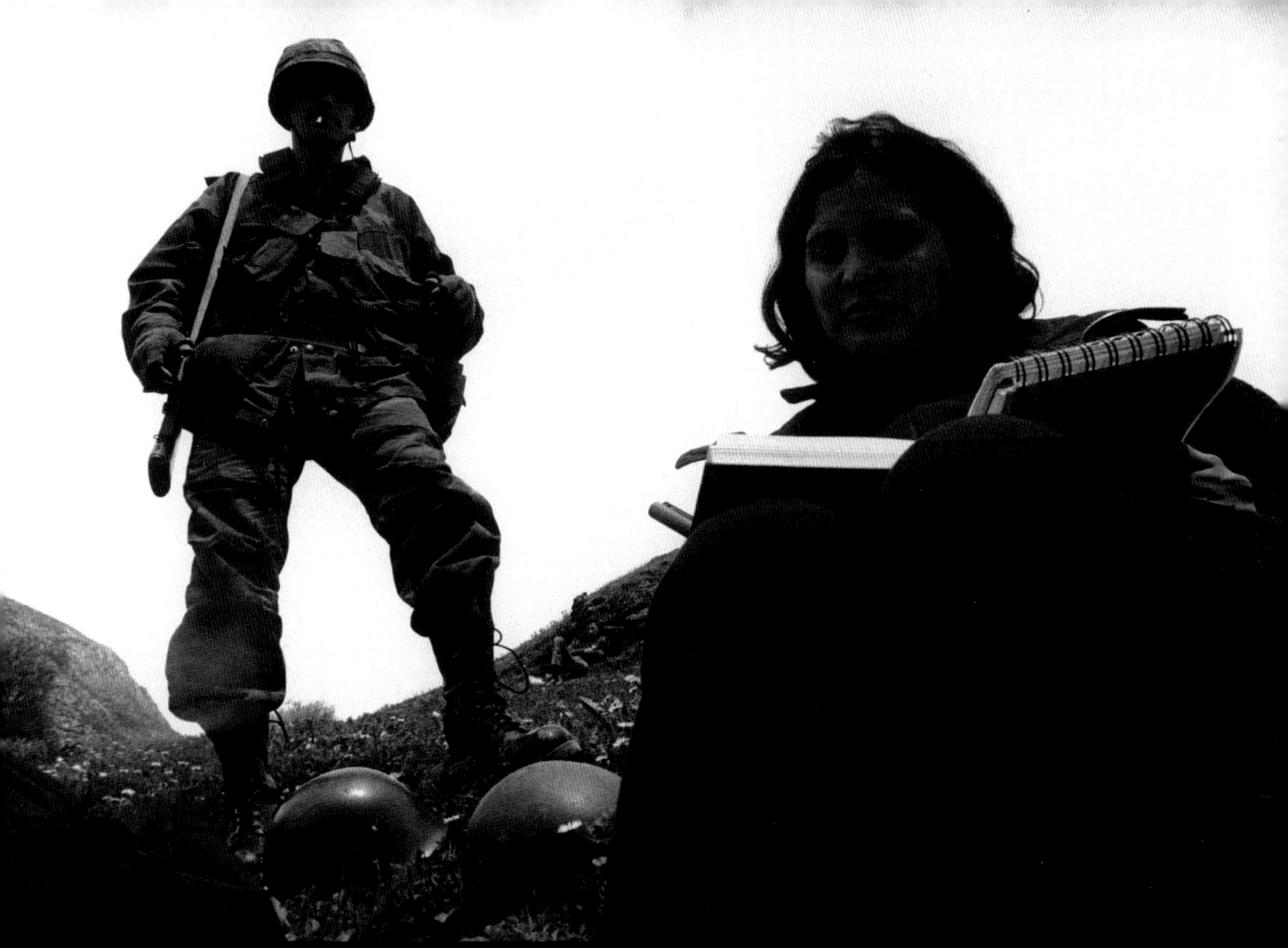

Padesh, Kosovo: The author with KLA soldiers, 1999

house because it was farther from the street and thus safer from errant shrapnel or snipers' bullets.

Courage is my old interpreter Mona in Baghdad, who stuck by my side through the darkest days of the Saddam times and during and after the invasion.

Courage is the man who drove through Russian tanks to bring me out of Grozny after he heard my newspaper reports aired on Russian television, and he knew that if Russian soldiers found me, they would probably kill me.

Courage is all of these people and a million more who are embedded forever in my notebooks. Ordinary people. The bravest souls are the ones who keep families together during war, who manage to continue their lives without going mad.

No, a reporter's role is to bear witness. And if we have the ability to do so—the financial backing of a paper or a TV company, the guts and the vision—then we have an obligation more than anything. Martha Gellhorn once wrote about loving only one war, and the rest being duty. I still feel like that—Bosnia was the war that took and broke my heart in a million little pieces. But Africa, the Middle East, Asia, the rest of the world, the places I will go and bring back a story that I hope someone will read, and then go to bed that night thinking "Thank God I don't live in Mogadishu" and gain some kind of insight, some kind of compassion—that to me is my responsibility. ■

Janine di Giovanni is a senior foreign correspondent for *The Times of London* and author of such books as *Madness Visible: A Memoir of War*. She is the recipient of two Amnesty International awards, the National Magazine Award, and other honors.
This article is reprinted by permission from *Nieman Reports* (Summer 2006): 61–63.

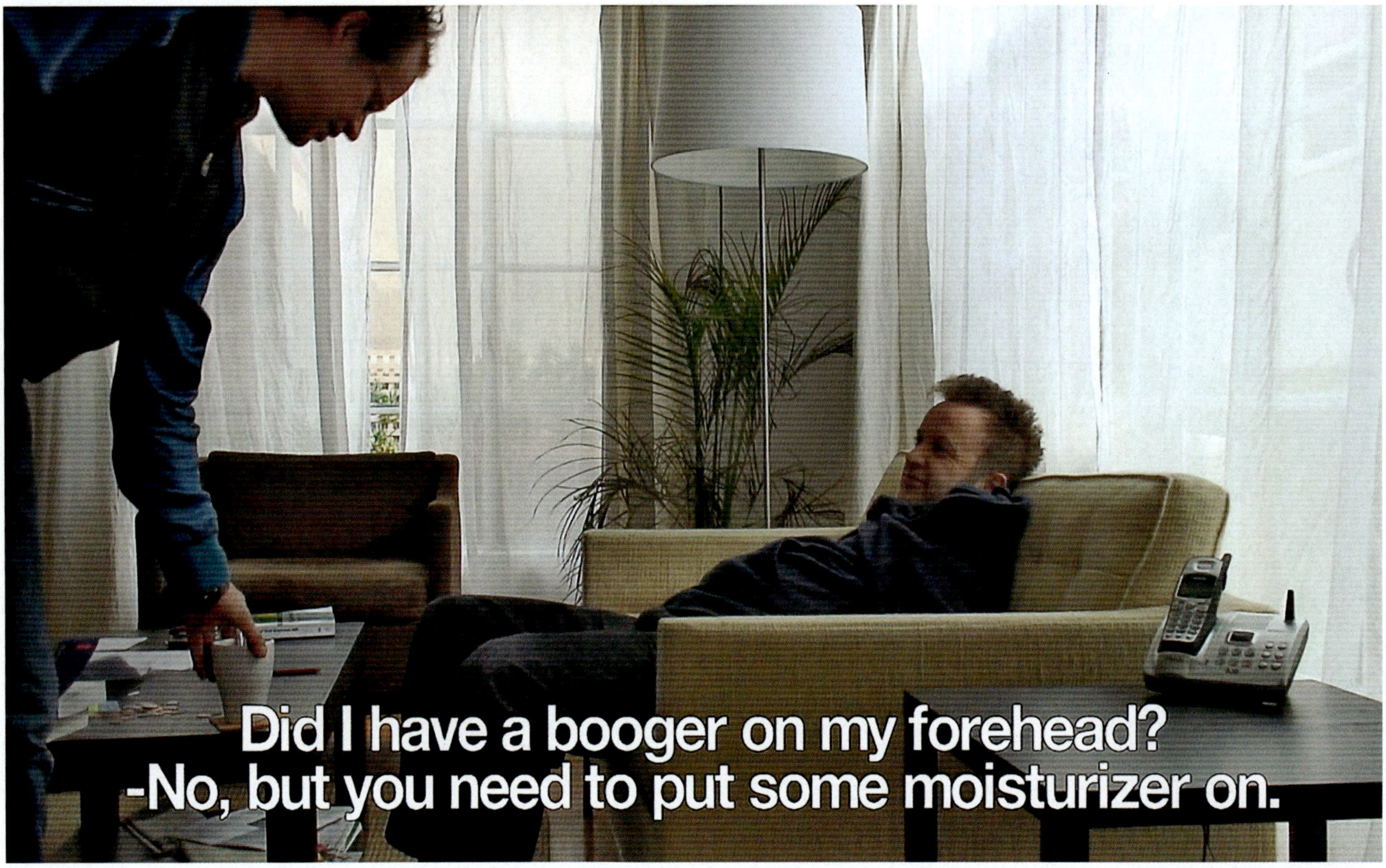

Still from *Guantánamo Baywatch, Part 1* 2007 video transferred to DVD (color, sound); 17 minutes Collaboration with Core van der Hoeven

LESSONS IN BUFFOONERY AND BRAVADO: ERIK VAN LIESHOUT

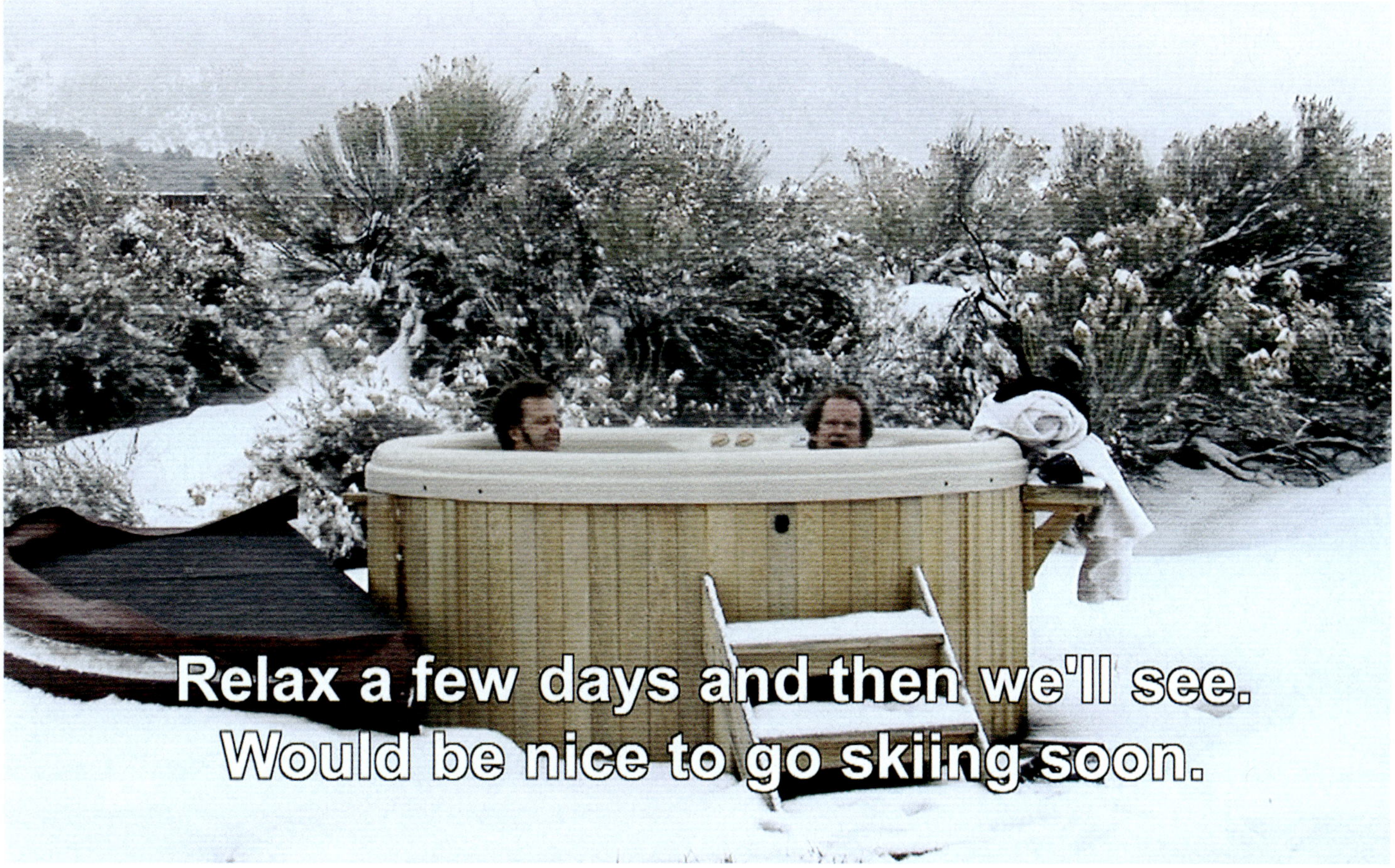

Still from *Guantánamo Baywatch, Part 2* 2007 video transferred to DVD (color, sound); 24 minutes Collaboration with Core van der Hoeven

Born in the Netherlands, 1968. Lives and works in Rotterdam.

As engaged as a postmodern moral philosopher with pragmatic issues of consensus and as embarrassingly funny as a slapstick comedian, Erik van Lieshout works in various mediums to present vulnerable encounters in which he and his audience confront the foreign or the forbidden. These meetings are imbued with risks, fears, and instabilities, bringing us to the edge of possibility and change. In recent projects, he entered communities of Ghanaian rappers, the nouveau riche, Moroccan immigrants, and a psychiatric hospital to record documentary-like social satires. Although the interactions are unscripted, certain personal and social issues recur throughout the films: tensions caused by immigration, the rise of right-wing nationalism, sexual exploration, and capitalist hypocrisies. These are hot-button issues in the artist's homeland, and their analysis drives his work: "Sometimes . . . it is better to look at subjects . . . as they relate to oneself first, before saying anything about other people. That is why I appear so frequently in my films."[1]

Van Lieshout's distinctive artistic practice, which combines artwork in two, three, and four dimensions, came together in the late 1990s when he began making interactive environments from salvaged building materials. In 1999, he made the video installation *EMMDM*, a play on the white emulation of hip-hop fashion and violence. To view it, visitors were required to crouch inside a cardboard box in which the video was projected. Since that time, van Lieshout has followed in the tradition of Dan Graham and Hélio Oiticica in designing expanded cinemas that physically engage viewers with installations and moving images. By displaying his videos in an architecture that forces visitors to move around other people in order to see the small projections or monitors, he encourages the viewer to undertake, on a small scale, the kind of social negotiations that he challenges himself with in his projects. The artist's functional structures are built on the physicality and frank immediacy of the drawings and paintings he has been making since his graduation from Ateliers '63, Haarlem, in 1992. Using the visual language of pornography and advertising, his works on paper now introduce the concepts behind each installation, record the brainstorming sessions for his videos, and provide a means to work through their inevitable emotional aftermath.

For this exhibition, the artist debuts the third section of his latest trilogy, *Guantánamo Baywatch* (2007), made in collaboration with his friend and video editor Core van der Hoeven, which explores the idea of America as an almost alien culture. Part 1 was made in Los Angeles; Part 2 was shot in New Mexico; and Part 3 of the trilogy was completed in Israel. As with earlier works, this series mixes the brutal honesty of first-person documentaries with the rhythm of MTV-style editing and music, a combination that has led many to compare his videos to reality television. But although they may be stylish, his broken narratives nonetheless resist neat packaging and surpass clichés. The artist has said that he left Europe for the United States in order to find the war in Iraq, and certain allusions to that conflict keep popping up in these three videos.[2] However, the troubling implications of war are not overt. Van Lieshout entertains us, but at the same time, the psychic residue he stirs up disturbs: "People ought to be overwhelmed by my work, and confused, because it is cheerful, intimate, and yet somber; they can then enjoy the latent humor. Nonetheless something should linger so that they can head straight for the pub to drink away the uncomfortable associations."[3]

RH

1. Rein Wolfs and Miriam Varadinis, "Cut the Performance in the Edit," in *This Can't Go On (Stay with Me)*, exh. cat., Museum Boijmans Van Beuningen, Rotterdam; Kunsthaus Zürich; Städtische Galerie im Lenbachhaus, Munich (Zurich: JRP/Ringier, 2006), 74–75.

2. Erik van Lieshout, interview with Ali Subotnick, in "Hammer Projects: *Eric van Lieshout*," http://www.hammer.ucla.edu/exhibitions/126/.

3. Kees Twist, et al., *Erik van Lieshout: Naughty by Nature, not because I hate you . . .*, exh. cat. (Groningen, the Netherlands: Groninger Museum; Rotterdam: NAi Uitgevers, 2002), 85.

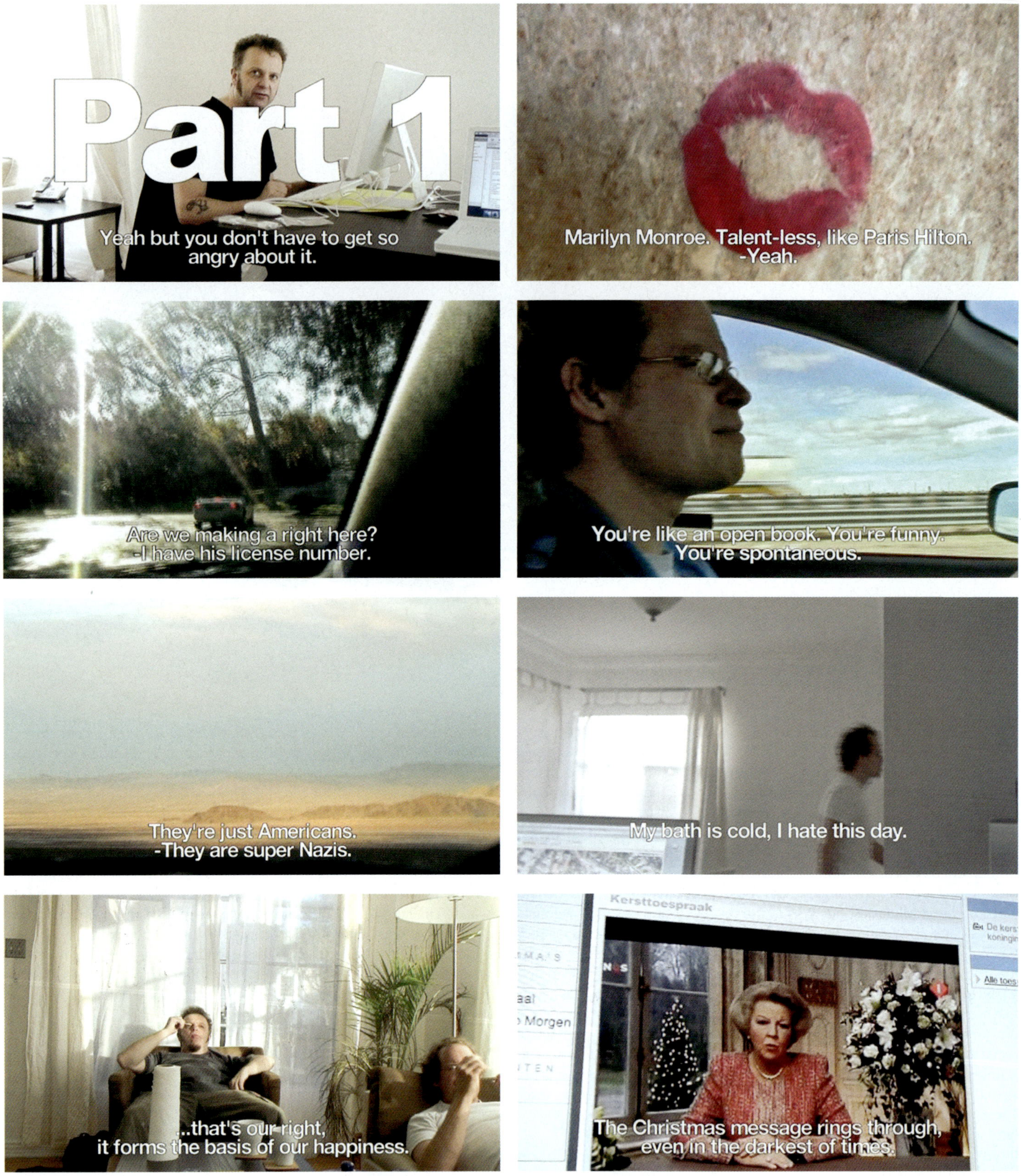

Stills from *Guantánamo Baywatch, Part 1* 2007 video transferred to DVD (color, sound); 17 minutes Collaboration with Core van der Hoeven

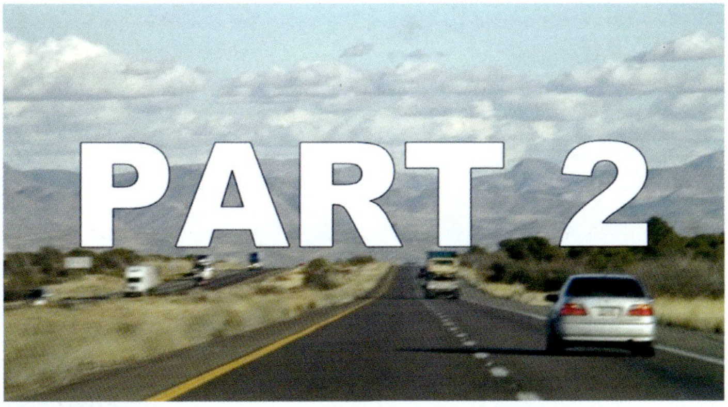

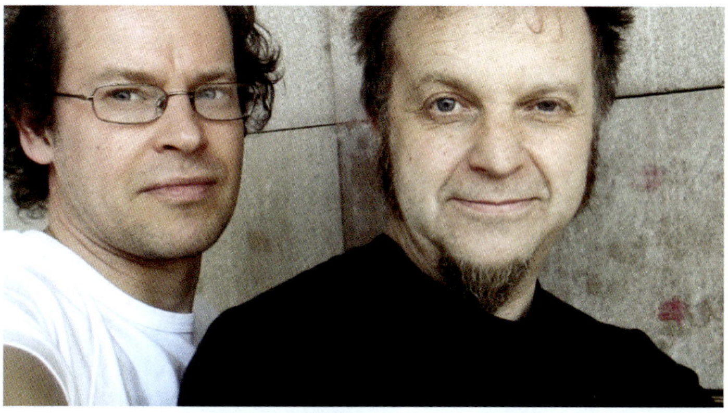

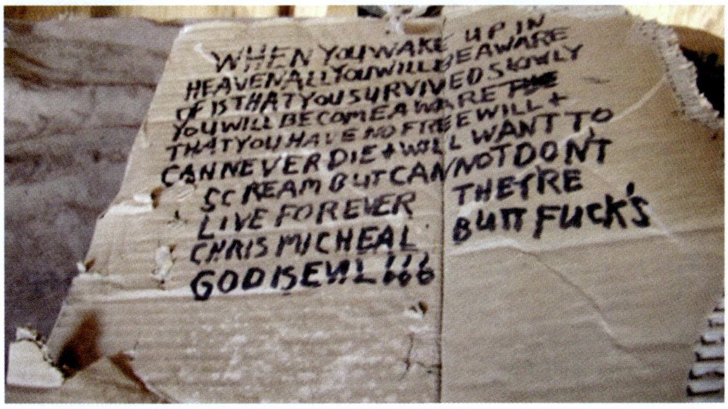

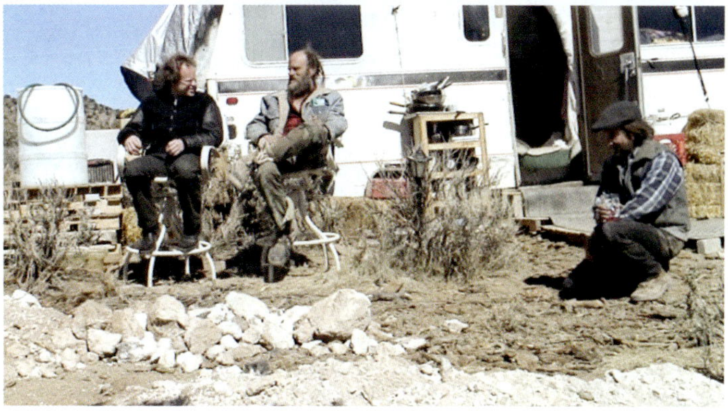

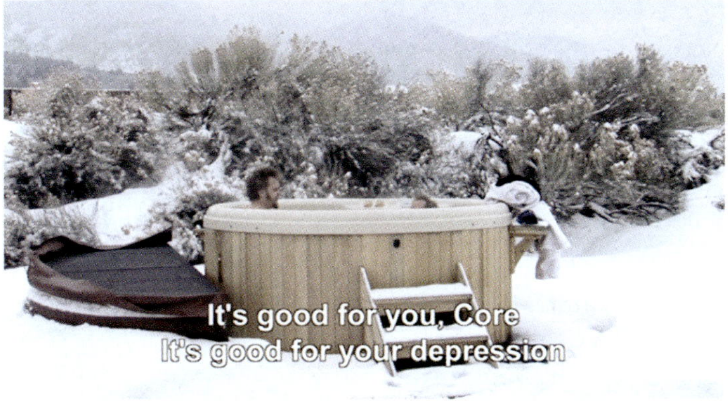

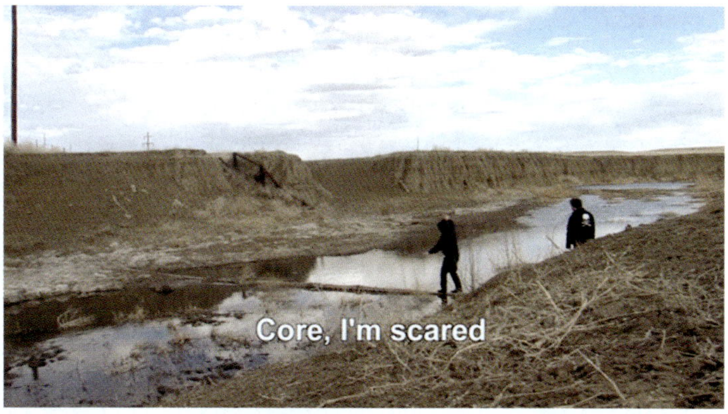

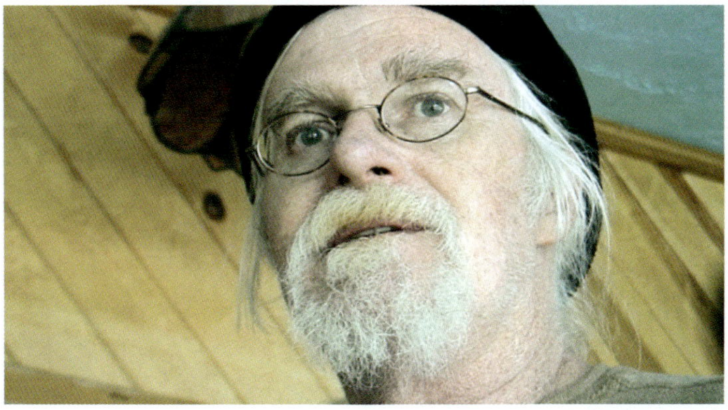

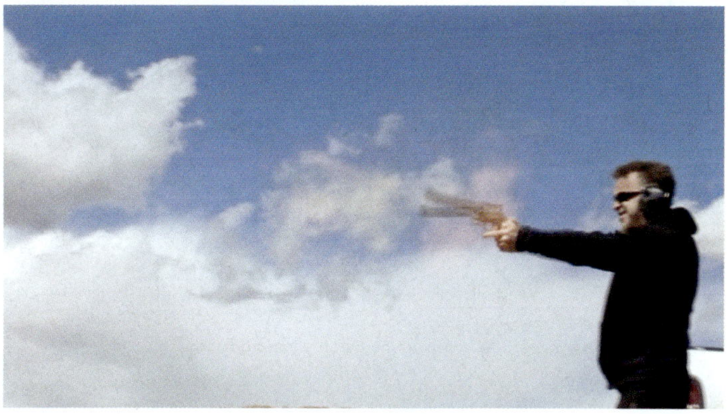

Stills from *Guantánamo Baywatch, Part 2* 2007 video transferred to DVD (color, sound); 24 minutes Collaboration with Core van der Hoeven

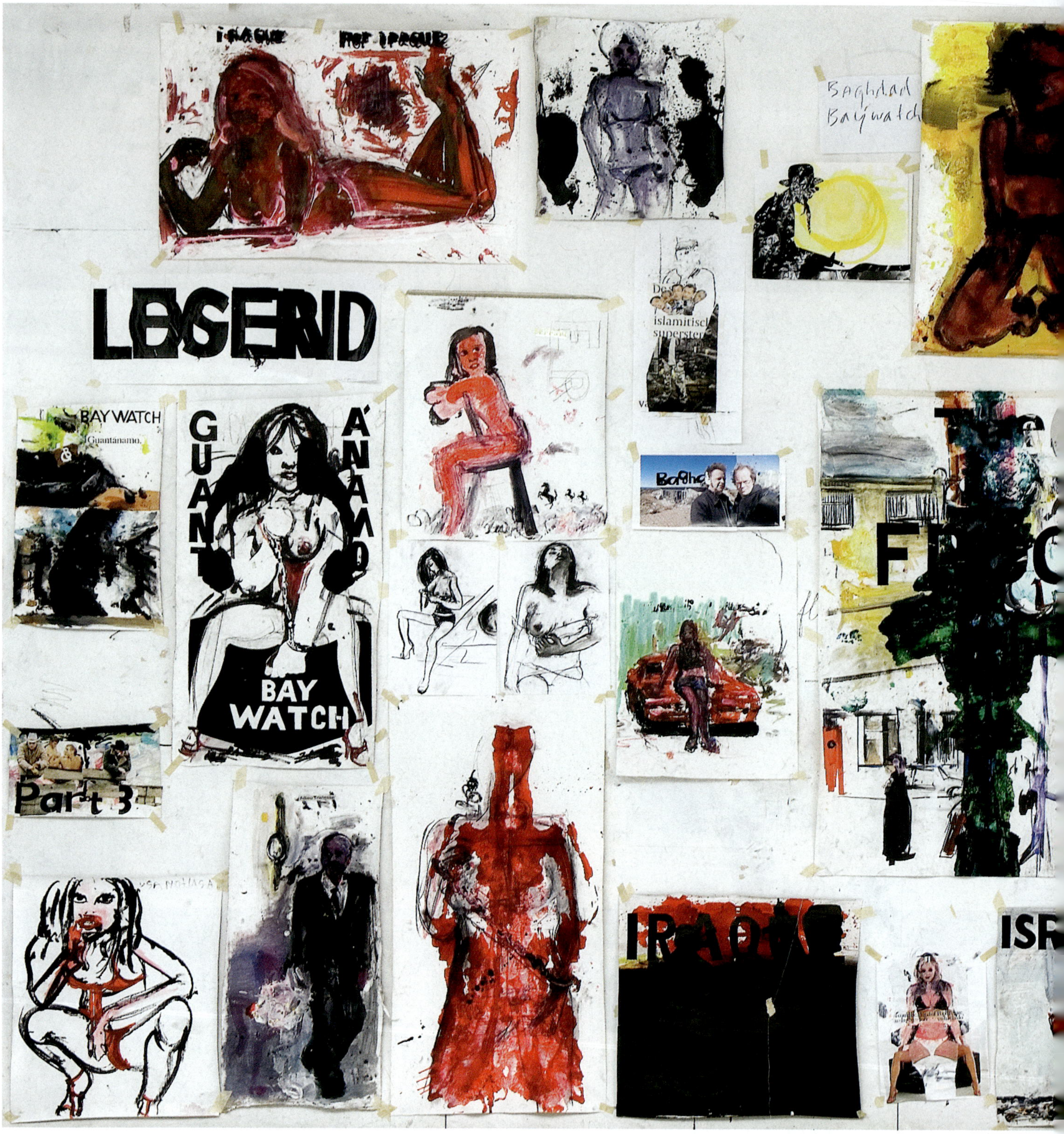

Guantánamo Baywatch 2007 mixed media on paper and canvas

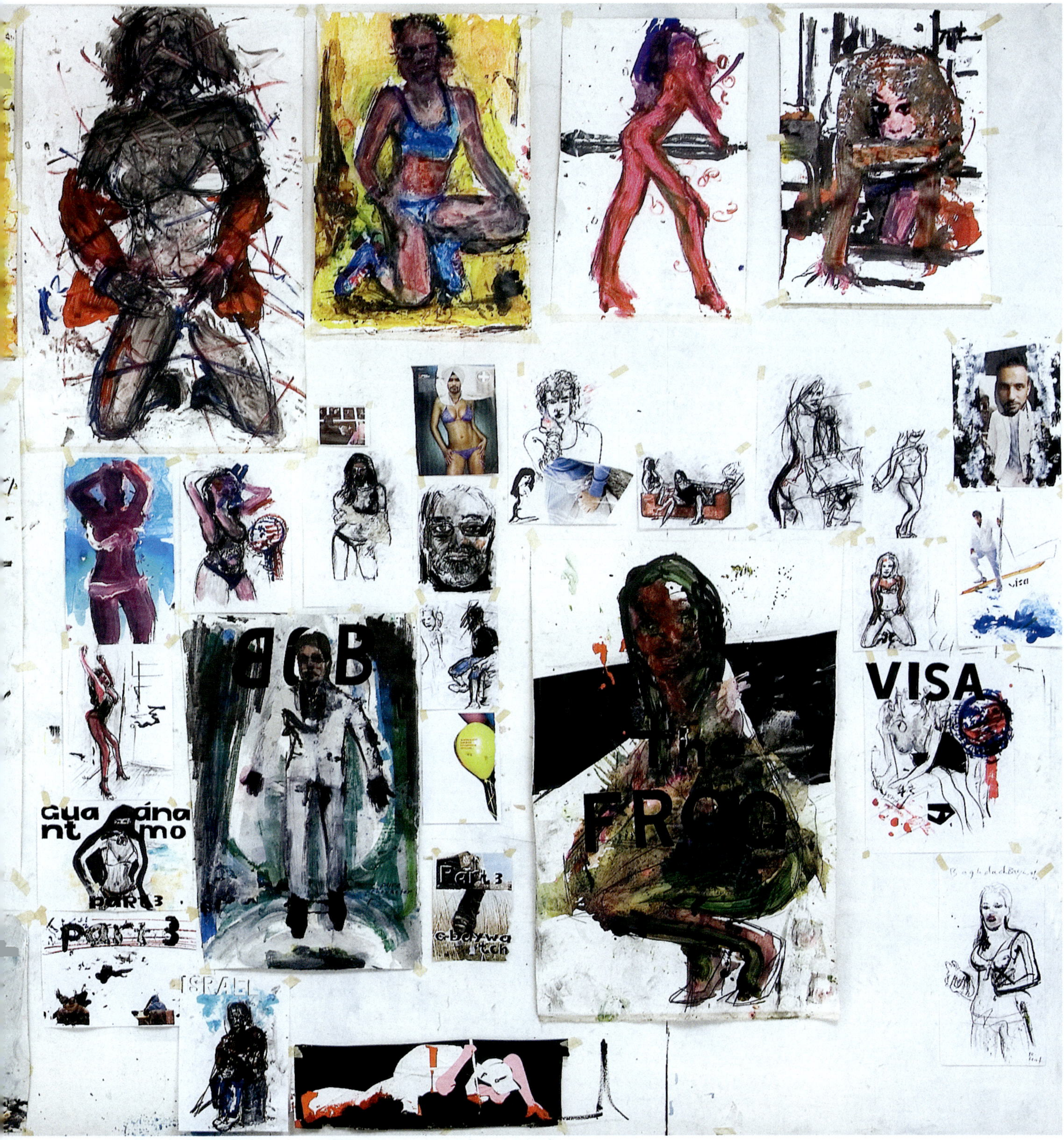
VISA
Part 3

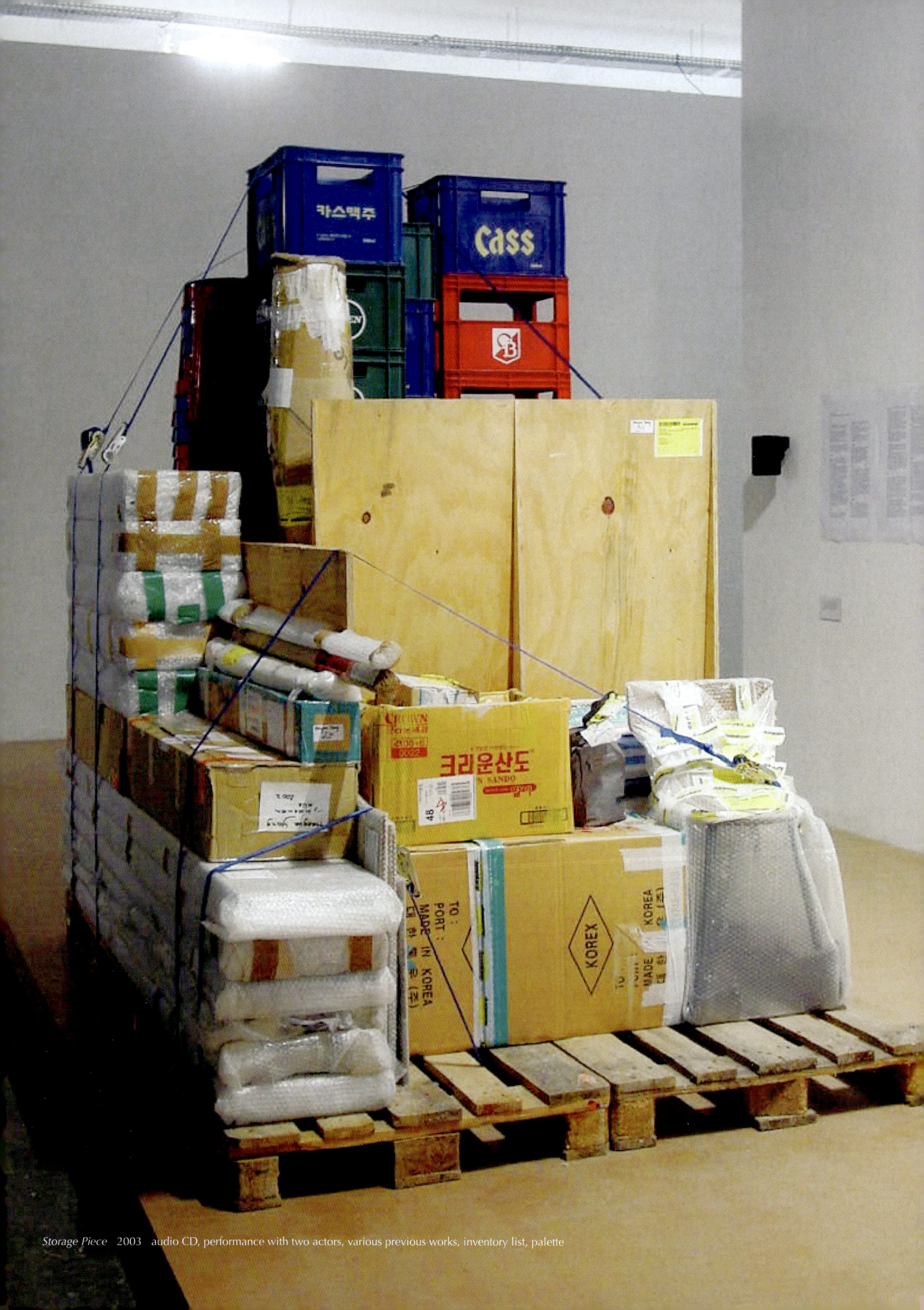

Storage Piece 2003 audio CD, performance with two actors, various previous works, inventory list, palette

TERRITORY OF A POET-ACTIVIST: HAEGUE YANG

Born in South Korea, 1971. Lives and works in Seoul and Berlin.

In 2003, Haegue Yang completed a work titled *Storage Piece*, a sculpture that consists of plastic crates for beer bottles, cardboard boxes sealed with green duct tape, and many flat objects soft-packed in bubble wrap, all held in place by rope and situated atop a big wooden pallet. The materials — or contents, to be more precise — of this sculpture were components in many of Yang's earlier works. The crates, for instance, had been stacked vertically in two columns on a gently ascending ramp in *Tilting on a Plane* (2002), a work about "everyday tension" inspired by the artist's memory of seeing a precarious method of transportation in Korea.[1] Yang, who studied at the Städelschule in Frankfurt-am-Main, Germany, often works with commercially available objects. She rearranges and resituates the items she finds or purchases in subtle ways that reconfigure her location and her viewers' notions of the social organization of things and the economy of artistic valuation. *Storage Piece* grew partly out of necessity when many of the artist's previous works were returned to her at the close of various shows and she had nowhere to store them. At the same time, she was being offered a space to exhibit, so the natural (or artful) solution for her was to make a new work out of these earlier pieces. This collision of the vagaries of life and the almost compulsive production required of an artist (especially one who is increasingly in demand) also highlighted for Yang the challenge of her more conceptually inclined methodology and her diasporic, continuously mobile life.

In 2004, Yang embarked on her video trilogy. The first two parts, *Unfolding Places* and *Restrained Courage* (both 2004) were made in places such as Frankfurt, Amsterdam, London, and Seoul. For the third installment, *Squandering Negative Spaces* (2006), Yang made a conscious decision to go to Brazil in search of what she calls, per Georges Bataille, a "community of absence."[2] Shot with a handheld camera in a casual manner and with melancholy languor, the videos each comprise a sequence of images of mostly insignificant moments — the sort that occupy, in actuality, most of our physical and perceptual space but fall out of our visual or mental perusal. Yang's camera is focused on stray objects and various examples of light reflection — puddles, raindrops, street lamps. They are things and spaces that are an irrelevant and "unintentional" surplus to the logic of urbanism, modernization, and the structural forces of capital and labor. Inspired, in particular, by the cinematic methodology of Paris-based filmmaker Chris Marker, whose *Sans Soleil* (1983) is a mosaic of parallel contemplative visuals and narratives, Yang features different voices in her videos reading texts seemingly unrelated to the composite images. The speakers ruminate on the pathos of living in this world: being alone, lost, and vulnerable; constantly losing oneself; negating distinctive territories; and lacking courage. While these are clearly and at times painfully private sentiments, the voices allude to the failure to relate to and connect with others also as a willful political act of evading the strictures and requirements of social relations. "I keep a kind of territory where my position could not be fully definable or cultivated, therefore instrumentalized by anyone else," she says. "It is a 'territory' where one can become a 'poet-activist' whose potential is to act radically."

Since the completion of the trilogy, which Yang considers an important turning point in her practice, she has developed a series of installations in which the videos are shown. First realized as *Series of Vulnerable Arrangements (Version Utrecht)* in 2006, the installation may be described as both a rudimentary and complex ecology of objects — commercially available electrical devices, such as scent machines, lamps, heaters, and air conditioners, all connected with electrical cords in a space demarcated and punctuated with industrial blinds. The installation has been realized in São Paulo, Seoul, Cologne, and now Minneapolis, with certain elements exiting and new ones entering the stage. The materials in the piece may be seen as surrogates for human beings and their subjectivities, and the mechanically motored operations as allusions to emotional or psychological states. At the same time, the sum of these objects may very well be no more or no less than their constituents—what counts here is the system of their relations, which constantly shifts and is recalibrated with each evolutionary iteration. Whether we would view the components as singular beings or a collective, these two oppositional readings can be thought of in a nonparadoxical way. Yang interprets a "community of absence" as a "community of the plural that shares nothing but ongoing self-examination and a strange kind of optimism."[3] Indeed, Yang's installation invites and integrates the viewer into an ecology, if only temporarily, in which the viewing subject can become one of the work's many objects, and these may transform into equal subjects in a community of pregnant solitude.

DC

1. Haegue Yang, *Industrie und Technik: Haegue Yang 20.02* (Frankfurt-am-Main: Axel Dielmann-Verlag, 2002), 45.

2. All citations in this paragraph and following are from Binna Choi and Haegue Yang, "Community of Absence: Conversation with Haegue Yang," in *Unevenly* Newsletter 2 (Utrecht: BAK basis voor actuele kunst, 2006).

3. Lars Bang Larson, "Community Work: Space and Event in the Art of Haegue Yang," in Binna Choi, ed., *Community of Absence—Haegue Yang* (Utrecht: BAK, basis voor actuele kunst, 2007), 30–31.

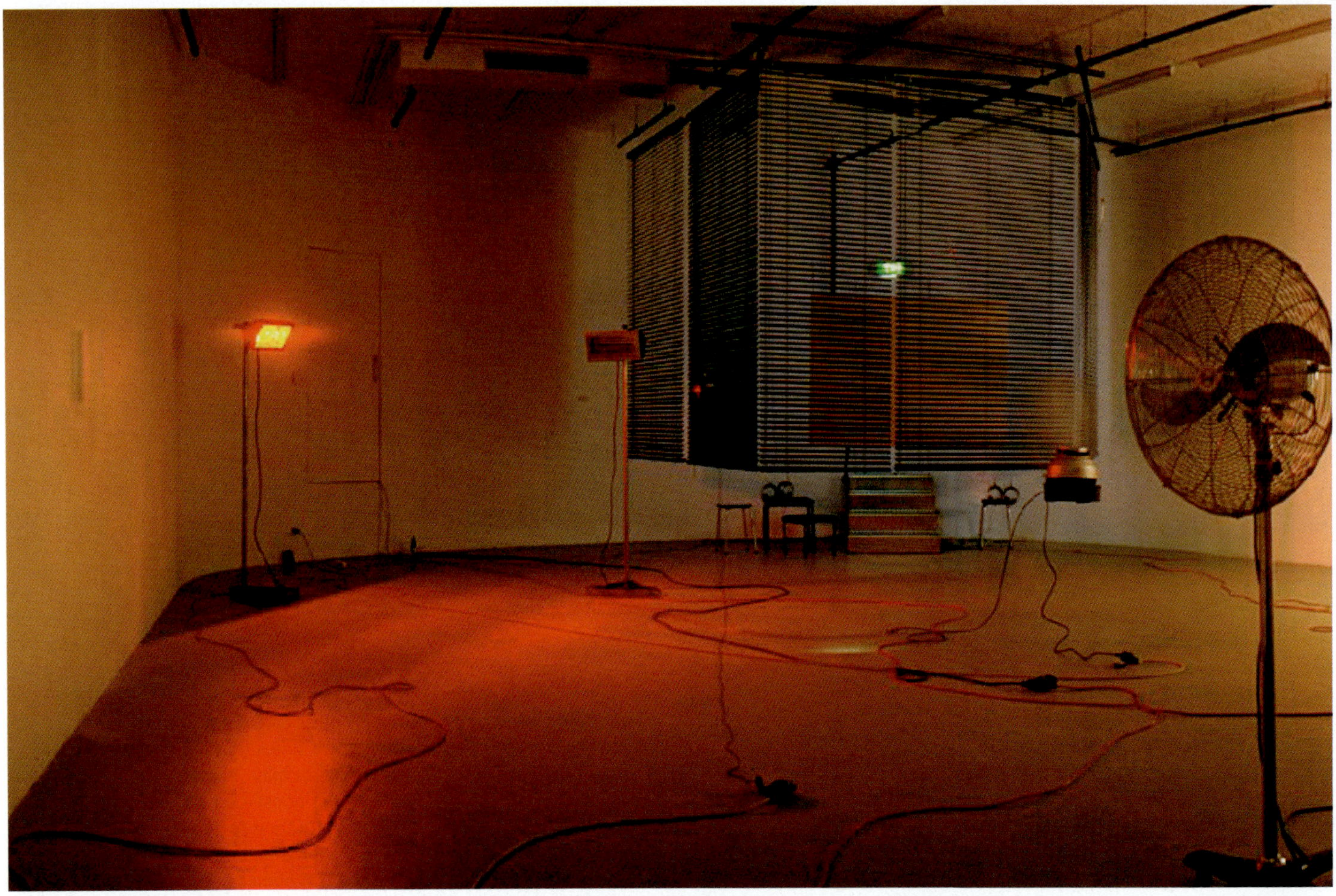

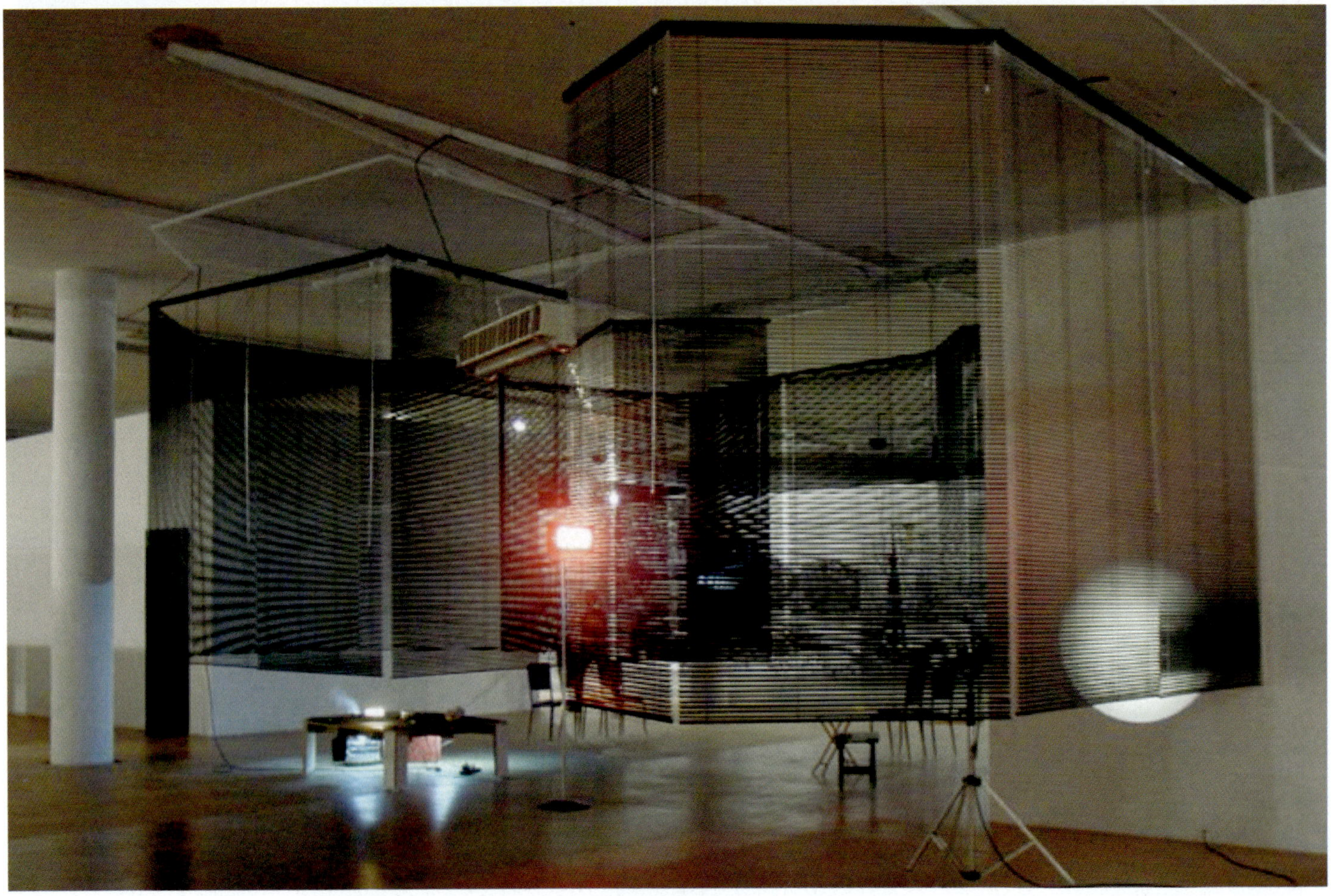

top: *Series of Vulnerable Arrangements, Version Utrecht* 2006 mixed media Installation view at BAK, basis voor actuele kunst, Utrecht, the Netherlands, 2006
bottom: *Blind Room* 2006 mixed media Installation view at the 27th São Paulo Biennale, São Paulo, Brazil, 2006

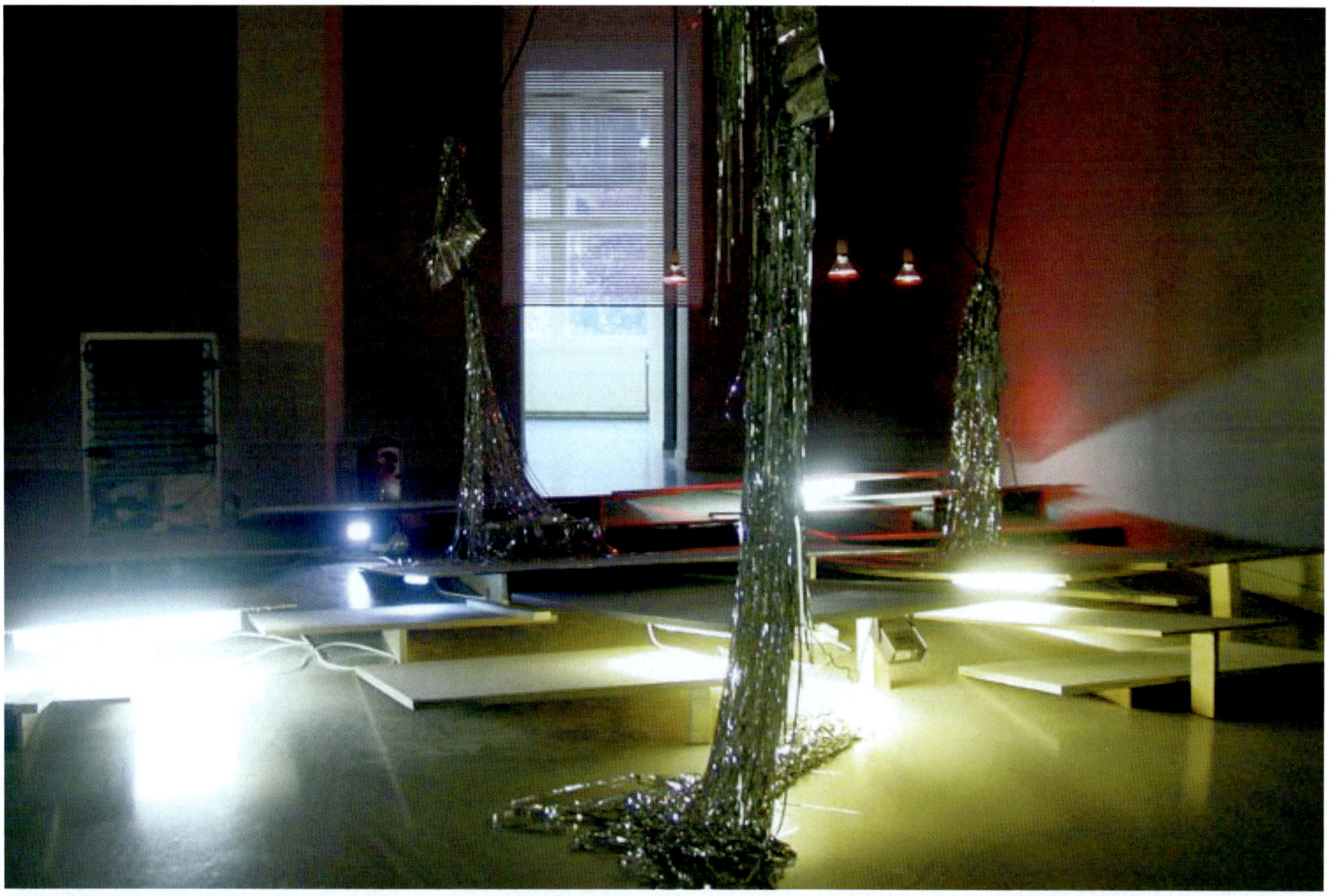

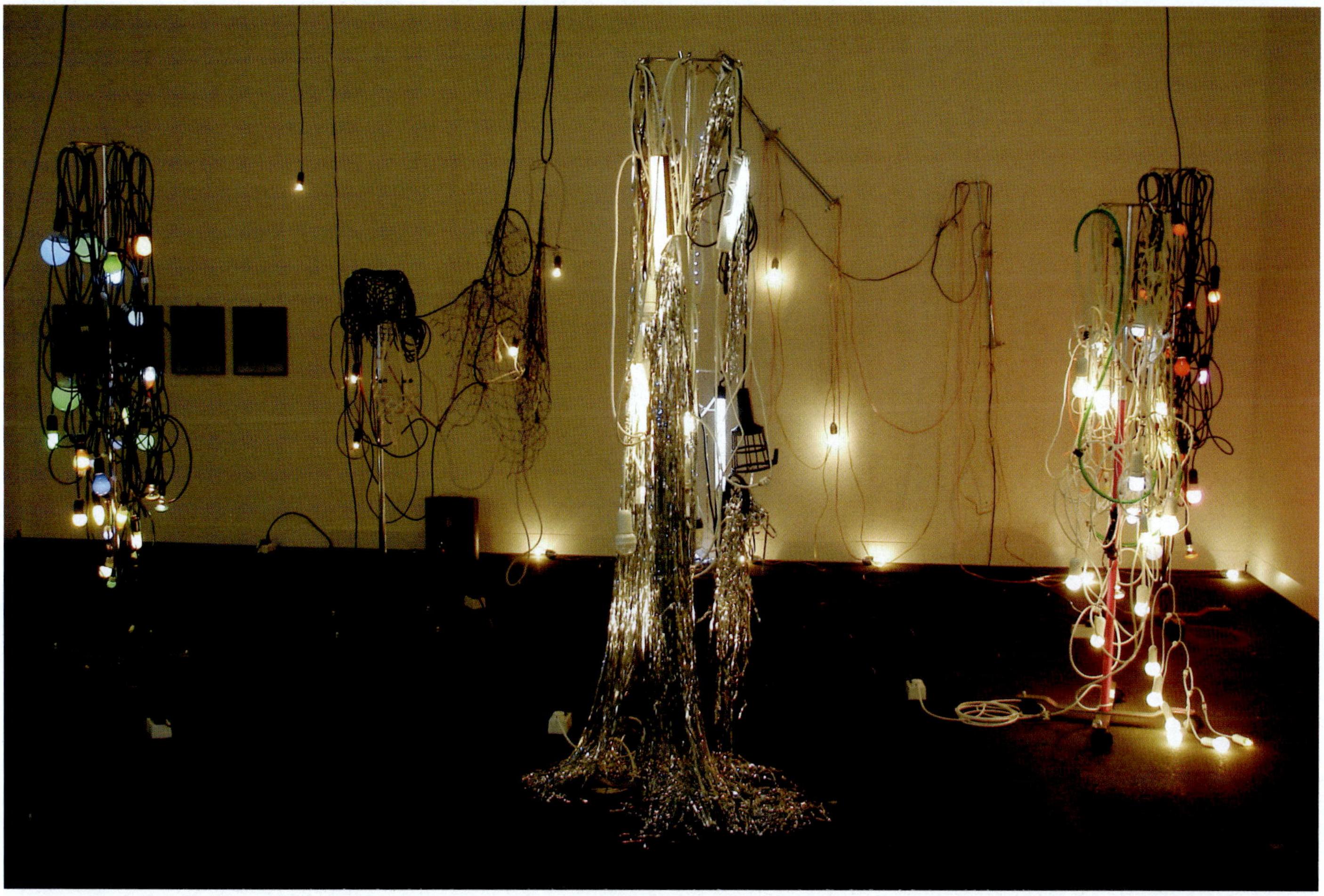

top: *Afterimage* 2006 mixed media Installation view at DeAppel Foundation, Amsterdam, 2006 bottom: *Series of Vulnerable Arrangements—Seven Basel Lights* 2007 mixed media Installation view at Art Basel, Switzerland, 2007

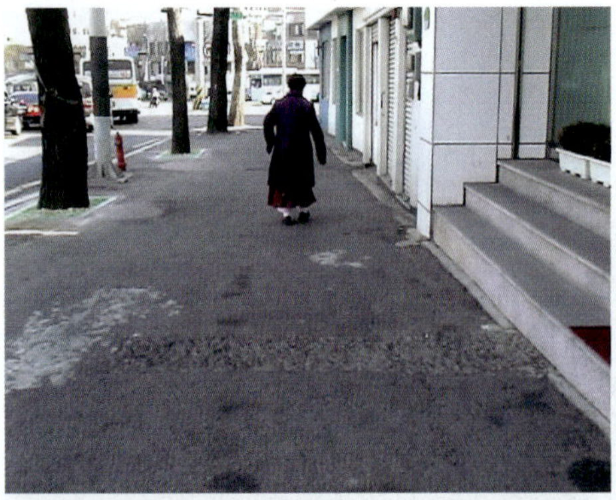
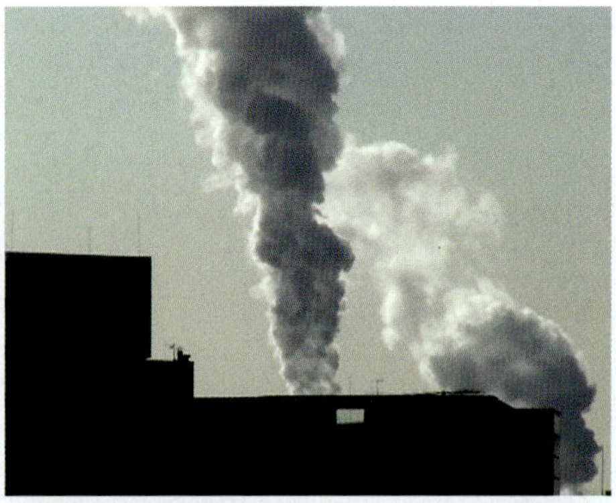
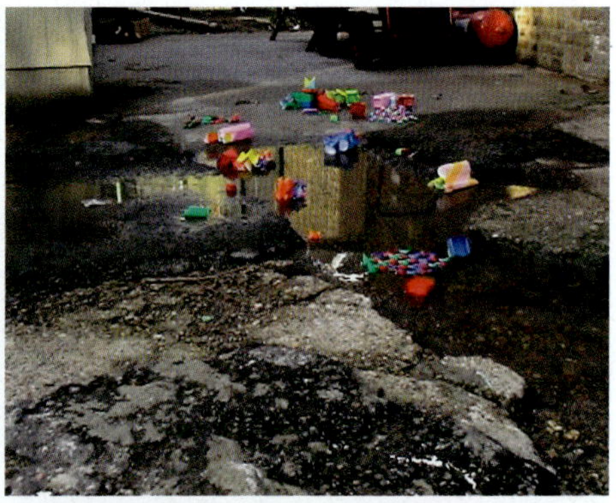
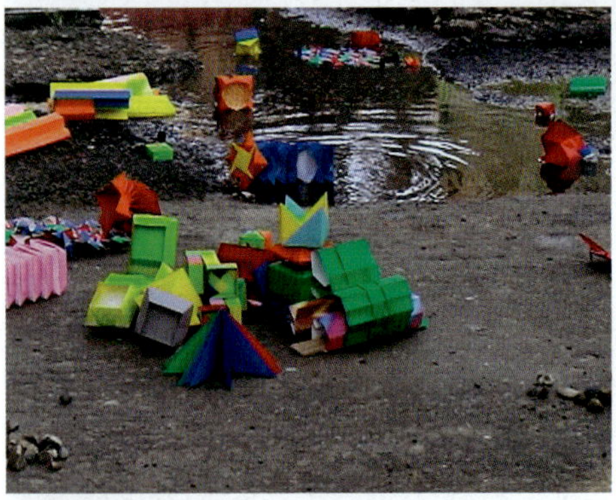
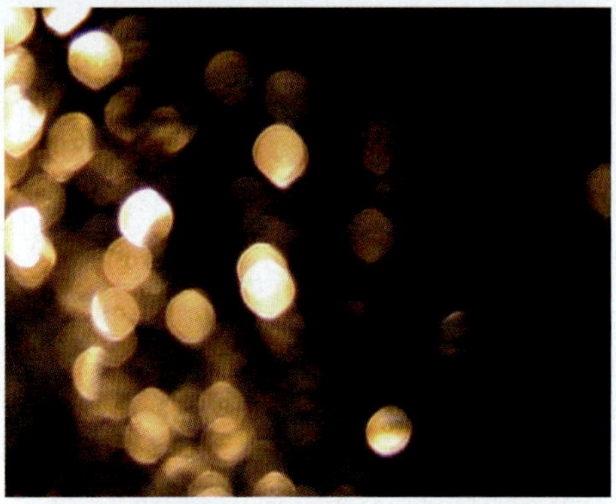
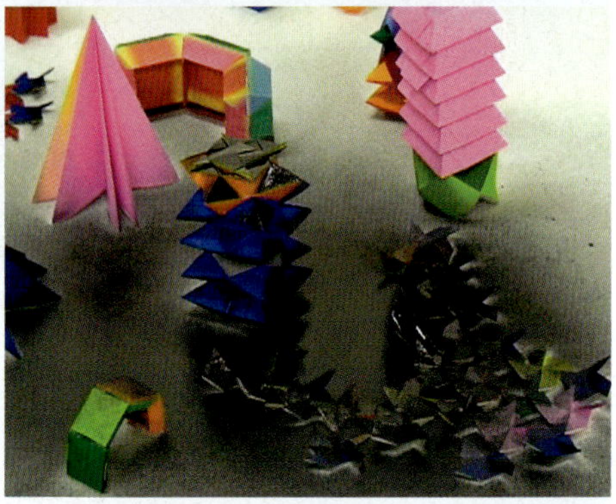
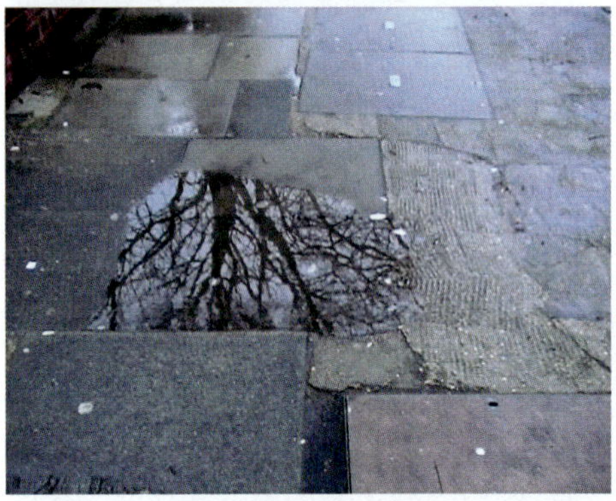
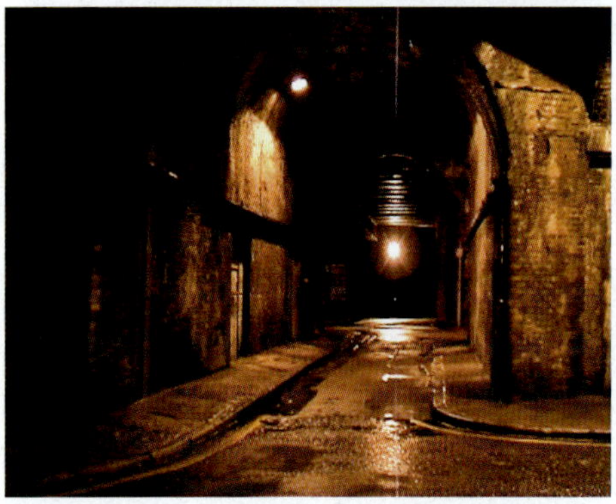
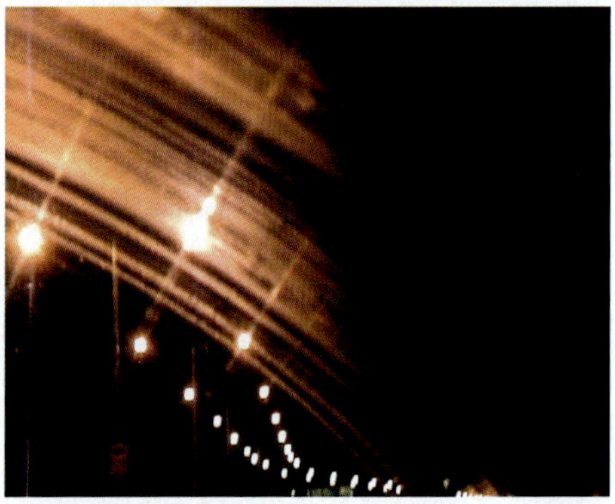
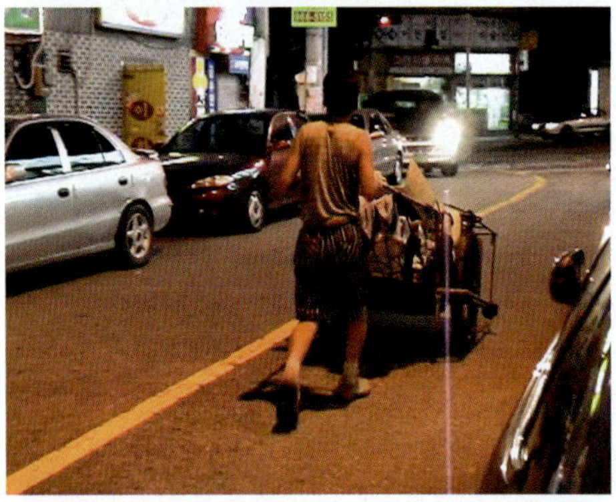
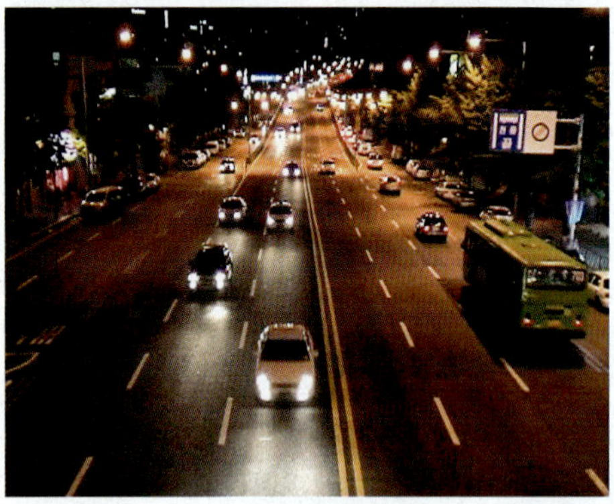
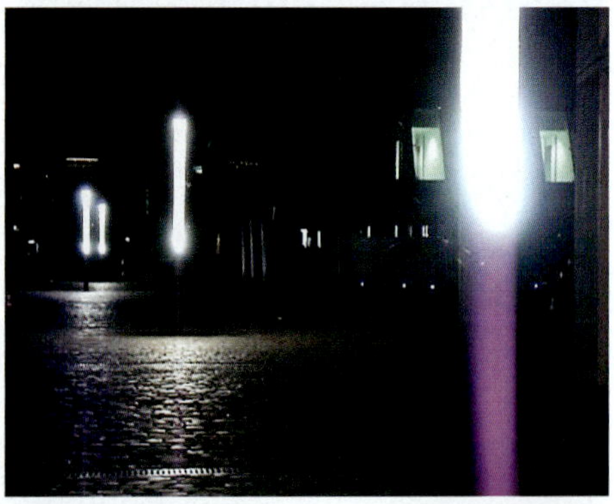
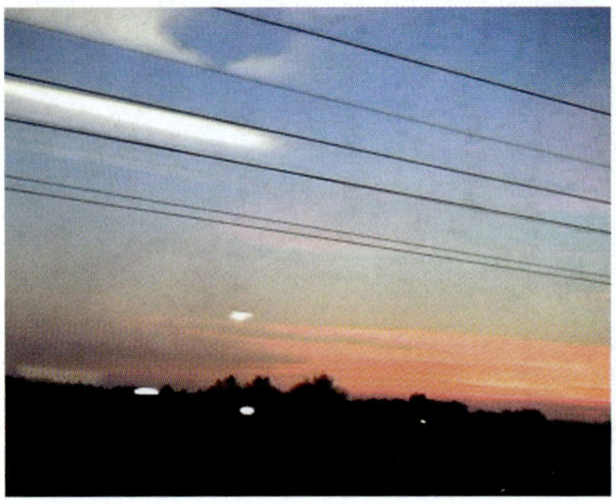
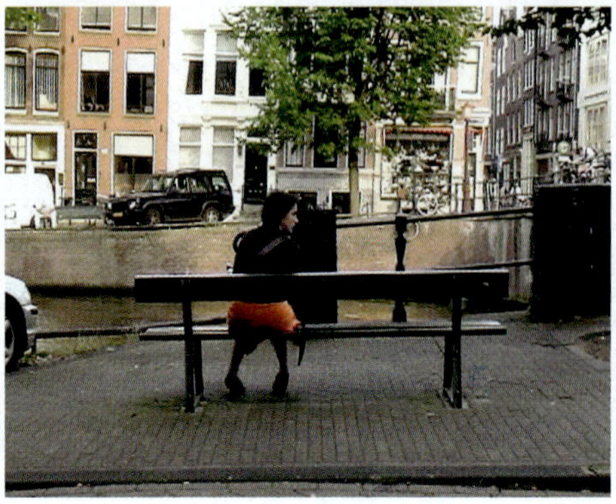
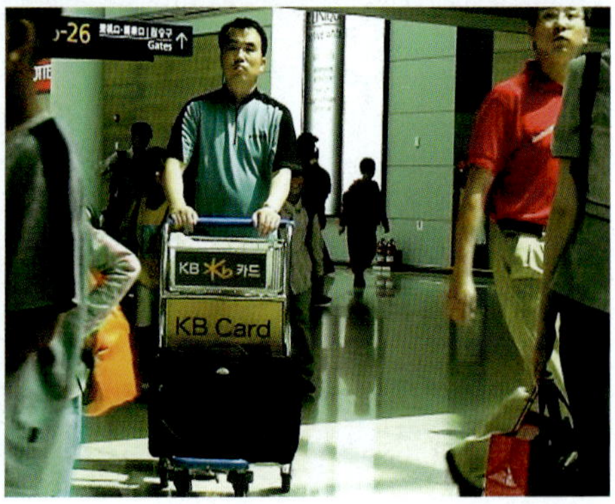
KB Card

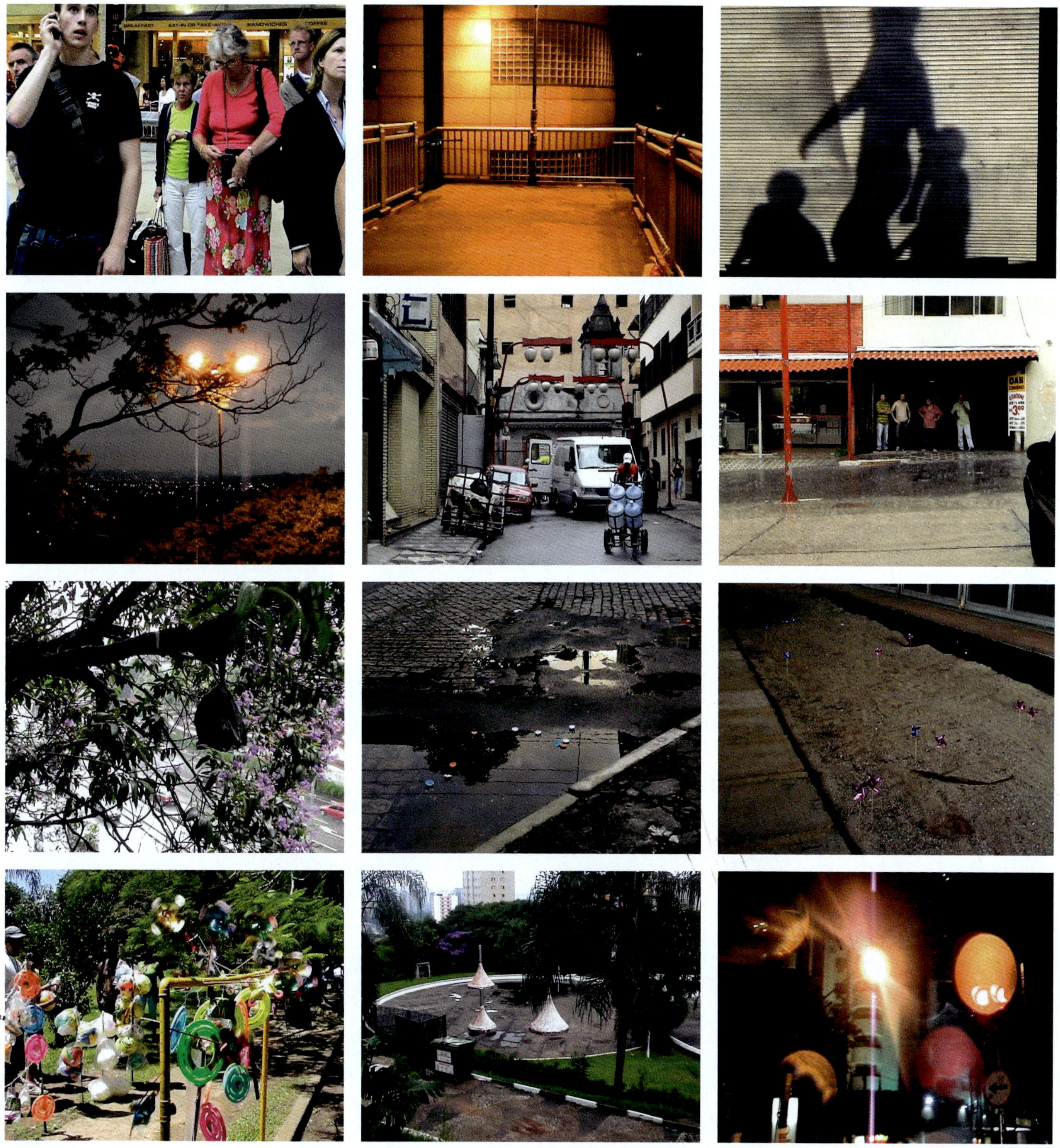

rows 1–3 (from top left): *Unfolding Places* 2004 DVD (color, sound); 18:11 minutes rows 4–6: *Restrained Courage* 2004 DVD (color, sound); 18:37 minutes rows 7–9: *Squandering Negative Spaces* 2006 DVD (color, sound); 27:54 minutes following pages: *Sadong 30* 2006 mixed-media site-specific installation in an abandoned house, Incheon, South Korea, 2006

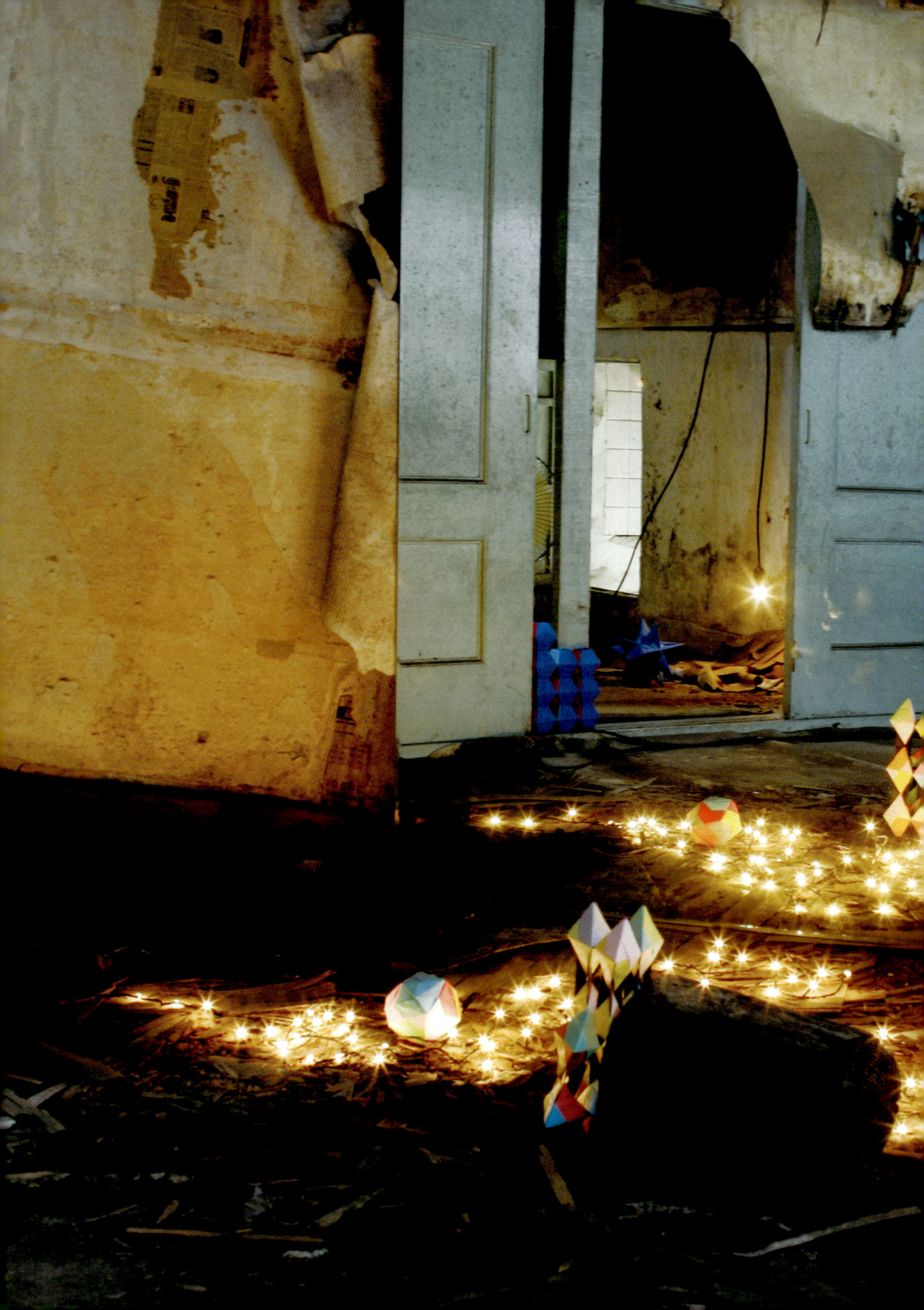

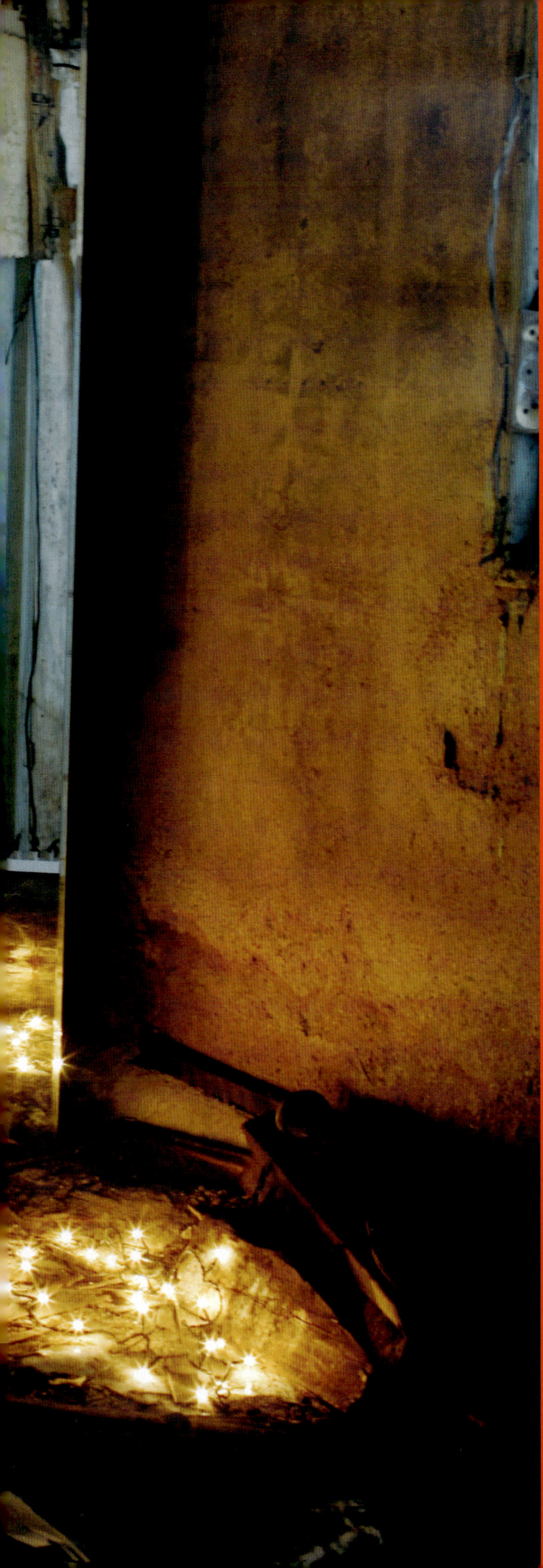

REGARDING THE PAIN AND THE HAPPINESS OF OTHERS

HU FANG

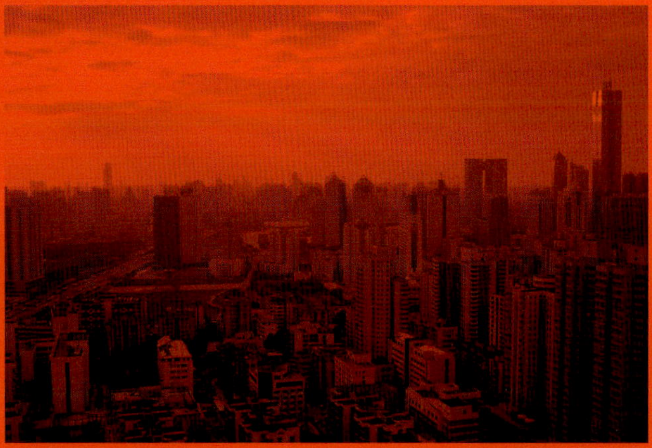

Being a spectator of calamities taking place in another country is a quintessential modern experience, the cumulative offering by more than a century and a half's worth of those professional, specialized tourists known as journalists. Wars are now also living room sights and sounds.
—Susan Sontag, Regarding the Pain of Others (2003)

My mother has walking problems due to seriously deformed joints, and hooking up to the Internet has become part of her daily ritual. The following is the content of my chat with her one day:

> I am watching TV—or, in fact, listening to the TV—at the same time as I am playing on the computer; this has become a habit.
>
> Daddy is already asleep; he generally goes to bed around eight o'clock and gets up around six in the morning. He doesn't watch much TV. He boils water after getting up in the morning, in an electric kettle.
>
> I generally go to bed around nine o'clock. Lately, I have been using a digital camera to reproduce old photos, which I find quite meaningful. While doing this, I have also learnt something about photography, and have remembered the days gone by, and had a lot of pleasure.

> As we get older, our life also gets more difficult. It was after that operation that I began to feel the "difficulty." [Note: she had an operation for breast cancer.] Sometimes to get to places not too far away, Daddy can still manage it; as for me, I have hardly gone out lately except to go to the hospital. I move around a bit at home, and spend some time on the computer; my main concern now is to make sure that I don't fall down, that I take care of myself, to try to avoid trouble for myself and my family.

At the end, she said:

> Daddy and I are doing well, don't worry!

Telling each other that all is well is the ending she and I often use.

Living in different cities, communication between us is done more over the Internet; she keeps in touch with the world through the Internet and TV.

Speaking of TV and the Internet, I remember an e-mail that my poet friend Andrew Brewerton sent from Britain in July 2005:

> I was in London last Thursday/Friday in the immediate aftermath of last week's bombing incident, and my hotel was within one of the police cordon areas. The street was closed, and I was escorted to the hotel by a police officer. In the hotel bar I was watching the BBC news reporter speaking to the camera on the TV screen, and through the window I could see the back of the same reporter talking to the BBC camera outside the hotel.

On the morning of January 2, 2007, aboard a flight to Bangkok, my wife and I watched the news report about the six explosions that had taken place in and around the city. The day after our arrival, while we were passing by a high-class shopping mall in the eastern part of the city, a group of policemen sealed off the area. It was rumored that an unidentified object had been found in a telephone booth nearby, that it was suspected to be a bomb.

Every day, we are surrounded by too many news reports about violence and pain. And yet, as the individual's living experience becomes increasingly abstract, these reports all become like background music in a restaurant—it is almost a tough question of daily life as to how to react to the reports about other human beings' pain.

> We see people fighting wars, and houses being consumed by fire, but we only have the strength to worry about our backaches and pimples.

The famous Taiwanese variety show host Kevin Tsai has converted our embarrassing situation into "entertainment" this way:

> We watch others playing football, yet we ourselves just sit in front of the screen, being couch potatoes.
>
> We witness people of all races and of all countries engaging in obsessional and long-lasting love relationships right in front of our eyes, yet we ourselves can be terribly lonely.
>
> Television is nothing but the crystal ball on the Gypsy fortune-teller's table; through it, we see some things about others, and that's it.

Other people's lives are like songs sung in karaoke bars: they are all other people's.

If the joy transmitted through the media always looks conspicuously cheap and becomes a lifeless revelation—it is converted into, so to speak, "entertainment news," as Susan Sontag has pointed out: "In the rich part of the world . . . news has been converted into entertainment"—with regard to the reports about pain, what can we do if not ignore them?

Coming back to my mother, I always forget that the physical pain she has to endure every day is something I cannot imagine, because she never complains about it. Only from time to time, when I myself feel pain in my joints from head to foot because of a cold, do I remember that this type of pain is actually part of her daily life.

The Chinese often say: It can be called life only when all of the five basic taste sensations (sweet, sour, bitter, spicy, and salty) are there. Bitterness is part of life. With my mother, I know that there is always optimism in her will to survive; thus, pain and happiness are only within thoughts.

If human beings' painful experiences today can only be known and shared by people through the media, news reports about pain are ever more related to audience ratings and their own eye-catchingness. By the same token, we are also removed from authentically joyful experiences, and we even forget that pain and joy have always been mutually interchangeable.

Nobody can decide beforehand whether someone is agonizing or happy.

Reality does not equal the reality shown in the media. Reality is "reality," not the portrayal of reality. We need the world as seen through the eyes of the media, but it doesn't mean that the world only exists in the form of "media reality."

Touching, feeling, and acting are the ways to reestablish a normal relationship with the world.

"Man, the measure of all things, speaks here through my mouth and narrates in my own language that which my eyes have seen." These are Che Guevara's first words in the book The Motorcycle Diaries. These words once again kindle our longing for the high-speed sensual life. Although we were once fed up with too many T-shirts printed with his portrait and too many restaurants and bars named after him, Guevara has always been the person who constantly grew from the trials and tribulations of travel and illness, who brought together philosophical theses and humble desires such as simply wanting a bowl of soup, who was an asthmatic explorer and his own grave-digger. He is the "I" that we once were—the "I" who was wide open and direct that we have gradually forgotten.

We are constantly going back and forth between one company and another in the city, between one office building and another where the companies are, between one shopping mall and another near the office building, and between one article and another displayed in the shopping mall, until one day when, looking down upon all living creatures through a glass-panel wall from a hundred meters up, we are suddenly conscious that we have already become a "traveler" in our own life and that we keep a perfunctory safe distance from life, as the meaning of life is being removed from this line of sight. It seems that our eyes long to see different things, but very soon, this impulse will disappear from the safe "travel route" of everyday life.

Do we still remember the last time we had a strong impulse to throw ourselves into life?

> If he works only for himself, he may perhaps become a famous man of learning, a great sage, an excellent poet, but he can never be a perfect, truly great man. . . . If we have chosen the position in life in which we can most of all work for mankind, no burdens can bow us down, because they are sacrifices for the benefit of all; then we shall experience no petty, limited, selfish joy, but our happiness will belong to millions, our deeds will live on quietly but perpetually at work, and over our ashes will be shed the hot tears of noble people.

A friend sent me these extracts from Karl Marx's essay "Reflections of a Young Man on the Choice of a Profession." This friend worked at the Party's newspaper in the past, and is now a freelancer. He didn't want to disclose his name, and didn't make any comment on these passages either. Did he want to express his nostalgia for the revolutionary utopia of the old days or his critique of the loss of values in China today? Or did he simply want to have a dig at me?

It is just as film director Krzysztof Kieslowski said: "How necessary and how difficult it is to tell a moral story today!"

In one of my novels, I created the character of a film director, and he comments on who is struggling with the conflict between imagination and reality this way: "I feel that the situation of a filmmaker is like a person who is enjoying the pleasure of making love on the couch and who suddenly sees an SOS appeal for sick children that appears on the TV screen. Life is full of metaphors, but it is very difficult if you want to spell them out clearly. Very often, because of ego, budget, or desire, we lose the courage to act."

Without any doubt, the same perplexity will also extend to virtual life because it is also a world created by men.

> Some younger friends have been talking about Second Life with great enthusiasm lately. Through playing this game, you can do many things that are possible or not in real life; for example, having a meal, dancing, shopping, singing karaoke, driving a car, traveling, making friends with the opposite sex, going across a strait, buying real estate, etc. You can design your own image, and choose your sex and social status however you want. There is an Internet currency called the Linden Dollar, and this virtual currency is even exchangeable for real currency: 250 Linden Dollars can be converted to one U.S. dollar. In addition, through this virtual life, you can communicate or trade with residents of Second Life throughout the world. In fact, the world of Second Life is strikingly similar to and has a close relationship with the real world. A poor musician friend of mine bragged to me how he had started to buy land and to possess virtual currency in Second Life. He believed that the game not only simulated life, but also allowed him to do things that he was not able to achieve in life. For him, it was the real life. As a result, I was enticed into visiting Second Life's home page and registered a new name for myself: China Tracy. I picked up a wild girl who looked like the offspring of a Chinese and an American couple. Ha-ha, my adventure was just about to start. The first thing I saw was that I was flying in Second Life . . .

There is nothing odd about the fact that so many people are joining the Second Life that artist Cao Fei described to me. Nevertheless, I think that Cao has understood well that virtual life as another reality is now penetrating the shrinking imagination of artists and forces you to respond to it. At the same time, I am also touched by what artist Zheng Guogu declared: "People don't die in a game, but they do in reality."

It is the one-timeness of life (life cannot be repeated) and the irrevocability of time (even in virtual life!) that fascinate me.

If we all agree that existing cities are not the destination of human life and it is only by chance that we make encounters with the world at certain moments and in certain places, perhaps we will see a moment such as this:

> I see the pastoral countryside shrinking rapidly in the setting sun's rays,
> Like the healing these past two days of the inflamed and ulcerated wound on my shin.
> Bright windows, humans' ardent melancholy.
> A young mother-to-be hanging out clothes, arms akimbo.
> An old couple walking through the living room, supporting each other by the arms.

And you, hiding in the shadow of September, are never original.

I took notes quickly: poetry flashes and disappears.

This is a moment that my poet friend Ling Yue revealed to me. I know that at this moment, he is working as an ordinary teacher at a school that fosters talent for the state machine. But who knows? Perhaps amidst the intense flows of the inner heart, every thinking man finds himself on the battlefield of daily life.

In that split second, I saw the transparent relationship between quick note-taking and the movement of reality; this transparency will transcend all of the present gulfs that exist between pain and joy, between us and the world in the same way that invisible sunlight and air do. ■

Translated by Yu Hsiao Hwei.

IMAGES

page 225 Guangzhou city view

page 229 Nansha New City public square, Guangzhou

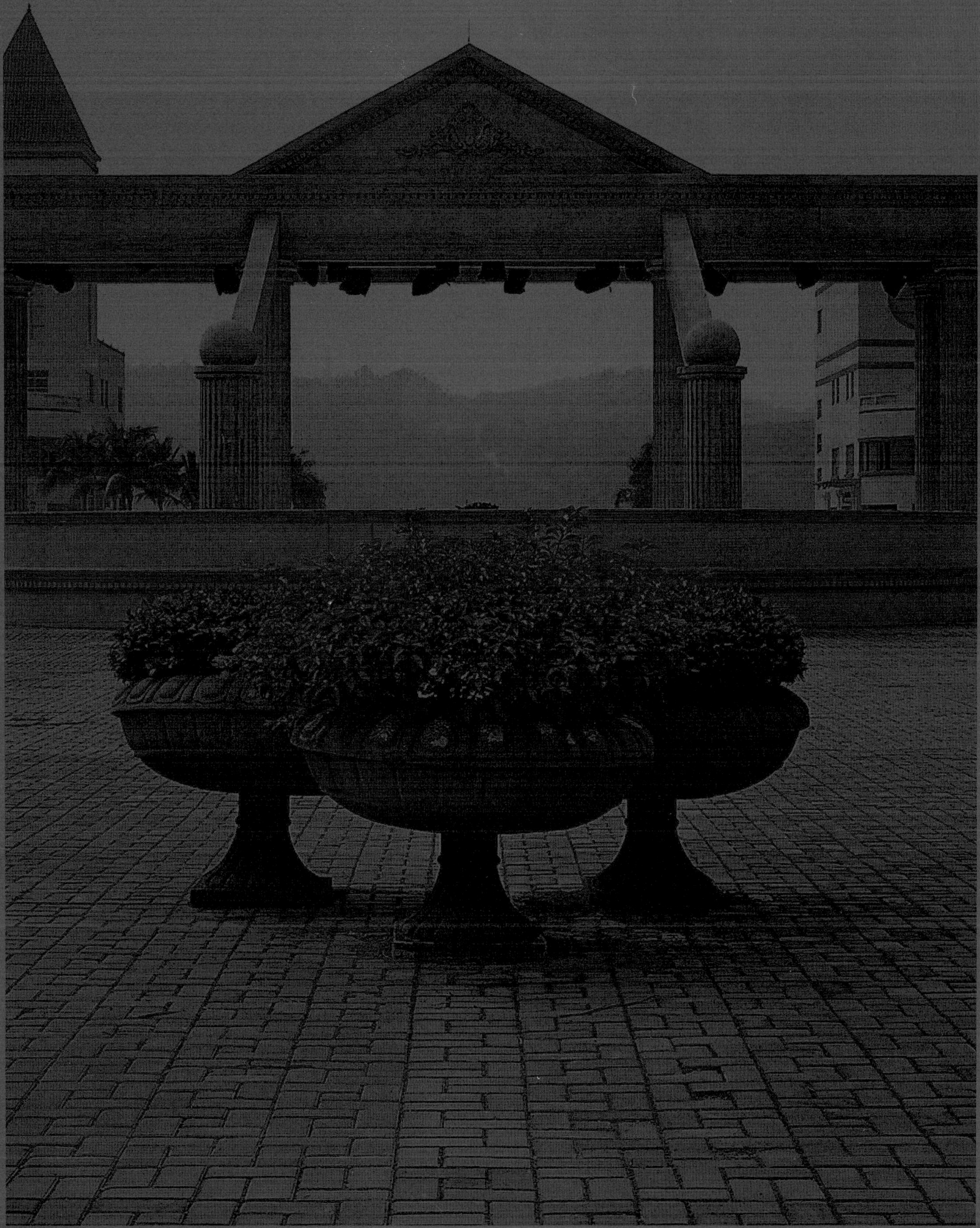

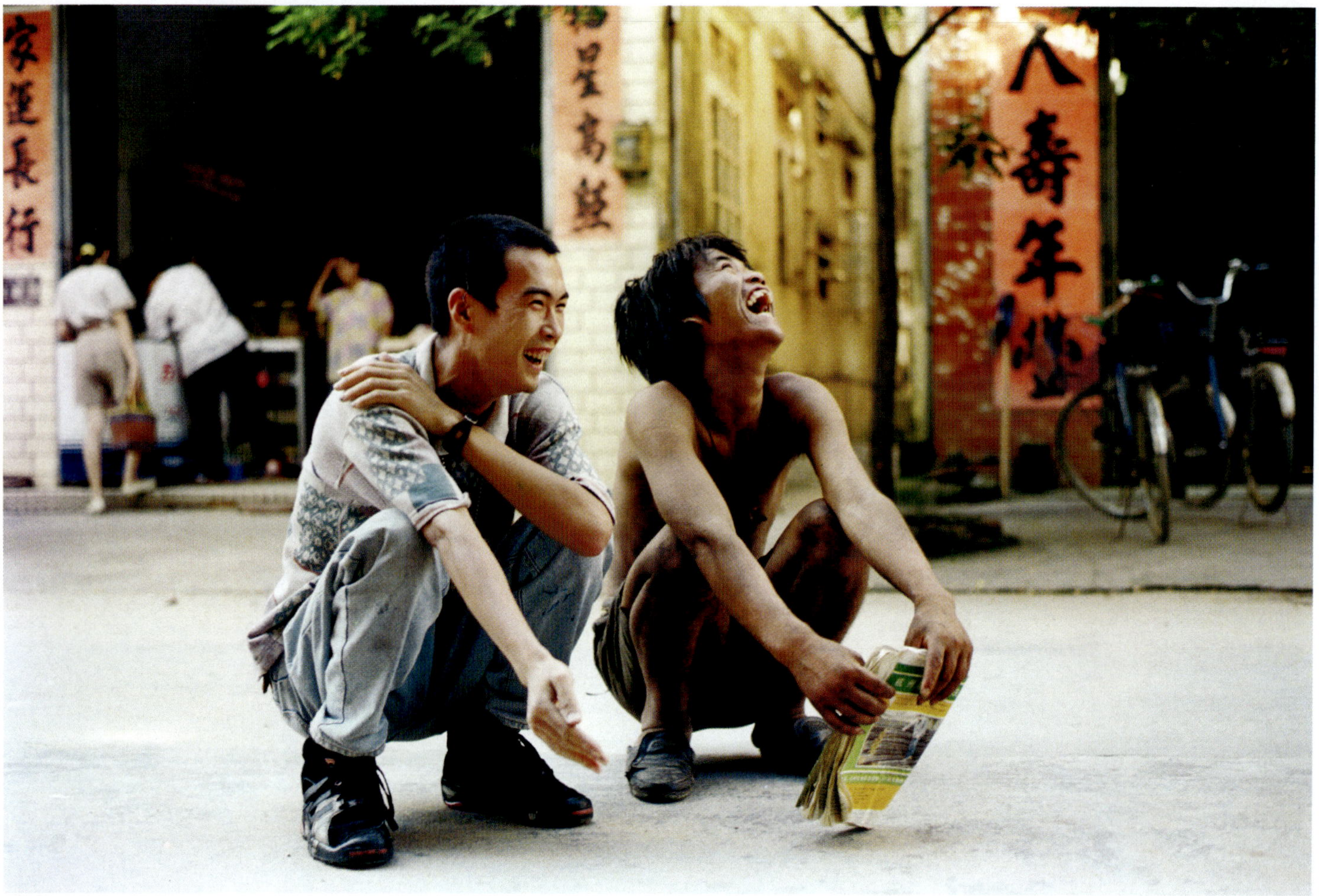

Me and My Teacher 1993 color photograph

ZHENG GUOGU'S POSITION IN THE WORLD

Born in China, 1970. Lives and works in Yangjiang, China.

One of the most unclassifiable yet respected Chinese artists working today, Zheng Guogu is also a conceptualist whose multifaceted body of work blurs the boundaries between life and art. This description, of course, has lost much of its efficacy in recent years from overuse, but is still relevant to an understanding of Zheng's prolific, organic artistic output, which is closely tied to his location. Yangjiang, where he was born and continues to live and work, is a coastal town in the Guangdong province in southern China. The city is far from notable as a cultural center, let alone as a locus of contemporary artistic production, so it is against such a backdrop that his early photographic works become particularly remarkable. In 1995, he asked the woman he was courting to pose as his bride at a local wedding photo studio. *My Bride* (1995), a group of almost saccharine images embodying the idea of Westernized, bourgeois romance, departs little from the conventions of staged studio photography, an increasingly popular means of expressing status in today's China. Although Zheng's female collaborator later rejected his marriage proposal, he found a bride the following year and produced with her another series of photographs. The highly intimate snapshots that constitute *Honeymoon* (1996), in contrast to *My Bride*, convey the couple's genuinely tender bond.

At the same time that he turned himself into the subject of autobiographical accounts and fantasies, the artist also began to commit those around him to film. *The Vagarious Life of Yangjiang Youths* (1996) consists of many images of his roguish friends acting out glamorized violence. They are seen wielding guns and knives, mock-torturing one another, and generally reveling in thuggish behaviors. Their feigned acts of aggression were, in fact, inspired by stylized representations in the TV programs and computer games they were watching and playing, and the illusion concocted by these assumed identities is corroborated by the artist's statement: "I'm a director who can't direct, and they are actors who can't act."[1] Zheng's casual, unplanned, and immediate approach here is quite distinct from the popular tendencies in much of contemporary Chinese photography to monumentalize urbanism or theatricalize the everyday. Even though the subjects in this series are "actors" and the depictions cannot be taken at face value as a sociological study, they do reflect and embody the fact that the city of Yangjiang is located in close proximity to Hong Kong and all its commodities. Zheng's work, then, is an expression of a subjective, individualized reception of localized cultural (re)production vis-à-vis a globalized culture. Such consumer goods have informed and shaped his construction of objects

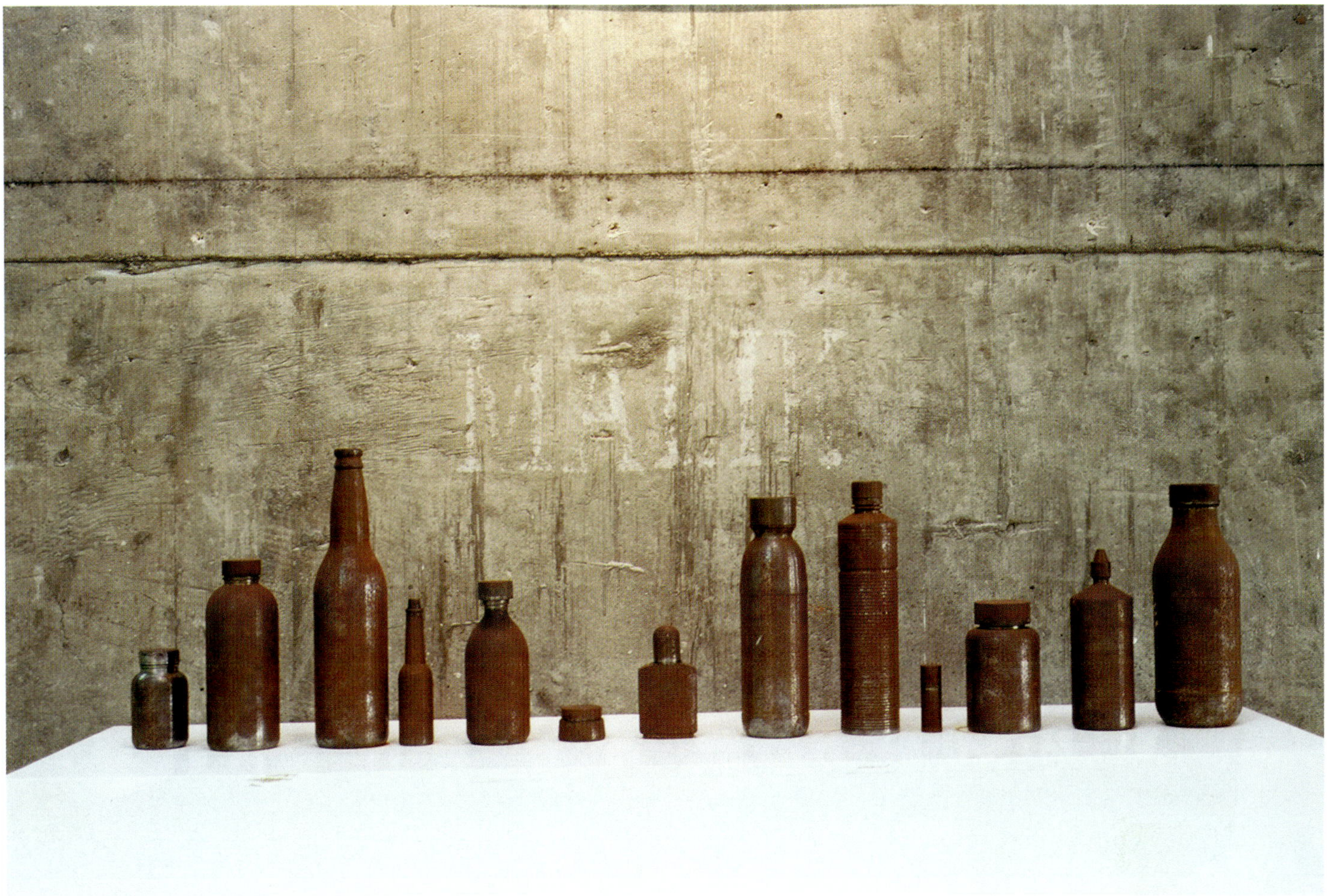

AD 2000, Rust Another 2000 Years I 1999–2000 cast-iron objects

as well. In *AD 2000, Rust Another 2000 Years I* (1999–2000), the artist cast in iron items that he found in local supermarkets, which were increasing in number and changing due to a transforming economy, as a "response to the heavy memories of the commodity exchanges of my childhood."[2]

Zheng's work addresses consumption not only as he and those around him experience it but also as the basis for a new relationship between himself as an art-maker and those of the monied and sophisticated class who purchase his works. *Ten Thousand Customers* (1997–present), a grid of photographic images printed in the same size as their contact strips, trumps the principles of multiple production of an identical artwork by proposing an edition of ten thousand. This yet-to-be-completed work is in fact not an edition at all, as each one, individually assembled from a blend of photographs of TV screens and manufactured goods, is different from the next.

For this exhibition, Zheng presents a new installation titled *My Home Is Your Museum* (2007), conceived and realized in collaboration with curator and writer Hu Fang.[3] An evolving and changing environment that adapts to different venues, the work in this particular iteration consists of a type of garden, with a new version of *AD 2000, Rust Another 2000 Years* emerging out of a floor covered in gravel and hexagonal bricks, and surrounded by a photographic mural and two paintings. *Me and My Teacher* (1993/2007) is a blown-up snapshot of the artist side-by-side with a disheveled, scantily-clad, unbathed man. The two are pictured squatting in the street and having a hearty laugh. The "teacher" had apparently gone mad and was wandering the city, but Zheng says he learned a lot from the man's direct, unmediated relationship with the world. The paintings *MOMA I Party No. 1* (2006–2007) and *Landscape of the Age of Empire No. 1* (2006) are both photorealist works done by a professional painter: the former is based on a scene shot by the artist of an opening party at the Museum of Modern Art, New York; and the latter is an idealized scene of a water-and-rock garden he's constructing at his home in Yangjiang. The depictions of art-world glitterati and a utopian landscape provide a stark conversational counterpoint to the image of the innocent and simpatico affinity existing between the artist and a social outcast. Both paintings are also embedded with clipped headlines from popular Hong Kong magazines. Their sensationalized, trivial meanings are wholly incongruous to the subjects pictured, but the uncanny overlaying effectively alludes to the motherboard of circuitry operating in the mind of an artist who freely shuttles between several incommensurate spheres inside a fluid world of information and transactions. This *gesamtkunstwerk* is a recombined mosaic of a creative mind defining its position in the world vis-à-vis realms of human relationships, cultural status, commodity exchange, and even built and natural ecologies.

DC

1. Zheng Guogu, quoted in Hans van Dijk, "The Relationship between the Fake and the Real Is Very Subtle," in *Zheng Guogu: Cross Back and Forth Quickly* (Shanghai: ShangART and Timezone 8 Ltd., 2003), 85.

2. Zheng Guogu, unpublished interview with Hu Fang, 2007.

3. Hu Fang, also a contributor to this catalogue, has written about Zheng Guogu numerous times and worked closely with him on curatorial projects. This essay has greatly benefited from my conversations with Hu and has been informed by his writings.

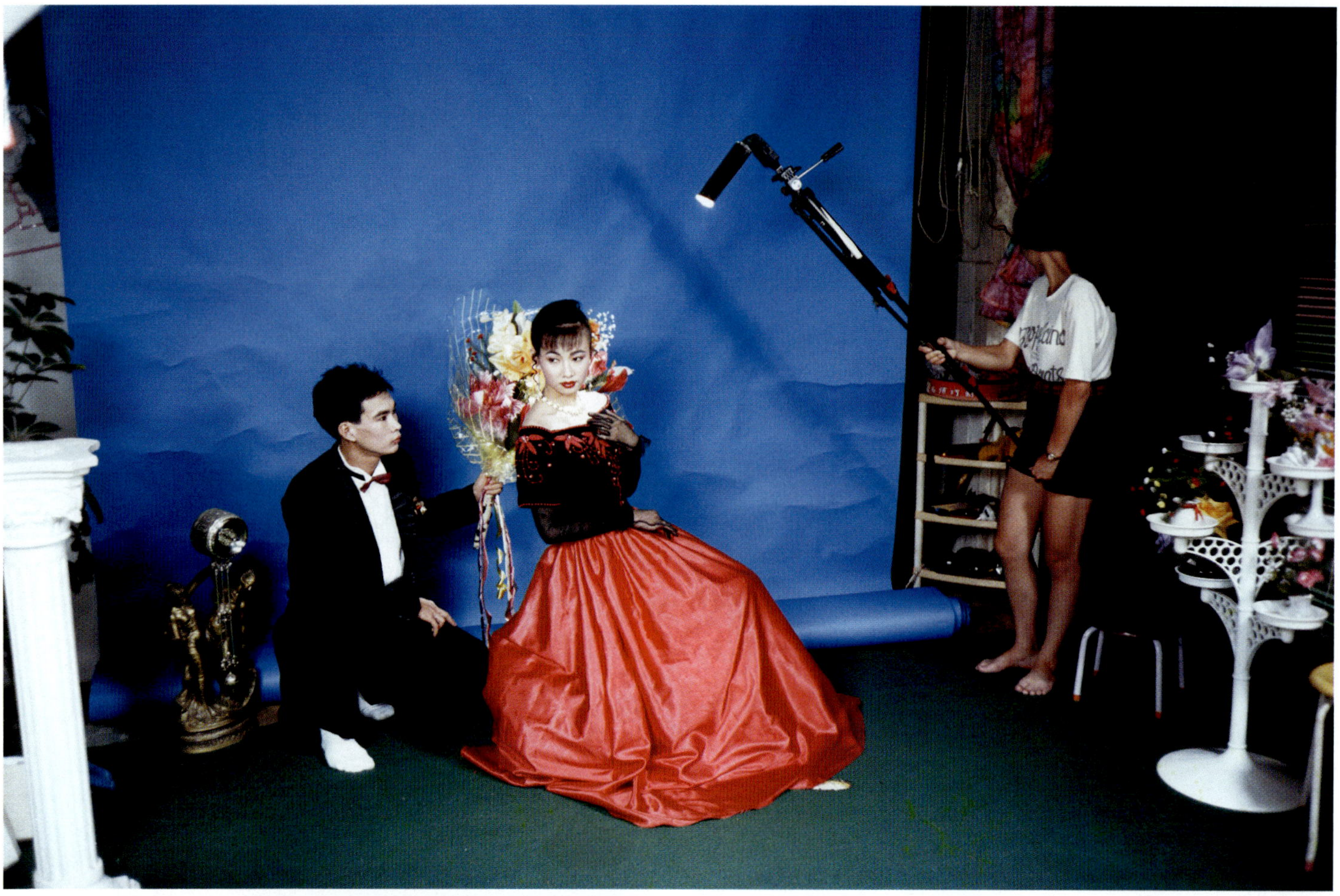

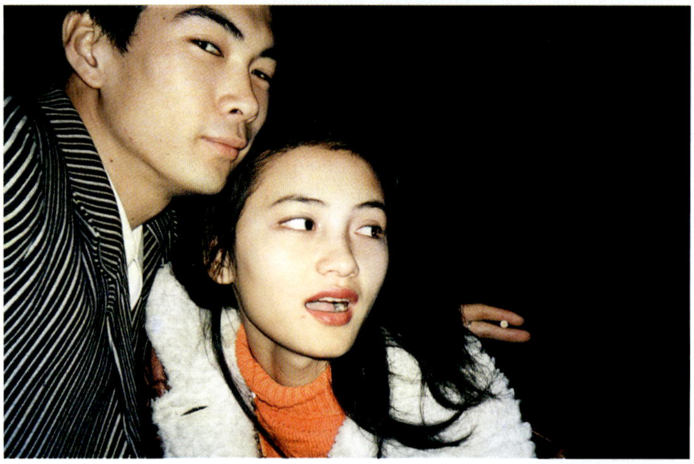

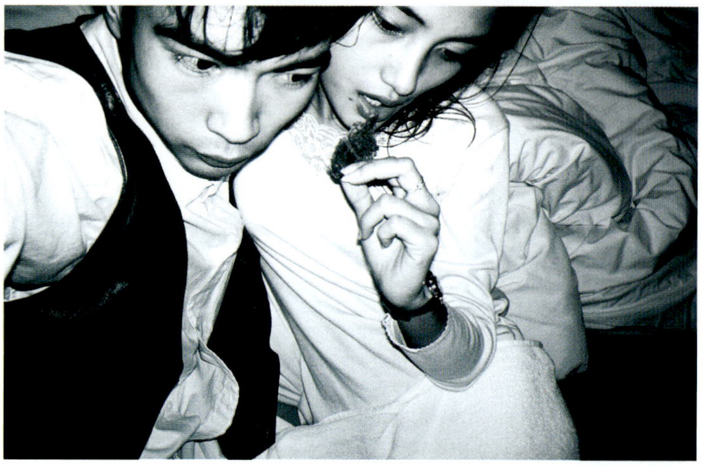

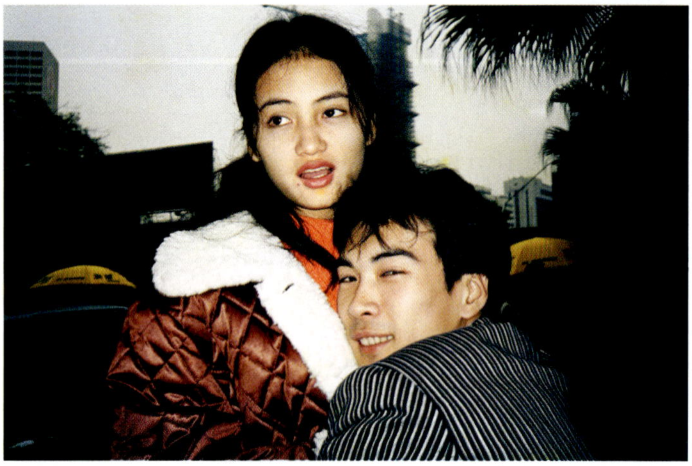

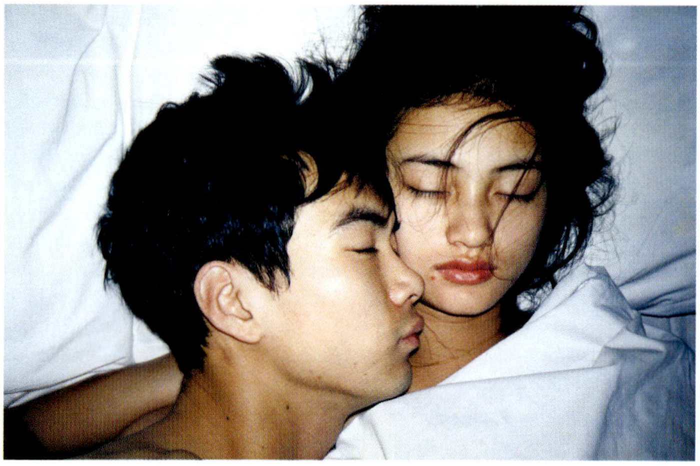

top: *My Bride* 1995 color photographs bottom rows: *Honeymoon* 1996 color photographs

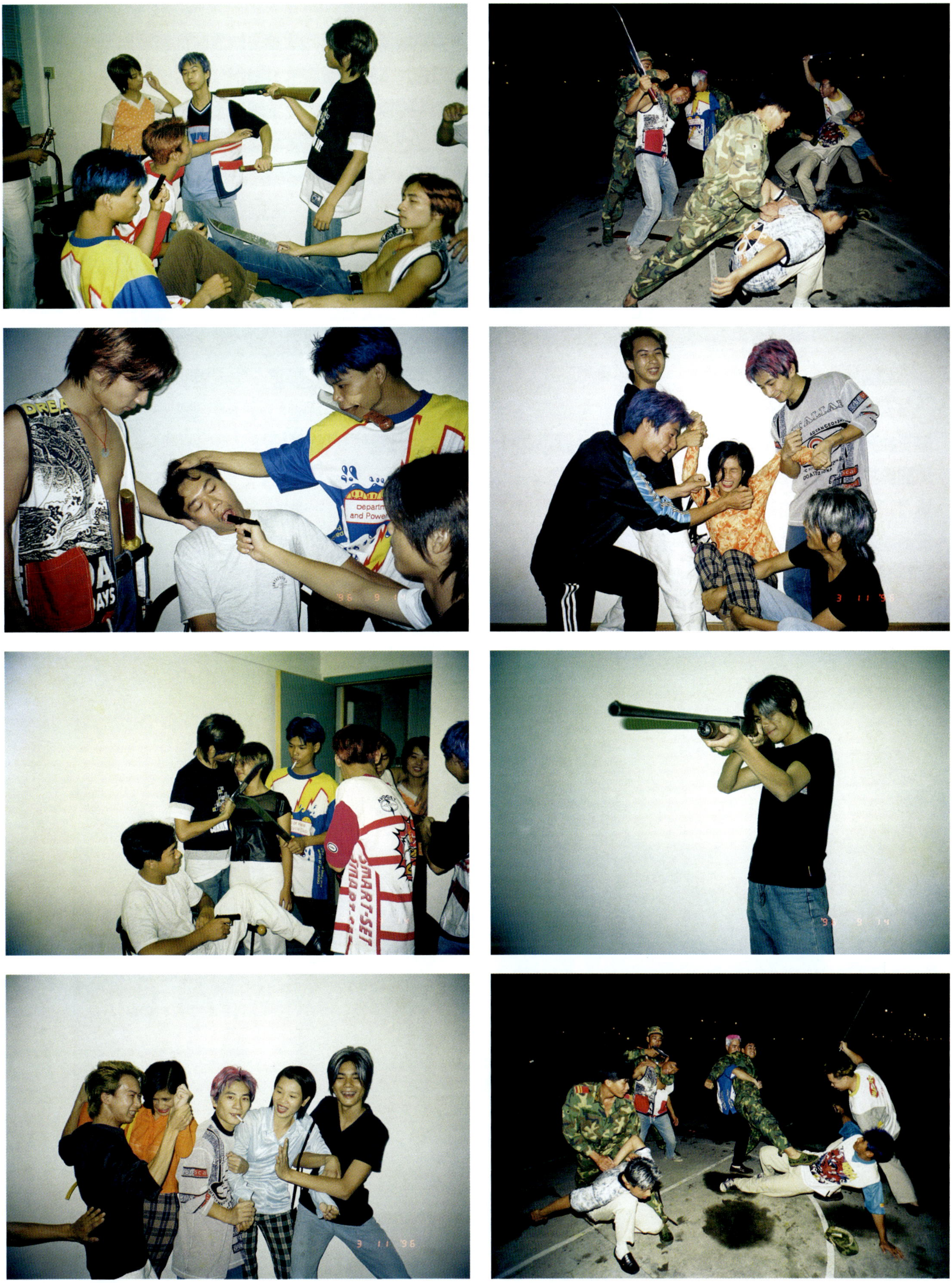

The Vagarious Life of Yangjiang Youths 1996 color photographs

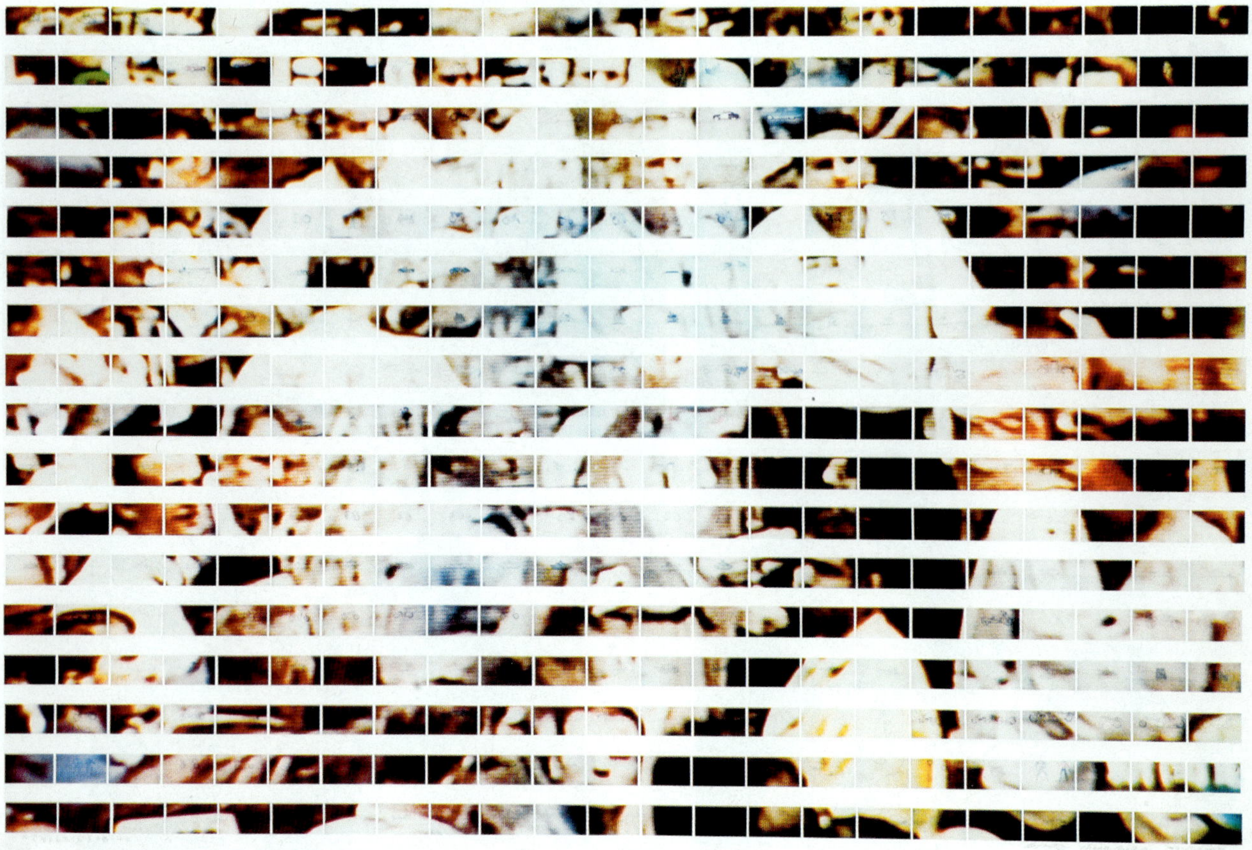

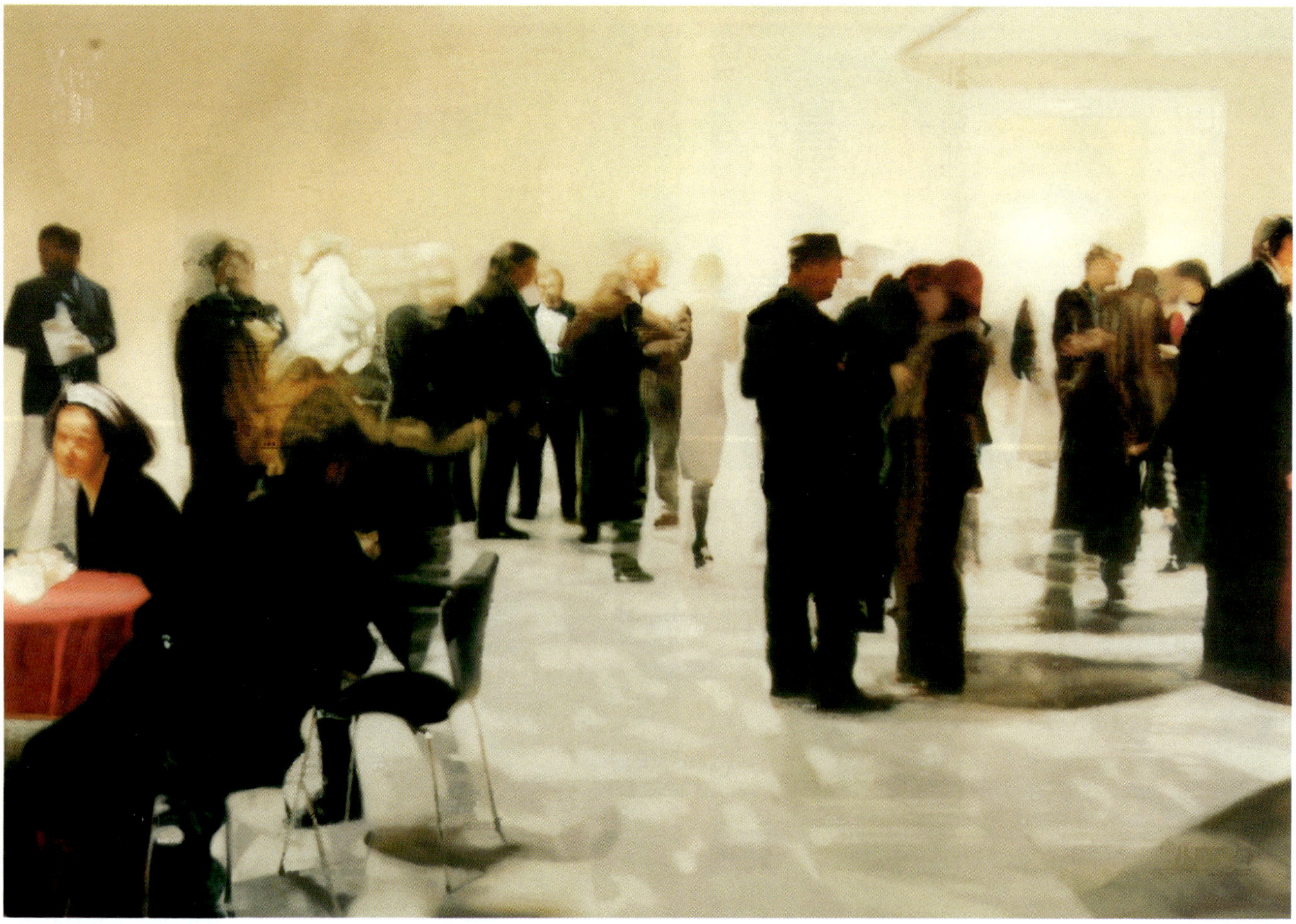

top: *Ten Thousand Customers, 213/10000* 1997–2005 photographs bottom: *MOMA I Party No. 1* 2006–2007 oil on canvas

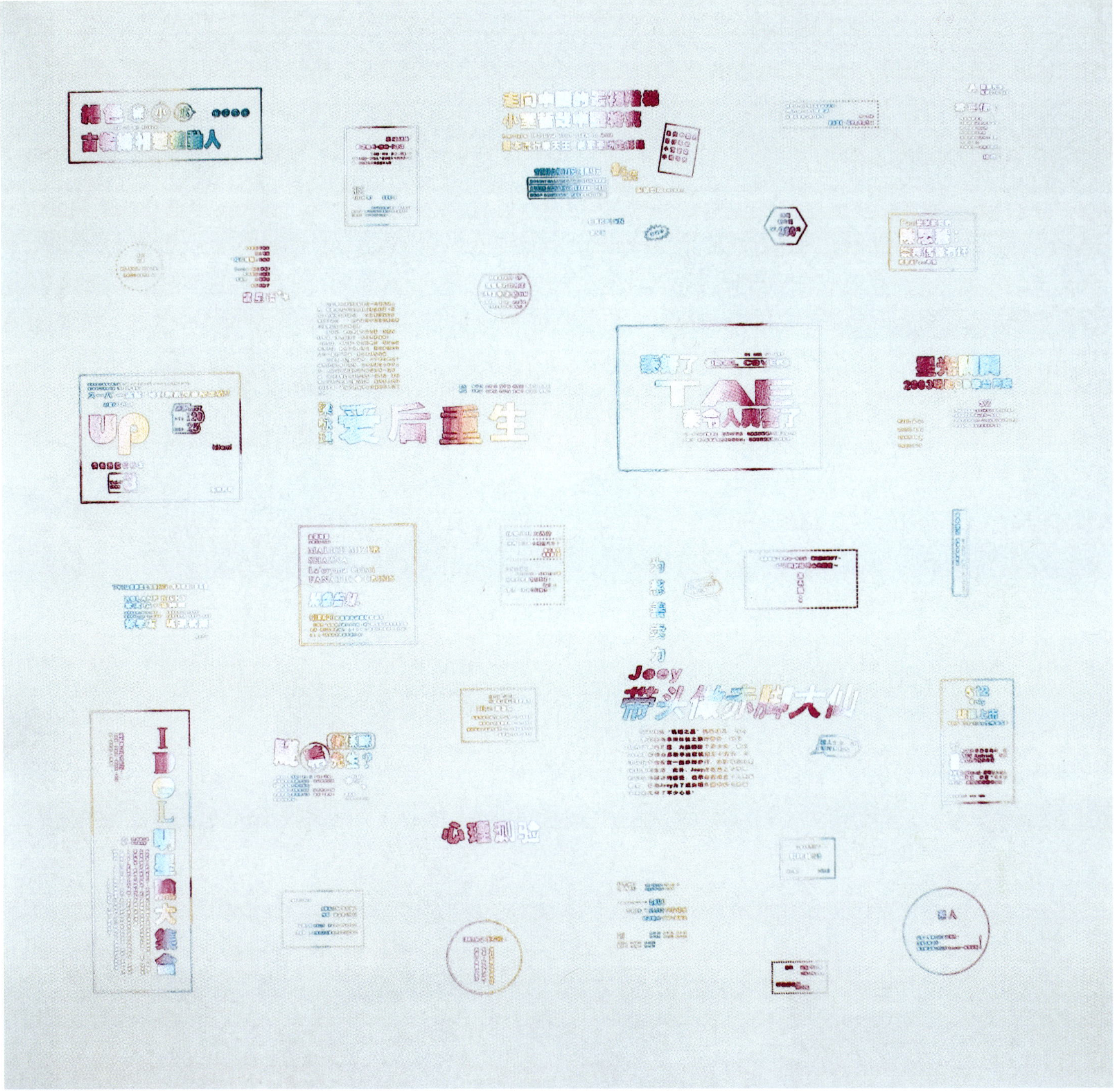

Computer Is Controlled by Pig's Brain—79 2006 oil on carpet

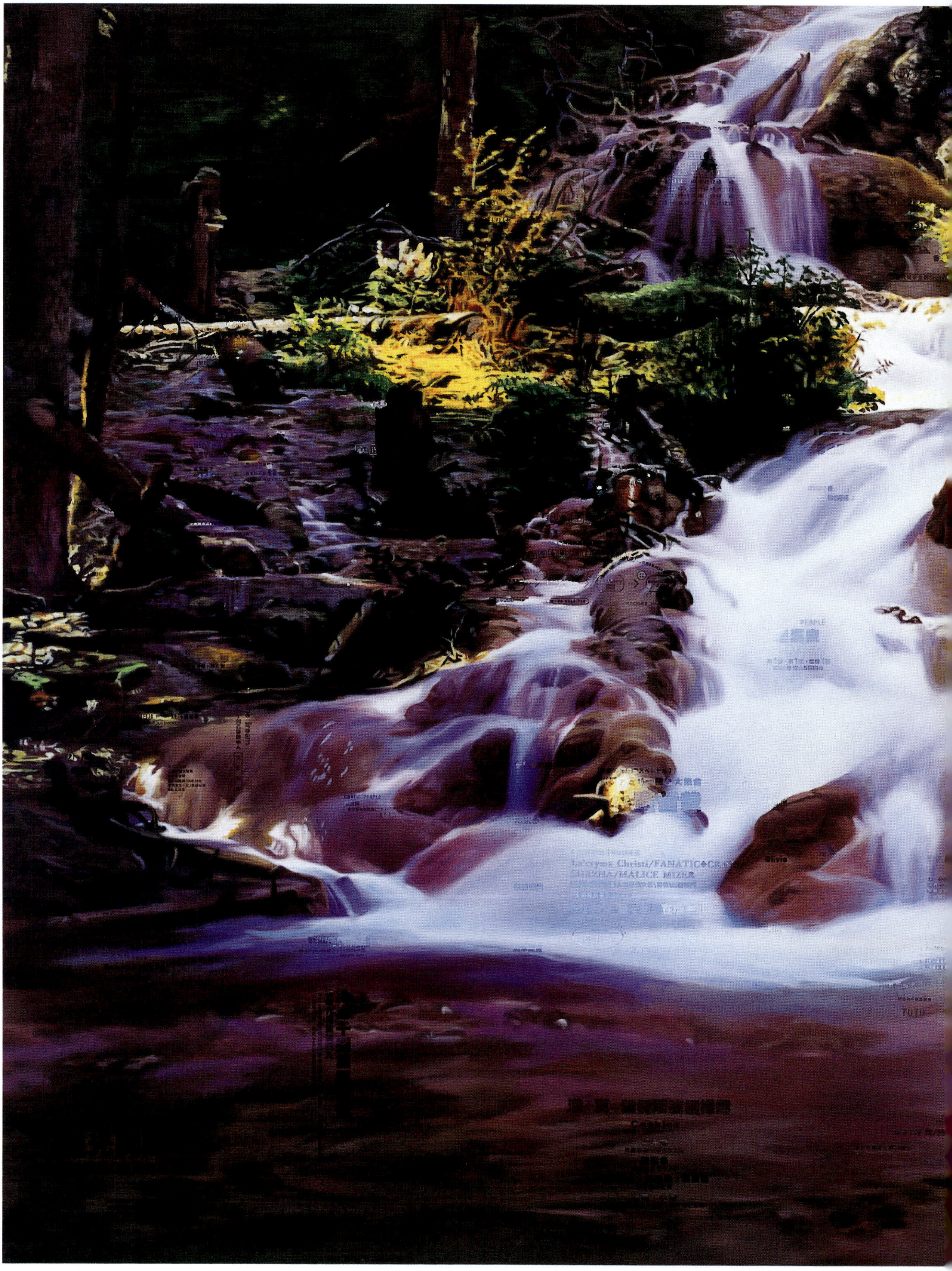

Landscape of the Age of Empire No. 1 2006 oil on canvas

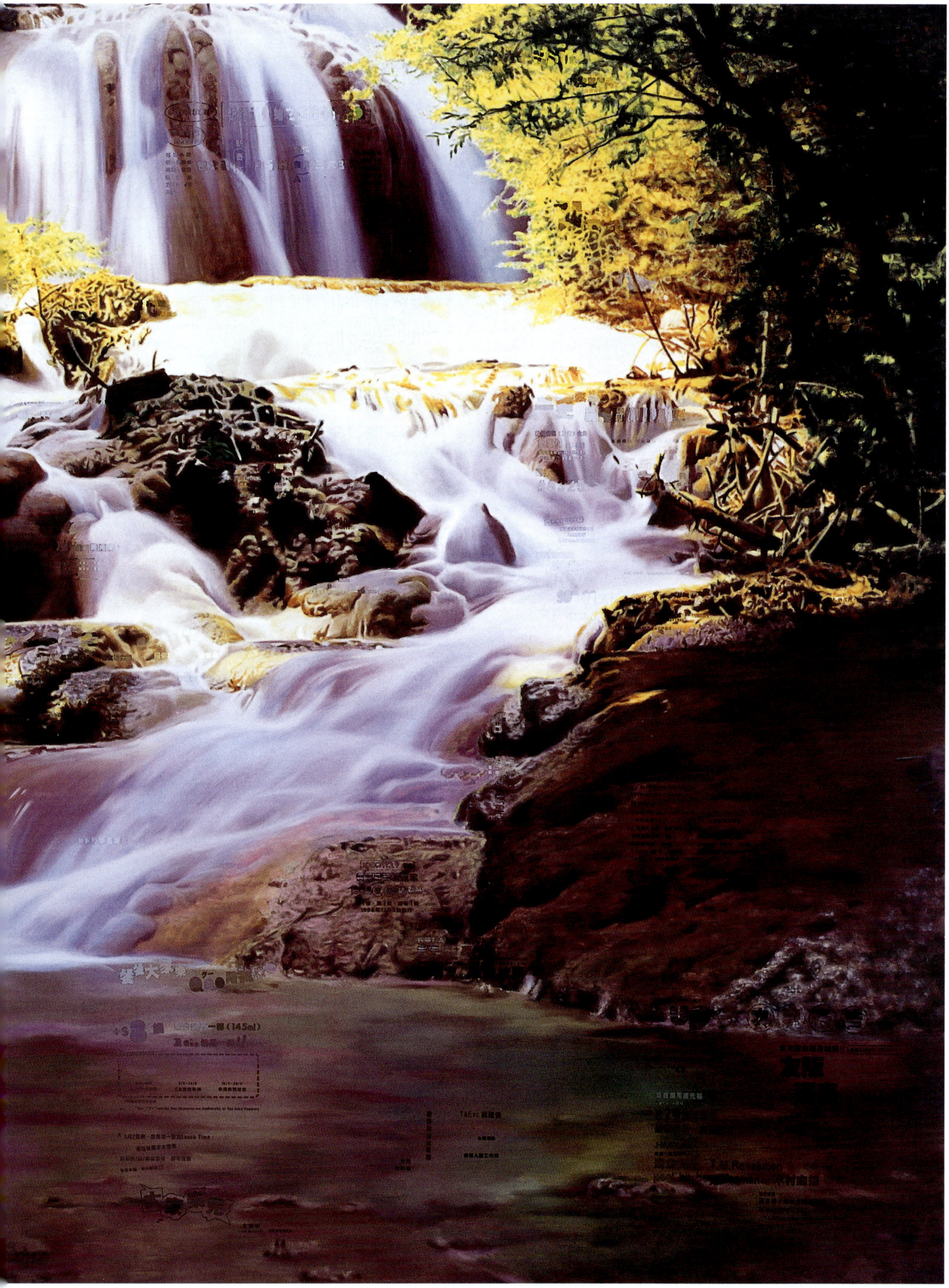

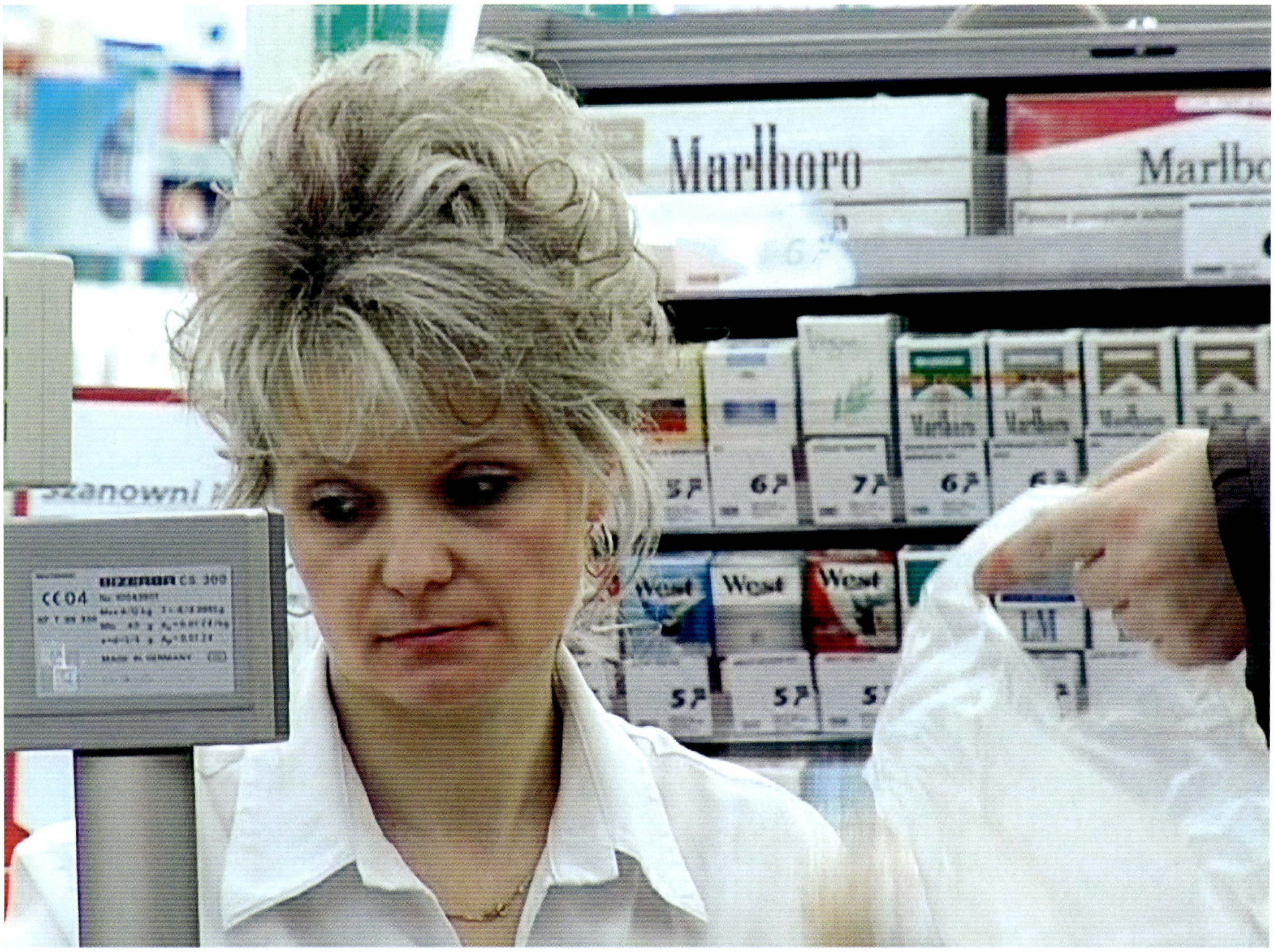

Still from *Dorota* 2006 video transferred to DVD (color, sound); 15 minutes

SUBTLE SHIFTS: ARTUR ŻMIJEWSKI

Born in Poland, 1966. Lives and works in Warsaw.

Since the mid-1990s, Artur Żmijewski has been creating anxious, strange, and beautiful films and videos with an intensely emotional impact. Most of his projects examine spiritual and physical aspects of human psychology. The stories Żmijewski tells map the mentality of his main characters in such a way that we are compelled to accept their autonomy and renegotiate our own thinking in response. He has stated that his ultimate goal is to subtly shift our thoughts so that we might reconsider how we treat people who are marginalized by society, lonely, or disenfranchised, and that the central question driving his work is, "Will the viewer dismiss what he sees and retain his own view, or will he allow the work to violate him and introduce into his brain a revelation?"[1]

One way in which the artist reveals certain ingrained ideas and prejudices to his viewers is through revisiting historical traumas. He has explored the therapeutic potential of invoking past injuries in his films *Game of Tag* (1999), in which Polish men and women play tag naked in a concentration-camp gas chamber, and *Repetition* (2005), a study of the psychological conditions of authoritarianism in a re-creation of the Stanford Prison Experiment originally conducted by American psychologist Philip Zimbardo in 1971.[2] Both films reawaken the psychic wreckage of World War II, as does *Pilgrimage* (2003), a documentation of a Polish Catholic group's visit to Israel that uncovers the group's anti-Semitism, and *Our Songbook* (2003), in which elderly Israelites who had spent their childhood in Poland before the war were asked to sing any Polish songs they could remember. By taking on the subject of the Holocaust, Żmijewski turns a collective memory into a game that diffuses the present traumatic effects of historical prejudices.

Danuta, *Dorota*, and *Halina* (2006) are three roughly fifteen-minute-long videos. Each shows us a day in the life of the Polish working-class woman after whom the piece is titled. The project began with a newspaper advertisement posted by the artist seeking employed persons who would agree to be filmed for an entire day. He interviewed and selected a laundress, a factory worker, and a supermarket cashier, and then followed each with a camera for a full twenty-

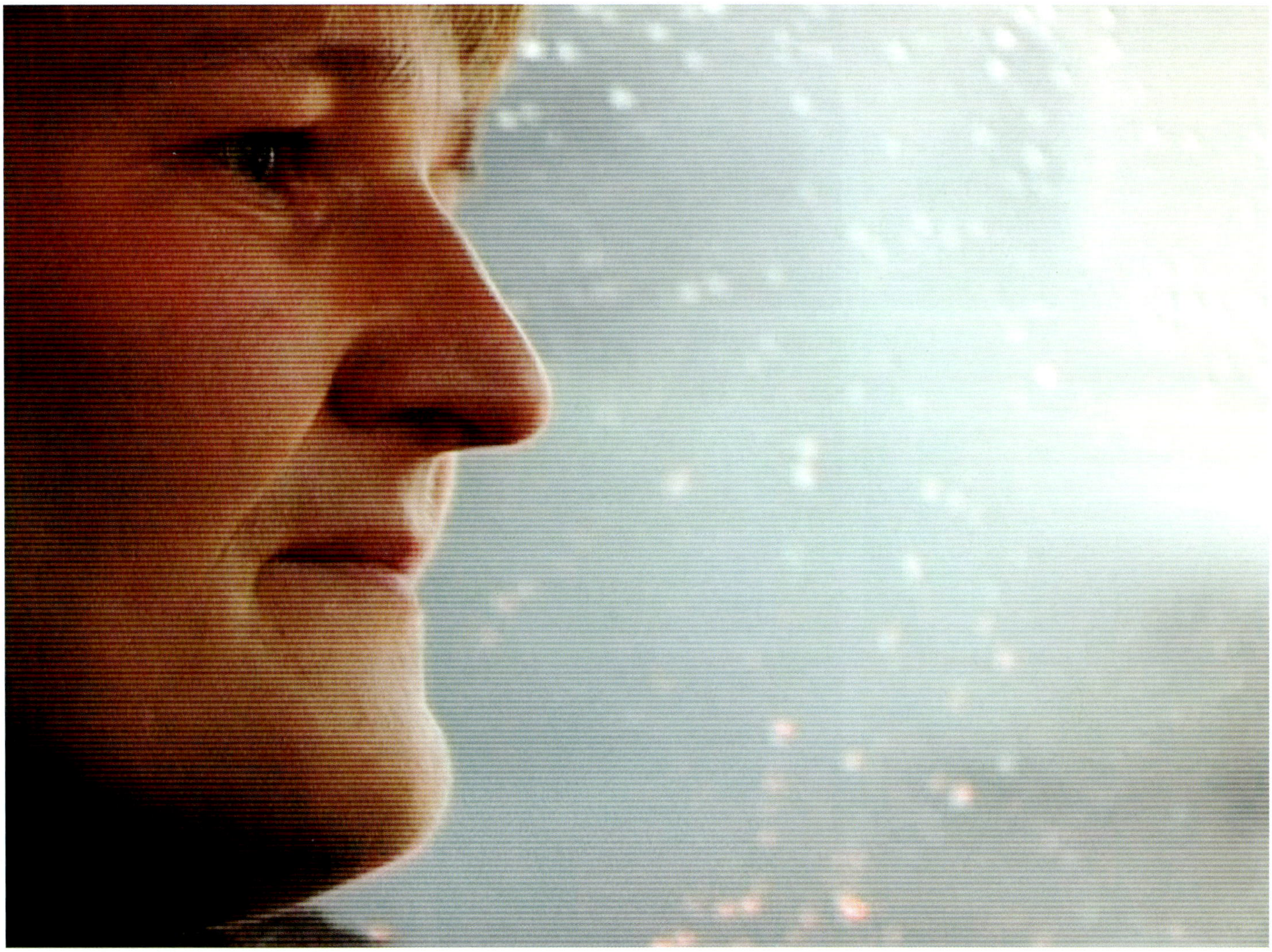

Still from *Halina* 2006 video transferred to DVD (color, sound); 15:32 minutes

four hours. The footage was edited to reveal the strict structure of the women's lives: riding the bus to work, repeating their habitual job routines, preparing meals for their family, and taking care of their homes. Although the day's events are out of sequence, the slow pacing and minimal dialogue convey a feeling of lonely monotony.

The narratives of these women suggest another reconsideration of the historical record—this time of Poland's more recent Communist past. The worker was a galvanizing figure in Polish history. From the Polish United Workers' Party's control in the Communist era to its end in the early 1980s brought about by the Solidarity trade union led by Lech Wałesa,[3] the worker has been the source of modern social reforms and power in Poland. For Żmijewski, to invoke this figure is therefore to reawaken both the optimism and distress of the Communist era. However, the artist shifts our understanding of the standard proletariat hero. By approaching the figure from the perspective of individual women, he repositions the worker on the margins of power. Thereby, he juxtaposes old icons with new and ultimately unchanged routines of labor, even amid the economic ideals of the European Union, which Poland joined in 2004.

RH

1. Artur Żmijewski, "A Favorite Theory of Art," master's thesis for Warsaw University, in *If It Happened Only Once It's As If It Never Happened*, trans. Marzena Guzowska, exh. cat. (Warsaw: Zachęta National Gallery of Art for the Polish Pavilion at the 2005 Venice Biennale), 158.

2. For the experiment conducted at Stanford University, Zimbardo re-created the physical trappings and psychological aura of a prison. He randomly assigned half of his student volunteers the role of prisoner and the other half that of guard. He used these findings to conclude that physical abuse is part of the psychological condition of authority in such an environment. However, Zmijewski's film contradicts Zimbardo's conclusion: in the artist's film, one of the "prisoners" manages to manipulate a "guard" into calling off the experiment. Zimbardo eventually had to halt the simulation because of the violence that ensued between the two groups.

3. Recipient of a 1983 Nobel Peace Prize, Wałesa served as president of the Republic of Poland from 1990 to 1995.

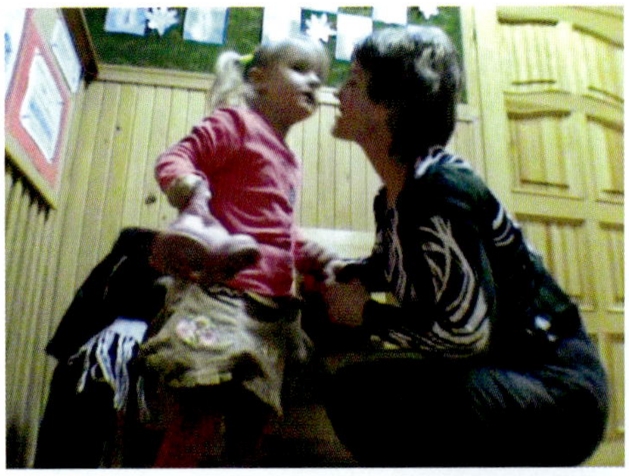
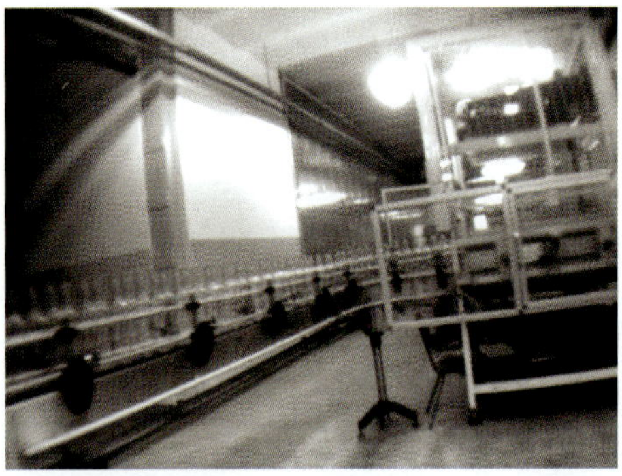
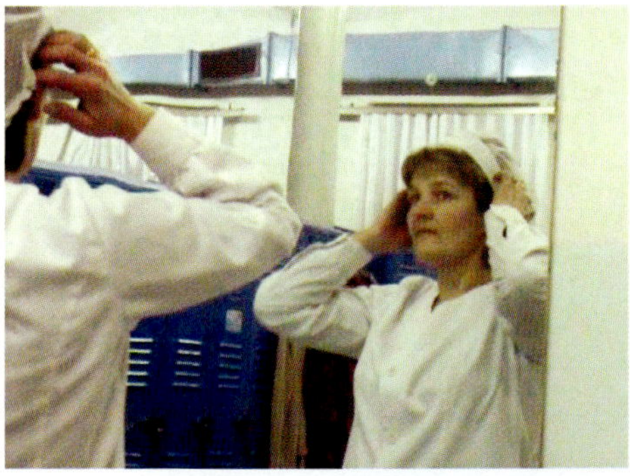
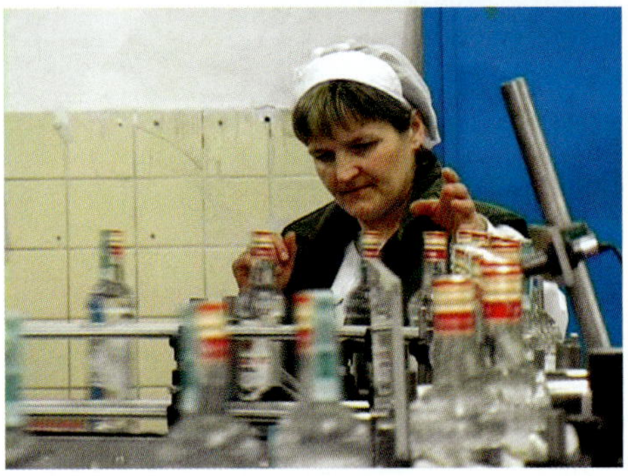
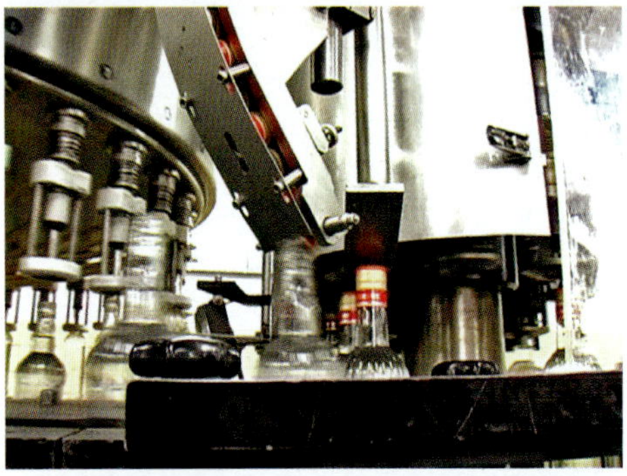
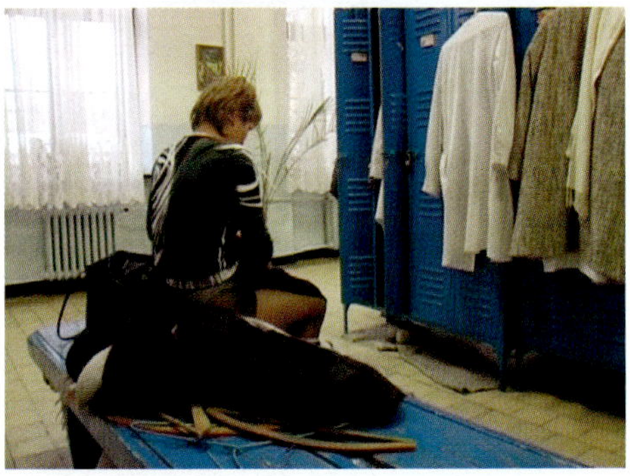
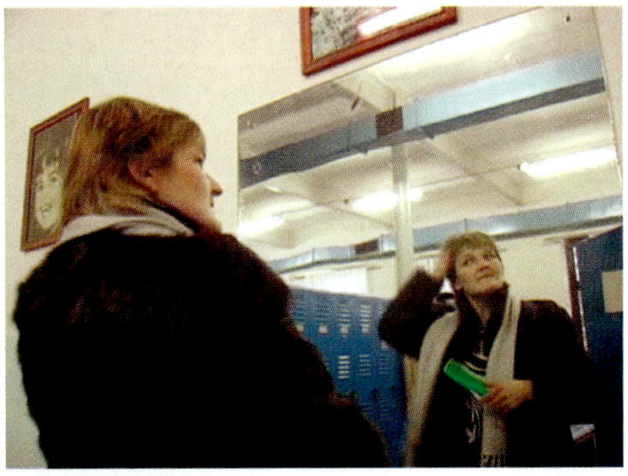
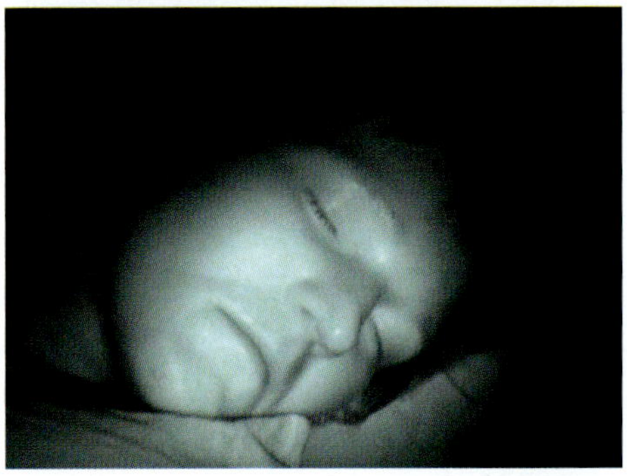
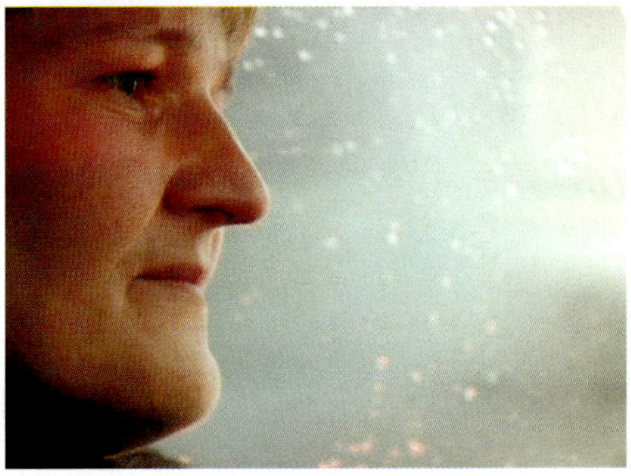
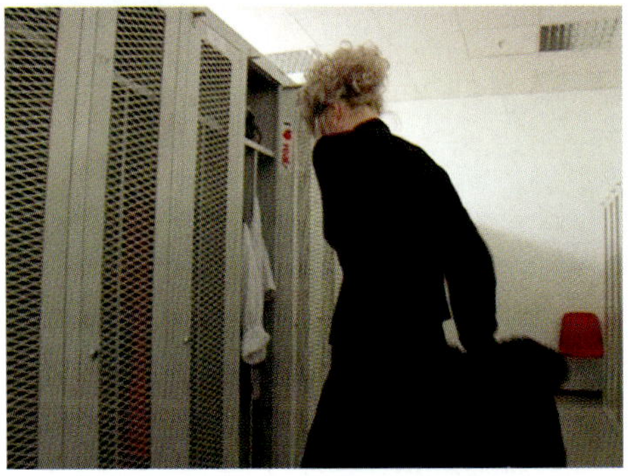
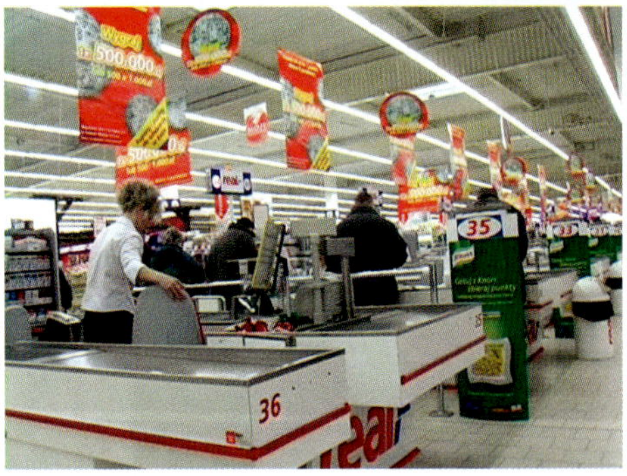
500.000
36
35
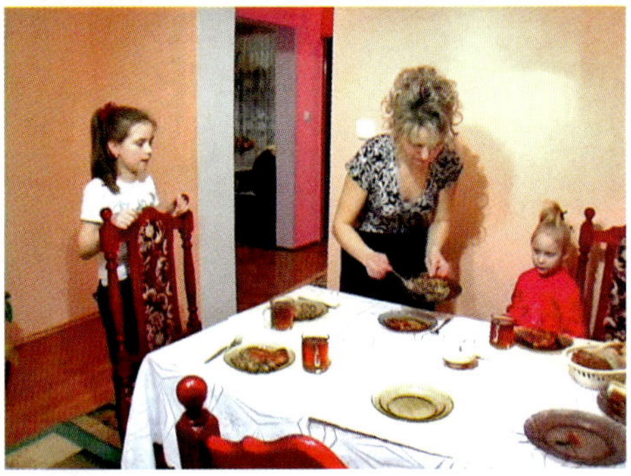
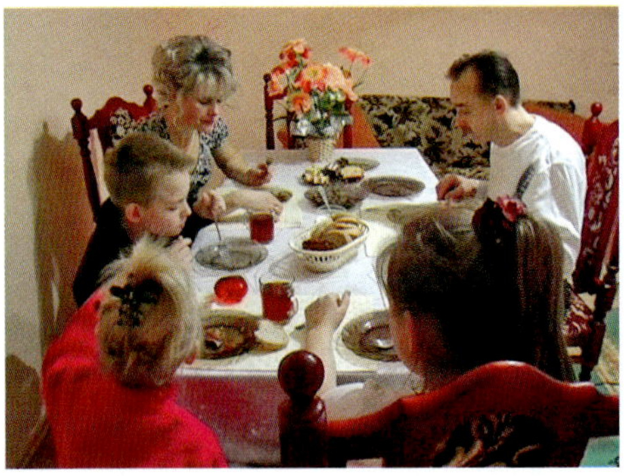
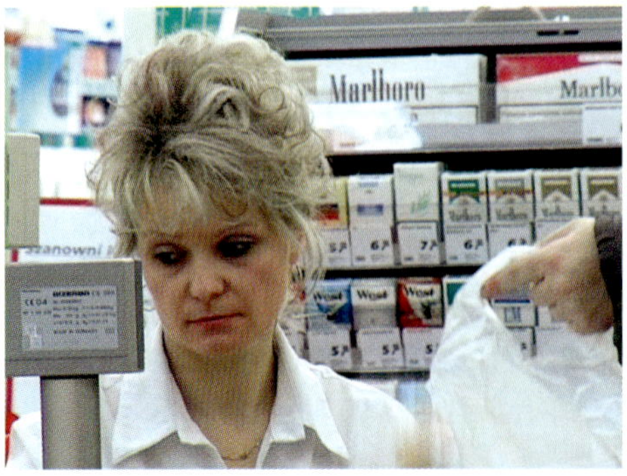
Marlboro
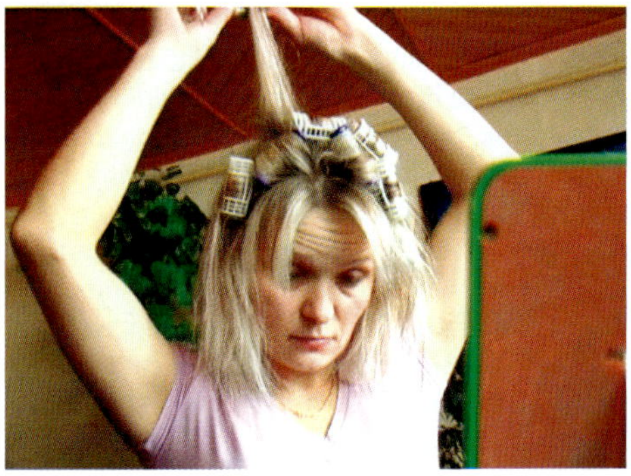

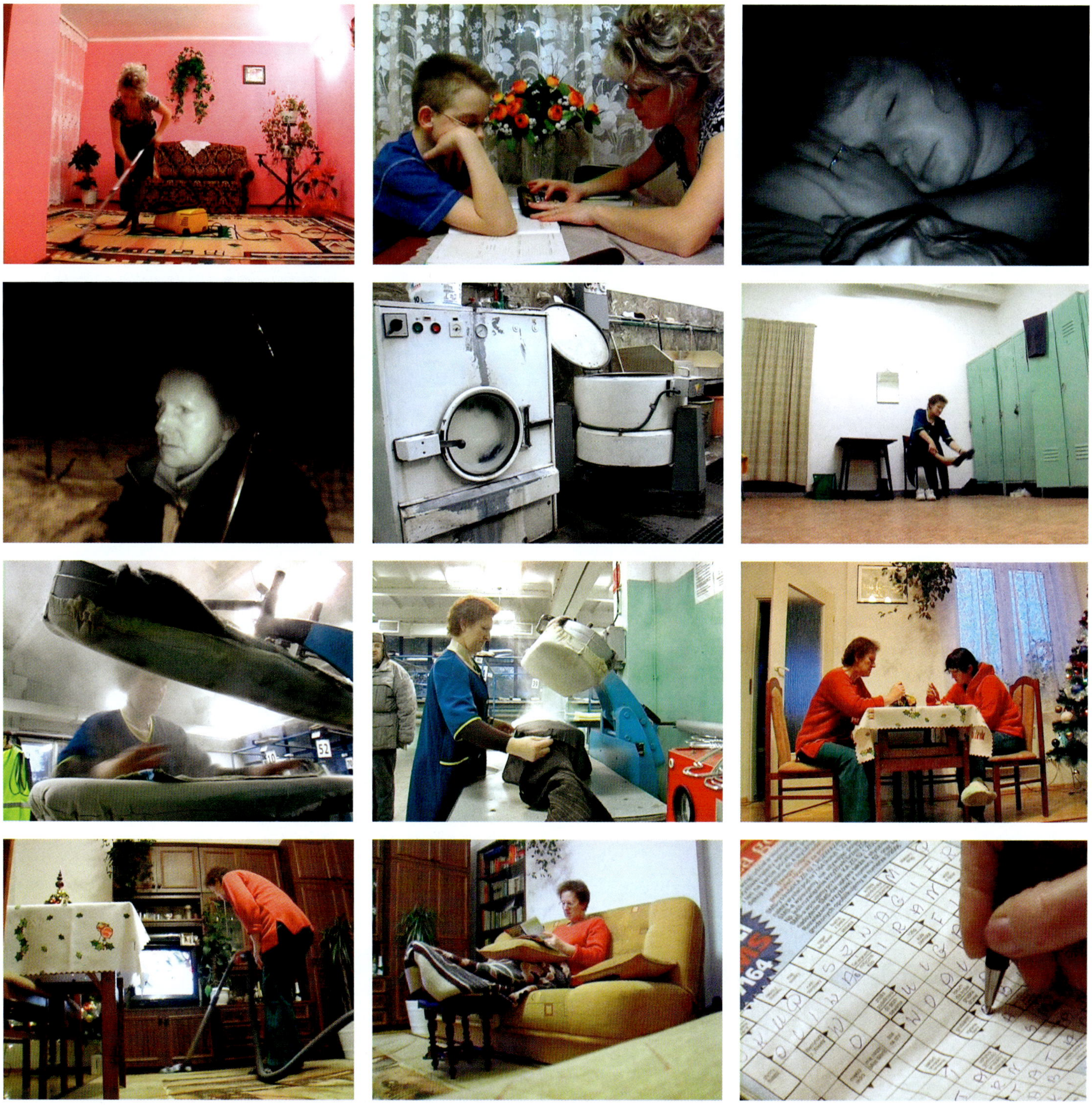

rows 1–3 (from top left): Stills from *Danuta* 2006 video transferred to DVD (color, sound); 13:30 minutes rows 4–6: Stills from *Dorota* 2006 video transferred to DVD (color, sound); 15 minutes rows 7–9: Stills from *Halina* 2006 video transferred to DVD (color, sound); 15:32 minutes

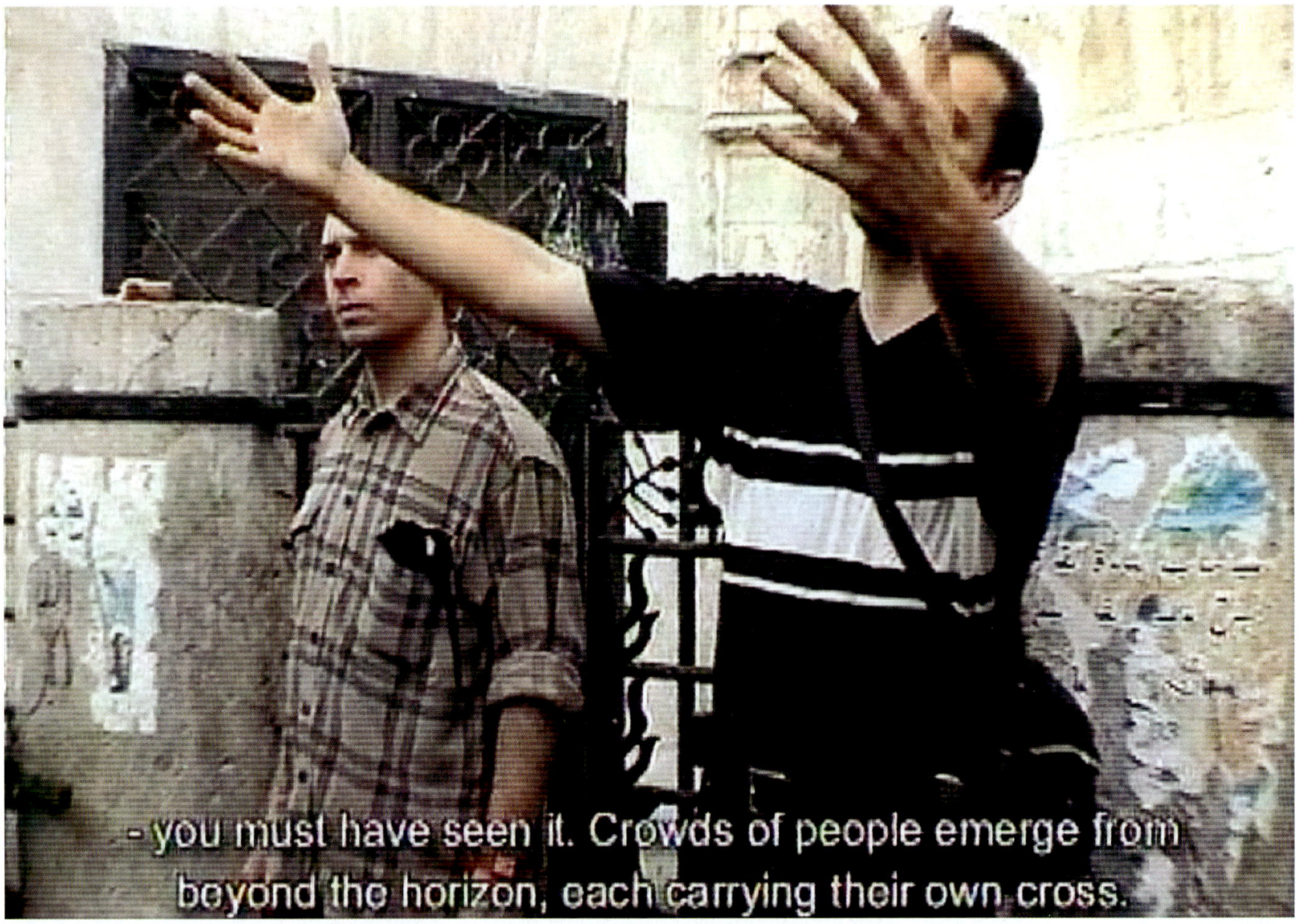

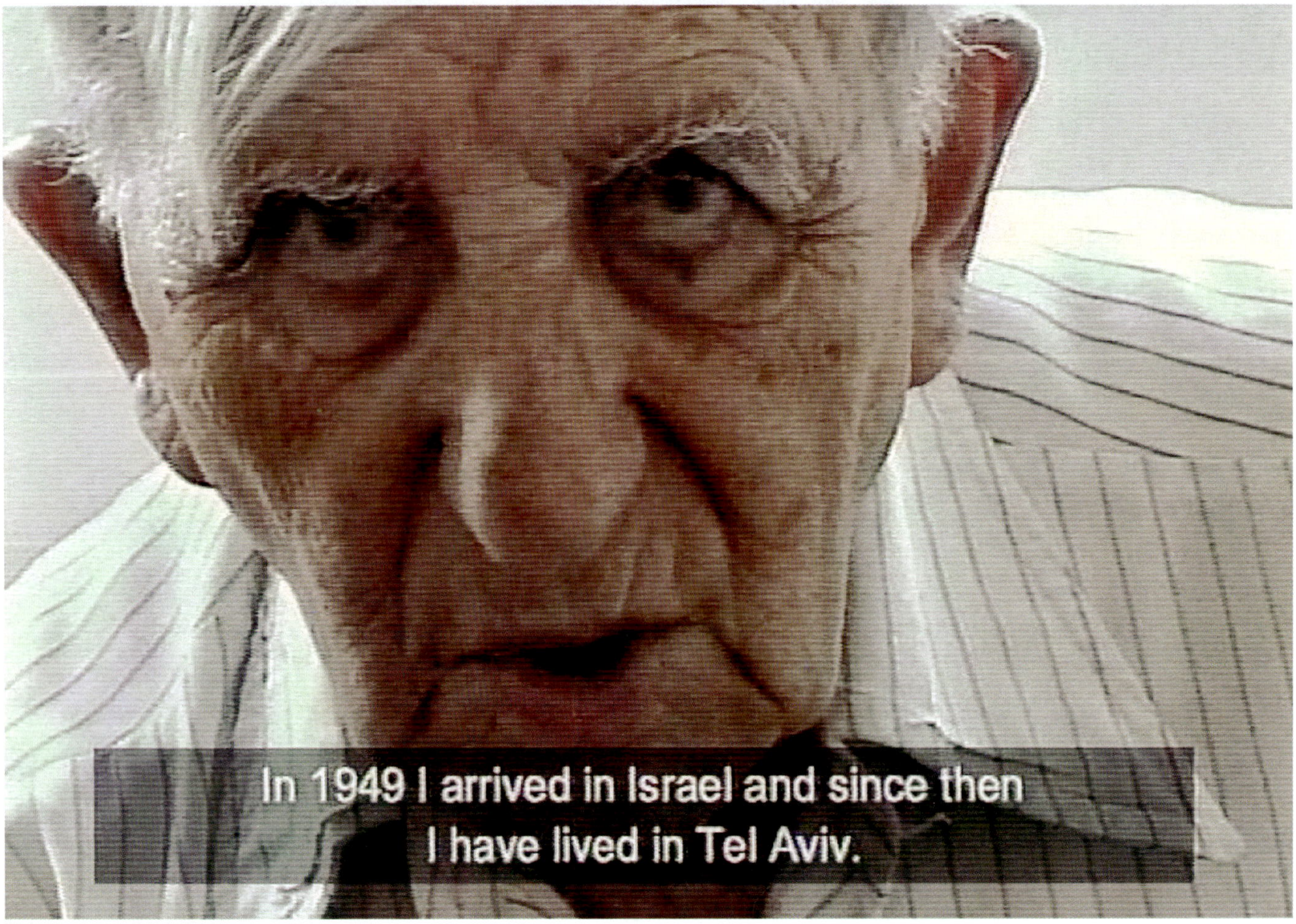

top: Still from *Pilgrimage* 2003 video transferred to DVD (color, sound); 29:30 minutes bottom: Still from *Our Songbook* 2003 video transferred to DVD (color, sound); 11 minutes

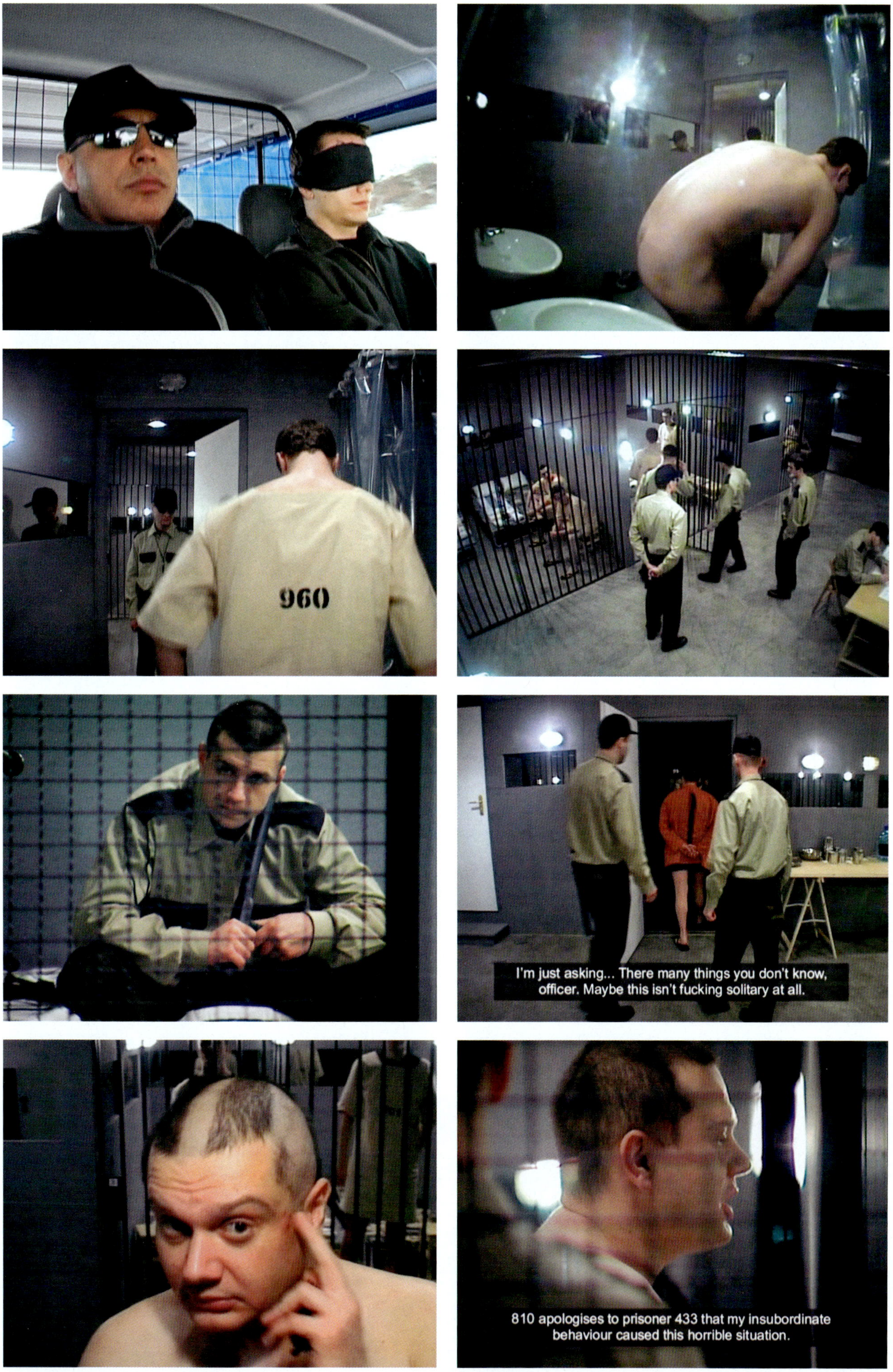

Stills from *Repetition* 2005 video transferred to DVD (color, sound); 75 minutes

Lia Perjovschi: *Subjective Art History*

In this chronicle of images, Lia Perjovschi writes her own history of modern art from 1826 to 2004, meticulously compiling, over the course of some fourteen years, reproductions of her favorite artworks along with pictures and documentation of inspiring events and influential artists. As the title suggests, subjectivity is both the organizing principle and the defining characteristic of the project. She originally printed this time line in a newspaper format and distributed it to the Bucharest/wider-Romanian art community for free out of her studio, which she dubbed the *Contemporary Art Archive/ Center for Art Analysis* (*CAA*). Now a historical document itself, this work is a testament to an extraordinarily inquiring and generous mind that ceaselessly questions what it means to be an artist in today's world.

caa
(center for art analysis)

subjective
Art History

From Modernism to present day.
Art and its context

Modernism/Modernity - (tendencies)
"Master Narratives and Metanarratives of history, culture and national identity,
Myths of cultural and ethnic origin;
Faith in "Grand Theory" - (to represent all knowledge and explain everything).
Progress through science and technology.
Myth of, social and cultural unity.
Individualism unified identity;
Family as central unit of social order;
Hierarchy, order, centralized control.
Big politics (Nation-state, party);
Faith in "Depth" (meaning, value, content, the signified) over "Surface" (appearances, the superficial, the signifier);
Faith in the "real";
Dichotomy of high and low culture (official vs. popular culture);
Mass culture, mass consumption, mass marketing;
Knowledge mastery- the Encyclopedia;
Phallic ordering of sexual difference"

As an art historical term - "refers to a period dating from roughly the 1860 - 1970
A radically new attitude toward both the past and the present
Urban, industrial society
Glorification of speed and movement (Futurism, the use of scientific models of thinking by artists.)
Expression of primitivism in Post Impressionism, Cubism, German expressionism, contact with Asian, African, Oceanic...cultures
Abstract art - progress toward purity in painting From Impressionism, to Post Impressionism, to Cubism, Constructivism, Expressionism, DADA, Abstract Expressionism, Pop Art, Minimalism)
"Innovation was the use of odd new art making materials (found objects, debris, natural light, high-tech equipment, the earth itself, new processes and media video computer art, new forms abstraction, appropriation, installation, performance art" *Harold Rosenberg*

Timeline

1826 Niepce (the first world photography)

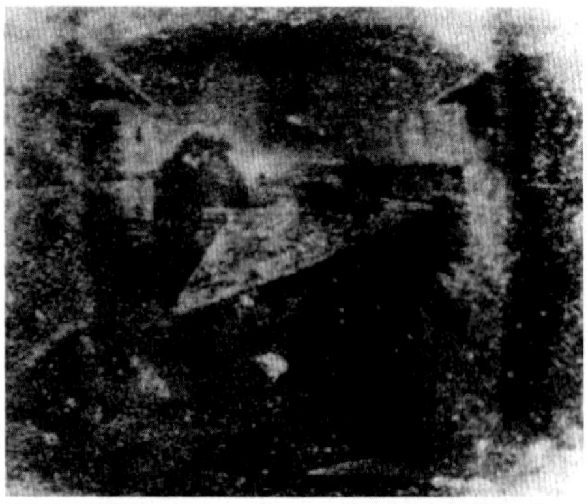

1879-1905 Hauterives France **Ferdinand Cheval** builds his **"Palais ideal"**

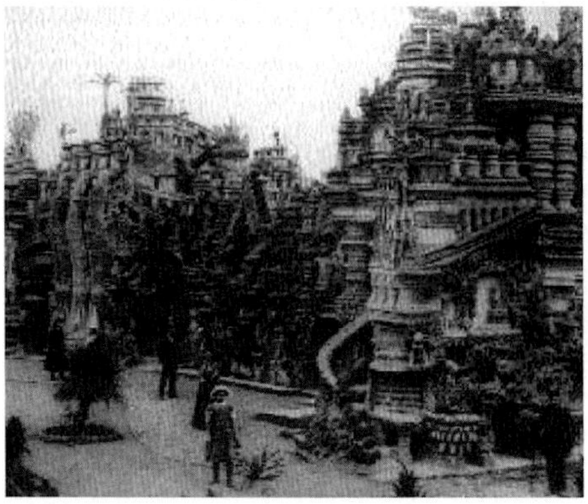

1881 **Edouard Manet** "A Bar at the Folie Berger" **(rejected the depiction of historical events in favor of portraying contemporary life)**
Crucial was the breakdown of traditional sources of financial support from the church, state, aristocratic elite.

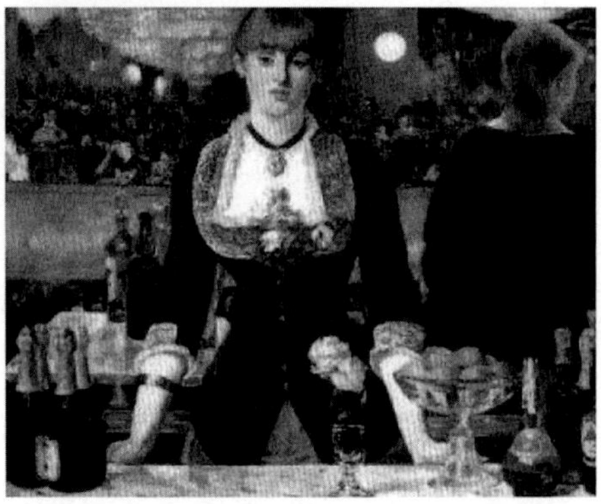

1884 **Etienne Jules Marey** (a scientist and physician) movement

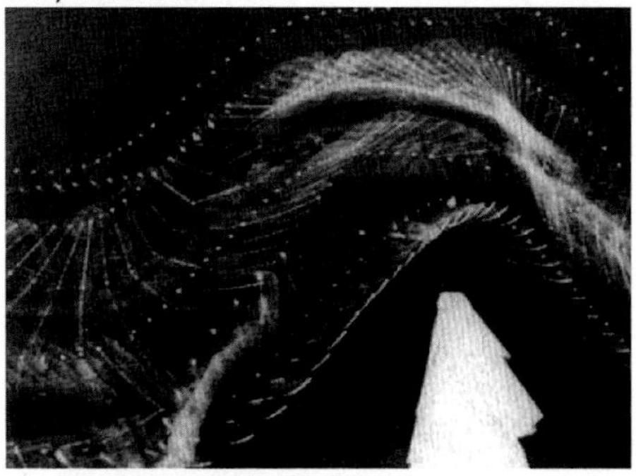

1889 **Universal exhibition** Paris

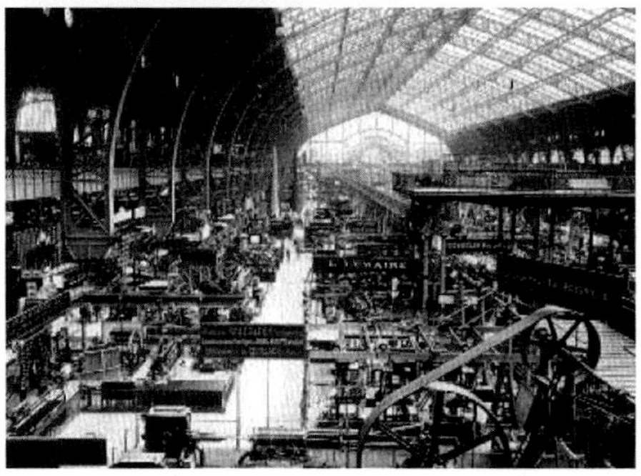

1896 **Lumiere** brothers (had projected filmed images onto screens)

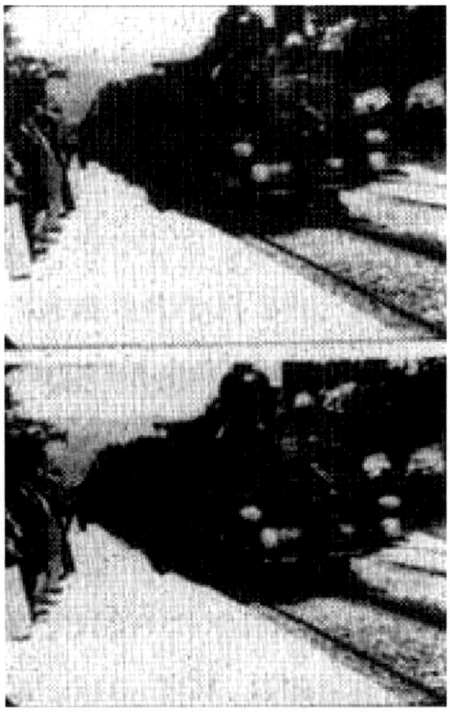

1904 Fauvism **H. Matisse**

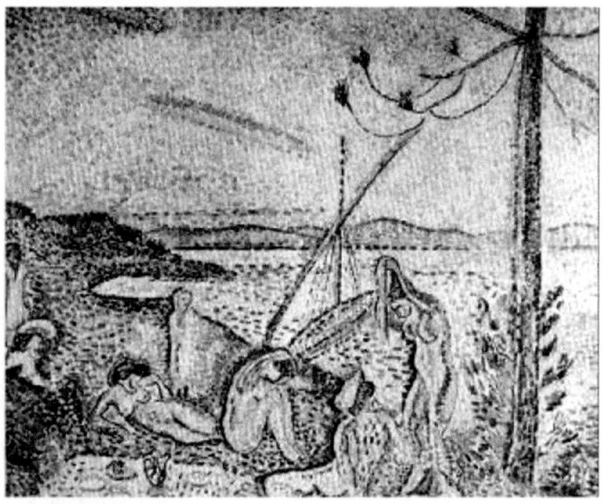

1905 **A Derain**

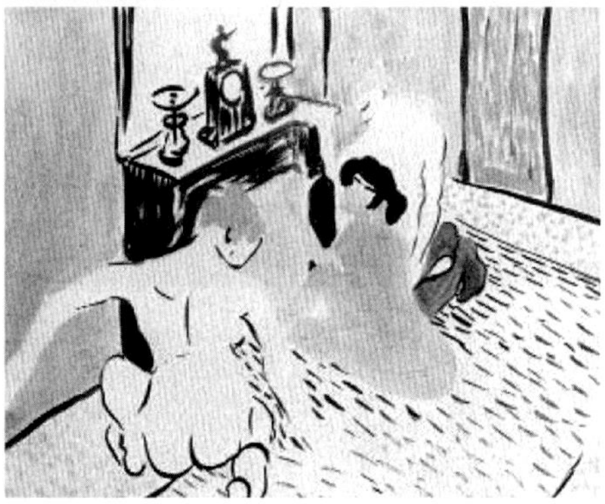

1907 **Pablo Picasso**

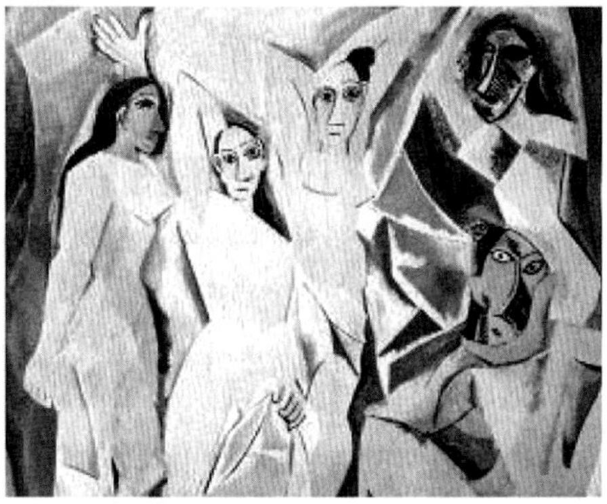

1909 **El Kirchner**

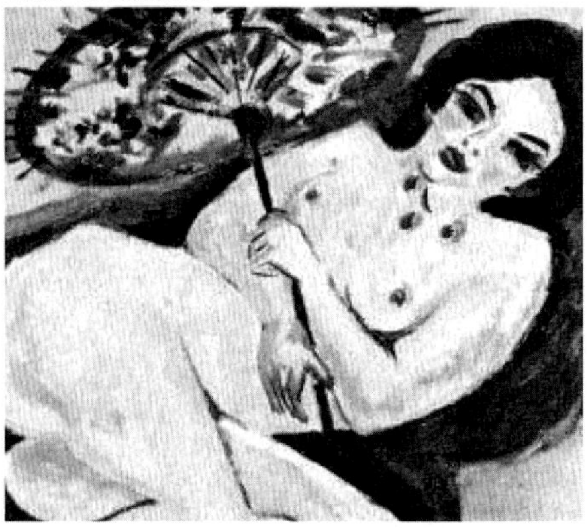

1909 Paris Marinetti the Manifesto of **Futurism** **(Glorification of speed and movement)**
1910 **Jacob Mohir** "Proofs"

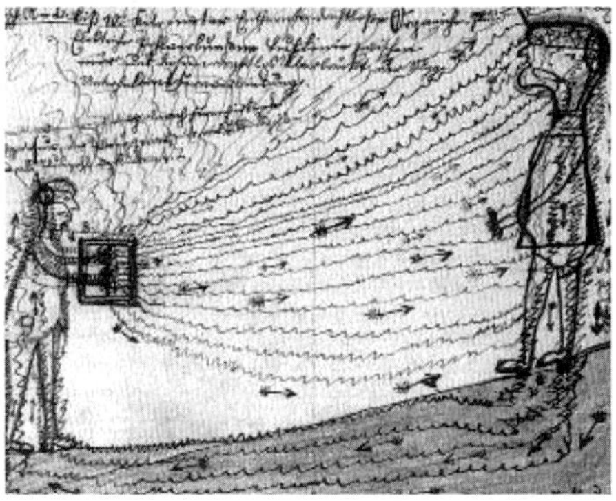

1913 **Marcel Duchamp** First readymade: a bicycle wheel mounted on a kitchen stool.
"His intention was to emphasize art's intellectual basis and in the process, to shift attention away from the physical act or craft involved in its creation."
"Art is a concept: it does not exist as a precisely definable physical type of thing, as elephants or chairs do. Since **it became self-conscious, aware that it was a special category, art has often played with this "conceptual" status.'**

1913-'20 URSS **Constructivism - Art in relation to science and technology**

1914 **Kasimir Malevich** "Art beyond its painting possibilities is forced to theory and logic"

1915 **Marinetti** "Feet" (photography with only the feet of performers and the objects)

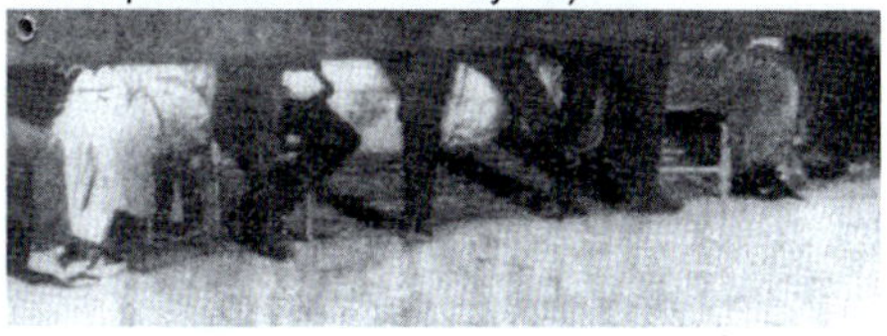

1915-1923 **DADA** "Means a variety of things in a variety of languages. **Is a world view**
Citizen - **provocateurs - incendiary public events, aggressive absurdity, anti-art form**, notable also for its **attitude on the nature of the exhibition."**
1915 **Vladimir Tatlin**

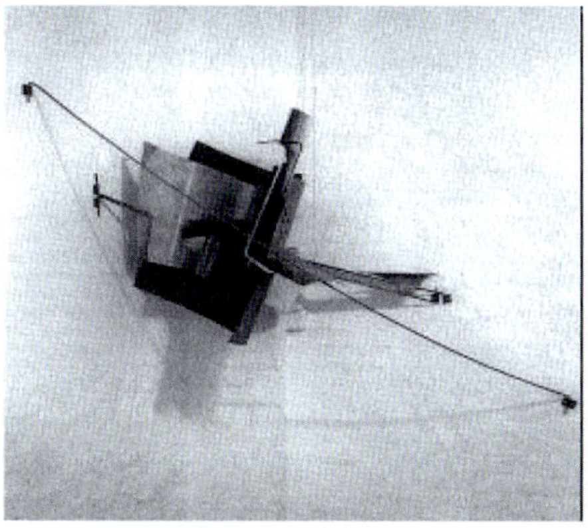

1916 **Francis Picabia** "Machine Tournez Vite"

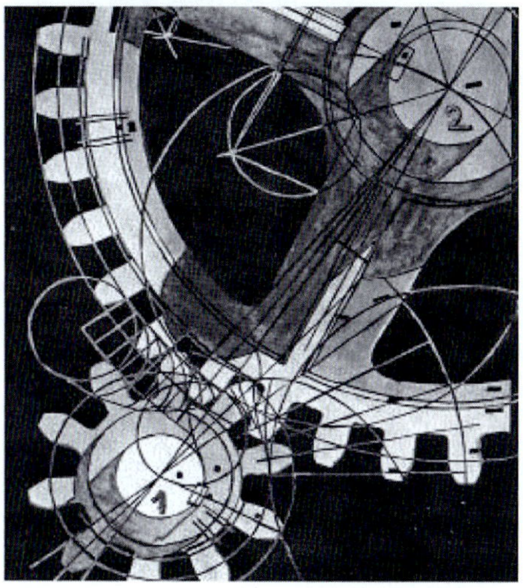

1916 **Robert Gie** "Central Machine"

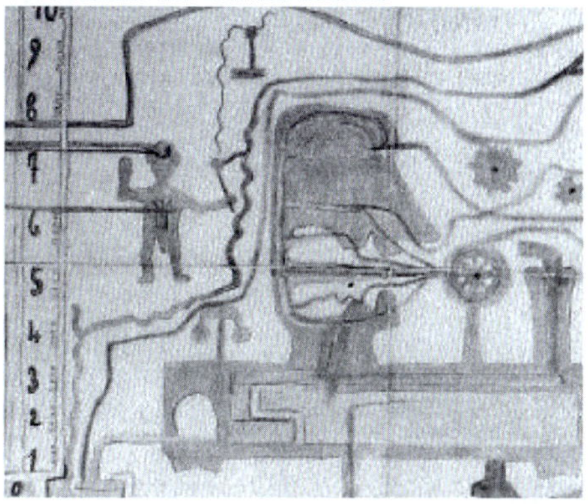

1917 **Piet Mondrian**

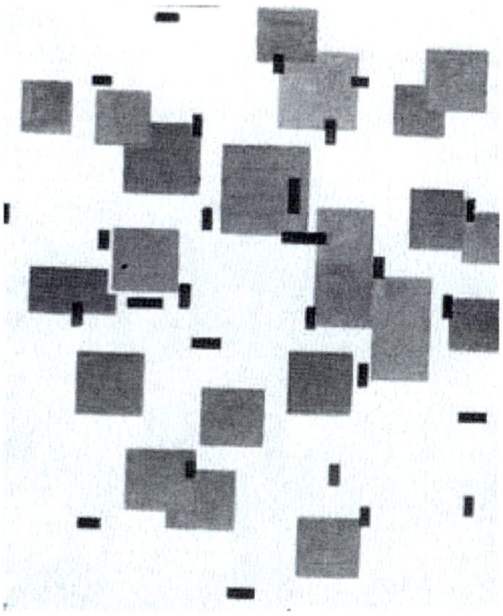

1917 **Marcel Duchamp**

Found Object **(Readymade)**- **"An art that consistently put itself forward as art while at the same time questioning exactly what "art" was.**
An existing object- is given a new identity (as an artwork)
Whether old or new, a found object infuses an artwork with meanings associated with its past use or intended function"

Marx "Objects cannot just be objects in our society; we overload them instinctively with meaning and significance" - (fetishism)
Freud show us how "objects in this world can be uncanny (rooted in the displacement and repression of what was once familiar. - to be found in the everyday, or symptomatic of how we understand the world at large"

Fountain that most notorious of ready-mades
"A group of New York artists and sympathetic collectors had set up the Society of Independent Artists to organize an annual exhibition.
In a true democratic spirit they decided that there would be no jury and no censorship that any artist who paid the fee of six dollars could exhibit.
This was an attempt to circumvent the conservatism of such institutions as the National Academy of Design. (..)
Before the opening, Marcel Duchamp bought a urinal from the showroom of the J.L. Mott.
He placed it on its back, signed it "R Mutt" and dated it. (..)
He then submitted it to the society to be exhibited. A vote was taken not to exhibit the work.
One intention of Duchamp had been to see whether the organizers would stick to their principles, (:they had not.)
The directors, by way of justification, told the press that it was "by no definition a work of art"
(..) Scandal was what Duchamp expected. It was an anti-authoritarian object, because it questioned the definition of art
The purpose of the work was to test standards and the behavior of the Society's directors. **It was meant to initiate a debate.**
Questioning the very nature of art and culture.
Crisis of authority (not just a political matter: it was also religious, sexual, (patriarchal) and cultural.)

Art, even Modernist art, it was believed, stood for certain things: culture, decency and high aspiration. Fountain has been put up not only for exhibition, but also for sale, and hence also **raised question about objects as commodities, and way we collect."**
Walter Benjamin said **Collecting**-and perhaps the drive to collect is inherent in all people living in culture-it about giving special significance to certain objects.

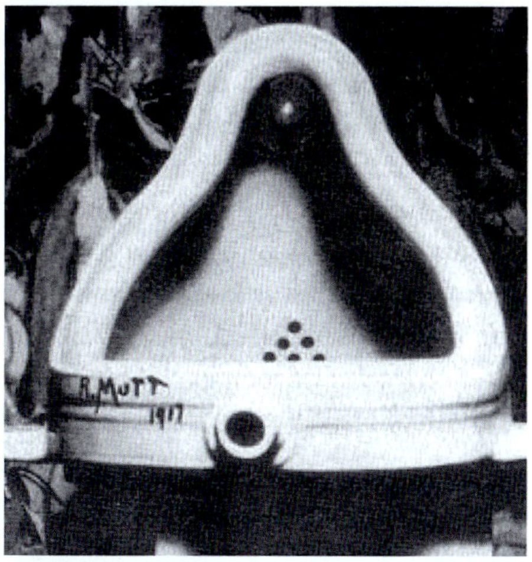

1918 **Katharina Detzel** (Male stuffed dummy of her own making) PH collection

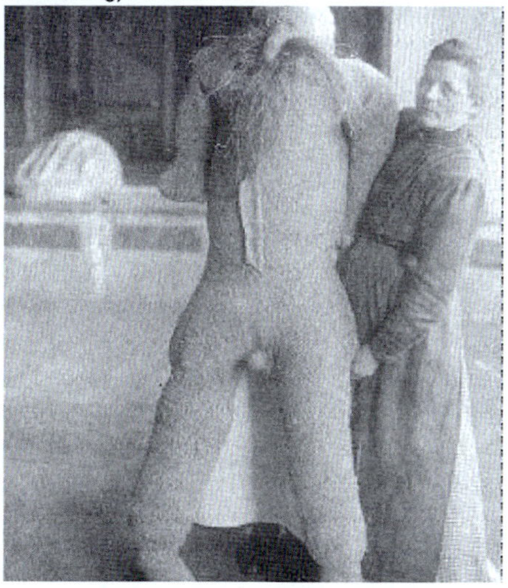

1919 **Agnes Richter** (hand sewn jacket embroidered with autobiographical and other texts)

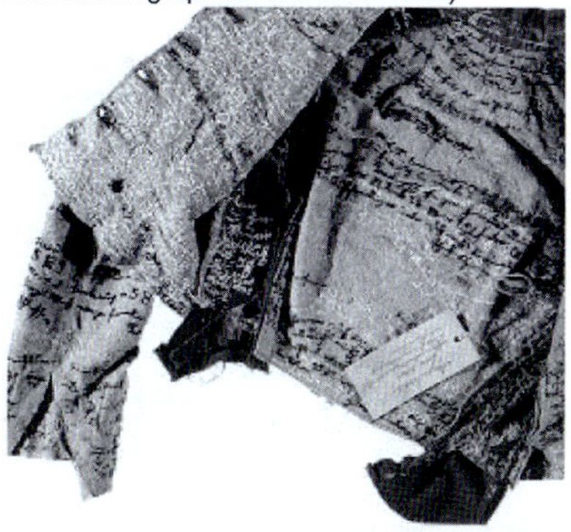

1919 Walter Gropius founds the **Bauhaus** in Weimar (closed in 1933)

1919 **Vladimir Tatlin**

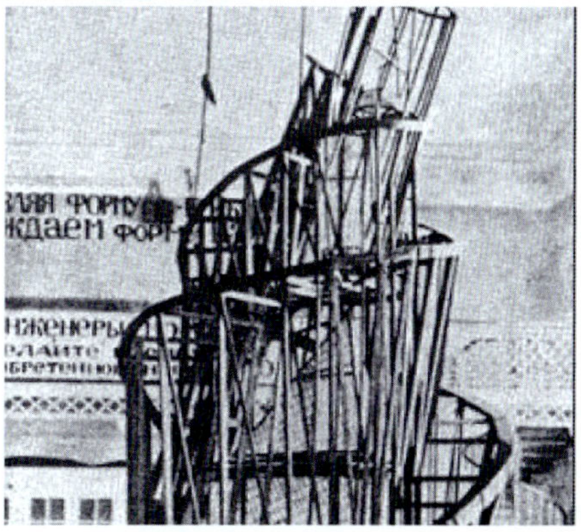

1920 First **DADA fair**

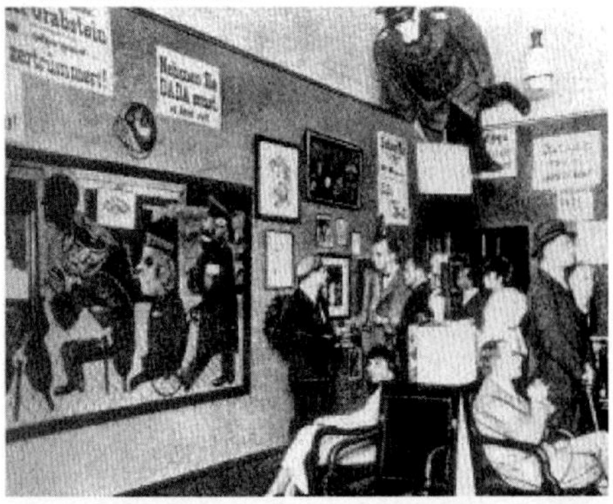

1920 Hanover **Kurt Schwitters** begins first **Merzbau** (Cathedral of Erotic Woes)

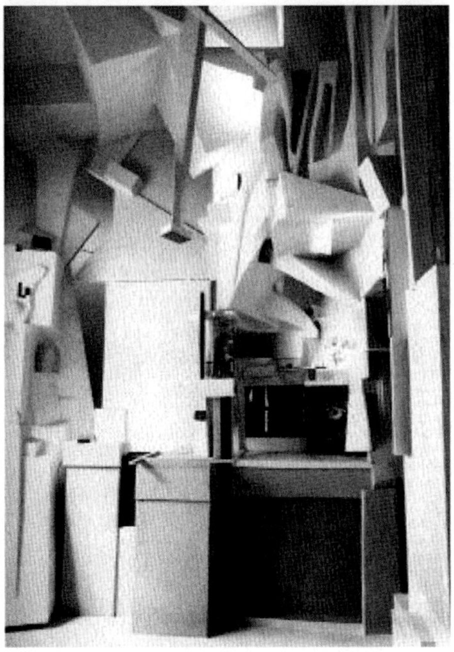

1920 Man Ray

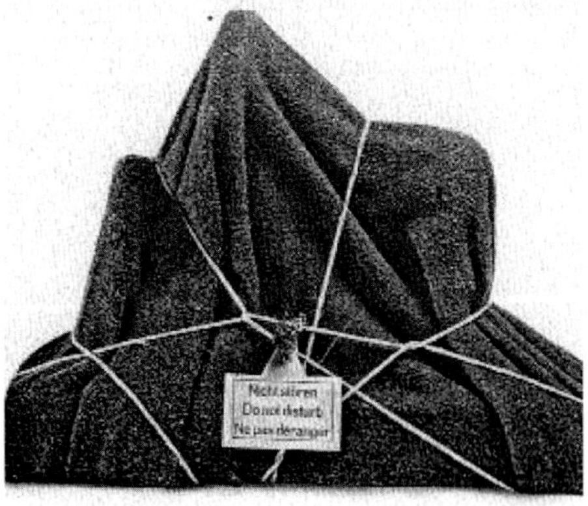

1921 **El Liszitzky**

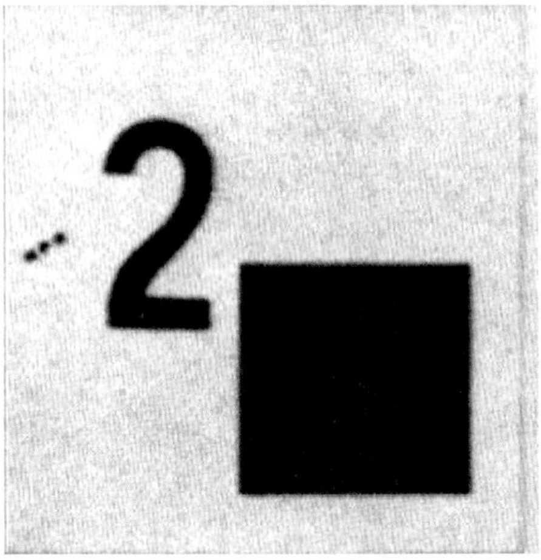

1922 Stuttgard Germany First performance of Triadic Ballet by **Oskar Schlemmer**
Hans Prinzhorn - Art Brut 'raw art", (**art of children, naïve artists,. mentally ill**)The art of the insane…
1923 First exhibition of the Proun environment by **El Lissitzky**

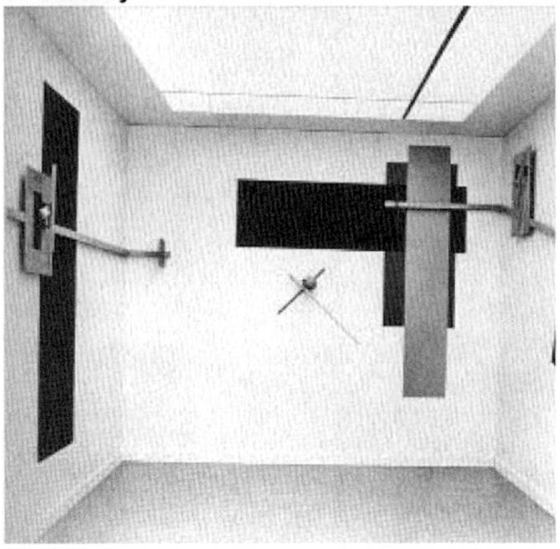

1923 **Forregger** "Mechanical dance" (dance initiated a transmission)

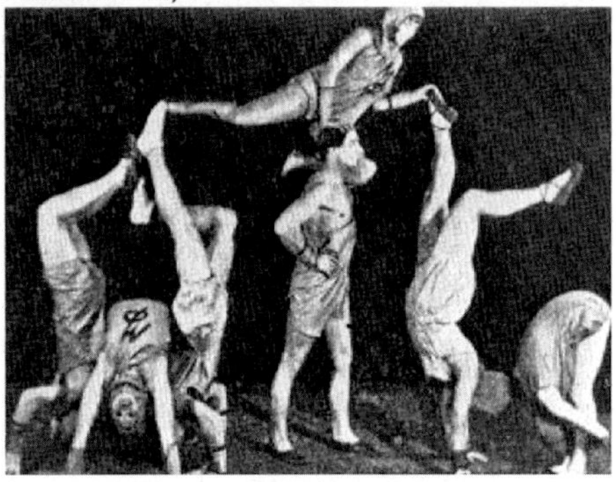

1923 **Marcel Duchamp** "Missing"… poster

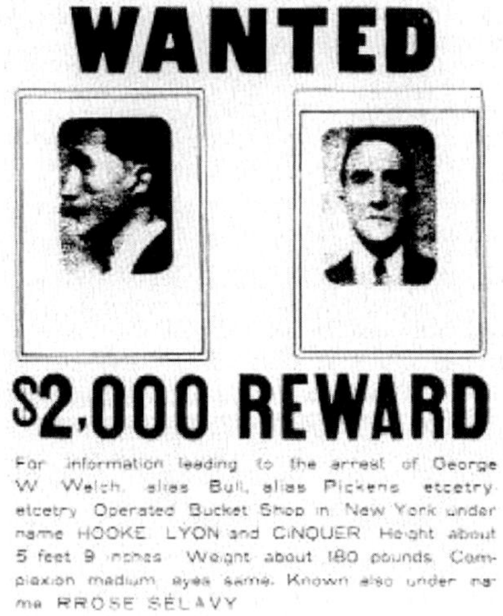

Marcel Duchamp

1924 **Surrealism** 1924 -'45
Breton this was "**the crisis of the object, sexualized, made strange**, taking as back to our past and our fantasies "
"Pure psyche automatism by which it is intended to express…the true function of though.
Though dictated in the absence of all control exerted by reason and outside all aesthetic or moral preoccupations".
"Freudian fascination with **sex, dreams, and the unconscious.**
Bizarre, hallucinatory dream images.
Dream imagery entered the popular imagination - through **art, film, fashion, advertising.** (extended deconstruction of the bourgeois exhibition. .the way art was exhibited and experienced…)

Objects can hold strange and disturbing meanings.
Objects and places seem to have their own "language" and history"

1926 **Oskar Schlemmer** "Diagram for Gesture Dance"

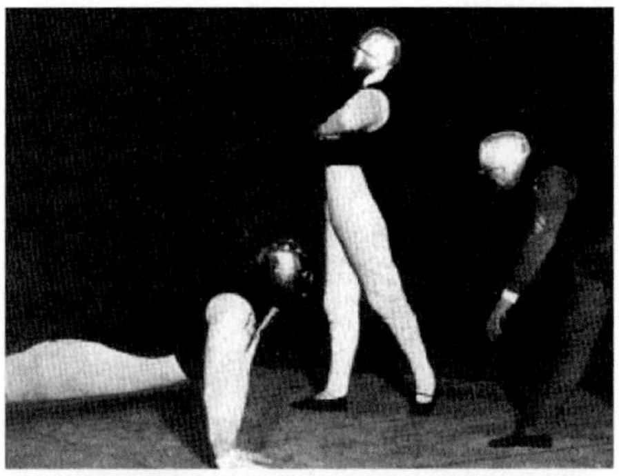

1927 Paris **Marcel Duchamp** creates "Porte" (11 Rue Larrey)

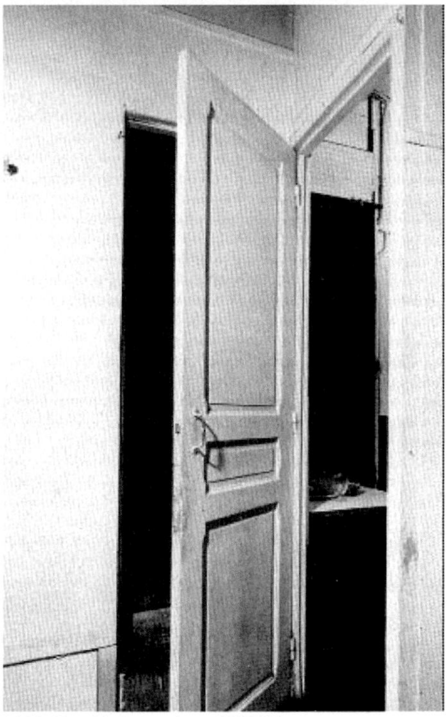

1929 New York opening of MOMA
1929 **Rene Magritte** - "Ceci n'est pas une pipe" Translation of the images.

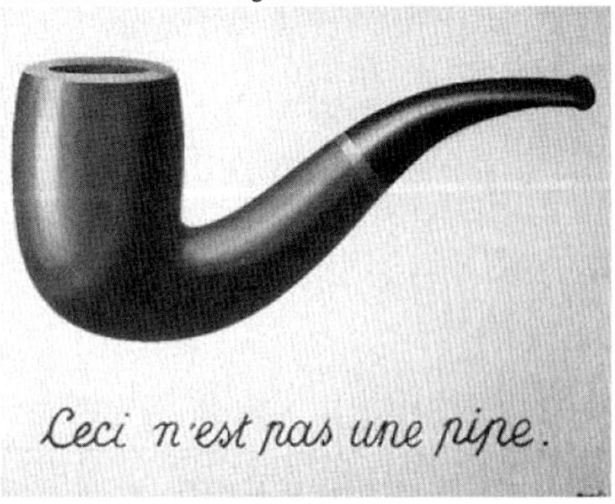

1935-38 Tirgu Jiu Romania **Constantin Brancusi** - sculptural environment. "Gate of Kiss", "Table of Silence", "Endless Column"

1938 Paris International Exhibition of Surrealism organized by Duchamp
1938 **Frida Kahlo**

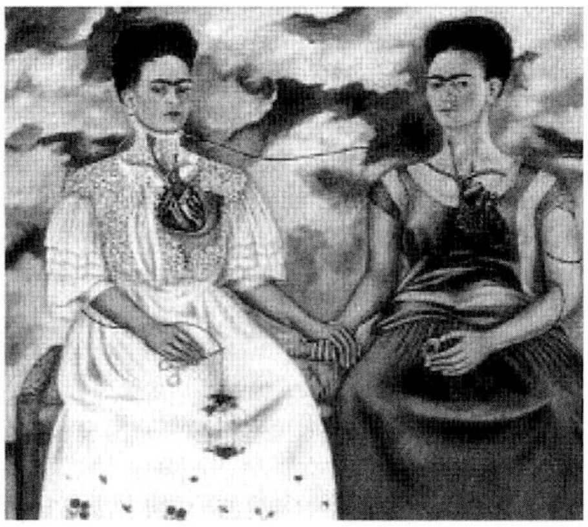

1939 New York, Solomon R **Guggenheim Museum.**
World War 2 beggins.
1940 **Book on love positions**

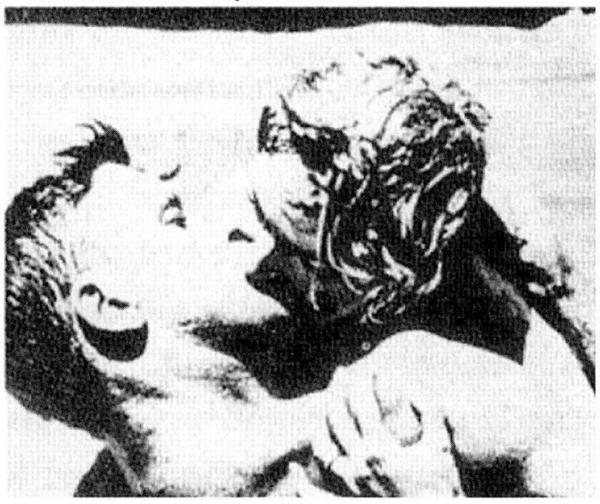

1941 Paris Marcel Duchamp completes his own "**museum in miniature**" La Boite en valise; 69 reproduction or miniatures of his works. New York, Mile of Strings....
1943 Milan **Lucio Fontana** first "Ambiente Spaziale"

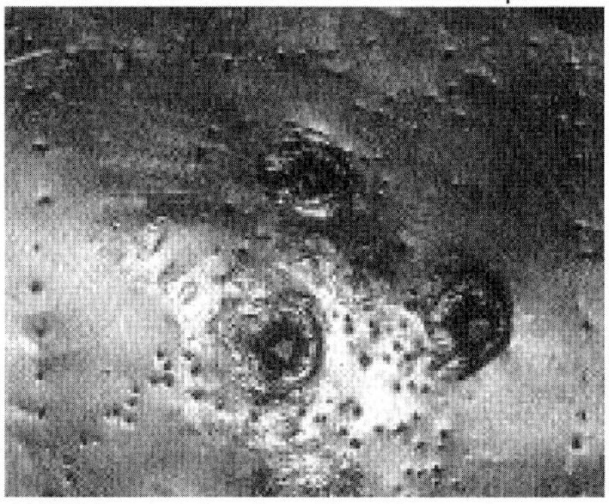

1945 **US atomic bomb on Hiroshima and Nagasaki**

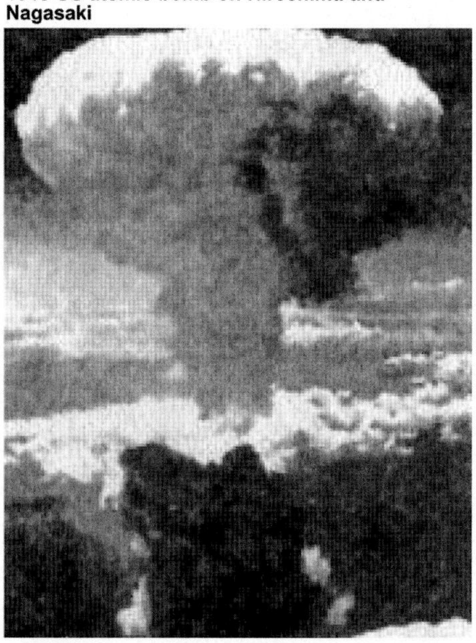

1945 Roberto Roselini "Open City" neorealism in film; Jean Dubuffet - term Art Brut
1946 French war in Vietnam begins.
Nuremburg trial -conviction of fourteen Nazi war criminals.
Xerography is invented
1947 India becomes independent from United Kingdom and is partitioned into India and Pakistan;
ICA London is founded
1948 The Marshal Plan for Europe - 17 billion USD
State of Israel is founded;
Transistor is invented
1949 **NATO** is established; PR China;
USSR tests its first atomic bomb;
Apartheid is enacted in Sud Africa.
Simone de Beauvoir - The Second Sex.
George Orwell 1984.
First Cobra exhibition.
Hambourg prostitutions

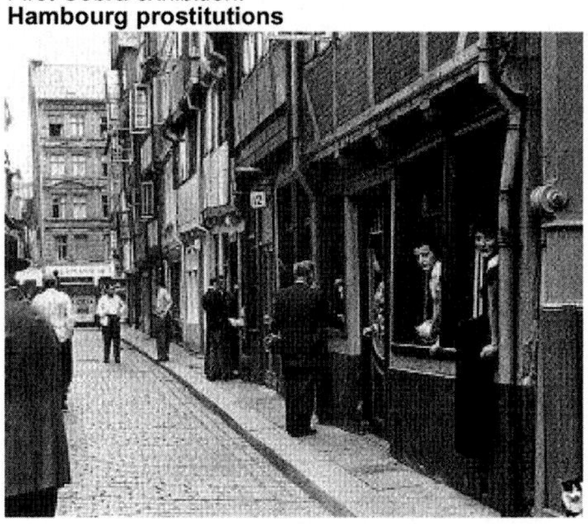

1949 **Abstract expressionism** NY Jackson Pollock

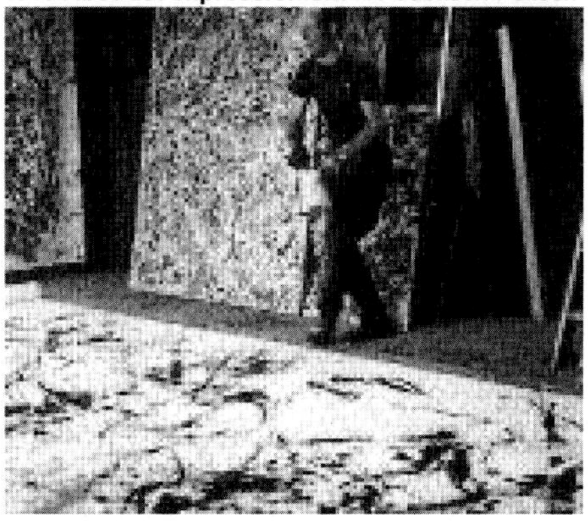

1950 **East EU Ion Grigorescu** secret service agent

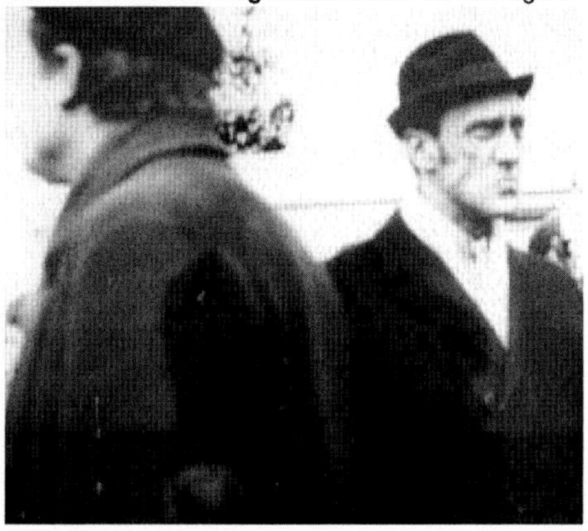

1950 Korean War begins
1950 Mc Carthy the communism hunting
USA First **Color TV**;
Film: Francois Truffaut Jean Luc Godard, Wim Wenders ...
Junk Sculpture "assemblages fashioned from **industrial debris**, the production of industrial refuse on a grand scale. Cesar - dumps and automobile graveyard - favorite hunt
The use of discarded materials - comments on the "throwaway " mentality of postwar consumerism"
Neo-Dada (1950-'60)
Jasper Johns Dada like sense of paradox and ambiguity, **targets, numbers, maps**
Nouveau Realism 1950-'60 Pierre Restany
Everyday life Manifesto **"new approaches to the perception of the real"**
Junk and found object -They turned to what they describe as **"a sociology of the world that was being created around them"** 'The passionate adventure of the real perceived in itself."
Arman..

1950 **Daniel Spoerri** - affixed the **remains of meals** to wooden panels"

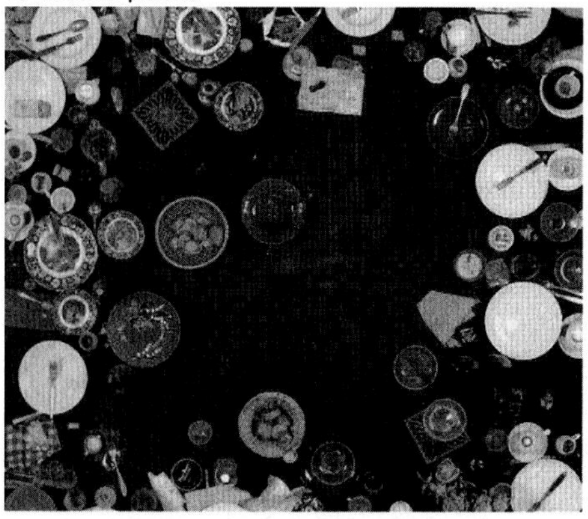

1950 **James Dean** - Rebel without a cause

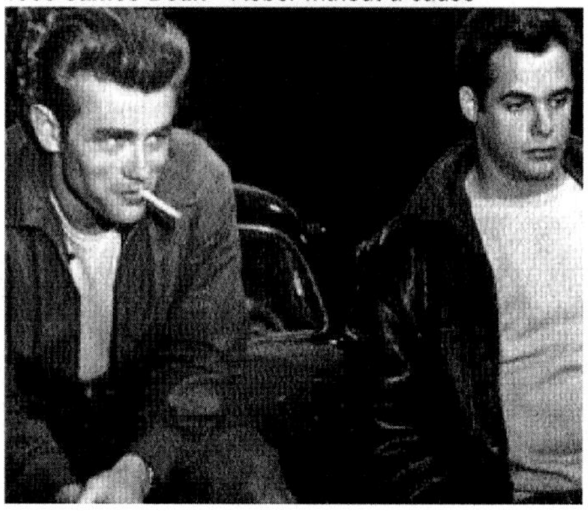

1951 Rachel Carson - The Sea around Us.
Lettriste group Isidore Isou 1951,
Guy Debord 1952
1952 ICA London **"A Parallel of Art and Life -** Man, Machine and Motion "
US explodes first hydrogen bomb
Samuel Bekett - Waiting for Godot
Michel Tapie -Another Art - **Art Informel**
Aaron Rosenberg Action painting (Abstract expressionism)
Independent art group - ICA London
Richard Hamilton collage "Just What is it That Makes Today's Home So Different So Appealing "
First Pop Art work
Pop art 1950-'60 "was **a celebration of post war consumerism**
Playful and ironic approach to art and life
Made up of a multitude of forms of cultural communication - **illustrated newspapers, movies, jazz, pop music, radio, advertising, comics, detective novels, tv"**

1952 **John Cage** (experimental composer)
"Silence" 4'33" "The pianist, lifted his hands as if to begin, but never a note he played. Silence - surprisingly **noisy**. Cage was asking people to listen to the sounds that were all around them, at all times.
Nothing could be everything"

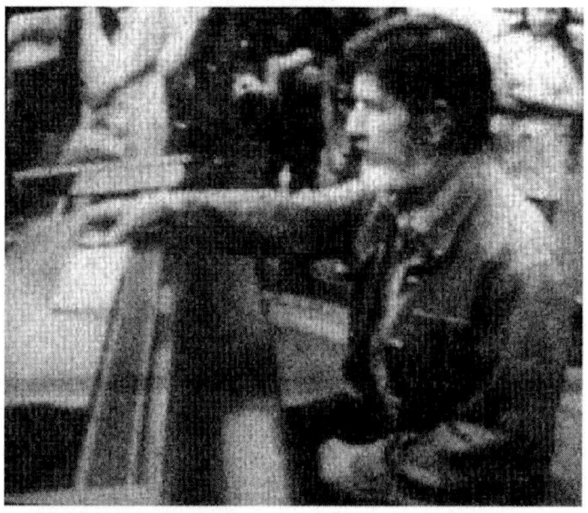

1953 **Double helix structure of DNA is discovered**
Alfred Kinsey - Sexual Behavior in the Human Female
Hug Hefner - Playboy magazine
First Sao Paulo Biennial
Robert Rauschenberg "unmodulated white painting"
Aware that these would get dirty, hi arranged in later years for a studio assistant to repaint them
Touch of the artist? What they revealed? "They had to do with shadows and projection of things onto the blank whiteness";

"Rauschenberg approached **Willem de Kooning** (an artist whom he especially admired), and told that he would like to make an **artwork in reverse**, that is, **by rubbing it out** De Kooning drawing. De Kooning agreed. **A joke**? That we now see enclosed in a gold frame? It is **a ghost** of a De Kooning drawing or a completed Rauschenberg drawing? **Destruction is creative too**?" Leo Stainberg " my first realization that **art** could take on this new modality **spinning like a satellite through consciousness, rather than being physical fact**."

1954 **Agostino Bonalumi**

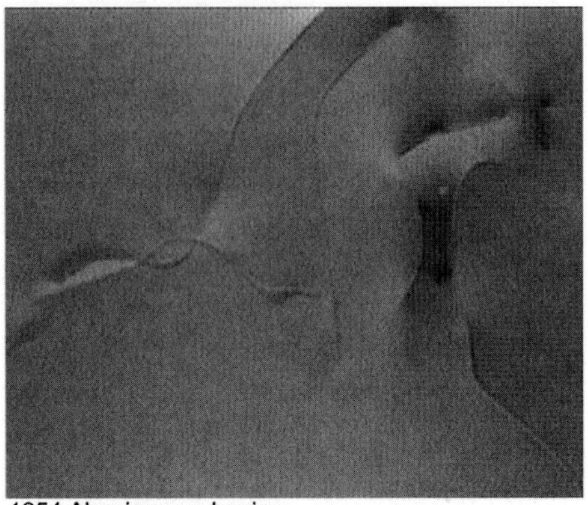

1954 Algerian war begins
Vietnam is divided, US involvement begins
Gutai group founded in Osaka Gutai group Tokyo - Paris **Wolf Vostell** - first **Decollages**
1955 **Kazuo Shiraga Challenging Mad**

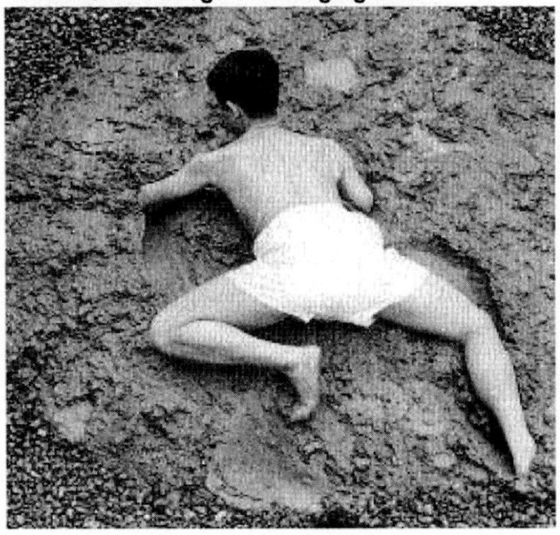

1955 Kassel First Documenta exhibition
Dusseldorf Founding of **Grouppe Zero (to stimulate dialogue between artists and scientists)**.
Leo Castelli Gallery
Paris Gaston Bachelard "Poetique de l'espace"
"The Family of Man" (we are all one) exhibition NY
1955 **Pierre Avezard** "Le Manege"

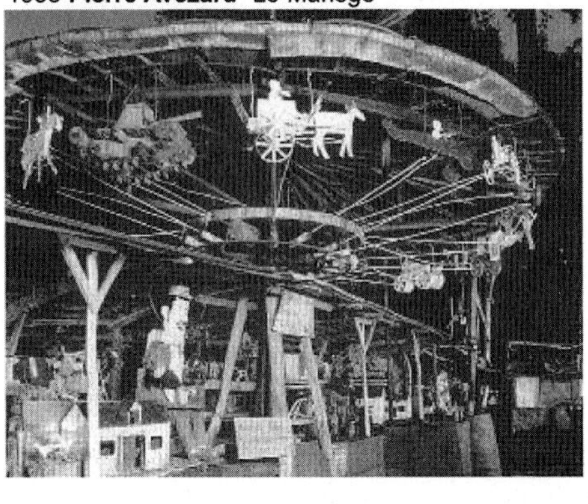

1956 **USSR crushes resistance in Poland and Hungary**
Transatlantic cable telephone inaugurated
Allen Ginsberg "How I" (tried for obscenity)
GB John Osborne's play "Look Back in Anger"
Angry Young Men
Frank Loyd Wrigh builds Solomon R. Guggenheim Museum NY
London **"This is Tomorrow"** White Chapel Gallery
Elvis Presley - **rock' n roll**

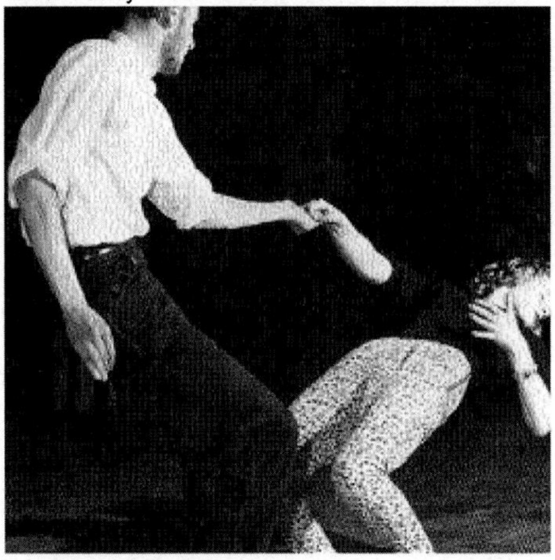

1957 **European Common Market** - is established
USSR - Sputnik 1 and 2 **- first satellites**
Jean Paul Sartre **anti novel (a non narrative**, avant- garde **form**)
Situationist International 1957 -72 (Guy Debord, Asger Jorn, GP Gallizio Spur Group)
"Emerged from **an analysis** of Western society that indicated **capitalism for its transformation of citizens into passive consumers of the depoliticized media spectacle that had replaced active participation in public life.**
Radically disrupting conventional, bourgeois life. Interest in the concepts of **detournement (diversion or displacement)** derive (drift) and urbanism unitaire (integrated city life)
Urbanism unitaire and urban environments as locales for situations, or **meaningful social interactions**. Were trying to create a new urbanism where people could be free, not ideological slaves.**Not a rush from home to work and back, but an adventure, through the city**, open to all its possibilities-a derive..
An art that was critical and self-critical could emerge." Asger "Art into pure existence, into social life, into urbanism, action, into thinking which was regarded as the important thing"
"It was an attempt to extend the notion of **parody, plagiarism and collage**.
Experimental activity, self-discovery, .Provocations.
"Revolution must happen inside us before it is achieved in reality"
By the mid '60 SI art making had largely given way to theoretical writing and political organizing.
The French general strike of May 1968 owed much to Situationist ideas."

1958 NASA is established in the US
Xerox - first copying machine
Claude Levi Strauss publishes **"Structural Anthropology"**
Yves Klein "The Void" -Iris Clert Gallery Paris
"Created a "void'- or "**zone of invisible pictorial sensibility**"-by removing all the furniture and painting the walls white. Before entered, visitors to the private view were given a blue cocktail (gin, Cointreau and methylene blue) as a result of which they would urinate blue for days, afterwards "
"Dematerializing the art object"
Paris **Christo** makes first **wrapped object** (empaquetages)
Audiosonic Research
1958 **Robert Filliou**

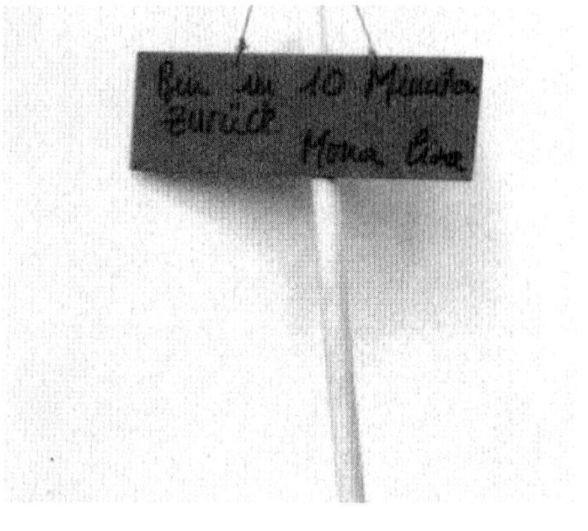

1958 **Ben Vautier**

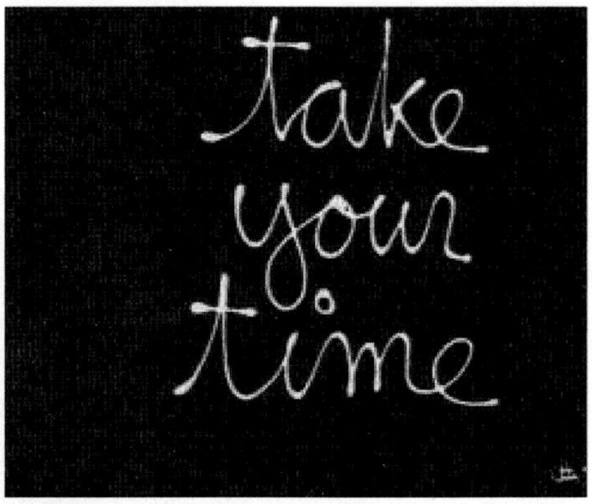

1959
French New Wave cinema
Allan Kaprow 18 Happenings in 6 parts
Happening - precisely choreographed, formally arranged **events that eluded explicit interpretation,a way of escaping the gallery and museum...The rest of the world has become endlessly available** "
"Assemblage of events performed in more than one time and place"), (Jim Dine - car Crash, Claes Oldenburg NY, LA Ed Kienholz Concept Tableaux)
"**As an environmental artwork activated by performers and viewers"**. (John Cage)
"Mixing media and concern for everyday life" Piero Manzoni

1960
Art in the '60 prone to **sudden change**
Wittgenstein - "many exhibits seemed to be visual presentation of ideas, the activity more conceptual than aesthetic"
Action/Actionism (1950-'70) "Live works presented in door or out door. **Artist desire for direct political action outside the art gallery"**
Body art (1960-'70)
The artist's body is the medium
Performance art.
"An activities that are presented before a live audience **To communicate more directly with viewers.** In gallery or outdoor sites, lasted **from a few minutes to a few days**, rarely repeated"
Feminist art
"The counterculture of the '60 inspired new and progressive social analyses
The mainstream was no longer regarded as ideologically neutral. Art history art "system" had institutionalized sexism just as the patriarchal society at large had done. Rasial minorities, lesbian, gays, they re-studied and reinterpret history. Patriarchal "male-gaze" female- the other
Narrative, autobiography, popular culture"
1960 **Yves Klein** Leap into the Void

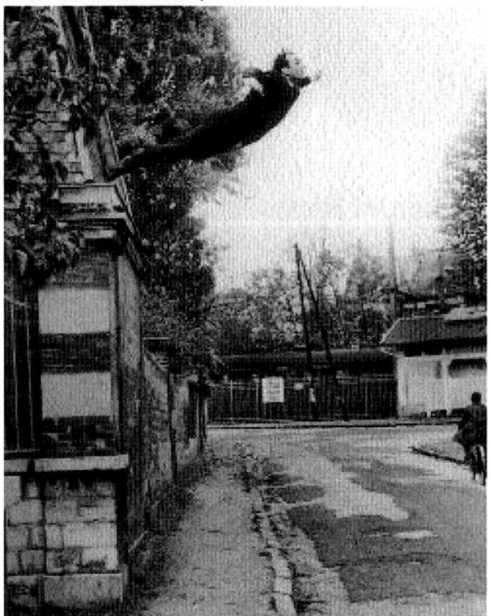

NarrativeArt
"Narrative **or story art** represents **events taking place over time** - compressed into a single image that implies something that has **already happened or is about to take place.**
Psychological self-examination and the investigation of the role-playing"
Minimalism
(1960-'70) **"Reducing painting and sculpture to essential**. Clarity and severity. As single unified image. Primary structures. New forms...

Art from the root is artificial- is unreal, constructed, invented, predetermined, intellectual, make believe, objective, contrived, useless.
The works were so "ordinary" that the viewer was made to think about the uncertain distinction between things in art and things in the world
Made viewers first consider their immediate environment, as much as the object per se, and then consider themselves.
They represent an experience that begins as a concept in the artist's head, and culminates inside the viewer's head as self- reflection"
The term **Postmodernism** - in Daniel Bell's End of Sociology
Pierre Restany - the term Nouveau Realisme
Frank Stella "Shaped Canvases" NY
GRAV (**art science interaction**) Paris
Yves Klein - nude woman as "brushes" Paris "**live painting**"
George Brecht "from 1960 (he wrote **instructions for events** on cards end sent them to friends.
Direction "Arrange to observe a sign indicating direction of travel. Travel in the indicated direction. Travel in another direction)"

1961
Yuri Gagarin USSR - orbits Earth in **the first manned space flight**
Alan Shepard makes the first American manned space flight
Berlin Wall erected
Birth control pills become available
Claes Oldenburg The Store (the studio) (transformed common place objects)
Henry Miller " Tropic of Cancer" US
The term **FLUXUS** - - George Maciunas
"**Social goals, short and enigmatic events**.
Diverse activities involved from an open-ended poetic sensibility (Zen, Dada, Beat elements)
Open up the question "**What could be art**?"
The term **Concept Art** by Henry Flynt
"Idea art - Idea not the object...
Against the increasingly commercial art world ' 60, formalism of postwar art
Used aspects of semiotics, feminism, popular culture
Performance, video art **- documentation"**

60 ties. **What is an art work**?
Bruce Nauman "What does an artist do?"
Believing that an artist must have a studio, just as a doctor has a surgery or a gardener has a garden, he found a studio His work began to evolve from that starting point
What is art**? Art is what an artist does**, just sitting around the studio.There was nothing in the studio because I didn't have much money for materials. So **I was forced to examine myself and what I was doing there.** Part of a **commitment to the everyday** in Conceptual art **to look at, and live with, failure.** Nauman's studio had become the space of a **do it yourself philosopher**. His mind, the body and its experience were central to his approach. Activity involves making something, and sometimes the activity itself is the piece.Thinking, moving and making were all activities. Coffee thrown away because it was too cold - photographs

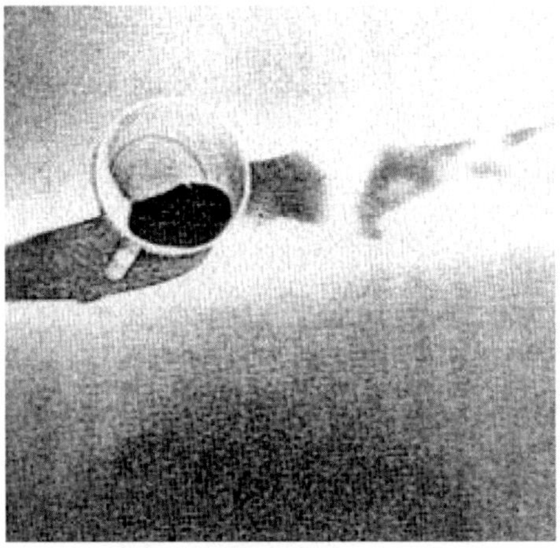

Obsessive documentation...socially engaged
Any activity or thought is a potential work of art...
Allan Kaprow - "Conceptual art as an interactive form of communication, especially in the wake of visual competition from spectacular, non art events..."
An interest in **story telling**, in **politics,** and in **images from art history and popular culture**...
What is art?
"If a work of Conceptual art begins with the question "What is art" one could argue that it is completed by the proposition "**This could be art**"
Piero Manzoni Cans of Artist's shit, The Artist's Breath...

1961 **George Brecht** for the group exhibition Environment, Situations, Space in NY placed an ordinary chair in the gallery under a spotlight, another in the toilet and one outside the front door.
The artwork was a modest intervention, sitting on the chair too, could become a modest and undemonstrative work of art"

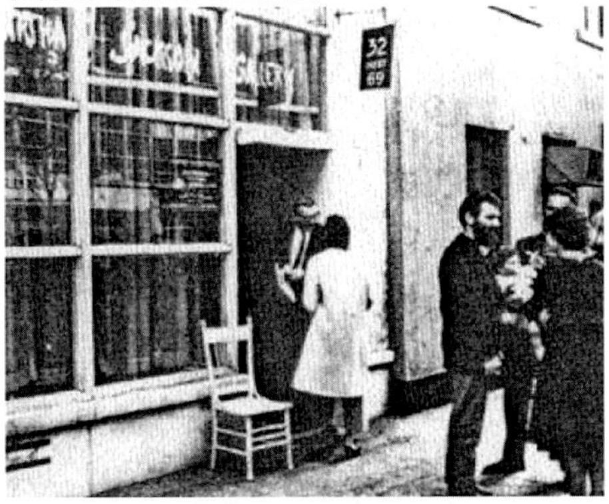

1962 NY The New Realists exhibition
1962 **Andy Warhol** "200 Campbell Soup Cans"

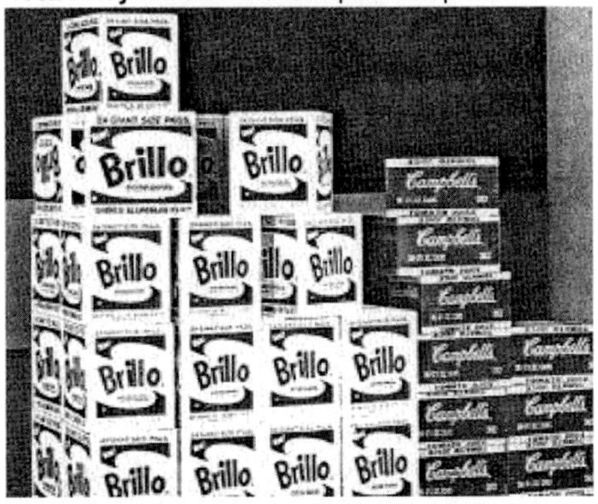

1962 **Andy Warhol** "Do-it-Yourself Flowers"

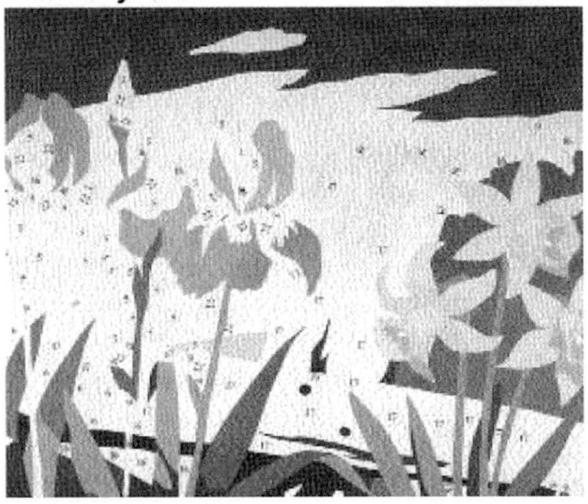

1962 **Daniel Spoerri** "Table pictures" (the plates, bottles and glasses would be left on the table at the end of a meal and fixed). "**Anecdoted Topography of Chance book**". He analyzed, partly as an explorer would, partly as a collector of memorabilia would, the hundred and one objects that happened to be on his table on 21 February 1962 at 8-07 pm
Wien Actions 1962-81
Rome, Luciano Fabro "Habitat" Galleria Mario Peroni
The sedative thalidomide is linked to thousands of birth defects
1962 Paris **Ben Vautier** sells himself as a **"Living Sculpture"** Gallery 1 London; "Magasin de Ben"

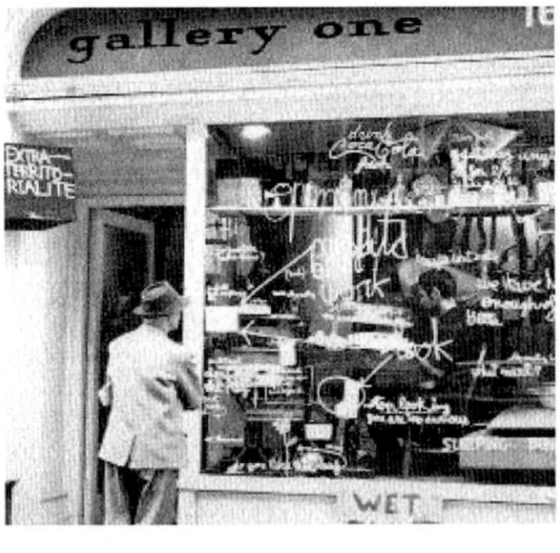

1962 **Bert Stern** "Marlyn Monroe"

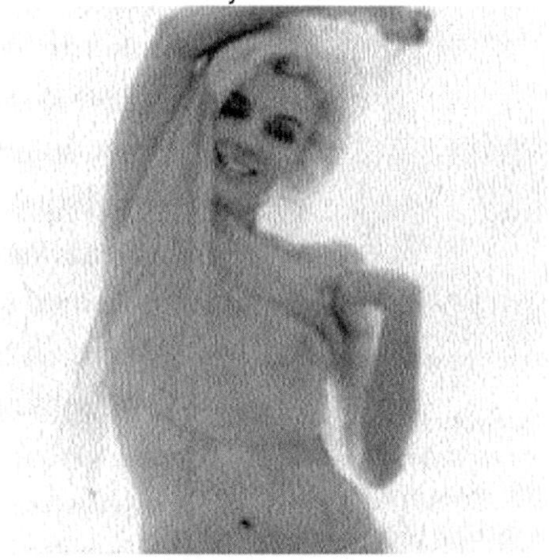

1962 **Milan Knizak** Small Environment on the street

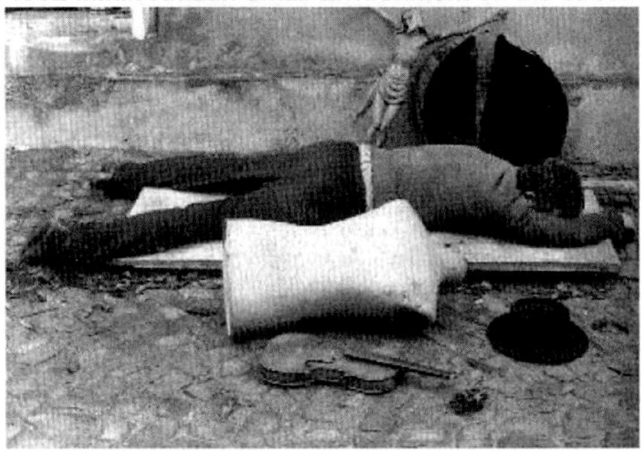

Process Art (1960-'70) -
Eva Hesse (unstable materials, slowly decomposing over time.
1963 NY **Haans Haacke** begins his "**Water plus Wind Sculptures**"(Plexi glass cube, or weather boxes -water condenses and evaporates in response to the changing levels of light and temperature in the gallery)

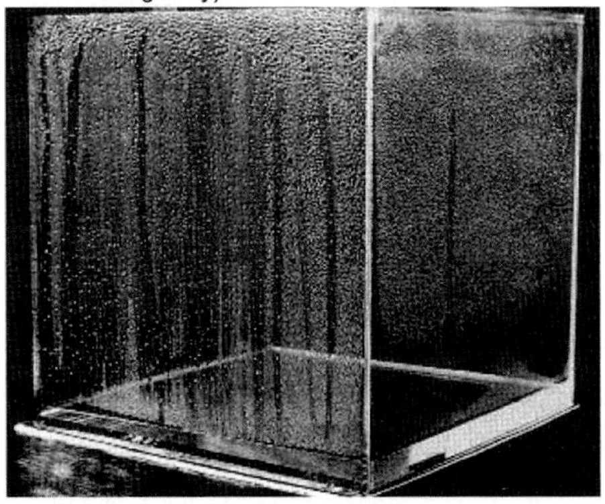

1963 Jannis Kounnellis; Robert Morris
"The means count more than the ends. Experience for its own sake. **The artist sets a process in motion and waits the result. Non precious works"**. Cologne Germany **Joseph Beuys** his first use of fat as a substance during a lecture.
JFKennedy assassinated in Dallas
Civil rights demonstrations Alabama - Freedom Marchers Washington DC. Michael De Bakey - first uses an artificial heart during surgery
First exhibition of **TV sculptures**
1963 **Nam June Paik** Germany Wuppertal, **the single line on tv** screen- reflected the very first image to appear on the first tv set in the late '30s

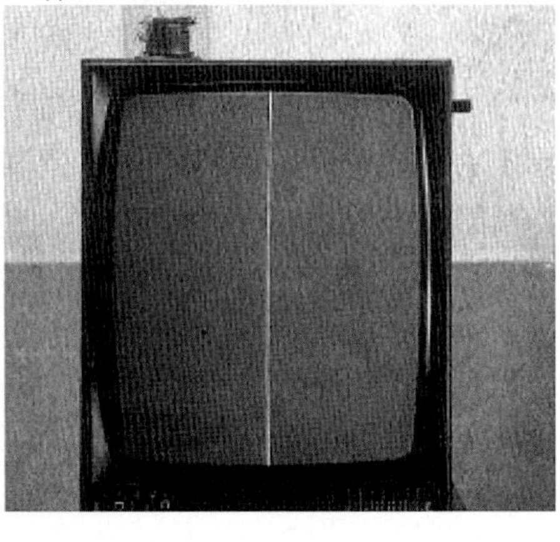

1963 **Andy Warhol** - began to call his studio "**The Factory**" (there was where he got workers to come and make his paintings. **Films** "Empire" we watch the **Empire State Building** for **eight hours.**(photo)

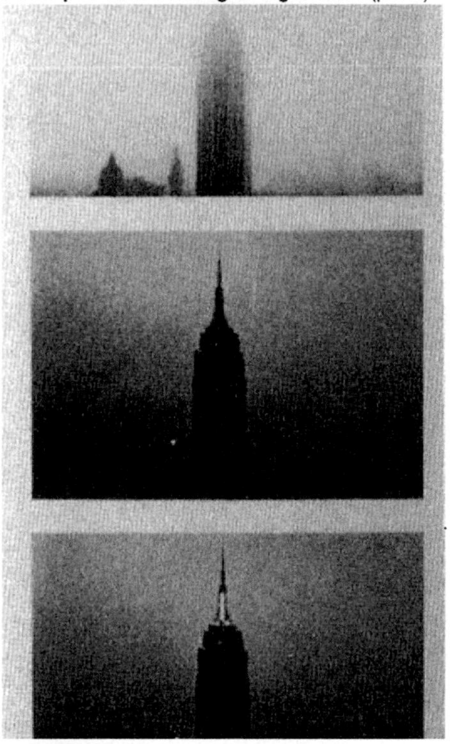

1963 **Wolf Vostel**, De-collage (happening)

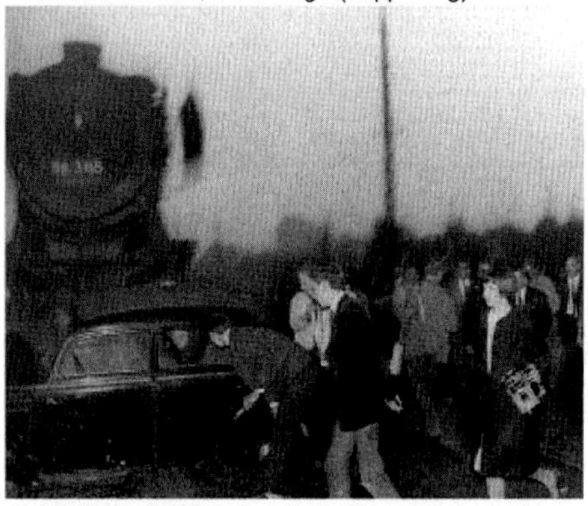

1963 **Warhol. Sleep** first film...we watch a sleeping man for **six hours**, **Kiss...Disasters**, "Saturday Disaster")
1963 **Larry Clark** "**Tulsa**" ('71) photographs and some film sequences from the years '63, '68, '71 depicting the life of his friends in Tulsa Oklahoma. Clark documents their longing to escape from their contines and their attempts to widen their con-sciouness, mainly through sex and drugs. Also show the side-effects of his hippie utopia, such as prostitu-tion, crime and violence" (photo)

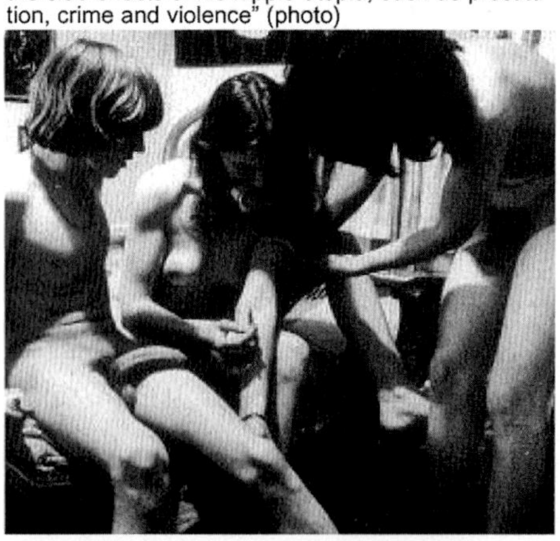

1964 **China explodes its first atomic bomb**
Free Speech movement begins in Berkeley California
Music become international language of youth
The Beatles..
Marshall McLuhan "Understanding Media The Extension of Man"
Op Art
NY Andy Warhol "Brillo Boxes"

1964 **Cy Twonbly**

1964 **Hi Red Center "Be clean"** (cleanup of the Metropolitan)

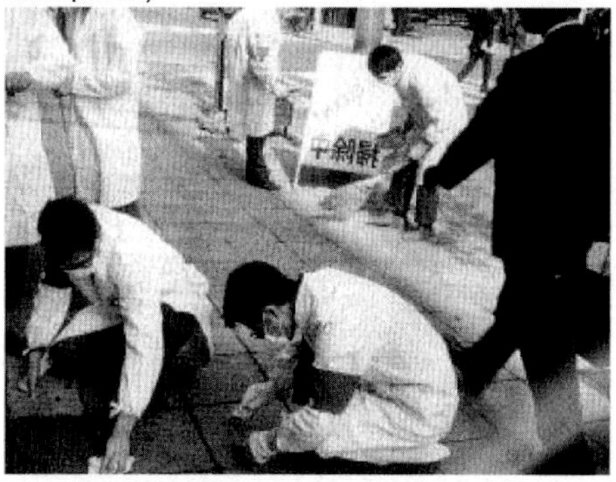

1964 **Hi Red Center** Drop Dropping event

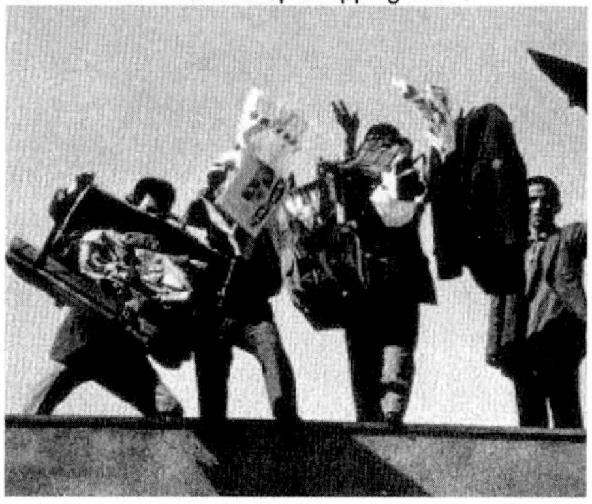

1964 NY Carolee Schneeman "Meat Joy" Judson Memorial Church; Kassel Germany Documenta 3 "**Museum of the 100 Days**"
1964 **Joseph Beuys** installation

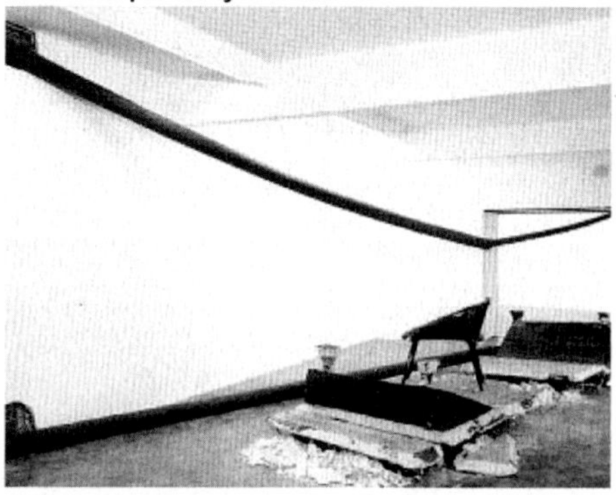

1965 **Lucio Fontana**

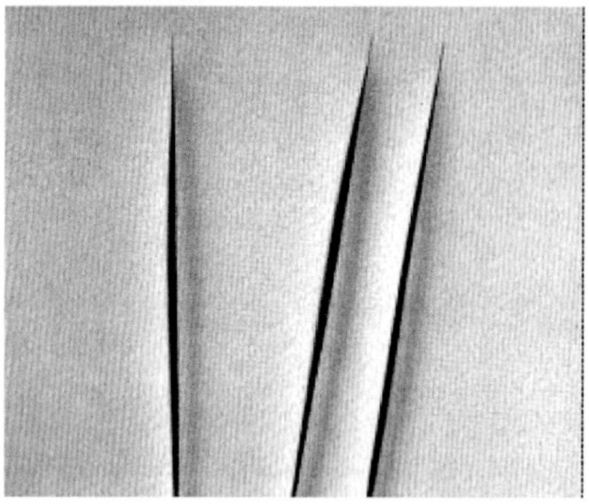

1965 **Andy Warhol Electric Chair**

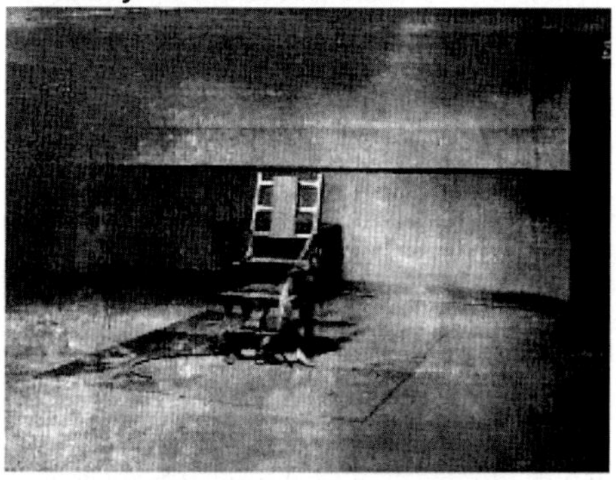

1965 **Joseph Kosuth** "One and Three Chairs "

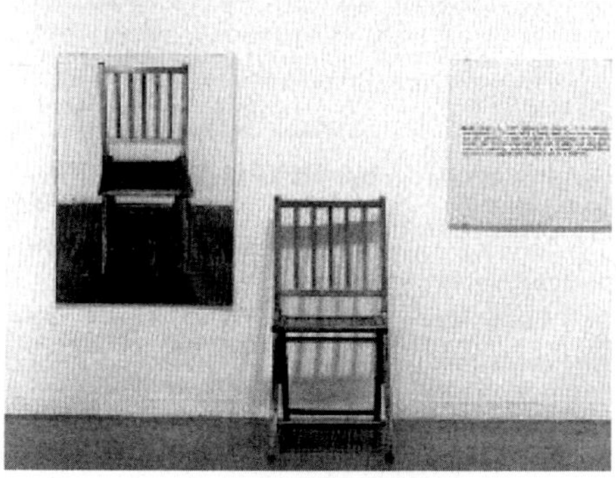

1965 **Roman Opalka** paint in white on a gray back-ground the series of numbers **from one towards infinity**. (Also photographed himself each day))

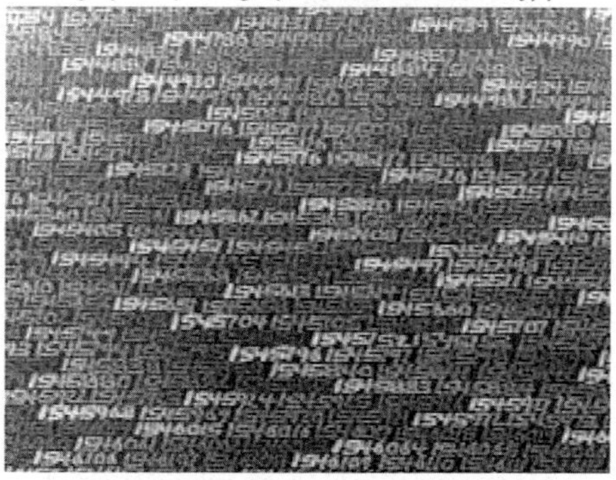

1965 **Yoko Ono** "Cutting piece" Tokyo

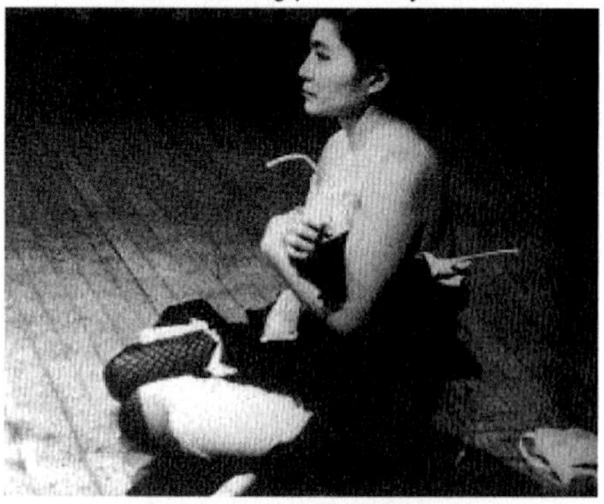

1965 **Daniel Spoerri** "**Restaurant**" 1966-'68

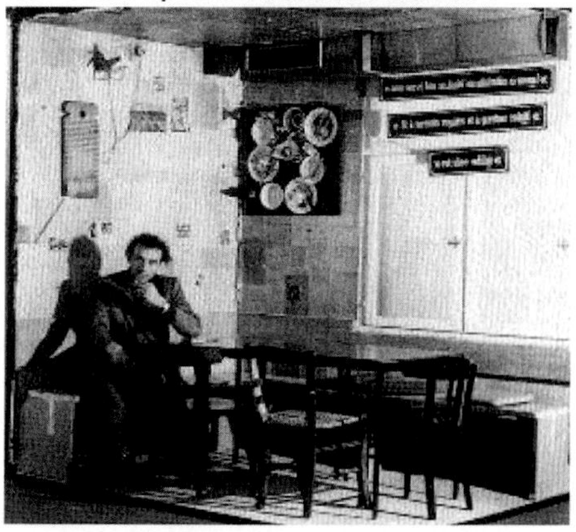

1965 Wien **Rudolf Schwarzkogler 'self mutilations'**)

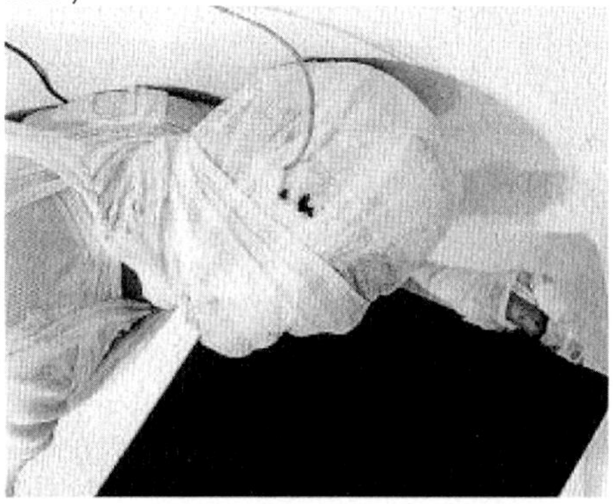

1965 Wuppertal Germany Joseph Beuys 24 hours happening: Stockholm "Inner and Outer Space" by Pontus Hulten
India and Pakistan fight for control of Kashmir
The Black Muslim leader Malcolm X is assassinated in NY
First artist's video by Nam Jun Paik NY

1966 Basic act of **counting. On Kawara**
(He is never photographed or interviewed , and he does not even attend his own exhibitions.
He has periodically sent **telegrams** to friends with the enigmatic message "**I am still alive**")

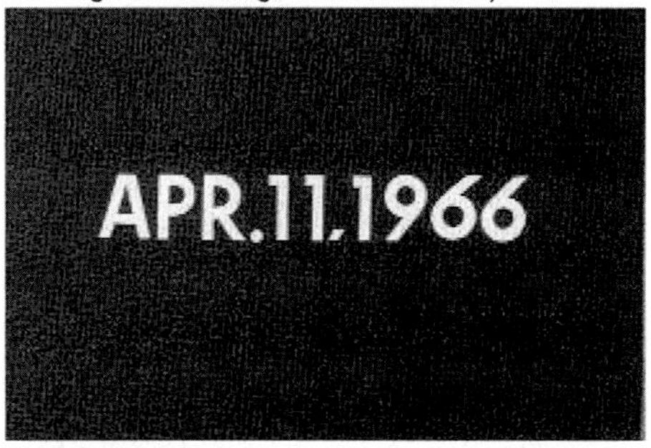

1966 **Lygia Clark**, Air and Stone.

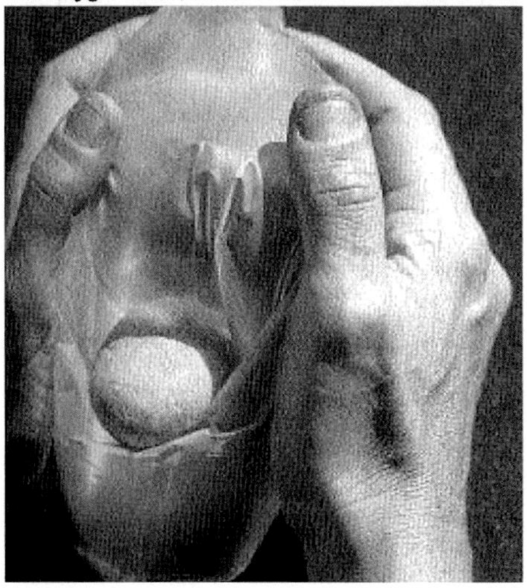

1966 **EAT - Experiments in Art and Technology - founded in NY**
Rudolf Schwarzkogler 6 th Action (actions only for the photo camera); Bruce Nauman Self Portrait as a Fountain 1966-'70; Eva Hesse Hang Up
Claes Oldenburg

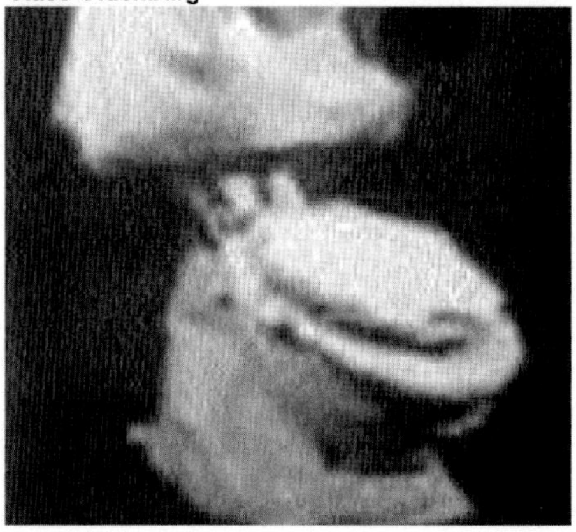

1967 Six Day War between Israel and Arab countries; Bolivian troops kill Cuban revolutionary Ernesto "Che" Guevara; **China explodes its first hydrogen bomb; Christian Bernard - first heart-transplant operation**
Mass media being what The Marxist philosopher **Louis Althusser** called **an "ideological state apparatus".**
"Television, controlled by the state and big business allowed for a new type of colonialism, an inner colonialism whereby the population was duped and controlled, not with weapons but with a glossy, false picture of the world."
The spectator feels at home nowhere, for the spectacle is everywhere."
1967 **Guy Debord** The Society of the Spectacle

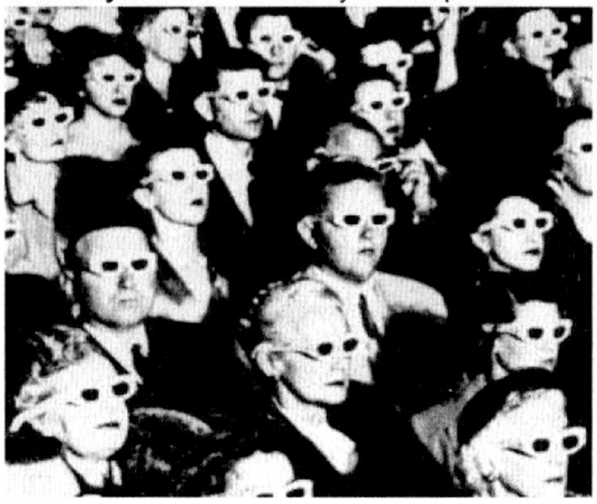

1967 **Tadeusz Kantor** "Sea Happening"

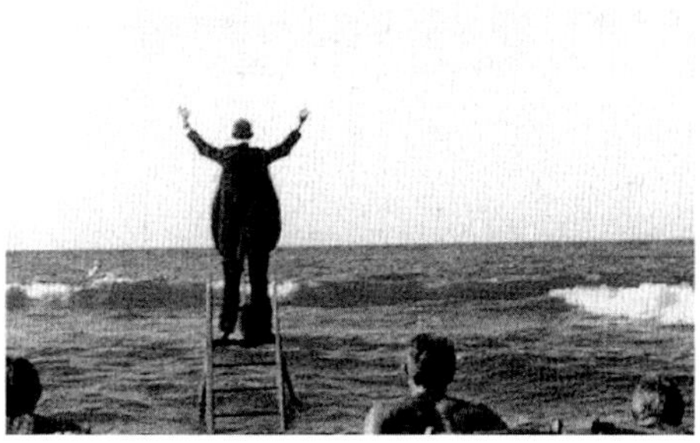

1967 Michelangelo Pistoletto "Venus of Rags"
Rolling Stones
The term **Arte Povera** by Germano Celant
"Poor Art art created from everyday materials (nature, history, or contemporary life).JC Amman "art that aspire to the technological world, end expresses the message by the simplest means."
NY **Claes Oldenburg** "**invisible sculpture**" (digging and refilling a trench)
1967 **Gilbert &George** call themselves "The Human Sculptures (**everything they do is a sculpture**)

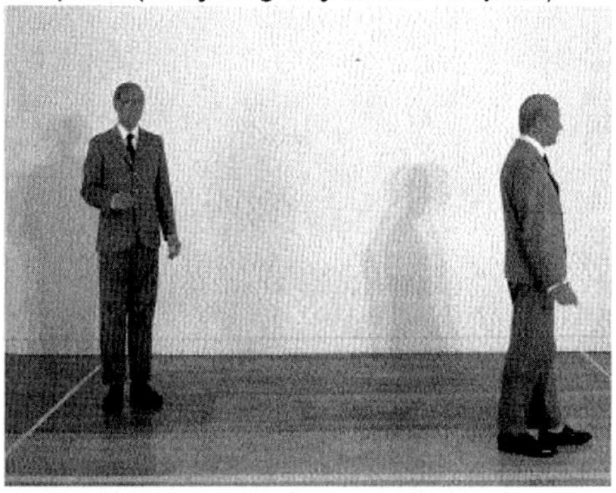

1967 Washinghton DC **'Scale as Content"**
NY Paul Thek "The Tomb Death of a Hippie" Stable Gallery. Joseph Kosuth "Art as Idea as Idea"
NY "Normal Art" Museum of Normal Art
Michelangelo Pistoletto Venus of Rags
1967 **Gerhard Richter**

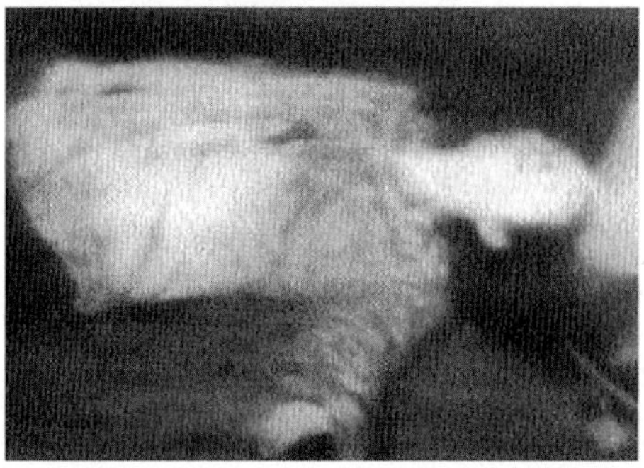

1968 **On Kawara** counting

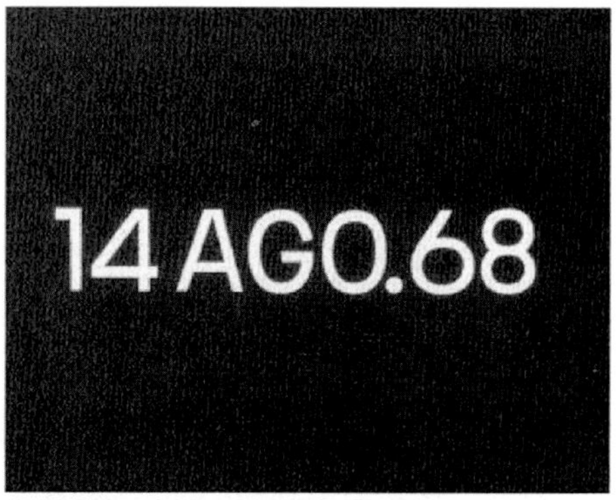

1968 Robert Irwin and **James Turrell (**undertake research on perception with Dr Edward Wortz)
Light and Space Art (art focus on sensory perception - redefine space)
NY Seth Siegelaub organizes first **exhibition** (by Douglas Hueble) **in catalogue form only**
USSR invades Cechoslovakia
Student uprising in Europe and US general strike.
1968 **Garry Winogrand** Demonstration in New York

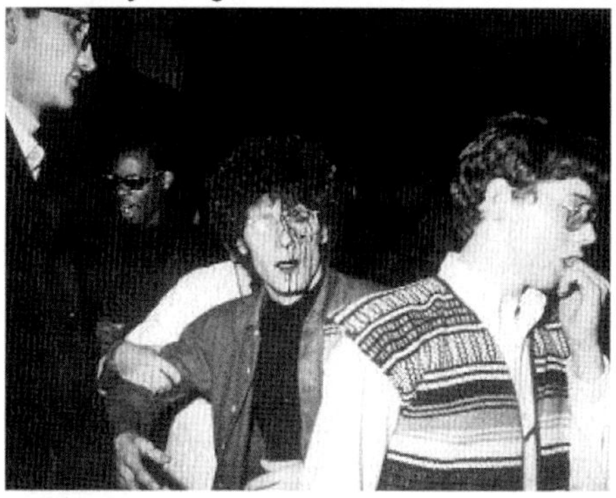

1968 **Eddie Adams** Vietnam

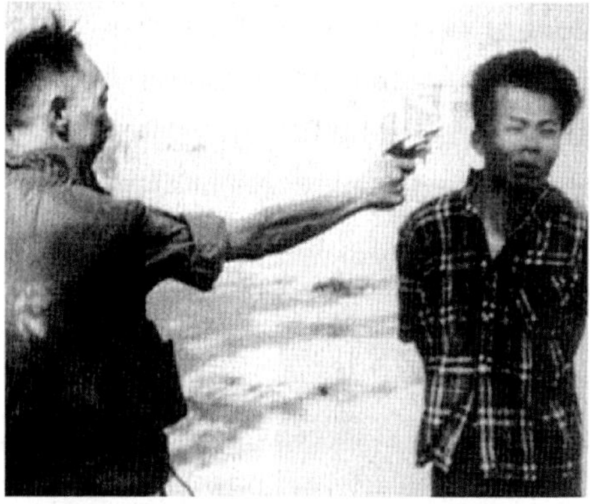

1968 Martin Luther King Jr. is assassinated
"Cybernetic Serendipity" **The Computer and the Arts** ICA London; "The Machine as Seen at the End of the Mechanical Age" MOMA NY; Andy Warhol - shot by Valerie Solanis; Bruce Nauman Slow Angle Walk; Rudolf Schwarzkogler.
Earth Art or Environmental art - **the rejection of the commercialization of art,** and the **support of the emerging ecological movement**
Marcel Duchamp dies - last work Etant donnes
Bruce Nauman "Wall/Floor Positions"
Wien Kunst und Revolution
1968 **Valie Export** and **Peter Weibel** "**Dog map"**

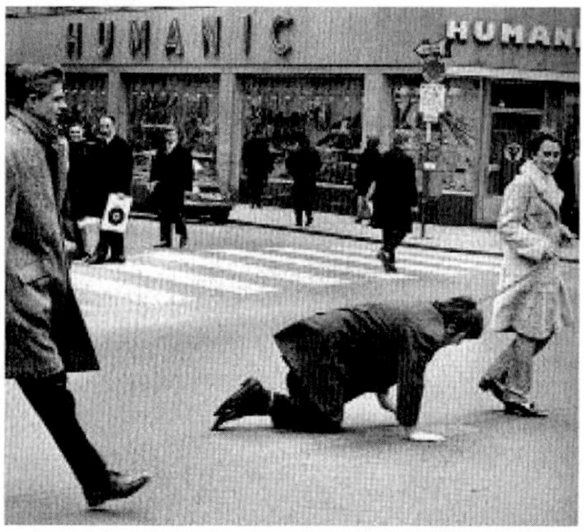

1968 **Paul Neagu** Boxed in

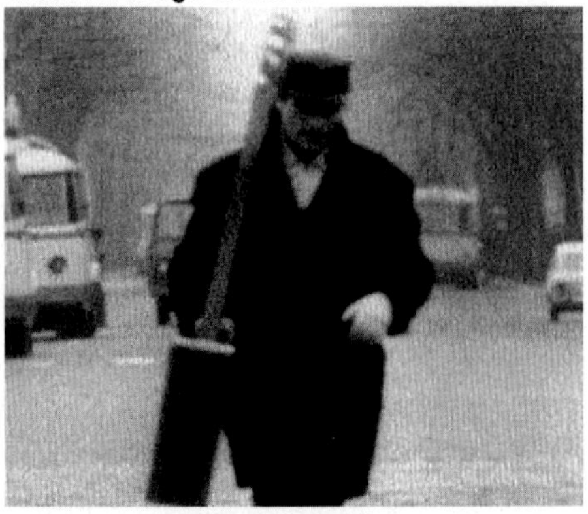

1969 Violent riots in N Ireland between Protestants and Roman Catholics
US Apollo 11 lands on moon, Neil Armstrong first man on the moon

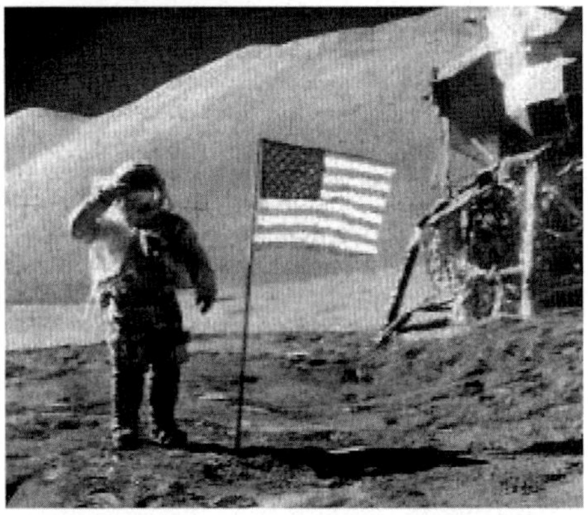

1969 **Art and Technology** - "the enthusiasm generated by the moon landing, but soon technology came to be associated with environmental destruction , nuclear danger..."
Human ovum is success-fully fertilized in vitro
Woodstock - music festival
"When Attitudes Become Form" - Berne Kunsthalle by Harald Szeeman
1968 **Joseph Kosuth** Swiss newspapers containing information for Space

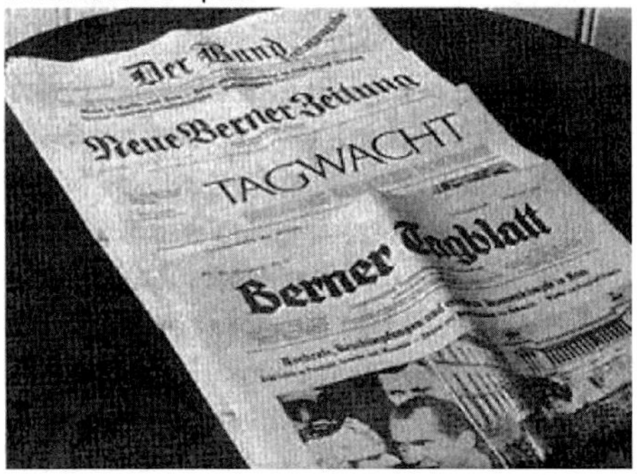

1969 **Stephen Kaltenbach** Tell a Lie, Start a Rumor Artforum;
Judy Chicago founds **first feminist art program** at California State University
First alternative space open in NY
Berne Switzerland **''Plans and Projects as Art"** Kunsthalle;
London Gilbert & George first 'Singing sculpture "
1969 **Christo and Jeanne -Claude** Wrapped Coast, Little Bay Australia Sydney One Million Square Feet

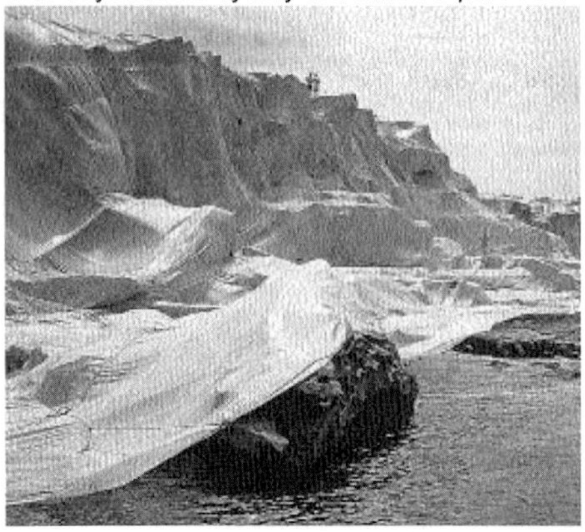

1969 NY 'Anti-Form" by **Robert Morris**
"Continuous Project Altered Daily" (photo)

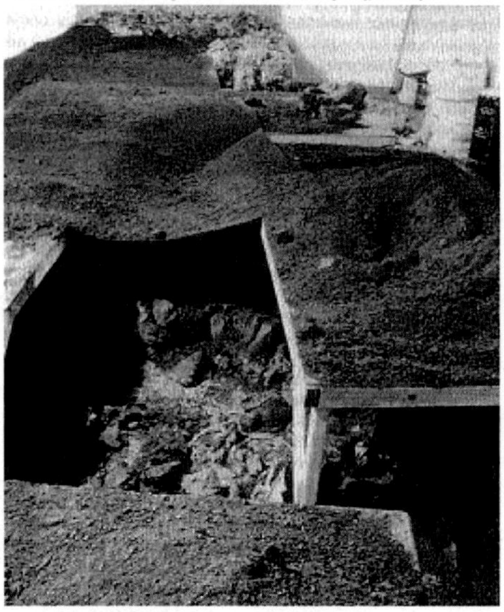

1969 **Robert Barry**

ALL THE THINGS I KNOW
BUT OF WHICH I AM NOT
AT THE MOMENT THINKING—
1:36 PM; JUNE 15, 1969

Robert Barry

1969 NY **''Anti-illusion"Procedures/Materials** WMAA; Rome Jannis Kounellis "Cavalli" (Horses) Galleria L'Attico; Valie Export Genital Panic
Yayoi Kusama opens **fashion boutique** NY
1969 **Marce Broodthaers** (The place of the subject) litteraire autour de Mallarme

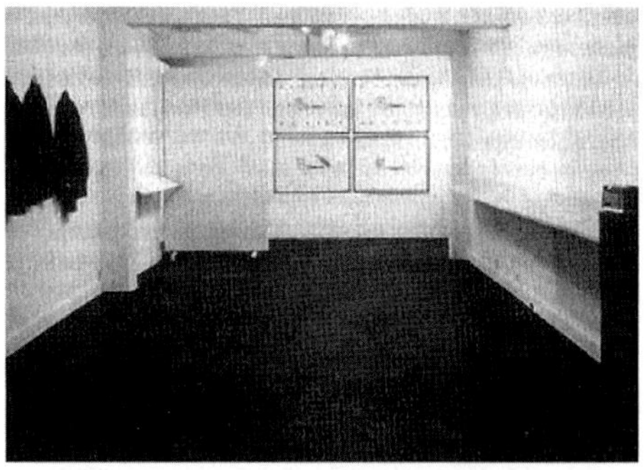

1969 **Ana Lupas** Identity shirt

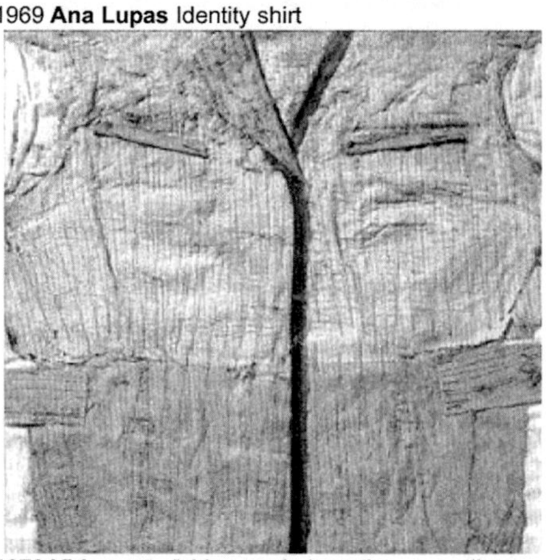

1970 **Video art** - "video made by artist - a medium not a style, documentation, issue the unsolved relationship of art - video - tv
Raises disturbing questions about our increasingly mediated - or direct, media derived experience of reality"
Sound Art exhibition NY;
London ''Idea Structure'
Kate Miller Sexual Politics

1970 **Museum of Conceptual Art** - founded by **Tom Marioni** at San Francisco. Organization of salon-style gatherings and exhibition at the Museum. "The Act of Drinking Beer with Friends is the Highest Form of Art" (photo). In 1971 stages a dinner, then leaves remnants on view California.
1970 **Duane Hanson** Supermarket Lady

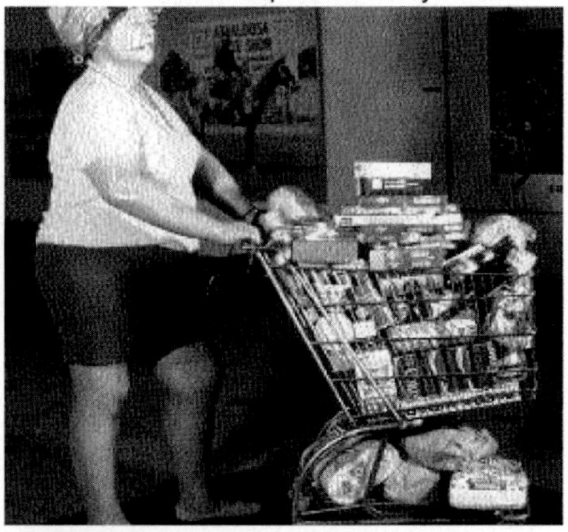

1970 **Richard Hamilton** Ken State

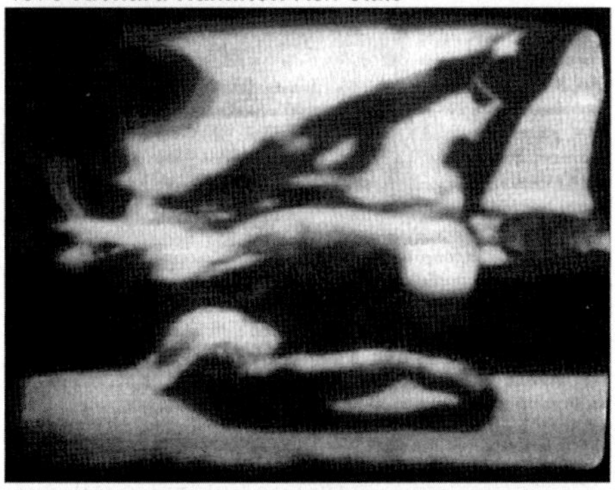

1970 **Cildo Meireles** Project Coca Cola insertions series. Message with white ink (invisible only when the bottle were emty, filled in the factory the information become legible)

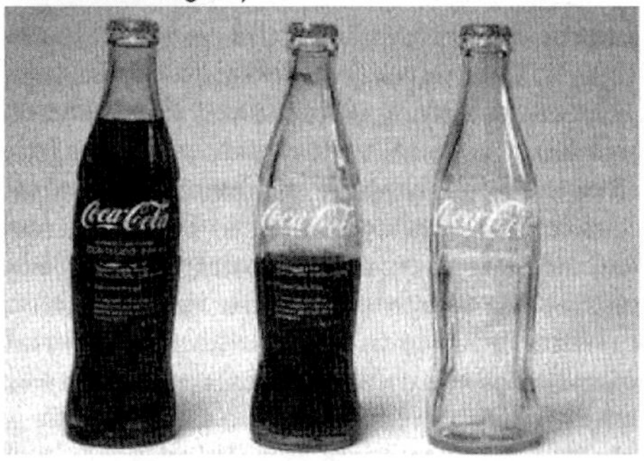

1970 **Jozef Robakowski**, The Market MCA L.

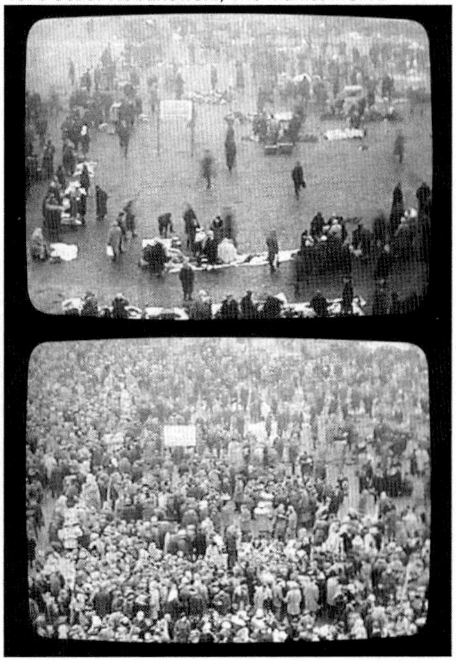

1970 **Joseph Kosuth,** Time

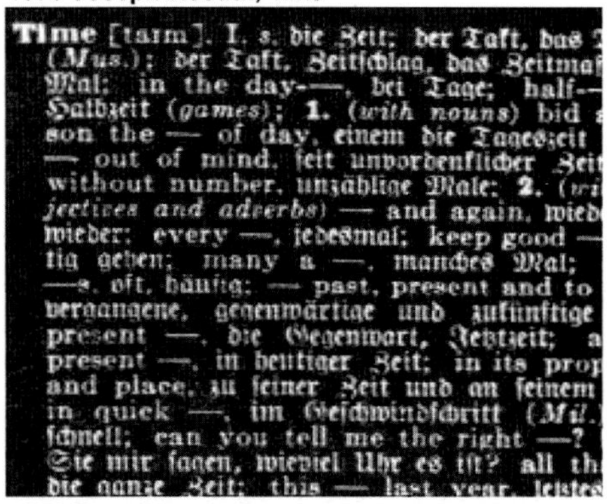

1970 **Terry Fox,** Cellar

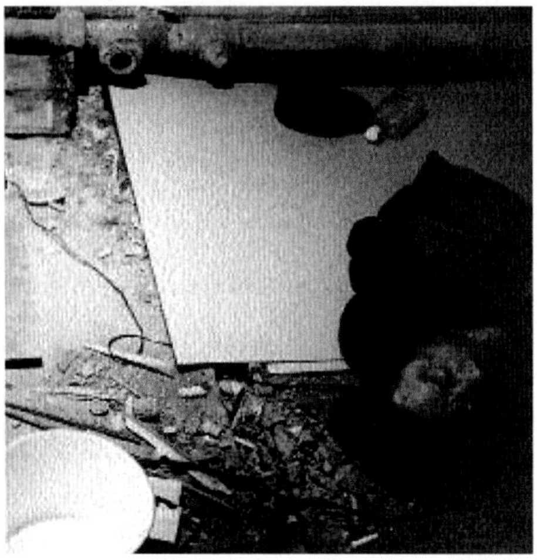

Astronomers confirm the "black hole" theory

1971 **Hans Haacke**- exhibition about NY "Manhattan Real Estat A Real-Time" Social Systeme ownership (is canceled by Guggenheim Museum NY)
"Artists with political agendas - Some art intervention certainly had an effect in raising consciousness about specific issues. If art was everyday, than **art could be made in everyday situations "**

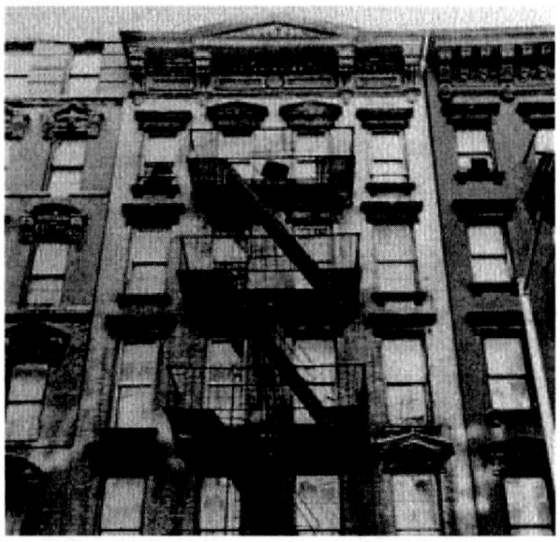

Walter de Maria **Lighting Field** 1971-77; Vito Acconci "Second hand performance"
1971 California Santa Ana **Chris Burden** - the 5 Day Looker piece...and let himself **Shoot**

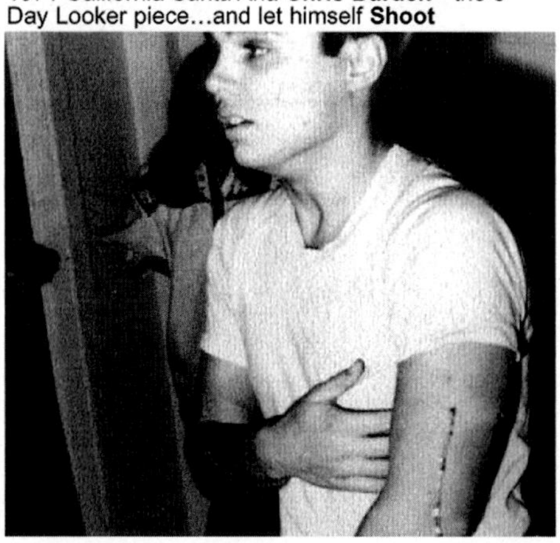

ICA New York founded by Alanna Heiss
1971 **Robert Morris** Minding the body at Tate

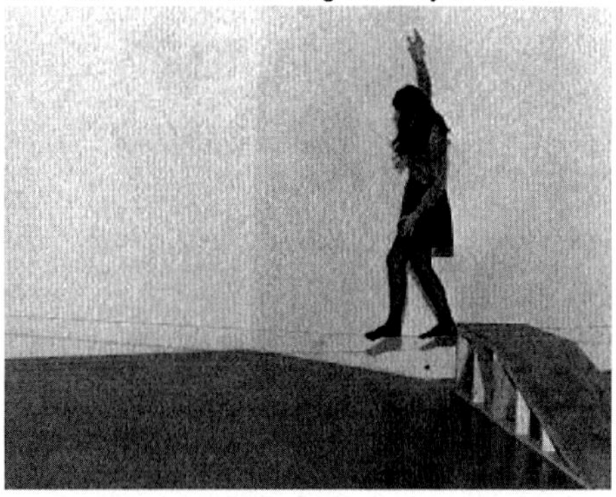

1971 **Ladislav Novak** Circle

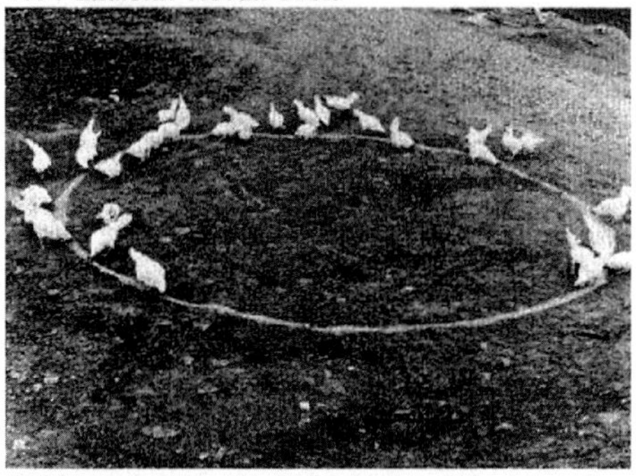

1972 London "And for Today Nothing" 2 week action by Stuart Brisley at Gallery House
US Supreme Court rules the death penalty unconstitutional
Arab terrorists kill two Israeli Olympic athletes in Munich, take nine others hostage all of whom are killed in shoot-out with police and military
1972-2000 **Jurge Klauke**

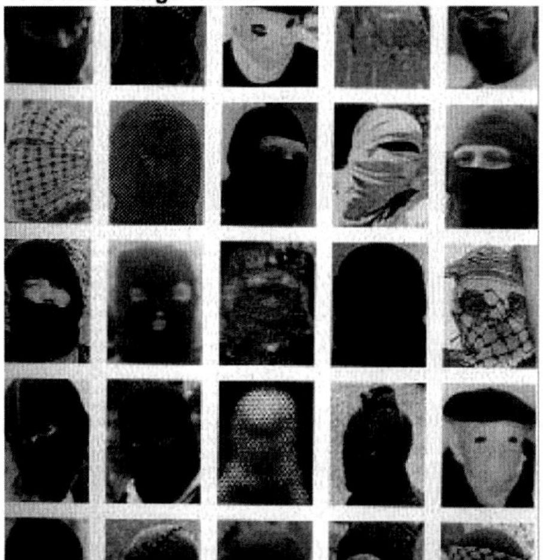

1972 Documenta 5 Photo-Realism
Gilbert and George All my life I give you nothing and still you ask for more
Sots art - Komar and Melamid - Moscow "**on communication and on how people behave"**.
Chris Burden TV Hijack during interview on cable television
1972 **Faith Wilding, Waiting**/Womanhouse

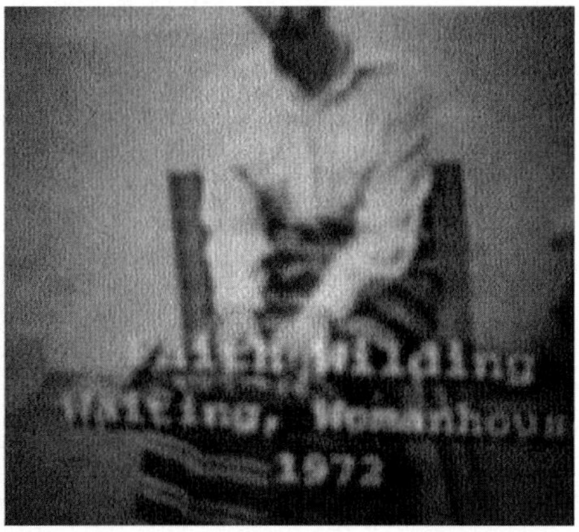

1972 **James Turrel,** Roden Crater, Arizona

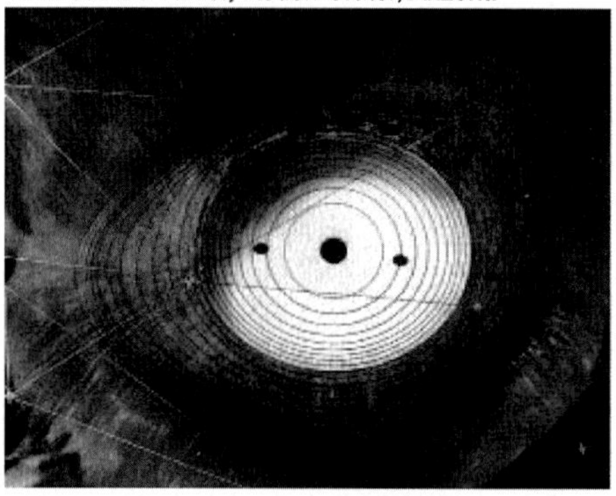

1972 **Ion Grigorescu,** Report from Gorj

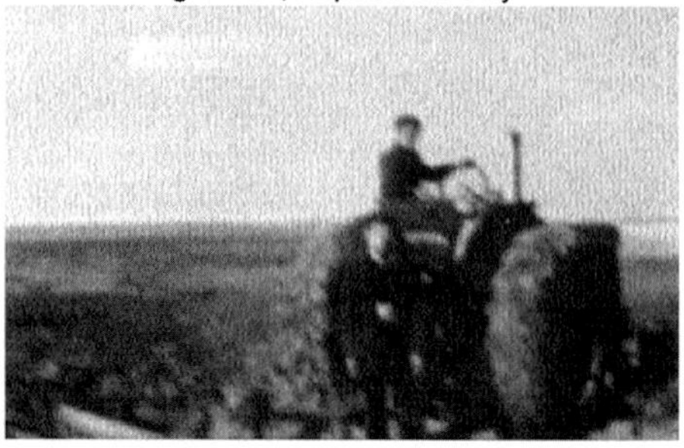

1972 **Jaroslaw Kozlowski** Physiks.

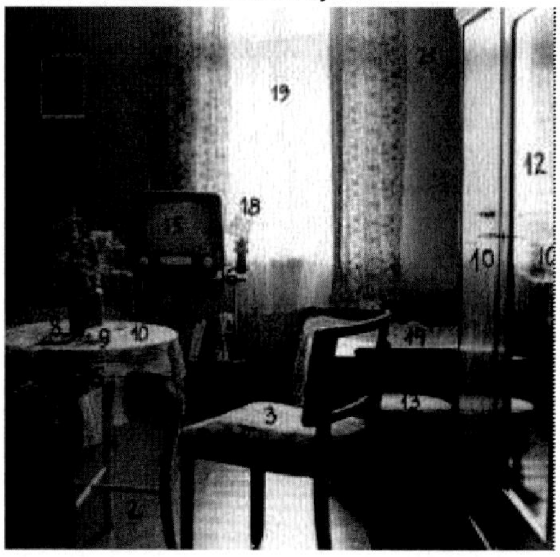

1972 **Tom Marioni**

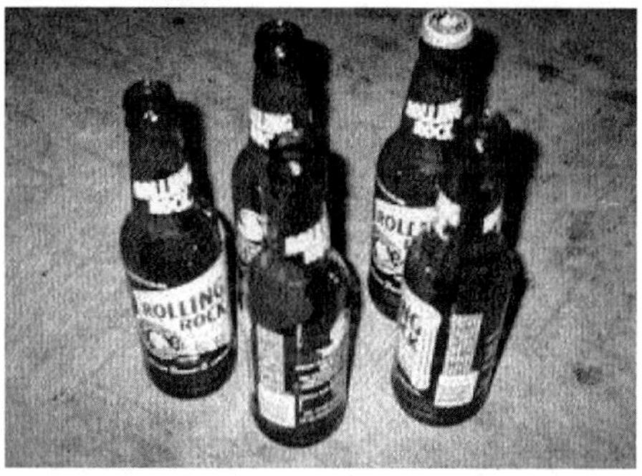

US Supreme Court rules a state may not prevent a woman from having an abortion.
1973 **Linda Montano and Tom Marioni handcuff four days** (later with Hiech handcuff 1 year)

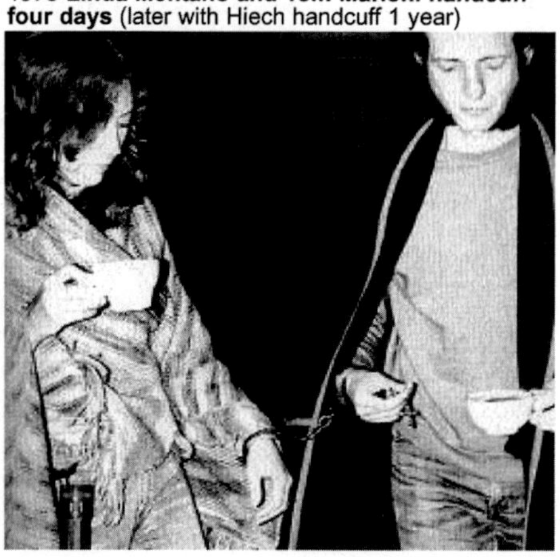

1973 **Stelarc** inside my Stomach.
Mel Bochner Axion of Indifference

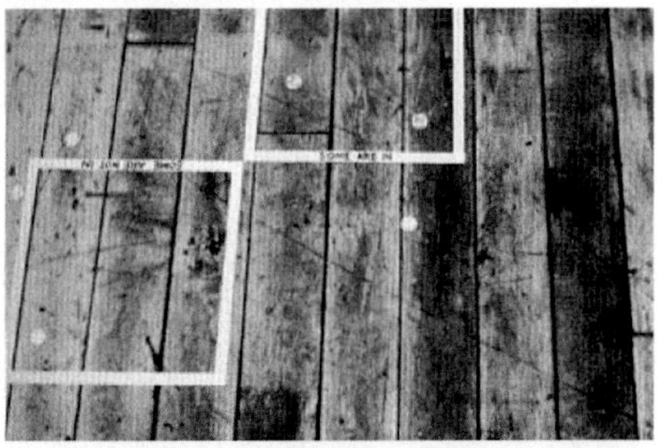

1973 **Marcel Broodthaers** The Manuscript Found in a Bottle. Bordeaux wine bottle, transparent glass marked "The Manuscript 1833" wrapped in printed tissue paper, in a cardboard box with a legend in 3 languages.

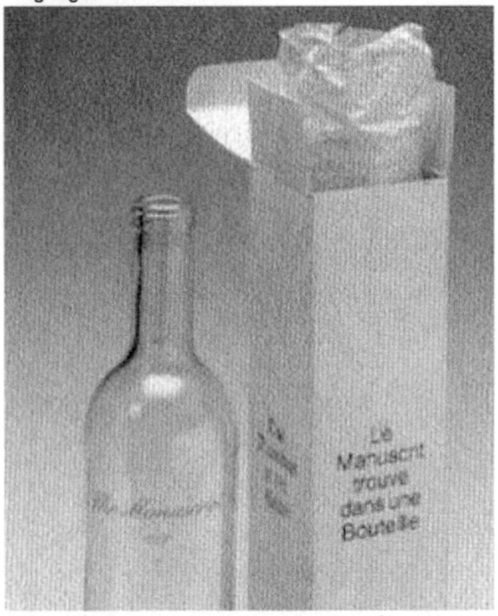

1973 **Mary Kelly** Post Partum Document ('73-'79)

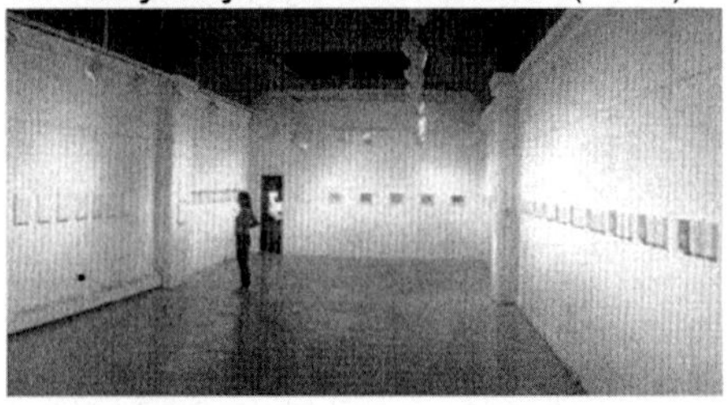

1973 **Oyvind Fahlstrom**

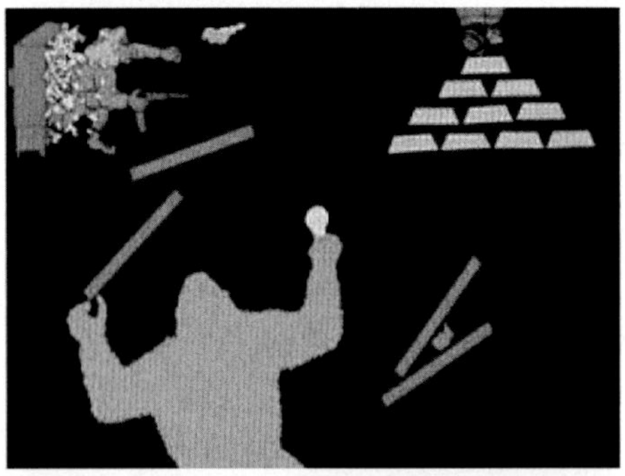

1973 **Manfred Mohr, P 159A** plotter drawing

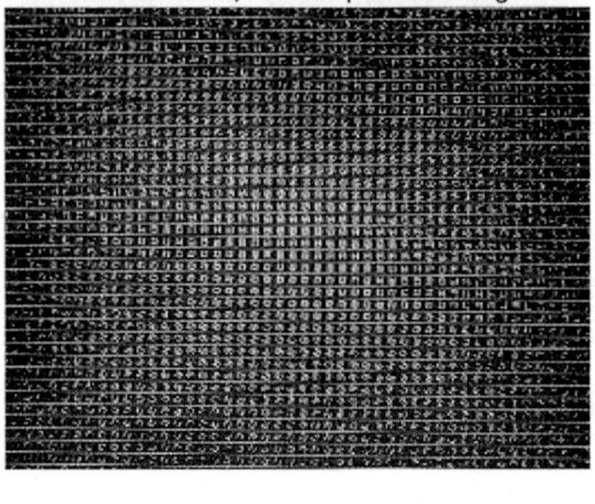

1974 Worldwide inflation and recession
FF **Copola** The Conversation

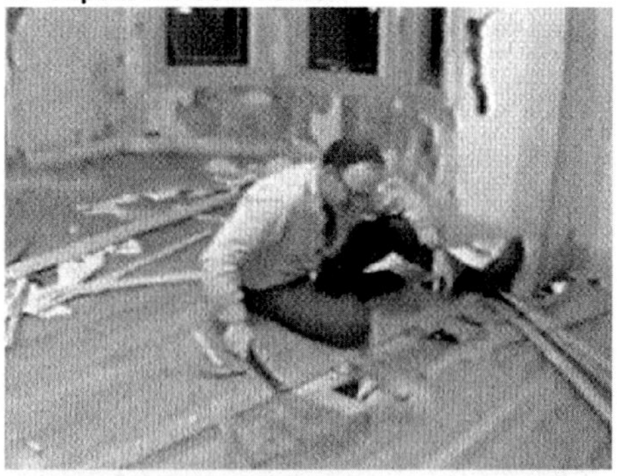

1974 **Dennis Oppenheim** Aging

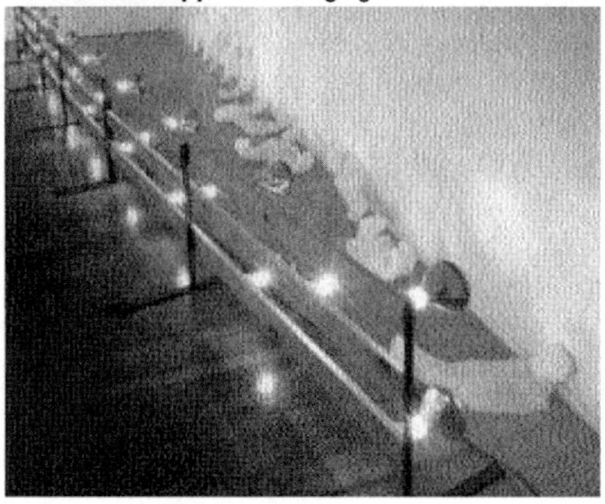

Vito Acconci Command performance - (a way to move from the page to an outside physical space.)
1974 **Carl Andre** Weather Deck

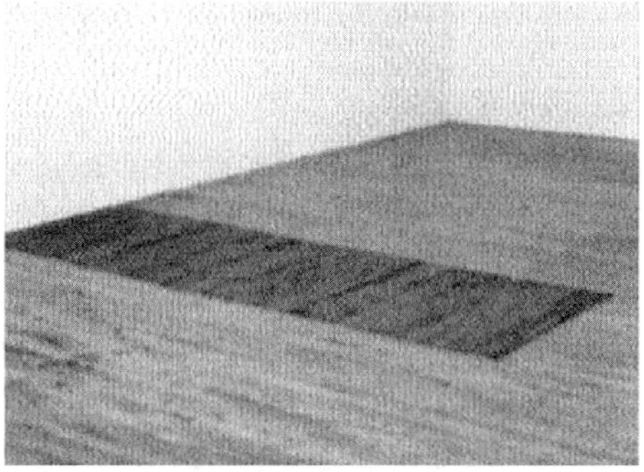

1974 **Joseph Beuys** New York 5 days with a Coyote "I like America and America likes Me'

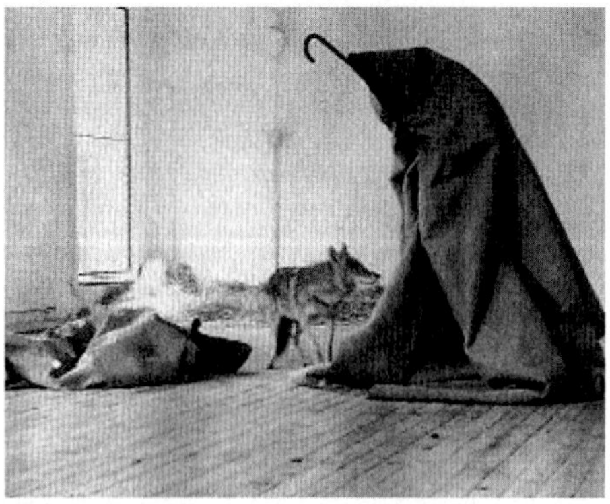

1974 **Geta Bratescu** No to violence

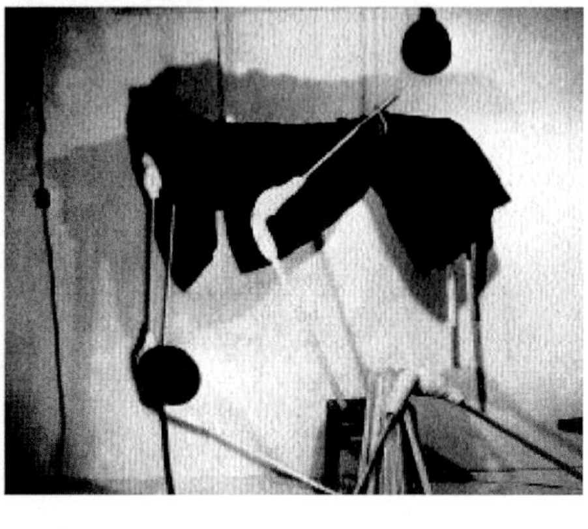

1974 **Marina Abramovic** Italy

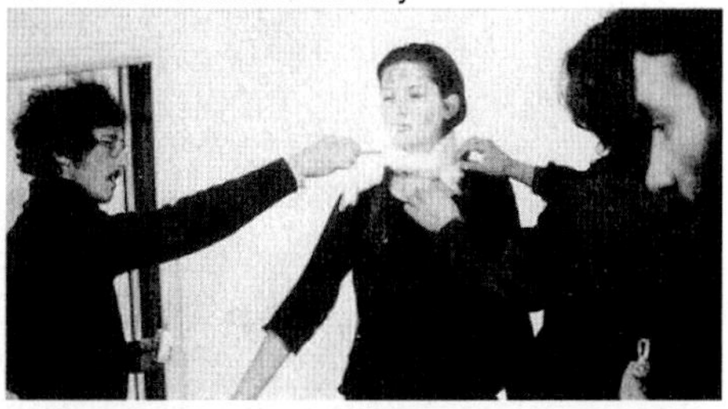

NY PS1 Museum opens **"Rooms"** exhibition.
Darmstadt Germany **Walter de Maria The Large Earth Room** at the Hessische Landesmuseum
1974-77, Permanent installation at Dia Center NY

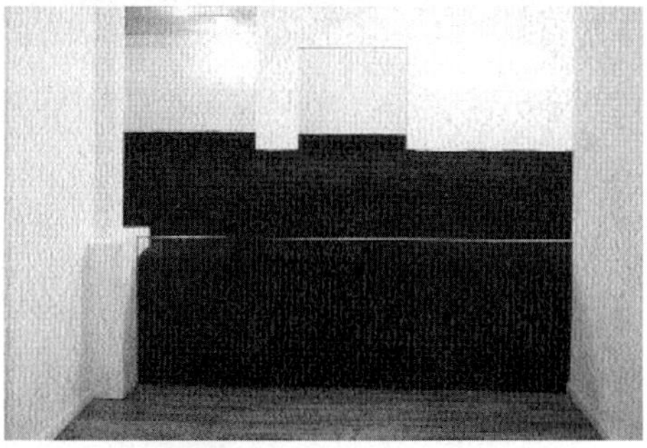

1974 Robert Wilson A Letter for Queen Victoria
Eleanor Antin begins public performances **in characters of a King, a Ballerina, a Black Movie Star, a Nurse** California
1974 **Dan Graham Present Continuous Past**(s) John Gibson Gallery New York

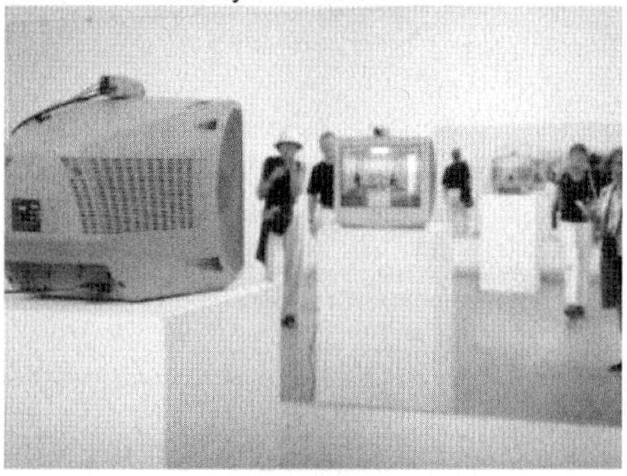

1974 **Gordon Matta Clark** Splitting

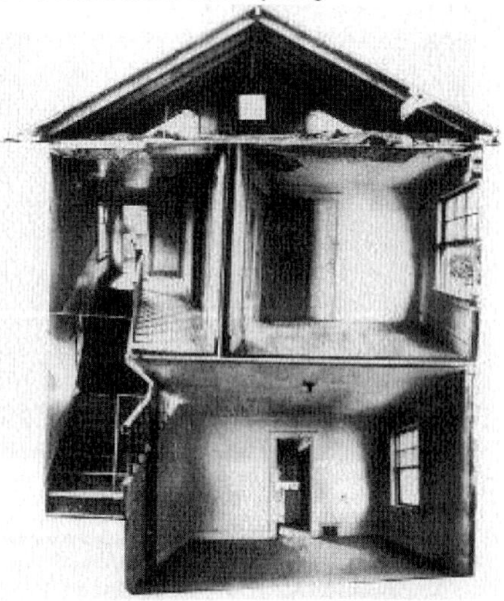

1974 **Michael Ascher**

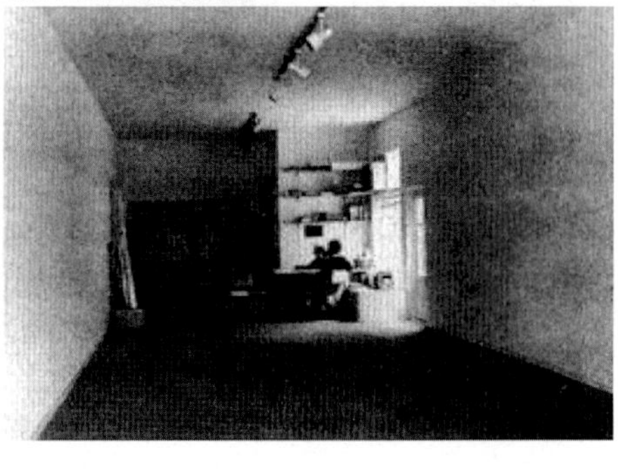

1975 Civil wars in Lebanon, Angola, and Ethiopia
First exhibition of **Graffiti** Art Artist Space NY - "scratch" it the plural form are drawings or images scratched into the surfaces of walls. Illicit graffiti (of the "Kilroy was here" variety) soon after aerosol spray paints in cans became readily available - NY subway trains were subjected to an onslaught of exuberantly colored graffiti. Streetwise teenagers. Unusual aesthetic and sociological import. Vandalism? Urban folk art? Anarchic manifestation of social freedom
Body works at ICA Chicago
1975 **Marina Abramovic** Amsterdam

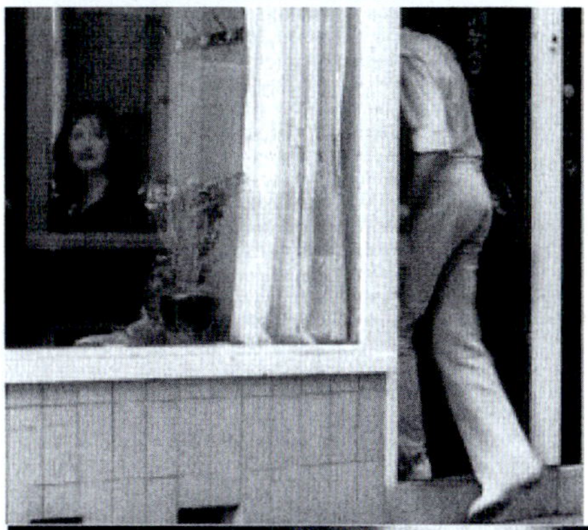

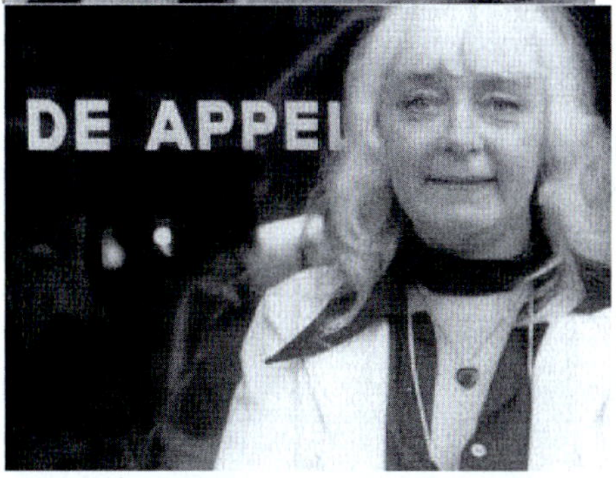

1975 **TR Uttico and Ant Farm The Eternal Frame** (Abraham Zapruder' amateur 8 millimeters film of Kennedy' assassination **)- frame by frame**

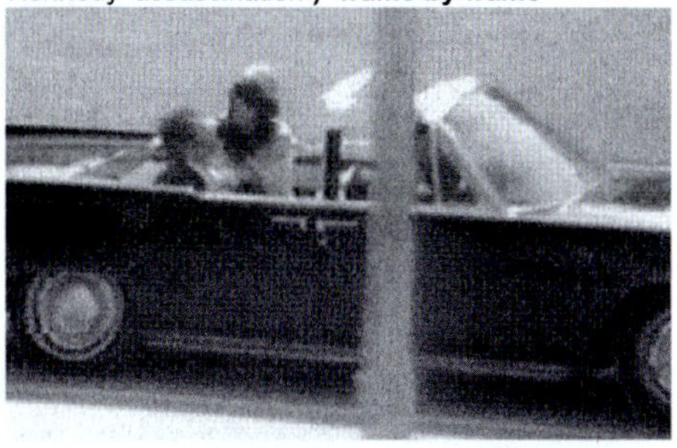

1978 Paris **Marcel Broothaers** La Salle blanche CNAC

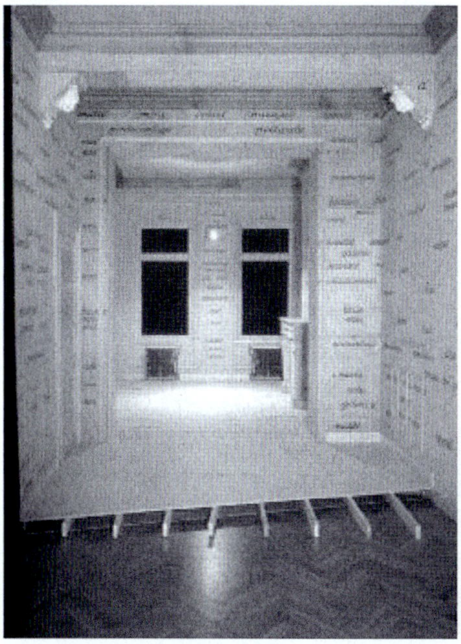

1975 **Maya Ying Lin, Vietnam Memorial** Washington DC

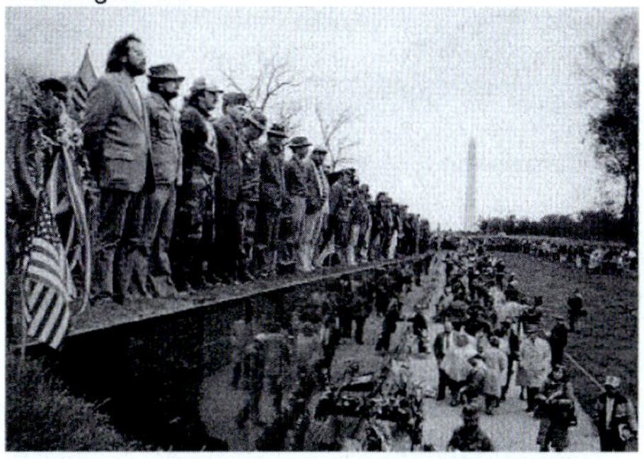

1976 **Brian O'Doherty** "Inside the **White Cube**"
First functional synthetic genre constructed at Massachusetts Institute of Technology Cambridge
1976 **Paul Neagu** Ramp Hyphen

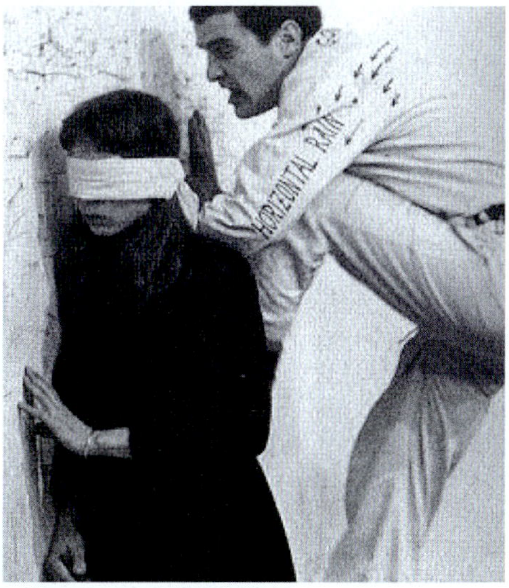

1977 **Disco** craze - Saturday Night Fever
George Pompidou (Beaubourg) opens in Paris
Jan Micoch The Classic Escape

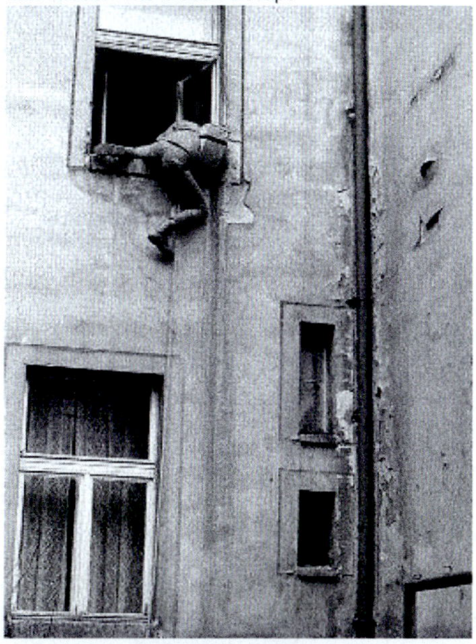

1977 **Gary Hill** Electronic Linguistics

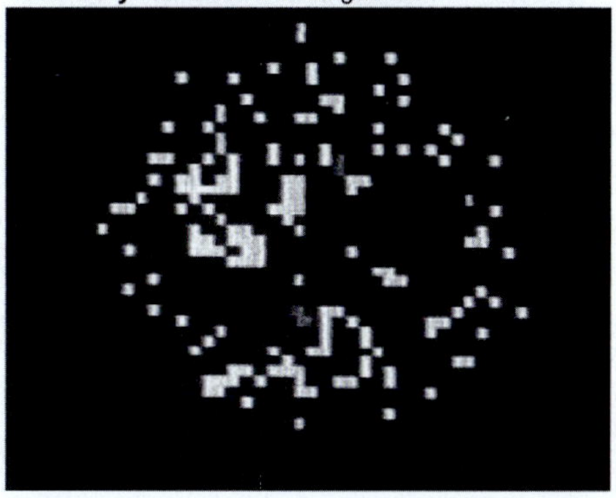

1977 London Ting (Theatre of **Mistake**s A Waterfall performance). **Documenta 6, Art and Media**
Ion Grigorescu Boxing

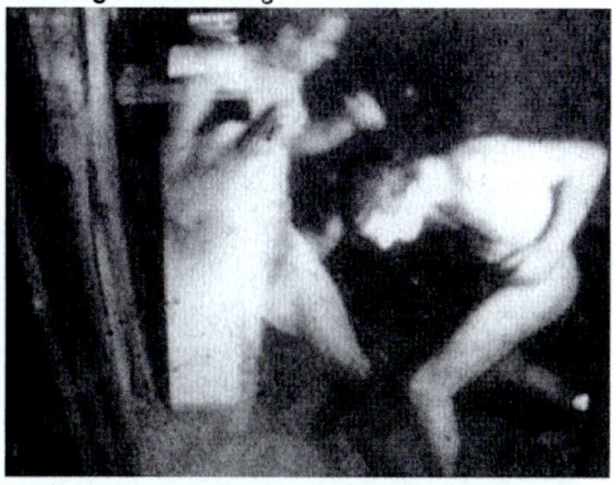

1978 **First "test-tube baby " is born in GB**
African Art - Gana leaders

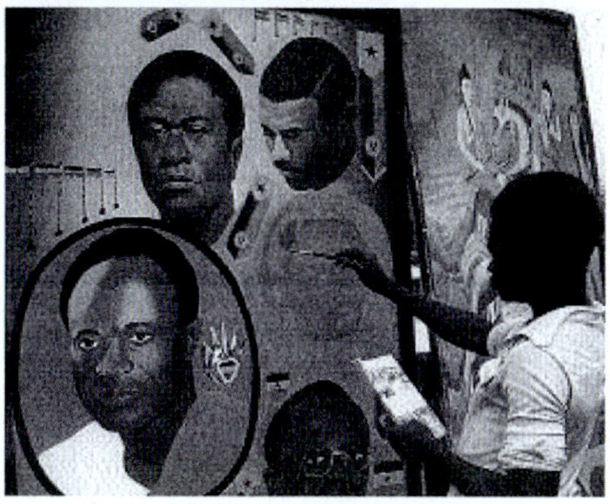

1978 **Stelarc** Event for Lateral Suspension Tokyo

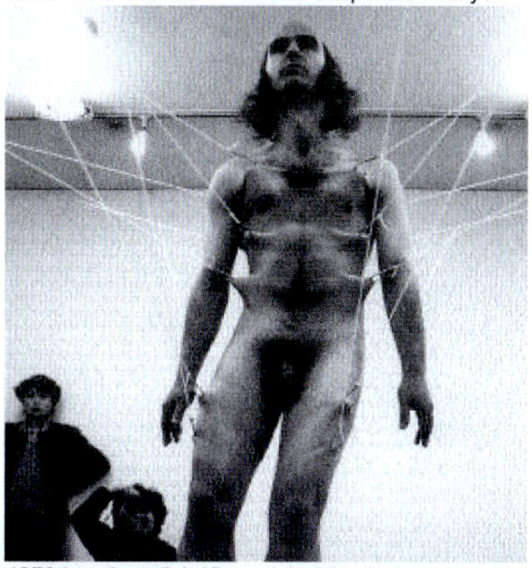

1979 Iran Ayatollah Khomeini - Islamic government
Christopher Lasch the Culture of Narcissism - about the "me generation"
1979 Zagreb **Sanja Ivekovic** Triangle

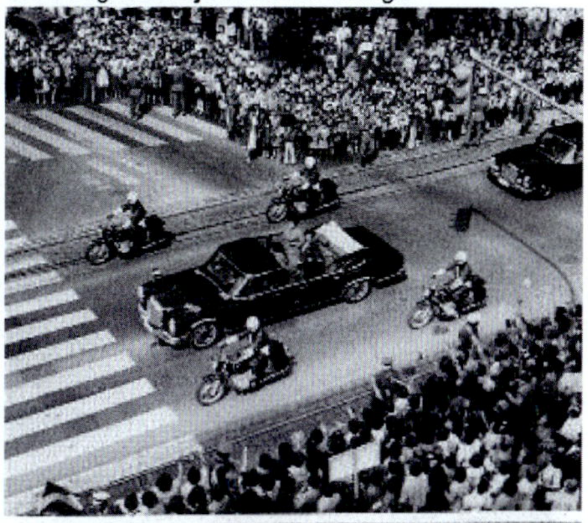

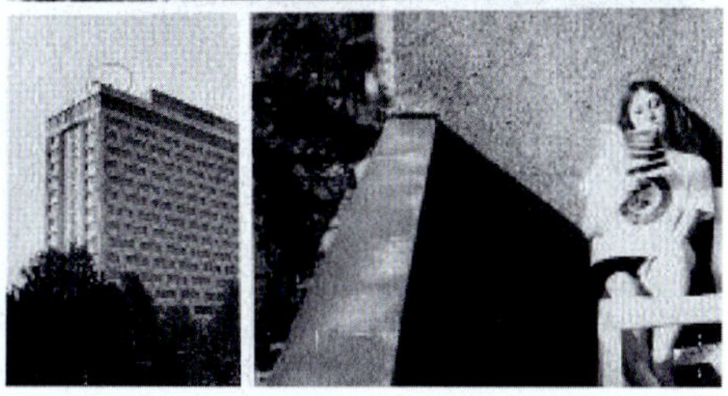

1980 **East EU Ion Grigorescu** (secret service agent)

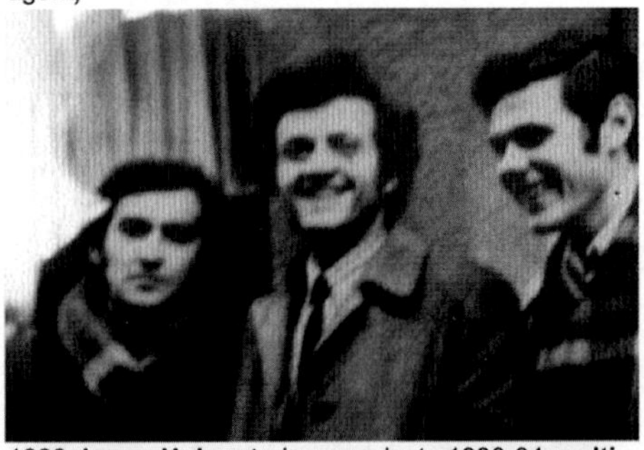

1980 **Jenny Holzer** truisms projects 1980-94 **multiple** (Produced in quantity relative low-priced works of contemporary art)

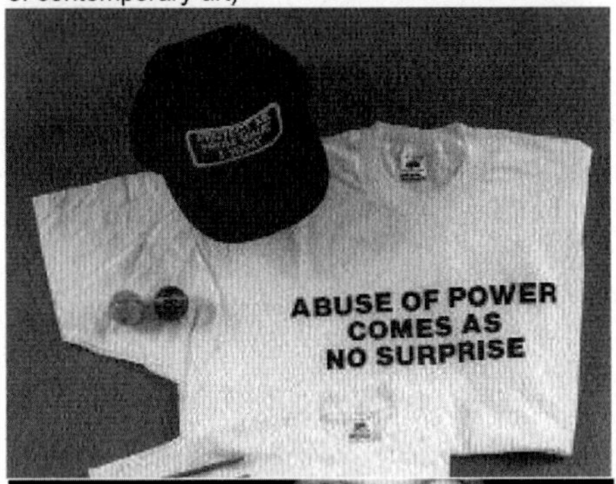

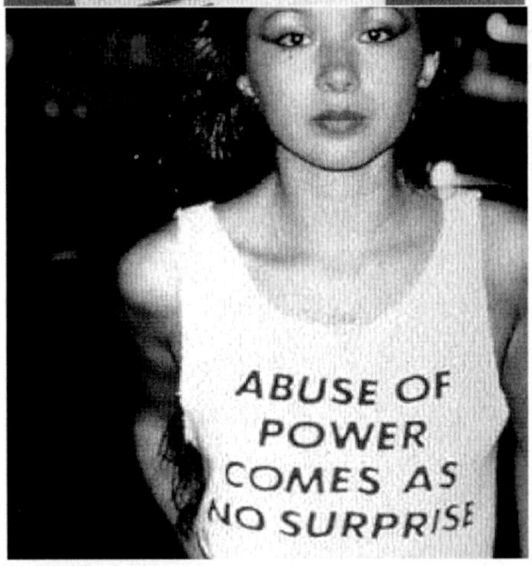

1980 **Marry Duffy Venus (performance** The effect of sedative thalidomide - birth defects)

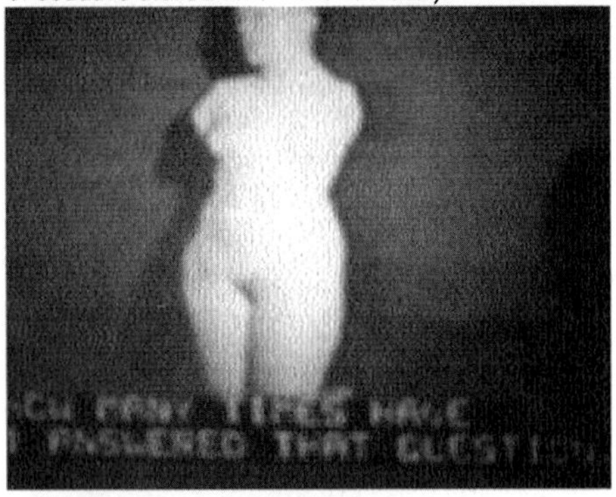

Berlin Bureau - experimental art space.
1980 **John Duncan** Blind Date

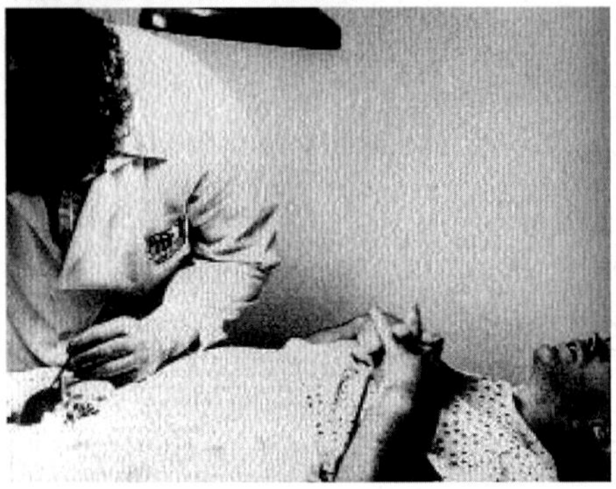

1980 **Ulay Marina Abramovic** Rest Energy

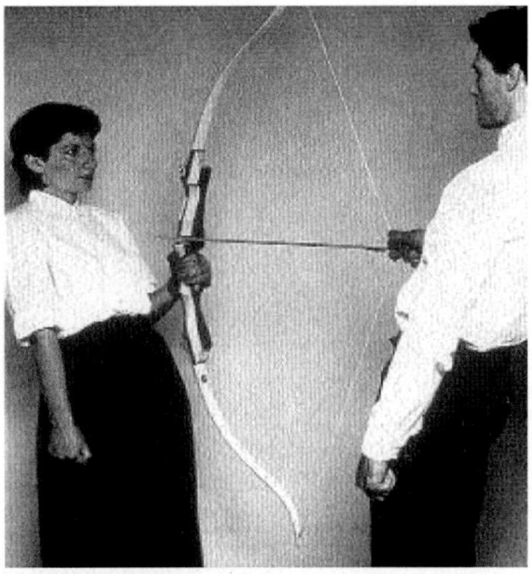

1980 **Nan Golding**

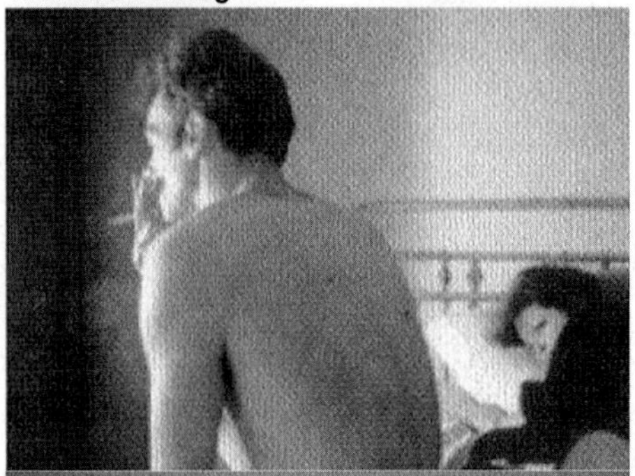

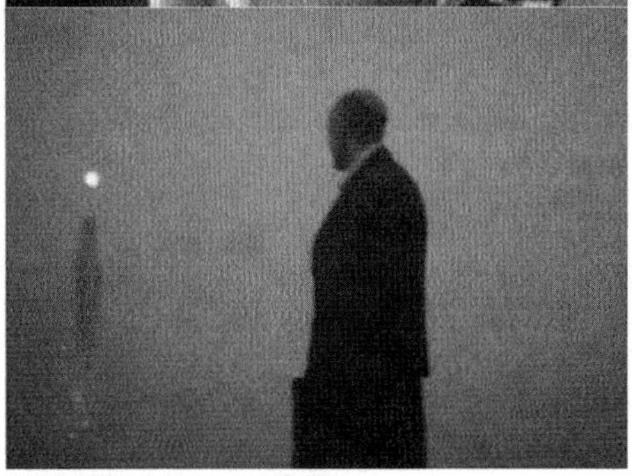

1981 **MTV** debuts on US TV
Berlin "**Zeitgeist**" exhibition - "spirit of the time" suggests the mood and thinking of a given era or, "what's in the air"
Appropriation to borrow. Is the practice of creating a new work by taking a pre-existing image from another context - art history, advertising, and the media? (photo). The postmodern appropriator redraw repaints re photographs it. ? On originality Is a technique or a method of working? Celebratory and critical. What constitutes a masterpiece, a master, art history itself. **Elaine Sturtevant**.

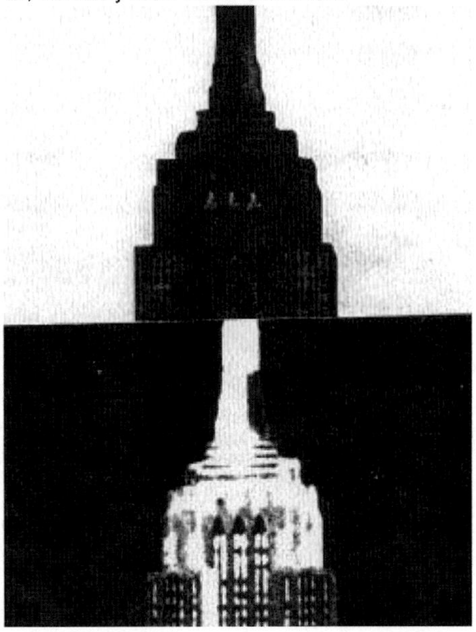

1980 **Sherrie Levine** (after Walker Evans 1936)

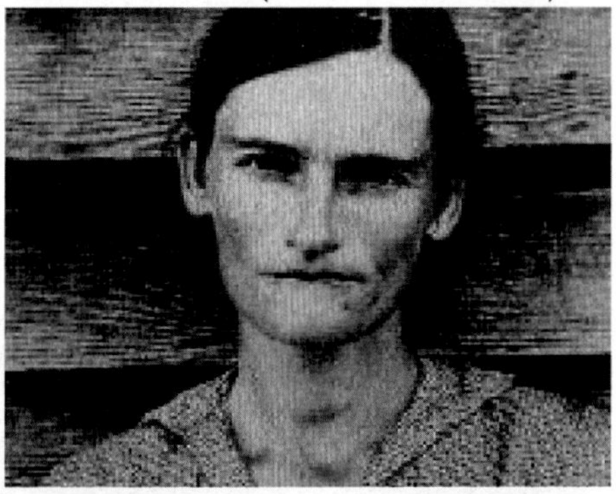

1982 **AIDS** - named by the US Centers for Disease Control. "Extended Sensibilities, Homosexual Presence in Contemporary Art", New Museum of Contemporary Art NY
1982 **Keith Haring** graffiti .

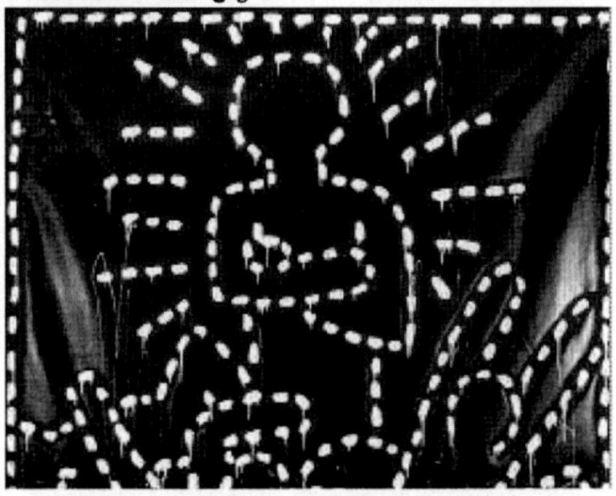

1982 **Werner Herzog** Fitzcaraldo

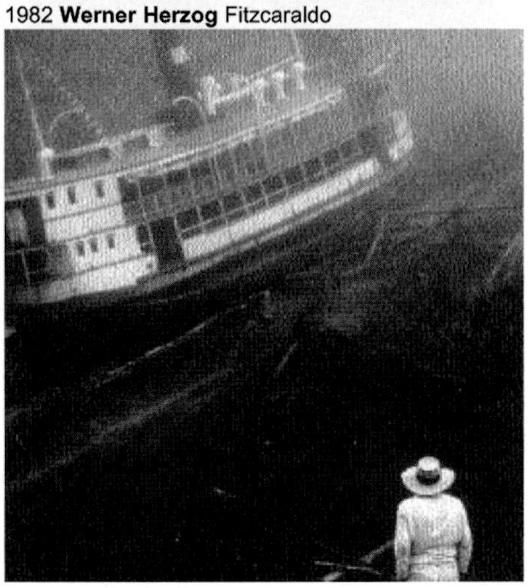

1983 **Jean Michel Basquiat**

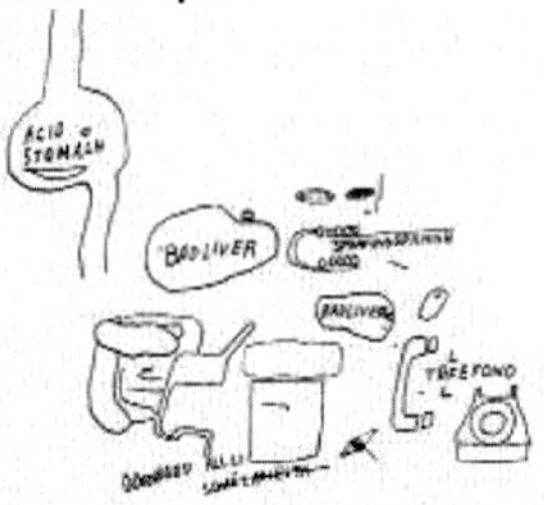

1983 **Jenny Holzer** Survival, Times Square NY 83-85

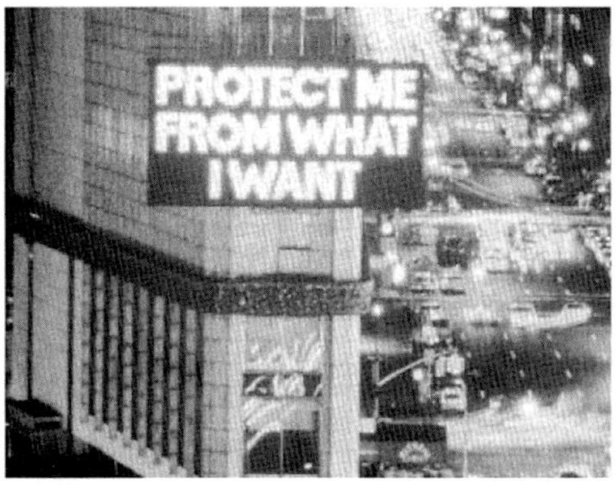

1983 **Sub-urb**

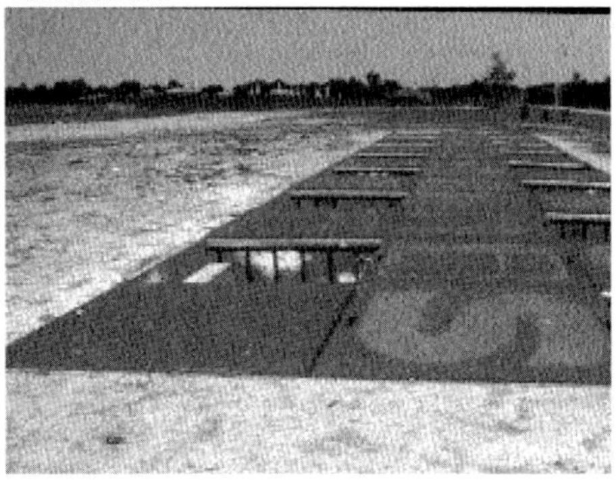

1984 Difference On Representation and Sexuality NMCA NY. Washington DC "**Content**": A Contemporary Focus 1974—84
St Louis Missouri Alice Aycock **The 100 Small Rooms**;
Stelarc Street Suspension
1984 **Group Material**

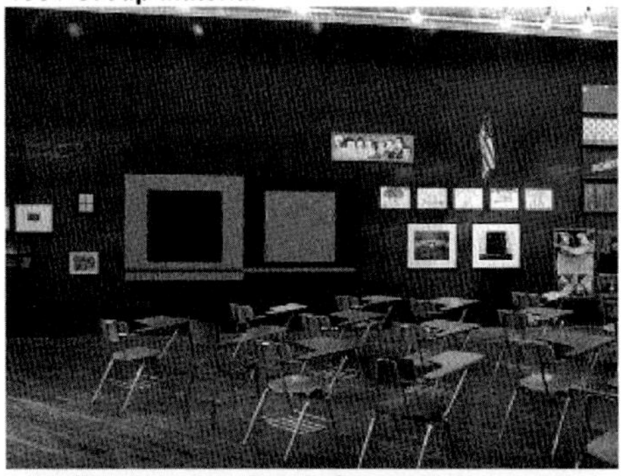

1985 The Japanese **Butoh** Group in NY

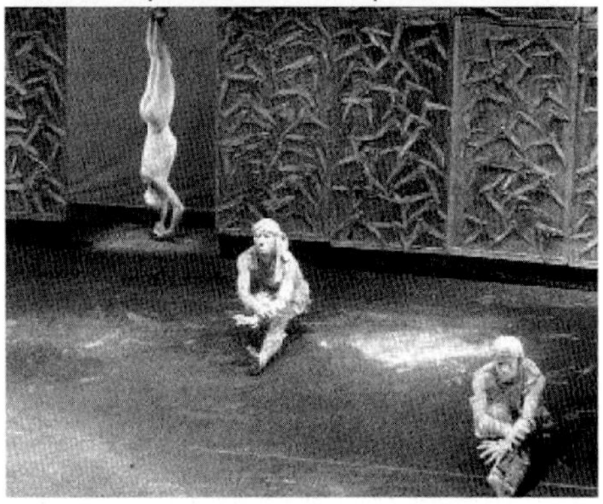

1985 **M Gorbachev** Perestroika and Glasnost
Jeff Koons One Ball Total Equilibrium Tank

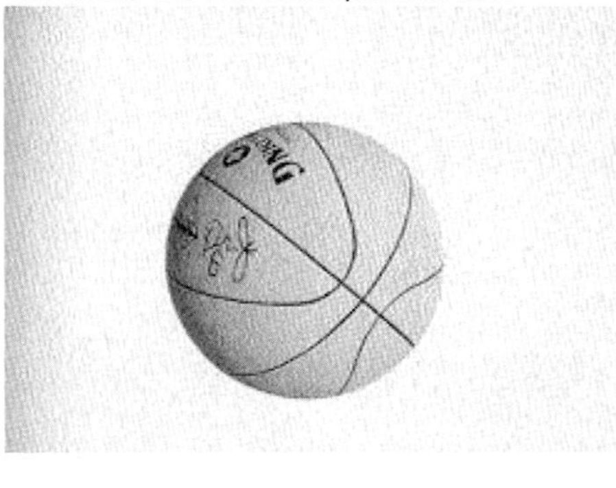

1985 LA "**The Artist as Social Designer** Aspects of Urban Art."NY "The Art of Memory the Loss of History" The New Museum
1985 **John Schlesinger**

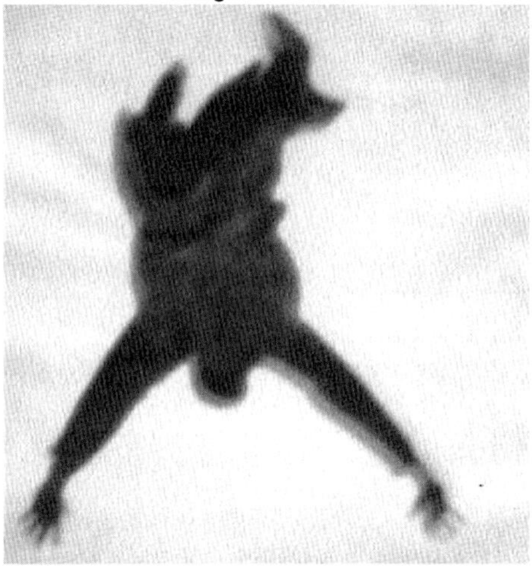

1985 **Peter Fischli/David Weiss** Der Lauf der Dinge

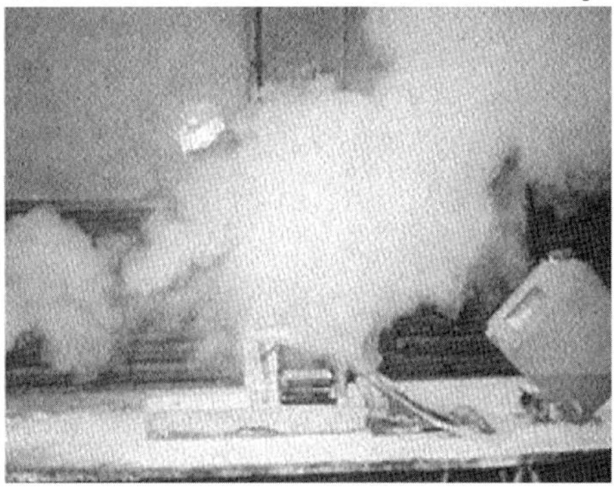

Lia&Dan Perjovschi AP art, meeting place Oradea
1985 **Gregor Shneider** House

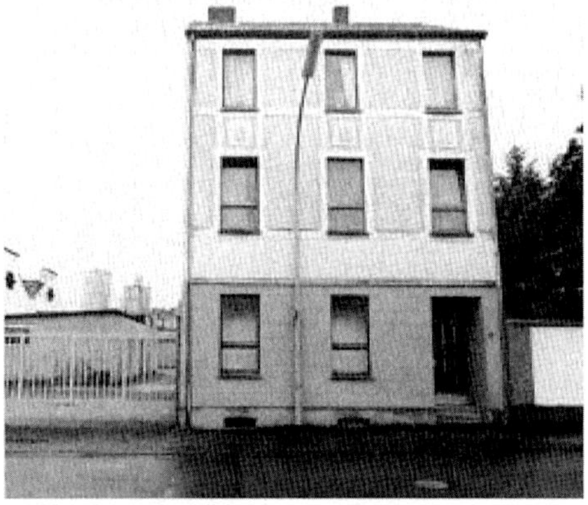

1986 US bombs Libia in response to terrorism in the Middle East. **Nuclear accident at Chernobyl**
1986 **Jeff Koons** Rabit

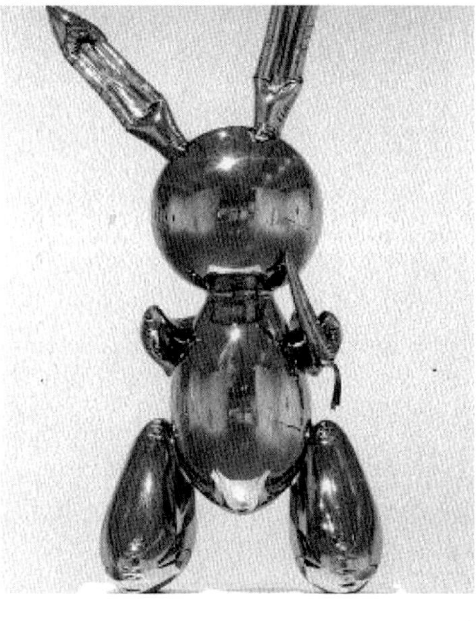

1986 US Space shuttle Challenger explodes
Ghent Belgium "**Chambre d'amis** - 50 installations **in domestic locations in the city**
Pittsburgh, Lothar Baumgarten, Vacuum
" **Arts and Leisure**" curated by Group Material, the Kitchen, New York**.**
Pipilotti Rist "I am not the girl who misses much

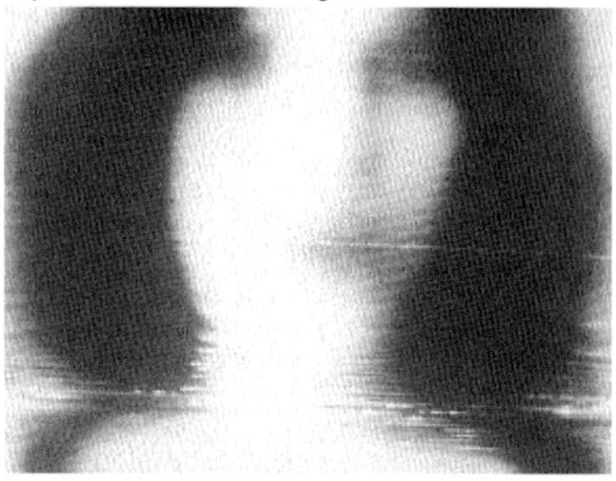

1986 **Black Audio Film Collective**

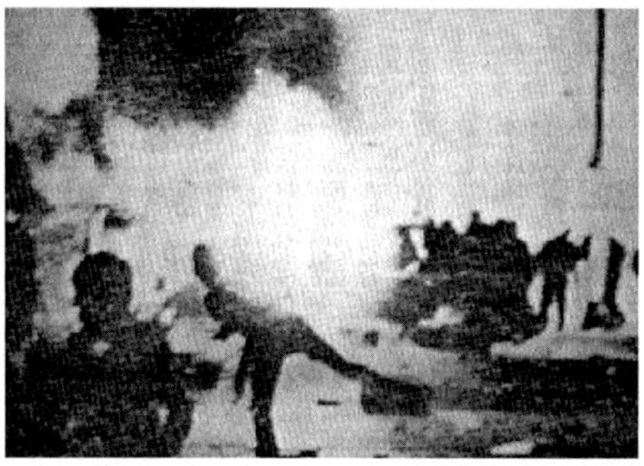

1986 **Sophie Calle** Les Aveugles

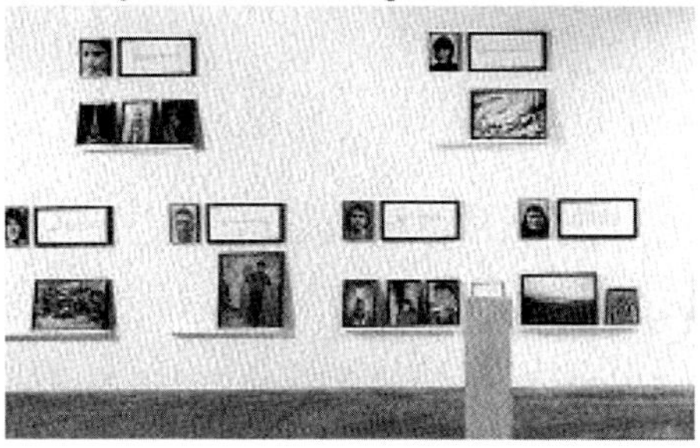

Madonna

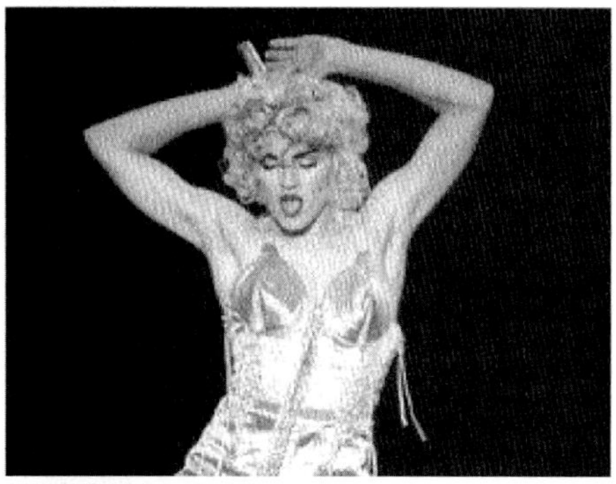

1986 **Wolfgang Robbe**

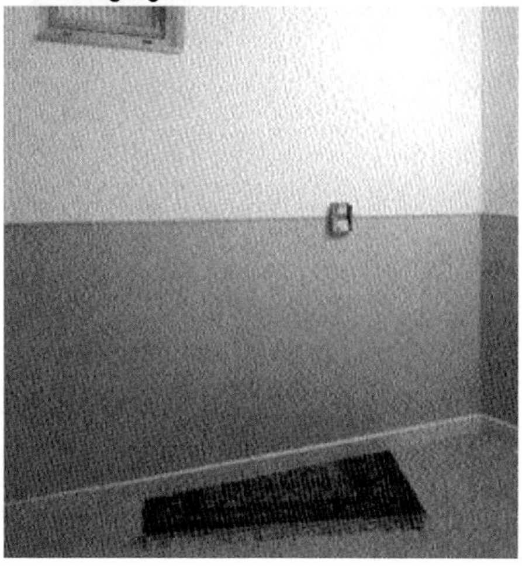

1987 Stock market crashes in NY
NY **"This is Tomorrow Today'** at Clocktower Arnhem, Barbara Bloom Lost and Found.
Largest gay-lesbian demonstration for civil rights Washington DC
1987 **Names Project Quilt**, devoted to those who have died of AIDS - Washington Mall DC

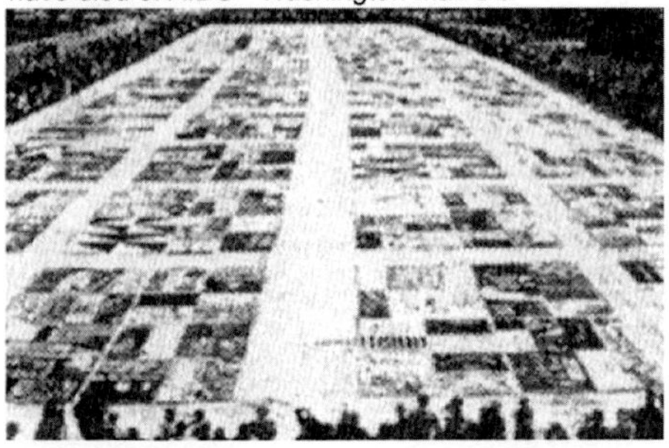

1987 **Chris Burden** US submarines

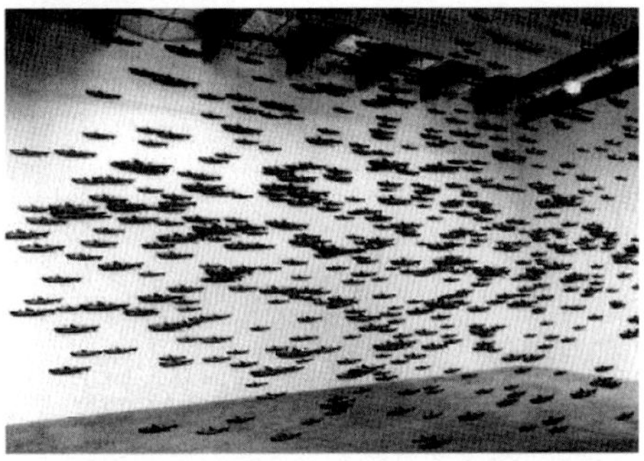

1987 **Robert Campbell** Death in custody

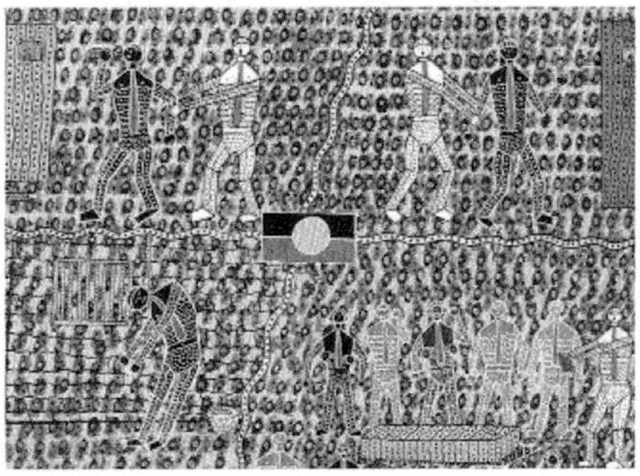

1987 **Timm Ulrich** x-ray images

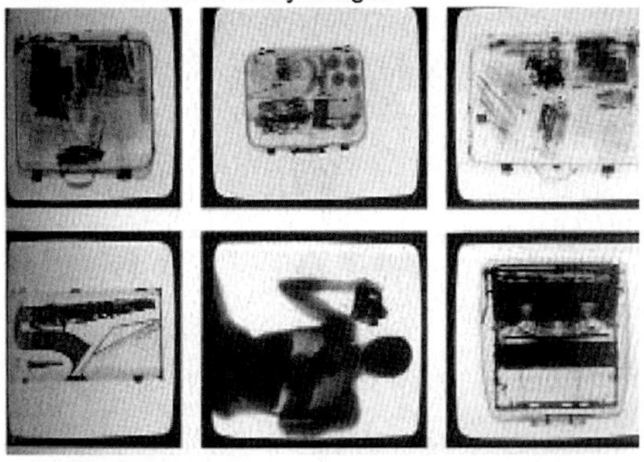

1987 **Andres Serrano** Piss Christ

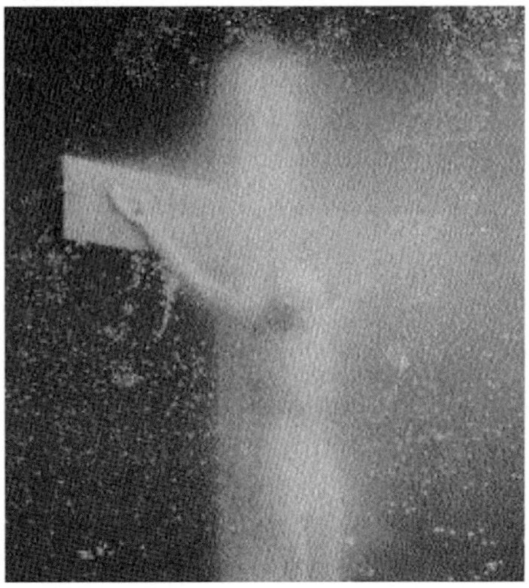

1987 **Felix Gonzalez-Torres**. Photographs printed on puzzles, stacks of posters, **piles of candy** (given away), **curtains of blue fabric**, **intimate images in public spaces**. A festive atmosphere, positive energy, precarious existence, loss and death. Pleasure as a form of ultimate struggle against denial and death. "Macro-history" and "micro-history". Being together. Idea of celebration, the need for desires the innocence of pleasure, the beauty of sharing. "The inclusion of the other in oneself" Charles Arthur Boyer.
Portrait of Marcel Brien 90 kg wrapped candies

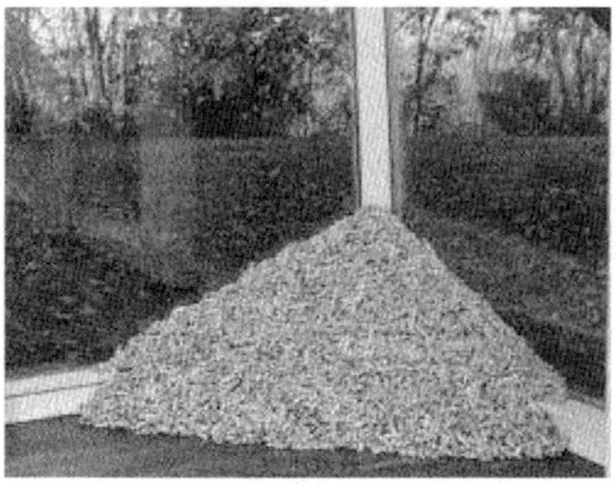

1987**Felix Gonzalez-Torres** Perfect Lovers

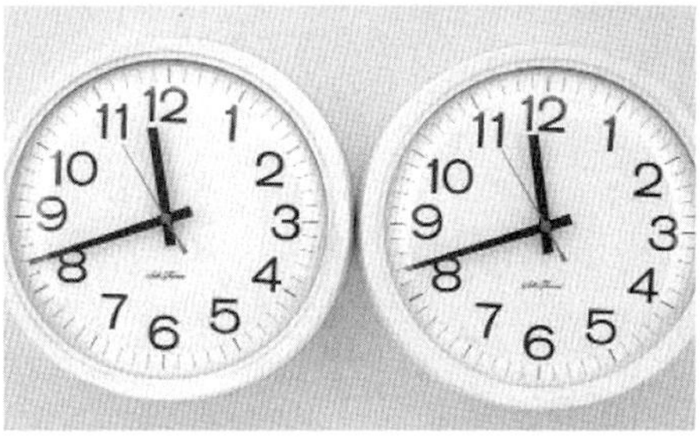

Sonsbeek - **site specific projects** in the city of Arnhem
1988 **Krysztof Wodicszko Unit** for homeless

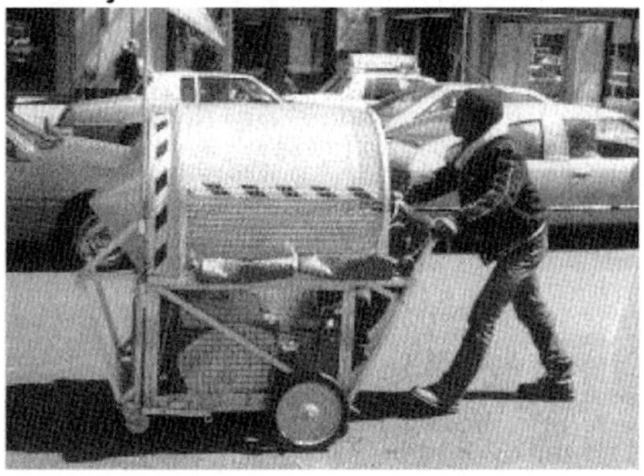

1988 **Katharina Fritsch** Company at Table

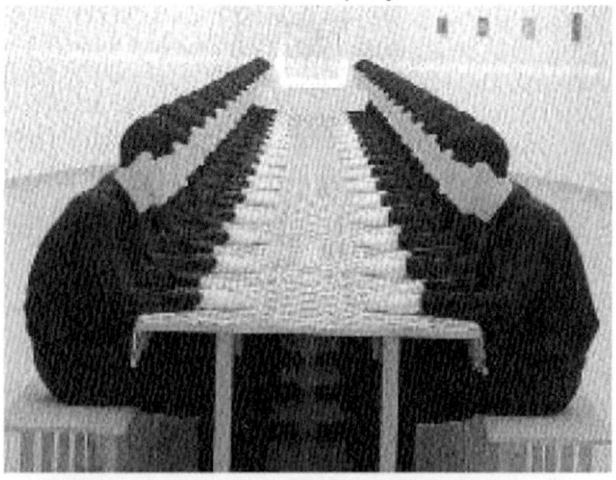

1988 **Joseph Kosuth** A grammatical remark

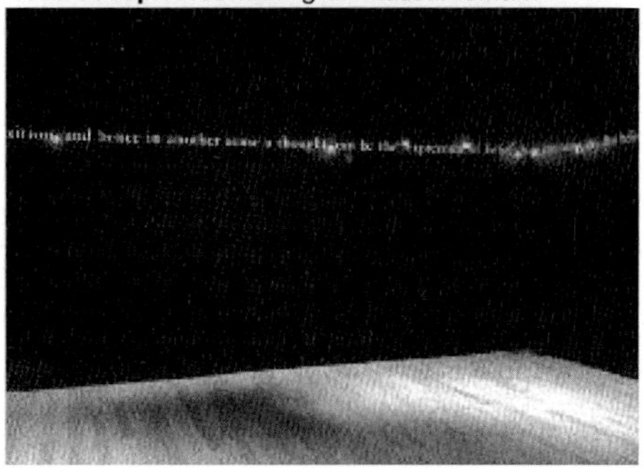

1988 **Michael Elmgreen & Inger Dragset**
Powerless structures

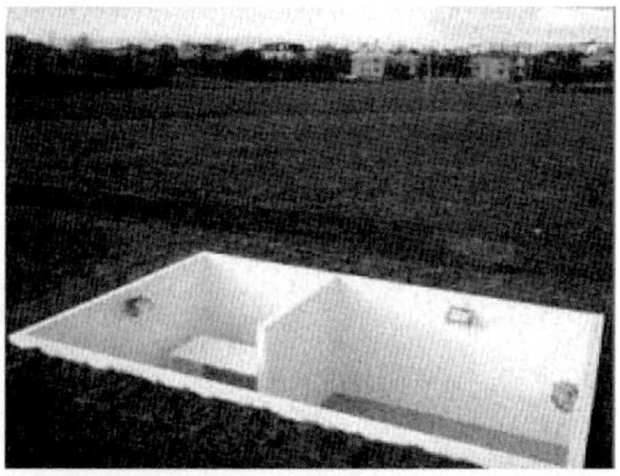

1989 **Ilya Kabakov**

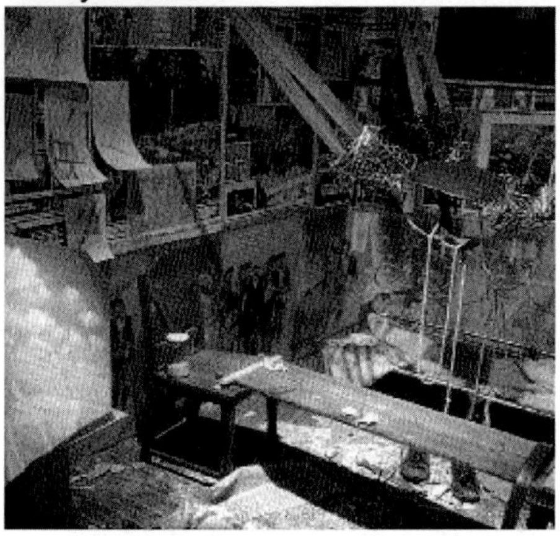

1989 **Fall of Berlin Wall. The fall of communism in East Europe**
Jeffrey Show the Legible City 1989-93 interactive work

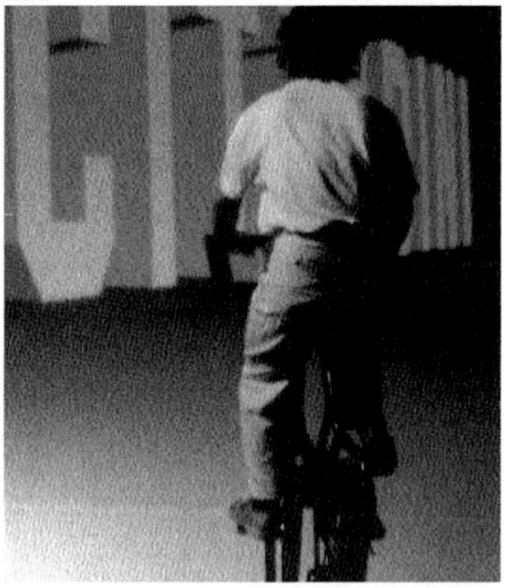

1989 **Damien Hirst** Medicine Box

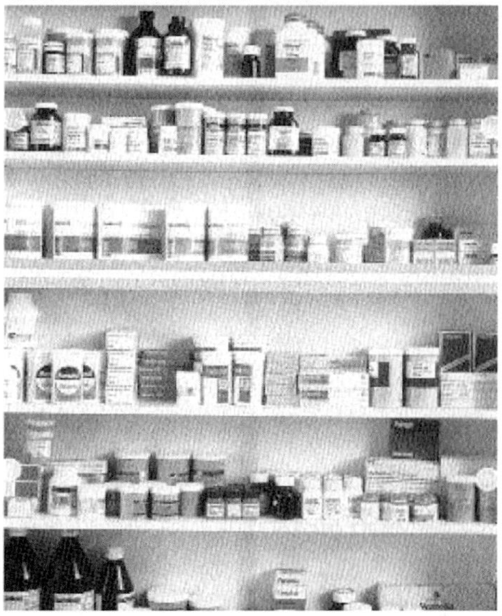

1989 **Dani Karavan**

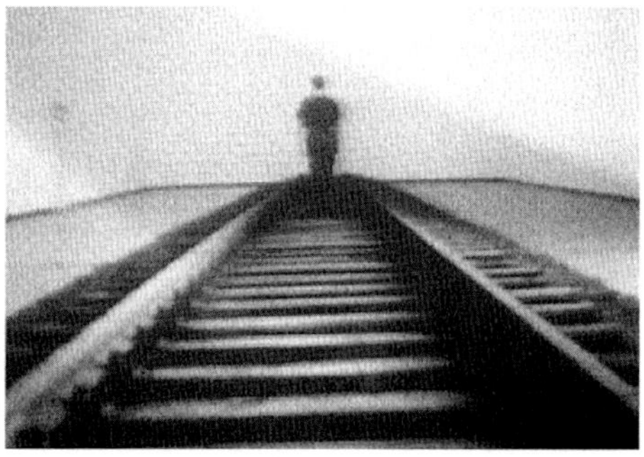

1989 **Christian Boltanski**

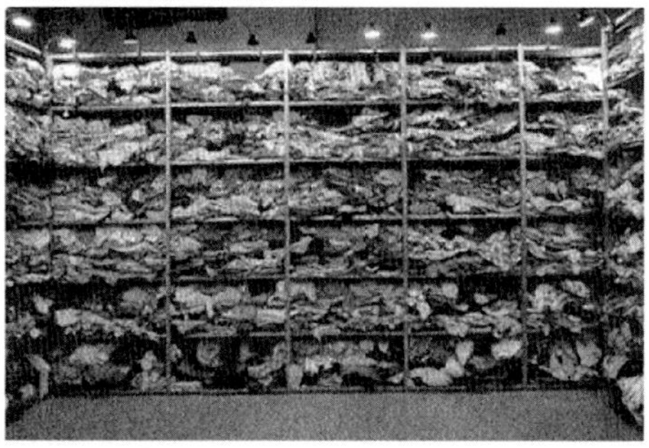

1989 **Kane Kwei** Airplane coffin

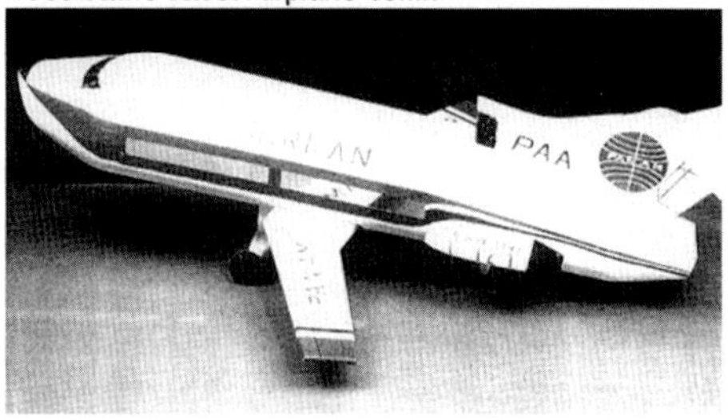

1989 **Feher Laszlo**

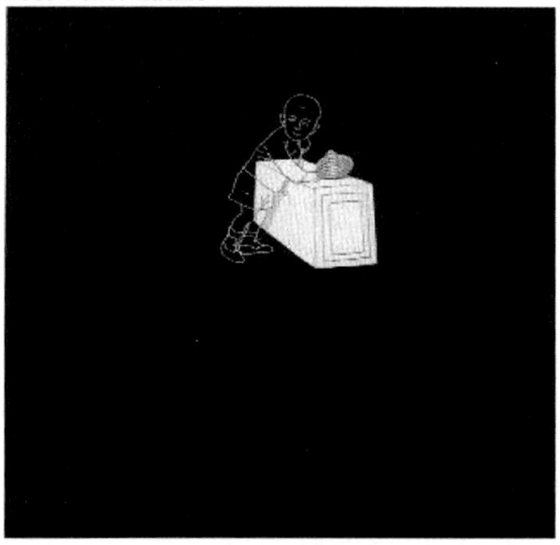

1989 Antwerp Belgium "Beyond the Everyday Object" by Florent Bex and Rita Compere
LA " A Forest of Signs" MCA

1989 **Matthew Barney** Field Dressing. Post human "Matthew Barney invents a world filed wit dream creatures, drag queens, satyrs and fairies. An expert in hybrids ignores the human/animal, feminine/masculine genres. Video -Hallucinatory, sex maniacs simulate a rape in the back of a limousine. An unconventional, ambiguous narcissist " Denis Angus

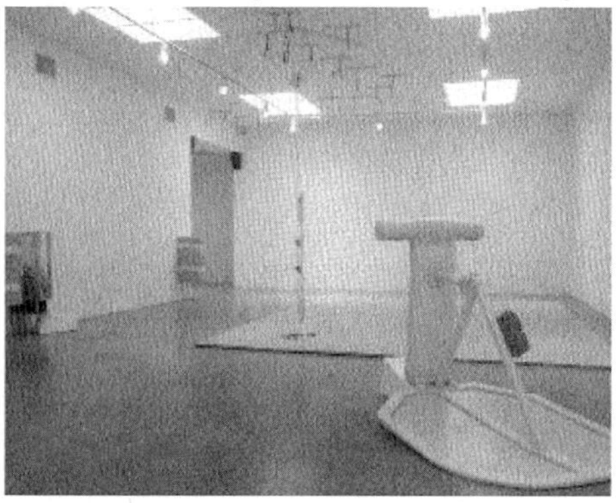

1989 **Robert Gober** Drawn

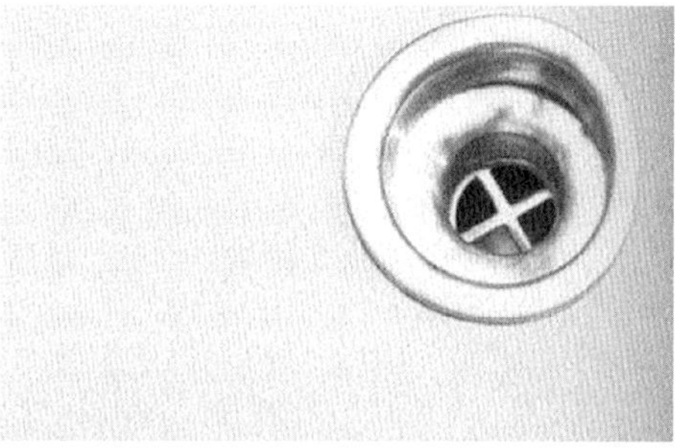

1989 **Jeff Wall** passerby

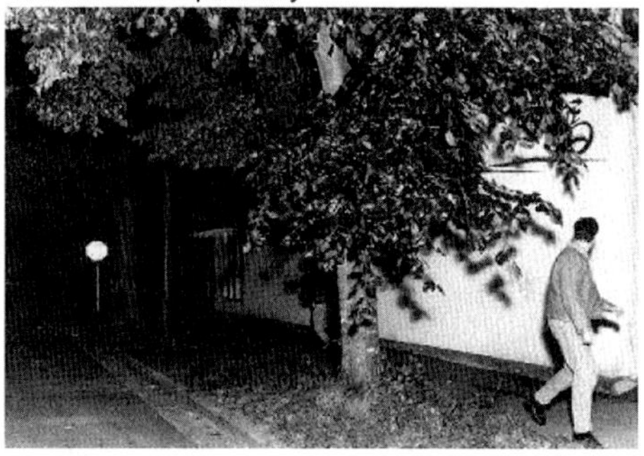

1989 **On Kawara**

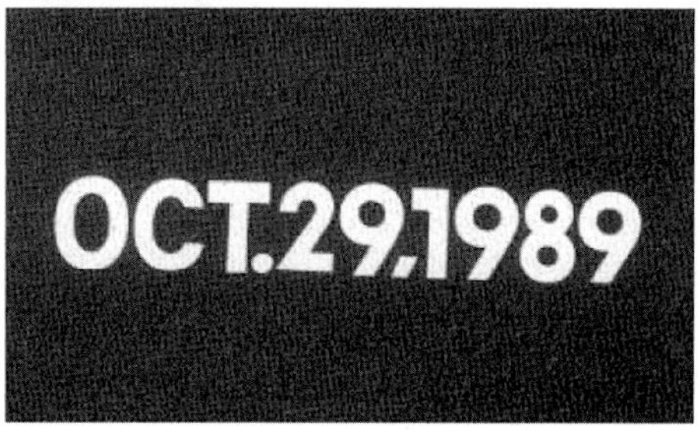

1990 Chicago "**Conceptualism Postconceptualism**
The 1960's to the 1990's"
MCA London **Museum of Installation**
1990 **Harum Faroki** Fotogrammes from a

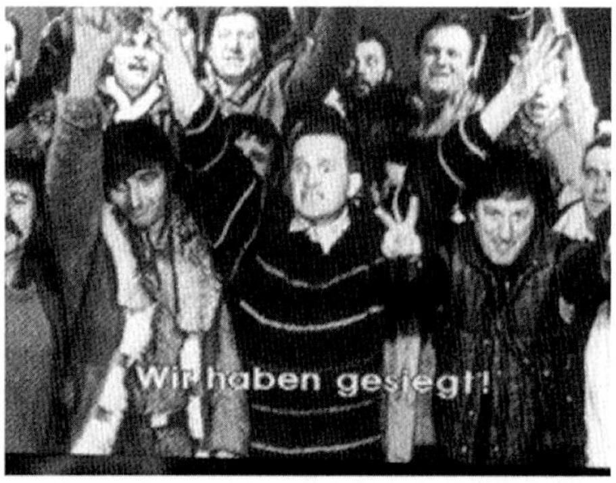

1990 **Felix Gonzalez Torres** Death by Gun prints
Offset print on paper, endless copies
Reproduces on each of its sheets the name, ages, and faces of 464 people who were killed by bullet wounds in the US in one -week period

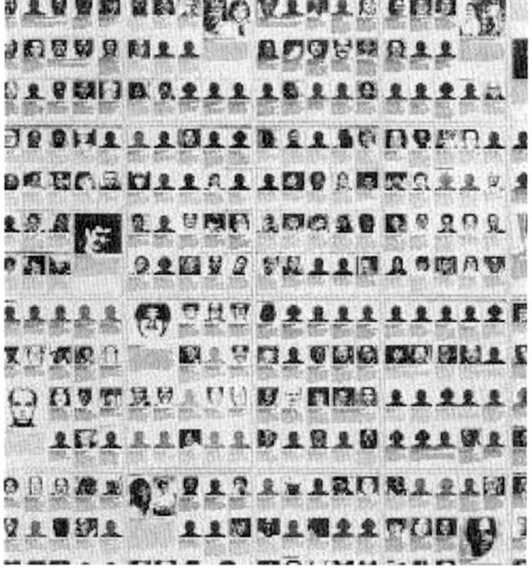

1990 **Akira Kurosawa** Dream
Dara Birnbaum Square Break in Transmission

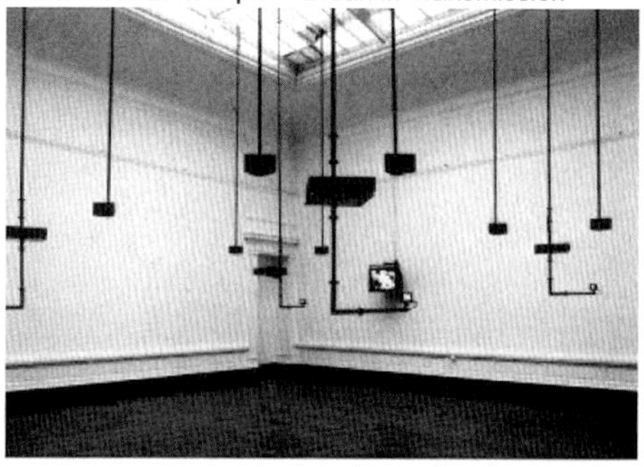

1990 **Sherrie Levine** La Fortune after Man Ray

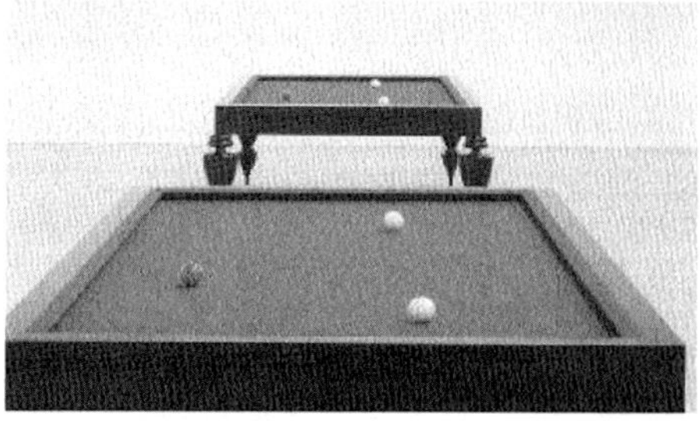

London "Seven Obsessions" at White Chapel Gallery. Columbus Ohio "New Works for New Space"
1990 **Yvonne Rainer** "Privilege"

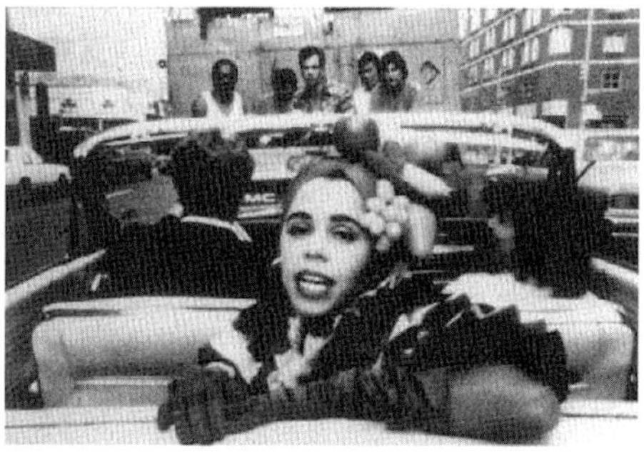

1990 **Jack Pierson** Lost

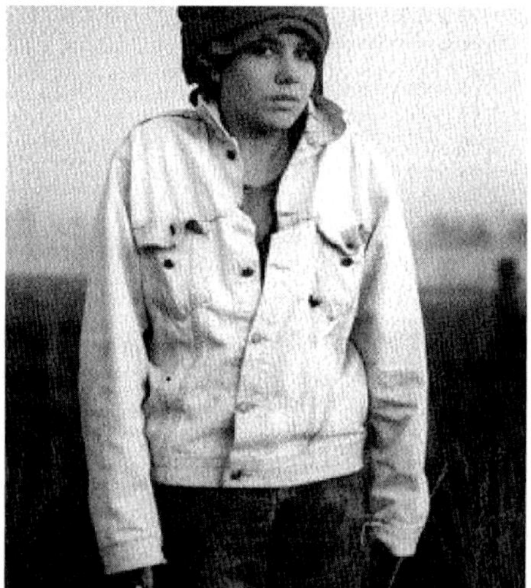

1990 **Felix Gonzalez Torres**

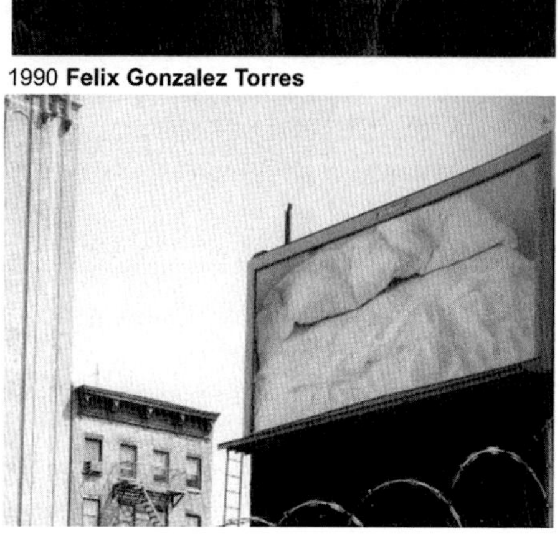

1990 **Lia Perjovschi** starts endless collections: plastic bags East EU, Globe, Angel)
Orlan aesthetic surgeries - as art
1990 **Aziz&Cucher** Crist

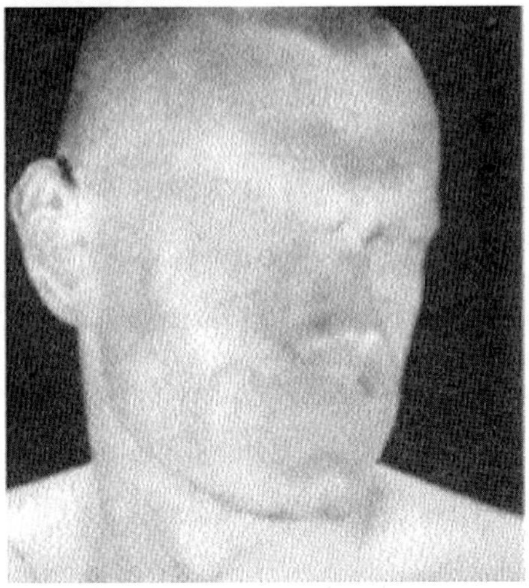

1990 **Manga** culture

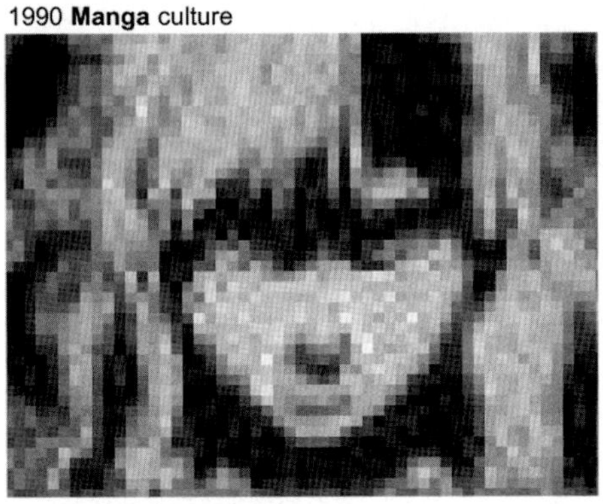

1991 **Mike Kelley** Dialogue)

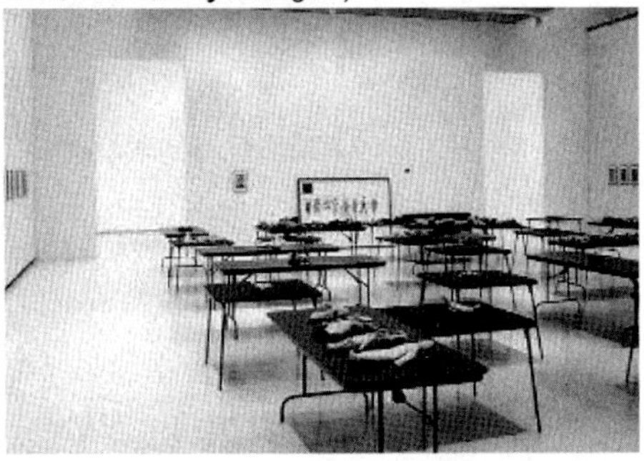

1991 **Dan Sandin** The Cave (VR) Chicago

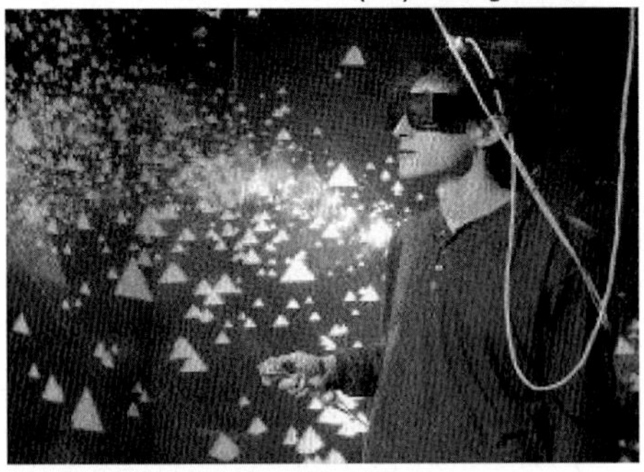

Charleston SC "Places with a Past
1991 **Damien Hirst** Out of Love

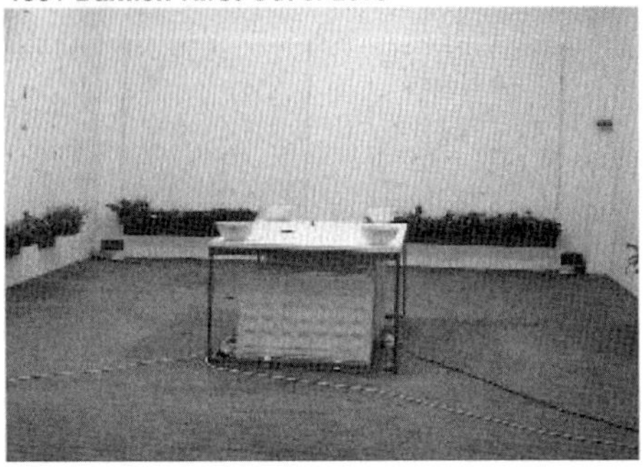

1991 **Barbara Kruger**

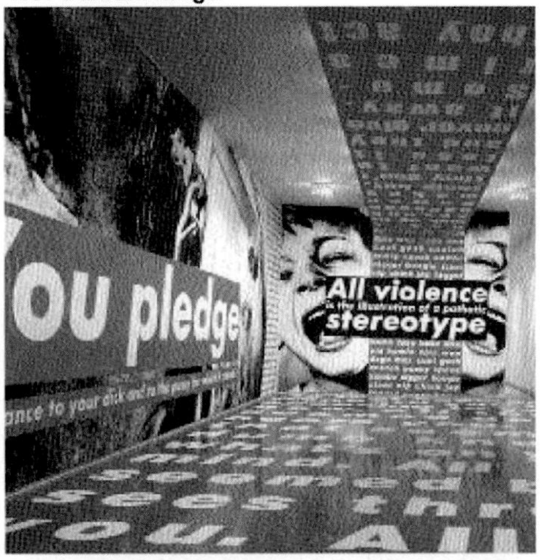

1991 **David Tremlet**

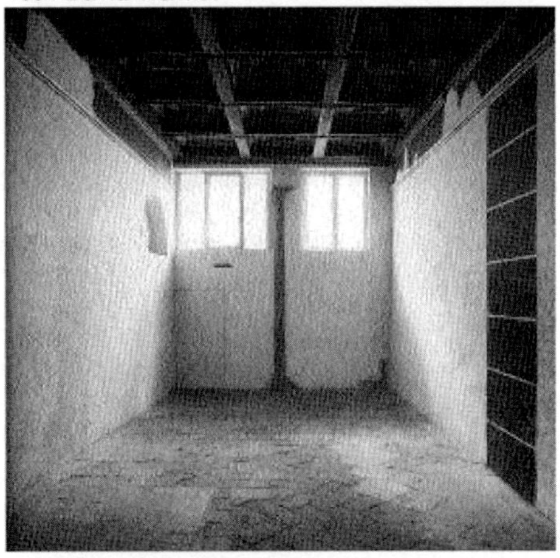

1991 **Felix Gonzalez Torres**

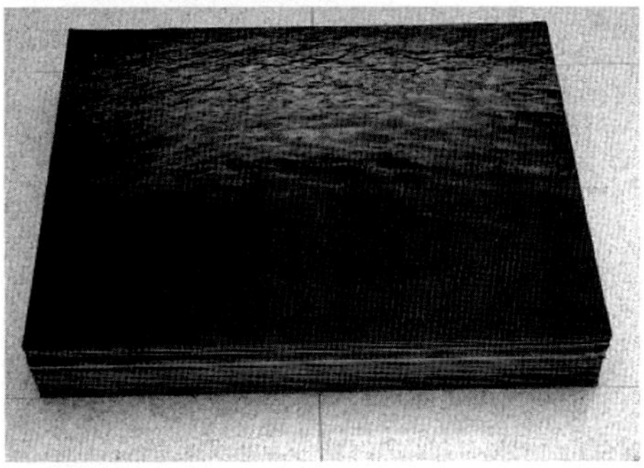

1991 **Simon Ungers**

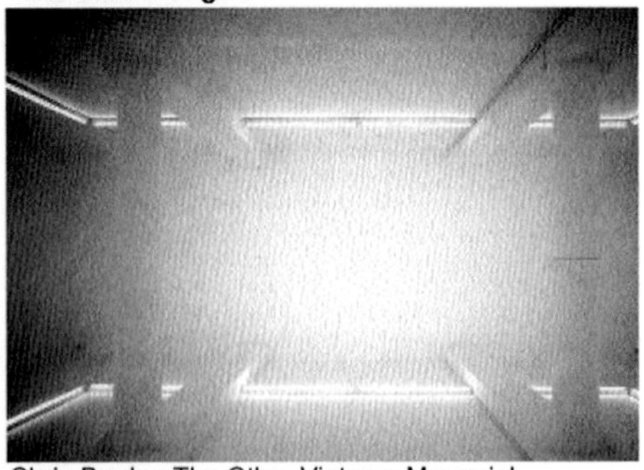

Chris Burden The Other Vietnam Memorial
1991 **Dan Perjovschi** from '91 political drawings in public space 22 magazine Bucharest

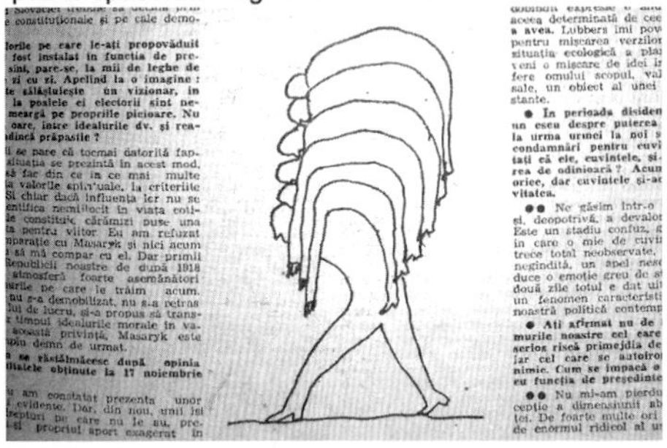

1991 **Caa** Lia & Dan Perjovschi (open studio)
Kristine Stiles

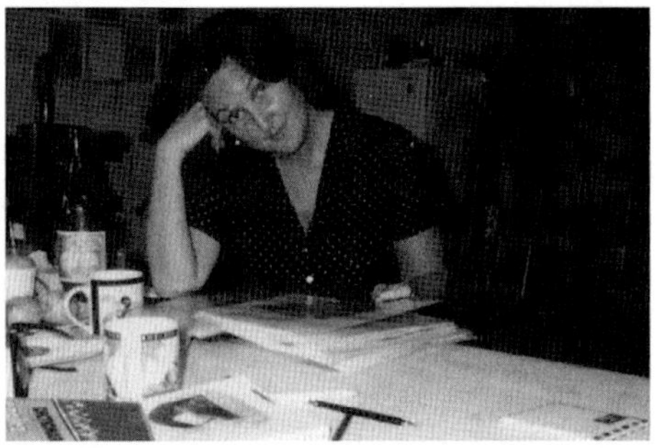

1991 **Sturtevant**

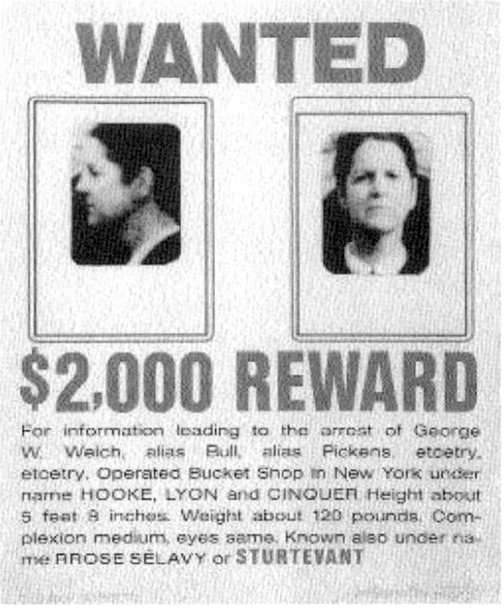

1992 **Rirkrit Tiravanija**
"A room no longer means anything at all if it cannot be used". My work is less about things in the gallery and more about the people I've met, had a conversation with, talked about things with, and looked at things". Whether he organizes dinners in museums, bars or rehearsals studios, he always invites the public to make use of his work
303 gallery he put all of the things found in the storeroom and office into the gallery itself including the director, forced to work in public. Meanwhile, in the storeroom, he cooked curries, for the visitor to the gallery. The leftovers, kitchen utensils and used food packets became the art whenever he was not there."

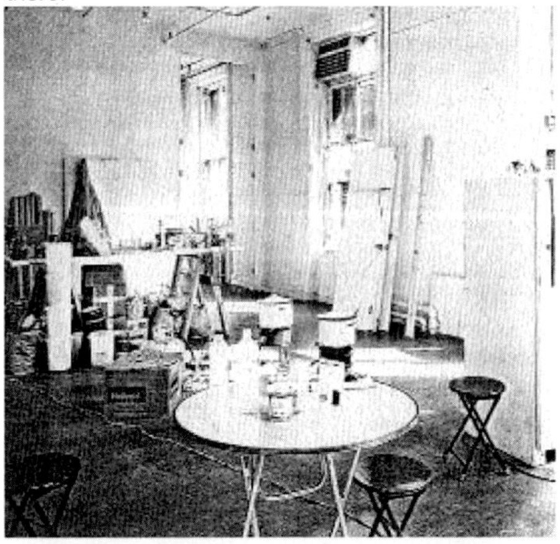

1992 **Christopher Bucklow** Solar image **MOMA**

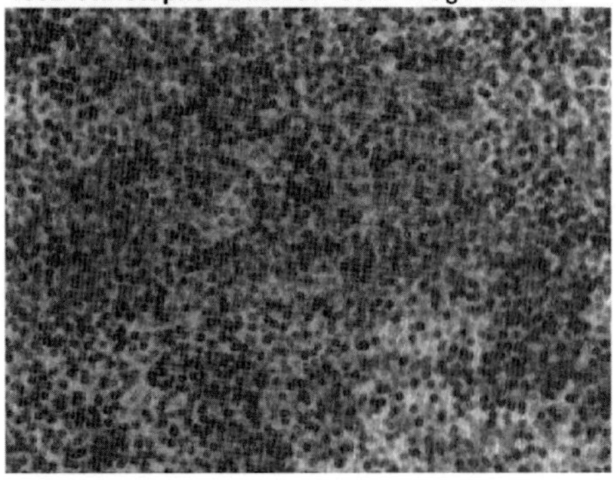

1992 **Mark Dion**

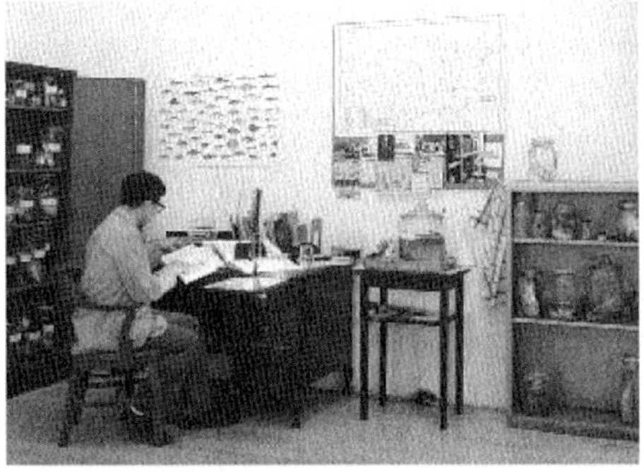

1992 **Bill Viola** triptic

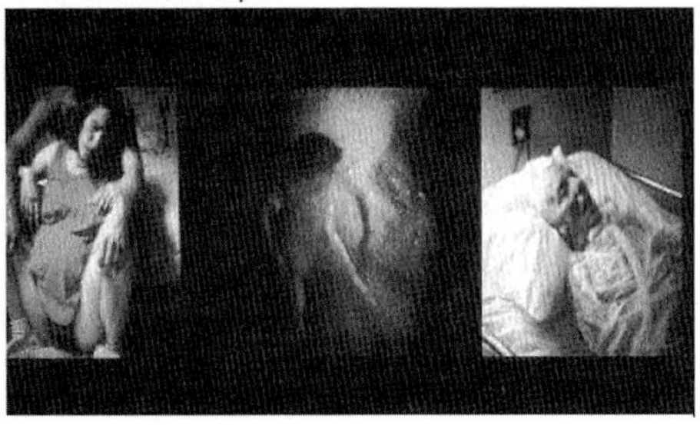

1992 **Yayoi Kusama** Pink boat

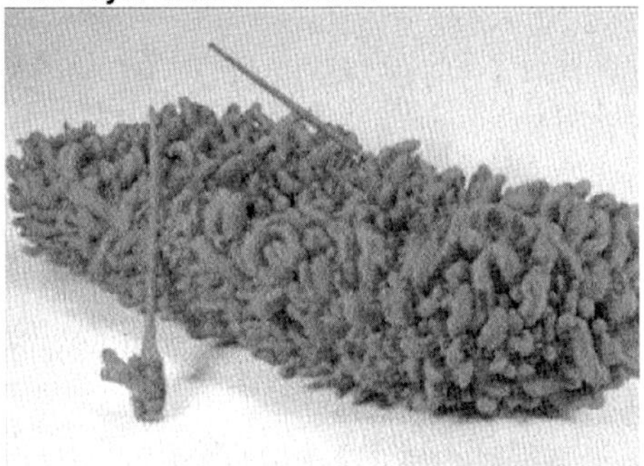

1992 **Peter Fischli & David Weiss**

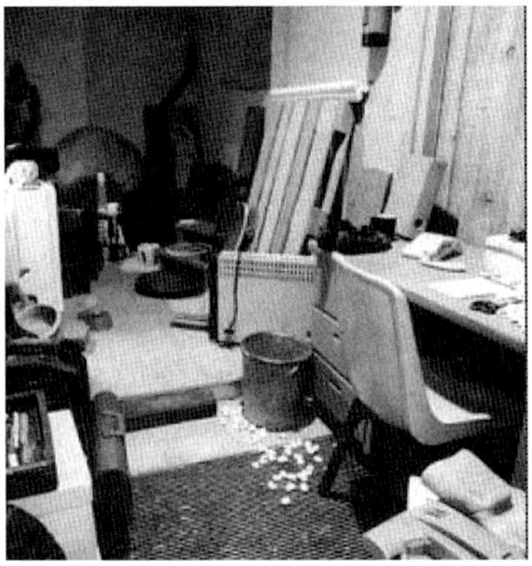

1992 **Luc Tuymans**

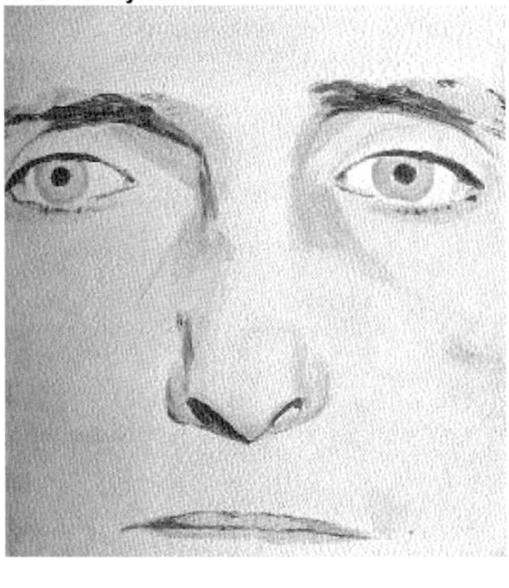

1992 **Gary Hill** Tall Ships, interactive technology

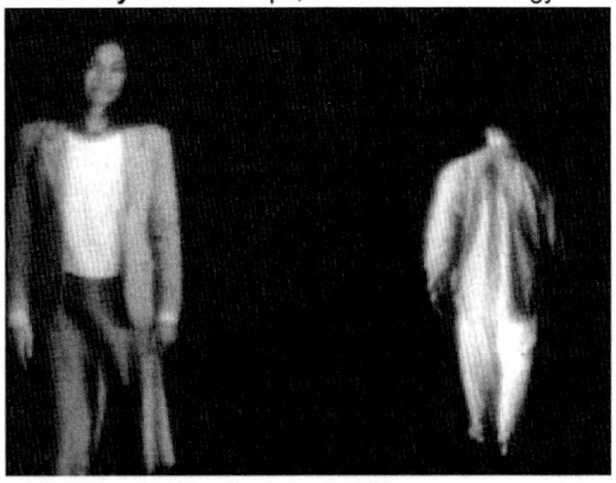

1992 **Michael Landy** closing down sale

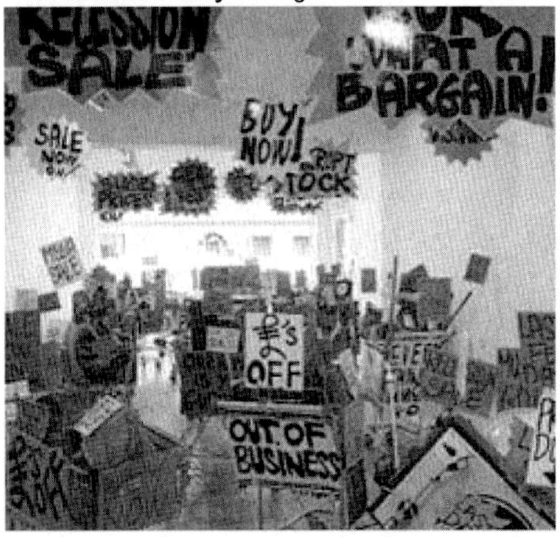

1992 **Paul Sermon** Telematic Dreaming

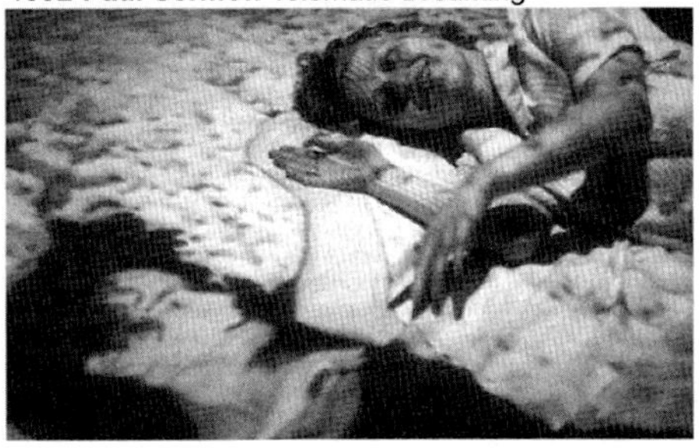

1992 **Gabriel Orozco** Maria, Maria, Maria

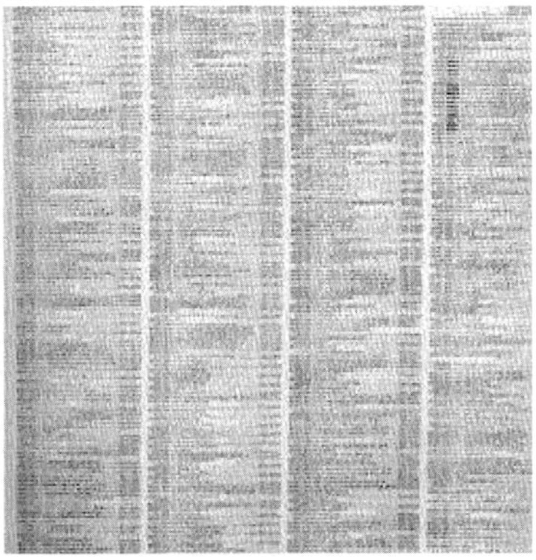

1992 **Ilya Kabakov** Incident at the Museum of Water Music NY

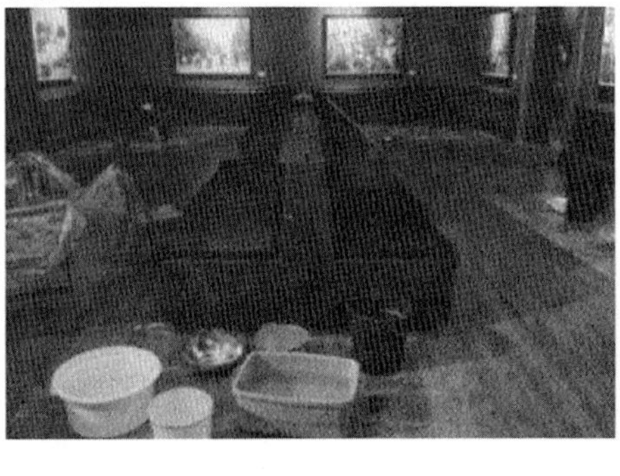

1992 **Abu Bakarr Monsaray** Sierra Leone Hell Extinguisher

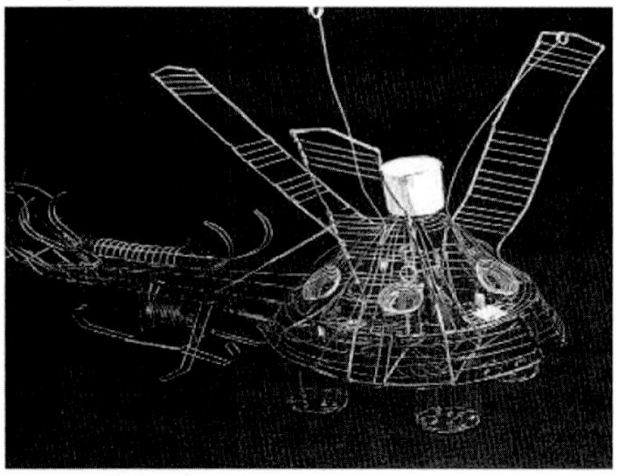

1992 **Ion Grigorescu**

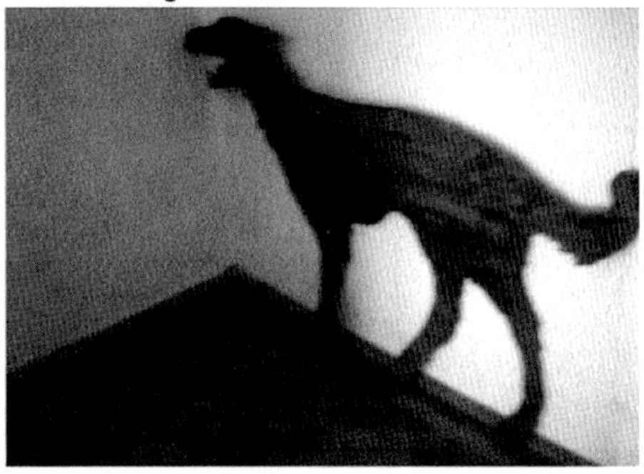

1993 **Stelarc** Amplified Body

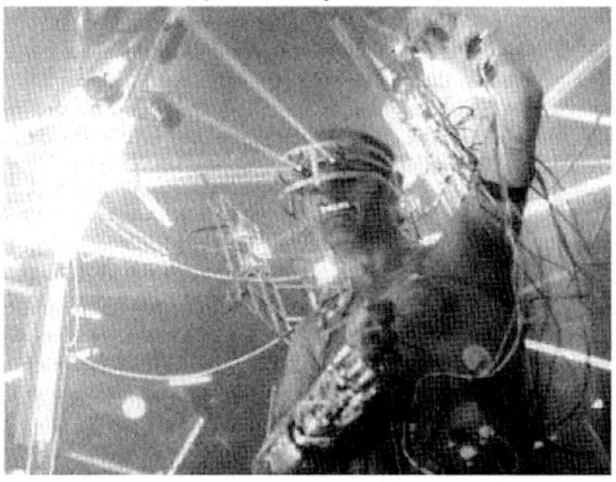

1993 **Absalon** Cellule

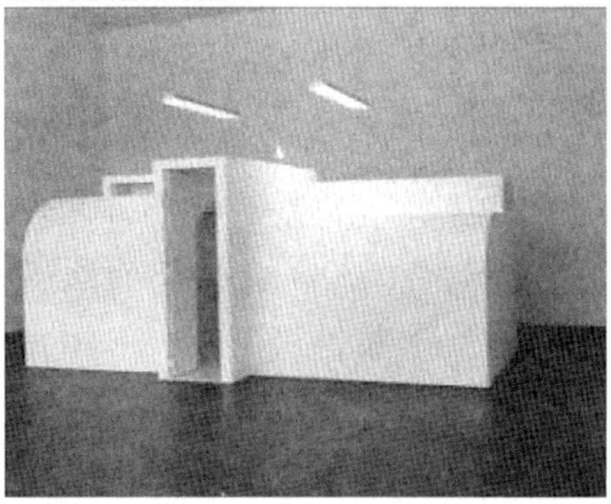

1993 **Gabriel Orozco** Transformed car
"The real question is; what is a space? Moving the knight. Citroen DS, refitted as single-seated, is an unrivaled piece.For Orozco, art is similar to an exercise in framing-as illustrated in one of his recent videos by an image of the precise moment when strollers crossing a square in Mexico seemed to be players on an immense game in which the artist's job is to make the rules." Nicolas Bourriaud.

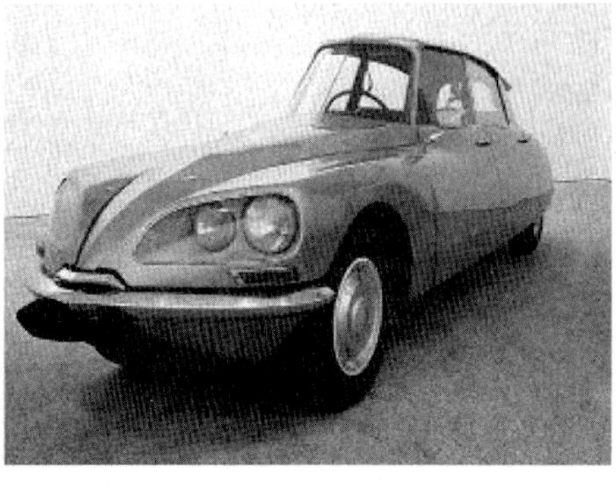

1993 **Rachel Whiteread** House

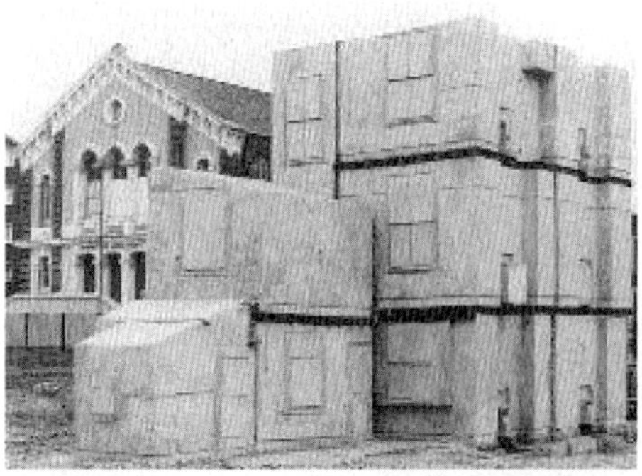

1993 **CNN** Bosnia

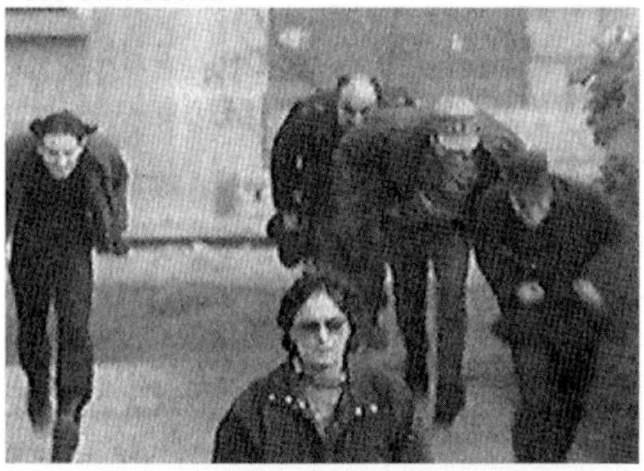

1993 **Hans Haacke** German Pavillion Venice

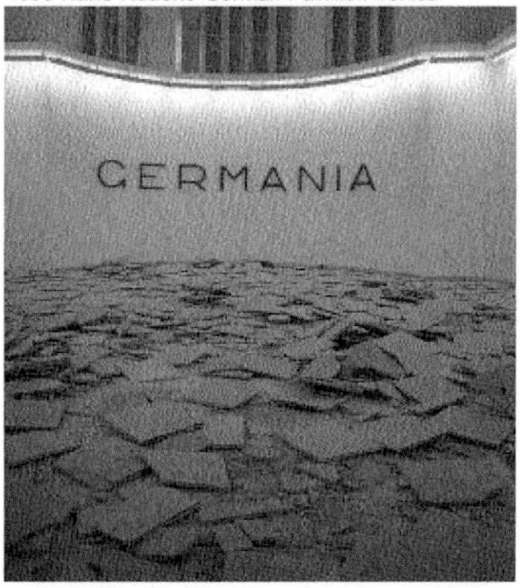

1993 **Hughes Brothers**

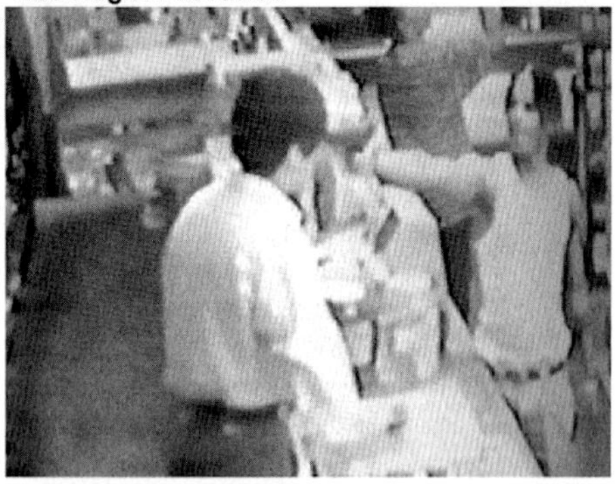

1993 **Antoni Muntadas** The file room

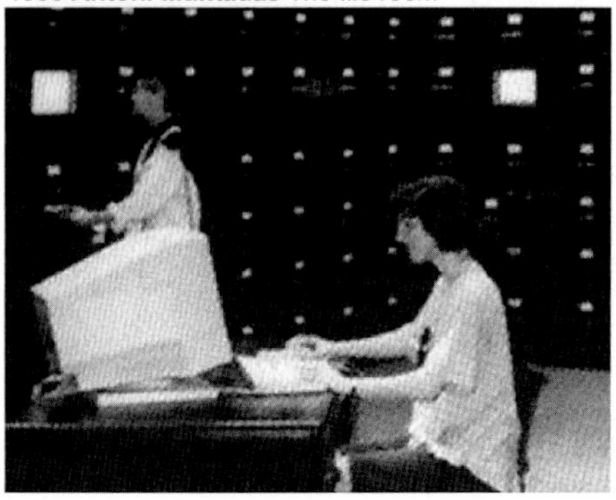

1993 **Rudolf Bone** stops making art
Lia Perjovschi I fight for my right to be different.
First Zone Performance Festival Timisoara

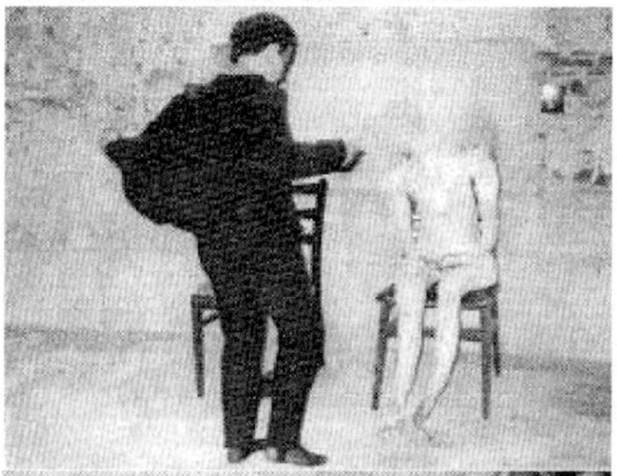

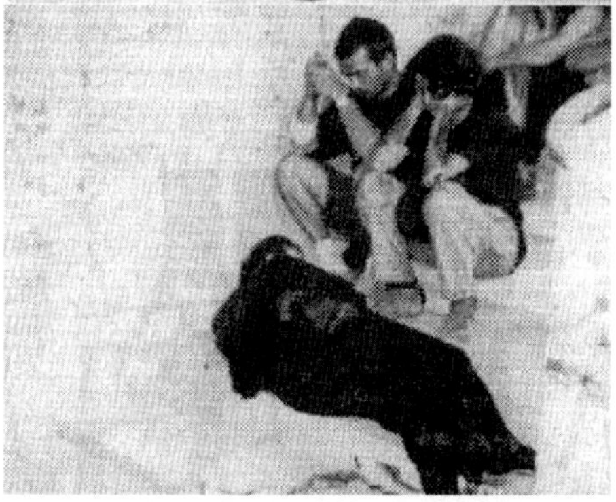

1993 **Dan Perjovschi** "Romania" (**tattoo** on his shoulder laser erased 1993

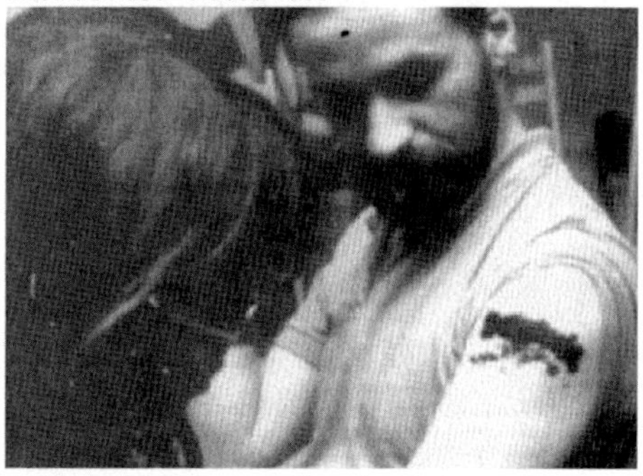

1993 **Douglas Gordon** "Psycho hitchhiker Glasgow (photo)"I can make specific investigations into territory to do with memory (or the malfunction of memory). **Psycho**
" Douglas Gorgon's work most often sends the viewer into a latent, semi-lethargic, half conscious state. When he projects Hitchcock's Psycho-in slow motion and for an entire day-it is so that we can better see the film, but also to immerse us in a total psycho-cinematic experienceHe explores his own memory in search of improbable stories and gestures that he then reactivates, and he draws up lists of people he has met. Memory-with its lapses, reflection, duplications, and sense of distance becomes, irremediably, a screen." Jean Max Colard

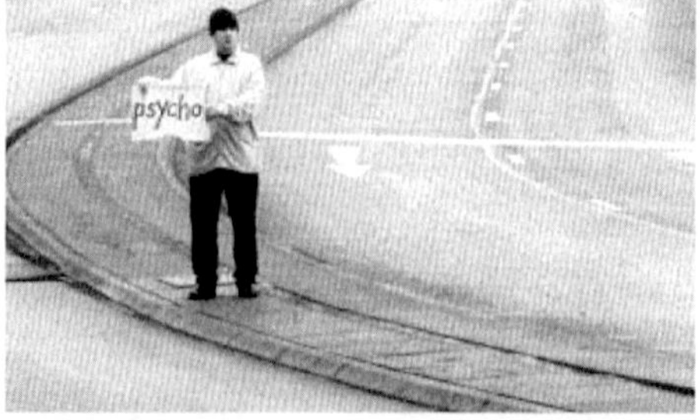

1993 **Creg Carvey**

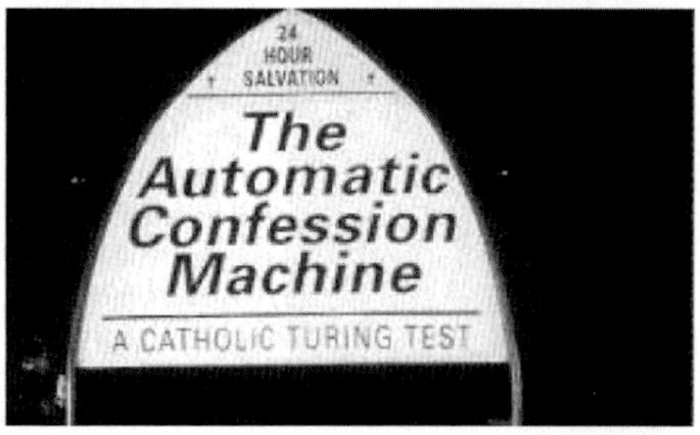

1994 Springer(in) Wien

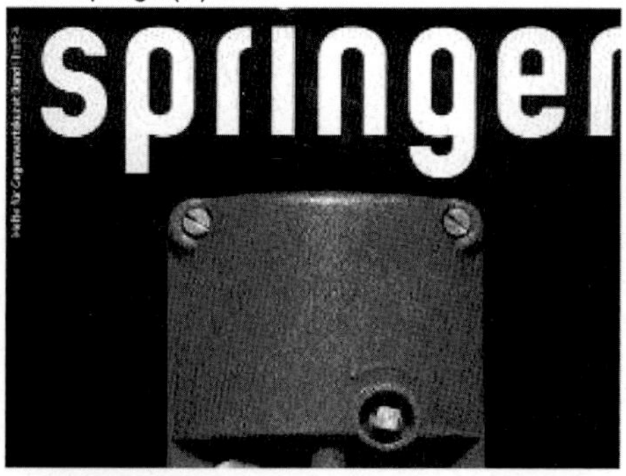

1994 **Mark Manders**

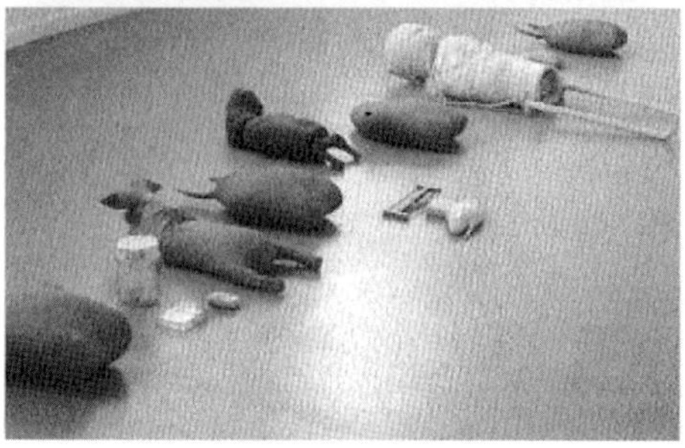

1994 **Roza El Hassan**

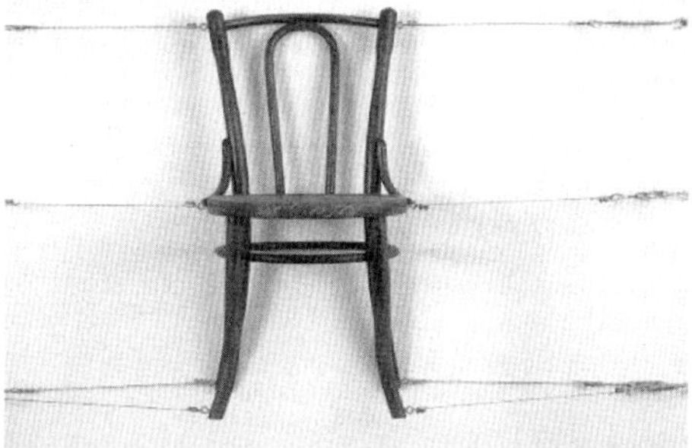

1994 **Mike Nelson** Trading Station

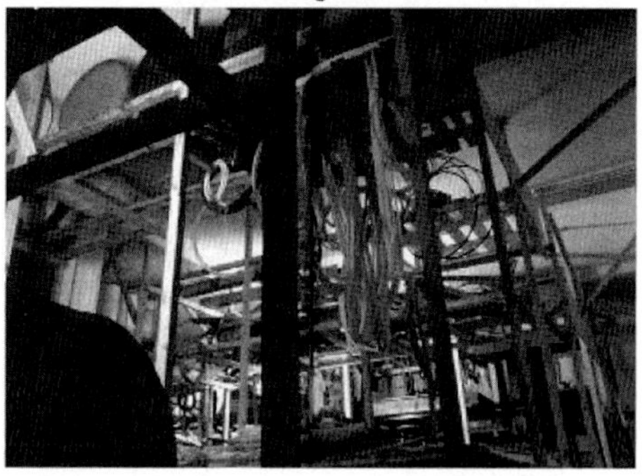

1994-95 **Damien Hirst** medicine boxes
"He opened a spot in London; it was a restaurant with a pharmaceutical theme, with waiters dressed in white and waitresses as nurses. Bloody and crazy world, rarely equaled darkness. In his installation, insects die gradually, cuts up animals are steeped in formaldehyde, and gas bottles can kill. His is an art of the scalped, reproducing with an impeccably cold style the clean, white and clinical form of contemporary death." Denis Angus

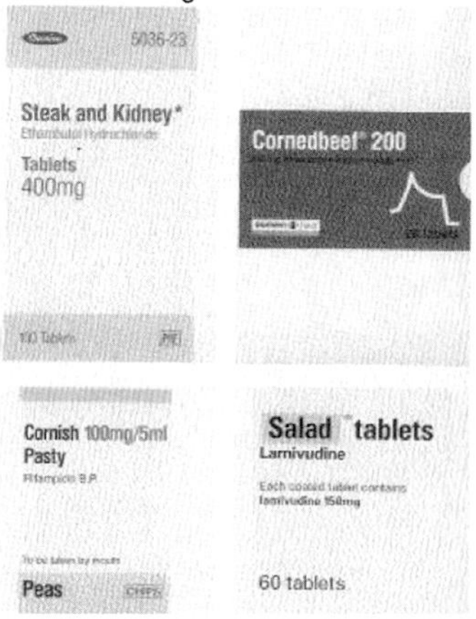

1994 **Andrea Zittel** Living unit a hybrid, a cross between a design agency, a utopia laboratory and a government sponsored behavioral control department" Jean Max Colard

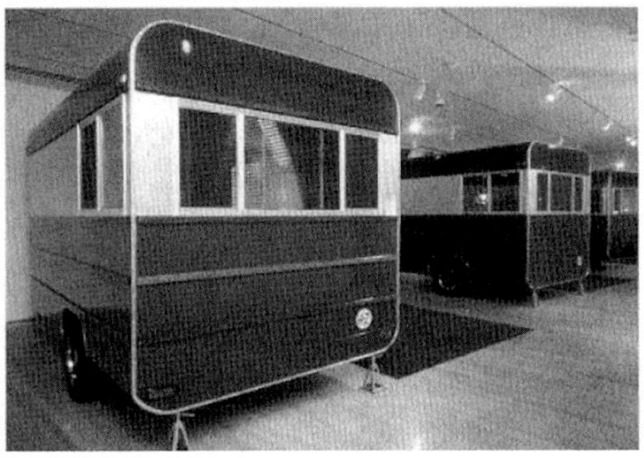

1994 **Pipilotti Rist** Selfless in the bath of Lava

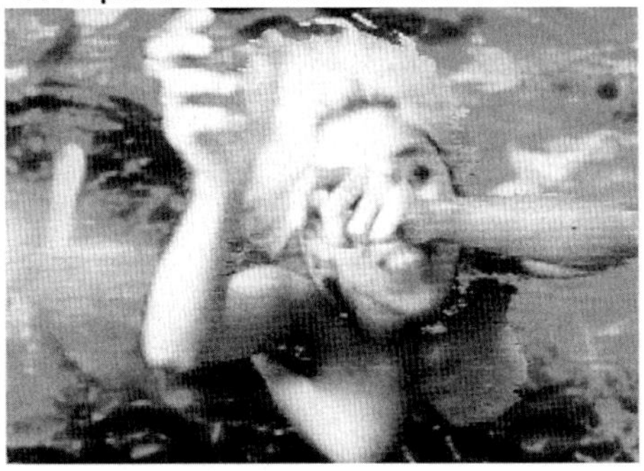

'94 **Oladele Ajiboye** Bonyboye Spells for Beginners

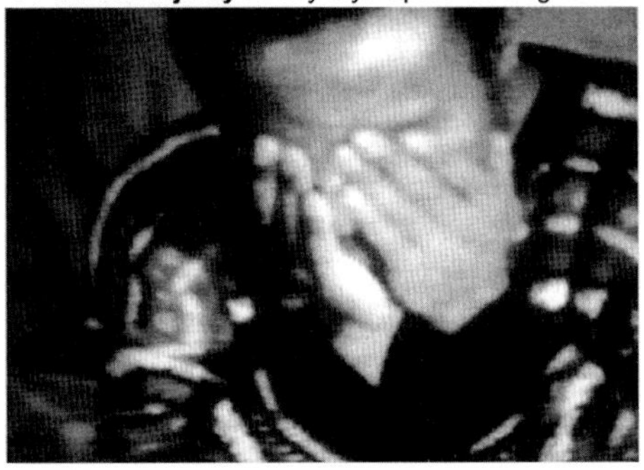

1994 **Tony Oursler** Horror

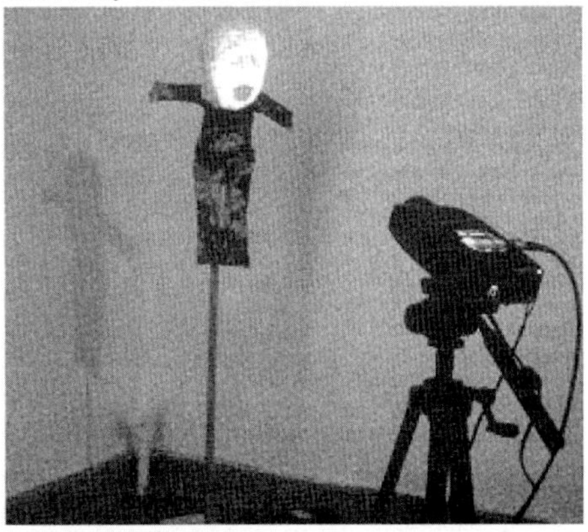

1994 **Stelarc** body connected to Internet
Mathew Barney Cremaster 4

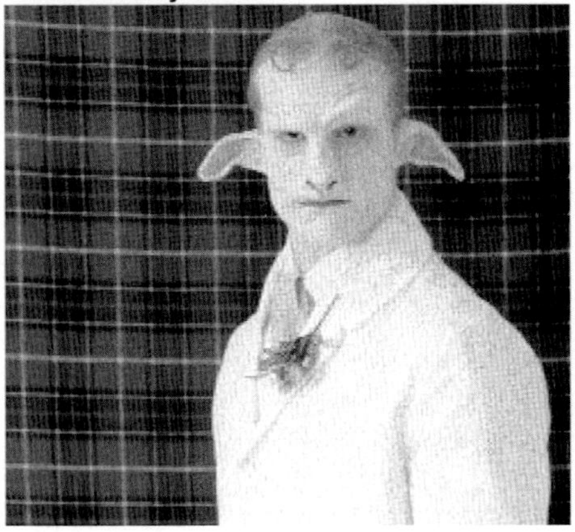

1994 **Pierre Huyghe** Sub-title "What is shown goes hand in hand with how it is shown. Reconfigure the form of art history and our social/cultural practices by making each of his works an open "proposal". Is always about the interpretation and the role of images in our behavioral setup". Nicolas Bourriaud.
Re-make

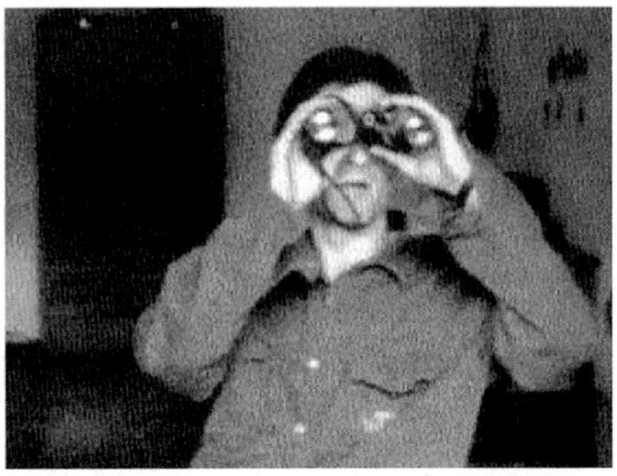

1995 **Teiji Furuhashi** Lovers, interactive installation

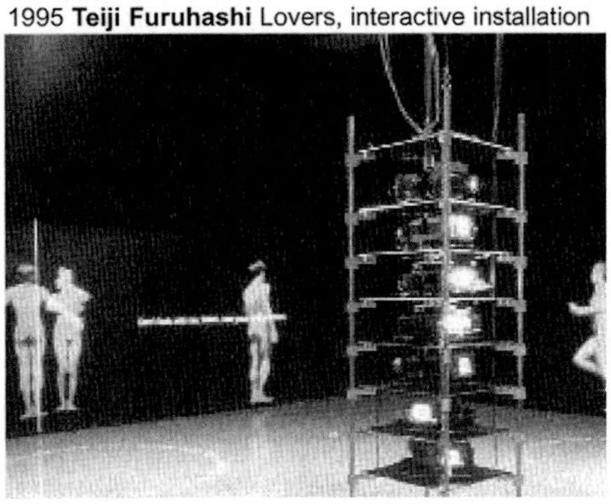

1995 **Bill Viola** Stations (5 channel installation)

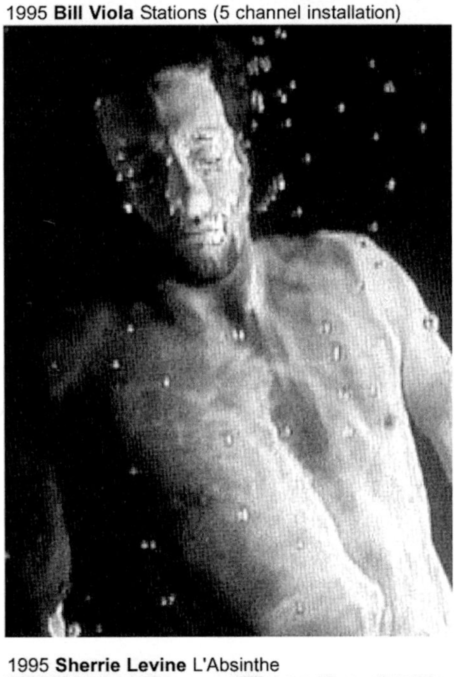

1995 **Sherrie Levine** L'Absinthe

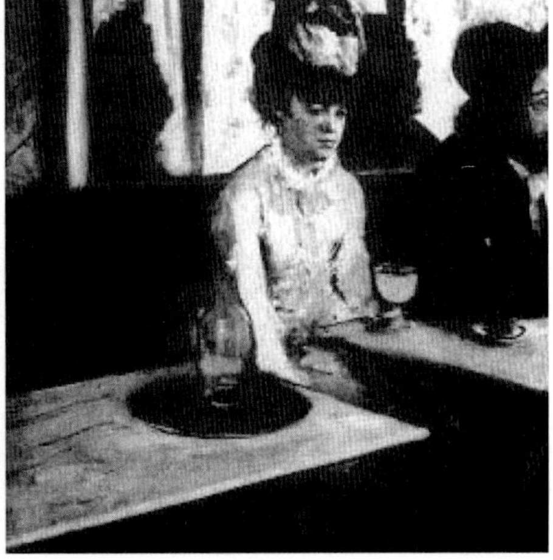

1995 **Yuri Leiderman**

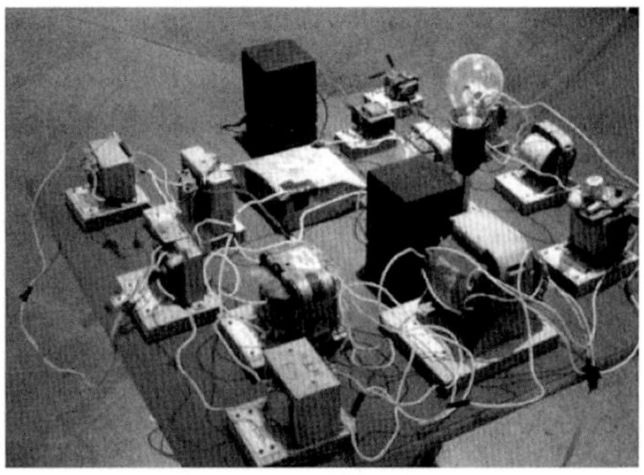

1995 **Depot** Wien (initiated by Stella Rollig)

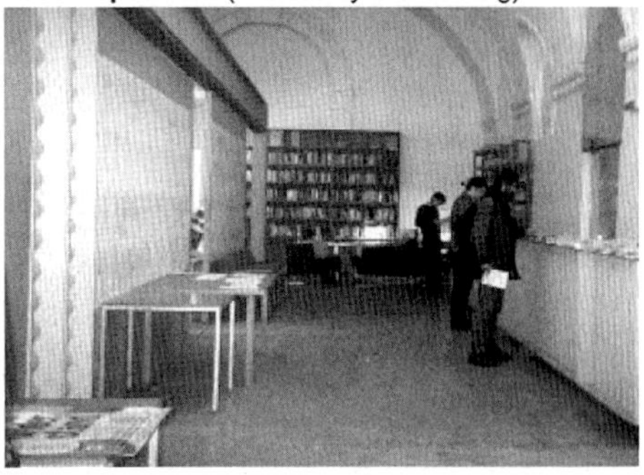

1995 **Ruth Motao** Daily Life Soweto

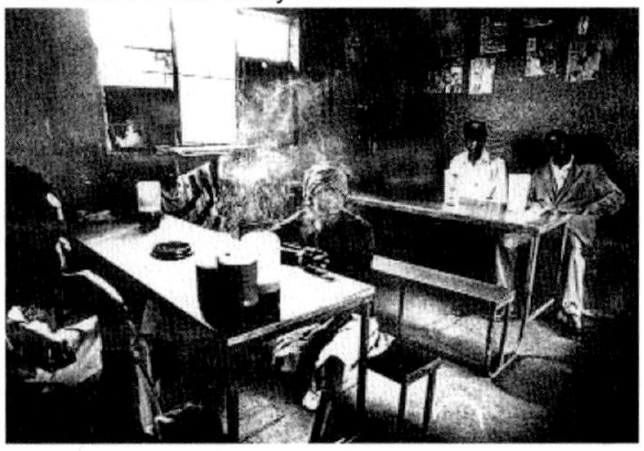

1995 **Pawel Althamer**

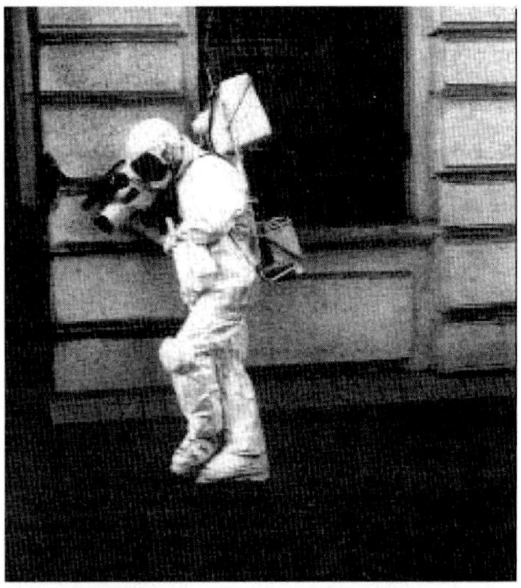

1995 **Rassim** (2 years body building. East body sponsored by west sponsor)

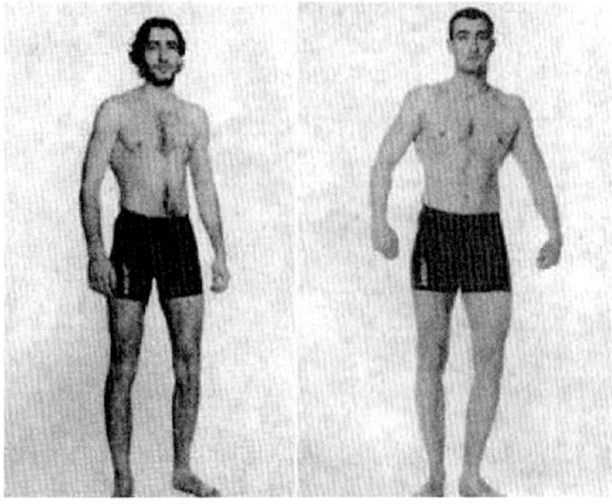

1995 **Lia Perjovschi** Calender

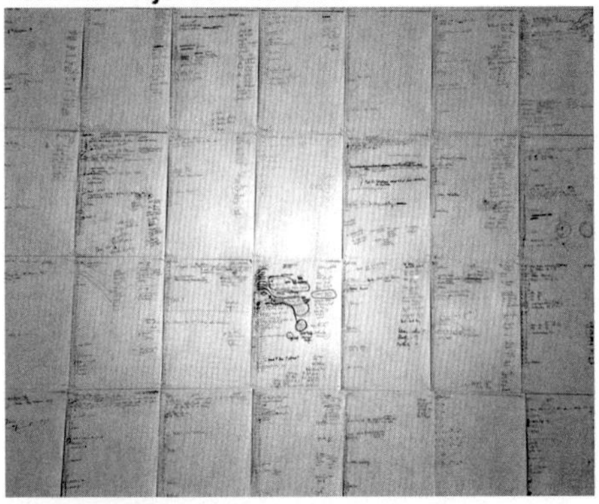

1995 **Kay Hassan**

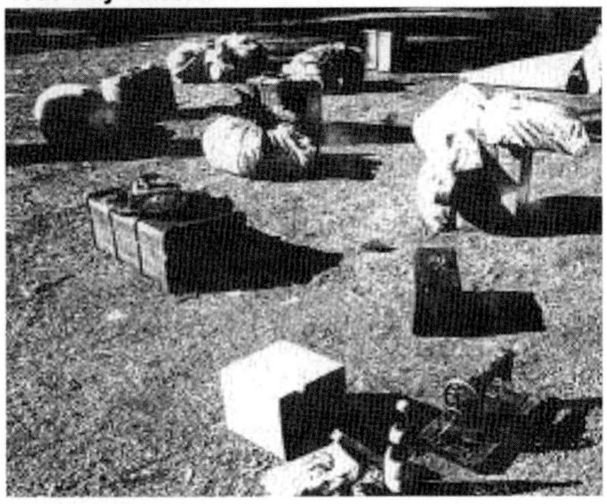

1995 **Tom Friedman** Sculpture

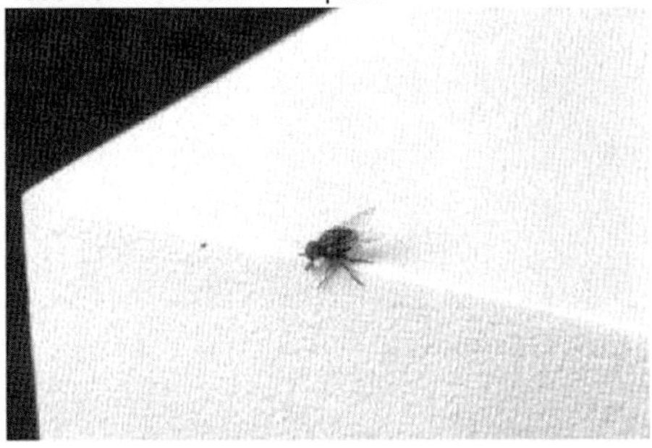

1995 **Goran Petercol** Negative

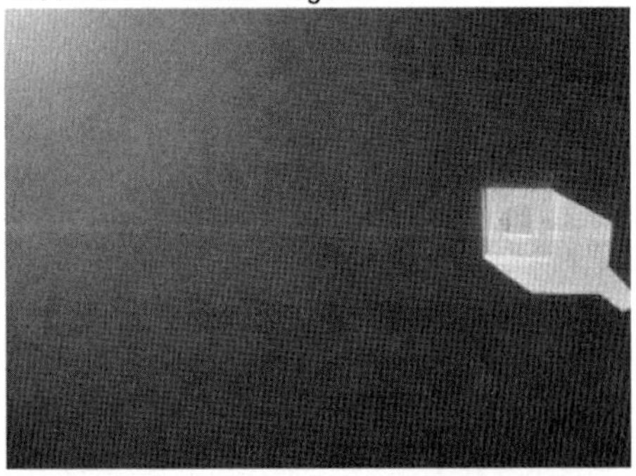

1995 **Robert Longo** Johny Pneumonic

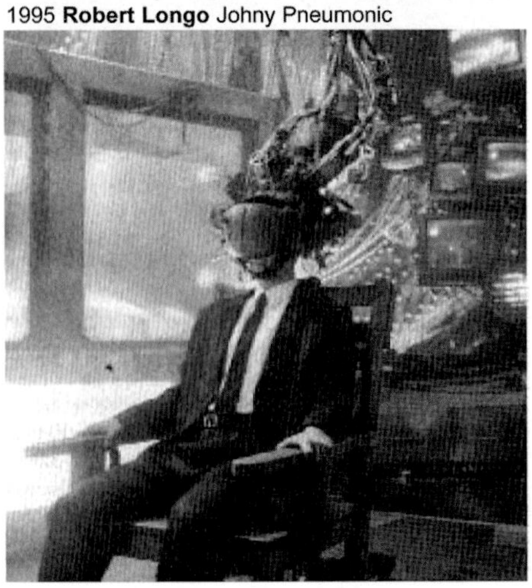

1995 **Andreas Gorsky** Prada

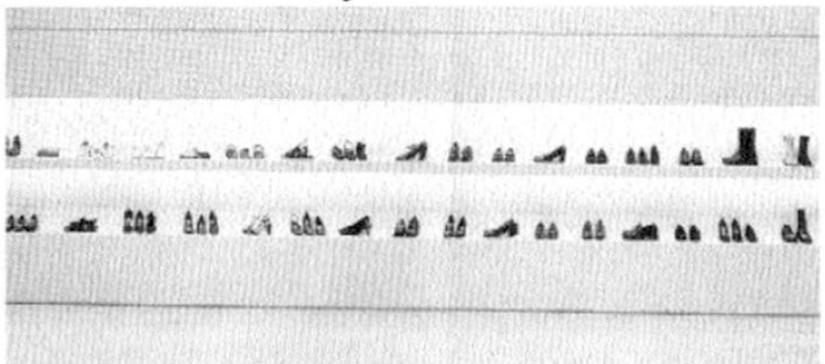

1995 **Christian Marclay** 95 telephones video

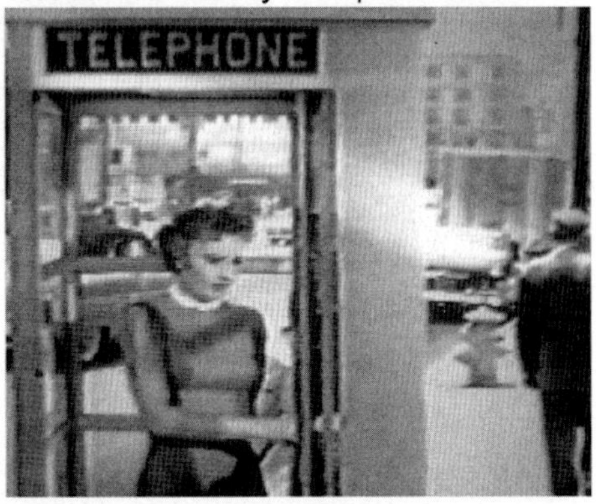

1995 **Christo et Jeanne -Claude** Wrapped Reichstag Berlin (1971-95)

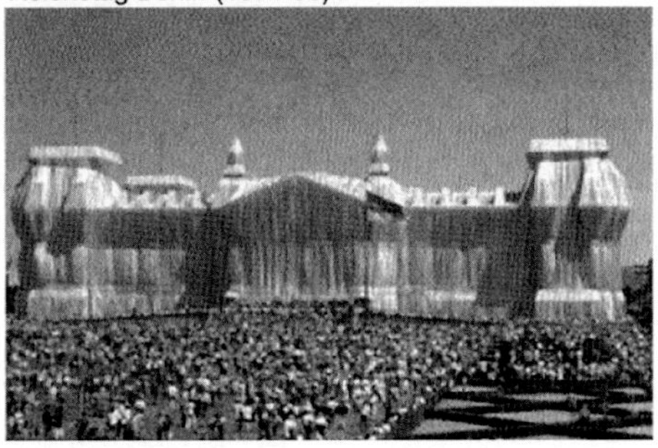

1995 **Charlie Cho** Love crimes

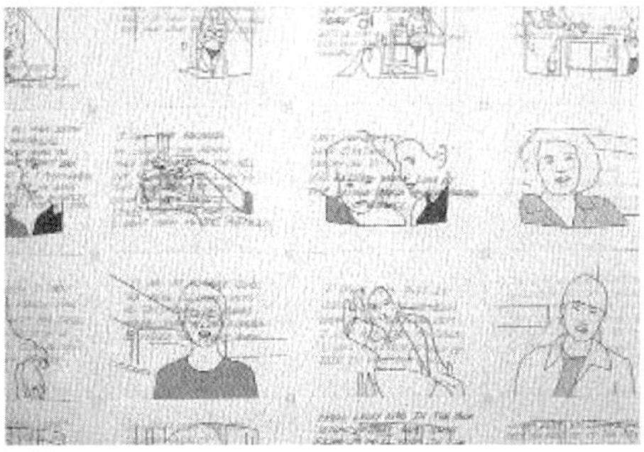

1995 **Joe Scanlan** Free Assembly

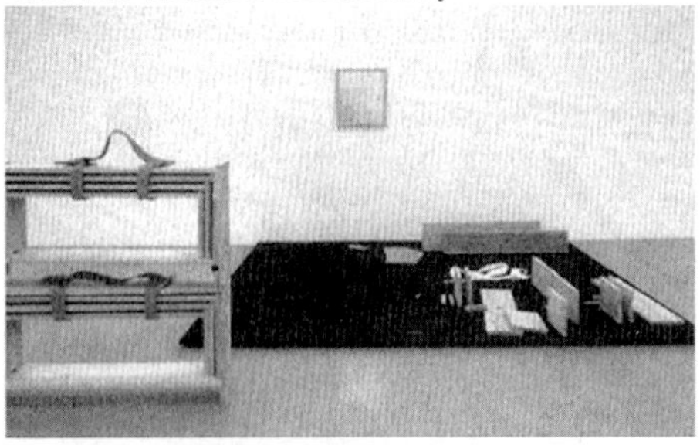

1995 **Douglas Gordon** Hysterical

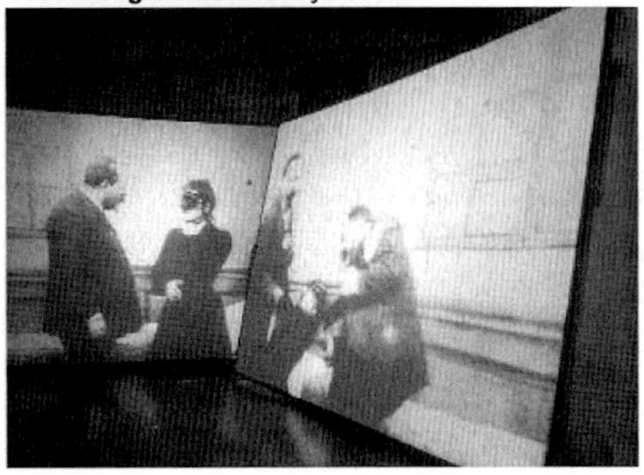

1995 **Komar & Melamid** komeranmelamid

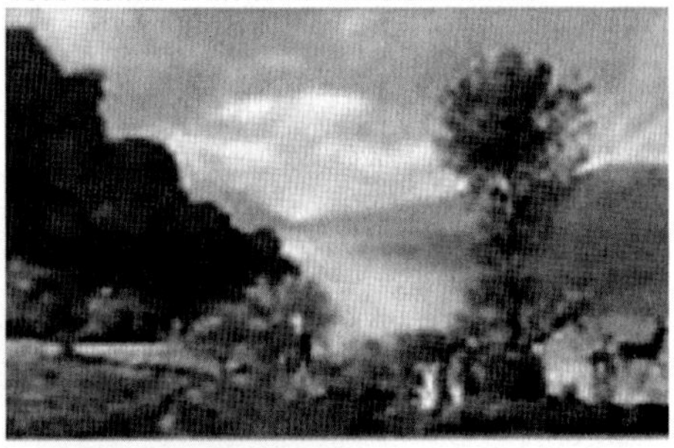

Generali Foundation Wien

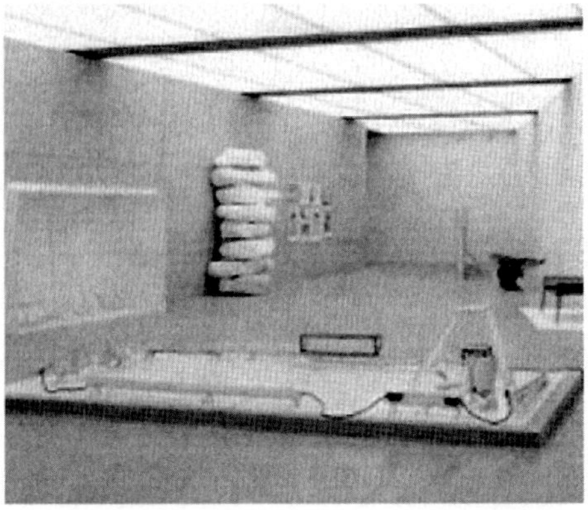

1995 **Thomas Demand** Archive

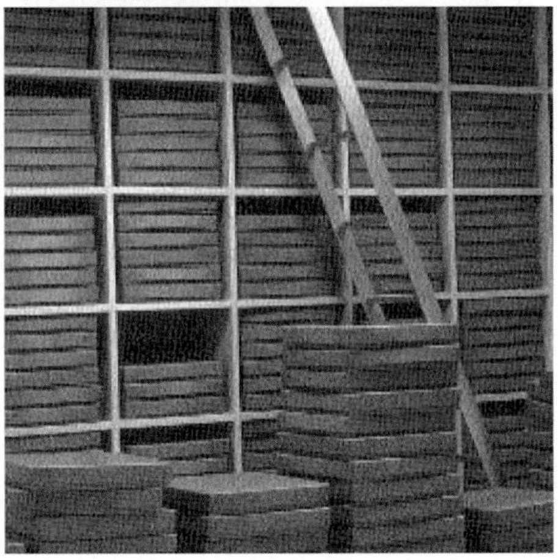

1996 **Lars von Trier "Breaking the Waves"**
"I don't care what films are about: what counts are that they're alive, that they shimmer with life"
"This Danish filmmaker stands out as a kind of contemporary artist in the film world, given his highly experimental approach to cinema; his film Dimension- which is being shot over a 30 year period of time A mix of strange images and sounds LVT sees the cinema as a fertile laboratory opting for imagination over reason and symbolism over talk. His art is founded on such themes as intrigue, networks and multiplicity and revolves around the conflicts arising over rules and the transgression of these rules, control, and chaos, semblance and truth.
Dogma ' 95 has become a manifesto for a new kind of filmmaking. He is blurring the parameters of filmmaking by always creating something new. To wit: this uncategorizable filmmaker currently swears that he is no longer even "an artist" Jacques Morice

Emily Watson (Bess) in Breaking the Waves

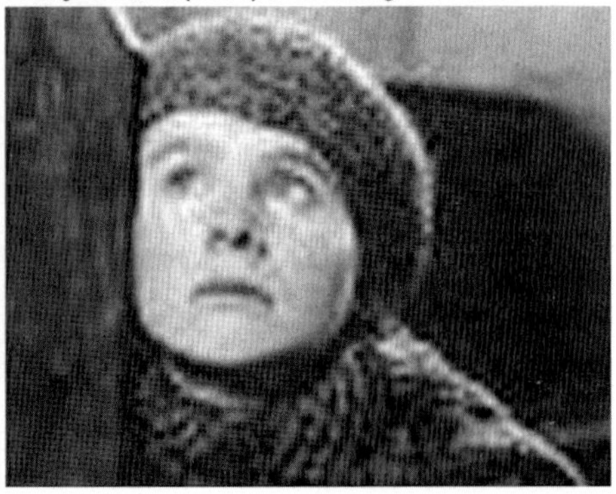

1996 **Lia Perjovschi** Hidden objects

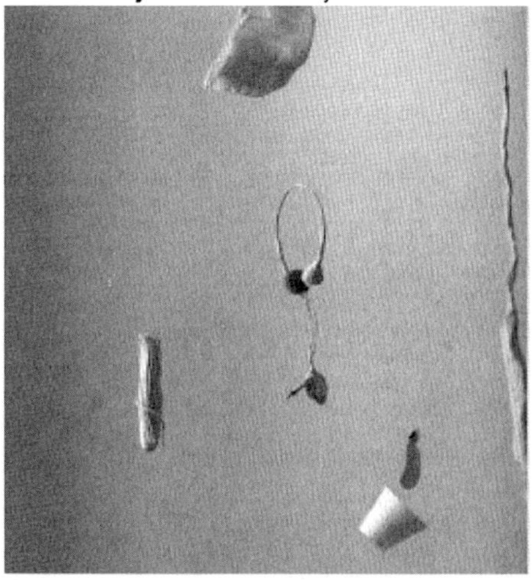

1996 **Lyal Silvan** - Ruanda

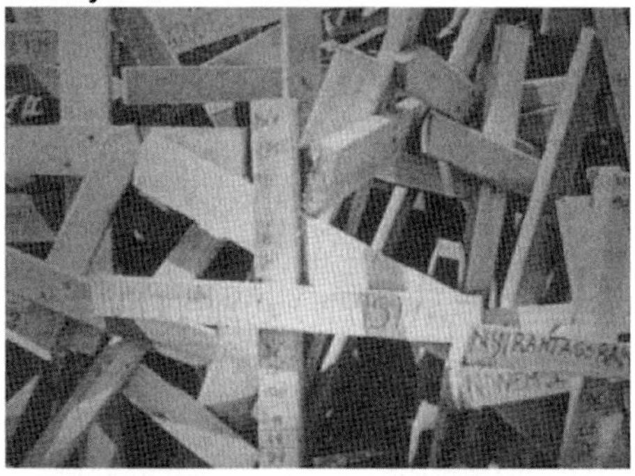

1996 **Mike Nelson**

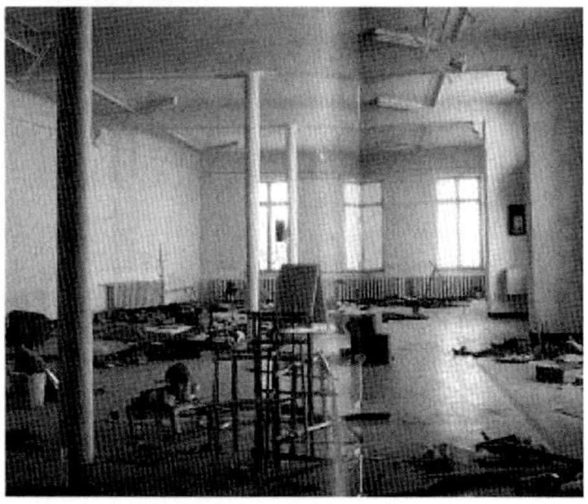

1996 **Louise Bourgeois**

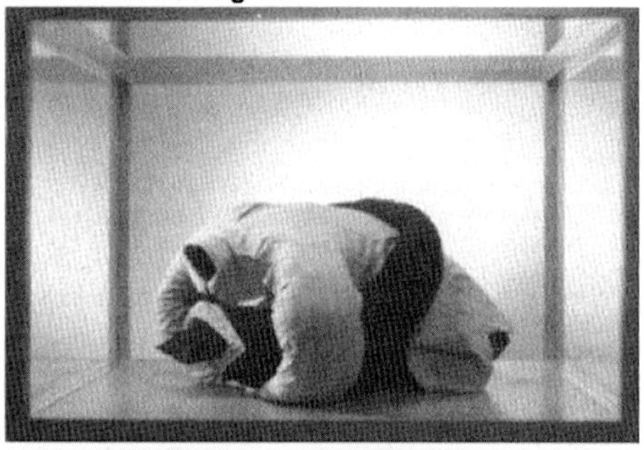

1996 **Marico Mori**

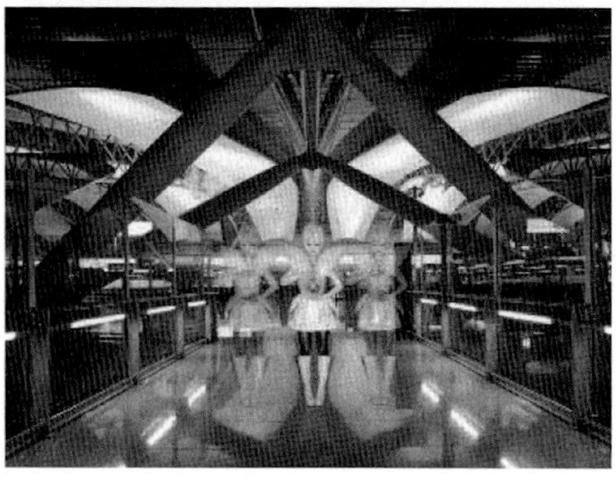

1996 **Joachim Schonfeldt**

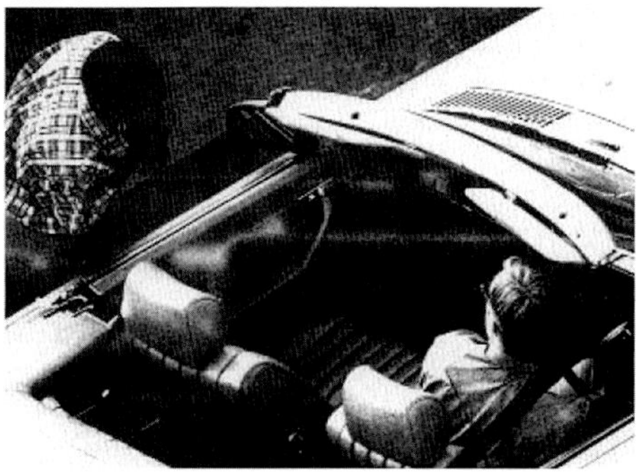

1996 **D Peschke /D Milohnic** Pool Essen KZKK '01

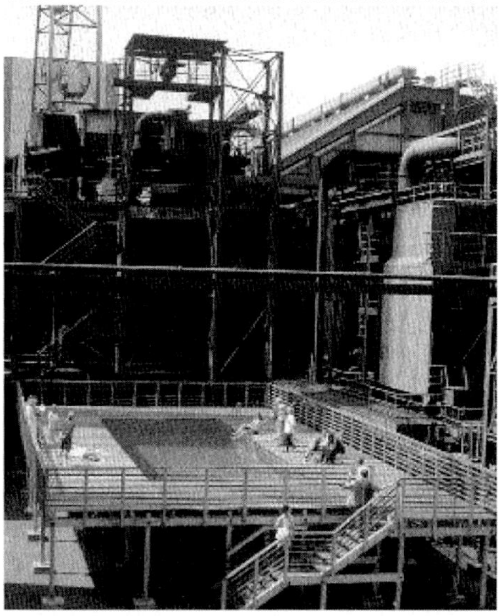

Jason Rhoades "To play God like in the universe" The big mess. " JR works like a project manager on a building siteTo build his immense installation, he combines all the arts and techniques, buying, assembling and constructing conceptual, physical, audible, and chaotic sculpture. For Rhoades, creativity means construction, and the artist is a mason. Fascinated by cars as symbols of the triumph of capitalism, the artist offers the visitor a short drive or the exchange of his Caprice for a Fiero. Whether his installation looks like a race course or a pulsating penis, Rhoades portrays our consumer and automobile society by integrating ideas of purchasing, money, flow and exchange into his creative process." Denis Angus

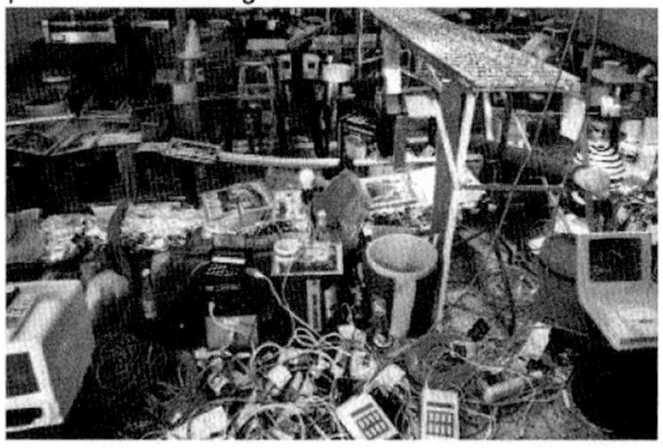

1996 **Maurizio Cattelan**

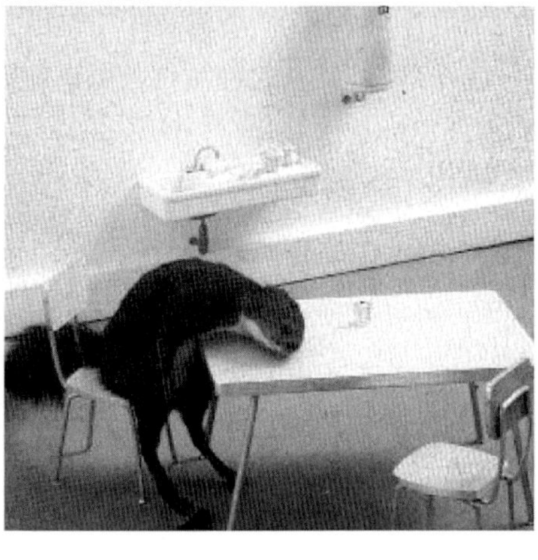

1996 **Giorgiana Starr** So long babe

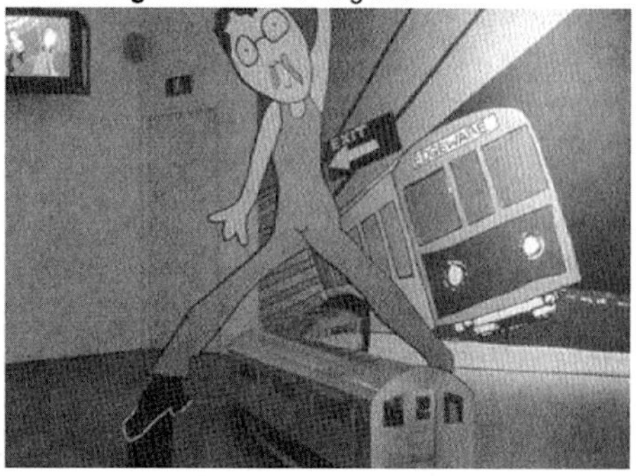

1996 **Henrik Plenge Jakobsen,** Everything is wrong

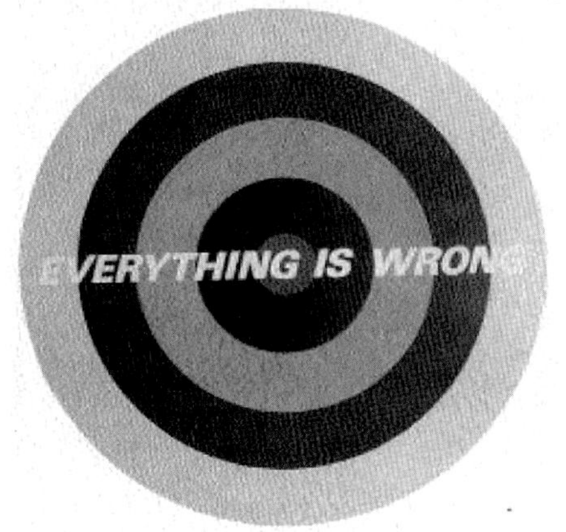

1996 **Yusumasa Morimura** Vivien Leigh

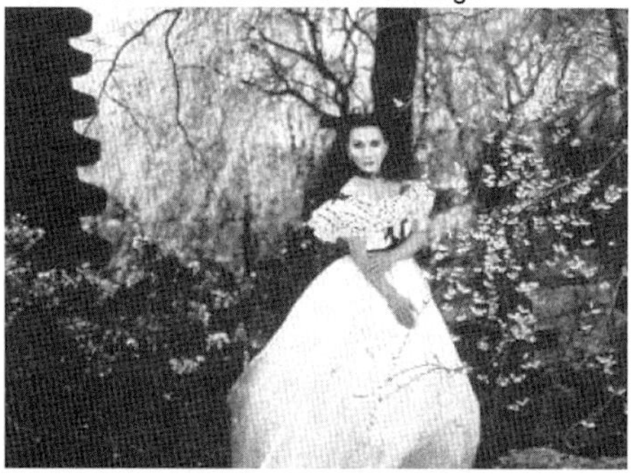

1996 **Nevin Aladag** Fliegerkuss

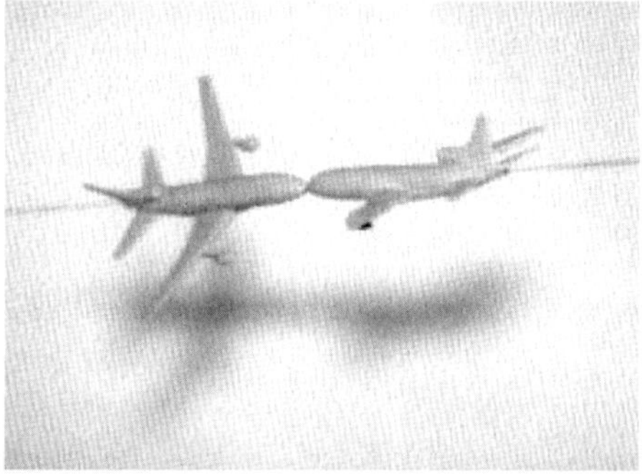

1996 **Ally Mc Beal**

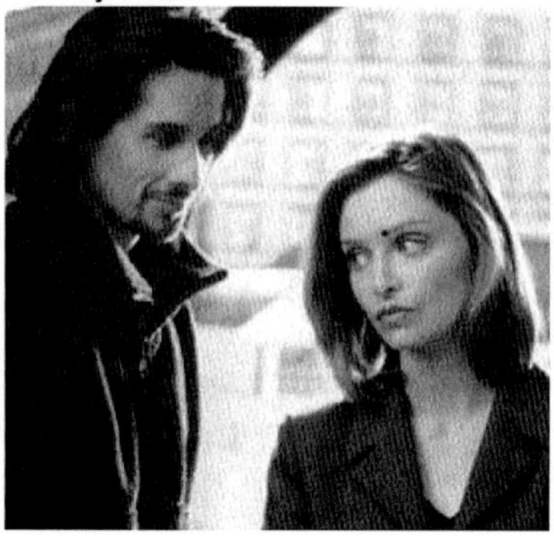

1996 **Caa** Lia & Dan Perjovschi Open **Studio**

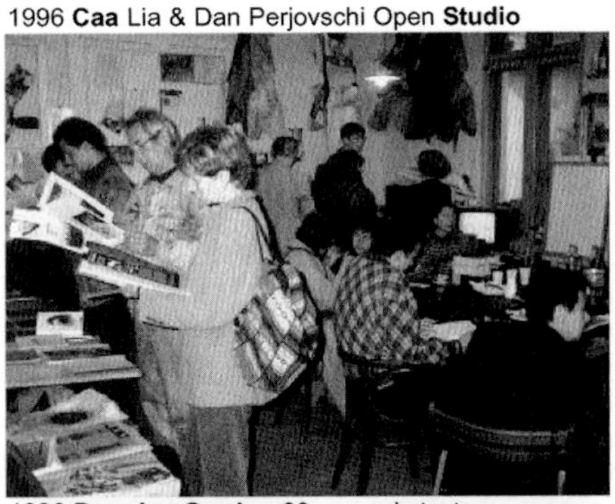

1996 **Douglas Gordon** 30 seconds text

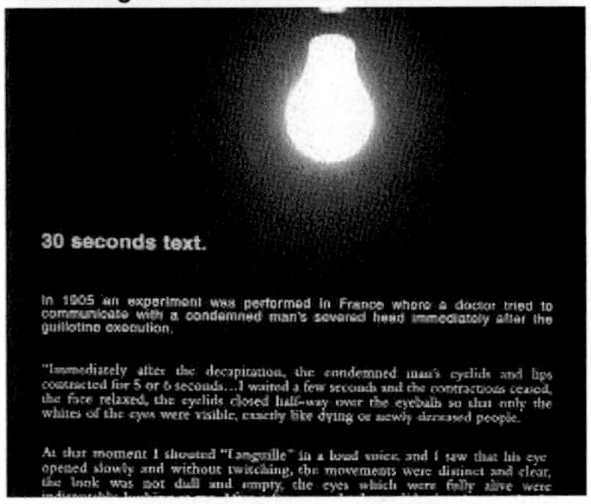

1996 **Paul Bush** The rumours of true things

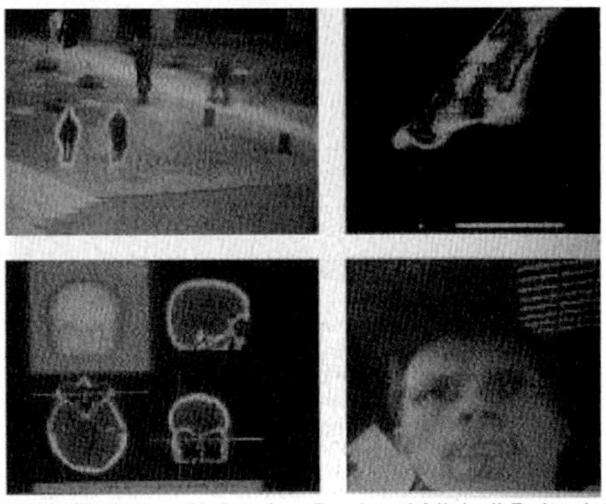

1996 **Christian H Cordes** Denkmal Michail Bakunin.

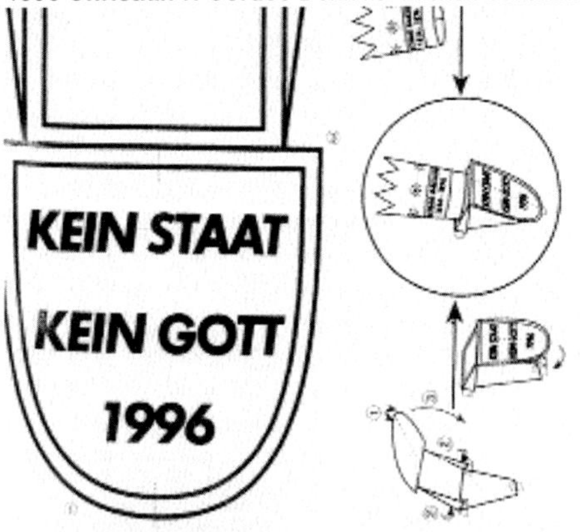

1997 **Lady Di** Last recorded images

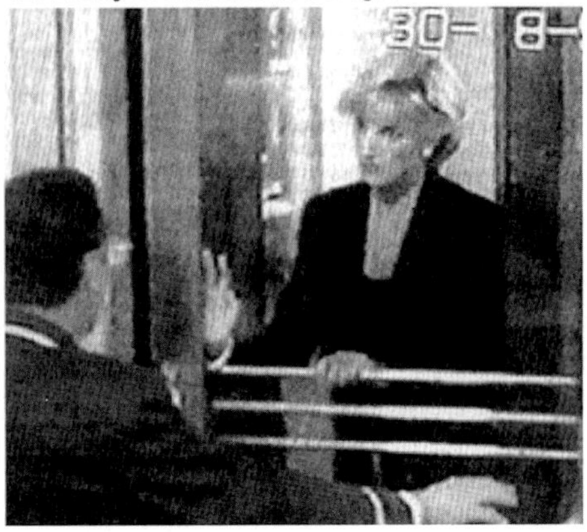

1997 **Marjetica Potrc** Water Roller

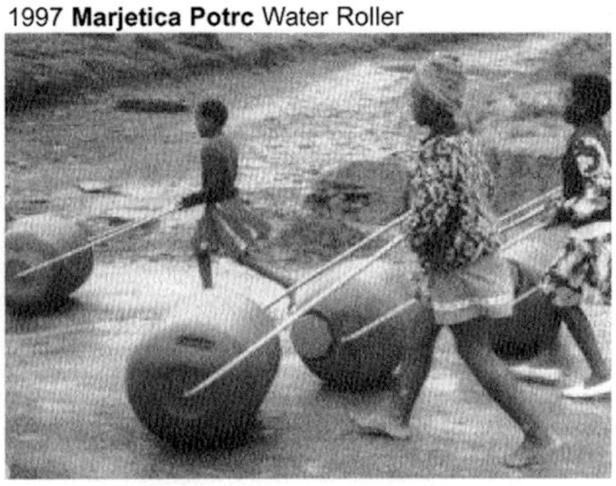

Maria Eichhorn "I prefer a type of activity that makes not distinction between artist and non-artists"
Walking away from art
"(..) When is it art?
Installation/Actions are often challenged as to whether they are really art in a gallery she placed a heap of fake letters on the floor, left there as if abandoned by their owner; she created furniture for children's art workshops, and she even held, in a soon-to-close museum, a garage sale which included works from previous exhibition - demonstrating her interest in the status of objects as both artwork and debris. She makes a more subtle, discreet and poetic use of artistic institutions. Working as a designer, fictions post office employee, librarian and occasional journalist, orchestrates the gradual disappearance of artist as such." Jean Max Collard
1997 **box**

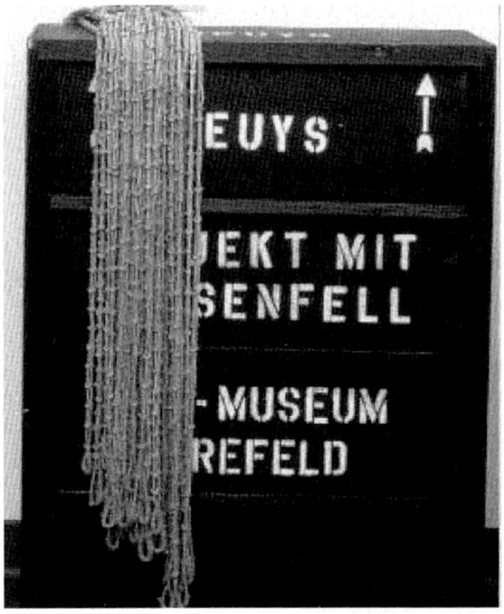

1997 **Nevin Aladag** California Sun

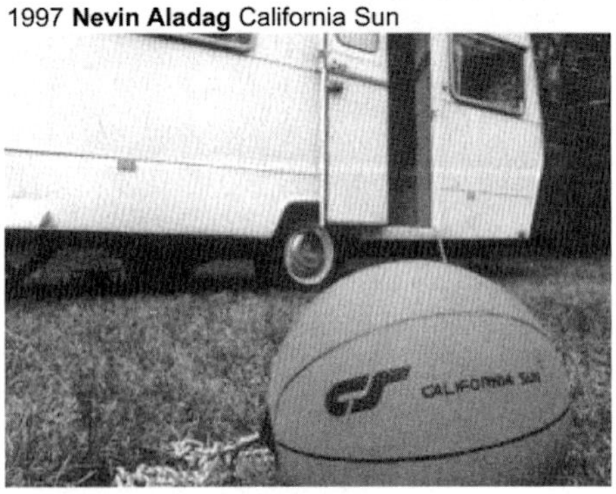

1997 **Christine Irene Hohenbuchler**

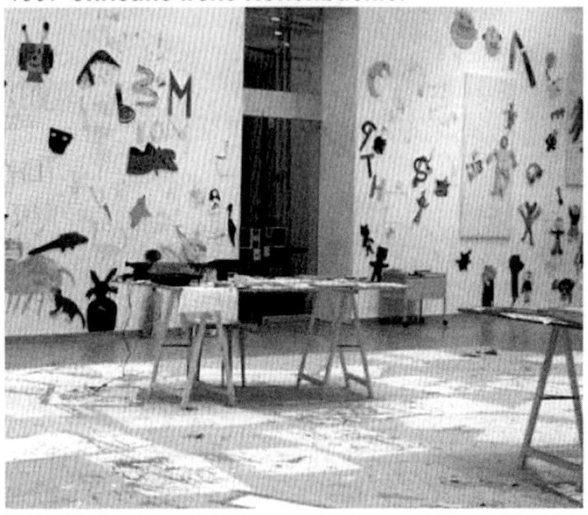

Maurizio Cattelan "I try to remain underground in everything I do"
Illegal traffic. "He prefer solution that are specific to the context of the exhibition, playing with expectation and altering the notion of "artwork". Uses black humor as a way to demonstrate how the art market functions His visual vocabulary is taken from cartoons and comic strips, with which he composes sketches representing different attitudes of the artist: A series of sheets knotted together (escape), a squirrel that has committed suicide (despair)-at least when he is not representing himself in a series of police pictures, self portraits of the artist as a criminal" Francois Piron
1997 **the hole in the gallery**

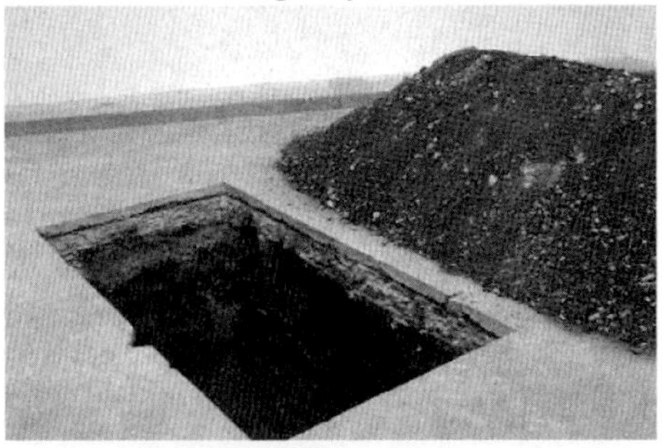

1997 **Andrea Zittel** Deserted clouds

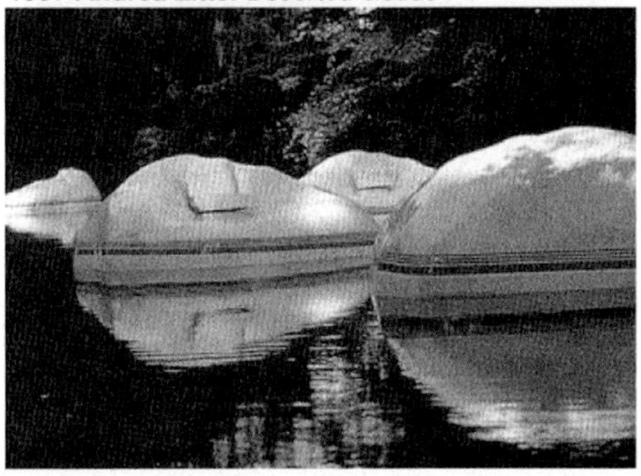

1997 **Graham Gussin** Studio

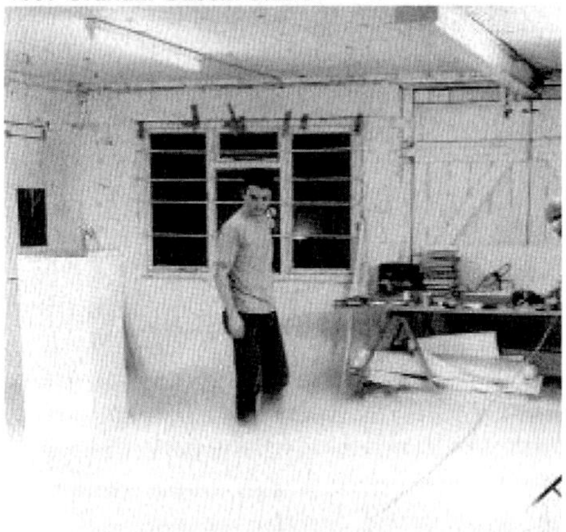

Vanessa Beecroft
"Frustration is the bedfellow of desire. You can watch these dream girls, but you cannot touch-and certainly not possess.
A kind of collective spirit binds the girls
They come into being before the crowd, proud of their femininity.
Pin-up girl or a character out of a film.
Identical look. They are like living, breathing sculptures, move very slowly, create an impression of near-fixity." Denis Angus

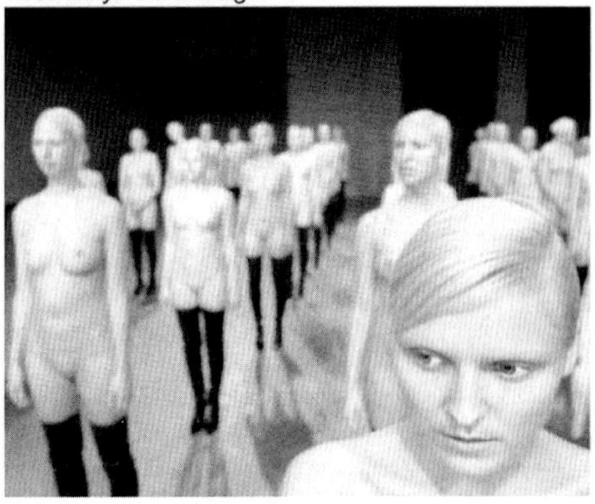

1997 **KunstHalle** Zurich supermarket

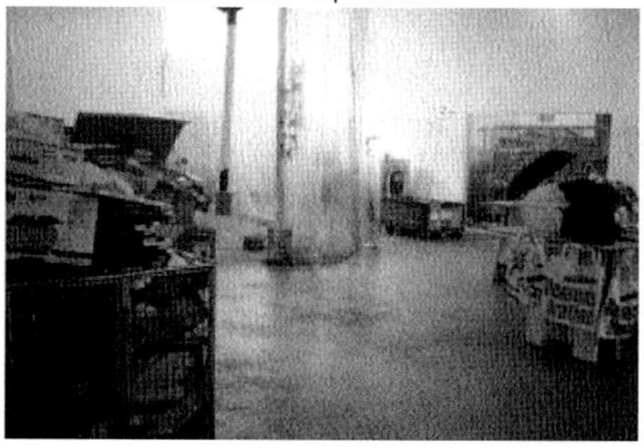

1997 **CAA (Archive of contemporary art)**

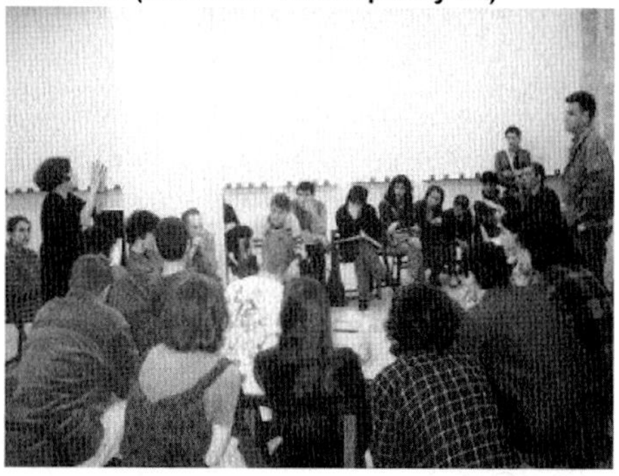

1997 **Jessica Stockholder**

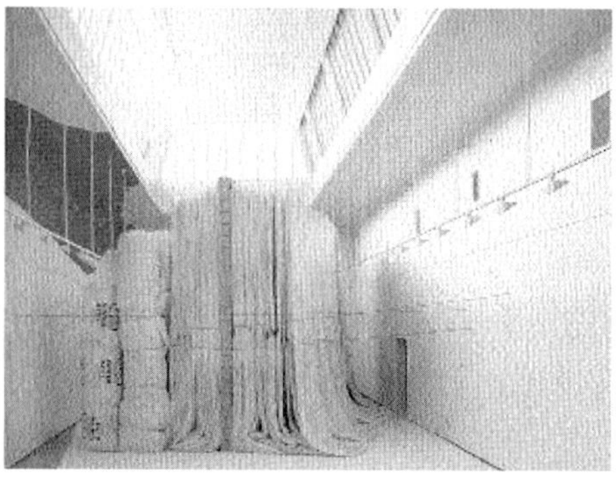

1997 **Jon Benet Ramsey** murder case

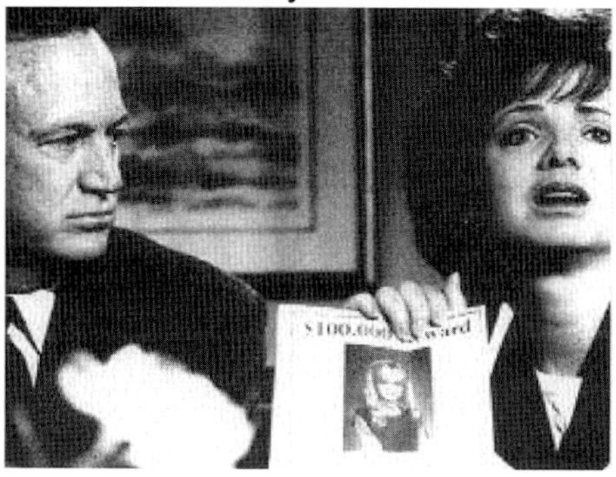

1997 **Heavens Gate** the suicidal cult

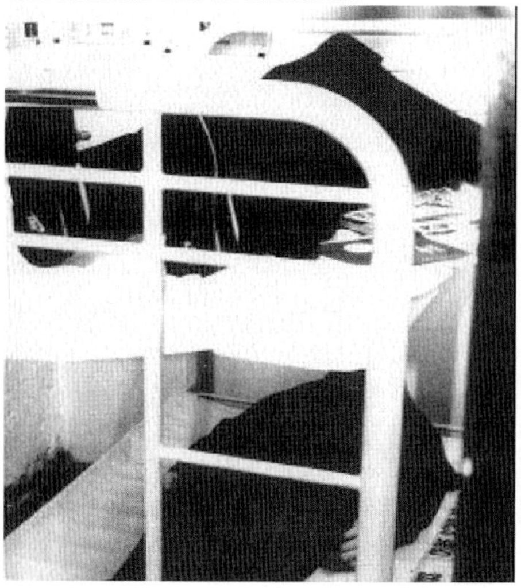

1997 **John Simon "Every Icon"** never ending succession of calculated visual tricks

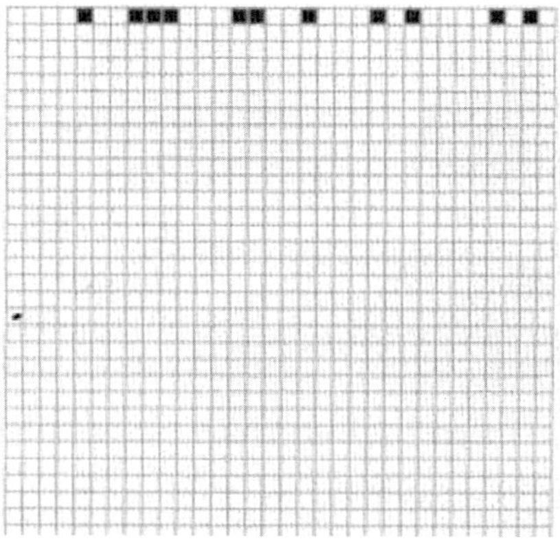

1997 **Sarah Lucas**

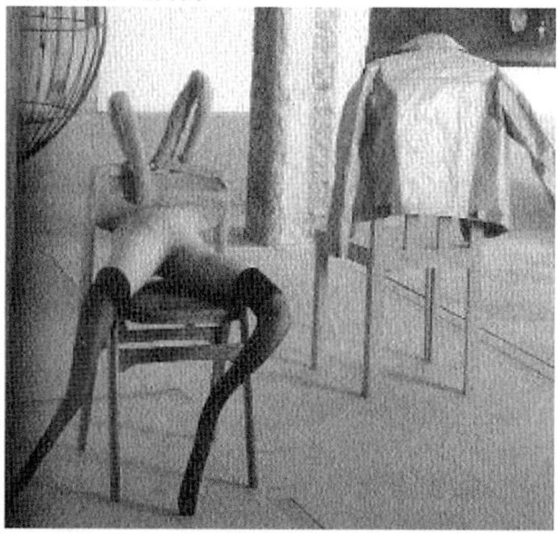

1997 **Mike Nelson** The Lion Heart

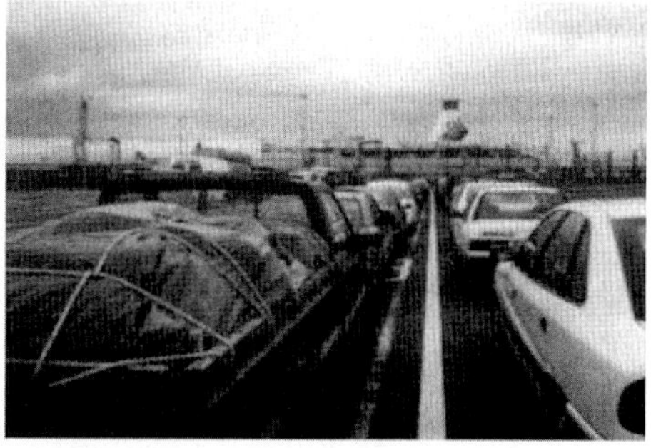

1998 **Andrea Zittel** Rough (landscape)

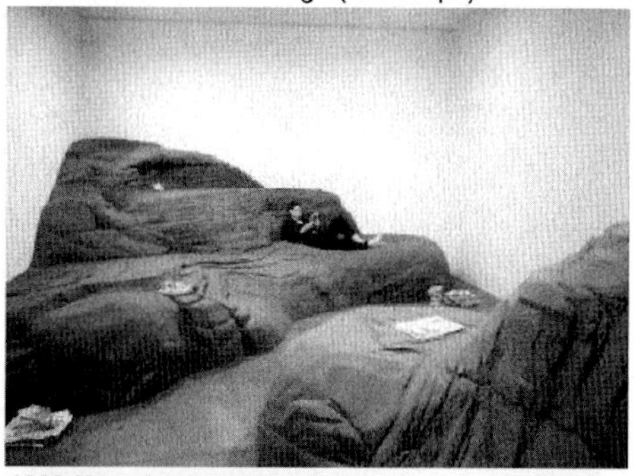

1998 **Knowbotic research**

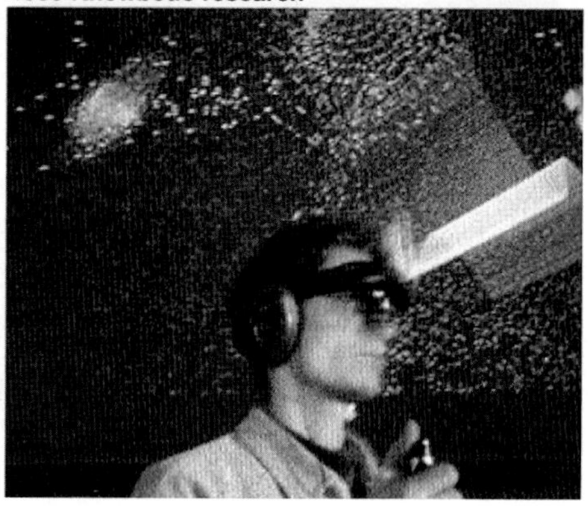

1998 **Destiny Deacon** pool

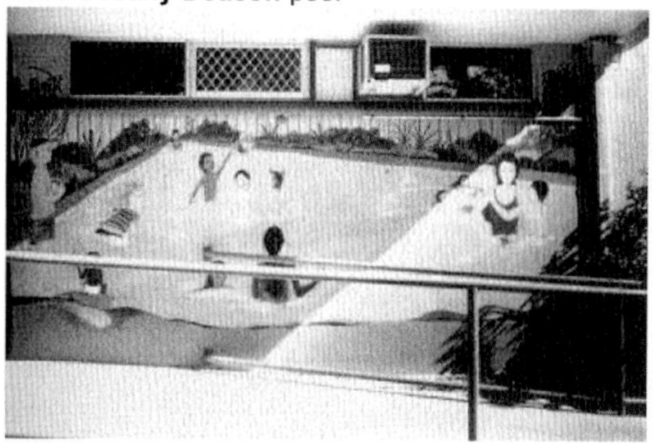

1998 **Peter Land** The staircase

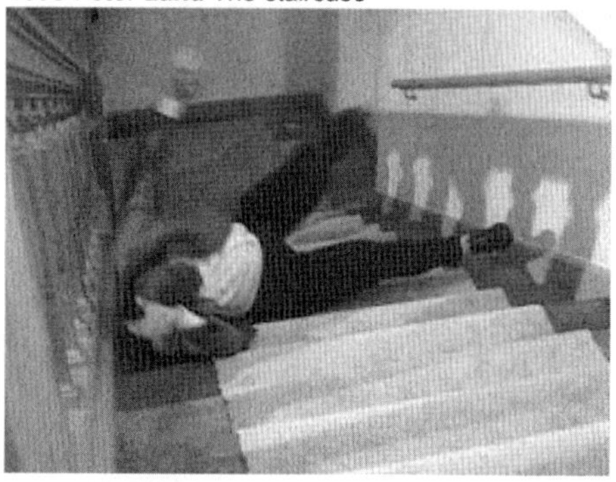

1998 **Peter Demand** The universe

1998 **Mona Hatoum**

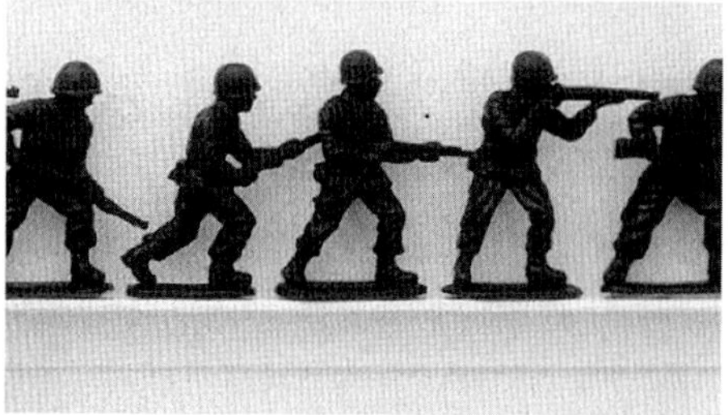

1998 **Nedko Solakov** Black and White

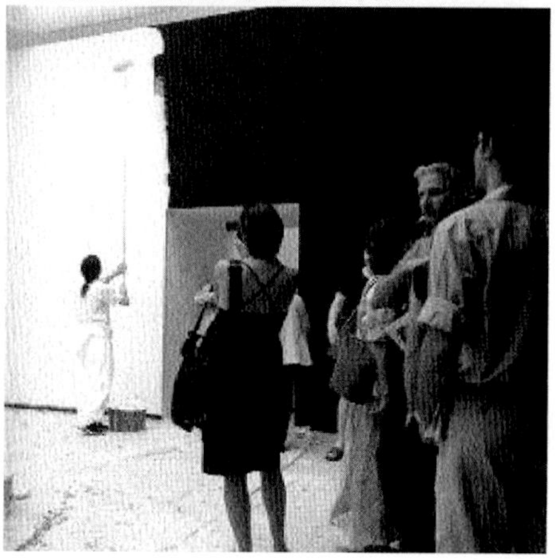

1998 **CAA** Dia pozitiv

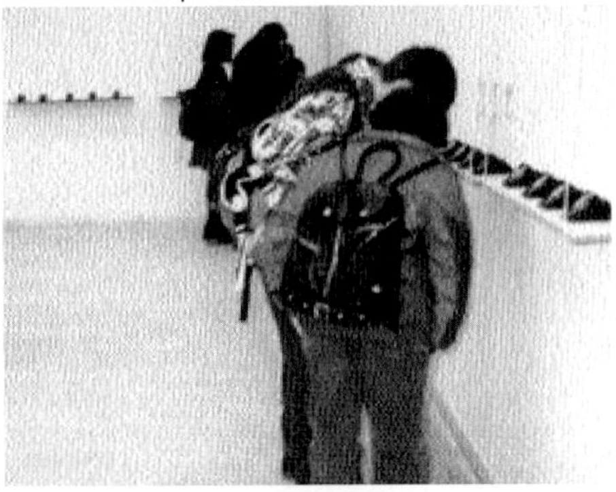

1998 **Marian Imre** (since 1996)

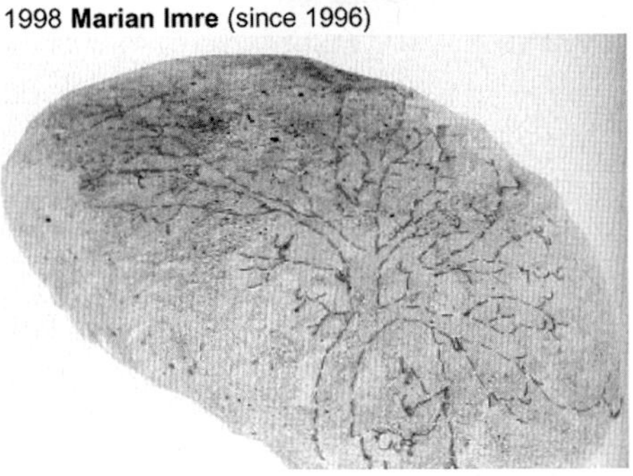

1998 **Orlan**

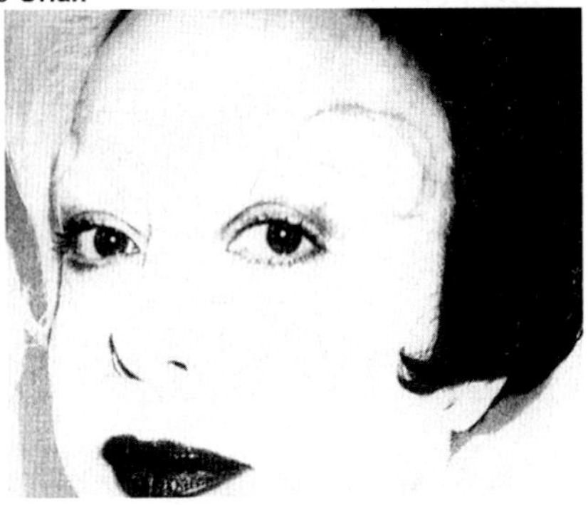

1998 **Sandor Bartha**

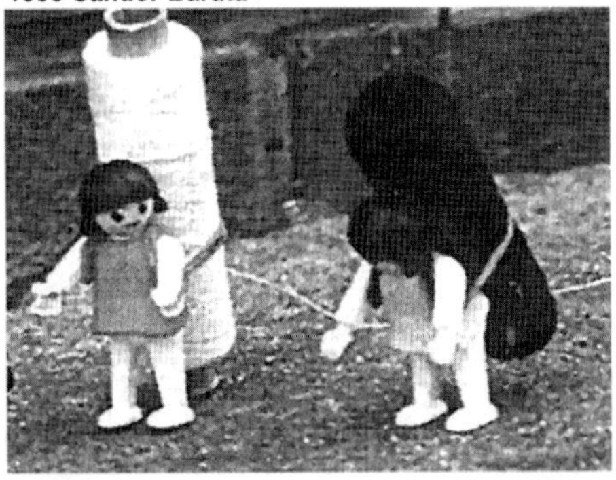

1998 **Sarah Lucas**

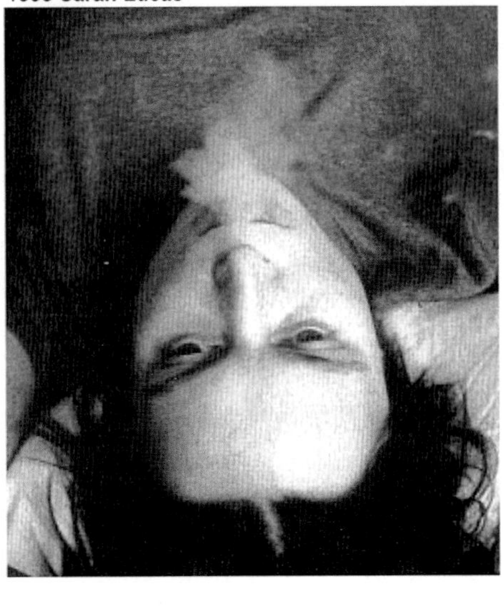

1999 **Matts Leiderstam**

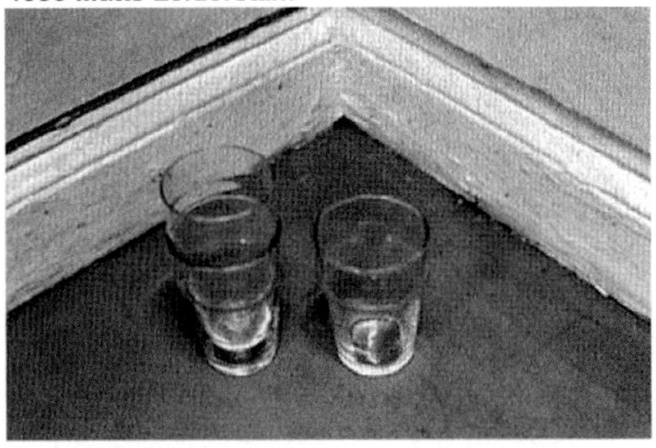

1999 **Ann Veronica Janssen** Belgian pavillion

1999 **Lia Perjovschi** art history, theory, criticism

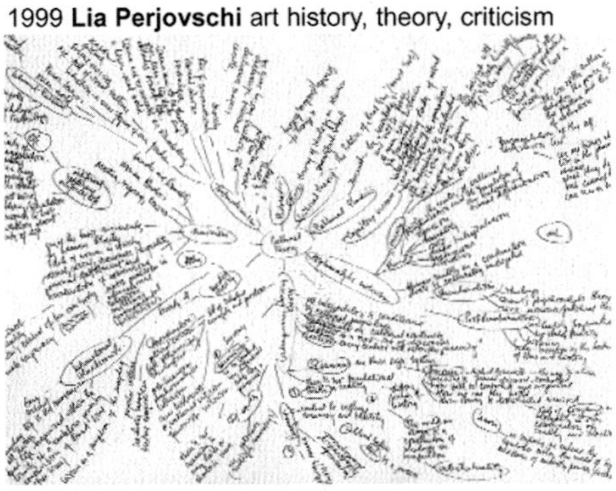

1999 **Balthasar Burkhard**

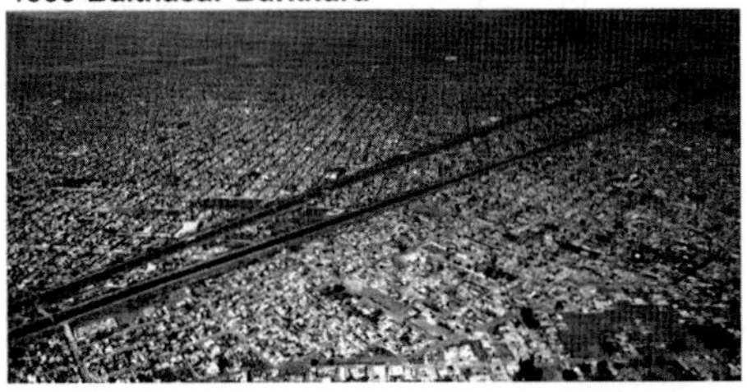

1999 **Bruce Nauman**

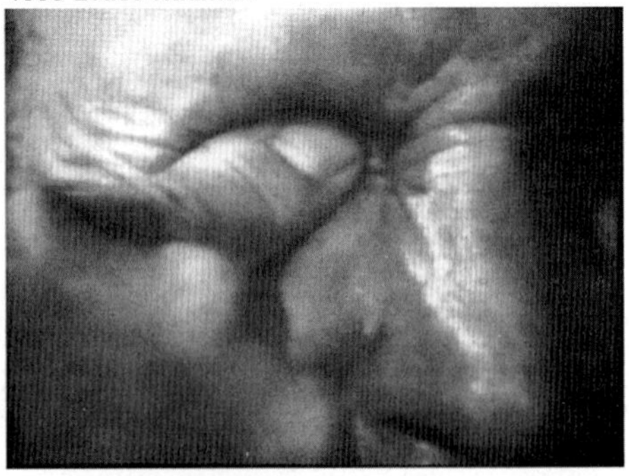

1999 **Gillian Wearing** Drunk

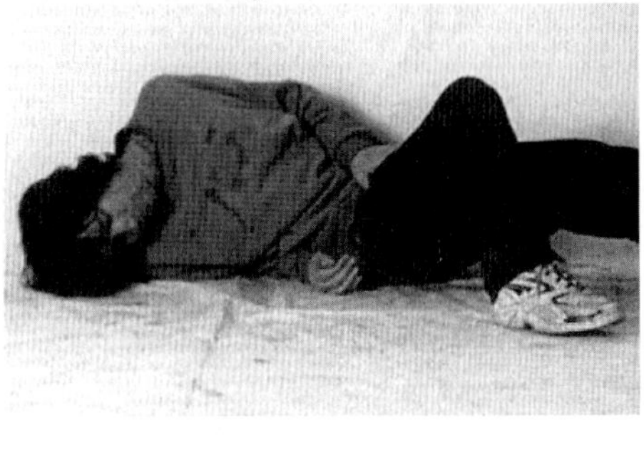

1999 **Thomas Hirschhorn** World Airport
"I spend all my energy fighting against the quality of the work. You shouldn't aim for improvement, but for deterioration. You shouldn't be better-but always less good." Artist, laborer, soldier
"(.) Exuberant and invasive, his works reflect the complexity of the world, with the daily flood of information, the multiple and contradictory points of views and the constant links.
His plastic vocabulary is deliberately rough."
Catherine Francblin

1999 **Anthony Gormley**

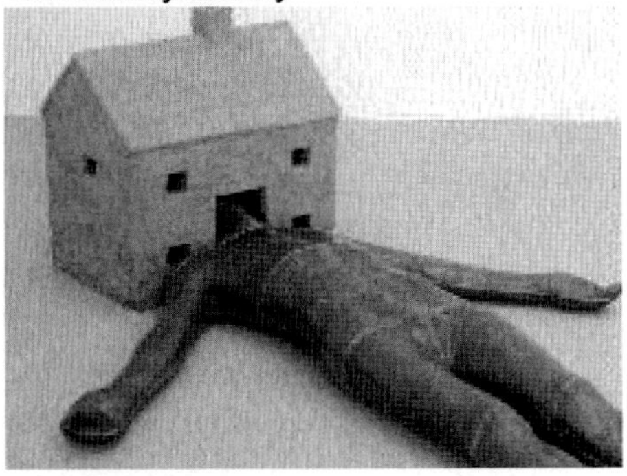

1999 **Dan Perjovschi** Romanian pavillion Venice

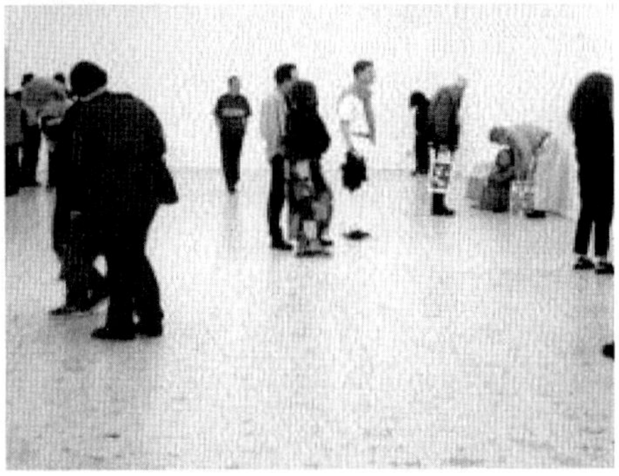

1999 **Ravi Agarwal** India

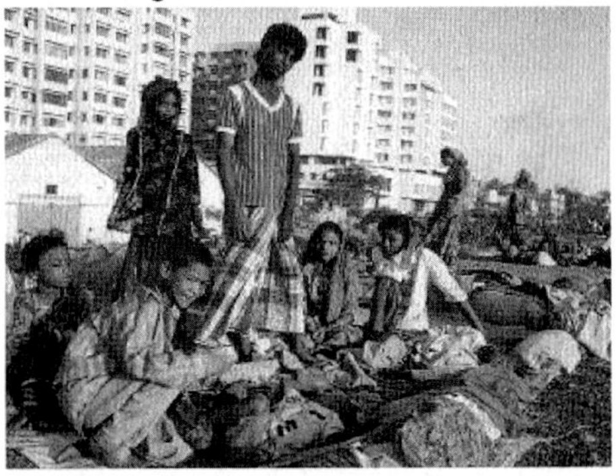

1999 **Roman Ondak** Chatting to a friend

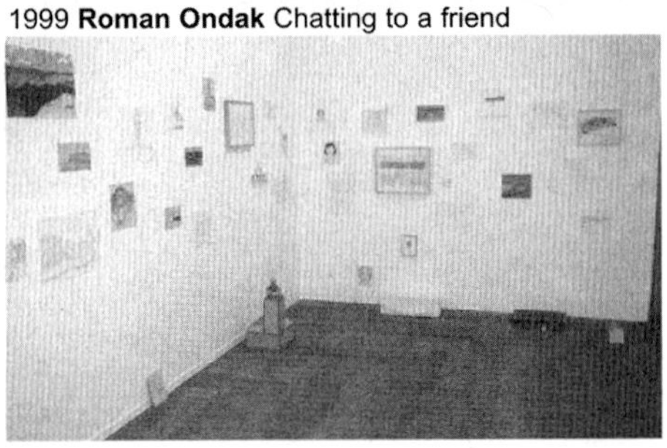

1999 **Luca**

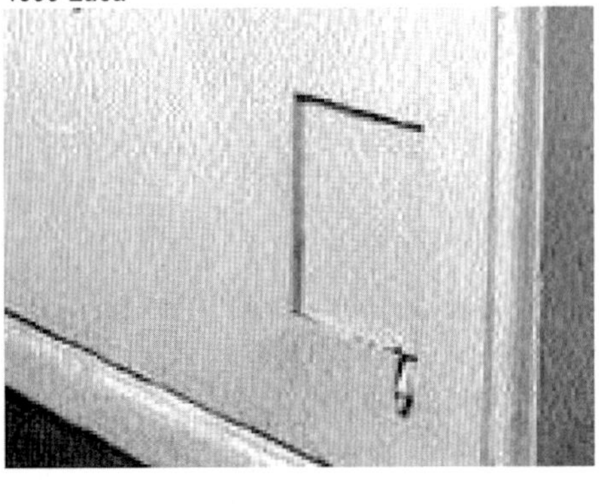

1999 **Doug Aitken** Continental drift
"(..)The art world is in competition with a certain number of other media-music, television and film-which are far more popular, but which lack one essential thing :content". Technological and media aberrations. Silent tragedies, images of a directionless urban youth, saturated by MTV. The price to pay for a high-speed world, which continues to express a naïve amazement in its own progress, until the body becomes afflicted or nature destroyed" Christine Marcel

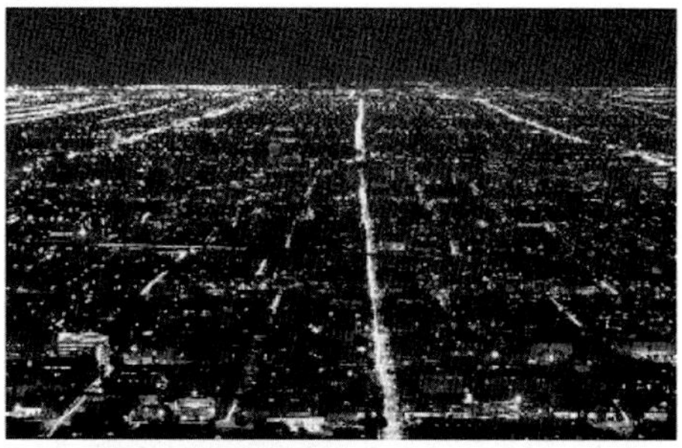

Doug Aitken Electric Earth

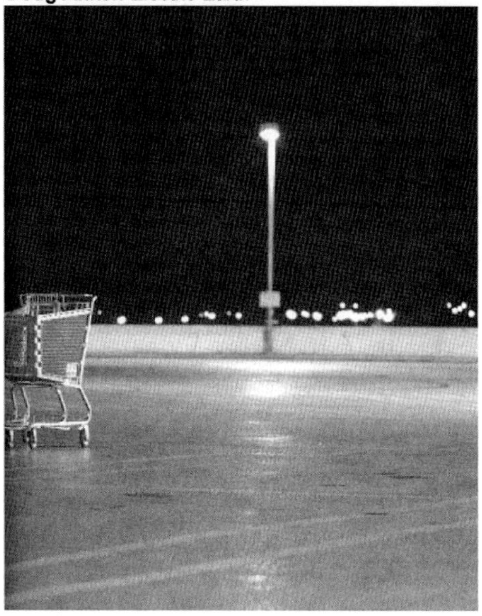

1999 **Frank Thiel** City TV

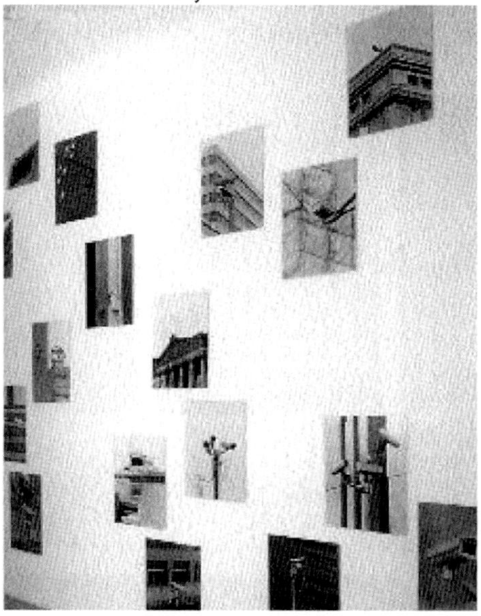

1999 **go away** artist and travel

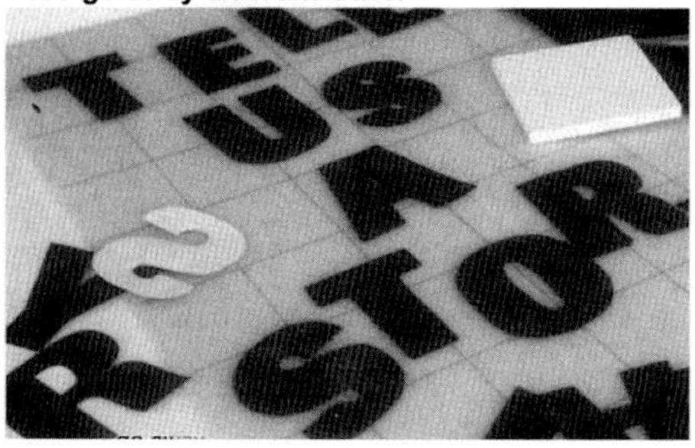

1999 **God's Army (soldier children)**

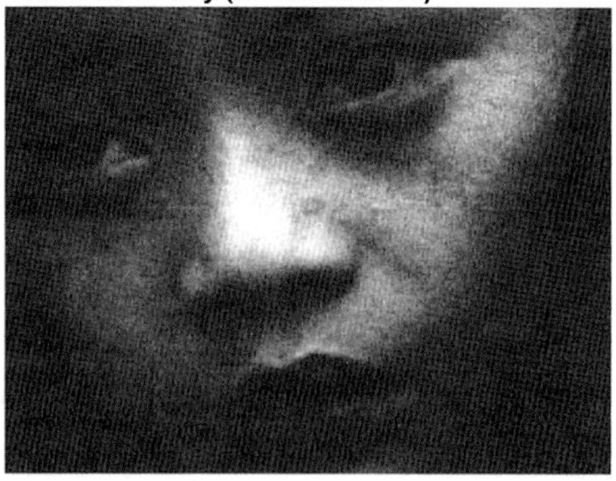

Olafur Eliasson Nature as experience
"Mainly using the powerful Icelandic landscape; his installations (or photographs) created from dampness, fog, plants and water in all its form, try to let the viewer create a kind of self-portrait by actively experiencing the work. His handling of light reinforces the immateriality of his spaces. The ephemeral nature of his works have meaning only in relation to the position of the viewer (who give the deliberate absence of explicit, well defined symbols)" Geraldine Bretault

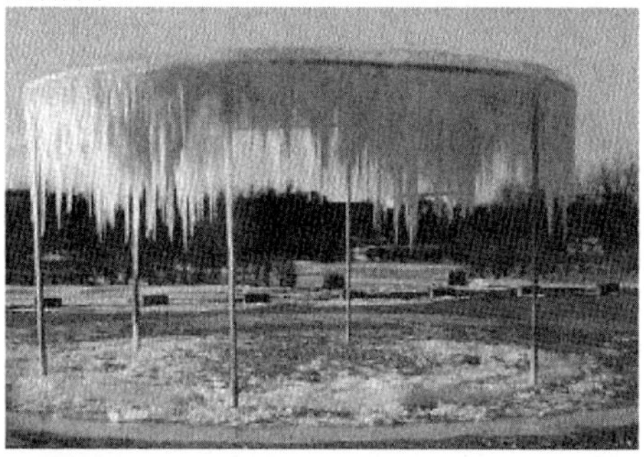

1999 **Rachel Lowe**

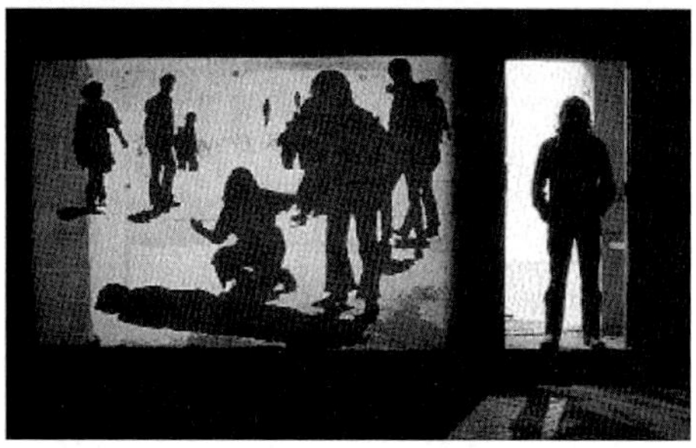

1999 **Miriam Backstrom** Museums

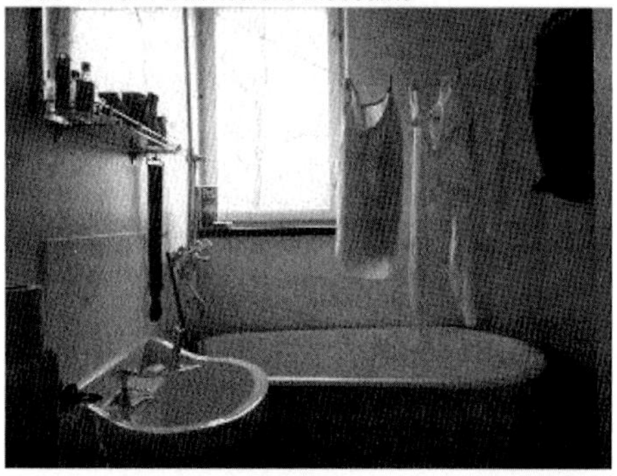

1999 **Joao Penalva** Kitsure

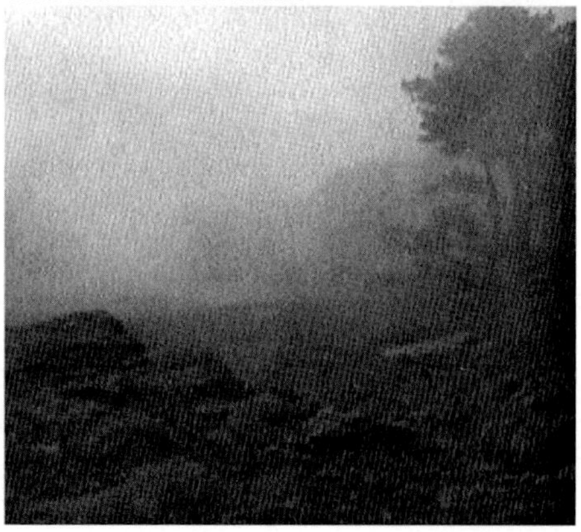

1999 **By the way** post cards re-exposed

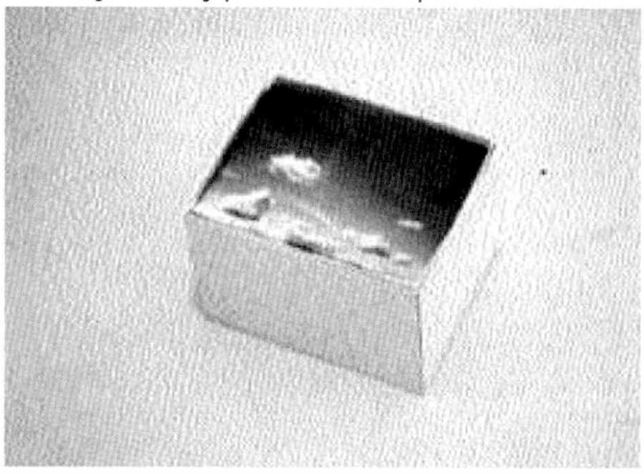

1999 **MAK** ine art India

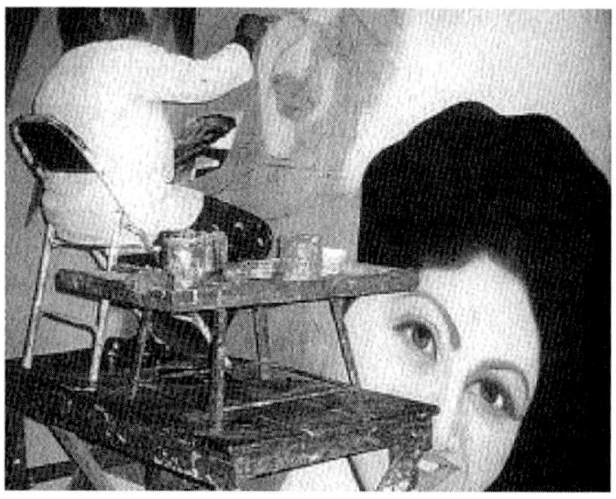

1999 **Ian Kiger**

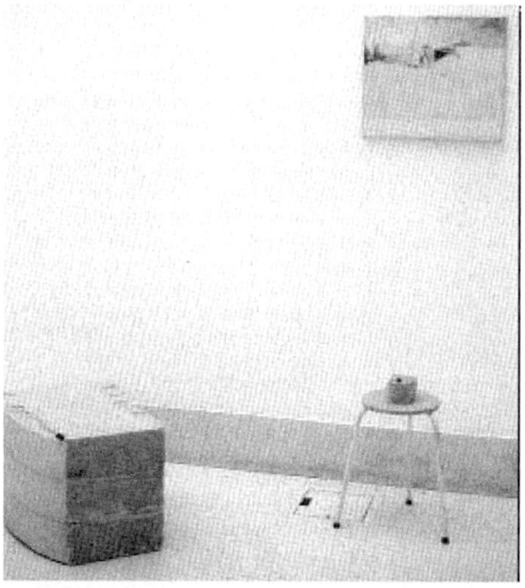

1999 **Mark Leckey Fiorucci** Made Me Hardcore

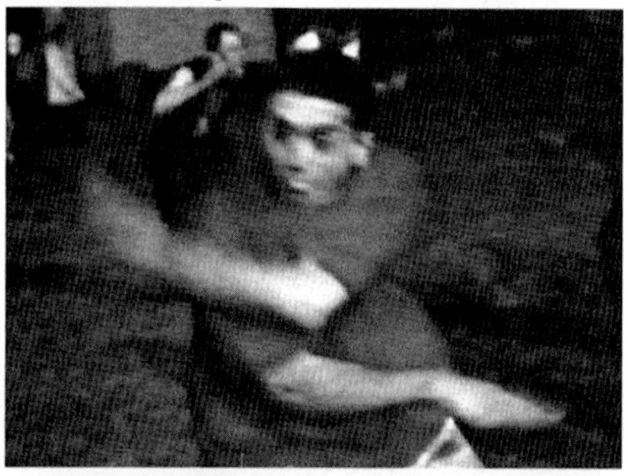

1999 **Shirin Neshat**

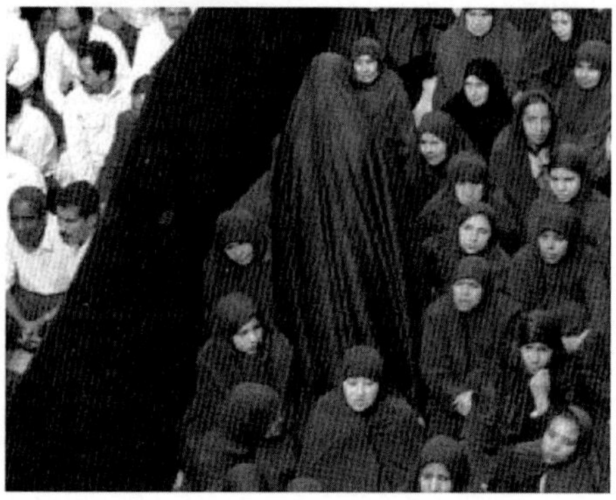

1999 **Michael Craig Martin** Modern Starts Things

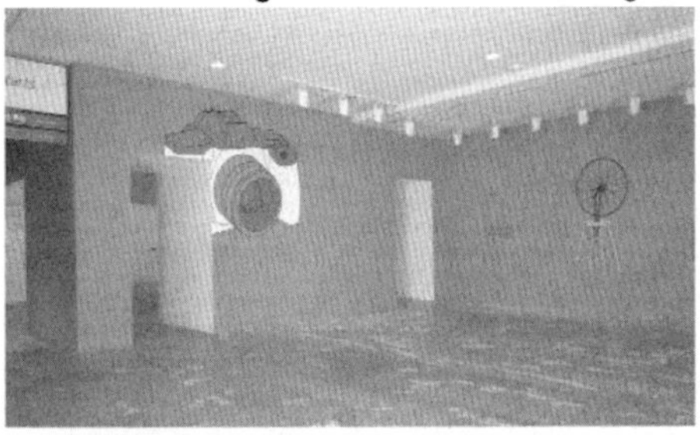

1999 **Mike Nelson** To the Memory of H.P. Lovecraft

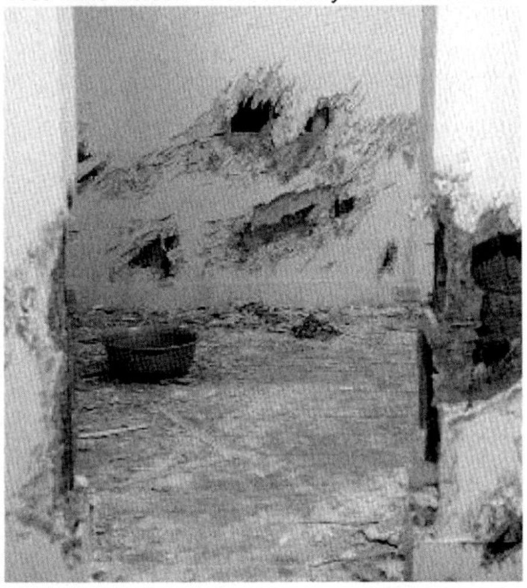

1999 **Pierre Huyghe** Secession exhibition

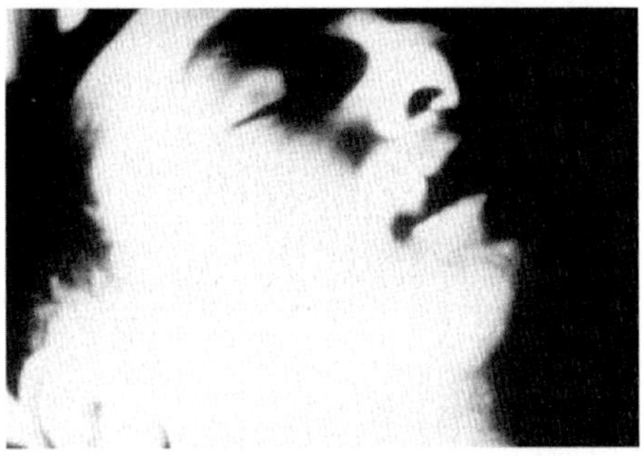

1999 **Oliver Musovik** Neighbours

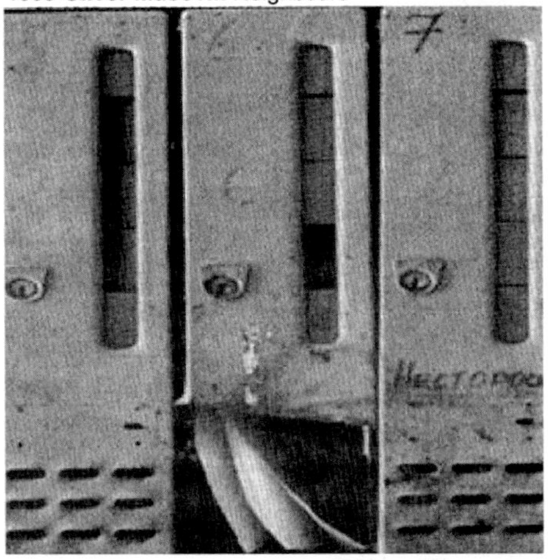

1999 **Roman Signer** Venice Biennial

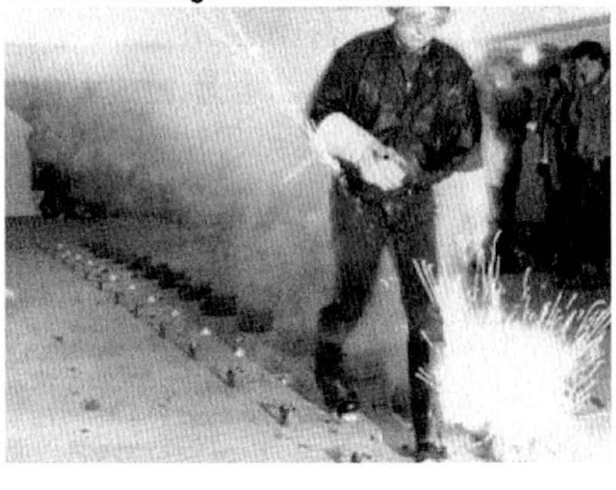

1999 **Roni Horn** Still Water

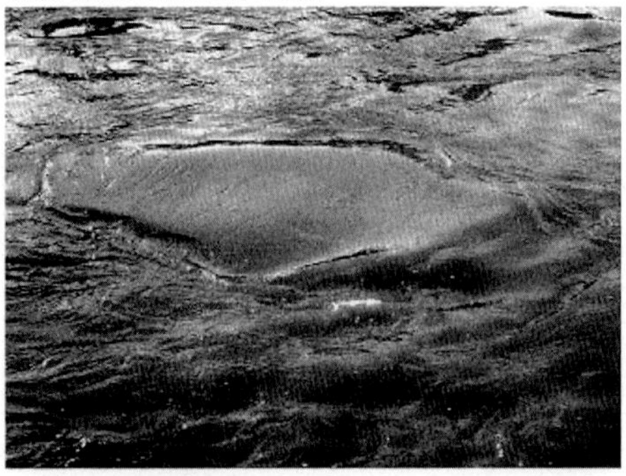

2000 **Alexej Shulgin**

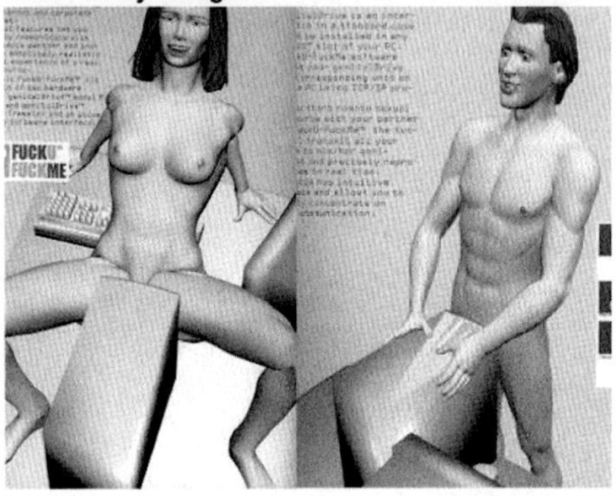

2000 **Santiago Sierra-** extreme actions 160cm line tattooed on 4 people; A person paid for 360 continuous working hours, 10 people paid to masturbate ephemeral actions - the use of other people as performers, emphasis on their renumeration - everything and everyone has a price - a grim meditation on the social and political conditions that permit such disparities in people's 'prices' to emerge: see, this is what some people will do for money, and this is what they are.

2000 **Michael Elmgreen & Ingar Draget** Between other Events

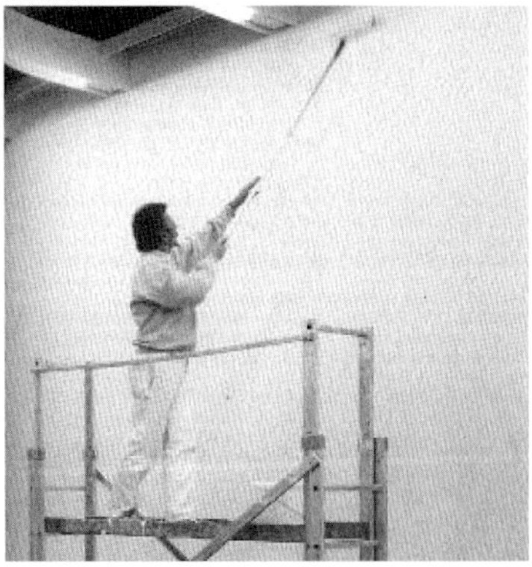

2000 **Dan Perjovschi**

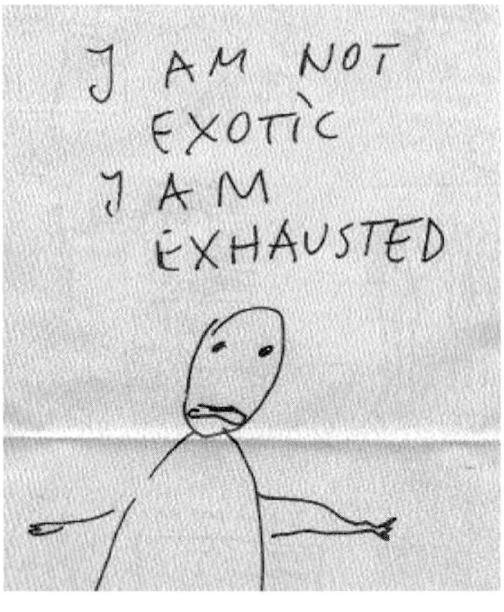

2000 **Dominique Gonzalez Foerster**

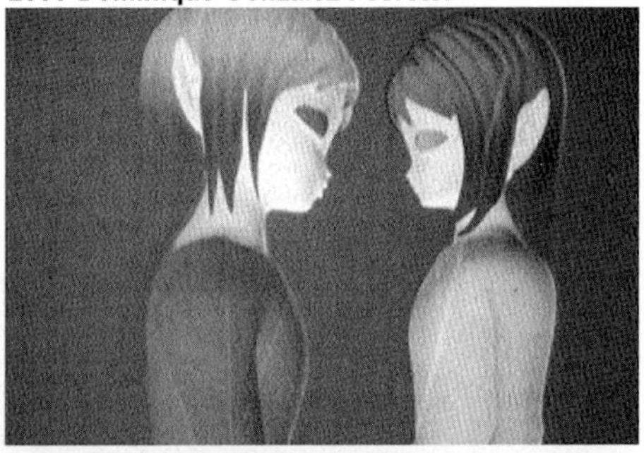

2000 **Arkady Nasonov**

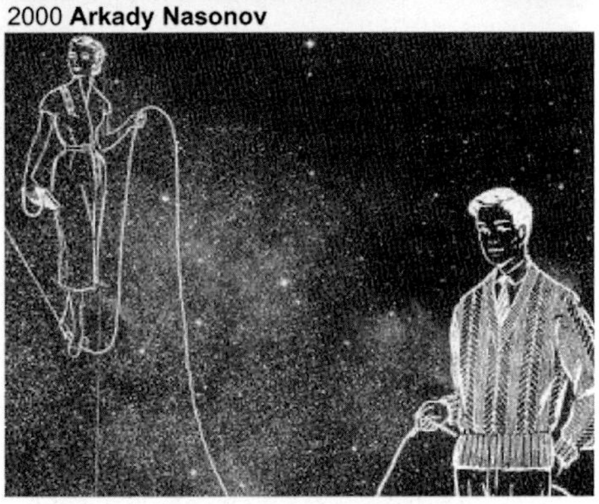

2000 **Big Brother TV**

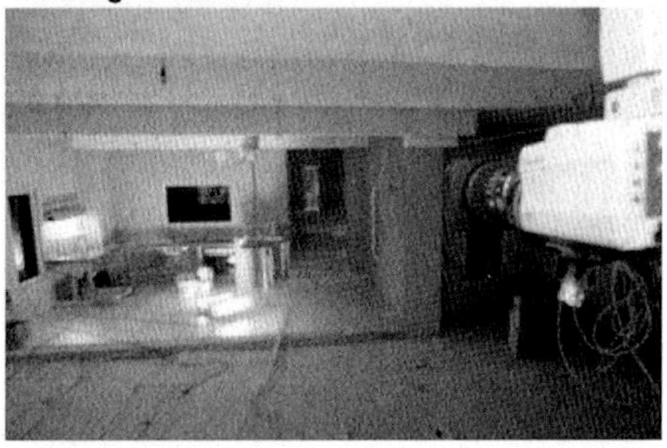

Cecilia Edefalk 2000-02

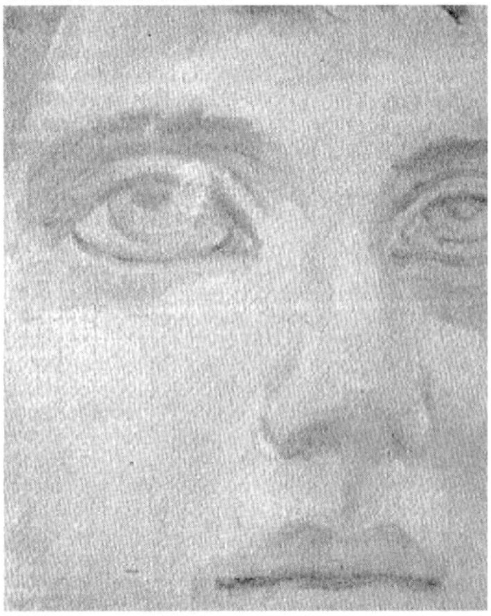

2000 **Ene Liis Semper**

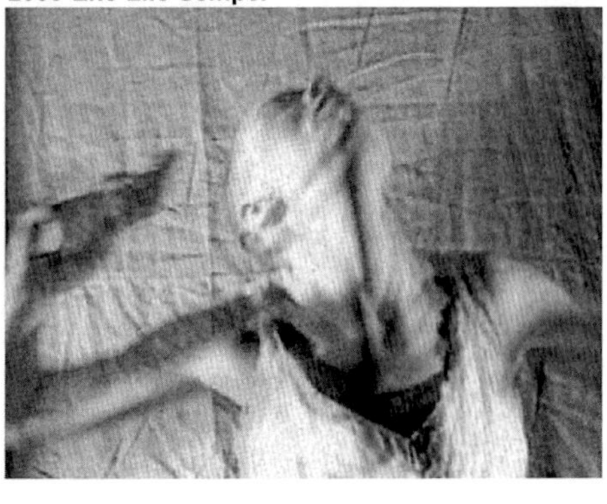

1999 **Mark Manders** (photo)

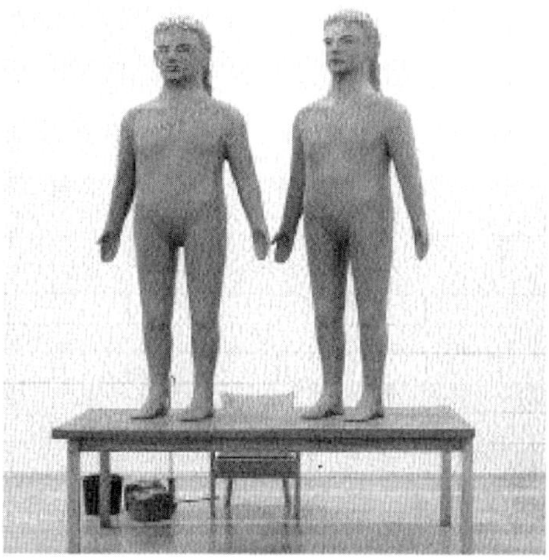

2000 **Daniel Knorr**

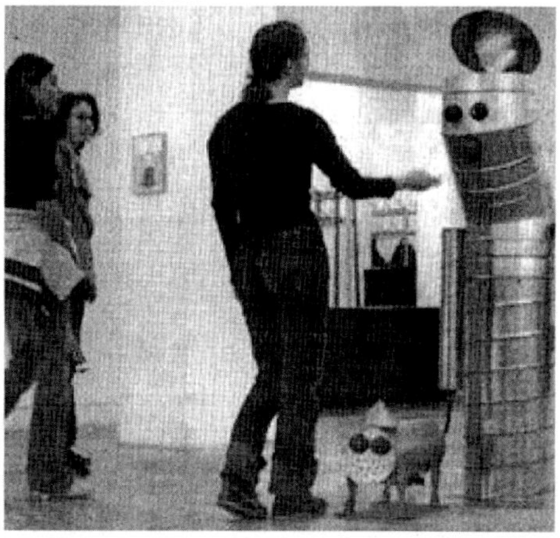

2000 **Peter Land** Nordic Art Kunsthalle Wien

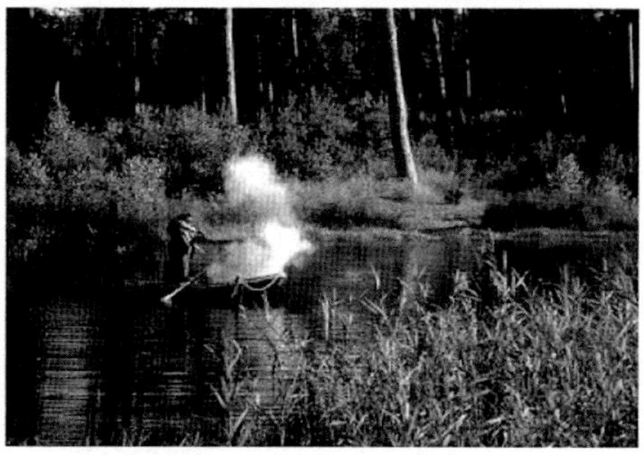

2000 **Koo Jeong a**

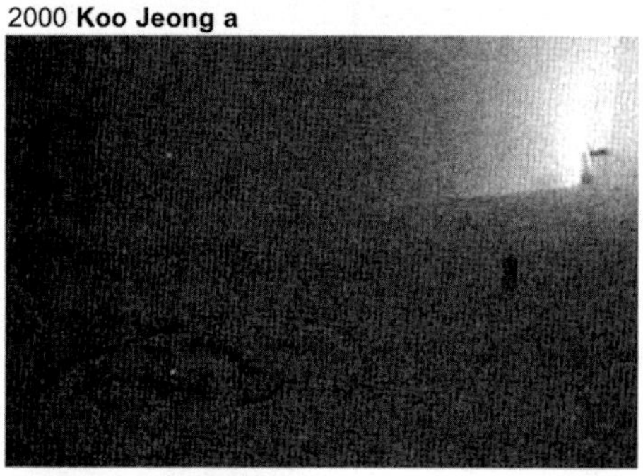

2000 **Surasi Kusolwong**

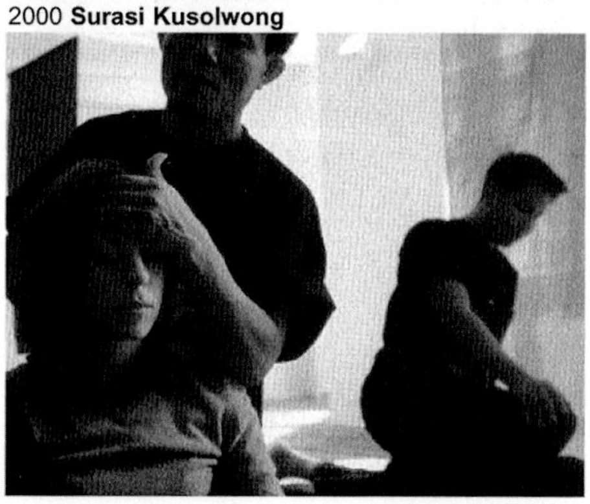

2000 **Utopia** exhibition Wien PL

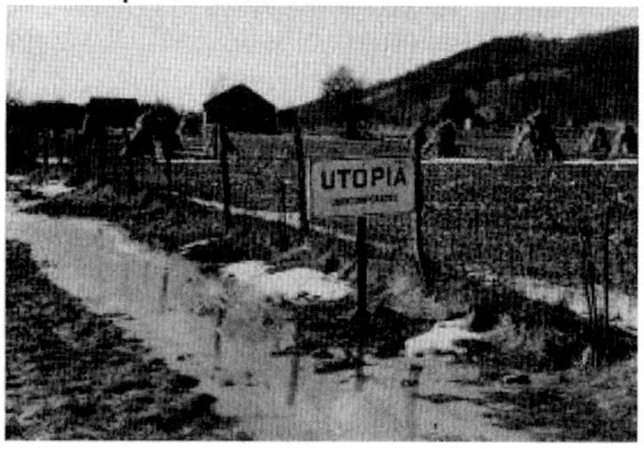

2000 **Vadim Fishkin** What's on the other side?

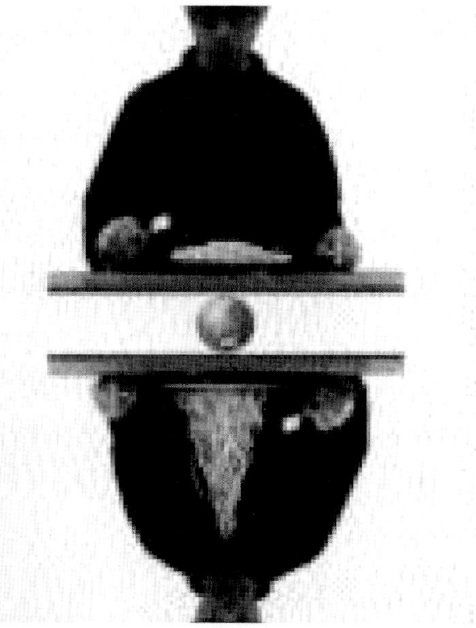

2000 **Oleg Kulik**

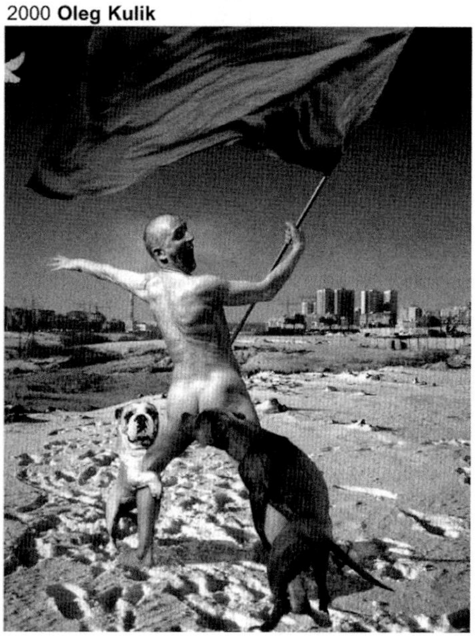

2000 **John Bock**

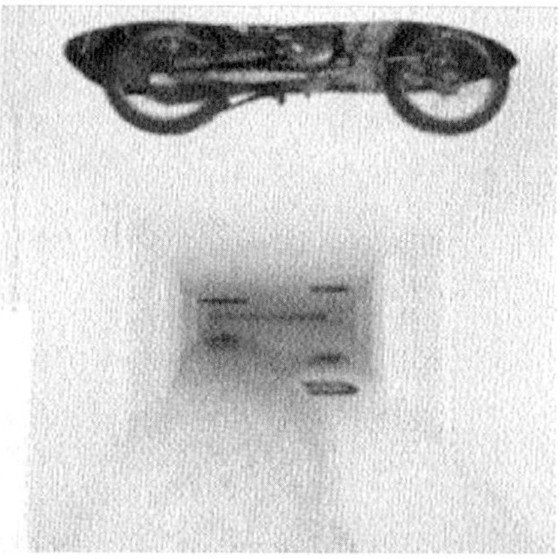

2000 **Richard Prince** cowboy

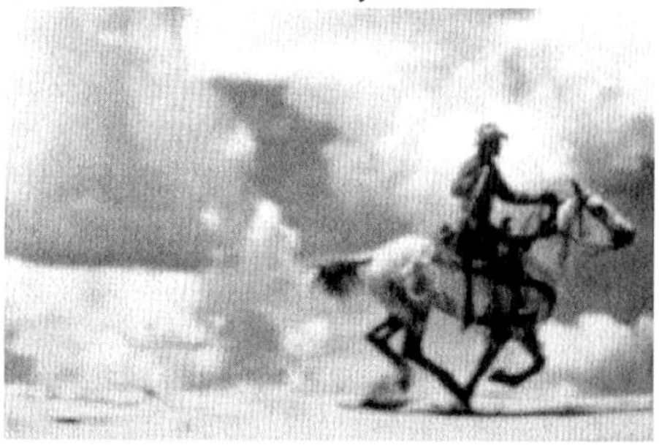

2000 **Caa** (Center for Art Analysis) Dizzydent from dizzy (critical attitude) Lia & Dan Perjovschi and Detective in contemporary art **Lia Perjovschi**
LIA & Dan Perjovschi moderating Everything on sight, live showont National TV Ro

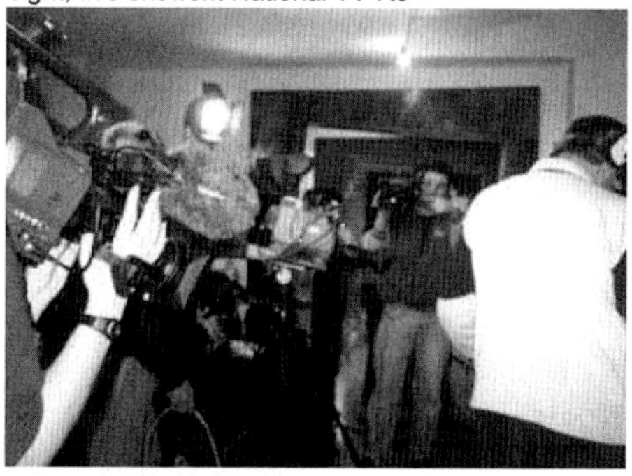

2001 Position Romania in MQ

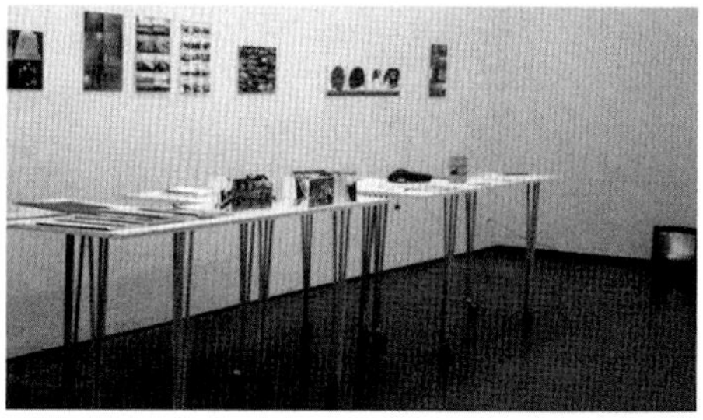

2001 **CAA** ViD (visual ID)

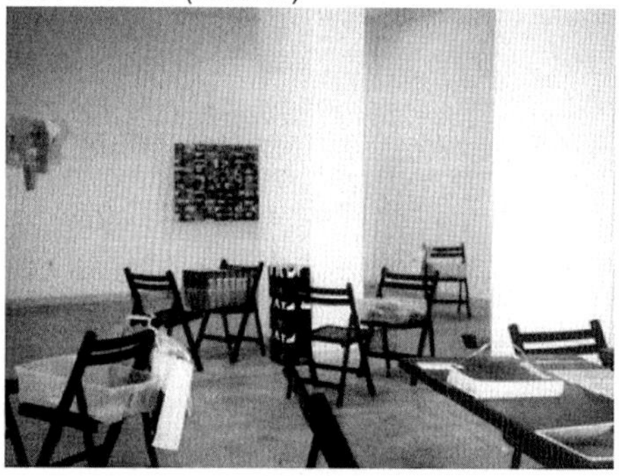

2001 **Silke Wagner,** Kokerei Zollverein Essen

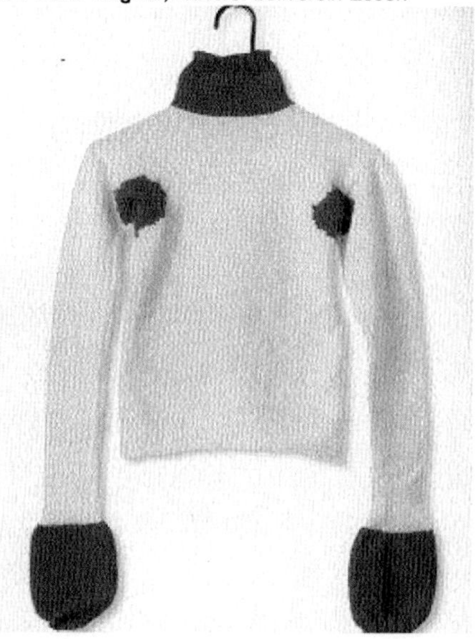

2001 **Anri Sala** Uomoduomo

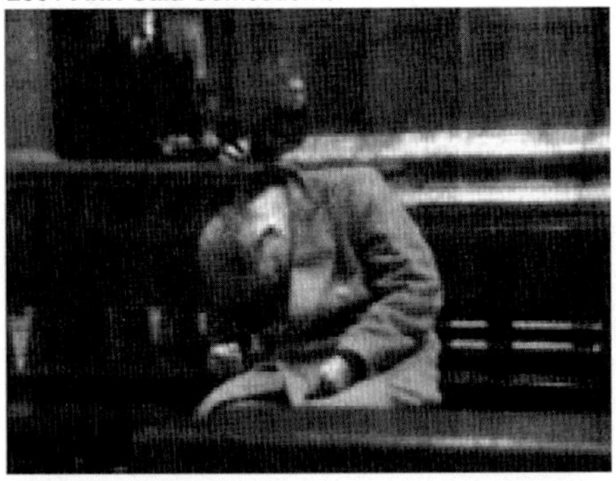

2001 **Attila Tordai** Mistake book, Protokoll studio

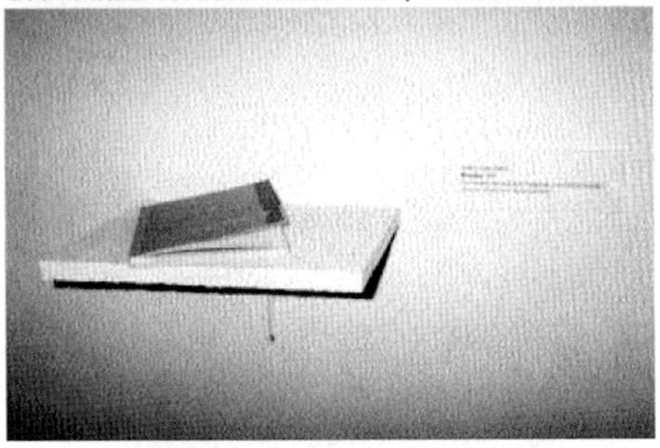

2001 **Barry mcGee, Stephen Powers, James Todd**

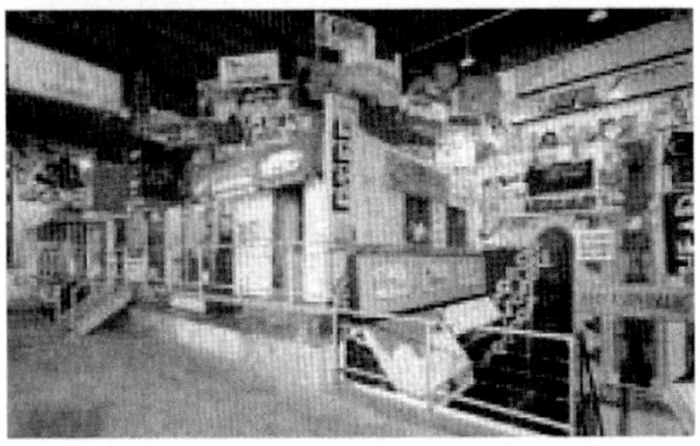

2001 **David Claerbout** Vietnam '68

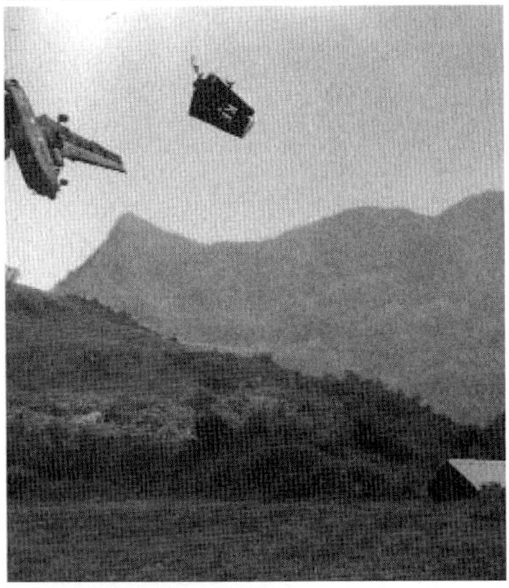

2001 **Laura Kurgan** 911 NY

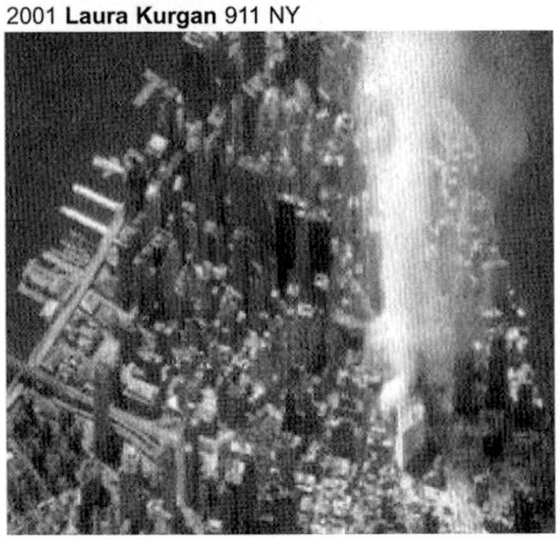

2001 **Emilio Lopez,** Menchero

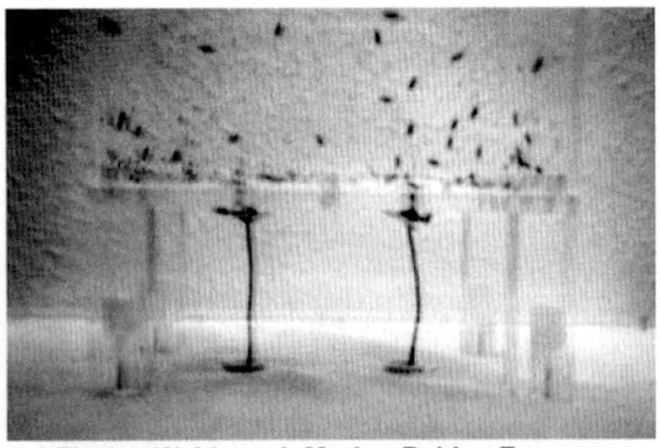

'01 **Florian Waldvogel, Marius Babias** Essen Kokerei, Zeitgenossische Kunst und Kritik 5 year

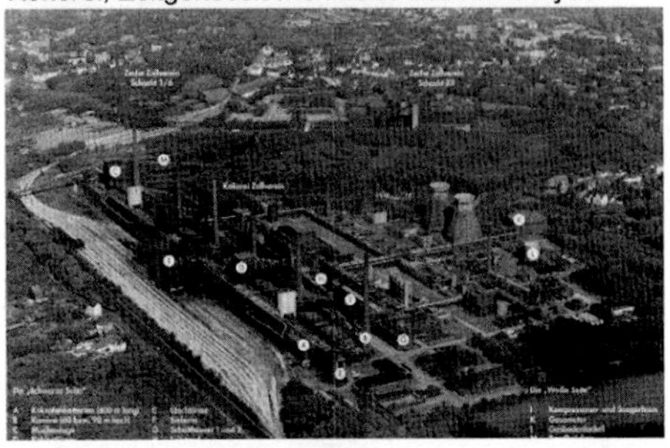

2001 **Maria Eihorn,** Courtain

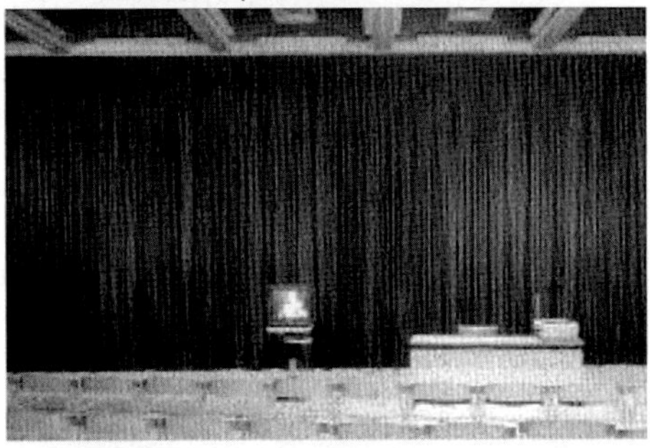

2001 **Marieta Potric** Upgrade

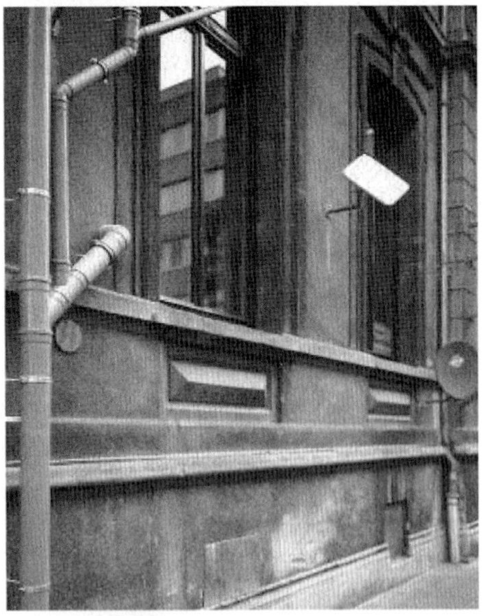

2001 **Robert Moreau**

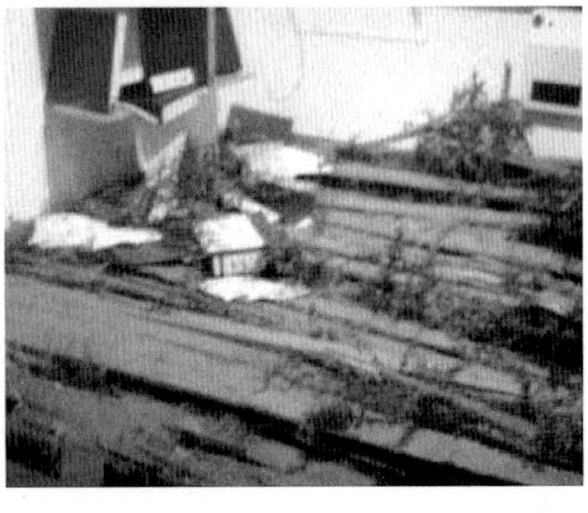

2001 **Michael Elmgreen & Ingar Dragset**
Powerless Structure

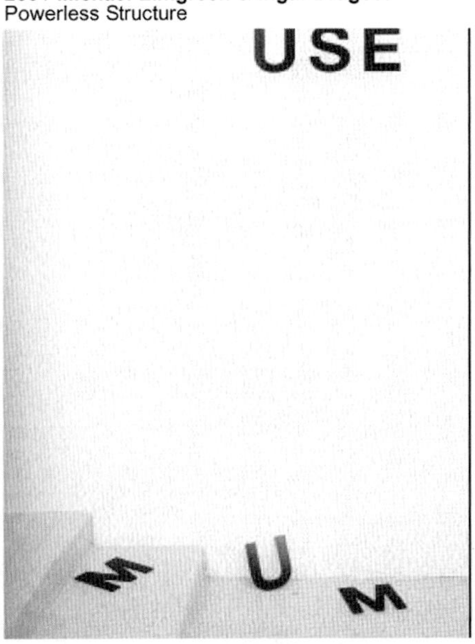

2001 **Vanessa Beecroft** Kunsthalle Wien

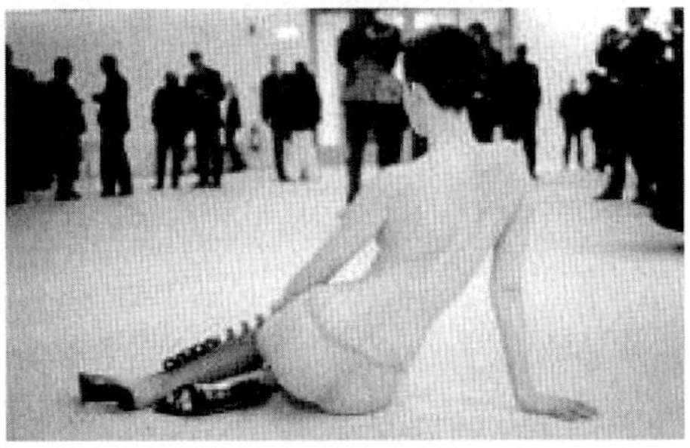

2002 **Kutlug Ataman** at Documenta 11

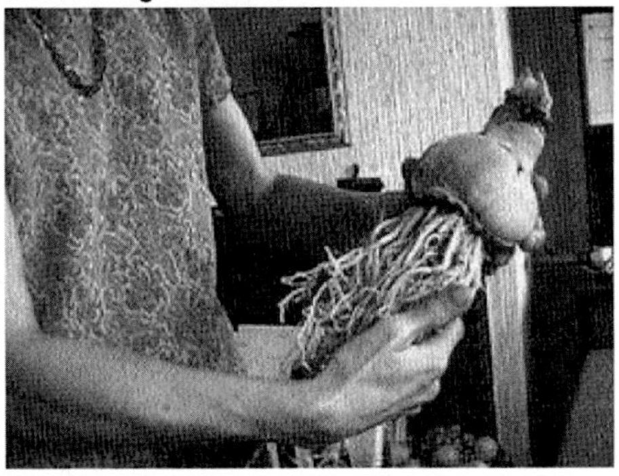

2002 **Chantal Akerman** at Documenta 11

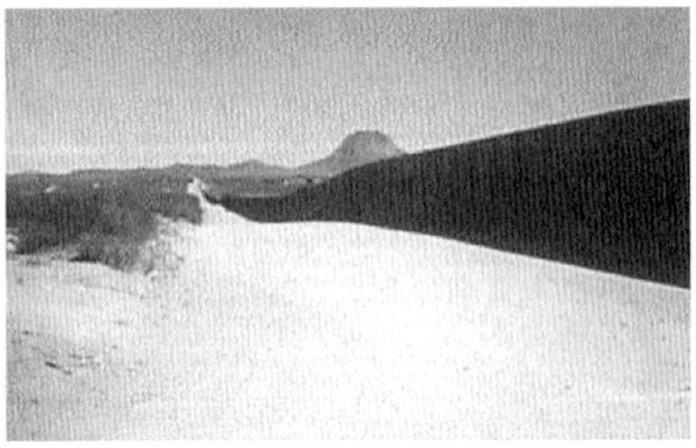

2002 **Kalin Serapionov** Cetinje Biennial reporter

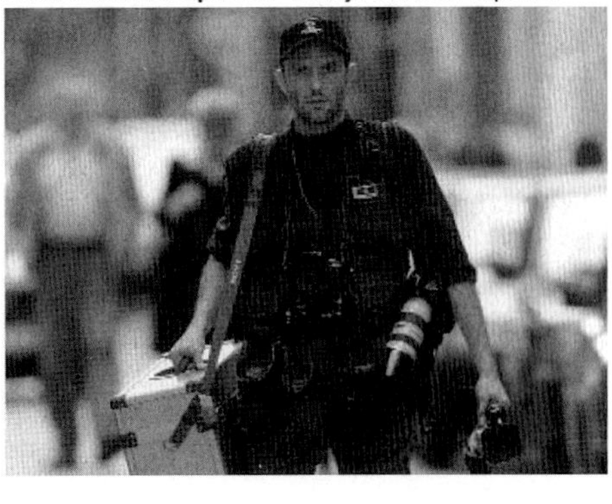

2002 **Bodys Isek Kingelez** Documenta 11

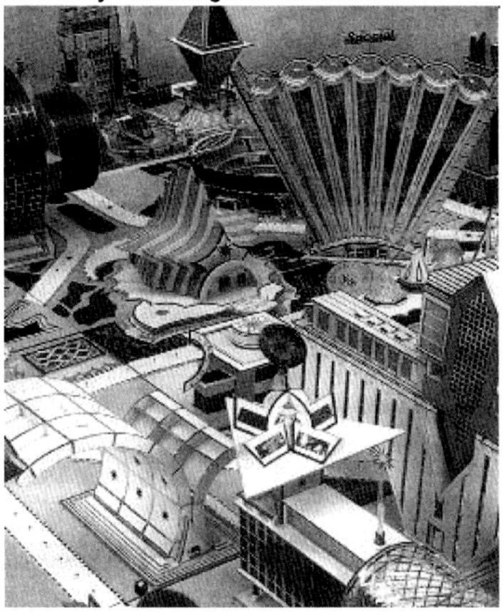

2002 **Mark Manders** at Documenta 11

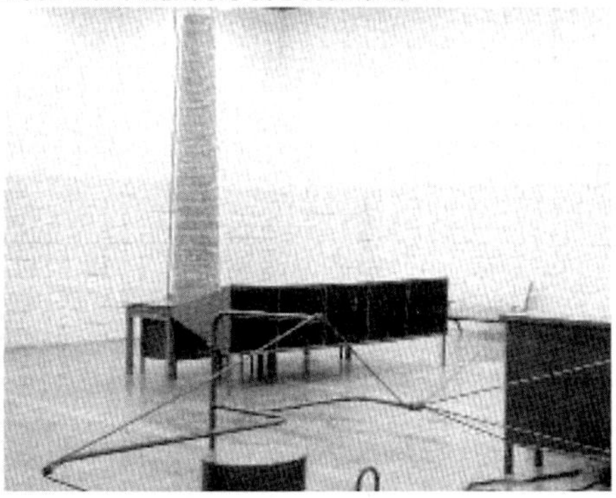

2002 **Pavel Braila** at Documenta 11

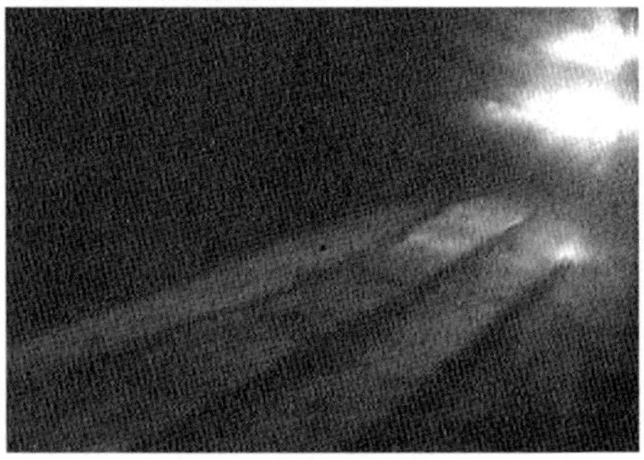

2002 **Nedko Solakov** A life

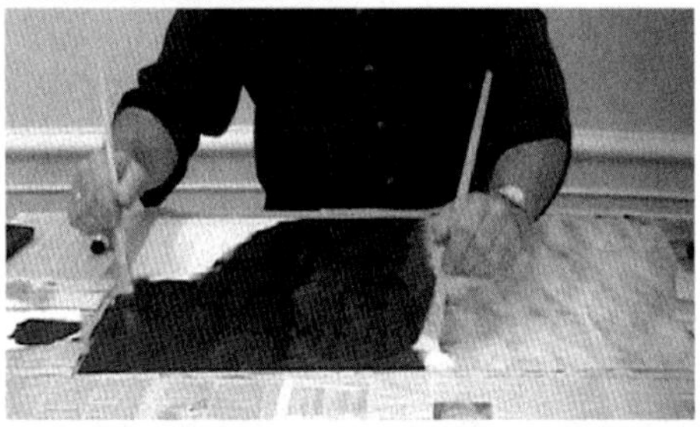

2002 **Sean Snyder**

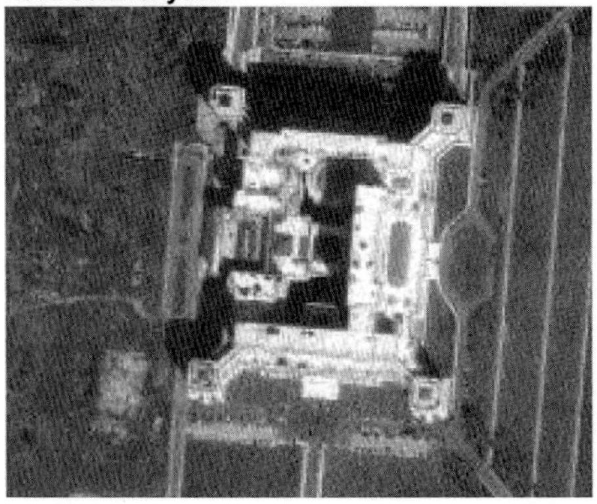

2002 **Thomas Hirschhorn**
Bataille Monument Documenta XI made in a suburb of Kassel comprised three installations in large makeshift shacks (constructed from materials of cheap timber, foil, plastic sheeting and brown tape), erected on a lawn between two housing estates, a bar run by one of the local families, and a sculpture of a tree.
The first housed a library of books and videos grouped around five Bataillean themes (word, image, art, sex, and sport) - a Turkish cab company who were contracted to ferry Documenta visitors to and from the site. - visitors feel like hapless intruders. Not 'zoo effect" "I want to do an active work. To me, the most important activity that an artwork can provoke is the activity of thinking."
Socially - engaged public art projects - public art 1980s

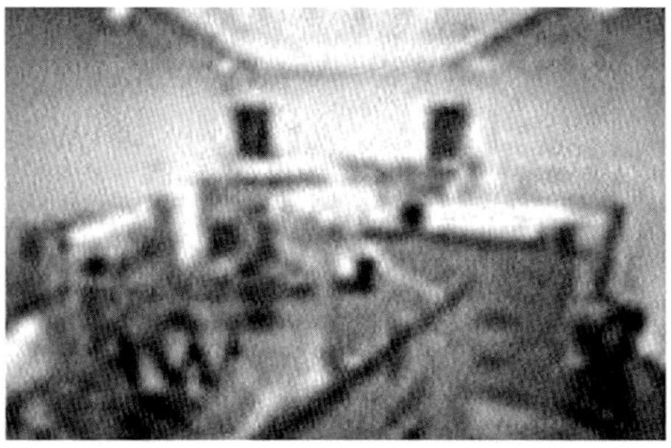

2002 **IRWIN** (artist group) create a map history of counter Art in East Europe (artists, artefacts events) An orientation tool in the still undefined field of the art of the East

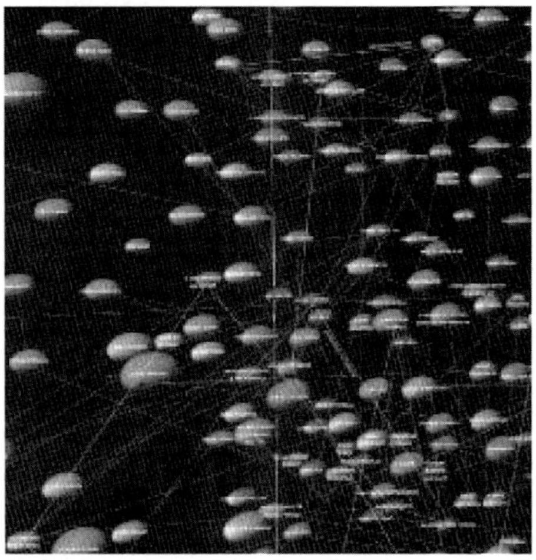

2002 **Carsten Nicolai** Telefunken.

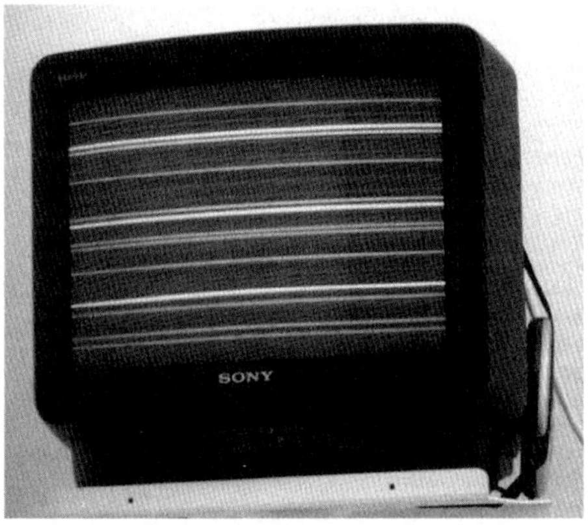

2003 **Monica Sosrowska** at Venice Biennial

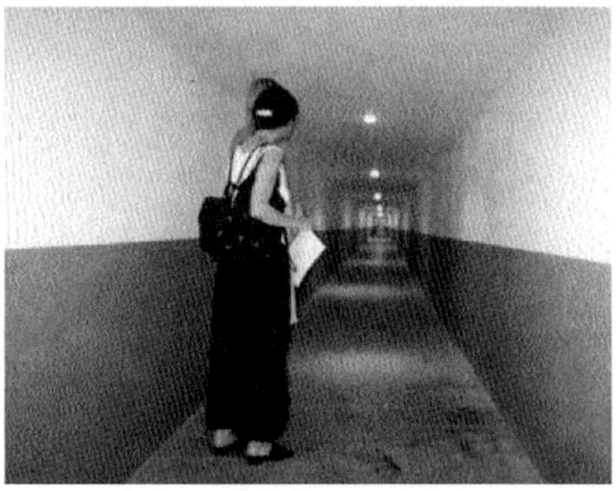

2003 **Aydan Murtezaoglu** Thermo Couples

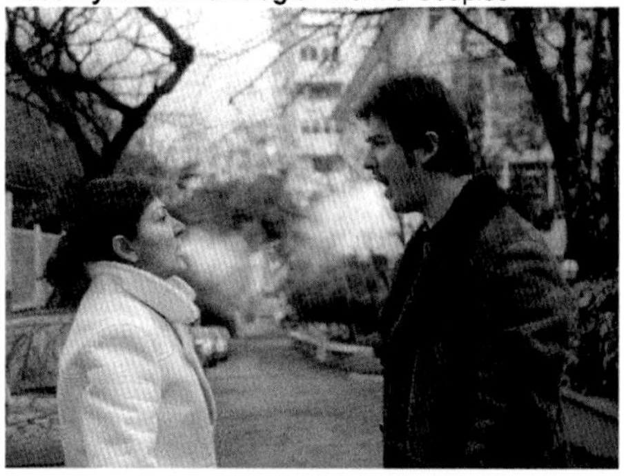

2003 **Yoko Ono** Venice Biennial

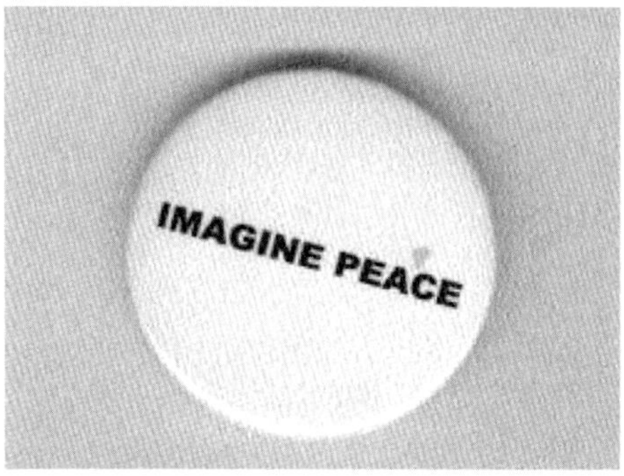

2003 **Alfredo & Maria Aquilizan**

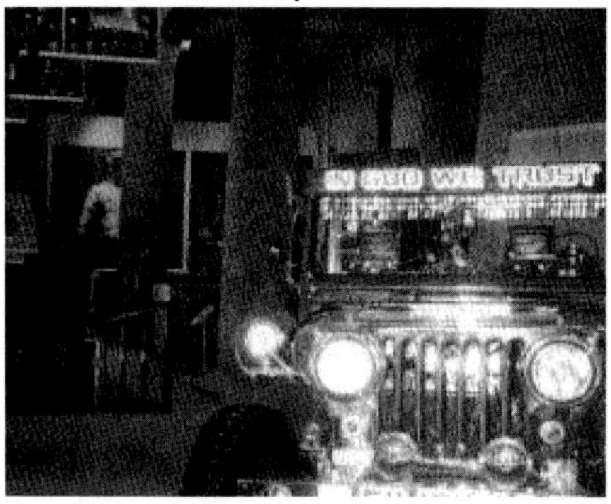

2003 **Peter Fischli & David Weiss** Venice Biennial

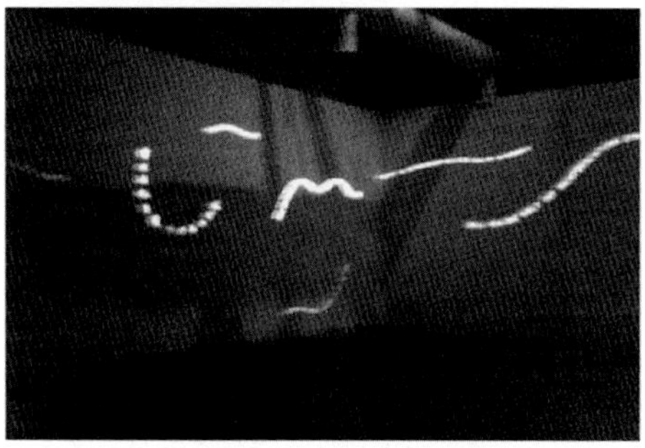

2003 **Sylvie Fleury** Space girl
"The fashion world was just as inventive as the plastic arts and the works were valued in the same way She attended Documenta and fashion shows. Her comprehension and fascination with these combined domains inspired her work, which features an infinite vocabulary of forms; photographs, videos, sculpture, installation, performances and more." Denis Angus

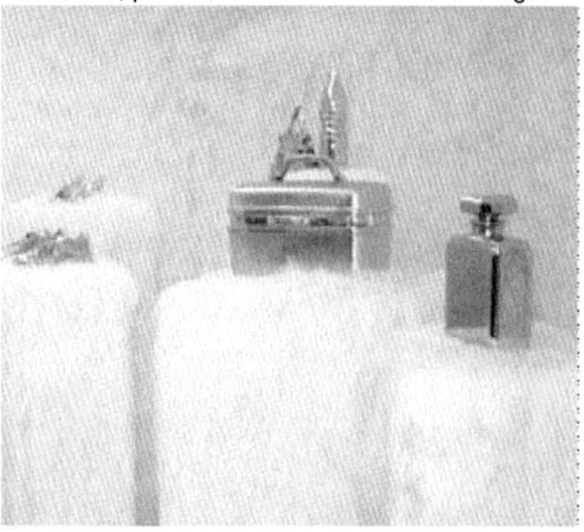

Dogville

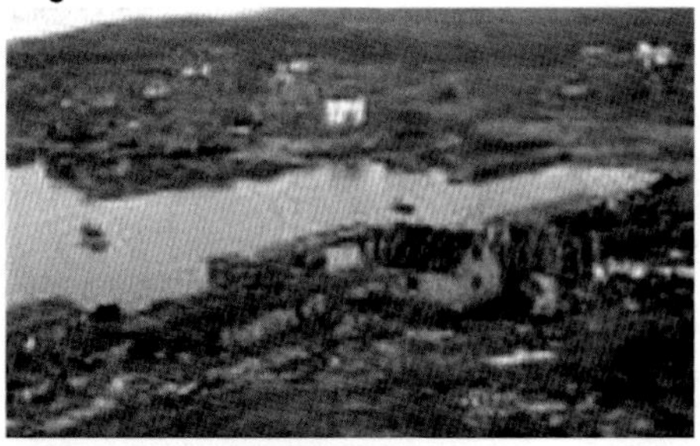

2003 **Lars von Trier** Dogville

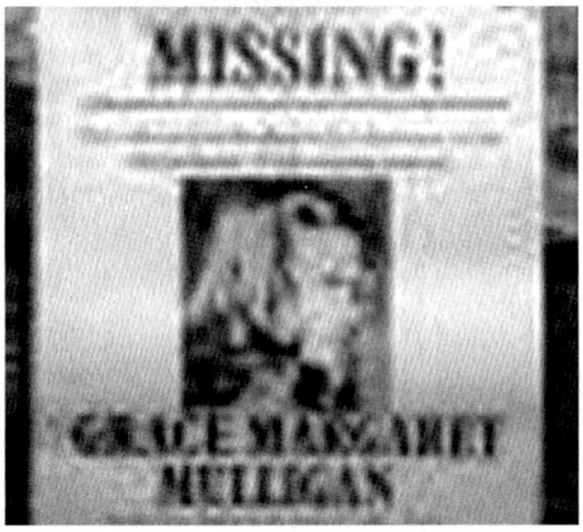

Lars von Trier Dogville, Nicole Kidman (Grace)

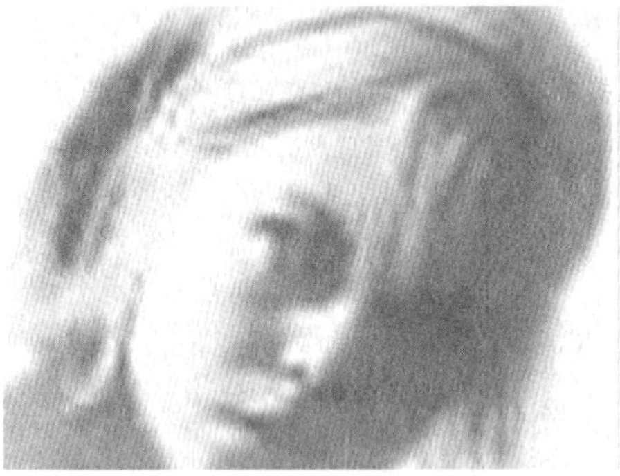

2003 **Supernova**

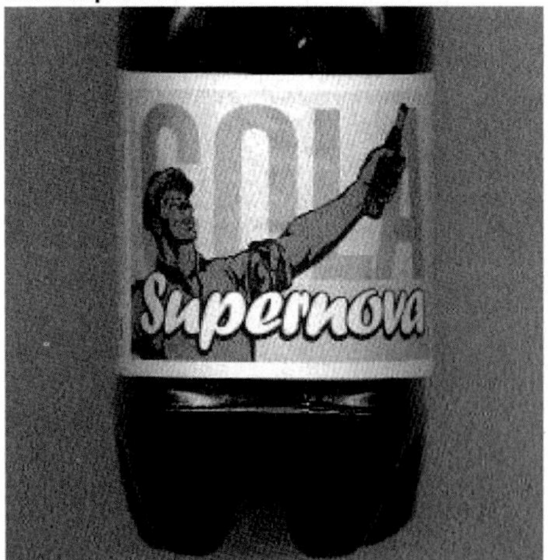

2003 **Chen Shaoxiong**

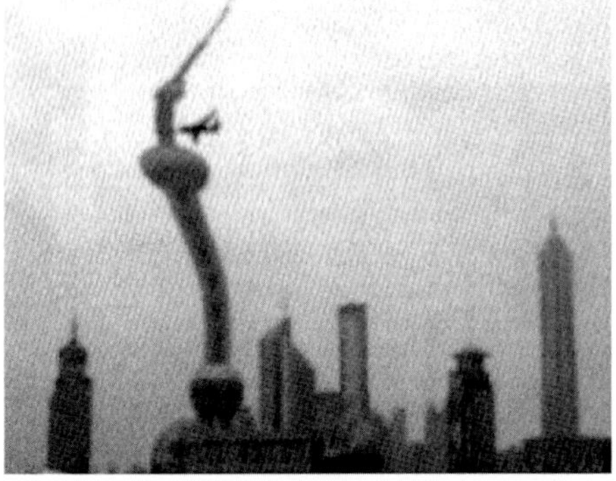

2003 **Bureau d'etudes Hommispheres.**

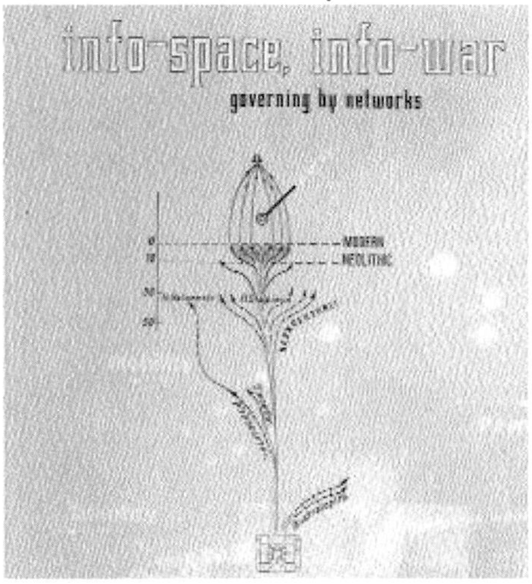

2003 **Ilya & Emilia Kabakov** Palais of Projects

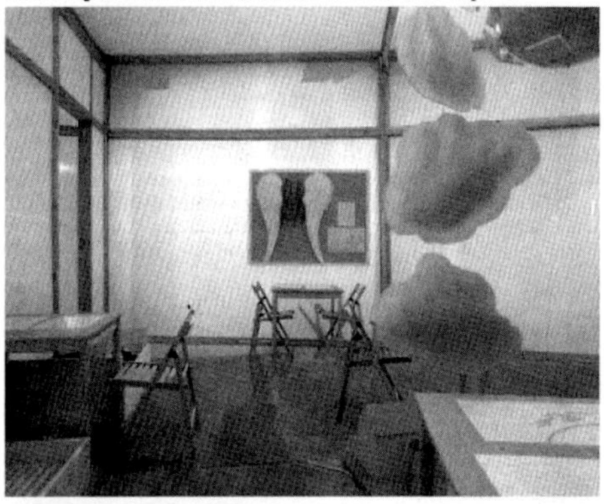

2003 **Venice Biennial**

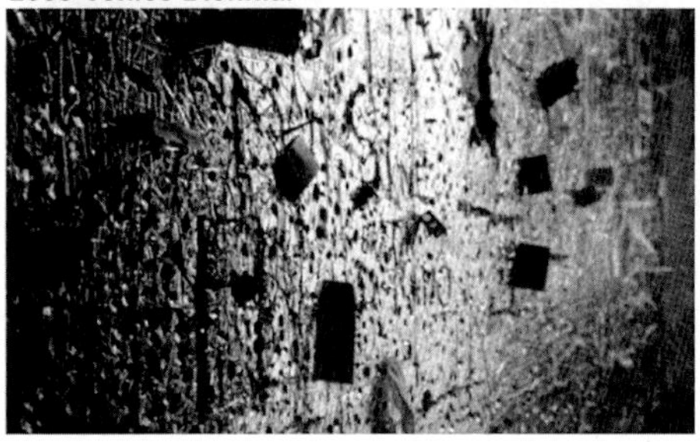

2003 **Jorinde Voigt Indonesia II 1-12.**

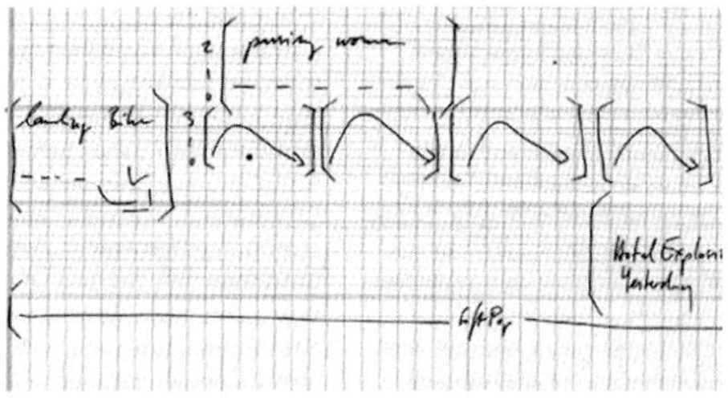

2003 **Jorge Macchi** Istanbul Biennial

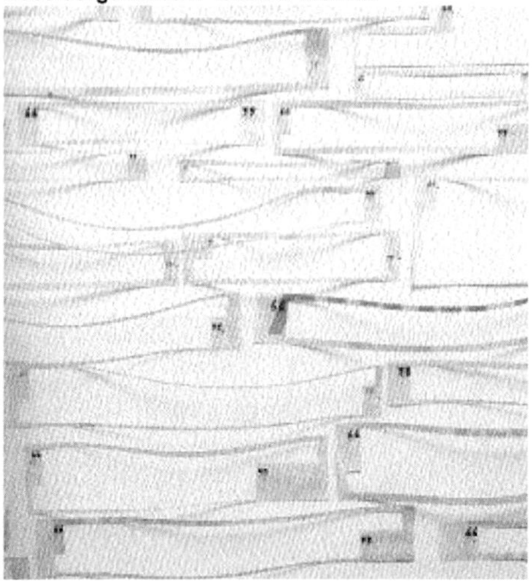

2003 **Lia Perjovschi, Endless Collection**

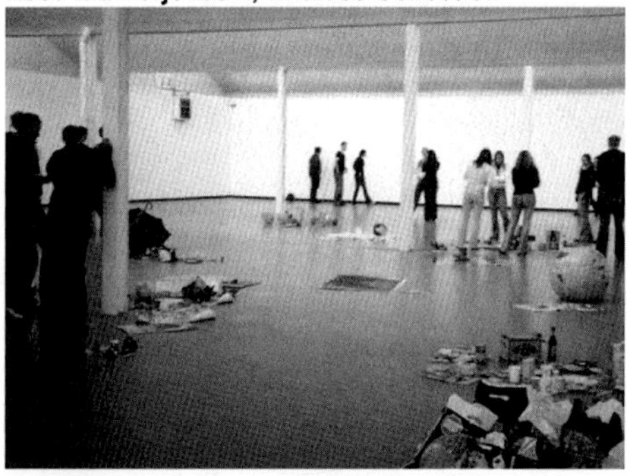

2003 **Rirkrit Tiravanija** Venice Biennial

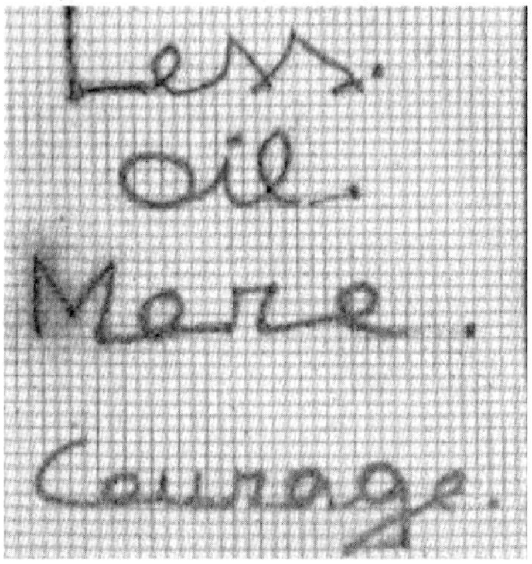

2003 **Suo Do Ho** Istanbul Biennial

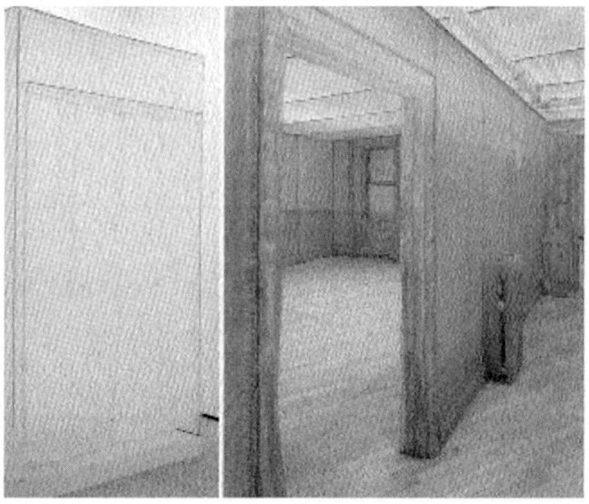

2003 **Tomas Bayrle**

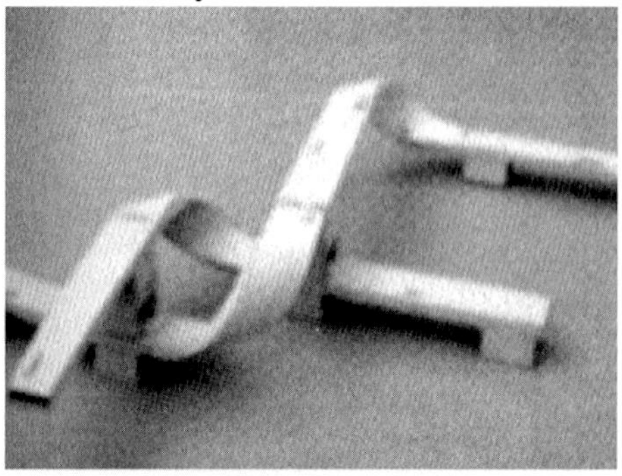

2003 **Annika Eriksson** Periferic Biennial

2003 **Thorvadur Thorsteinsson** Wanted (for Romanian future) Periferic Biennial

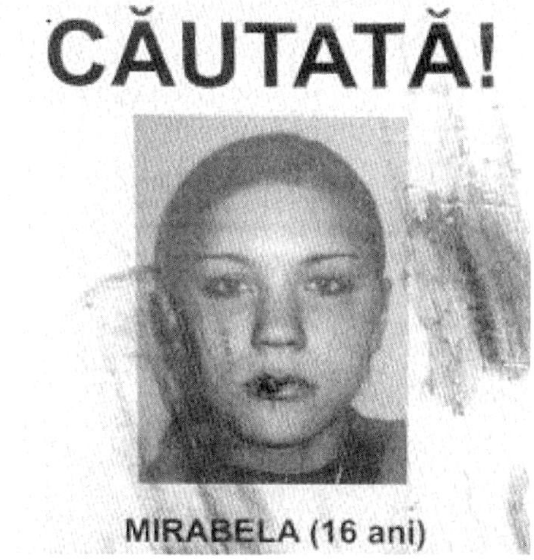

2003 **IDEA Art & Society**

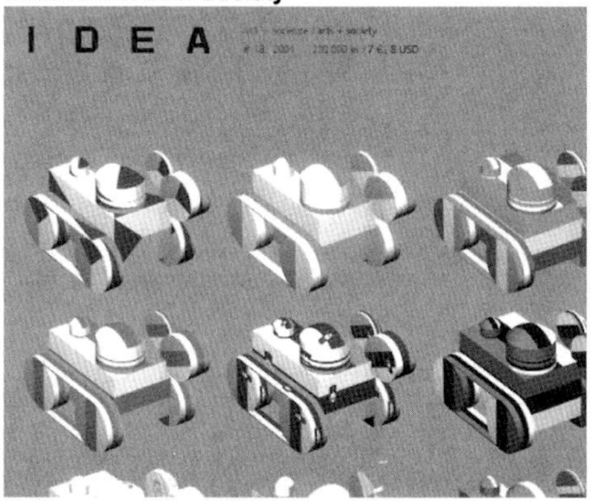

2004 **Susanne Neuburger & Hedwig Saxenhuber** MUMOK Wien

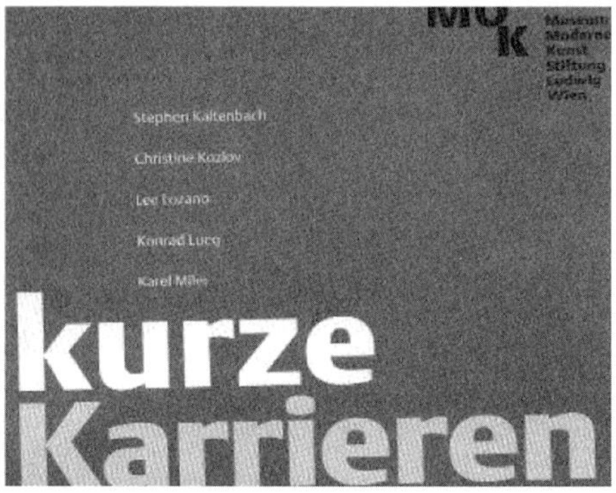

2004 **www.incepem.ro** chat list
www.e-cart.ro on line magazine

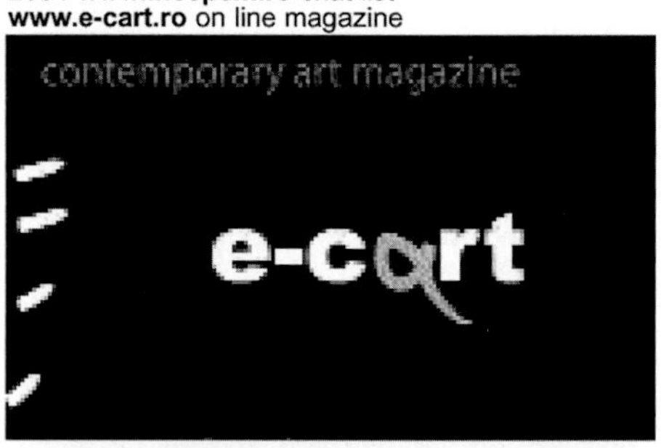

2004 **Florian Waldvogel** Nizza Transfer Project

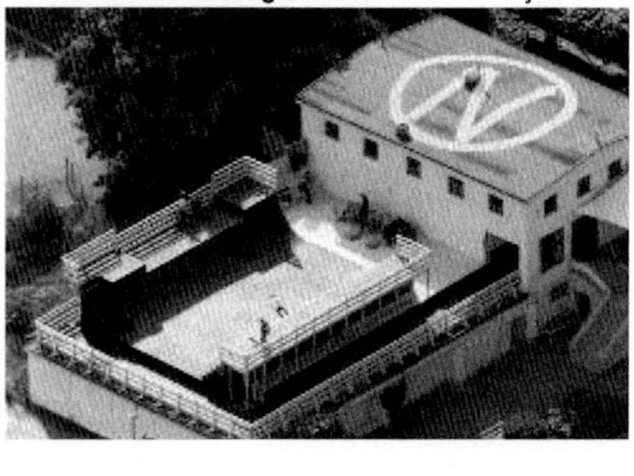

2004 **Ciprian Mursan**

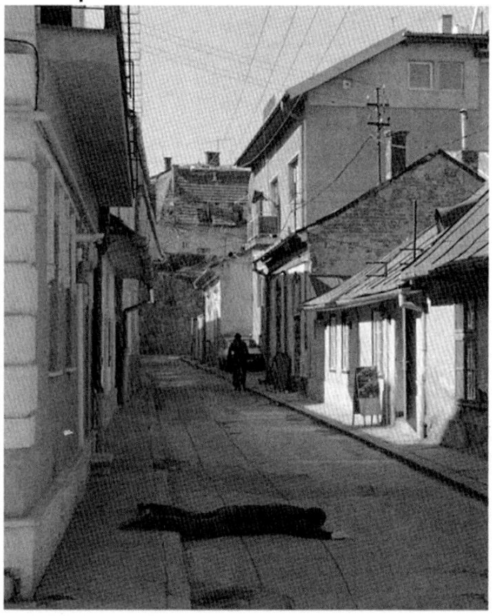

2004 **CAA** Center for Art Annalysis, Bucharest

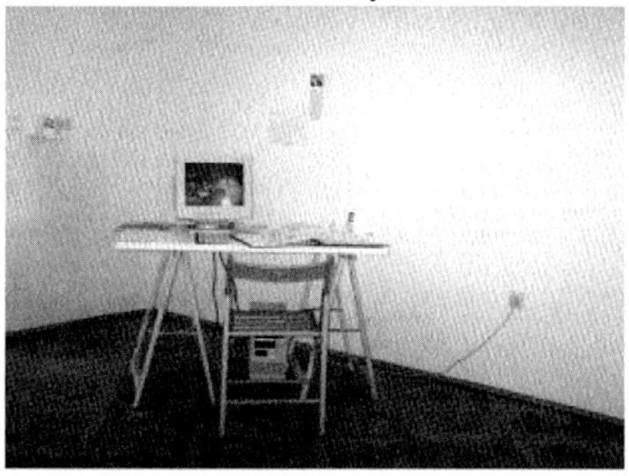

Postmodern/postmodernity Suspicion and rejection of Master Narratives, of totalizing theories.
Social and cultural pluralism;
Skepticism of progress, anti-technology reactions;
Sense of fragmentation and decentered self, multiple conflicting identities,
Alternative family units - for couplings and childraissing;
Loss of centralized control, fragmentation;
Trust and investment in micro-politics, identity politics, local politics, institutional power struggles;
Rhizome/surface tropes.
Attention to play of surfaces, images, signifiers without concern for "Depth";
Hyper-reality, image saturation, simulacra more powerful than the 'real";
Images and texts with no prior "original" "as seen on TV and as seen on MTV" are more powerful than unmediated experience;
Mixing of popular and high culture.
"Art as process, performance, production, intertextuality.
Art as recycling of culture authenticated by audience and validated in subcultures sharing identity with the artist.
Navigation, information management, just -in - time knowledge.
The web; interactive; dispersal, dissemination, networked, distributed knowledge; indeterminancy;
Play, irony, challenge to official seriousness, subversion of earnestness.
Recombinant culture, intertextuality, pastiche;
Design and Architecture of LA and Las Vegas;
Cyborgian mixing of organic and inorganic, human, machine and electronic.
Androgyny, queer sexual identities, polymorphous sexuality, mass marketing of pornography;
Hypermedia. The Web or Net as information system"
www - *691 Collective Martin Irvine '98.*
Postmodern (the term) = after modernism, contra modernism (subverting, resisting, opposing, or countering features of modernism)
Equivalent to "late capitalism" (postindustrial, consumerist, and multi-and trans-national capitalism)
"Global village" phenomena: globalization of culture, races, images, capital ,products ("information age" a sense of a global mixing of cultures) (..)
Postmodern historians and philosophers question the representation of history and cultural identities: history as "what 'really happened"
Multiculturalism, History and identity politics
Walter Benjamin's recognition of the non -neutrality of history.
"There is no document of civilization which is not at the same time a document of barbarism."
"The transformation of reality into image" Debord and Baudrillard
"The fragmentation of time into a series of perpetual presents"
(high culture and mass or popular culture (Jameson) pastiche and parody; "in a world in which stylistic innovation is no longer possible, all that is left is to imitate dead styles"; No individualism or individual style, voice, expressive identity; illusion of individualism (ads)through images that define/create desired positions (being the one who's cool, hip, sexy, desirable, sophisticated)
Some features of postmodern styles
Nostalgia and retro styles**, recycling** earlier genres and styles in new contexts (**film/TV, internet images**, typography, advertising imagespop culture, fantasies of the past)
"The disappearance of a sense of history, **perpetual present, perpetual change** The information function of the media - would be to help us to forget (**amnesia**)" Jameson
Postmodernism
The term - Daniel Bell' End of Ideology 1960
From modernism to postmodernism signified art epochal shift in consciousness corresponding to momentous changes in the contemporary social and economic order.
Multinational corporation now control a proliferating system of information technology and mass media that renders national boundaries obsolete.
A consumerist vision
Loss of faith in technological progress - replaced by postmodern ambivalence about the effects of that "progress' on the environment
Modern culture - the industrial age.
Fueled by the desire for accommodation with the electronic age
Modernism - unyielding optimism and idealism
Emotional range of postmodernism..
Robert Venturi arhitecture - " elements - hybrid rather than "pure", compromising rather than clean, ambiguous rather than articulated perverse as well as interesting
Important to distinguish what is new about postmodernism from what is a reaction against modernism.
New aspect - is the dissolution of traditional categories - the divisions between art, popular culture, media - eroded
In term of theorizing about art, earlier distinctions between art criticism, sociology, anthropology, journalism - nonexistent in the work of Michel Foucault, Jean Baudrilard, Frederic Jameson
The clearest distinction between modern and post modern art involves the sociology of art world
The booming art market 1980 - undermined the modern image of the artist as an impoverished and altered outsider (Vincent van Gogh model of tormented artist) replaced by the pre-modern ideal of the **artist as a** (wo)man of the world a la Peter Paul Rubens the wealthy Flemish artist and **diplomat who traveled widely throughout EU society** 17th century,
The postmodern phenomenon of **retrospective exhibitions for acclaimed artists** in their **thirties puts heavy pressure on artists to succeed at an early age and frequently results in compromises between career concerns and artistic goals**, a problem unknown to the generation of modern artists who preceded them.

Colpitt "**art is** not about ideas in isolation, but **about being in the Word** If the paradigm for the conceptuaL **artist in the 1960 was the philosopher, that for the artist in the 1990 has been the researcher**
The key aspect of a Conceptual art today, would thus, lie not in object or space, but in **communality**, and an emphasis.

What is Art (today)?
Beaux Art magazine 1999
"An amazing adventure
Everything is always reinvented by artists.
Unique desires and obsessions"
Fabrice Bousteau
What is an artist (today)
"The artist is the stealth aircraft of culture: :undetectable by the radar of entertainment, but extremely efficient, as it always aims toward the sharpest edges, the most critical situations"
'Today, with television and brand names, **our entire society produces images. The studio has therefore lost its initial function of being the place where images are made. As a result, artist move around, going where images are made,** placing them selves as links in the economic chain, attempting to intercept them. **The studio** is thus no longer the accepted site of creativity, it is merely the place

where **images collected elsewhere are centralized.**
Furthermore, a studio is where raw materials are manipulated: a century ago, they were filled essentially with clay or tubes of color. Today, they may contain **magazine images, televisions, social situations, cars-anything at all."**
The new squatter
(..)"**The artist is permanently squatting every other Field**(..)
This is no longer creating, but rather **surfing on existing structures** (..)
At the same time, these squats are also shelters: art today has become a kind of general refuge for all manner of projects which are not immediately efficient or productive for industry or the consumer society"(..)
"Political action in my view, the most effective political action is when an artist demonstrates what can be done with what we are given, - reordering of forms and structures that we have been led to believe are eternal or "natural".
In other words :**"this is what we have; what can we do with it**? With this spirit, things can be indeed be changed much more radically"
The artist as director
(..)"The artist works exactly like a director who decides what will be filmed.
This, then, is the exhibition: a movie without a camera, a film which records an action, a shape. In exchange, the viewer can in some way organize his own exhibition sequence."(..)
The artist as storyteller
"Words are very good, it is important to be able to tell something. What links us all are stories"
(..)The keys to understanding artwork today are rarely provided by the work itself. This is what the general public finds so annoying, but this is also what is so fascinating: it is up to each individual to understand, like a detective, where a work comes from, how it was make"
Nicolas Bourriaud
Art work (today)
No style, no date. So, what else?
"(..) It seems that the criteria of style and date which have, up to now, been the basis of art history, must now be totally abandoned, in favor of the **indeterminate undefinable references which today characterize contemporary art**.(..)
There are no more style, no more dates and no more major trends to confort lazy minds: how hard is has become for a viewer today who looks at art with a systematic spirit. And how rich is this time for the person who exists in the present, without the nostalgia of romanticism or some vague idea of transcendence. The heterogeneous nature of art today is **more a reflection** than a new category indicating a **new eclecticism** It teaches nothing about art itself, but rather about the history of art whose existing forms are reaching their end"(..)
Redefining the commonplace
In a world in which banality has overcome the capacity to create, how to keep attempting to escape from the everyday and the commonplace (..)
The idea is this: to reoccupy and reinvent everyday life, because time is more than ever in the present, in the here and now, in a certain quest for pleasure.(..)
Micropolitics
How can we continue to question the foundation of political and social reality in a context in which the great ideologies no longer have any meaning? With the erosion of binary thought, artist are operating simply and uncynically in the interstices of reality, through immediate, even modest actions, in keeping with the idea of reoccupying the commonplace. The ecumenical undertaking, the trident declaration, the slogan and formality have been replaced by critical, sometimes ironical and in any case, non-insistent micropositions.(..)
Artist are re-introducing a paradoxical molecular dimension into fiction and social action."
Christian Marcel
Network and collectives in the 90s
(..) **"The artists of the 1990s have invented multiform collaborations that cross over into a variety of fields.**
Stephanie Moisdom-Trembley & Hans -Ulrich Obrist
"The artist have abandoned specialties and genres, and refuse to be strictly categorized. **Artist today are multidisciplinary, multimedia**; they work with every possible type of support, from postcard to canvasses, as well as video and watercolor. They may grow plants or create automobile prototypes or habitats. Before rejecting these forms which often appear to be incongruous and irreconcilable with the ideas we all have about a work of art, we should perhaps let them evolve, and let ourselves been convinced by their very strangeness. **If there is one thing that art requires of us, it is a clear and open mind, a momentary breakdown in our mental classifications- to finish with preconceived ideas about contemporary art once and for all"** *Jean -Max Colard*

Nicolas Bourriaud Postproduction
Culture as screenplay: How art reprograms the World
2000
"People produce works, and we do what we can with them, we use them for ourselves" Serge Daney
Postproduction is a technical term from the audiovisual vocabulary used in television, film, and video.
It refers to **the set of processes applied to recorded material: montage, the inclusion of the other visual or audio sources, subtitling, voice over, special effects.**
As a set of activities linked to the service industry and recycling, postproduction belongs to the tertiary sector, as opposed to the industrial or agricultural sector, the production of raw materials.
Since the early nineties - artworks have been created on the basis of preexisting works, more and more artists interpret, reproduce, re-exhibit, or use works made by others or available cultural products.
This art of postproduction seems to respond to the proliferating chaos of global culture in the information age
Eradication of the traditional distinction between production and consumption, creation and copy, readymade and original workworking with objects that are already in circulation on the cultural market
A typology of postproduction
Reprogramming existing works
1993 Maurizio Cattelan a canvas that reproduced Zorro's famous Z (Lucio Fontana) Sylvie Fleury glamorous world of trends offered by women's magazine - when she isn't sure what colors to use in her work, she uses the new colors by Chanel..
Making use of images
24 Hour Psycho 1997 Douglas Gordon Alfred Hitchcock's film slowed down.
Using society as a catalog of forms
Heger and Dejanov take every job they can in order to acquire "objects of desire" BMW project '99
Investing in Fashion and Media
Vanessa Beecroft from protocol of fashion photography
Already produced forms
Inscribe the work of art within a network of signs and signification's. ..in flows of production. "Things and thoughts"
The artistic question is no longer: "What can we make that is new?' but **" how can we make do with what we have?"**
How can we produce singularity and meaning from this chaotic mass of objects, names, and references that constitutes our daily life?
Ludwig Wittgenstein "Don't look for the meaning, look for the use".
DJs, Web surfers, postproduction artists "semionauts"..navigation.
New form of culture - the culture of use or a culture of activity - the art work like a narrative that extends and reinterprets preceding narratives—multiple scenarios. The artwork is no longer an end point but a moment in an infinite chain of contributions.
The use of objects
Marx A product only becomes a real product in consumption Because consumption creates the need to new production, consumption is both its motor and motive.
Michel de Certeau "to use an object is necessarily to interpret it"
What matters is what we make of the elements placed at our disposal.
Reading a book (film, music), we produce new material, we become producers. To organize this production new ways - remote controls,VCRs, computers, - to select, reconstruct, edit
Postproduction artists are agents of this evolution, the specialized workers of cultural reappropriation.
The use of the product from Marcel Duchamp to Jeff Koons
To choose one object among those that exist and to use or modify these according to specific intention.
'Marcel Broodthaers said that "since Duchamp, the artist is the author of a definition" which is substituted for that of the objects he or she has chosen.
Appropriation
Marcel Duchamp " the act of choosing is enough to establish the artistic process - to give a new idea to an object is already production - to create is to insert an object into a new scenario, to consider it a character in a narrative.
Aman (trash), Cesar(crushed, unusable automobile, at the end of its destiny as a vehicle), Spoerri (the poetry of table scraps)- the act of consumptionrelicsTo document a sociological phenomenon
The end result of the process of consumption.
The authors of the still lifes of industrial society.
Worhol, Oldenburg - on visual impetus - to acquire a product. To exploit new iconographic material. - advertising and its mechanics of visual frontality.
The visual conditioning (ads, packaging) that accompanies mass consumption.
Art work "absolute commodity
The object shown from the angle of the compulsion to buy, from the angle of desire midway between the inaccessible and the available. Marketing - the true subject of Simulationist works.
Sherrie Levine exhibited exact copies of works by famous artists
Jeff Koons displayed ads, salvaged kitsch icons.
Objects define personality of the owner , to fulfill desires
The artist consumes the world in place of the viewer, and for him.
The Flea market: the dominant art form of the '90
1980- 1990 the passage - shop windows, flea market or airport shopping mall
From Jeff Koons to Rirkrit Tiravanija to Jason Rhoades - the dominant visual model is closer to the open-air market, the bazaar, the souk - a temporary and nomadic gathering of precarious materials and products of various provenances. Recycling (a method) and chaotic arrangement (an aesthetic) have supplaned shopping store windows, and the shelving in the role of formal matrices.
The market - the omnipresent referent for the contemporary artistic practices. Represent - a collective form, a disordered, proliferating and endlessly renewed conglomeration, composed of multiple individual signs- flea market is the locus of a reorganization of postproduction - the flows and relationships(online shopping).is a place where products of multiple provenances converge, waiting for new uses. Here, past production is recycled and switches directions- an object is given a new idea
Dan Cameron used Claude Levi-Strauss - opposition "the raw and the cooked" artists who transformed materials and made them unrecognizable (the cooked) and artists who preserved the singular aspect of these materials (the raw)**Jason Rhoades** - industrial quantities of things- provincial junk fair for the dimension of Los Angeles - the experience of driving a car. Perfect World The space of the work is urban space, traversed at a certain speed the objects are enormous or reducedthe car the role of an optical tool allowing one to select forms.
Thomas Hirschhorn work relies not on spaces of exchange but places where the individual losses contact with the social and becomes embedded in an abstract background an international airport, a department store's windows, a company's headquarterswrapped vague everyday forms - made uniform-projected into monstrous, proliferating, tentacle-like form-networks.
Market - (Process of buying and selling) original status - as a negotiation between 2 people - a relationship Any transaction may be defined as "a successful encounter of histories., affinities, wishes, constrains habits, threats, skins, tensions" Michel Henochsberg
Art tends to give shape and weight to the most invisible processes.
Economic globalization- existence -in abstractio - the basic functions of our daily lives are slowly transformed into products of consumption (including human relations - artist rematerialize these functions and processes to give shape to what is disappearing before our eyes. As medium of experience - by striving to shatter the logic of the spectacle, **art restores the world to us as an experience to be lived.**
The use of forms
The '80 and the birth of DJ culture :toward a formal collectivism
New cultural; configuration- emblematic figures - the programmer and the DJ the remixer, the rave
Philippe Thomas - artwork belong to everyone - free access to works (communism of forms?)
1956 Guy Debord 'Methods of Detournement" The literary and artistic heritage of humanity should be used for partisan propaganda purposesAny elements, no matter where they are taken from, can serve in making new combinations"
Japanese musician Ken Ishiiii "the history of techno music resembles that of Internet Now everyone can compose musics endlessly (different genres based on everyone's personality.
DJ - proposing a personal orbit, sequences, atmosphere, reacting to the movements on the crowd.
Scratching or actions - filters, mixing level, adding sounds "assisted readymades" open network samples, play.
Deejaying implies a culture of the use of forms, which connects rap, techno
DJ Kool Herc '70 "breakbeat" isolating a musical phrase and looping- back and forth
Deejaying and contemporary art similar configurations
Pierre Huyghe 2 video - an interview with John Giorno and a film by Andy Warhol side by side.
1996 Douglas Gordon a selection of films censored

upon their release.
Rirkrit Tiravanija constructed a festive setting for the programming.
Soon Do-it Yourself will reach every layer of cultural production - the musicians of Coldout Let us play 1997 with a CD-ROOM - allows to remix the record yourself.
High culture - ideology of framing and the pedestal-codes of presentation.
Low culture exaltation of outer limits, bad taste, and transgression
When screenplays become forms: a user's guide to the world
Postproduction artists invent new users for works (of the past) also reed alternative scenarios.
historical or ideological narratives in .
Human society is strutured by narratives, immaterial scenariostranslated by lifestyles relationships to work or leisure, institutions, and ideologies.
"We are all caught within the scenario play of late capitalism" Liam Gillick
The artwork - the site of a negotiation between reality and fiction, narrative and commentary.
Rirkrit Tiravanija "lots of people" like a movie director- actors a specific attitude - relation aesthetic - mobility. - temporary campsites, bivouacs, workshops, encounters, and trajectories - the subject is nomadism, problematics of travel. Giving, or opening of a space
Precariousness is at the center of a formal universe in which nothing is durable, everything is movement. How to inhabit the world without residing anywhere.
Pierre Huyghe as a critique of the narrative models. Offered us by society
Michel Foucault - theory of the organization of power - a "micropolitics" reflects ideological fictions that prescribe ways of living and tacit organize a system of domination..
1996 Multiple Scenarios - casting.
(Godard of the militant years - he planned to re shoot Love Story and distribute cameras to factory workers in order to thwart the bourgeois image of the world, this falsified image that the bourgeoisie calls a "reflection of the real". - "the class struggle is the struggle of one image against another image and one sound against another sound."
As a monteur, or film editor. And montage (Godard) is a "fundamental political notion. An image is never alone, it only exists on a background (ideology) or in relation to those that precede or follow it"
Maurizio Cattelan - familiar elements dubbed.
1993 NY gallery crystal chandelier (horses Kounellis 69 Rome)Warning Enter at your own risk. Do not touch, do not feed, no smoking, no photographs, no dogs, thank you)
1993 occupied the entire gallery
1992 group show - he escape - "I let myself down from the window and I ran away"
A troublemaker, the eternal bad student
Felix Gonzalez Torres used historicized forms to revel their ideological foundations and to construct a new alphabet to struggle against sexual forms..
1993 he rented his exhibition space (Aperto Venice Biennial) to a cosmetics manufacture
The use of the world
Playing the world reprogramming social forms.
The exhibition is no longer the end result of a process, its "happy ending" (Parreno) but a place of production. An open stage between décor, film set, and information center.
Conceptual art, Pop art Anti-form, Junk art, design, cinema, economy, industry
Hacking, work, and free time
1999 **Swetlana Heger and Plamen Dejanov** - 1 year contractual relationship with BMW - space, visibility for rent, "pirate medium"(After the Wall)
Vienna- closing the gallery for the duration of their show, allowing the staff to go on vacation.
Pierre Huyghe " what do you do for a living?" " what are you doing with your life?"
How to inhabit global culture
(Aesthetics after MP3)
From Pop art to Minimalism and Conceptual art, the art of the sixties corresponds to the apex of the pair formed by industrial production and mass consumption - supermarket- visual frontality, seriality, abundance.
The contractual and administrative aesthetic of Conceptual art marked the beginning of the service economy- computer research
On Kawara One Million Years - data storage, index card classification, filling cabinetinto artistic practice.
The Author, the legal entity
Destroying the figure of the Author DJ - multiple names
More than a physical person, a name now designates a mode of appearance or production, a line, a fiction.
Multinationals
The art of '80 criticized notions of authorship and signatureif buying is an art, the signature of the artist-broker guaranteed a successful and profitable exchange. Art of displaydistinguish
Questioning the notion of the signature **Elaine Sturtevant, Sherrie Levine** - reproducing works of the past, but via very different strategies - to re-exhibit them, to arrange them according to personal principles, each creating a "new idea" After
Mike Bido constructs an ideal Museum, Sturtevant constructs a narrative by reproducing works showing radical moments in history, Levine copyst work, inspired by Roland Barthes- culture an infinite palimpsest. - the receiver becomes the central figure of culture.
'60 Umberto Eco "open work"
Levy "the emerging techno cultural environment encourages the development of new types of art that ignore the separation between transmission and reception, composition and interpretation.
Eclecticism and postproduction
Greenberg History must make sense. And this sense must be organized in a linear narrative.
Art represents a counterpower.
Today the official image of reality propagated by advertising discourse, relayed by the media, organized by an ultralight ideology of consumption and social competition. In our daily lives, we come across fictions, representations, and forms that sustain this collective imaginary whose contents are dictated by power. Art puts us in the presence of counterimage, forms that question social forms. In the face of the economic abstraction that makes daily life unreal, or an absolute weapon of techno-market power, artist reactivate forms by inhabiting them, pirating private property and copyrights, brands and products, museum - bound forms and signatures.
If the downloading of forms (samplings and remakes) - important concerns today - it is because these forms urge to consider global culture as a toolbox, an open narrative space. Instead of prostrating ourselves before works of the past, we can use thm. Art can be a form of using the world, **an endless negotiation between points of view**..
Art is an activity that produces relationship to the world and in one form or another makes its relationship to space and time material
Claire Bishop
Today, political, moral and ethical judgments have come to fill the vacuum of aesthetic judgment. Artistic experience is more adequate to the split, divided and incomplete subject of today. **Relational antagonism predicated not on social harmony, but on exposure of that which is repressed in contriving the semblance of this harmony, and thereby would provide a more concrete and polemical grounds for rethinking our relationship to the world and to each other.**

Glossary
Action, performance, Body Art - a type of work that appeared in the late 1960s; the artist uses his or her own body. The idea evolved toward the living painting (Vanessa Beecroft) or living characters in which people are used to interpret the work.
Anime - Japanese cartoon films, whose simply drawn figures and straightforward plots are based on Japanese manga comics. In the 1990s anime and their extravagant soundtracks became famous outside Japan
Appropriation art in Appropriation Art, objects, images and texts are lifted from their cultural context and placed unchanged in a new one . They thus become charged with a new significance.
Artist-run space - an exhibition space run by artists (glassbox)
Aura - Walter Benjamin - the immanence of the artwork, its sacred character and power.
Autonomy Condition of self reliance and independence. In art autonomy means freedom from any conditions by non-artistic, objectives.
Cinema - has supplied processes now used in the field of plastic arts. The concept of post-production, for example, which no longer uses the exhibition as a place to show work made elsewhere, but as a laboratory in which the work is conceived and created in real time.
Club culture The 1990's club culture was shaped by the aesthetics of techno-music. However, it was not confined to dance-floor activities but also found expression through a whole lifestyle, influencing fashion, design, and typography.
Code Sign system providing the basis for communication and conveying information..
Context art Criticises the art business and its institutions. Power structures are disclosed, distribution mechanisms and exhibition forms. Are investigated for their political functions. Various artistic means of expression are adopted to present this criticism, such as performances, installation and Object Art.
Contextual art - an art that is interdependent with the production or appearance
Crossover - the capacity to draw from different fields of experience and skill simultaneously;
refers to crossing the boundaries between art and popular culture and between different cultures, also to the inclusion of music, design and folklore etc in artistic work.
Cultural Studies studies that is concerned with the examination of popular culture. Cultural studies pay particular attention to the influence of racial, class or gender factors on cultural expression.
Curator - the person responsible for the selection of subject, artists and / or ideas that will be part of an exhibition. This curator may be associated with an institution or may work as a free - lance curator (independent curator);
decides what exhibitions are about, and selects the participating artists.
A means of interpretation that regards a work as an open and many -layered network of the most varied elements in form and content. These elements, their functions and contradictions, are revealed by deconstruction.
Eclecticism A common resort of postmodernism, characterised by extensive quotation from largely historical styles and other artists works.
Entropy A concept derived from heat theory signifying the degree of disorder in closed system. Total entropy would be reached when a system collapsed in chaos. By analogy , entropy indicates the informational value of news. The ultimate here would be a meaningless rushing noise.
Gender surfing the confusing game with sexual roles whose point is to mix them up to humorous effect.
Globalisation means that economic or cultural processes increasingly have wordwide impliations.
High and low culture A complex of themes concerning the influence of trivial culture (low art) on modern art (high art) . The concept derives from an exhibition assembled by Kirk Varnedoe in 1990 at the New York Museum of Modern Art.
Hybrid Of many forms, mixed, incapable of single classification.
Icon image or person venerated by a cult.
Iconography The language of images or forms that is typical of a particular cultural context, for example , the iconography of advertising, the western, post-modern architecture etc.
Iconology The interpretation of the content of a work of art, based on its iconography.
Installation art - a work that cannot be limited to a single element and may use several techniques simultaneously (Video, audio, objects,and so on) it forms a temporary site or even an environment (by extension contextual art)
Interface - a term borrowed from computers, designating an element that connects two different systems, creating a network.
Mainstream Predominant style reflecting the taste of the general public
Manga Comics and cartoon films, the most popular type of reading matter in Japan, where manga is produced and consumed in large quantities.
Micropolitics Political strategy based on intervention involving small social groups rather than overall **social change.**
Montage Joining together pictorial elements or sequences in photography, film and video.
Multiple in the 1960's the classical concept of a work of art came under fire. Instead of a single original, works of art were produced in longer runs as "multiple" The idea was to take art out of museums and galleries and make it more available.
New age A form of alternative culture that believed in the beginning of a new age.
Phenomenology A branch of philosophy which examines the way external reality appears to humans.
Pop culture finds its expression in the mass circulation of items from areas such as fashion, music, sport and film. The world of pop culture entered art in the '60 through Pop Art.
Post human A complex of themes centering on the influence of new technologies such as computers, genetic engineering etc. and the influence of a media-based society on the human body. "Post human" was the title of an exhibition put together by Jeffrey Deitch in 1992.
Post-conceptualism Aesthetic approach that like '60 conceptual art, concentrates more on the idea and concept of art than on its visual and perceptible form.
Postmodernism Unlike modernism, Postmodernism starts from the assumption that grand utopias are impossible. It accepts that reality is fragmented and that personal identity is an unstable quantity transmitted by a variety of cultural factors.
Postmodernism advocates an irreverent playful treatment of one's own identity, and a liberal society.
Post structuralism assumes that sign systems are always dynamic and open to change.
Process art idea of change ability of form, collaboration and incompleteness within the creative process.
Reactivate - an undertaking that consists of reusing

older forms or concepts, thought with new purposes.
Ready made - a manufactured object used as is. (Marcel Duchamp)
Relational aesthetics - this defines "an art that uses th sphere of human interactions and its social context as a theoretical horizon, rather than as an affirmation of a private and autonomous symbolic space" (nicolas Bourriaud) This artistic practice requires the spectator to occupy a key position, and the works are sometimes interactive.
Sampling Arrangement of existing visual or audio material with the main intention of playing with the material's form characteristics. Rather than quoting from the material whose sources are often unclear, sampling aims to reformulate it.
Scatter art installation art consisting of everyday objects, including objects trouves and junk scattered seemingly at random around exhibition spaces.
Simulacrum An illusionary image which is so seductive that it can supplant reality.
Social work Art here is understood as a service that quite deliberately accepts socio-political functions.
Stereotype A standardised, non-individual image that has become generally accepted.
Spectator - a term defining the individual intended to see the work. It stands in opposition to the concept of the public.
Urbanism The subject of town construction and living together in towns
Virtual reality An artificial world created on computer.
Techno - a musical style in which certain technics (similar to the principles of collage) are used in the field of the visual arts (mixing, sampling and so on) The artist as DJ - an artist who mixes and samples (shapes, concepts, etc.)
White cube The neutral white exhibition room which in modern times has succeeded older forms of presenting art. The white cube is supposed to facilitates the concentrated and undisturbed perception of the work of art.
Work in progress Work which the artist does not attempt to complete, focusing instead on the actual creative process.;
An evolving work that is transformed during the period of the exhibition. The opposite of the idea of art work as finished object.
Art Now Uta Grosenick & Burkhard Riemschneider Beaux Arts 1999

Bibliography

***Beaux Arts** 1999*
***Concepts of Modern Art** from Fauvismto Postmodernism by Nikos Stangos 1974*
***Performance Art** from Futurism to the present RoseLee Goldberg 1988*
***Art Speak** A Guide to Contemporary Ideas, Movements, and Buzzwords 1945 to the Present Robert Atkins 1990*
***Illuminating Video** an essential Guide to Video Art Doug Hall and Sally Jo Fifer 1990*
***Art in Theory** 1900 - 2000 An Anthology of Changing Ideas edited by Charles Harrison & Paul Wood 1993*
***Installation art** Nicolas de Oliveira Nicola Oxley Michael Petry Michael Archer 1994*
***Esthetique Relationelle** Nicolas Bourriaud 1995*
***Theory and Documents** of Contemporary Art a Source Book of Artist's Writings by Kristine Stilles and Peter Selz 1996*
***Petit Dictionaire des Artistes Contemporains** Pascale Le ThorelDavlot, Louise Bordas1996*
***Thinking about Exhibition** by Reesa Greenberg, Bruce W Ferguson, Sandy Naine 1996*
***Electronic Culture** by Timothy Druckrey 1996*
***Conceptual Art** Tony Godfrey*
Artsince 1960 Michael Archer 1997
***New Art** 1997*
***Avant -Garde and After** Rethinking Art Now by Brandon Taylor*
***L'Art Contemporain** depuis 1945*
***Out of Action** between performance and the object 1949-1979 Paul Schimmel 1998*
***The Digital Evolution** AD Coleman 1998*
***Net condition** art and globalmedia Peter Weibel /Timothy Druckrey 1998*
***New Media in late 20th century art** Michael Rush 1999*
***Outsider Art** Spontaneous Alternatives Art Colin Rhodes 2000*
Postproduction Culture as screenplay: How art reprograms the *World* **N***icolas Bourriaud* 2000
***Information Arts** intersection of art, science, and technology Stephen Wilson 2002*
Antagonism and Relational Aesthetics *text by Claire Bishop 2004*
Rewriting Conceptual Art *Michael Newman and Jon Bird*
2000 + Arteast collection *Liublijana Zdenka Badovinac*

Acknowledgments

An exhibition of this magnitude could not have been realized without the important contributions of many key individuals. We would like first and foremost to extend our deepest appreciation and admiration to the artists whose work helped inspire this exhibition and catalogue.

We express our sincerest gratitude to Ann M. Hatch and Peter and Annie Remes for their enthusiasm for the exhibition and for so generously underwriting this effort. A warm thank-you goes out to the Consulate General of the Netherlands in New York, and Robert Kloos, director for visual arts, architecture, and design, in particular, for providing support for artist travel.

We would also like to acknowledge all the lenders and the galleries whose commitment made the exhibition possible. Special thanks to:

Ruth Benzacar Galería de Arte, Buenos Aires, Argentina: Orly Benzacar and Solana Molina Viamonte

Tanya Bonakdar Gallery, New York: Tanya Bonakdar and James Lavender

Paula Cooper Gallery, New York: Paula Cooper, Anthony Allen, Steven Henry, and Amanda Parmer

D'Amelio Terras Gallery, New York: Christopher D'Amelio, Rachel Uffner, and Tatiana Kronberg

Elizabeth Dee Gallery, New York: Elizabeth Dee, Jenny Moore, and Tim Saltarelli

Foksal Gallery Foundation, Warsaw, Poland: Andrzej Przywara, Joanna Diem, and Aleksandra Sciegienna

Carl Freedman Gallery, London, England: Carl Freedman and Charlie Blightman

Glenn Fuhrman, New York

Annet Gelink Gallery, Amsterdam, the Netherlands: Annet Gelink, Floor Wullems, and Geer Oskam

Diane and Bruce Halle Collection, Scottsdale, Arizona: Diane and Bruce Halle and Beverly Adams

Collection Inelcom, Madrid-Xàtiva, Spain

Peter Kilchmann Gallery, Zürich, Switzerland: Peter Kilchmann

Gallery Koyanagi, Tokyo, Japan: Chie Fukasawa

Kurimanzutto, Mexico City: José Kuri and Mónica Manzutto

Yvon Lambert, New York: Yvon Lambert, Olivier Belot, Jayoon Choi, and Molly Klais

Lisson Gallery, London, England: Nicholas Logsdail and Silvia Sgualdini

Stella Lohaus Gallery, Antwerp, Belgium: Stella Lohaus

Lombard-Freid Projects, New York: Jane Lombard, Lea Freid, Cristian Alexa, and Jovan Erfan

Ebrahim Melamed Collection/Honart Museum, Tehran, Iran: Ebrahim Melamed

Galeria Franco Noero, Turin, Italy: Franco Noero

Orange County Museum of Art, Newport Beach, California: Aimee Chang and Tom Callas

Galerie Polaris, Paris, France: Bernard Utudjian and Anthony van Nooren

San Francisco Art Institute, San Francisco, California: Hou Hanru and Mary Ellyn Johnson

Jack Shainman Gallery, New York: Jack Shainman, Claude Simard, Judy Sagal, and Brooke Mellen

Sikkema Jenkins & Co., New York: Brent Sikkema, Michael Jenkins, and Ellie Bronson

Galerie Barbara Thumm, Berlin, Germany: Barbara Thumm and Berit Hummel

Rosalía and Humberto Ugobono, San Juan, Puerto Rico

Dean Valentine and Amy Adelson, Los Angeles, California

Vitamin Creative Space, Guangzhou, China: Zhang Wei and Hu Fang

White Cube, London, England: Alex Bradley, Vicki Thornton, and Sophie Greig

Barbara Wien Galerie and Bookshop for Art Books, Berlin, Germany: Barbara Wien and Wilma Luukatsch

Gallery Yuijro, London, England: Andréa Adcock, Dale Adcock, and Nicholas Dowdeswell

and private collections

We appreciate the kind and efficient help of artists' assistants and associates:

Sabine Eilers, Erica Love, Simona Schneider, Ewout Vellekoop, and Suzanne Weenink

We thank the following individuals who were so generous with their time and their ideas:

Simon Baier, Berlin, Germany

Marc Bembekoff, Frac Champagne-Ardenne, Reims, France

Tobias Berger and Christina Li, Para/Site Art Space, Hong Kong

Christine Böhler, DIE ERSTE österreichische Spar-Casse Privatstiftung, Vienna, Austria

Cecilia Brunson, Josefina Guilisasti, Isabel del Rio, and Bárbara Palomino, INCUBO, Santiago, Chile

Marina Buendia, Galeria Vermelho, São Paulo, Brazil

Cosmin Costinaş, *documenta 12* magazines, Vienna, Austria

Kris Douglas, Rochester Art Center, Rochester, Minnesota

Richard Flood and Eungie Joo, New Museum of Contemporary Art, New York

Douglas Fogle, Carnegie Museum of Art, Pittsburgh, Pennsylvania

Adrian Ghenie, Galeria Plan B, Cluj-Napoca, Romania

Lukasz Gorczyca and Michal Kaczynski, Raster Gallery, Warsaw, Poland

Claire Hsu, Asia Art Archive, Hong Kong

Máximo Jacoby, Casa de Arte Juana de Arco, Buenos Aires, Argentina

Zuzanna Janin, Agnieszka Rayzacher, Michal Suchora, Lokal 30, Warsaw, Poland

Magda Kardasz, Zachęta National Gallery of Art, Warsaw, Poland

Mami Kataoka, Mori Art Museum, Tokyo, Japan

Clara Kim, REDCAT, Los Angeles, California

Sunjung Kim, Samuso: Space for Contemporary Art, Seoul, South Korea

Robert Kloos, Consulate General of the Netherlands, New York

Vasif Kortun and November Paynter, Platform Garanti Contemporary Art Center, Istanbul, Turkey

Erden Kosova, Istanbul, Turkey

Marcin Krasny, Centre for Contemporary Art, Ujazdowski Castle, Warsaw, Poland

Marta Kuzma and Erikka Fyrand, Office for Contemporary Art, Oslo, Norway

Fernanda Laguna, Belleza y Felicidad, Buenos Aires, Argentina

Dr. Friedemann Malsch, Kunstmuseum, Lichtenstein

Victoria Noorthoorn, Buenos Aires, Argentina

Manu D. Park, Seoul, South Korea

John Rasmussen, Midway Contemporary Art, Minneapolis, Minnesota

Julia Rometti and Victor Costales, São Paulo, Brazil

Joan Rothfuss, Minneapolis, Minnesota

Alberto Sendros and Ana Gallardo, Galería Alberto Sendros, Buenos Aires, Argentina

Matthew Schum, Minneapolis, Minnesota

Claire Staebler, Pinchuk Art Centre, Kiev, Ukraine

Lilian Tone, The Museum of Modern Art, New York

Attila Tordai-S, IDEA arts + society, Cluj-Napoca, Romania

Pelin Uran, Istanbul, Turkey

Jochen Volz, INHOTIM Centro de arte contemporanea, Belo Horizonte, Brazil

This book is an attempt to both faithfully represent the exhibition and expand on its intellectual contents. It thus required complex planning and cooperation. We first thank our fiercely intelligent and committed correspondents: Max Andrews and Mariana Cánepa Luna (Barcelona, Spain); Cecilia Brunson (Santiago, Chile); Tone Hansen (Oslo, Norway); Hu Fang (Guangzhou, China), Mihnea Mircan (Bucharest, Romania); and José Roca (Bogotá, Colombia). We deeply appreciate the generous permissions from Kwame Anthony Appiah, Janine di Giovanni, and Arundhati Roy, who allowed us to reprint their writings.

We are also extremely grateful to the staff of the Walker's Design Department. Emmet Byrne has been a curators' dream designer, constantly urging us to clarify our vision and inspiring us with his tremendously creative, meticulous, and distinctive approach. Design director and curator Andrew Blauvelt was always ready to guide and advise through the journey of making this complicated endeavor a reality, and design fellow Layla Tweedie-Cullen lent an essential helping hand. Production specialist Greg Beckel applied his magic to the images in this book. Editors Kathleen McLean and Pamela Johnson made an elegant order out of the chaos of contents with amazing diligence, dedication, and a dose of wicked wit and good humor, while publications manager Lisa Middag guided its production from start to finish with a combination of grace and rigor.

We thank our visual arts colleagues, Lynn Dierks and Eileen Romain, who deftly handled many administrative details of the exhibition and publication, and curators Betsy Carpenter, Peter Eleey, and Siri Engberg, whose feedback and enthusiasm have been essential in the realization of the exhibition. We'd also like to thank performing arts curator Philip Bither and assistant curator Doug Benidt as well as film curator Sheryl Mousley and assistant curator Dean Otto for their support of our endeavors inside the galleries.

The experience in the galleries is the work of an amazing team of collaborators: chief registrar Gwen Bitz, who expertly accomplished the Herculean task of gathering, care, and safe handling of artworks from across the world and made it seem almost easy; associate registrar Joe King, senior registration technician Dave Bartley, and registration technician Evan Reiter were also instrumental with their able assistance. As always, we are deeply indebted to Cameron Zebrun, director of program services, and the eternally dedicated and good-humored crew led by Doc Czypinski, the exhibition crew chief, who unflappably came up with solutions for installing an exhibition with such a diversity of works. Peter Murphy and Brian Lesterberg deserve a special shout-out for managing the incredible amount of technical work for this very media-heavy exhibition. We thank education and community programs director Sarah Schultz and her staff, especially Freda Fair, Allison Herrera, and Sarah Peters for their brilliant input and for designing intriguing public programs that illuminate and enrich the exhibition. Robin Dowden and her talented staff in New Media Initiatives ensured that our message exists beyond gallery walls and printed matter. Our Walker colleagues from across the programming departments met with us in the early stages of this exhibition to discuss art in the context of recent political events, and their intelligence and dedication was a great source of encouragement. The group included Christi Atkinson, Joe Beres, Megan Leafblad, Lara Roy, Witt Siasoco, and Michèle Steinwald as well as many of the aforementioned individuals.

We would like to thank development director Christopher Stevens and his colleagues Marla Stack, Annie Schmidt, and others in the department for their unflagging efforts to make this exhibition financially possible. Thanks also go to the Walker's fiscal caretakers, chief operating officer David Steglich and chief financial officer Mary Polta. Marketing and public relations director Phillip Bahar, public relations associate director Karen Gysin, marketing associate director Paul Schmelzer, and their staff worked enthusiastically to widen the visibility of the exhibition. We would also like to thank librarian Rosemary Furtak for her always thorough assistance during the research for this exhibition.

Special thanks go to curatorial fellow Rachel Hooper, who made invaluable contributions to the exhibition and catalogue. She not only handled many challenging tasks—including writing artist essays as well as compiling and double- and triple-checking information on all works in the exhibition—with incredible efficiency and precision, but also became a congenial and committed interlocutor for us. We couldn't have done this project without her. Lastly, we would like to thank director Kathy Halbreich and deputy director and chief curator Philippe Vergne for creating an institutional environment that both values the experimental and gives a new meaning to the notion of worldliness.

Doryun Chong & Yasmil Raymond

Exhibition Checklist

1.
Armando Andrade Tudela
Camión 2003
35mm color slides, plexiglass stand;
15 minutes
13 7/8 x 19 11/16 in. (35.2 x 50 cm) image
Courtesy the artist; Carl Freedman Gallery,
London; and Annet Gelink Gallery, Amsterdam

2.
Armando Andrade Tudela
Fotograma solarizado #1 (*Solarized Photogram #1*) 2007
chromogenic print mounted on aluminum;
edition 1/2 + 1 AP
80 1/2 x 60 13/16 in. (204.5 x 154.5 cm)
Courtesy the artist; Carl Freedman Gallery,
London; and Annet Gelink Gallery, Amsterdam

3.
Armando Andrade Tudela
Fotograma solarizado #2 (*Solarized Photogram #2*) 2007
chromogenic print mounted on aluminum;
edition 1/2 + 1 AP
80 1/2 x 60 13/16 in. (204.5 x 154.5 cm)
Courtesy the artist; Carl Freedman Gallery,
London; and Annet Gelink Gallery, Amsterdam

4.
Armando Andrade Tudela
Fotograma solarizado #5 (*Solarized Photogram #5*) 2007
chromogenic print mounted on aluminum;
edition 1/2 + 1 AP
80 1/2 x 60 13/16 in. (204.5 x 154.5 cm)
Courtesy the artist; Carl Freedman Gallery,
London; and Annet Gelink Gallery, Amsterdam

5.
Armando Andrade Tudela
Fotograma solarizado #6 (*Solarized Photogram #6*) 2007
chromogenic print mounted on aluminum;
edition 1/2 + 1 AP
80 1/2 x 60 13/16 in. (204.5 x 154.5 cm)
Courtesy the artist; Carl Freedman Gallery,
London; and Annet Gelink Gallery, Amsterdam

6.
Armando Andrade Tudela
Untitled Film #2 (Space Niemeyer and Infra Red Light) 2007
16mm film transferred to DVD (double-screen
projection, color, silent); 8:30 minutes (loop)
Courtesy the artist; Carl Freedman Gallery,
London; and Annet Gelink Gallery, Amsterdam

7.
Yto Barrada
AUTOCAR Tangier, 2004, Figure #1 from
A Life Full of Holes: The Strait Project 2004
chromogenic print
24 3/16 x 24 3/16 in. (61.5 x 61.5 cm)
Courtesy the artist and Galerie Polaris, Paris

8.
Yto Barrada
AUTOCAR Tangier, 2004, Figure #2 from
A Life Full of Holes: The Strait Project 2004
chromogenic print
24 3/16 x 24 3/16 in. (61.5 x 61.5 cm)
Courtesy the artist and Galerie Polaris, Paris

9.
Yto Barrada
AUTOCAR Tangier, 2004, Figure #3 from
A Life Full of Holes: The Strait Project 2004
chromogenic print
24 3/16 x 24 3/16 in. (61.5 x 61.5 cm)
Courtesy the artist and Galerie Polaris, Paris

10.
Yto Barrada
AUTOCAR Tangier, 2004, Figure #4 from
A Life Full of Holes: The Strait Project 2004
chromogenic print
24 3/16 x 24 3/16 in. (61.5 x 61.5 cm)
Courtesy the artist and Galerie Polaris, Paris

11.
Yto Barrada
The Sleepers, Tangier 2006, Figure #2 from
A Life Full of Holes: The Strait Project 2006
chromogenic print
50 x 50 in. (127 x 127 cm)
Courtesy the artist and Galerie Polaris, Paris

12.
Yto Barrada
The Sleepers, Tangier 2006, Figure #8 from
A Life Full of Holes: The Strait Project 2006
chromogenic print
50 x 50 in. (127 x 127 cm)
Courtesy the artist and Galerie Polaris, Paris

13.
Yael Bartana
A Declaration 2006
video transferred to DVD (color, sound); 7:30
minutes
Sound track: Daniel Meir
Courtesy the artist and Annet Gelink Gallery,
Amsterdam

14.
Mark Bradford
Ridin' Dirty 2006
mixed-media collage on paper
109 x 336 in. (276.9 x 853.4 cm) overall of 79
panels
Collection Glenn Fuhrman, New York

15.
Fernando Bryce
Work in Progress 2005–2006
ink on paper
11 7/16 x 8 5/8 x 1 in. (29.1 x 21.9 x 2.5 cm)
each of 80
Collection Inelcom, Madrid-Xàtiva, Spain

16.
Mircea Cantor
Chaplet 2007
printer's ink, artist's fingerprints on wall
dimensions variable
Courtesy the artist and Yvon Lambert,
New York

17.
Mircea Cantor
Shadow for a While 2007
16mm film (black and white, silent);
2 minutes
Courtesy the artist and Yvon Lambert,
New York

18.
Mircea Cantor
Talking Mirror 2007
size 7 1/8 platinum "El Patron" from the Larry Mahan Collection by Milano Hats, polyester-resin tray, used motor oil, distressed pine
40 x 27 x 27 in. (101.6 x 68.6 x 68.6 cm)
Courtesy the artist and Yvon Lambert, New York

19.
Mircea Cantor
The Spring 2007
oil on canvas
14 x 9 in. (35.6 x 22.9 cm)
Courtesy the artist and Yvon Lambert, New York

20.
Cao Fei
Whose Utopia 2006–2007
multimedia installation, video (color, sound); 20 minutes
dimensions variable
Courtesy the artist and Lombard-Freid Projects, New York

21.
Banu Cennetoğlu
Determined Barbara 2002–2004
ink-jet prints on paper
7 5/16 x 10 1/16 in. (18.6 x 25.6 cm) each of 32
Courtesy the artist, Istanbul

22.
Gimhongsok
The Boat 2001
polyester-resin casting with urethane coating, audio equipment, kitchen utensils, water bottles, kerosene lamp, paddles, life floats, bucket, rope, fishnet, fishing pole, towel, seat cushion, parasol; consumer goods: beer, canned foods, instant noodles, snacks, vitamin pills, medicine bottles, suntan cream, magazines, CDs
47 x 53 1/8 x 98 7/16 in.
(119.4 x 134.9 x 250 cm)
Courtesy the artist, Seoul

23.
Gimhongsok
Mao Met Nixon 2004
wood, glass, brass
45 1/4 x 21 5/8 x 21 5/8 in.
(114.9 x 54.9 x 54.9 cm)
24 3/8 x 15 3/4 in. (61.9 x 40 cm) brass panel
Courtesy the artist, Seoul

24.
Gimhongsok
This Is Coyote 2006
foam rubber, fabric
77 9/16 x 32 5/16 x 25 9/16 in.
(197 x 82.1 x 64.9 cm)
Courtesy the artist, Seoul

25.
Runa Islam
Time Lines 2005
35mm film (color, sound); 17:05 minutes
Courtesy the artist and Jay Jopling/White Cube, London

26.
Gabriel Kuri
Overlapping Statistic (Blind Olives Eyelid) 2007
painted plywood, weatherproof roofing roll, painted glass, tissue box, painted jar, isolating roll
29 x 48 x 48 in. (73.7 x 121.9 x 121.9 cm)
Courtesy the artist and Kurimanzutto, Mexico City

27.
Gabriel Kuri
Overlapping Statistic (Color Chart Can) 2007
plywood, weatherproof roofing roll, aluminum drink can, cardboard color charts
29 x 48 x 48 in. (73.7 x 121.9 x 121.9 cm)
Courtesy the artist and Kurimanzutto, Mexico City

28.
Gabriel Kuri
Speculation III 2007
painted plywood, mixed media
29 x 48 x 48 in. (73.7 x 121.9 x 121.9 cm)
Courtesy the artist and Kurimanzutto, Mexico City

29.
Jorge Macchi
Nube 2006
postcard, 35mm slide, slide projector, base; edition 1/3
3 15/16 x 6 3/8 in. (10 x 16.2 cm)
Collection Mr. and Mrs. Alfredo Hertzog da Silva, São Paulo, Brazil

30.
Jorge Macchi
Nuevo Mundo 2006
paper collage
48 x 59 in. (121.9 x 149.9 cm)
Private collection

31.
Jorge Macchi
Tevere 2006
concrete; edition 1/3
4 1/2 x 275 9/16 x 78 3/4 in.
(11.4 x 699.9 x 200 cm)
Collection Diane and Bruce Halle, Scottsdale, Arizona

32.
Jorge Macchi
Untitled 2006
paper
47 1/2 x 59 in. (120.7 x 149.9 cm)
Collection Rosalía and Humberto Ugobono, San Juan, Puerto Rico

33.
Jorge Macchi
Atlas 2007
paper, string
47 1/4 x 47 1/4 in. (120 x 120 cm)
Collection Diane and Bruce Halle, Scottsdale, Arizona

34.
Jorge Macchi
Liliput 2007
paper collage
59 x 70 7/8 in. (149.9 x 180 cm)
Ebrahim Melamed Collection/Honart Museum Tehran, Iran

35.
Josephine Meckseper
March on Washington to End the War on Iraq, 9/24/05 2006
Super 8 film and video transferred to DVD (black and white/color, silent); 8:50 minutes
Courtesy the artist and Elizabeth Dee, New York

36.
Josephine Meckseper
The Children's Crusade 2006
aluminum, plexiglass, glass, lights, gouache on plastic sign, toilet brush, metal display stand, rabbit furs, chromogenic print, plastic mannequin hand
89 1/4 x 46 x 18 in.
(226.7 x 116.8 x 45.7 cm)
Collection Dean Valentine and Amy Adelson, Los Angeles

37.
Josephine Meckseper
Untitled (Cold War) 2006
wallpaper of color photocopies
dimensions variable
Courtesy the artist and Elizabeth Dee, New York
Exhibition copy

38.
Zwelethu Mthethwa
Untitled 2000
chromogenic print; edition of 3
38 x 51 in. (96.5 x 129.5 cm)
Courtesy the artist and Jack Shainman Gallery, New York

39.
Zwelethu Mthethwa
Untitled 2000
chromogenic print; edition of 3
37 1/2 x 50 1/4 in. (95.3 x 127.6 cm)
Courtesy the artist and Jack Shainman Gallery, New York

40.
Zwelethu Mthethwa
Untitled 2003
chromogenic print; edition of 3
33 5/8 x 40 in. (85.4 x 101.6 cm)
Courtesy the artist and Jack Shainman Gallery, New York

41.
Zwelethu Mthethwa
Untitled 2003
chromogenic print; edition of 3
33 5/8 x 42 5/8 in. (85.4 x 108.3 cm)
Courtesy the artist and Jack Shainman Gallery, New York

42.
Zwelethu Mthethwa
Untitled 2003
chromogenic print; edition of 3
61 3/8 x 79 1/4 in. (155.9 x 201.3 cm)
Courtesy the artist and Jack Shainman Gallery, New York

43.
Zwelethu Mthethwa
Untitled 2003
chromogenic print; edition of 3
61 1/2 x 79 1/4 in. (154.9 x 201.3 cm)
Courtesy the artist and Jack Shainman Gallery, New York

44.
Noguchi Rika
The Sun 2005–2006
chromogenic prints
17 13/16 x 25 11/16 in. (45.3 x 65.3 cm)
each of 18
Courtesy the artist; D'Amelio Terras Gallery, New York; and Gallery Koyanagi, Tokyo

45.
Dan Perjovschi
Minneapolis Drawing 2007
felt-tip pen ink on painted wall
dimensions variable
Courtesy the artist and Lombard-Freid Projects, New York

46.
Lia Perjovschi
Knowledge Museum 1999–present
mixed-media installation
39 3/8 x 137 13/16 in. (100 x 350 cm)
Courtesy the artist, Bucharest, Romania

47.
Walid Raad
Let's Be Honest, The Weather Helped
1984–2007
archival color ink-jet prints; edition 6/7 + 2 AP
18 1/4 x 28 1/4 in. (46.4 x 71.8 cm) each of 17
Collection Walker Art Center, Minneapolis
T. B. Walker Acquisition Fund, 2007

48.
Tomás Saraceno
attractive 2000
magnets, light fixture, screws, string; edition of 3 + 1 AP
dimensions variable
Courtesy the artist and Tanya Bonakdar Gallery, New York

49.
Tomás Saraceno
Flying Garden/Air-Port-City/32SW 2007
32 PVC pillows, black webbing; edition of 3 + 1 AP
20 1/16 in. (51 cm) diameter each of 12 pillows
24 in. (61 cm) diameter each of 20 pillows
66 15/16 in. (170 cm) diameter overall
Courtesy the artist and Tanya Bonakdar Gallery, New York

50.
Tomás Saraceno
untitled (drawing with arrows) 2007
laser prints on paper; edition of 5 + 1 AP
35 7/16 x 51 3/16 in. (90 x 130 cm) each of 3
Courtesy the artist and Tanya Bonakdar Gallery, New York

51.
Sean Snyder
Schema (Television) 2006–2007
video transferred to DVD (rear projection, color, sound), tables; 10 minutes
Courtesy the artist and Lisson Gallery, London

52.
Sean Snyder
Optics.Compression.Propaganda 2006–2007
LightJet prints
dimensions variable
Courtesy the artist and Lisson Gallery, London

53.
Erik van Lieshout
Guantánamo Baywatch 2007
mixed media on paper and canvas
installed dimensions variable
Courtesy the artist

54.
Erik van Lieshout, in collaboration with
Core van der Hoeven
Guantánamo Baywatch, Part 1 2007
video transferred to DVD (color, sound);
17 minutes
Courtesy the artist, with financial support from
the Hammer Museum, Los Angeles

55.
Erik van Lieshout, in collaboration with
Core van der Hoeven
Guantánamo Baywatch, Part 2 2007
video transferred to DVD (color, sound);
24 minutes
Courtesy the artist

56.
Erik van Lieshout, in collaboration with
Core van der Hoeven
Guantánamo Baywatch, Part 3 2007
video transferred to DVD (color, sound);
22 minutes
Courtesy the artist

57.
Haegue Yang
Restrained Courage 2004
DVD (color, sound); 18:37 minutes
Courtesy the artist and Galerie Barbara Wien,
Berlin

58.
Haegue Yang
Unfolding Places 2004
DVD (color, sound); 18:11 minutes
Courtesy the artist and Galerie Barbara Wien,
Berlin

59.
Haegue Yang
Squandering Negative Spaces 2006
DVD (color, sound); 27:54 minutes
Courtesy the artist and Galerie Barbara Wien,
Berlin

60.
Haegue Yang
Blind Room 2006/2007
mixed media (lightbulbs, stands, electrical cords,
window blinds)
dimensions variable
Courtesy the artist and Galerie Barbara Wien,
Berlin

61.
Zheng Guogu
Me and My Teacher 1993/2007
photographic mural
dimensions variable
Courtesy the artist and Vitamin Creative Space,
Guangzhou

62.
Zheng Guogu
Landscape of the Age of Empire No. 1 2006
oil on canvas
82 11/16 x 122 7/16 in. (210 x 311 cm)
DSL collection

63.
Zheng Guogu
MOMA I Party No. 1 2006–2007
oil on canvas
82 5/16 x 124 7/16 in. (209 x 316 cm)
Courtesy the artist and Vitamin Creative Space,
Guangzhou

64.
Zheng Guogu
AD 2000, Rust Another 2000 Years II 2007
cast iron
dimensions variable
Courtesy the artist and Vitamin Creative Space,
Guangzhou

65.
Artur Żmijewski
Danuta 2006
video transferred to DVD (color, sound);
13:30 minutes; edition of 3
Courtesy the artist and Foksal Gallery
Foundation, Warsaw

66.
Artur Żmijewski
Dorota 2006
video transferred to DVD (color, sound);
15 minutes; edition of 3
Courtesy the artist and Foksal Gallery
Foundation, Warsaw

67.
Artur Żmijewski
Halina 2006
video transferred to DVD (color, sound);
15:32 minutes; edition of 3
Courtesy the artist and Foksal Gallery
Foundation, Warsaw

Reproduction Credits

Courtesy AP/WIDE WORLD PHOTOS. © 2007 The Associated Press. All rights reserved: **70, 140, 142**
Courtesy the artist and Annet Gelink Gallery, Amsterdam: **3 (right), 46–51**
Courtesy the artist; Annet Gelink Gallery, Am[illegible]dam; and Carl Friedman Gallery, London: **2 ([illegible]), 28, 30–33**
C[illegible]tesy the artist; Annet Gelink Gallery, A[illegible]terdam; and Carl Friedman Gallery, London [illegible]007 Tate, London: **29**
[illegible]urtesy the artist, Bucharest, Romania: **14 [illegible]ight), 19 (right), 186–189, 246–281**
[illegible]ourtesy the artist, Buenos Aires, Argentina: **10 (left), 134–139**
Courtesy the artist, D'Amelio Terras, New York, and Gallery Koyanagi, Tokyo: **13 (left), 166, 168–173**
Courtesy the artist and Elizabeth Dee, New York: **11 (left), 144–149**
Courtesy the artist and Foksal Gallery Foundation, Warsaw: **19 (left), 238–243**
Courtesy the artist and Galerie Barbara Wien, Berlin, © Haegue Yang: **17 (right), 218, 220–224**
Courtesy the artist and Galerie Barbara Thumm, Berlin: **4 (right), 60, 62–69**
Courtesy the artist and Galerie Polaris, Paris: **2 (right), 35–42**
Courtesy the artist, Istanbul, Turkey: **8 (left), 108–115**
Courtesy the artist and Jack Shainman Gallery, New York: **11 (right), 150–155**
Courtesy the artist and Jay Jopling/White Cube, London © Runa Islam: **9 (left), 122–127**
Courtesy the artist and Kurimanzutto, Mexico City: **9 (right), 128–133**
Courtesy the artist and Lisson Gallery, London: **16 (left), 203–209**
Courtesy the artist and Lombard–Freid Projects, New York: **cover, 6 (right), 88, 90–93**
Courtesy the artist and Lombard–Freid Projects, New York © Dan Perjovschi: **13 (right), 175–177**
Courtesy the artist; Lombard–Freid Projects, New York; and the San Francisco Art Institute, Walter & McBean Galleries, San Francisco: **89**
Courtesy the artist, New York: **178, 183**
Courtesy the artist and Paula Cooper Gallery, New York: **15 (left), 190, 192–195**
Courtesy the artist, Rotterdam, the Netherlands: **17 (left), 213, 215–217**
Courtesy the artist, Seoul, Korea: **8 (right), 116, 118–121**
Courtesy the artist and Sikkema Jenkins & Co., New York: **54–57, 59**
Courtesy the artist and Tanya Bonakdar Gallery, New York: **15 (right), 196–201**
Courtesy the artist and Yvon Lambert Gallery, New York © Mircea Cantor: **6 (left), 78–79, 84–85**
Courtesy the artist and Vitamin Creative Space, Guangzhou, China © Zheng Guogu: **18 (right), 230–237**
Courtesy the artist with the financial support of the Hammer Museum, Los Angeles: **212, 214**
Courtesy Escuela de Arquitectura, Universidad Católica, Valparaíso: **163 (right)**
Courtesy FRAC Champagne-Ardenne, Reims: **80, 82–83**
Courtesy Magnum Photos, © Alex Majoli/ Magnum Photos: **211**
Alfred and Marie Greisinger Collection, Walker Art Center, Minneapolis; T. B. Walker Acquisition Fund, 1992 © 2007 Artists Rights Society (ARS), New York/VG Bild–Kunst, Bonn: **156–157**
Collection Inelcom, Madrid-Xàtiva, Spain: **4 (right), 60, 62–65**
Collection Contemporary Art Museum, Kumamoto / Sunjung Kim: **8 (right), 121**
Collection Diane and Bruce Halle, Scottsdale, Arizona: **10 (left), 134**
Collection Glenn Fuhrman, New York: **54–55**
Collection Lisa and Hunter Gray, New York: **57**
Collection Ebrahim Melamed/Honart Museum, Tehran, Iran: **136–137**
Collection MUSAC, Spain: **66–69**
Collection Saatchi Gallery, London: **146–147**
Collection Tate Gallery, London. Lent by the American Fund for the Tate Gallery, courtesy of the American Acquisitions Committee, 2006: **56**
Collection Rosalía and Humberto Ugobono, San Juan, Puerto Rico: **138–139**
Collection Dean Valentine and Amy Adelson, Los Angeles: **11 (left), 144**
Collection Walker Art Center, Minneapolis; Butler Family Fund, 2004: **58**
Collection Walker Art Center, Minneapolis; Justin Smith Purchase Fund, 1995 © Chantal Akerman and Lieurac Productions: **161, 163 (left)**
Collection Walker Art Center, Minneapolis; Justin Smith Purchase Fund, 2006: **93**
Collection Walker Art Center, Minneapolis; Clinton and Della Walker Acquisition Fund, 2007: **94–95, 97**
Collection Walker Art Center, Minneapolis; T. B. Walker Acquisition Fund, 1990: **103 (left)**
Collection Walker Art Center, Minneapolis; T. B. Walker Acquisition Fund, 1991: **159–160, 162**
Collection Walker Art Center, Minneapolis; T. B. Walker Acquisition Fund, 2006: **4 (left), 52, 81**
Collection Walker Art Center, Minneapolis; T. B. Walker Acquisition Fund, 2007: **15 (left), 192–195**
Formerly the collection of Otto Piene and Elizabeth Goldring, Massachusetts. Collection Walker Art Center, Minneapolis; T. B. Walker Acquisition Fund, 1992: **98**
Private collection, Puerto Rico: **135**

Photography Credits

Max Andrews, Barcelona, Spain: **43**
Wilfried Bauer, Kassel, Germany: **157**
Ela Bialkowski, San Gimignano, Italy: **10 (left), 134**
Doryun Chong, Minneapolis: **75, 86**
Hu Fang, Guangzhou, China: **225, 229**
Javier Galeano, Bogotá, Colombia: **70**
Glenn Halvorson for the Walker Art Center, Minneapolis: **103 (left), 159–160, 162**
Tone Hansen, Oslo, Norway: **103 (right), 107**
Ryan Hendon and Aaron Rosenstreich, San Francisco: **89**
Robin Holland, New York: **13 (right), 176–177**
Jhoeko, Rotterdam, the Netherlands: **17 (left), 216–217**
Herbert Knosowski: **140**
Gabriel Kuri, Brussels, Belgium: **129**
Gustavo Lowry: **135–139**
Alex Majoli: **211**
Pablo Mirando, Sebastian Pereira, Tomás Saraceno, Lucas di Stefano, and Alejandro Quiles: **198–199**
Aurelien Mole: **80, 82–83**
Karel Prinsloo: **142**
David Regen, New York: **85**
Tomás Saraceno, Frankfurt, Germany: **15 (right), 196–197, 200–201**
Cameron Wittig for the Walker Art Center, Minneapolis: **52, 98**

Afterword

Excuse me for my melancholy romanticism. These are trying times. It is difficult to retain the cool of cynical detachment when neither a sense of opportunity nor decline dominates, leaving our emotional (and consequently, political) choreography to be shaped by an uncertainty that radically tests our sense of balance. We don't know what to believe, but we suspect authority of all sorts. This is not all bad. Once upon a time curators imagined they knew enough about the world and its people to use their specialized expertise to make universal judgments about artistic quality and, consequently, truth as well as the values that buttress it. Many histories were all too casually overlooked or disregarded. Occasionally, when the creations that grew out of these histories were examined by the cultural elite, they were found to be wanting—too primitive, shamanistic, and hermetic, for example, or lacking in originality.

This ignorance gave birth to a contagious anger among some of those—a global majority—who realized the meaning they possessed and the images they made were so little understood by the authors of these limited fictions that the alternatives they provided were not respected enough to be either appreciated or feared. Only recently have the complexity and drama of our social, political, ethnic, cultural, and economic identities been recognized and translated by these curators and critics into a more circumspect and increasingly less colonial narrative form. As we move across a more accessible landscape, because of increasingly less expensive communication technologies and modes of transportation, that world counterintuitively expands and we begin to see an embroidered intricacy where once the patterns were more rigid and linear. It is perhaps no coincidence that the curatorial ranks also are becoming more geographically and generationally diverse, making the conversations around the table far less abstract but no less theoretical. The power of singularity is being replaced by pressures of the polymorphous and personal.

There is joy in these revolutions. Curators, who seek to better understand context to achieve a more intimate and pleasurable connection to meaning that may be unfamiliar, become less isolated in the process. Artists frequently underscore the freedom inherent in each viewer's ability to construct a private relationship with an artwork by, for instance, removing it from the wall and placing it in a shared position where active participation is possible. These guerrilla tactics—the use of ephemeral materials, temporary installations, recycled images, and even the photograph—bespeak a rupture with an institutional past in which precious objects were kept secure behind glass or under bonnets on pedestals. Similarly, museums encourage speaking in the galleries where once silence reigned. Interrogation, both of the self and the other, is now a curatorial necessity. As confusing as these times are, it appears to be possible, through this questioning, to resuscitate our humanity and, thus affected by each other, yearn for closer proximity.

Exhibition curators and editors of this book, Doryun Chong, born in Korea, and Yasmil Raymond, of Puerto Rican lineage, are the brave new curators who have helped me to grasp the breadth of artistic models and critical engagements reflected in this exhibition as a sign of hope. Expanding Aldous Huxley's original title to its plural form, they envisioned a platform from which to foreground a diversity of observations and obsessions as made visible in the work of the twenty-four artists in this exhibition, who are from cities as far apart as Beijing, Buenos Aires, Istanbul, and Warsaw. Together, their images form a portrait that critically proposes a collectivity based on a shared sense of responsibility toward one another. The Walker Art Center benefits enormously from the risks embraced by these curators and supported by its trustees; most importantly, our view of the world is expanded by the artists in this exhibition who dare to make work for and examine their practices in the new context of the Walker galleries. One of our main challenges as an arts institution is to invent and foster many ways for understanding the creative process—its mysteries, urgencies, and poetry.

In 2003, the Walker bolstered its commitment to the multidisciplinary and global nature of contemporary artistic practices and, simultaneously, to interpreting ideas beyond our national borders and the familiar West from multiple perspectives. Doryun and Yasmil have thoughtfully and elegantly tested this institutional commitment in order to expand our field of vision and the chorus of voices offering us pressing stories. In this and many other ways, they have been inspired and supported by Philippe Vergne, the deputy director and chief curator, who gave them carte blanche to conceive a group exhibition and challenged them through its development. They have made public a complicated world view that is at once seductive and serious, pointed and compassionate.

Kathy Halbreich, Director
October 2007

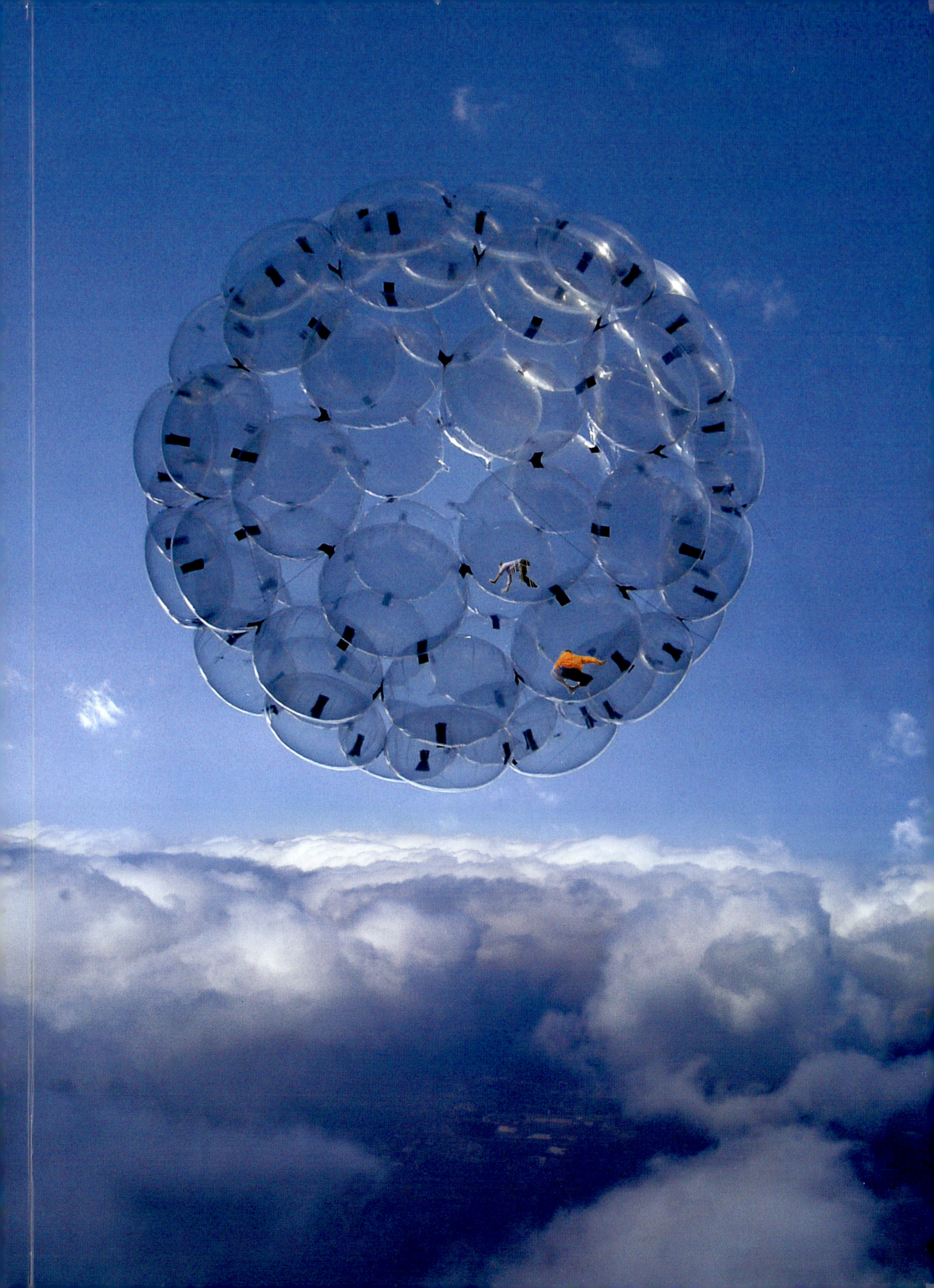

ARMANDO ANDRADE TUDELA

YTO BARRADA

YAEL BARTANA

MARK BRADFORD

FERNANDO BRYCE

MIRCEA CANTOR

CAO FEI

BANU CENNETOĞLU

GIMHONGSOK

RUNA ISLAM

GABRIEL KURI

JORGE MACCHI

JOSEPHINE MECKSEPER

ZWELETHU MTHETHWA

NOGUCHI RIKA

DAN PERJOVSCHI

LIA PERJOVSCHI

WALID RAAD

TOMÁS SARACENO

SEAN SNYDER

ERIK VAN LIESHOUT

HAEGUE YANG

ZHENG GUOGU

ARTUR ŻMIJEWSKI